PIANO SOLO

THE DEFINITIVE
Classical
COLLECTION

ISBN 0-634-03351-4

7777 W. BLUEMOUND RD. P.O. BOX 13819 MILWAUKEE, WI 53213

For all works contained herein:
Unauthorized copying, arranging, adapting, recording or public performance is an infringement of copyright.
Infringers are liable under the law.

Visit Hal Leonard Online at
www.halleonard.com

EVANSTON PUBLIC LIBRARY
1703 ORRINGTON AVENUE
EVANSTON, ILLINOIS 60201

THE DEFINITIVE Classical COLLECTION

Tomaso Albinoni
- 6   Adagio in G Minor

Johann Sebastian Bach
- 16   Air on the G String (from the Orchestral Suite No. 3)
- 11   Jesu, Joy of Man's Desiring
- 27   Prelude in C Major, from *The Well-Tempered Clavier*, Book 1
- 18   Sheep May Safely Graze (from Cantata 208)
- 22   Two-Part Invention No. 1 in C Major
- 24   Two-Part Invention No. 8 in F Major
- 30   Wachet auf, ruft uns die Stimme (Sleepers, wake), Excerpt

Ludwig van Beethoven
- 36   Für Elise
- 33   Minuet in G Major
- 40   Piano Concerto No. 5 ("Emperor"), First Movement Excerpt
- 42   Symphony No. 3 ("Eroica"), First Movement Excerpt
- 50   Symphony No. 5, First Movement Excerpt
- 54   Symphony No. 7, First Movement Excerpt
- 60   Symphony No. 7, Second Movement Excerpt
- 63   Symphony No. 9, Fourth Movement Excerpt ("Ode to Joy")
- 66   Turkish March (from *The Ruins of Athens*)
- 69   Violin Concerto, First Movement Excerpt

Georges Bizet
- 74   Habanera (from *Carmen*)
- 76   Toreador Song (from *Carmen*)

Alexander Borodin
- 79   Polovetzian Dances (from *Prince Igor*), First Theme

Johannes Brahms
- 82   Lullaby (Wiegenlied)
- 83   Piano Concerto No. 2, First Movement Excerpt
- 88   Symphony No. 1, Fourth Movement Excerpt
- 90   Symphony No. 3, Third Movement Excerpt
- 92   Symphony No. 4, First Movement Excerpt

Fryderyk Chopin
- 100   Mazurka in E Minor, Op. 17, No. 2
- 103   Prelude in A Major, Op. 28, No. 7
- 106   Prelude in B Minor, Op. 28, No. 6
- 114   Prelude in C Minor, Op. 28, No. 20
- 108   Prelude in D-flat Major ("Raindrop"), Op. 28, No. 15
- 104   Prelude in E Minor, Op. 28, No. 4
- 94   Waltz in A-flat Major, Op. 69, No. 1

Claude Debussy
- 115   The Girl with the Flaxen Hair
- 118   Prelude to the Afternoon of a Faun, Opening Excerpt
- 123   Rêverie

Léo Delibes
- 128   Pizzicato Polka (from *Sylvia*)

Antonín Dvorák
- 134 Slavonic Dance, Excerpt
- 131 Symphony No. 9 ("From the New World")
    Second Movement Excerpt

Albert Ellmenreich
- 138 Spinning Song

Gabriel Fauré
- 144 Après un rêve (After a Dream)

Friedrich von Flotow
- 141 M'appari tutt'amor (Ach, so fromm, from *Martha*)

César Franck
- 148 Panis angelicus

François-Joseph Gossec
- 151 Gavotte

Charles Gounod
- 156 Ave Maria (based on Prelude in C Major by J.S. Bach)
- 154 Funeral March of a Marionette, Themes

Edvard Grieg
- 161 In the Hall of the Mountain King (from *Peer Gynt*)
- 168 Morning (from *Peer Gynt*)
- 166 Solvejg's Song (from *Peer Gynt*)

George Frideric Handel
- 176 Air (from *Water Music*)
- 173 Allegro (from *Water Music*)
- 178 Allegro maestoso (from *Water Music*), Excerpt
- 188 Hallelujah (from *Messiah*)
- 192 Largo (Ombra mai fù, from *Serse*)
- 186 Pastoral Symphony (from *Messiah*)
- 181 The Trumpet Shall Sound (from *Messiah*)

Franz Joseph Haydn
- 208 Gypsy Rondo (from Keyboard Trio No. 23, in G Major)
    Third Movement Excerpt
- 194 The Heavens Are Telling (from *The Creation*)
- 198 Symphony No. 94 ("Surprise"), Second Movement Excerpt
- 200 Symphony No. 101 ("The Clock") Third Movement Excerpt
- 204 Symphony No. 104 ("London"), First Movement Excerpt

Scott Joplin
- 211 Maple Leaf Rag
- 216 Solace

Edward MacDowell
- 220 To a Wild Rose, from *Woodland Sketches*, Op. 51

Gustav Mahler
- 222 Symphony No. 1 ("Titan"), Third Movement Opening Theme
- 228 Symphony No. 2 ("Resurrection") Fifth Movement Choral Theme
- 224 Symphony No. 5, Fourth Movement Excerpt ("Adagietto")

Jules Massenet
- 229 Meditation (from *Thaïs*)

Felix Mendelssohn
- 232 "Fingal's Cave" Overture, or "*The Hebrides*" Themes
- 234 *A Midsummer Night's Dream*, Overture Themes
- 241 Symphony No. 4 ("Italian"), First Movement Excerpt
- 244 Violin Concerto, First Movement Excerpt

Jean-Joseph Mouret
- 248 Rondeau, Excerpt

Wolfgang Amadeus Mozart
- 250 Alleluia (from *Exsultate, Jubilate*), Excerpt
- 254 Ave verum corpus
- 263 Eine kleine Nachtmusik (A Little Night Music), First Movement Excerpt
- 256 Là ci darem la mano (from *Don Giovanni*)
- 260 Lacrymosa (from *Requiem*)
- 266 Piano Concerto No. 21 ("Elvira Madigan") Second Movement Excerpt
- 268 Symphony No. 29, First Movement Excerpt
- 272 Symphony No. 35 ("Haffner"), First Movement Excerpt
- 276 Symphony No. 38 ("Prague"), First Movement Excerpt
- 284 Symphony No. 40, First Movement Excerpt
- 279 Symphony No. 41 ("Jupiter"), First Movement Excerpt

Jacques Offenbach
- 294 Barcarolle (from *The Tales of Hoffmann*)
- 290 Can Can (from *Orpheus in the Underworld*)

Johann Pachelbel
- 300 Canon, Excerpt

Hubert Parry
- 297 Jerusalem

Giacomo Puccini
- 304 O mio babbino caro (from *Gianni Schicchi*)
- 306 Quando men vo ("Musetta's Waltz," from *La Bohème*)
- 308 Un bel dì vedremo (from *Madama Butterfly*)
- 312 Vissi d'arte (from *Tosca*)

Henry Purcell
- 315 Rondeau (from *Abdelazer*)

Nikolay Rimsky-Korsakov
- 330 Sadko (Song of India)
- 324 Sheherazade, Themes from Part 1

Gioachino Rossini
- 318 *William Tell* Overture

Camille Saint-Saëns
- 336 Aquarium (from *Carnival of the Animals*)
- 333 The Swan (from *Carnival of the Animals*)

Erik Satie
- 338 Gymnopédie No. 1

Franz Schubert
- 354 Ave Maria
- 341 Die Forelle (The Trout)
- 356 Serenade (Ständchen)
- 344 Symphony No. 5, First Movement Excerpt
- 348 Symphony No. 8 ("Unfinished"), First Movement Excerpt

Robert Schumann
- 359 The Happy Farmer Returning from Work
- 365 Ich grolle nicht (I bear no grudge)
- 360 Piano Concerto in A Minor, First Movement Themes
- 368 Widmung (Devotion)

Bedrich Smetana
- 373 The Moldau (from *Má Vlast*), Excerpt

Johann Strauss, Jr.
- 376 By the Beautiful Blue Danube, Themes
- 381 Emperor Waltz (Kaiser Walzer), Excerpt
- 392 The Fledermaus Waltz (from *Die Fledermaus*)
- 395 Tales from the Vienna Woods, Themes
- 398 Vienna Life (Wiener Blut), Themes

Pyotr Il'yich Tchaikovsky
- 410 Dance of the Reed-Flutes (from *The Nutcracker*)
- 407 Dance of the Sugar Plum Fairy (from *The Nutcracker*)
- 424 1812 Overture, Excerpt
- 429 Marche Slav, Themes
- 434 Piano Concerto No. 1, First Movement Excerpt
- 438 Romeo and Juliet, Fantasy Overture, Excerpt
- 440 Romeo and Juliet, Fantasy Overture, "Love Theme"
- 419 The Sleeping Beauty Waltz (from *The Sleeping Beauty*), Excerpt
- 444 Symphony No. 6 ("Pathétique"), First Movement Excerpt
- 414 Waltz of the Flowers (from *The Nutcracker*), Excerpt

Giuseppe Verdi
- 446 Lacrymosa (from *Requiem*)
- 450 La donna è mobile (from *Rigoletto*)
- 452 Triumphal March (from *Aïda*)

Antonio Vivaldi
- 456 Autumn (from *The Four Seasons*), First Movement Excerpt
- 458 Autumn (from *The Four Seasons*), Third Movement Excerpt
- 470 Mandolin Concerto in C Major, First Movement Excerpt
- 465 Spring (from *The Four Seasons*), First Movement Excerpt

Richard Wagner
- 478 Bridal Chorus (from *Lohengrin*)
- 474 Pilgrims' Chorus (from *Tannhäuser*)

Adagio in G Minor

Tomaso Albinoni
1671–1751
originally for organ and strings

Jesu, Joy of Man's Desiring

Jesus bleibet meine Freude
from Cantata No. 147, HERZ UND MUND UND TAT UND LEBEN

Johann Sebastian Bach
1685–1750
BWV 147
originally for choir and orchestra

Air on the G String
from the Orchestral Suite No. 3 in D

Johann Sebastian Bach
1685–1750
BWV 1068
originally for orchestra

Sheep May Safely Graze
from Cantata 208 ("Birthday Cantata")

Johann Sebastian Bach
1685-1750
BWV 208
originally for soprano,
2 flutes and continuo

Copyright © 2000 by HAL LEONARD CORPORATION
International Copyright Secured   All Rights Reserved

Two-Part Invention No. 1 in C Major

Johann Sebastian Bach
1685-1750

Two-Part Invention No. 8
in F Major

Johann Sebastian Bach
1685-1750

Prelude in C Major
from THE WELL-TEMPERED CLAVIER, BOOK 1

Johann Sebastian Bach
1685–1750

28

Wachet auf, ruft uns die Stimme
(Sleepers, wake)
from Cantata 140
Excerpt

Johann Sebastian Bach
1685-1750
BWV 140
originally for tenor,
strings and continuo

Copyright © 2000 by HAL LEONARD CORPORATION
International Copyright Secured   All Rights Reserved

Minuet in G Major

Ludwig van Beethoven
1770-1827

34

Für Elise
(For Elise)
Bagatelle in A minor

Ludwig van Beethoven
1770–1827
WoO 59

37

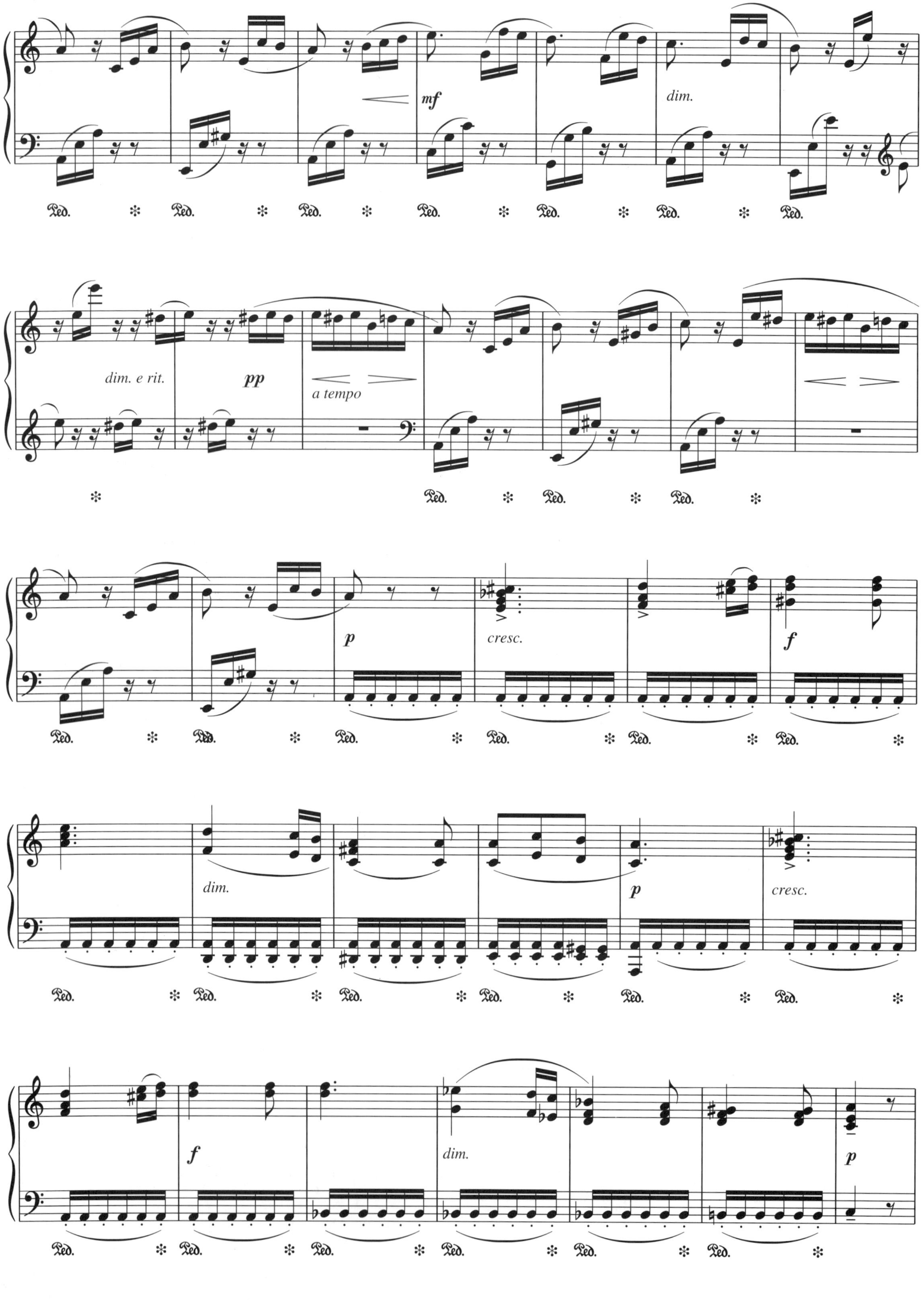
mf
dim.
dim. e rit.
pp
a tempo
p
cresc.
f
dim.
p
cresc.
f
dim.
p

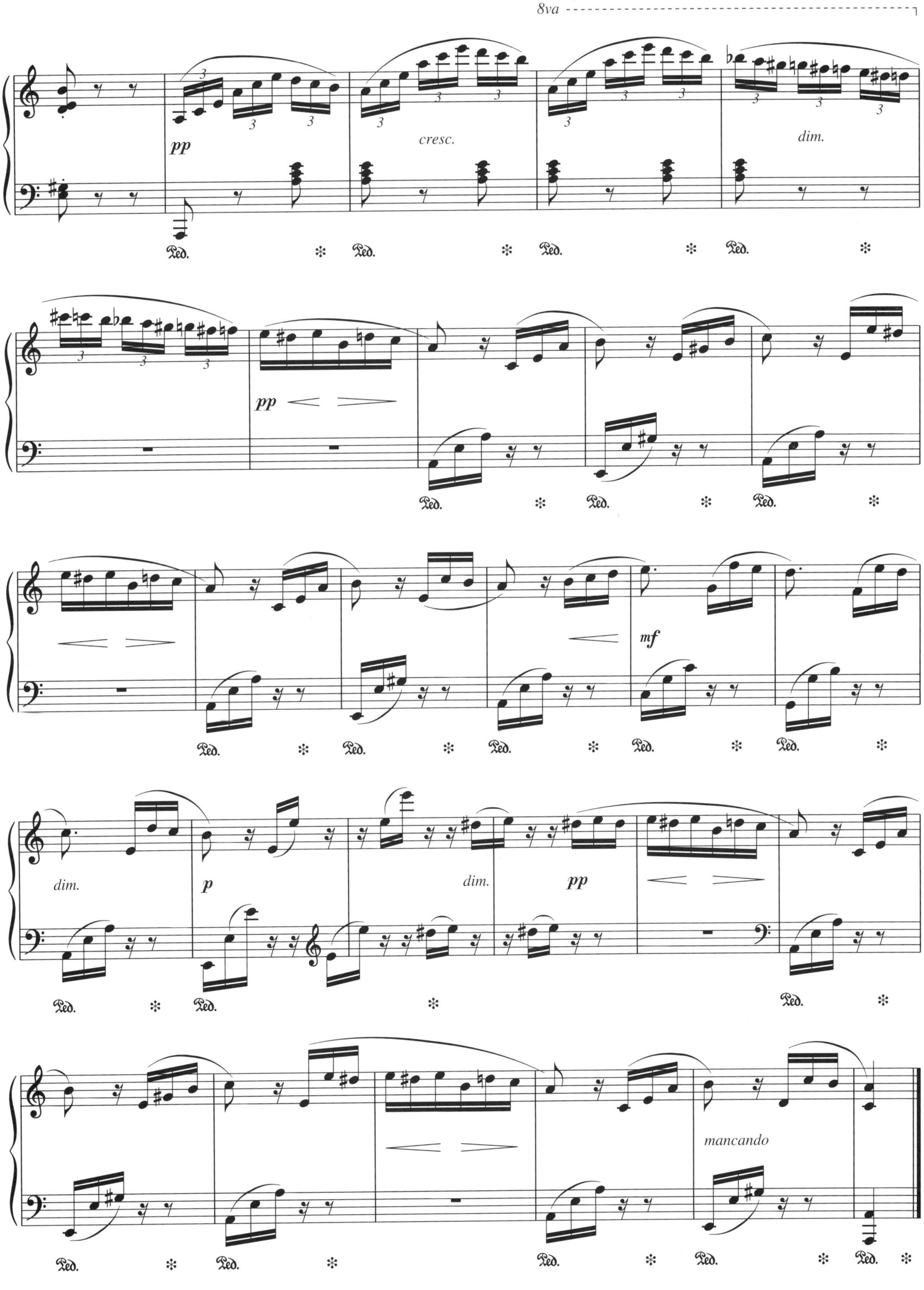
8va
pp
cresc.
dim.
pp
mf
dim.
p
dim.
pp
mancando

Piano Concerto No. 5

"Emperor"
First Movement Excerpt

Ludwig van Beethoven
1770-1827
Op. 73
originally for piano and orchestra

Allegro

original key: E-flat Major

41

Symphony No. 3
"Eroica"
First Movement Excerpt

Ludwig van Beethoven
1770–1827
Op. 55
originally for orchestra

Allegro con brio

original key: E-flat Major

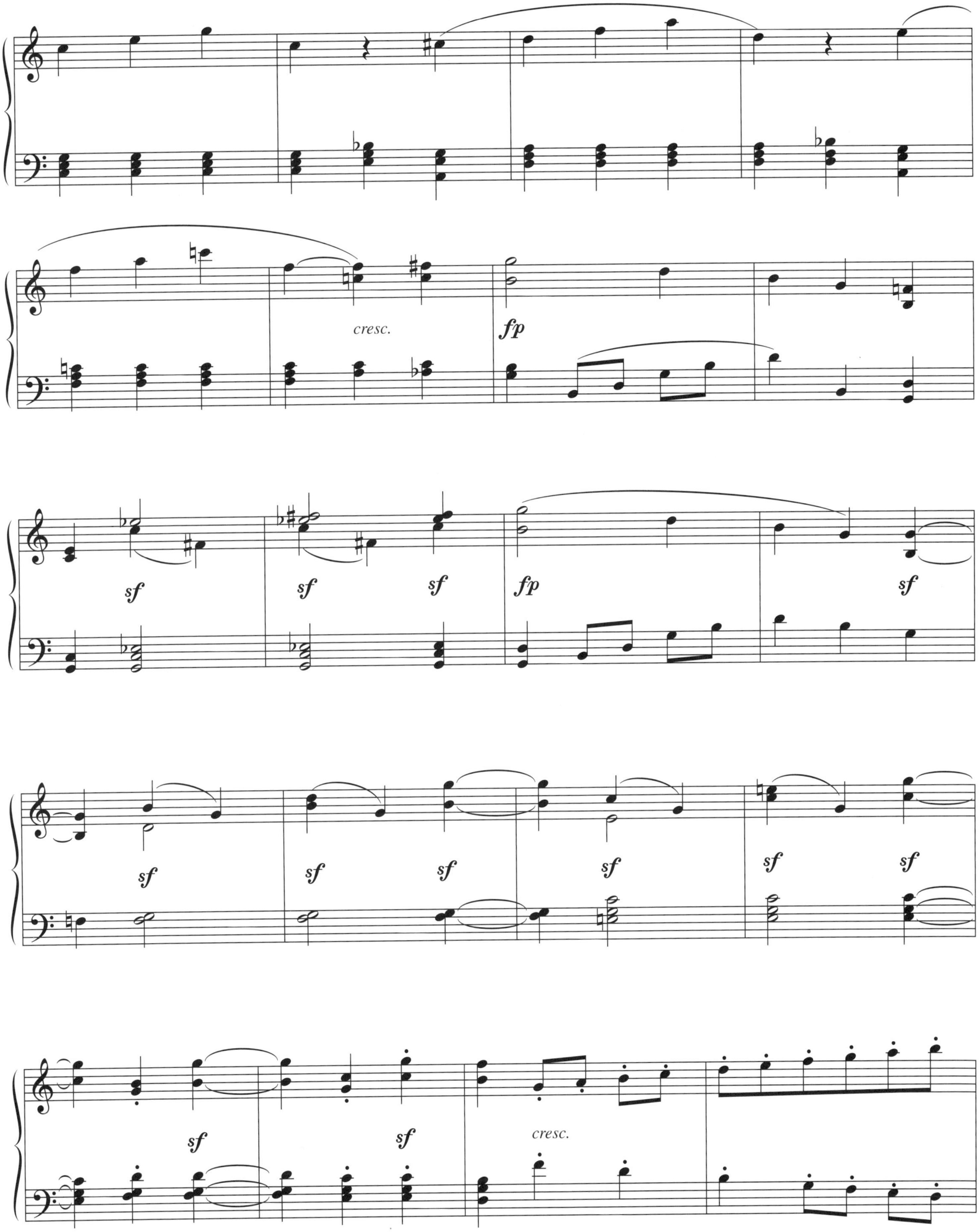
cresc.
fp
sf
sf
sf
fp
sf
sf
sf
sf
sf
sf
sf
sf
sf
cresc.

44

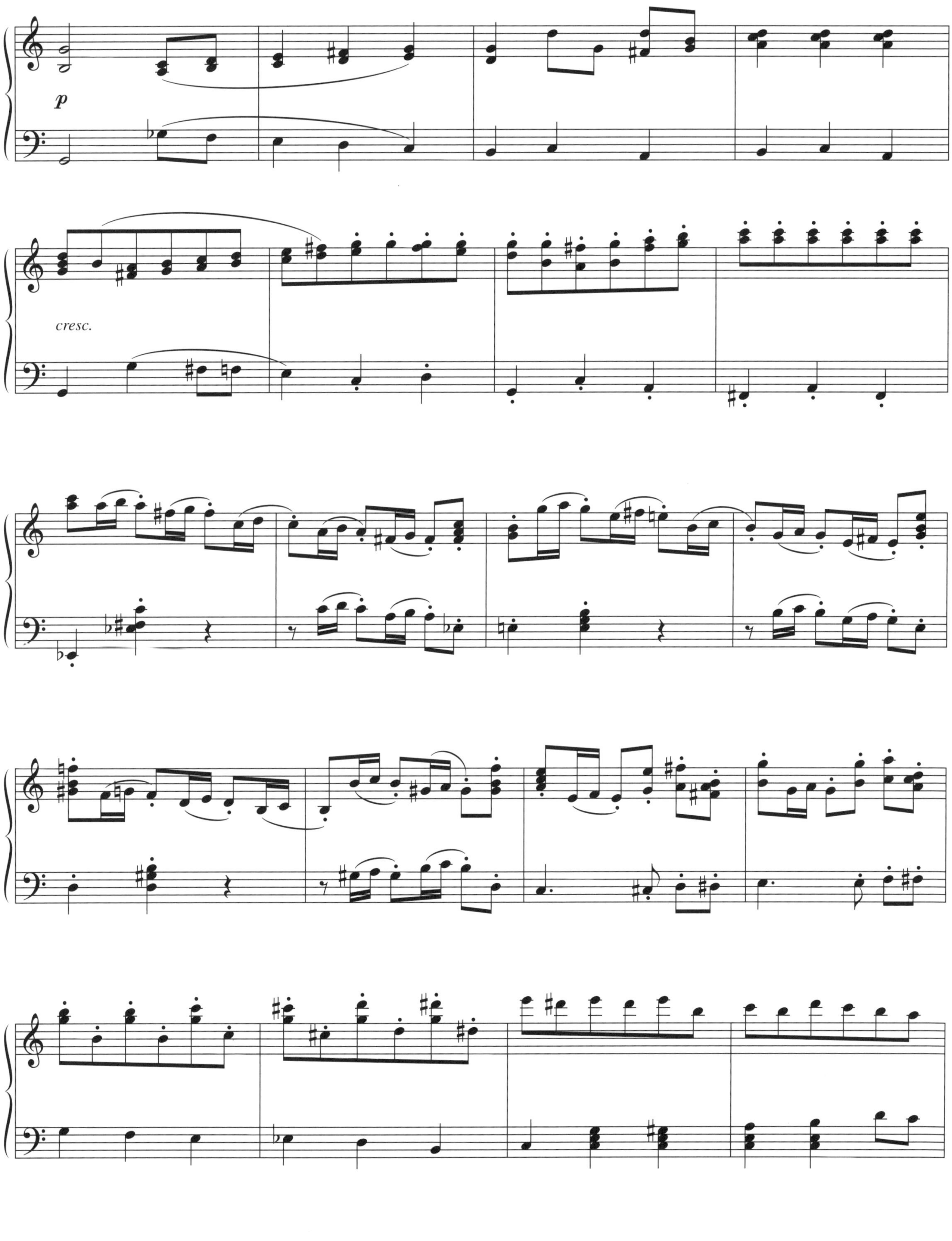
p
cresc.

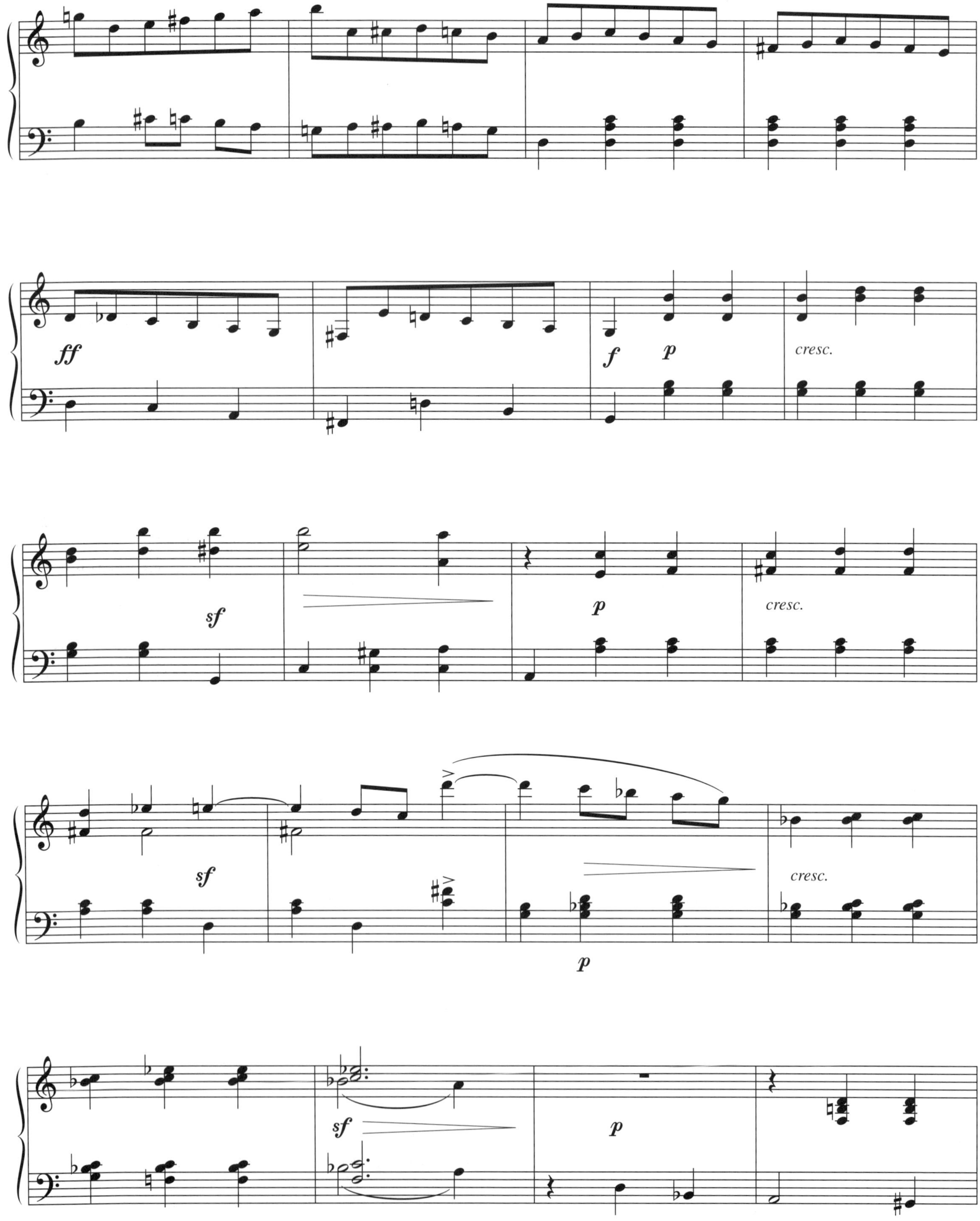
ff
f
p
cresc.
sf
p
cresc.
sf
p
cresc.
sf
p

47

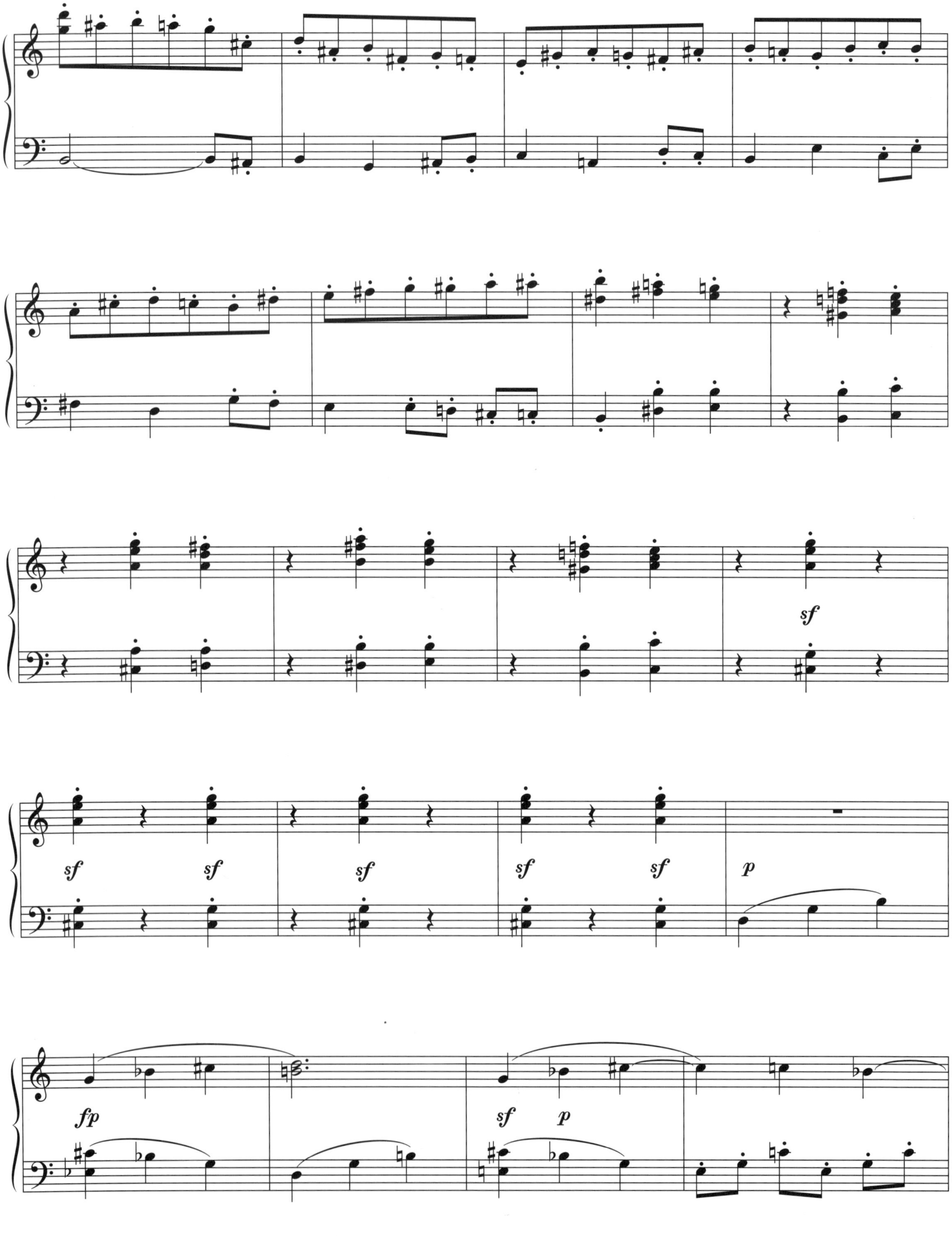
sf
sf
sf
sf
sf
sf
p
fp
sf
p

49

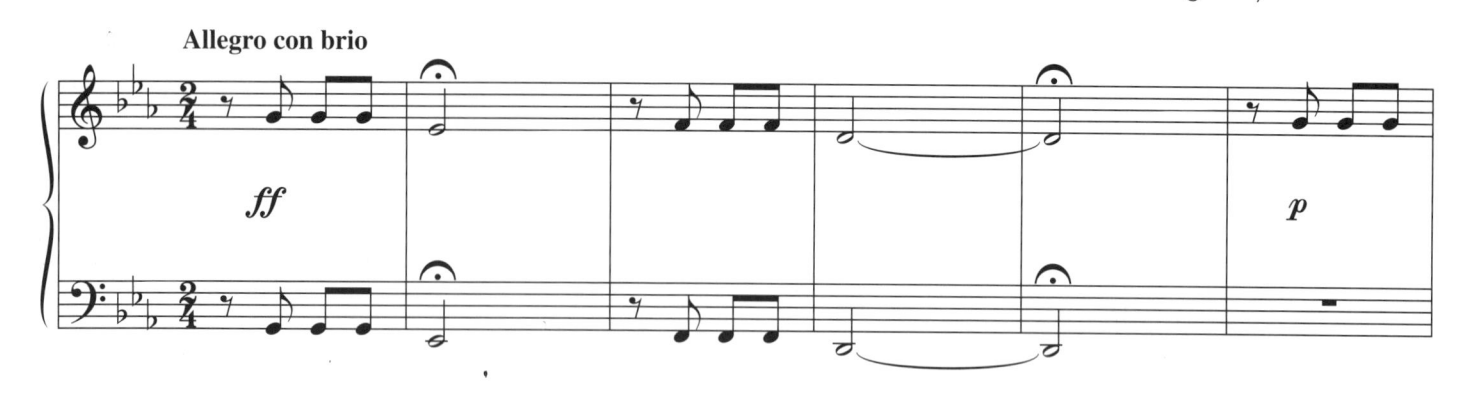

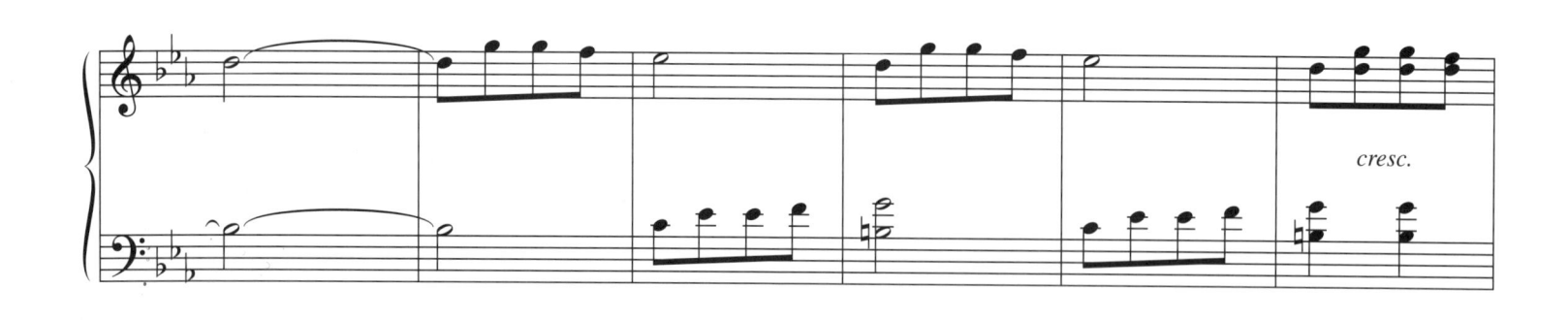

Symphony No. 5
First Movement Excerpt

Ludwig van Beethoven
1770–1827
Op. 67
originally for orchestra

Allegro con brio

51

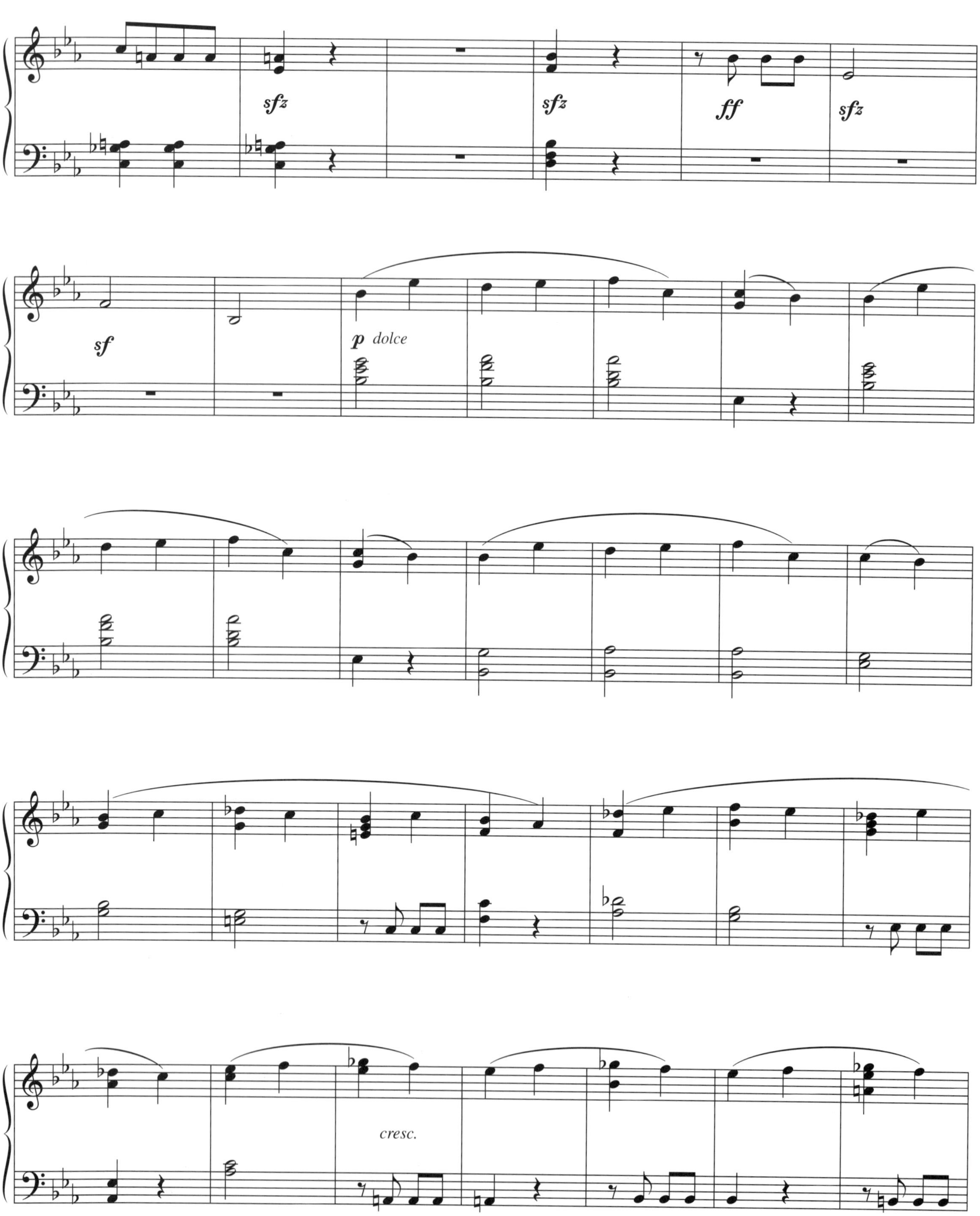
sfz
sfz
ff
sfz
sf
p dolce
cresc.

53

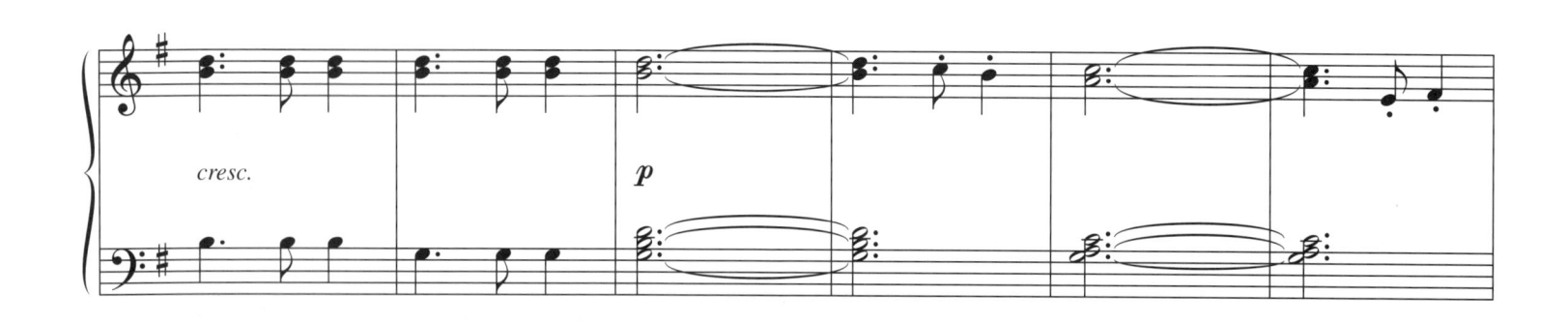

Symphony No. 7

First Movement Excerpt

Ludwig van Beethoven
1770-1827
Op. 92
originally for orchestra

original key: A Major

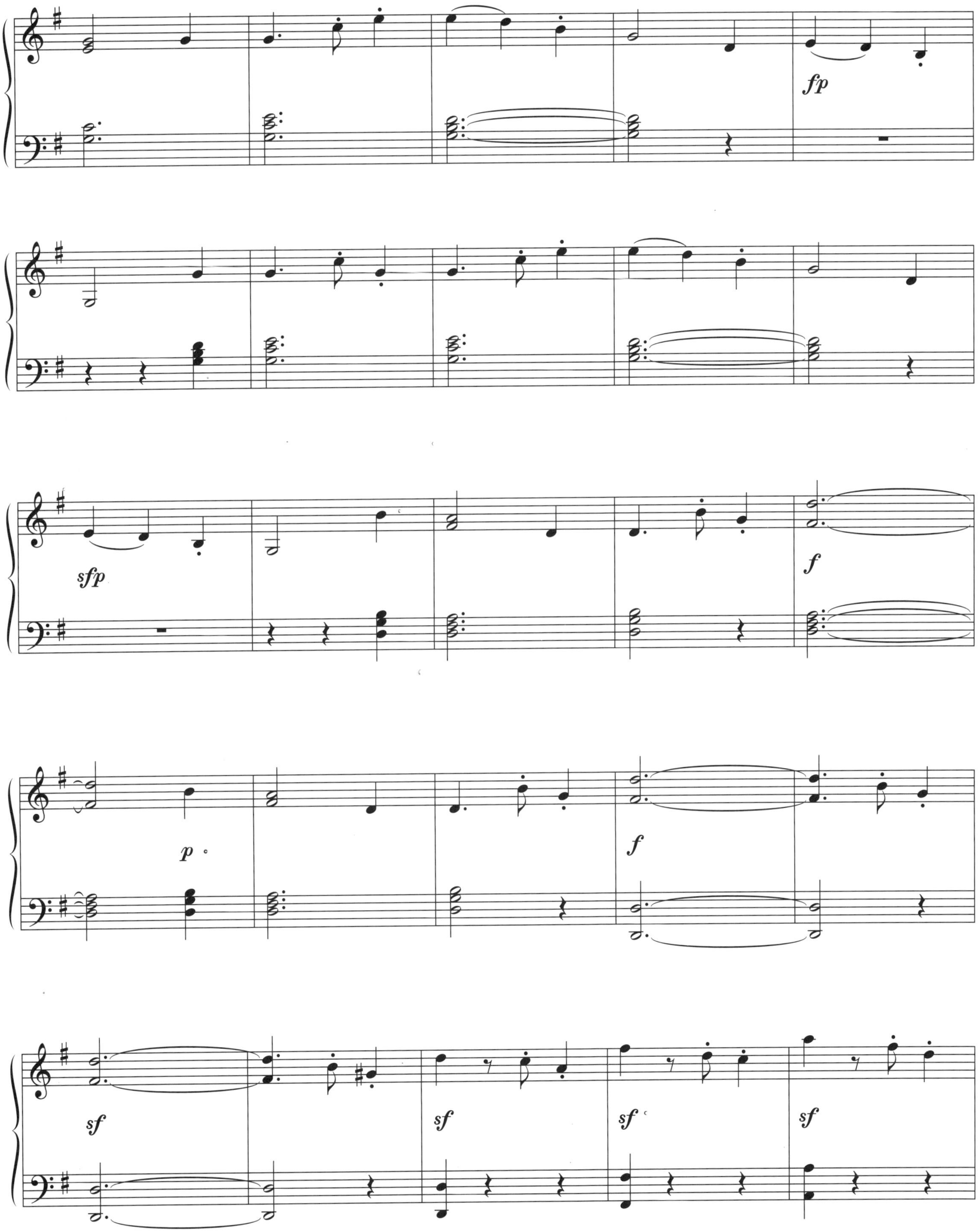
fp
sfp
f
p
f
sf
sf
sf
sf

56

57

58

59

Symphony No. 7
Second Movement Excerpt

Ludwig van Beethoven
1770-1827
Op. 92
originally for orchestra

Allegretto

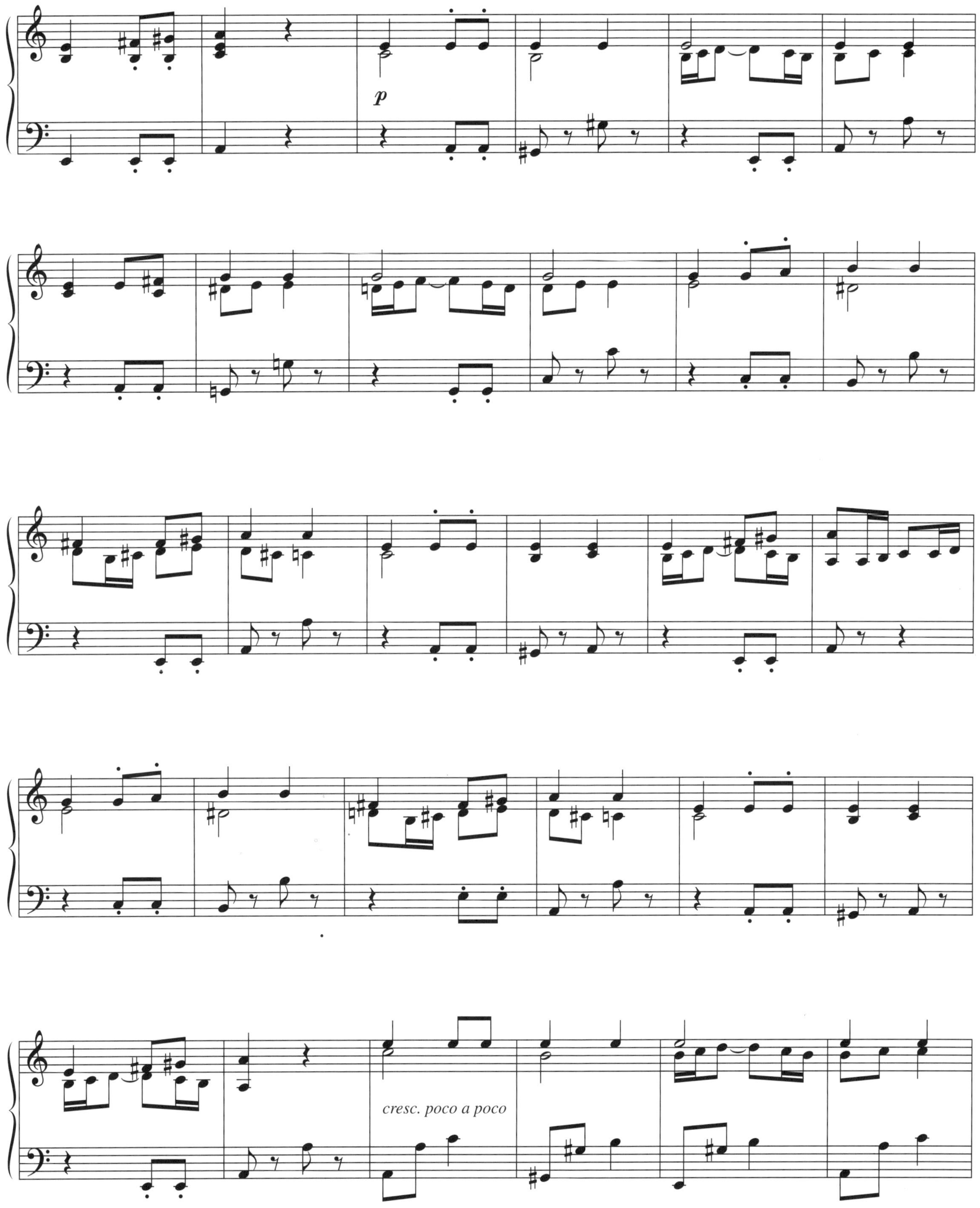
p
cresc. poco a poco

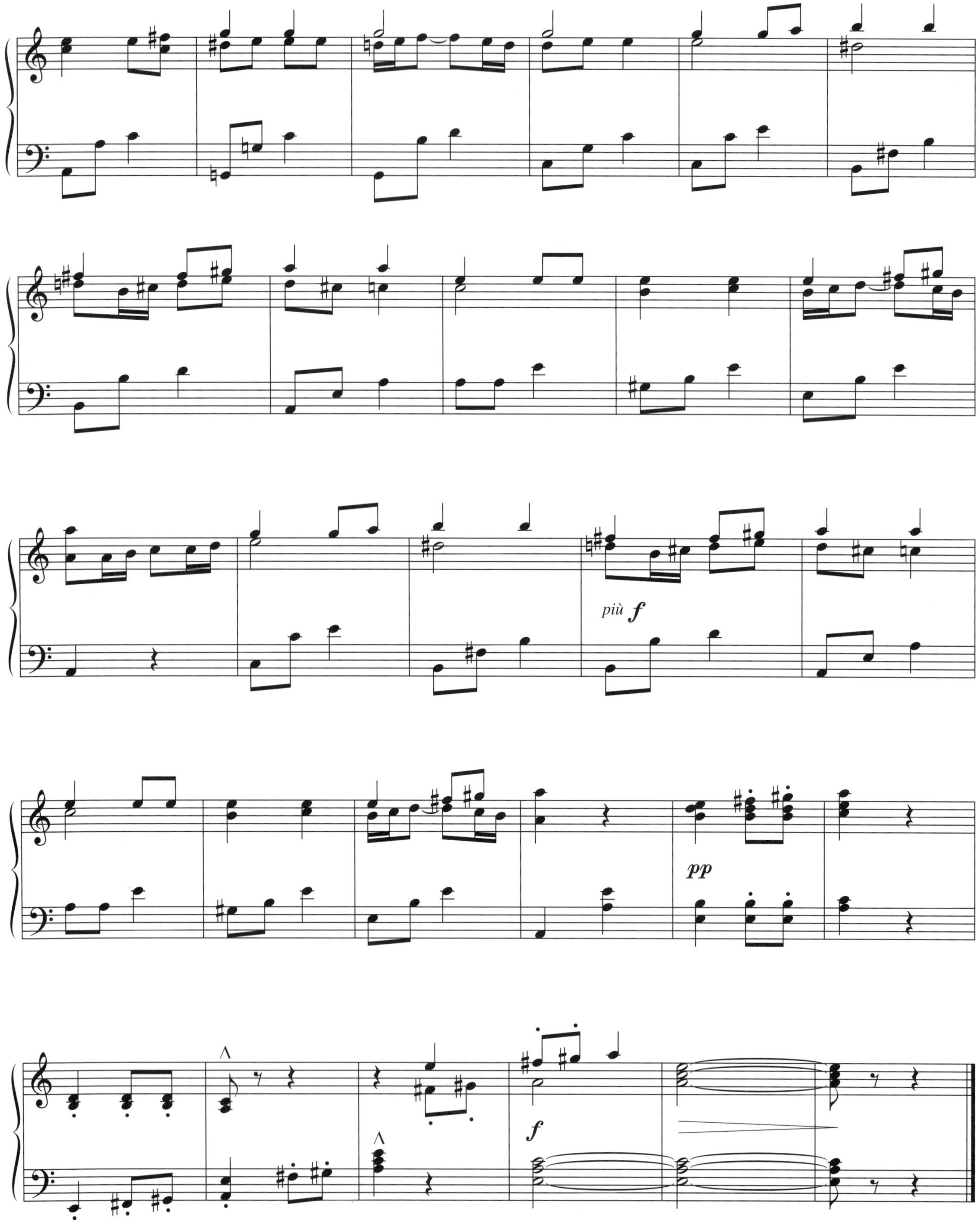
più f
pp
f

Symphony No. 9

Fourth Movement Excerpt
"Ode to Joy"

Ludwig van Beethoven
1770-1827
Op. 125
originally for chorus and orchestra

Allegro assai vivace

original key: D Major

Copyright © 2000 by HAL LEONARD CORPORATION
International Copyright Secured   All Rights Reserved

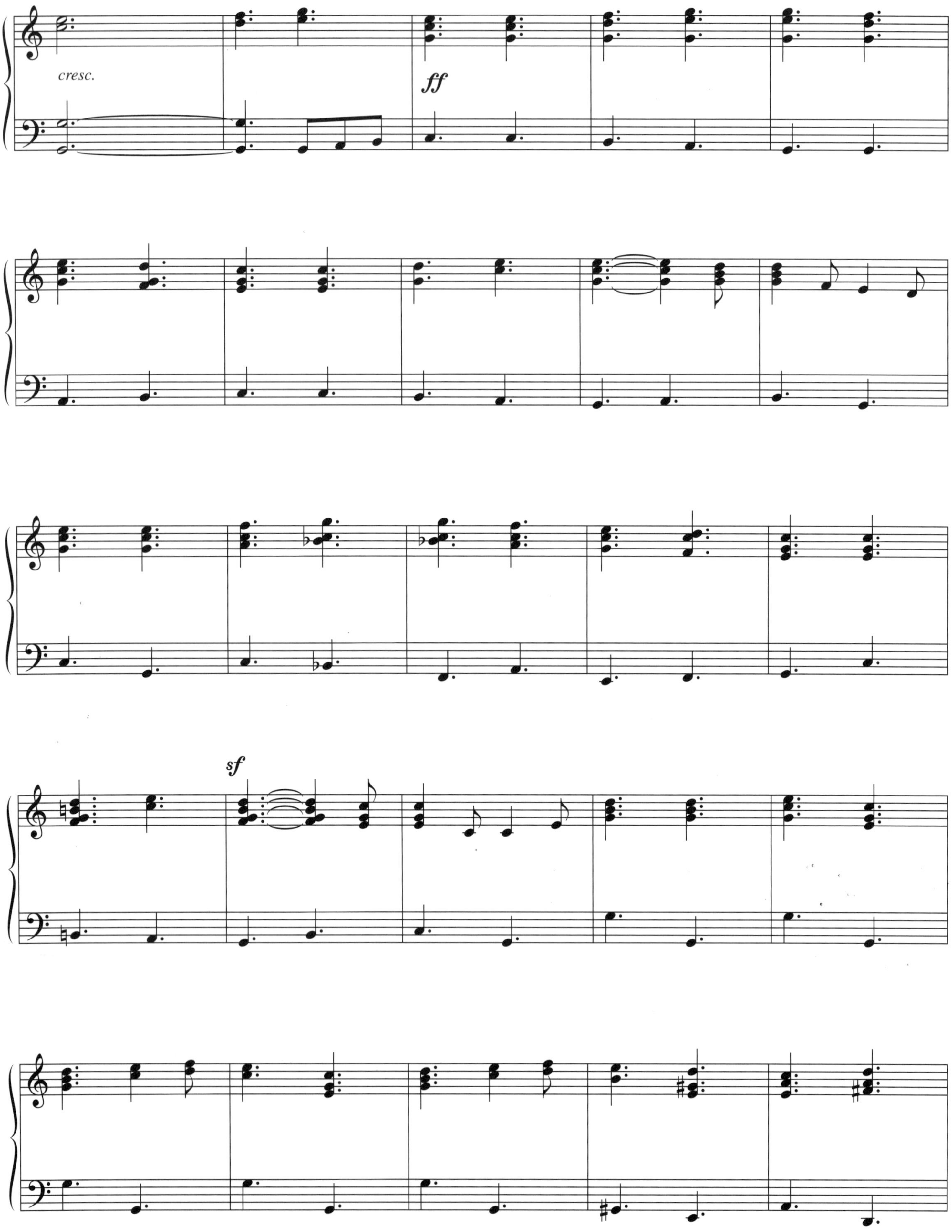
cresc.
ff
sf

65

Turkish March
from THE RUINS OF ATHENS

Ludwig van Beethoven
1770-1827
Op. 113
originally for orchestra

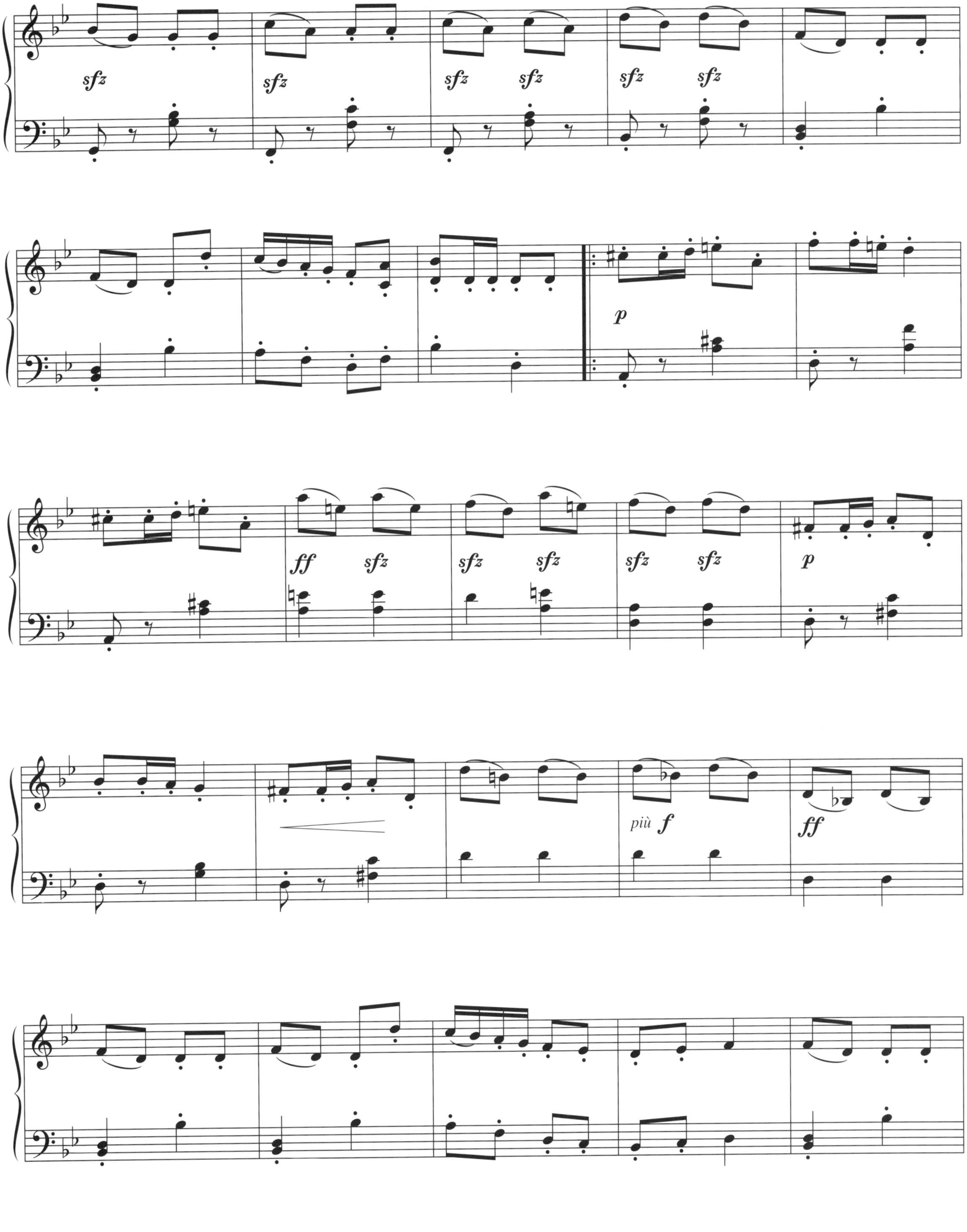
sfz
sfz
sfz sfz
sfz sfz
p
ff sfz
sfz sfz
sfz sfz
p
più f
ff

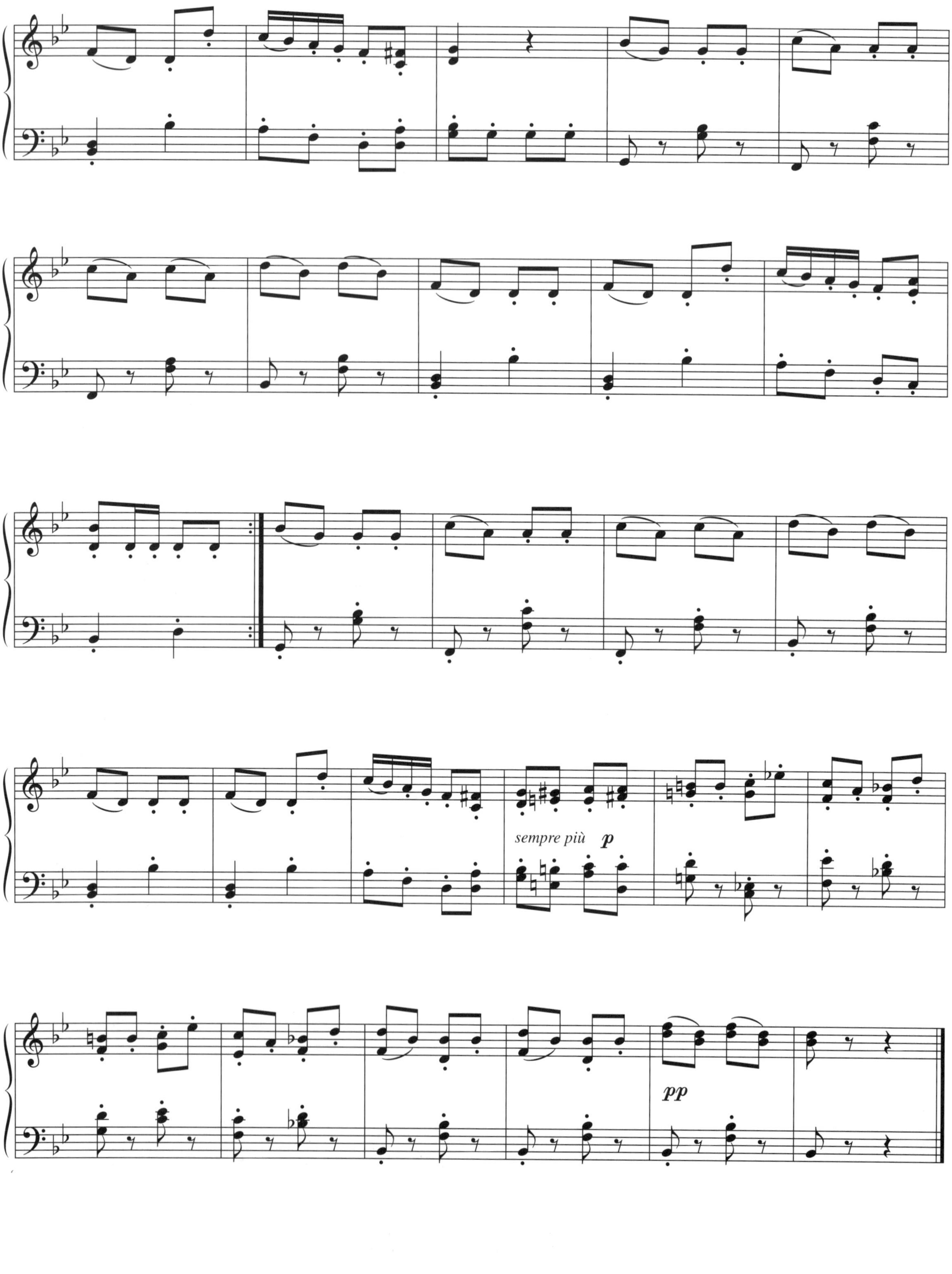
sempre più p
pp

Violin Concerto
First Movement Excerpt

Ludwig van Beethoven
1770-1827
Op. 61
originally for violin and orchestra

Allegro, ma non troppo

original key: D Major

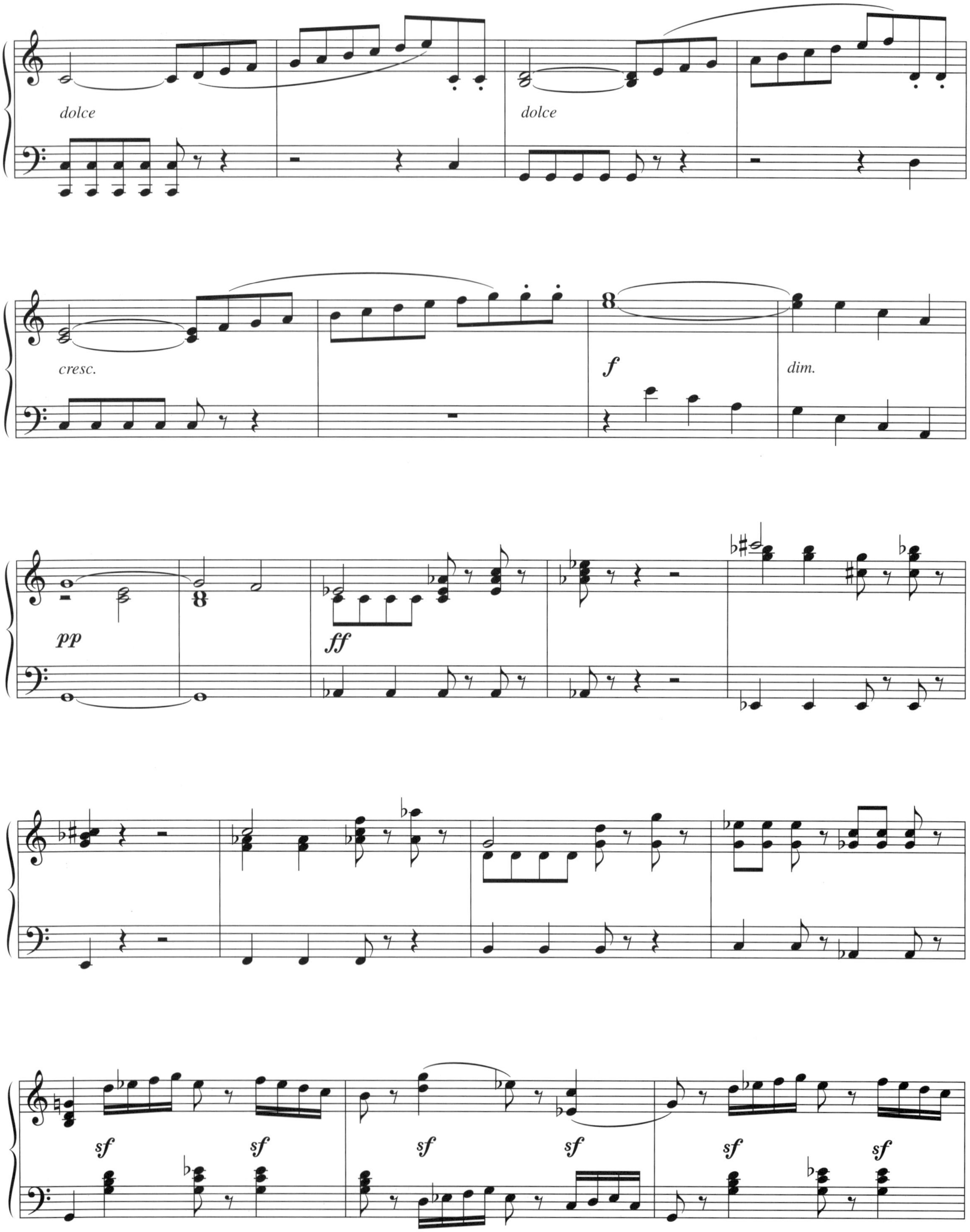
dolce
dolce
cresc.
f
dim.
pp
ff
sf
sf
sf
sf
sf
sf

71

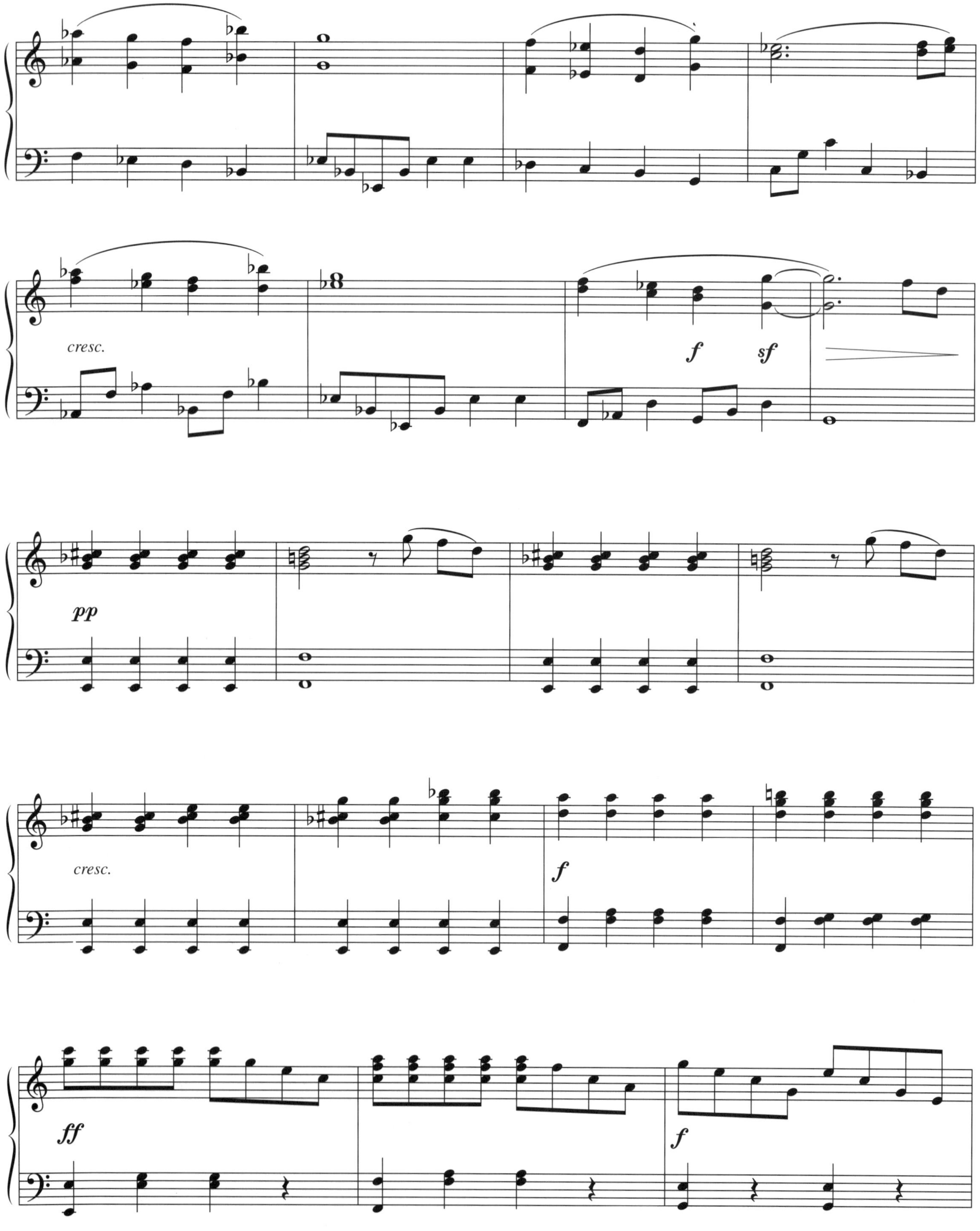
cresc.
f
sf
pp
cresc.
f
ff
f

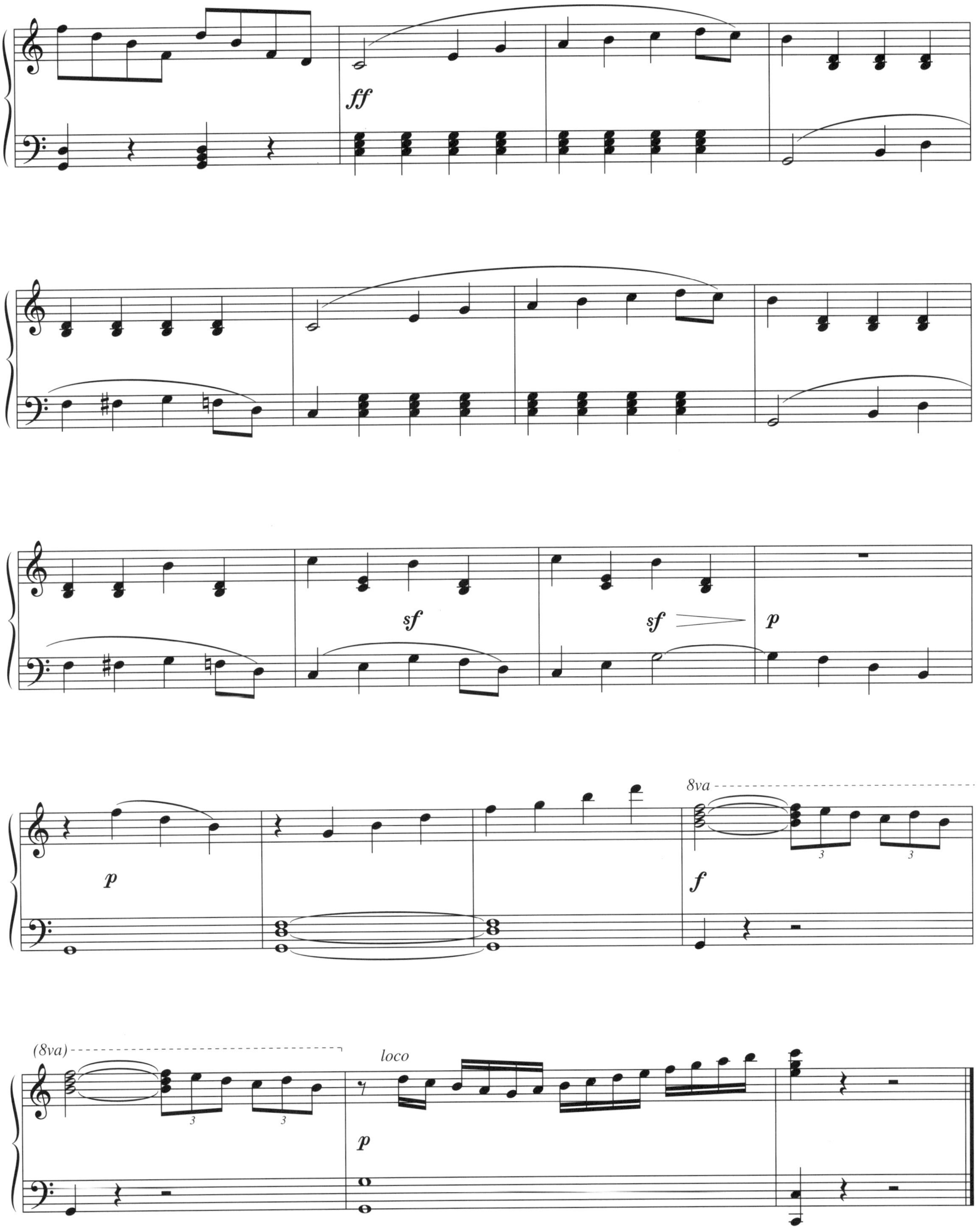
ff
sf
sf
p
p
8va
f
3
(8va)
loco
p

Habanera
from the opera CARMEN

Georges Bizet
1838–1875

75

Toreador Song
from the opera CARMEN

Georges Bizet
1838–1875

Allegro moderato

77

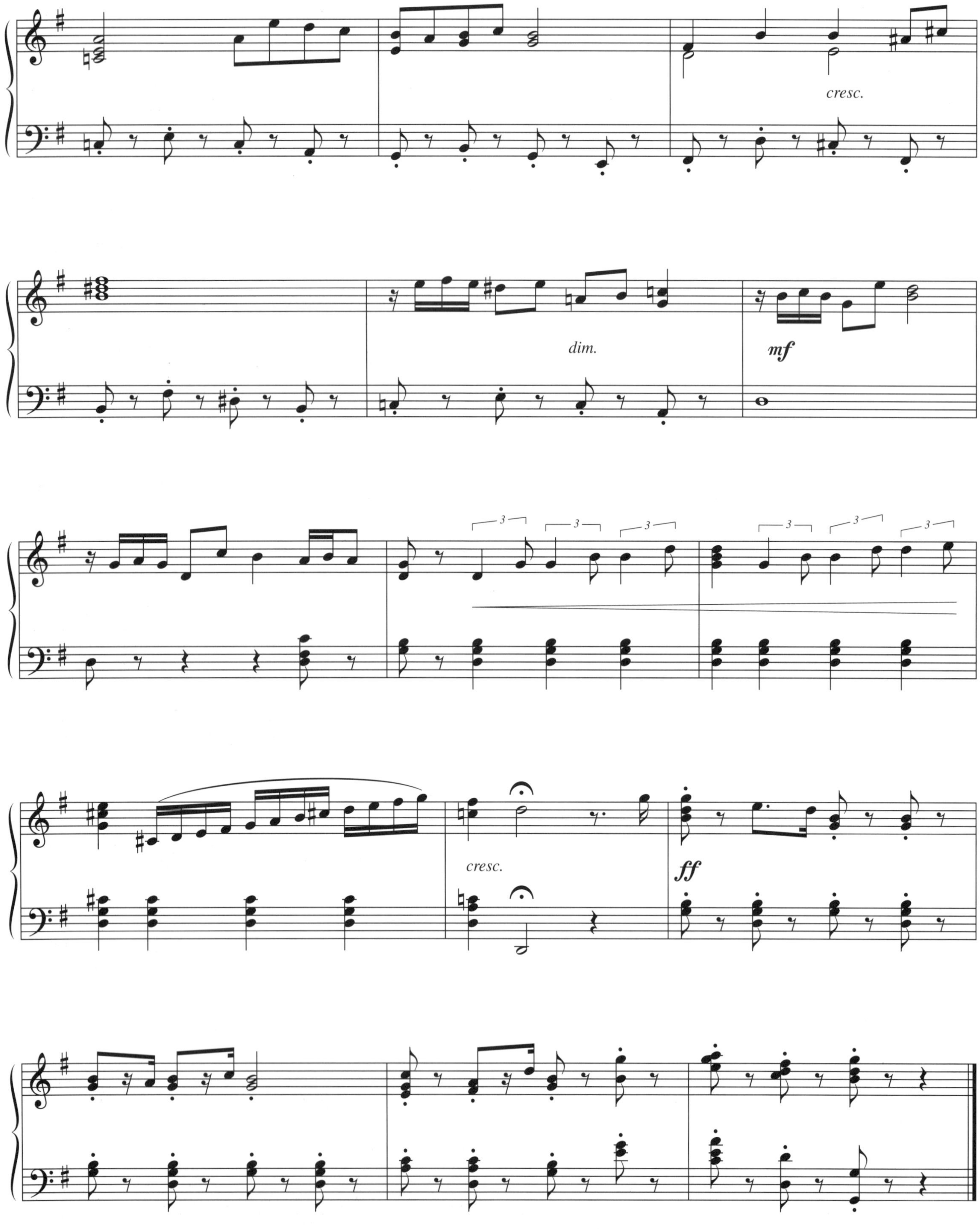
cresc.
dim.
mf
cresc.
ff

# Polovetzian Dances
from the opera PRINCE IGOR
First Theme

Alexander Borodin
1833-1887
originally for orchestra

original key: A Major

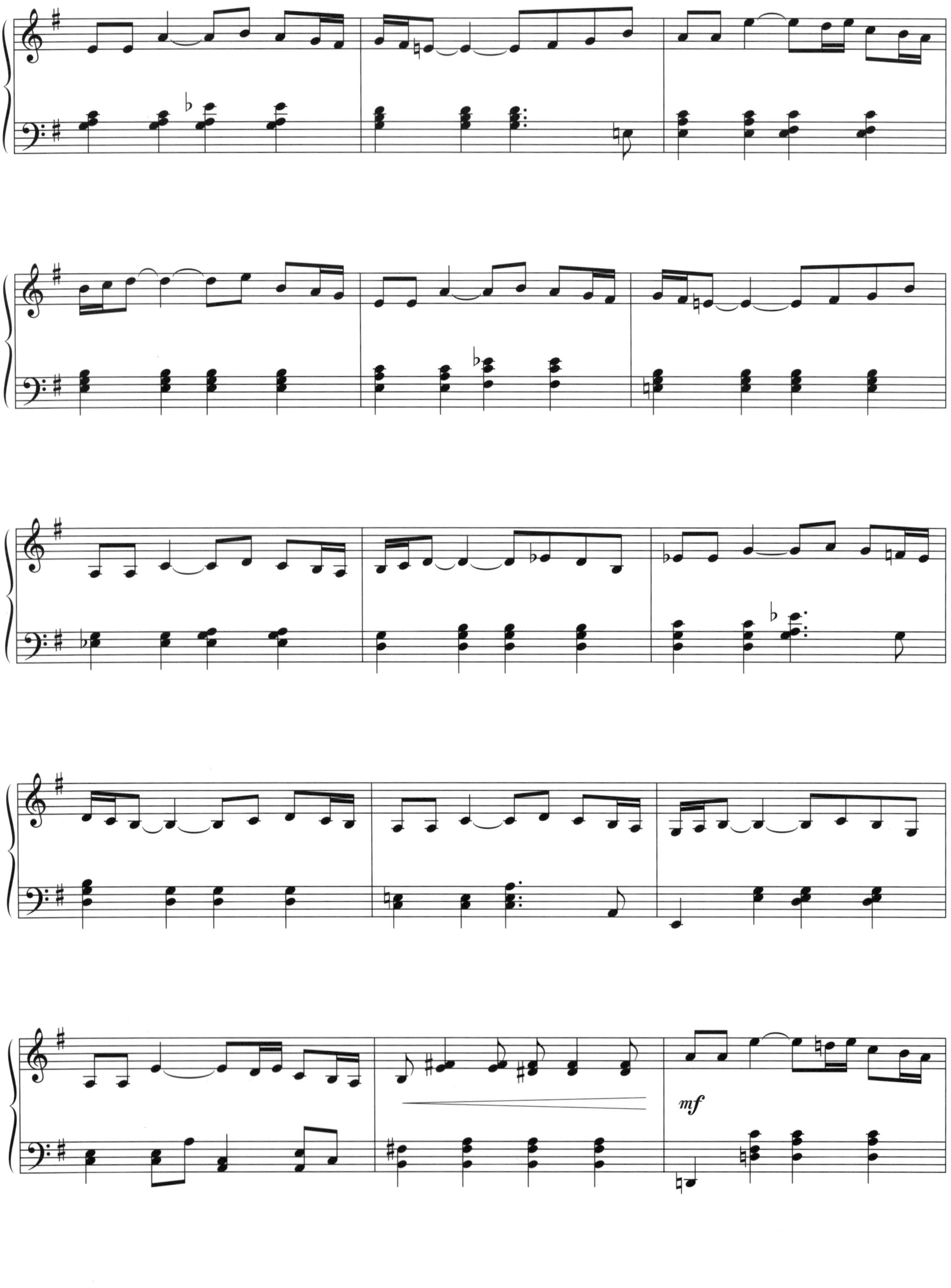
mf

81

Lullaby
(Wiegenlied)

Johannes Brahms
1830–1897
Op. 49, No. 4
originally for voice and piano

Dolce, con moto

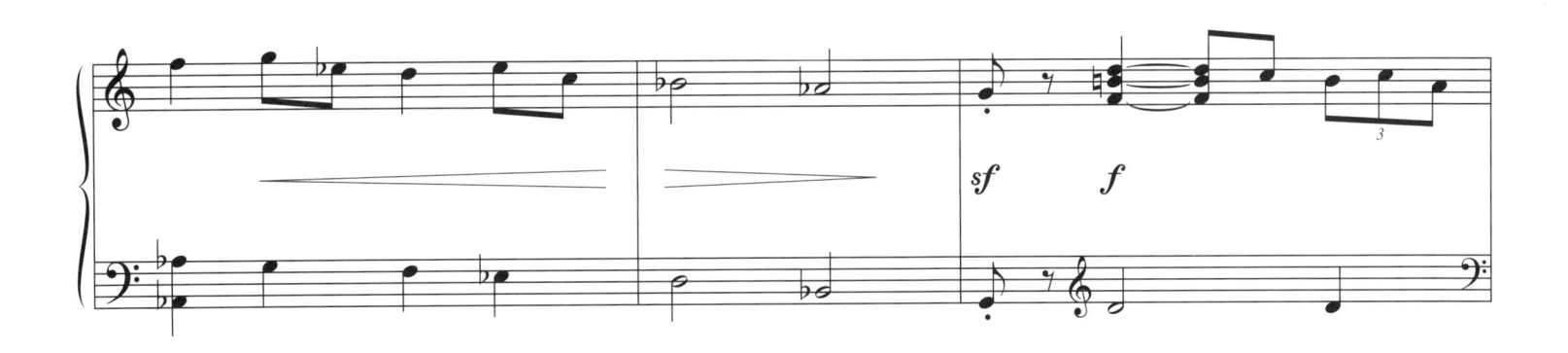

Piano Concerto No. 2

First Movement Excerpt

Johannes Brahms
1830-1897
Op. 83
originally for piano and orchestra

Allegro non troppo

original key: B-flat Major

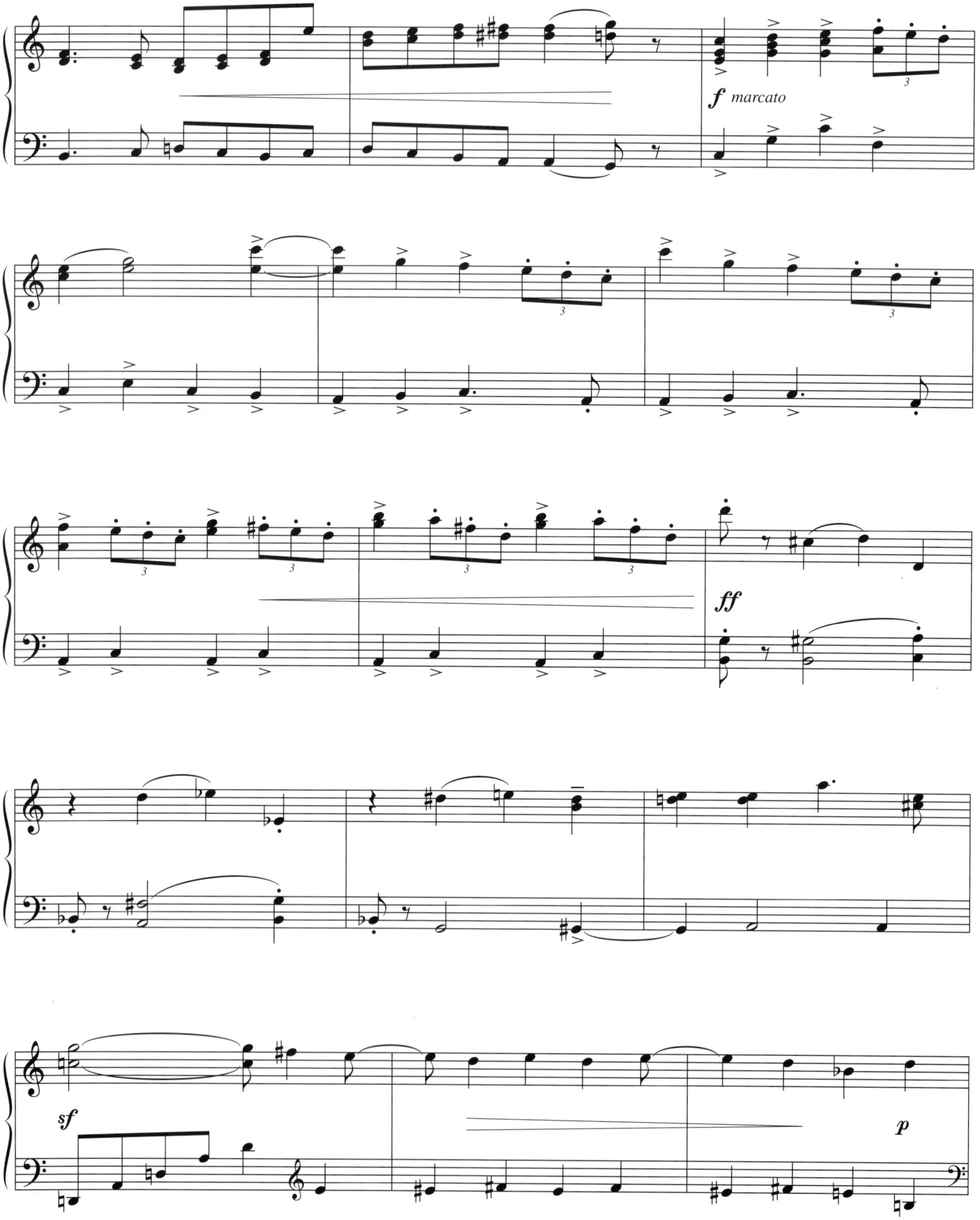
f marcato
ff
sf
p

85

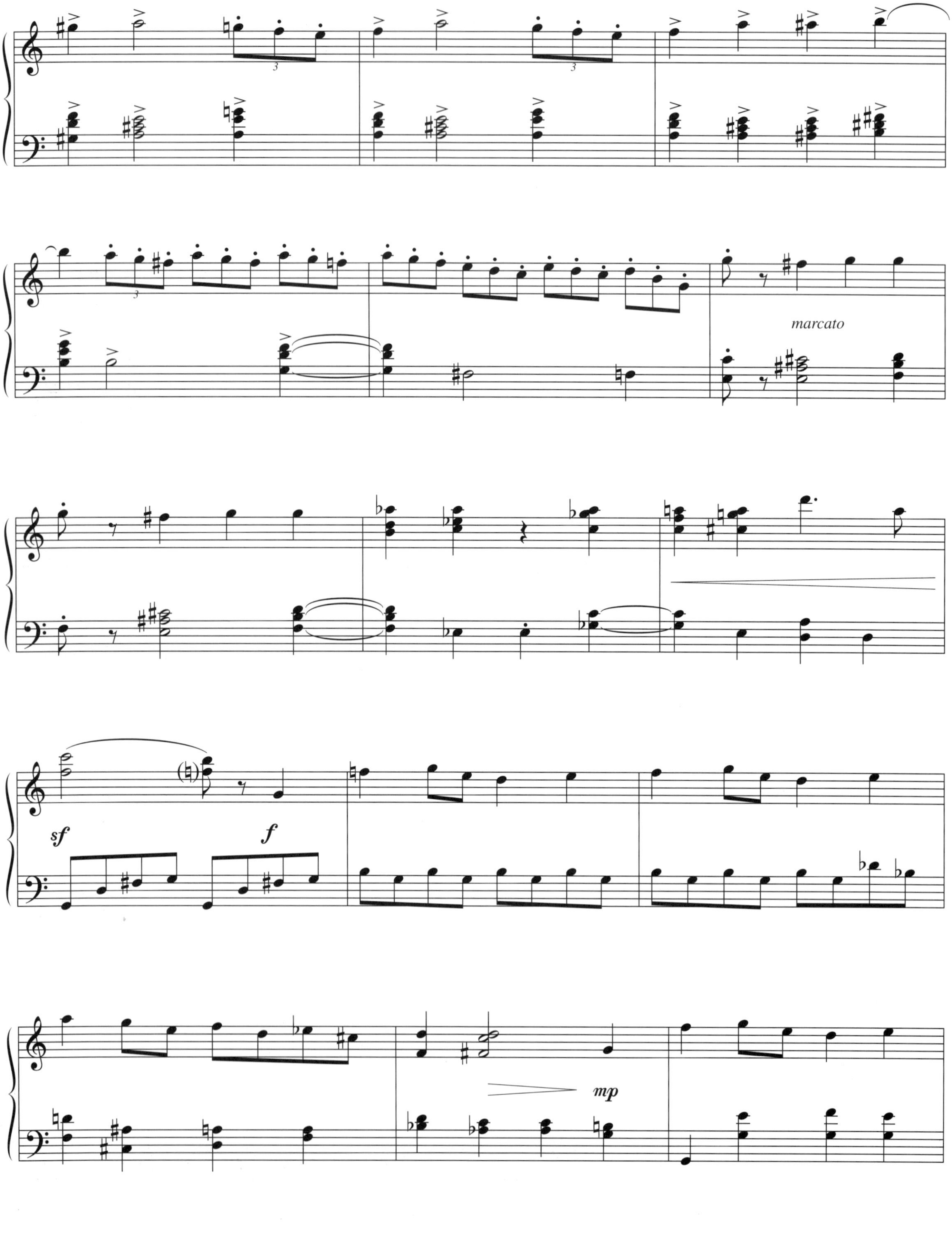

marcato
sf
f
mp

87

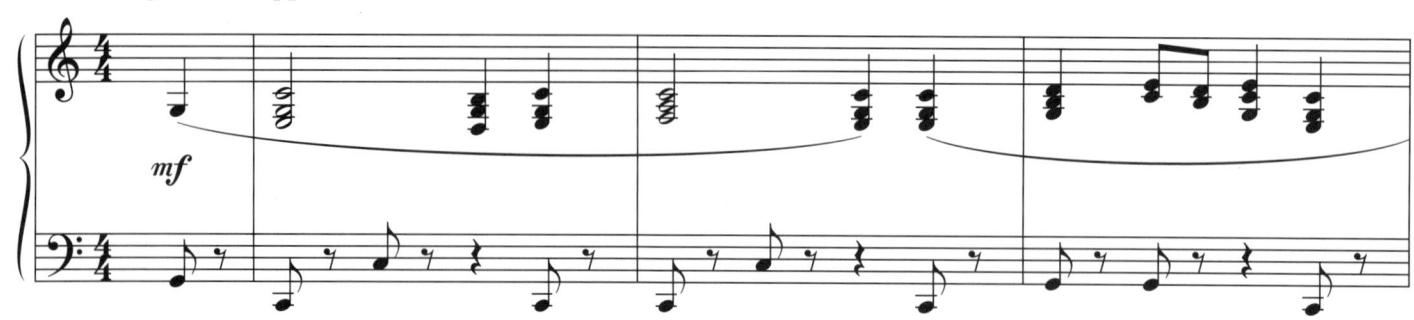

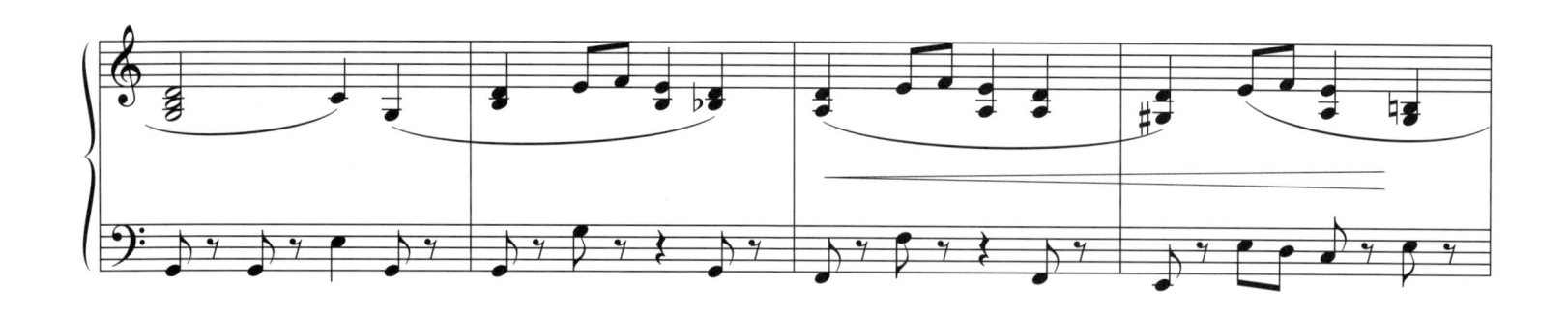

Symphony No. 1
Fourth Movement Excerpt

Johannes Brahms
1830–1897
Op. 68
originally for orchestra

Allegro non troppo ma con brio

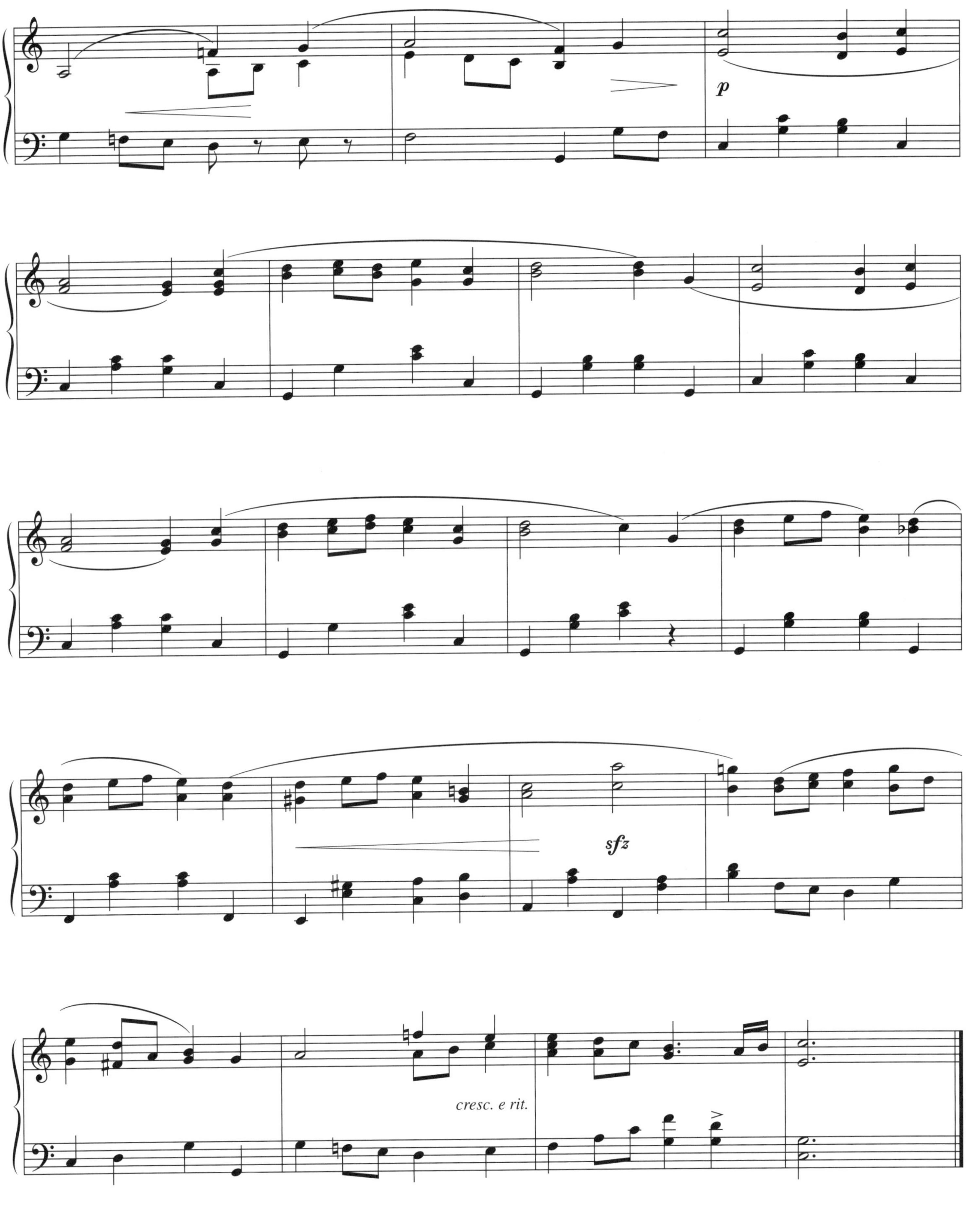
p
sfz
cresc. e rit.

Symphony No. 3
Third Movement Excerpt

Johannes Brahms
1830-1897
Op. 90
originally for orchestra

Poco Allegretto

original key: C Minor

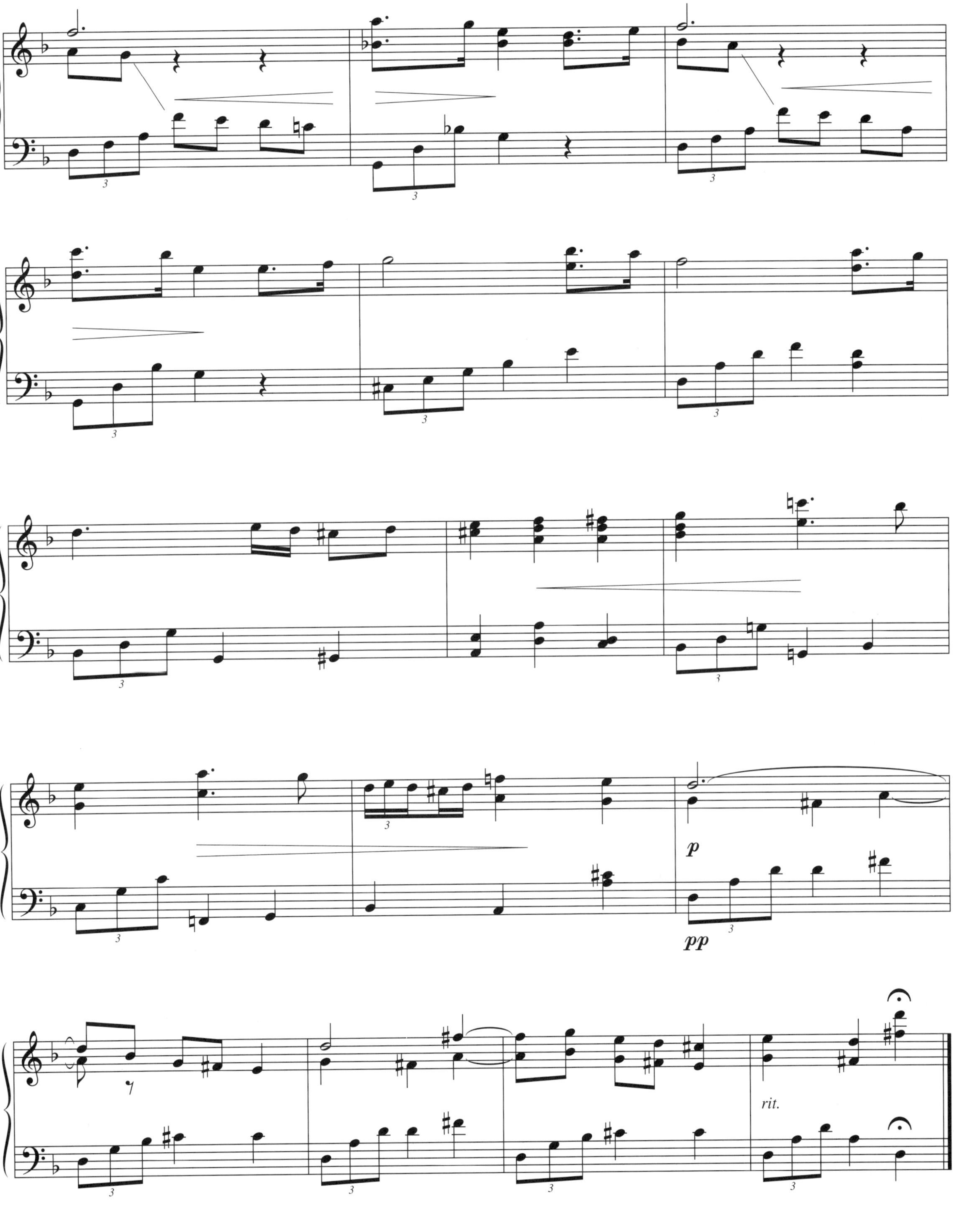
p
pp
rit.

Symphony No. 4

First Movement Excerpt

Johannes Brahms
1830-1897
Op. 98
originally for orchestra

Allegro non troppo

93

Waltz in A-flat Major

Fryderyk Chopin
1810-1849
Op. 69, No. 1

Lento (♩ = 138)

p con espressione

95

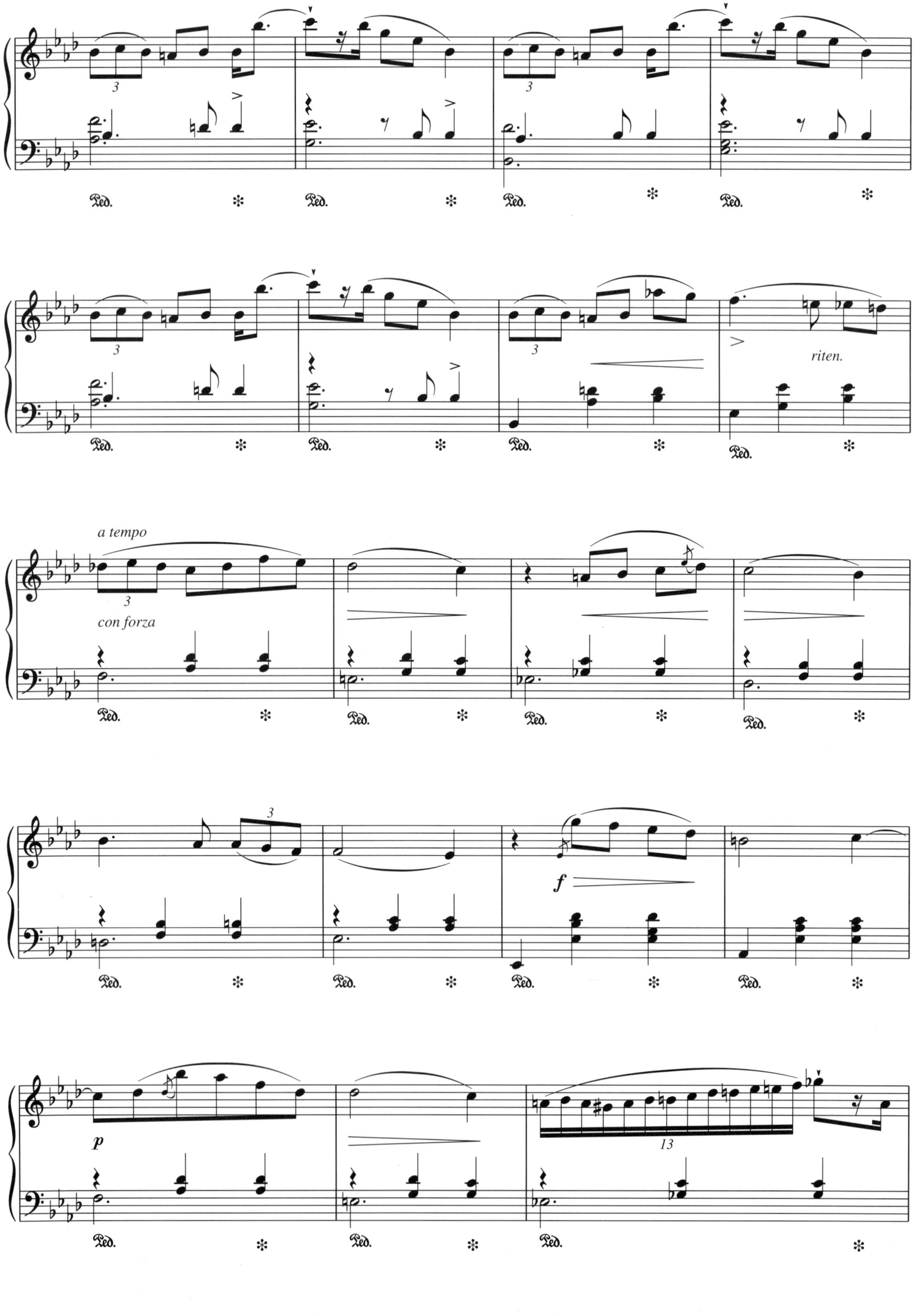

3
Ped.
riten.
a tempo
con forza
f
p
13

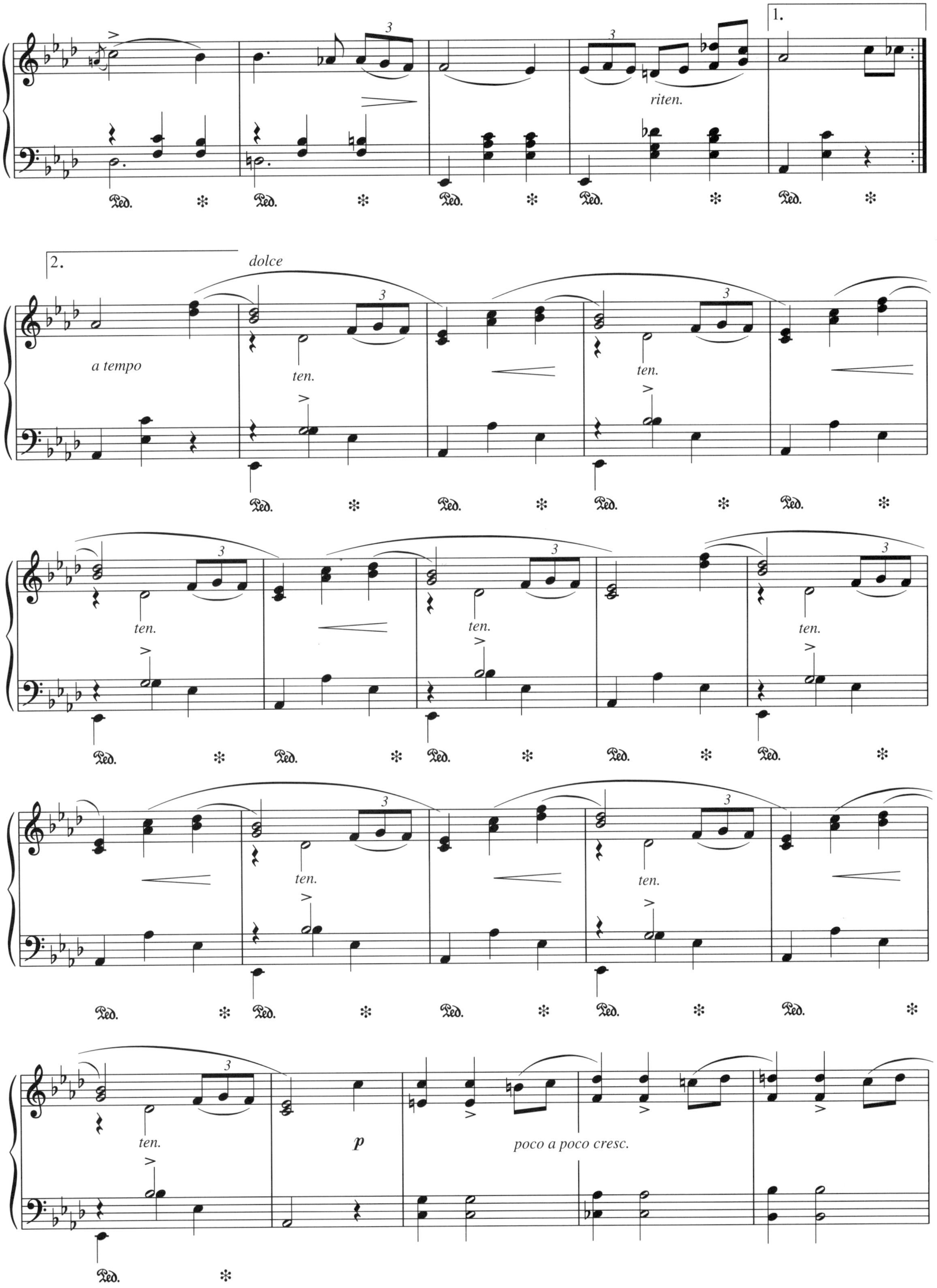
1.
riten.
2.
dolce
a tempo
ten.
p
poco a poco cresc.
Ped.

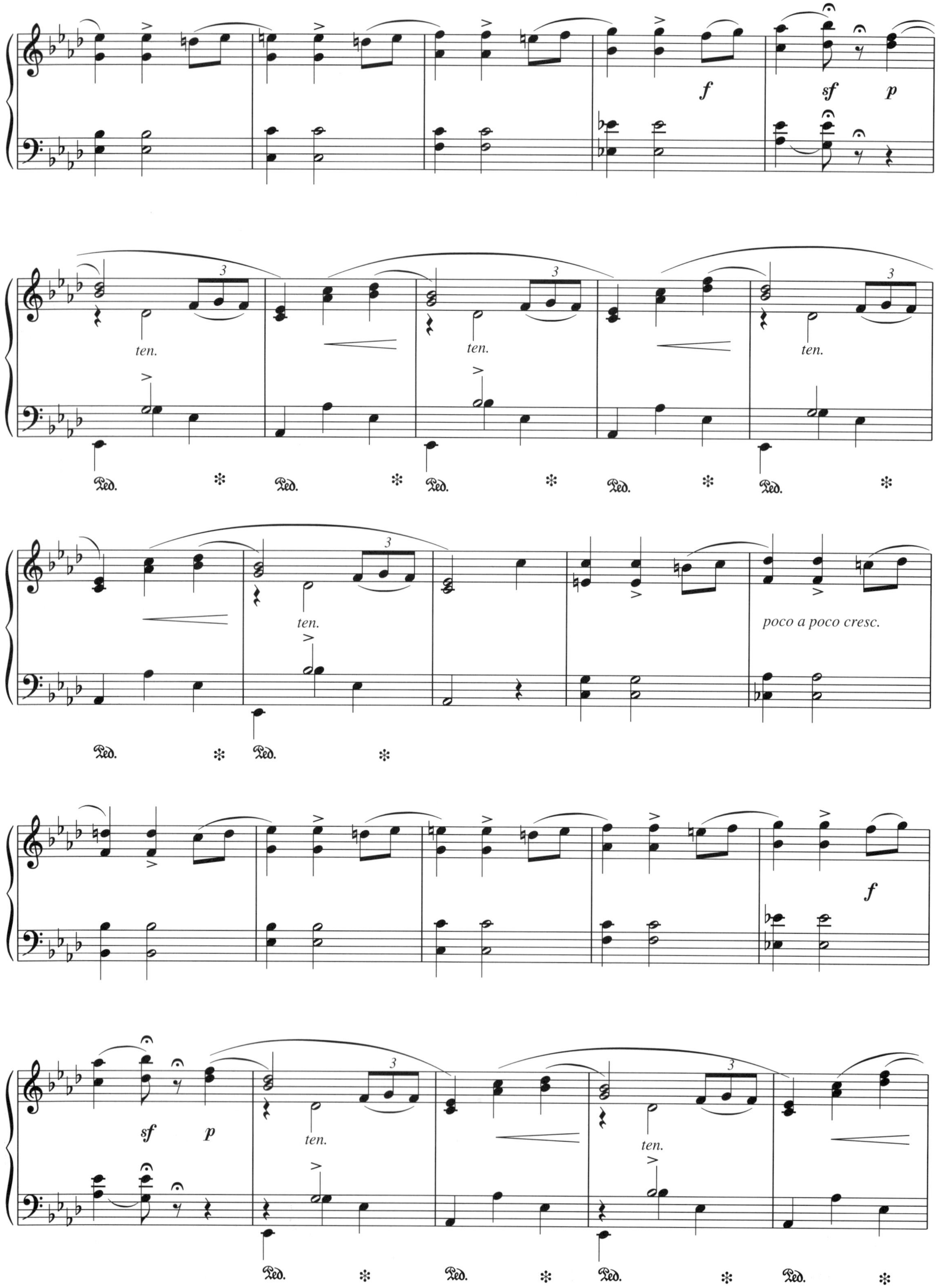
f
sf
p
ten.
Ped.
poco a poco cresc.

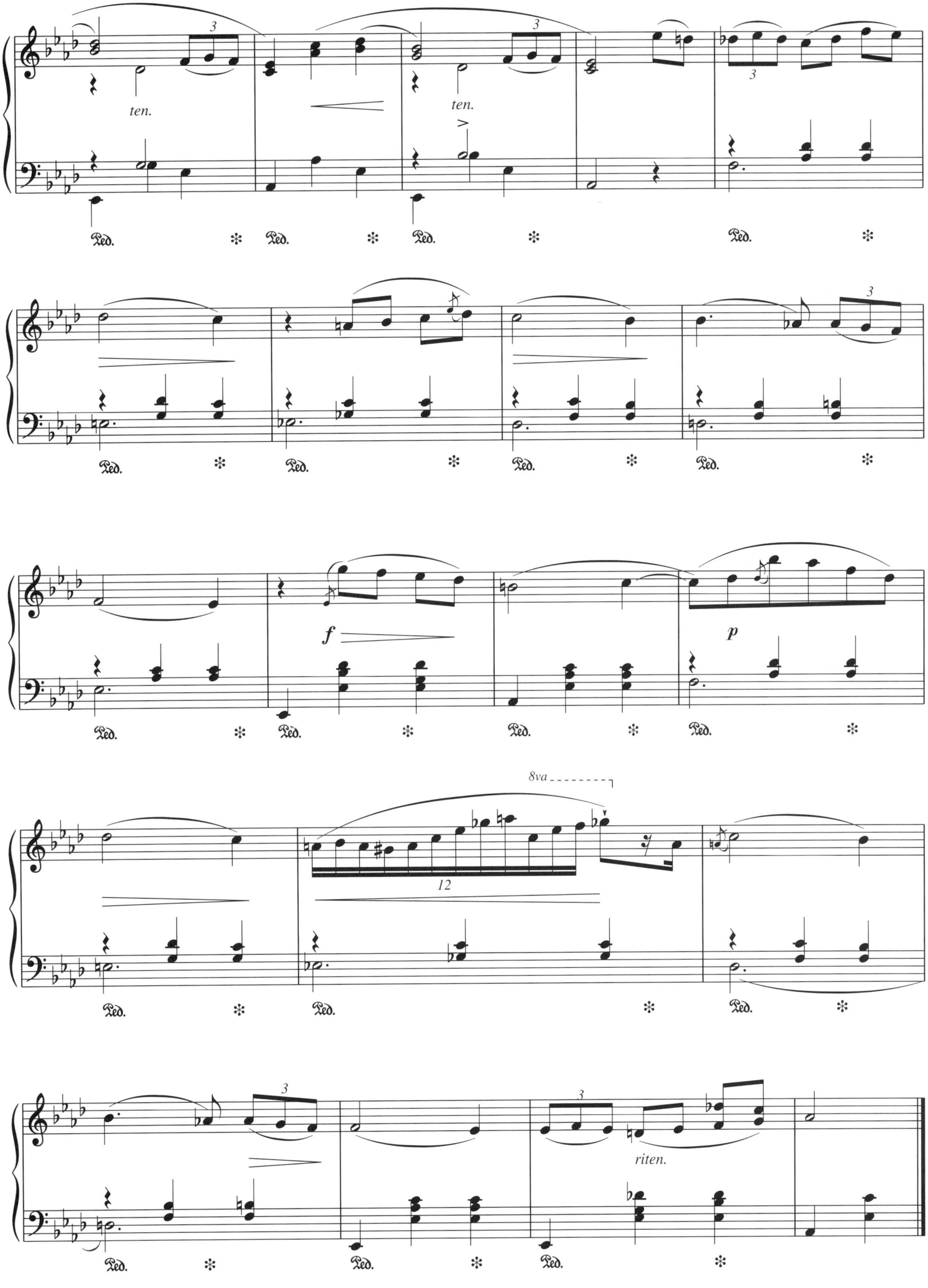
ten.
ten.
8va
riten.

Mazurka in E Minor

Fryderyk Chopin
1810–1849
Op. 17, No. 2

Lento, ma non troppo ♩ = 144

101

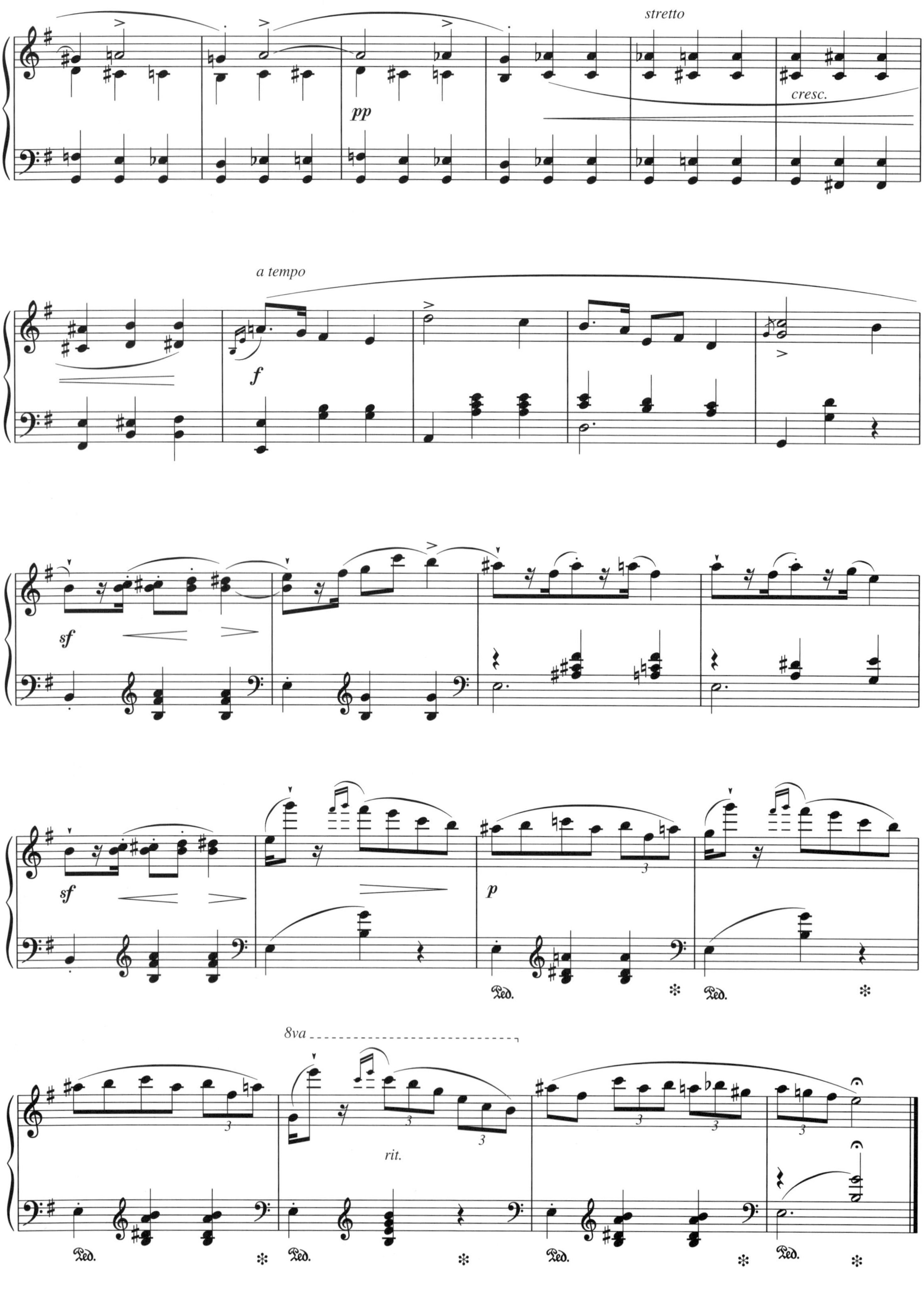
stretto
pp
cresc.
a tempo
f
sf
sf
p
Ped.
8va
rit.

Prelude in A Major

Fryderyk Chopin
1810–1849
Op. 28, No. 7

Andantino

Prelude in E Minor

Fryderyk Chopin
1810–1849
Op. 28, No. 4

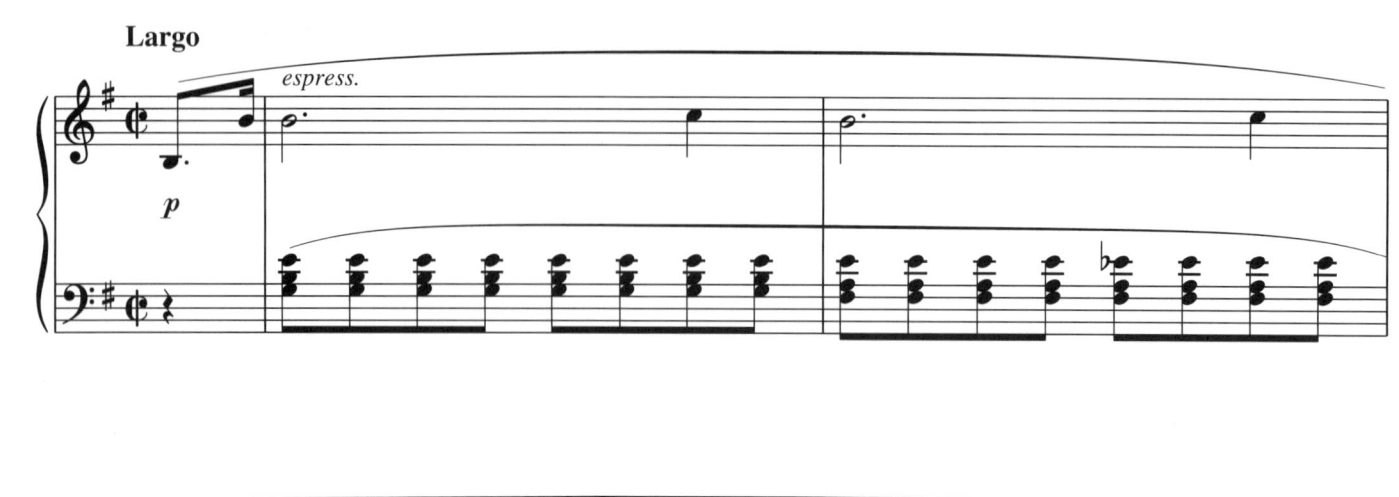

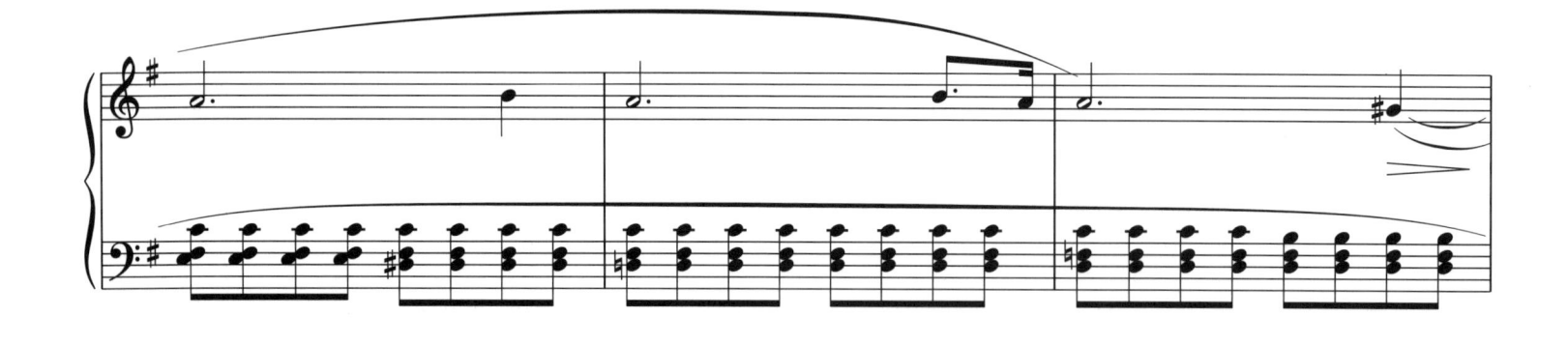

Largo

105

Prelude in B Minor

Fryderyk Chopin
1810–1849
Op. 28, No. 6

Lento assai

107

Prelude in D-flat Major
("Raindrop")

Fryderyk Chopin
1810-1849
Op. 28, No. 15

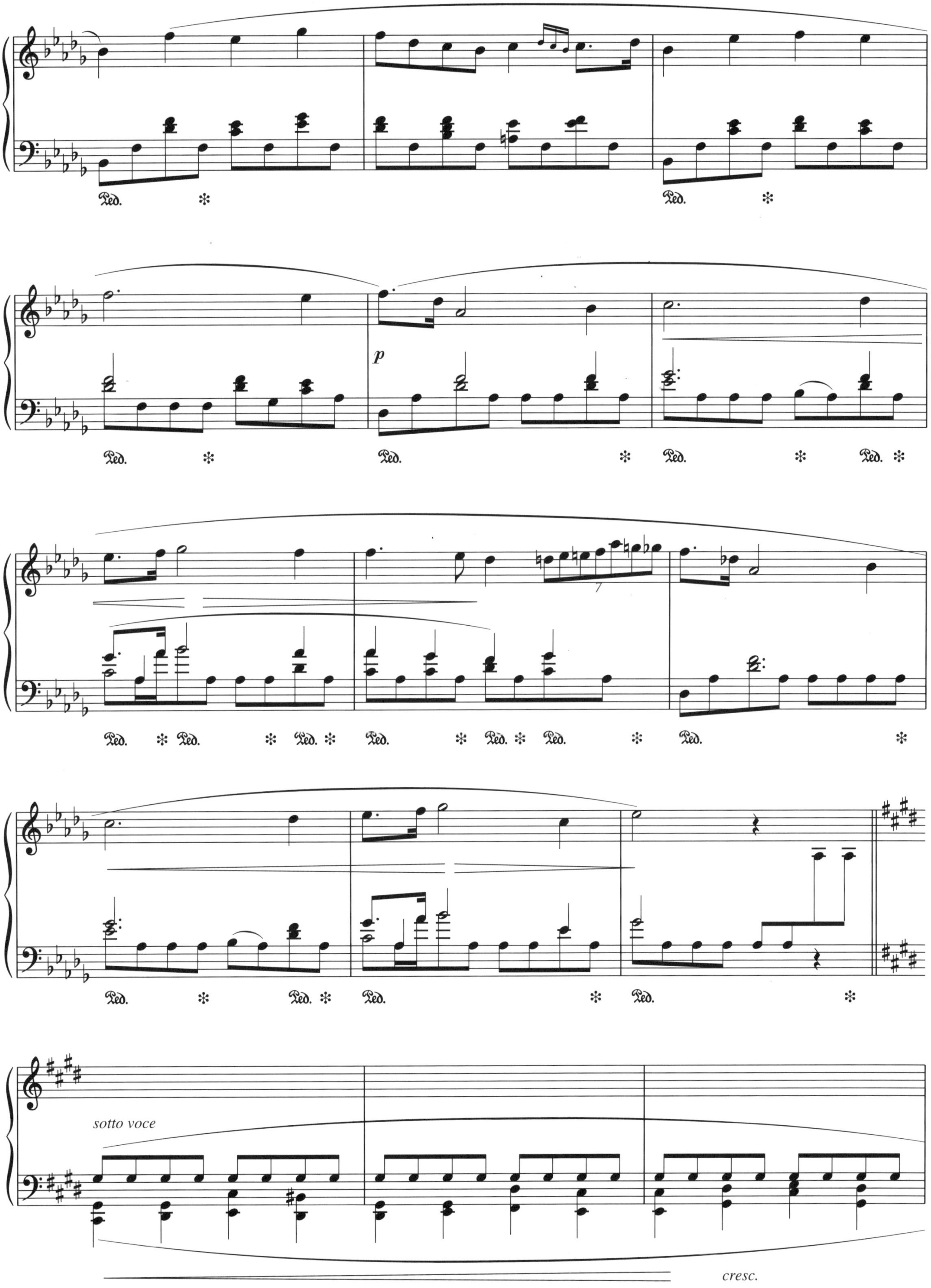
p
sotto voce
cresc.

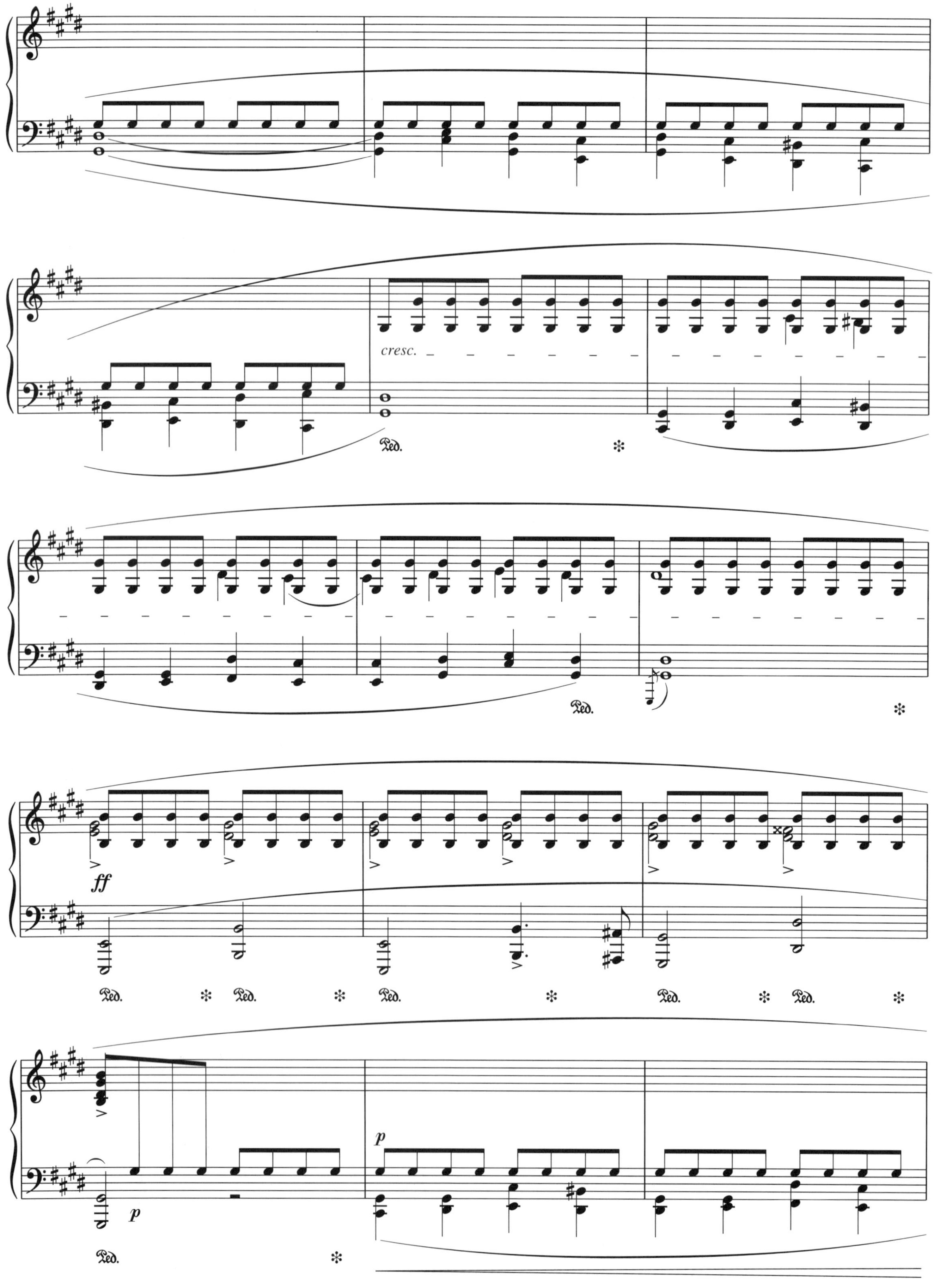
cresc.
Ped.
ff
p

111

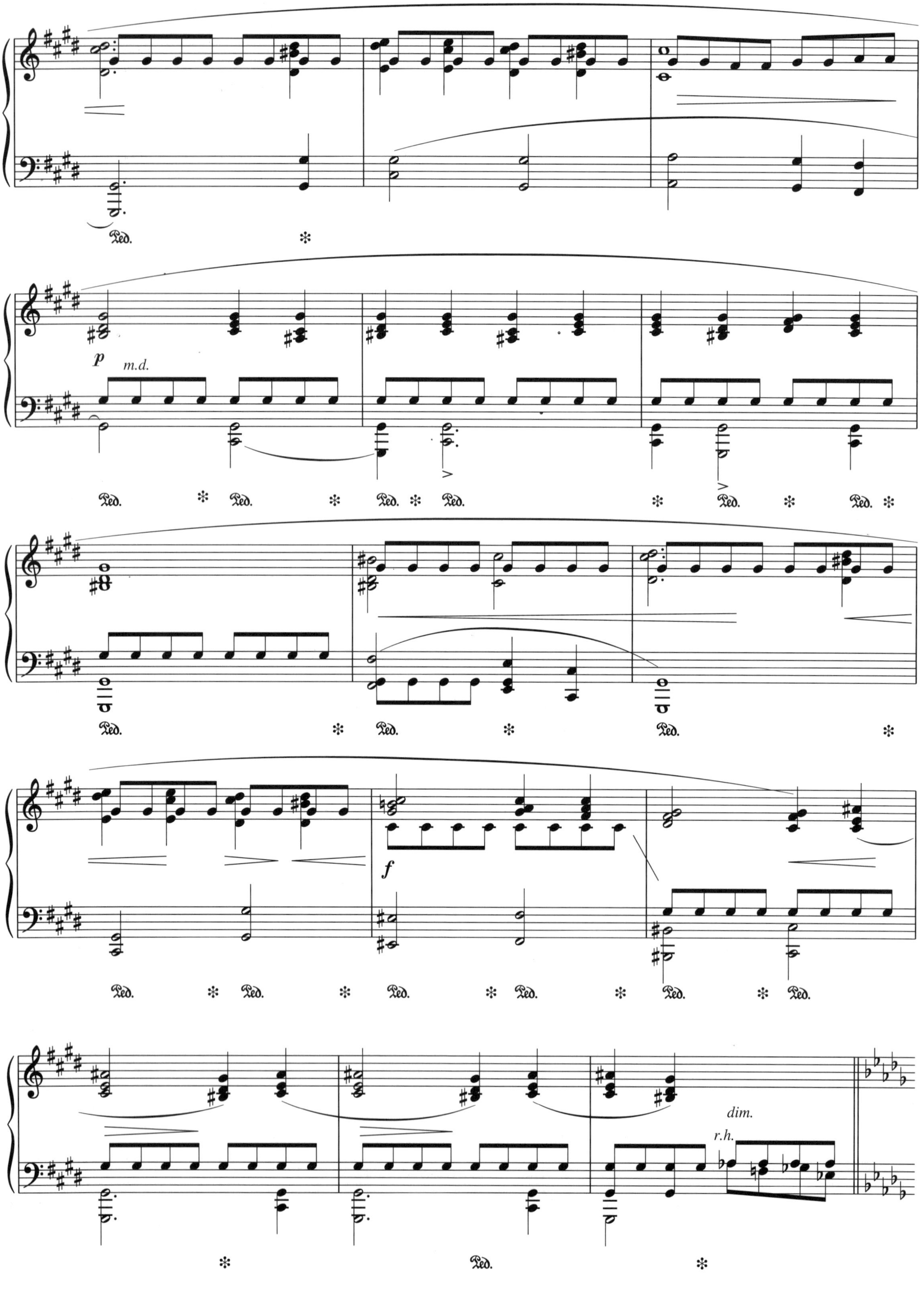
Ped.
p
m.d.
f
dim.
r.h.

113

Prelude in C Minor

Fryderyk Chopin
1810–1849
Op. 28, No. 20

The Girl with the Flaxen Hair
(La fille aux cheveux de lin)

Claude Debussy
1862–1918

*più **p***

(très peu)

p   *p*   *p*

un peu animé

p

mf

Cédez_ _ _ _ _ _ _ // au Mouv^t. (sans lourdeur)

pp

Cédez
au Mouv^t.
p
pp
très doux
Murmuré et en retenant peu à peu
pp
3
perdendosi
pp

Prelude to the Afternoon of a Faun
(Prélude à l'après-midi d'un faune)
Opening Excerpt

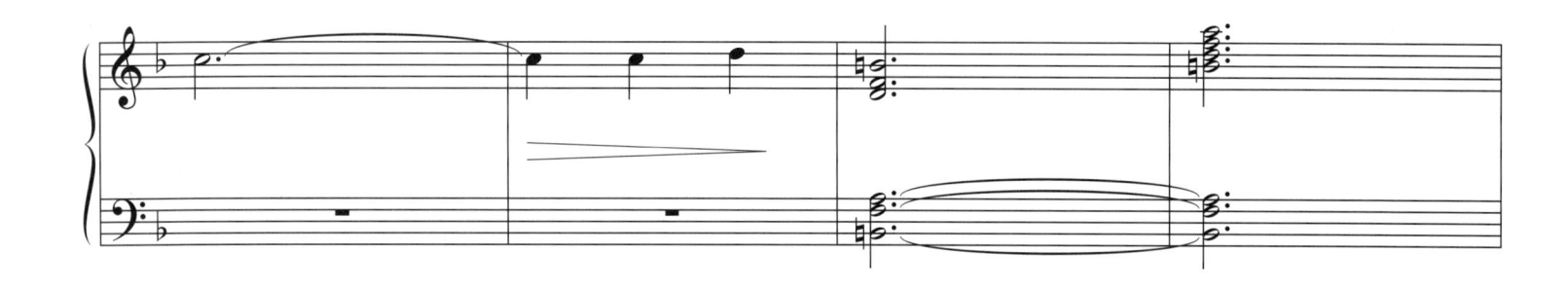

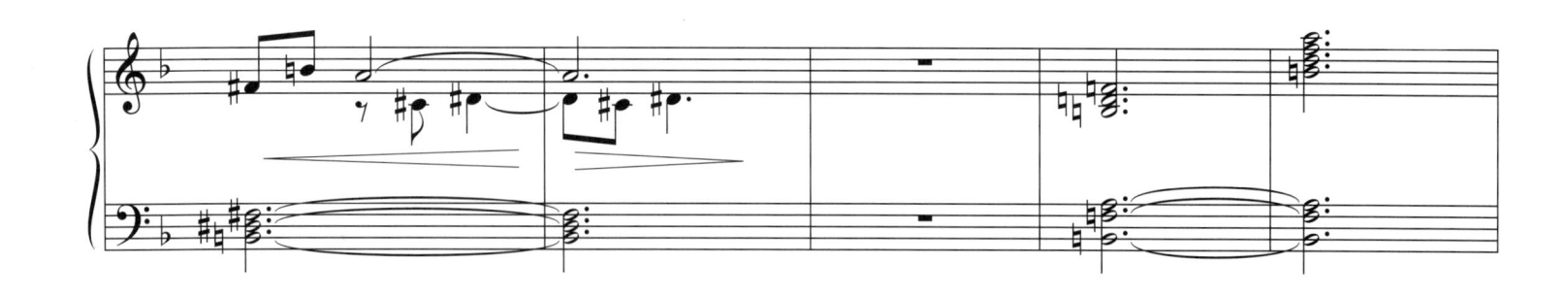

Claude Debussy
1862-1918
originally for orchestra

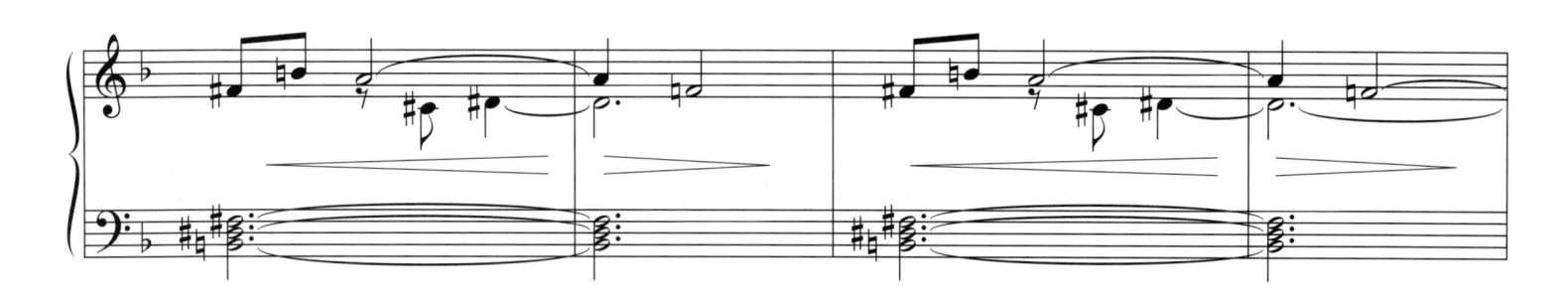

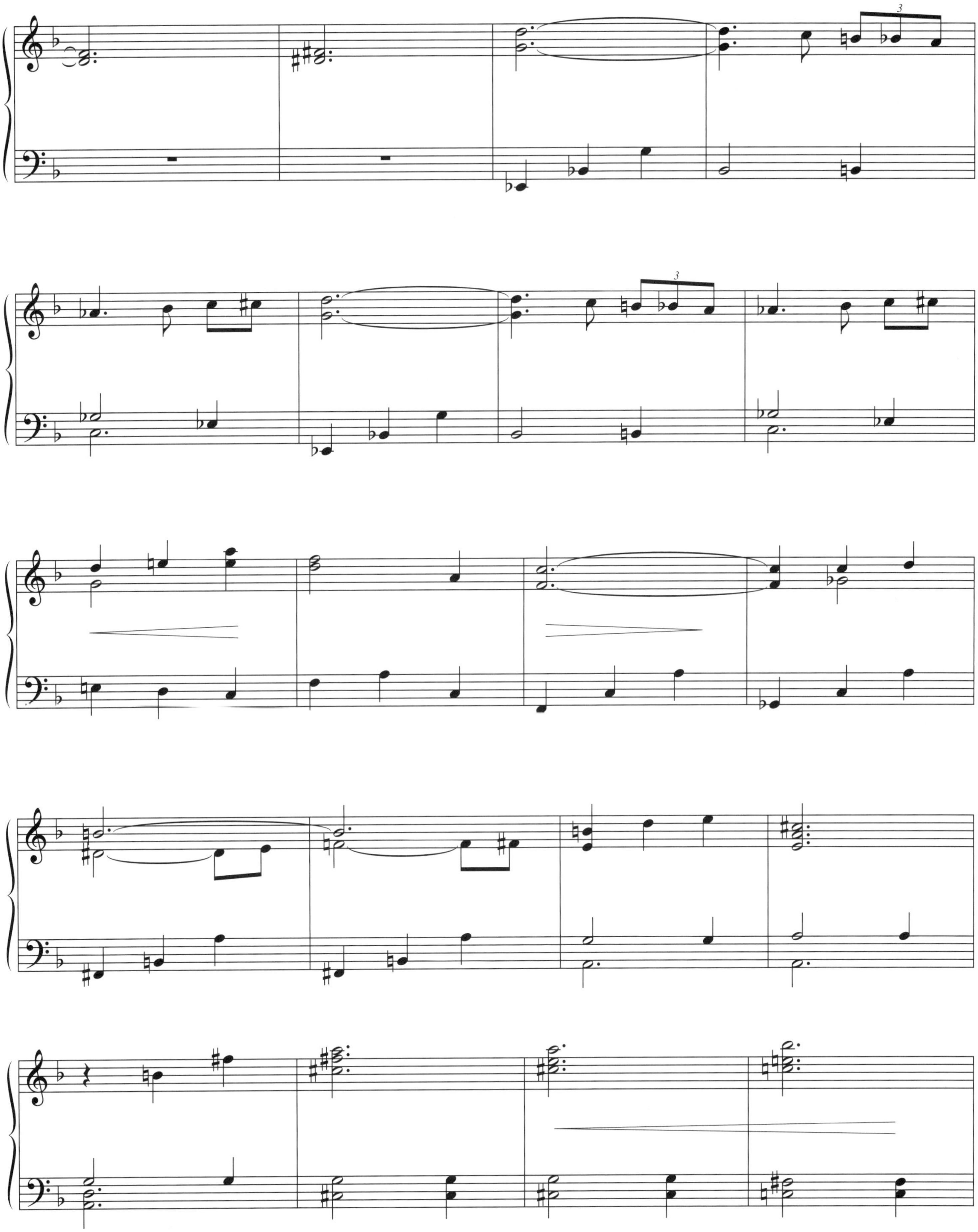
3
3

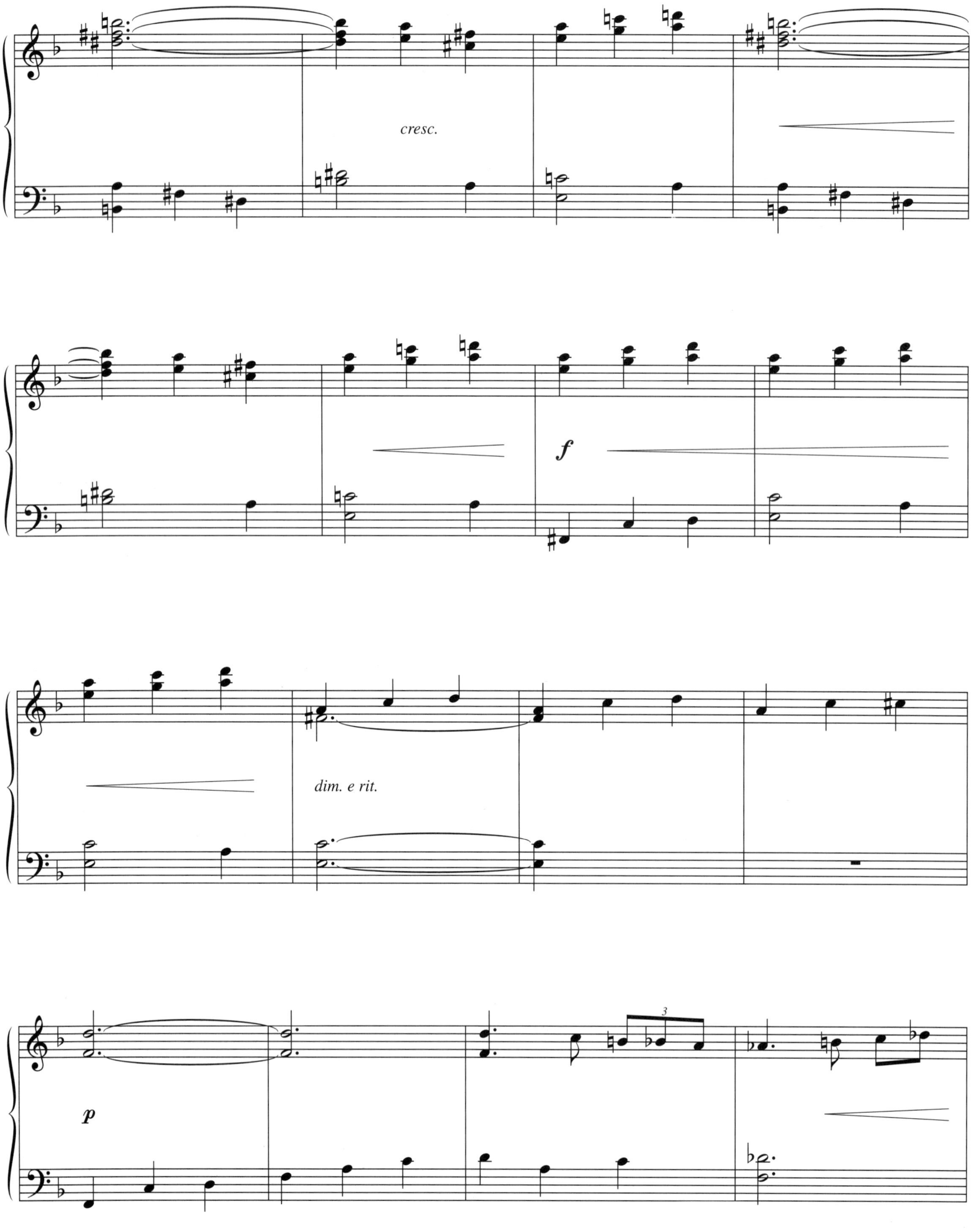
cresc.
f
dim. e rit.
3
p

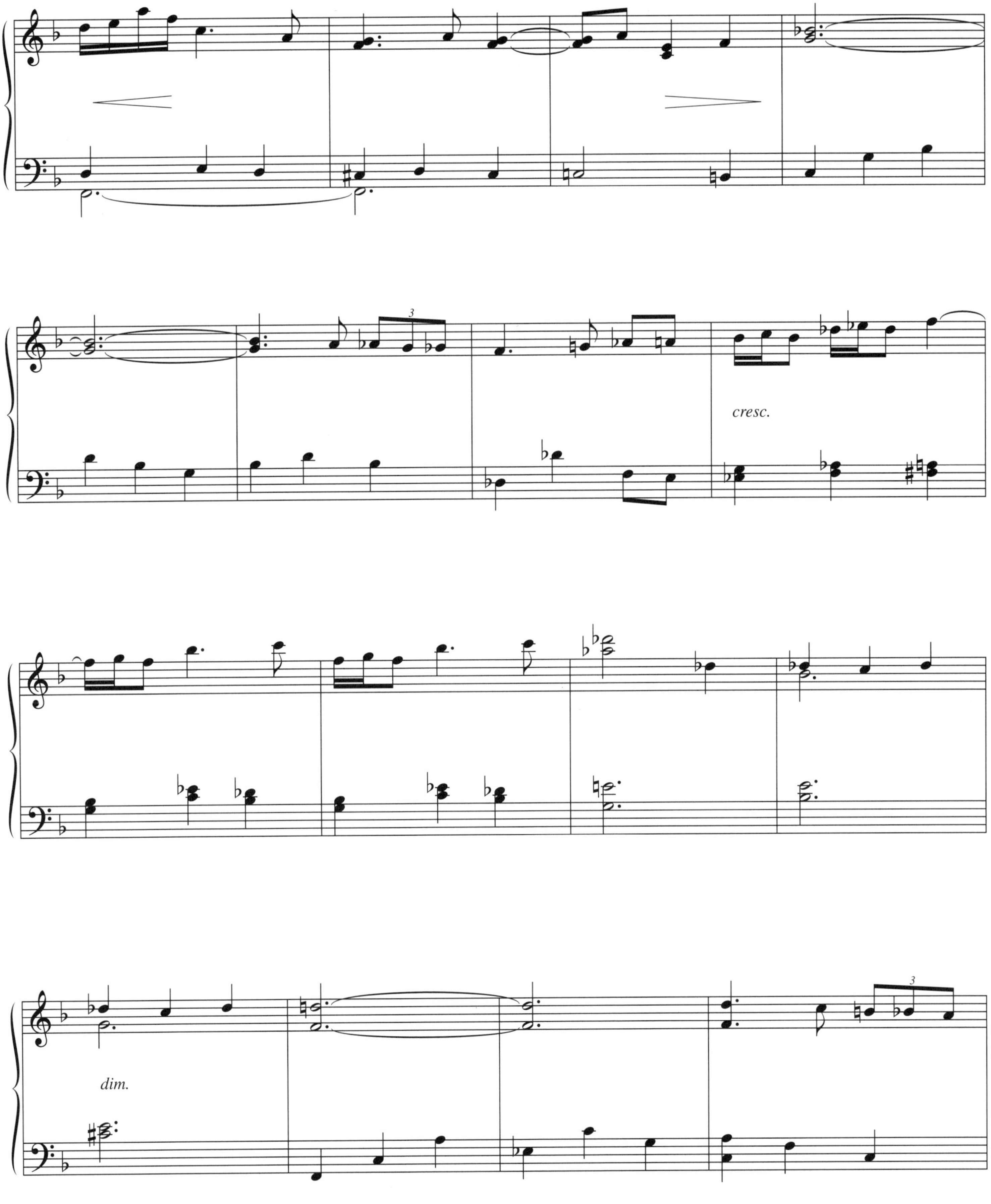
cresc.
dim.

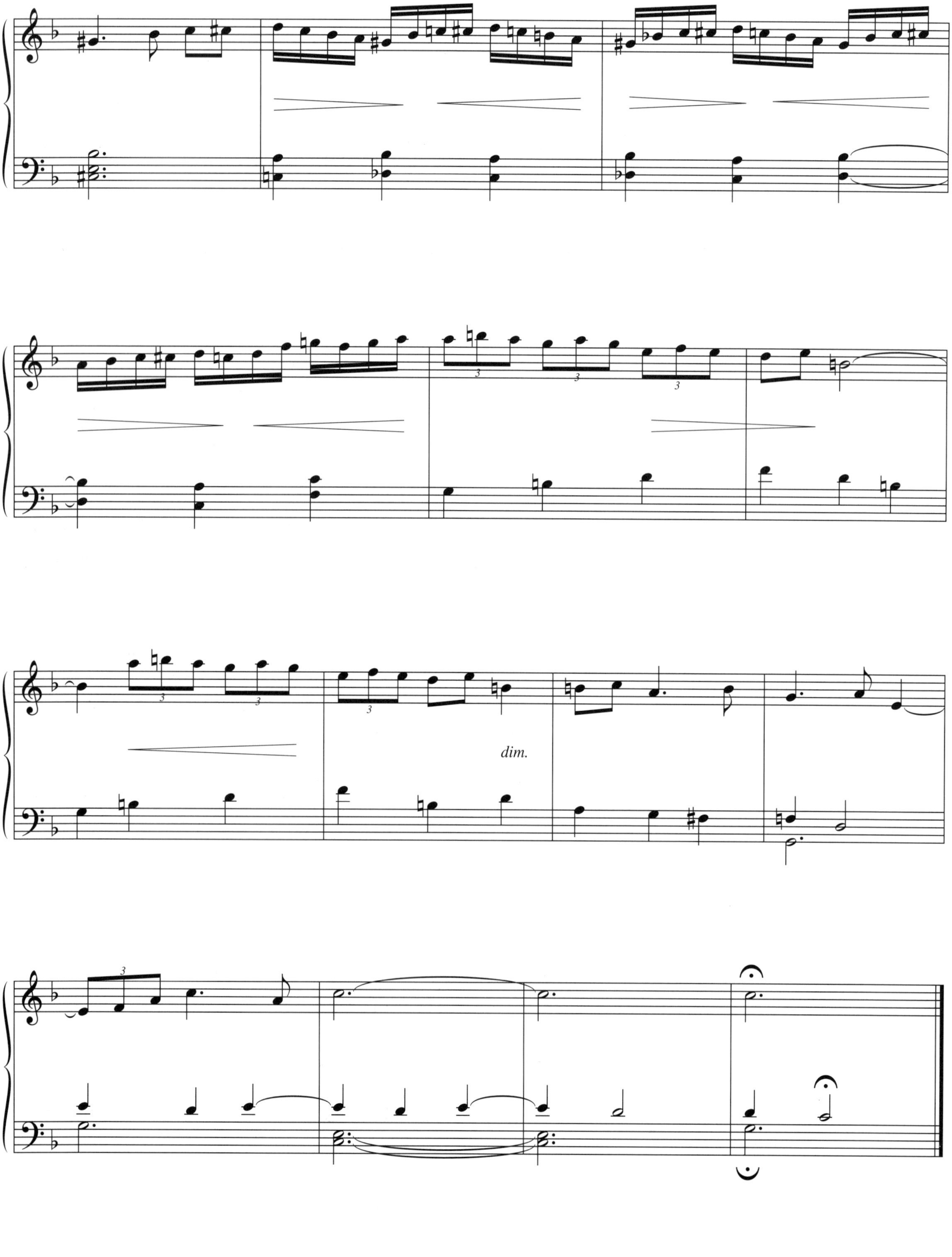
dim.

Rêverie

Claude Debussy
1862–1918

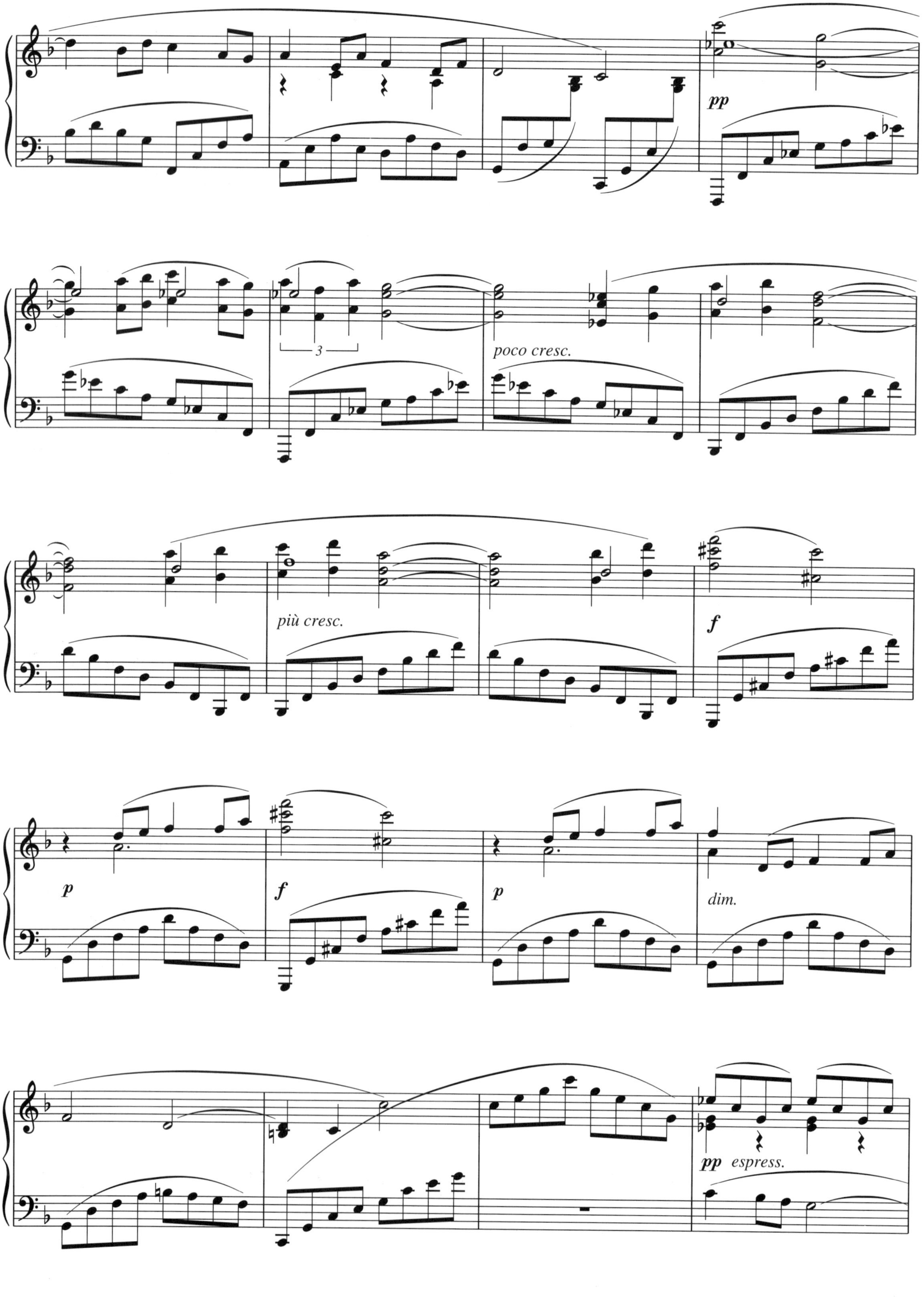
pp
3
poco cresc.
più cresc.
f
p
f
p
dim.
pp espress.

125

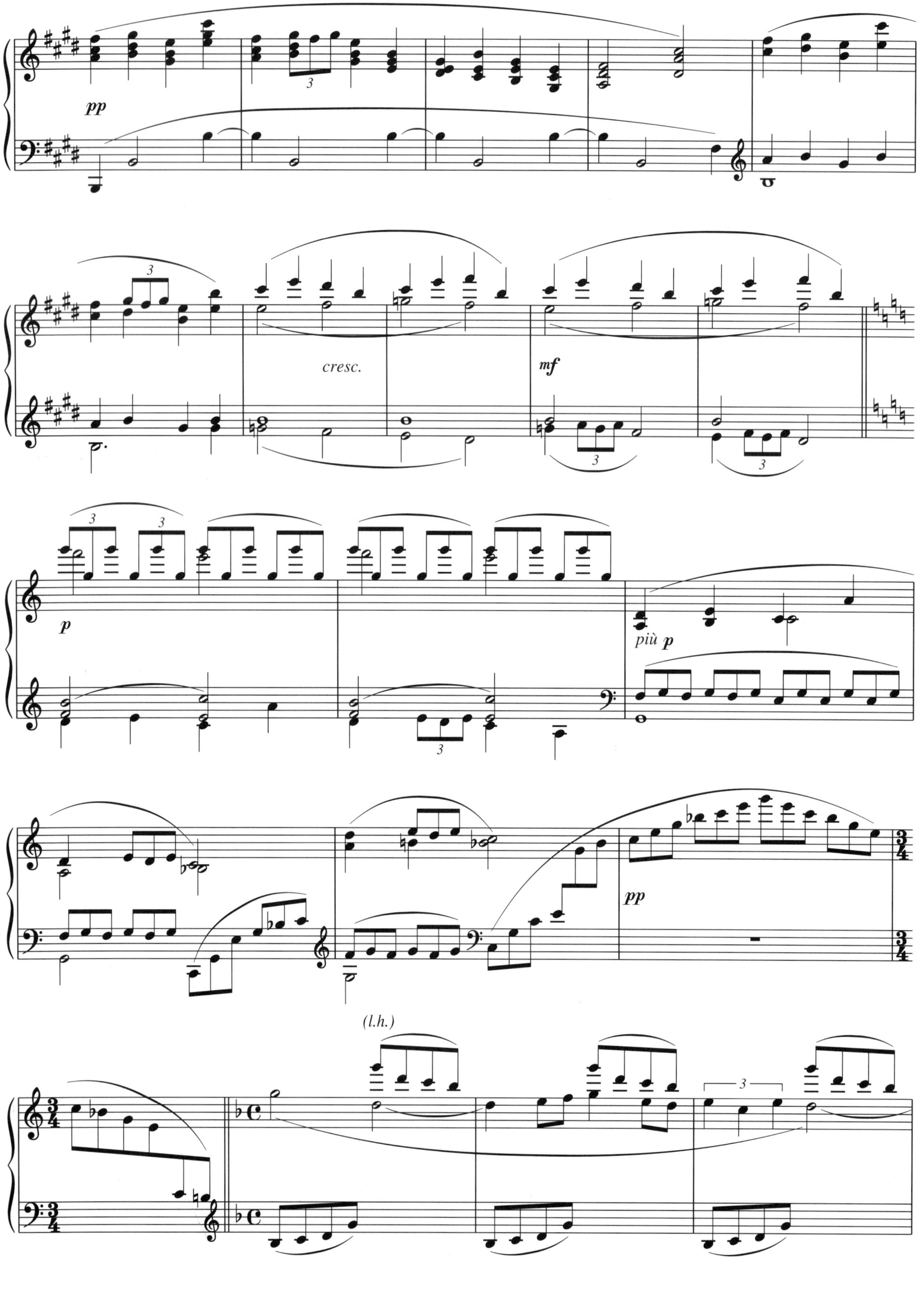
pp
cresc.
mf
p
più p
pp
(l.h.)

(l.h.)
meno p
p
p
p
un peu retenu
(a little slower)
p
3
più p
pp
rit. e
perdendosi
3

Pizzicato Polka

from the ballet SYLVIA

Léo Delibes
1836-1891
originally for orchestra

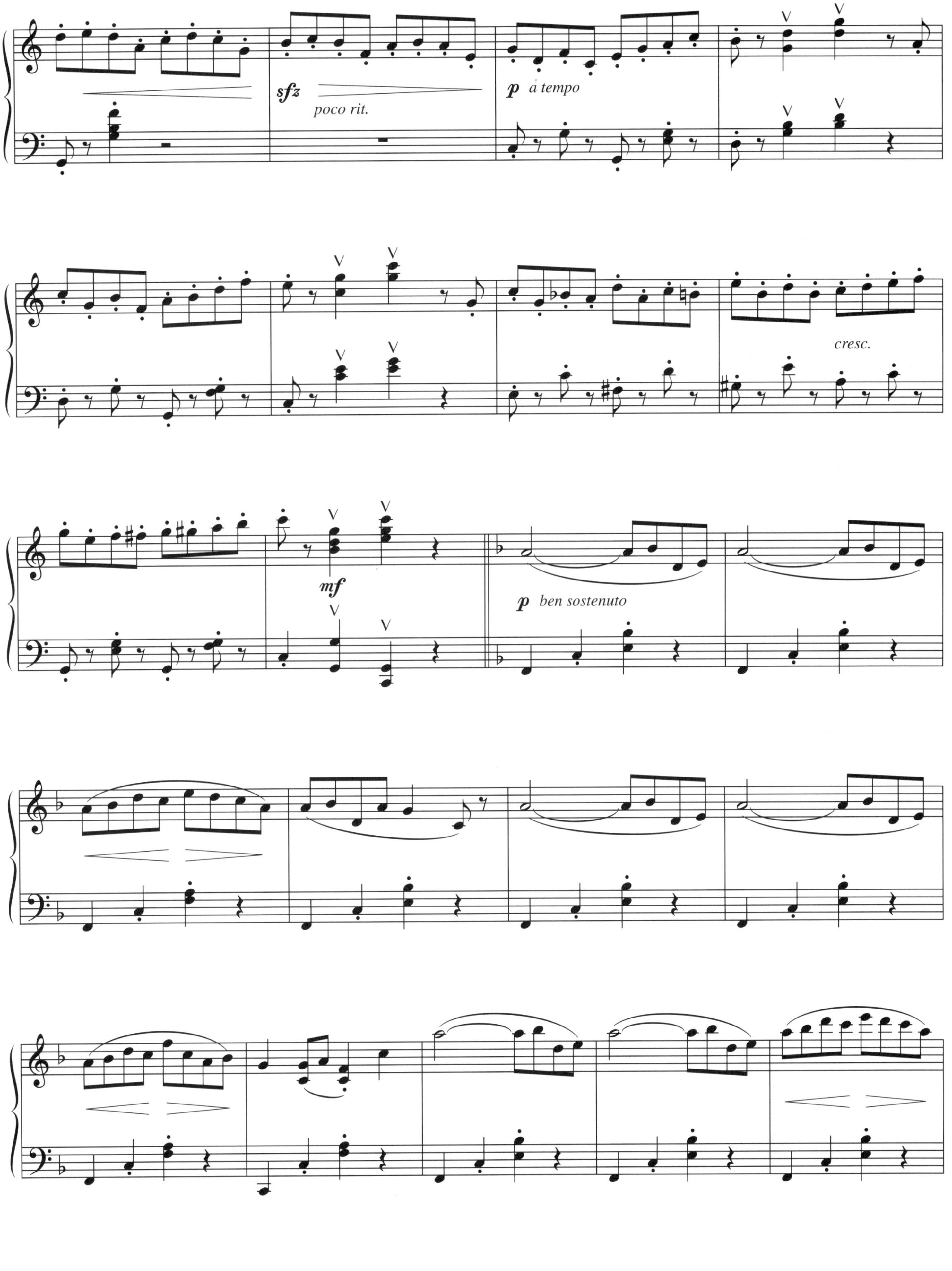
sfz
poco rit.
p a tempo
cresc.
mf
p ben sostenuto

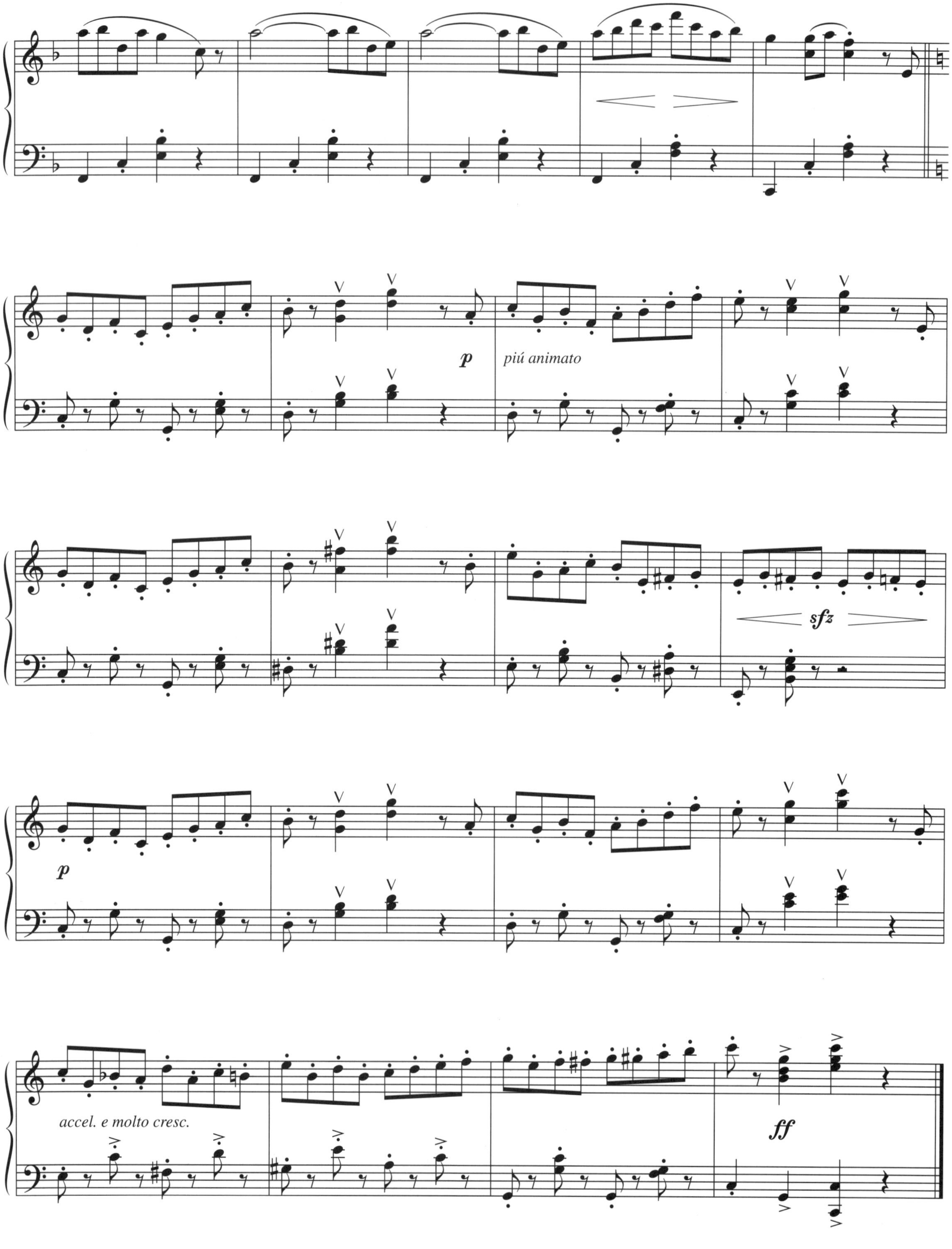
p
piú animato
sfz
p
accel. e molto cresc.
ff

Symphony No. 9
"From the New World"
Second Movement Excerpt

Antonín Dvořák
1841-1904
Op. 95
originally for orchestra

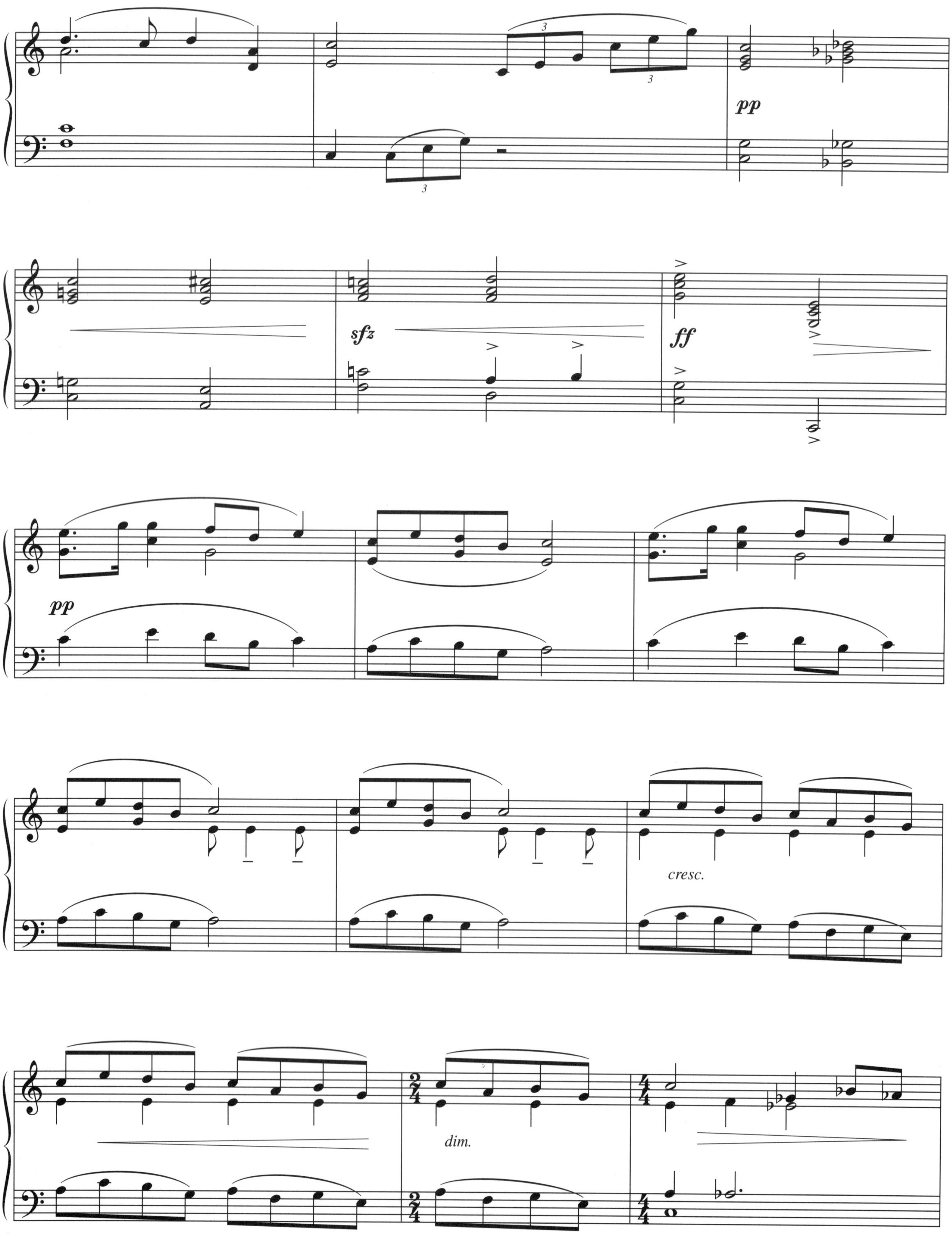

pp
sfz
ff
pp
cresc.
dim.

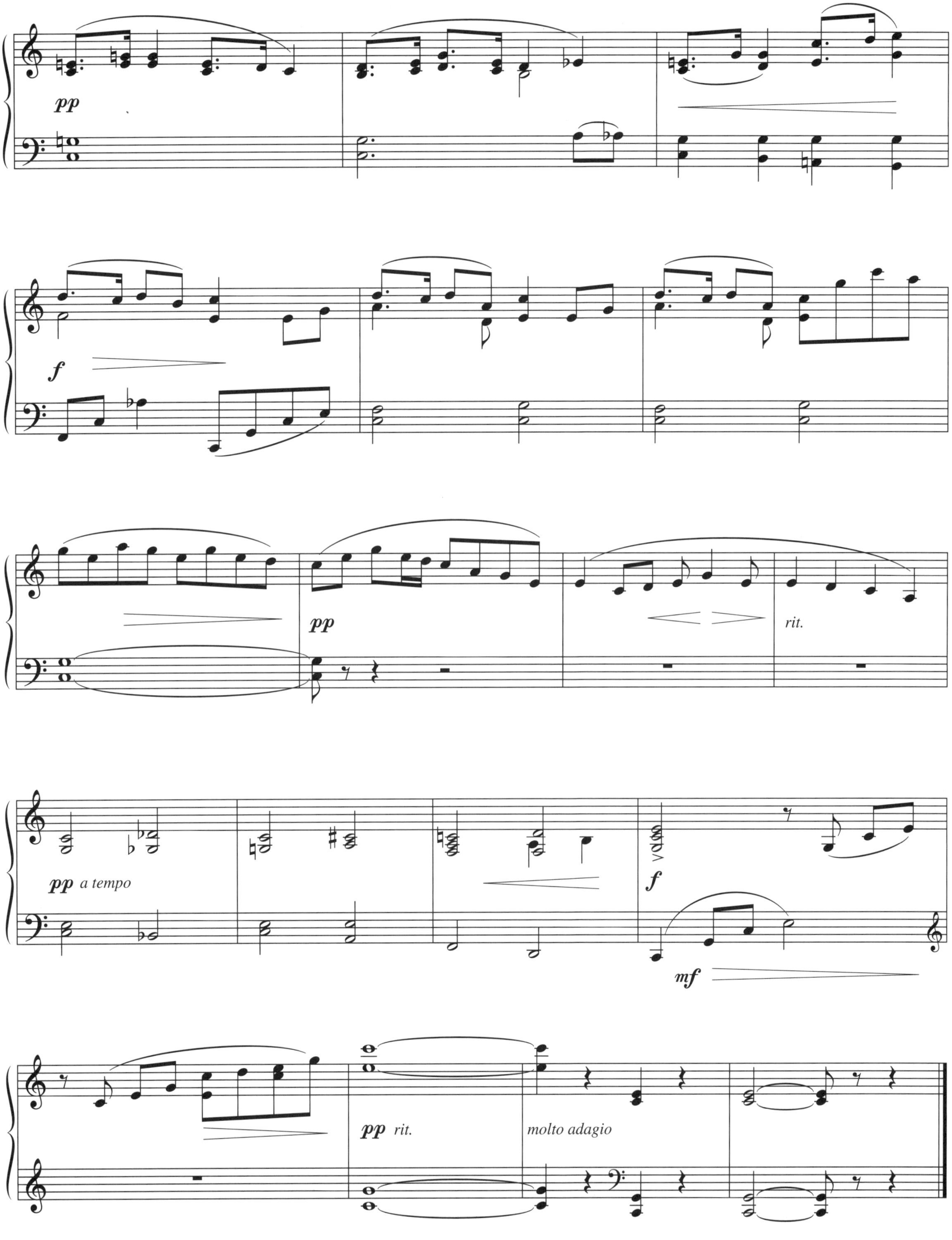
pp
f
pp
rit.
pp a tempo
f
mf
pp rit.
molto adagio

Slavonic Dance

Excerpt

Antonín Dvořák
1841-1904
Op. 46, No. 1
originally for piano, four hands
orchestrated by the composer

135

136

137

Spinning Song

(Spinnliedchen)

Albert Ellmenreich
1816–1905
Op. 14, No. 4

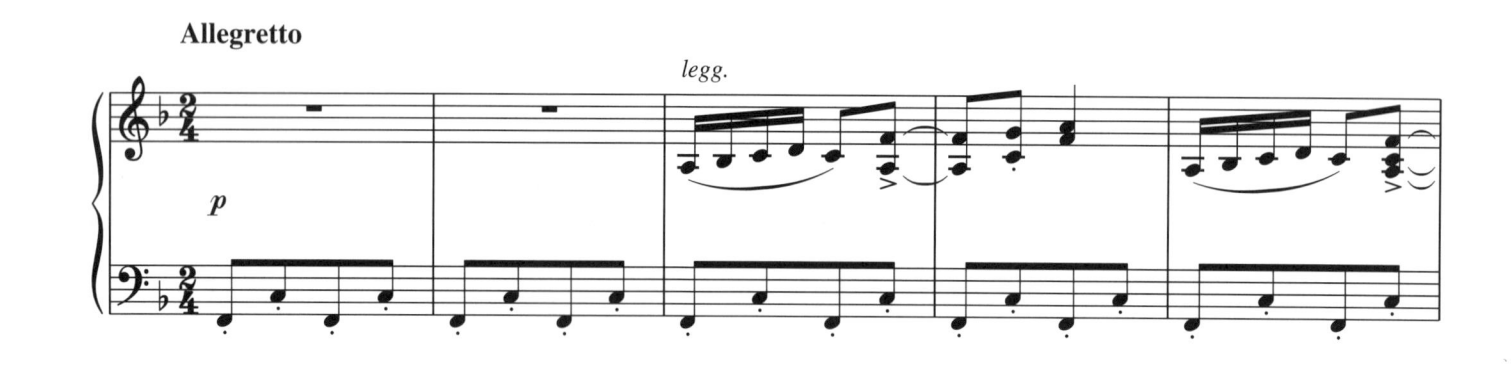

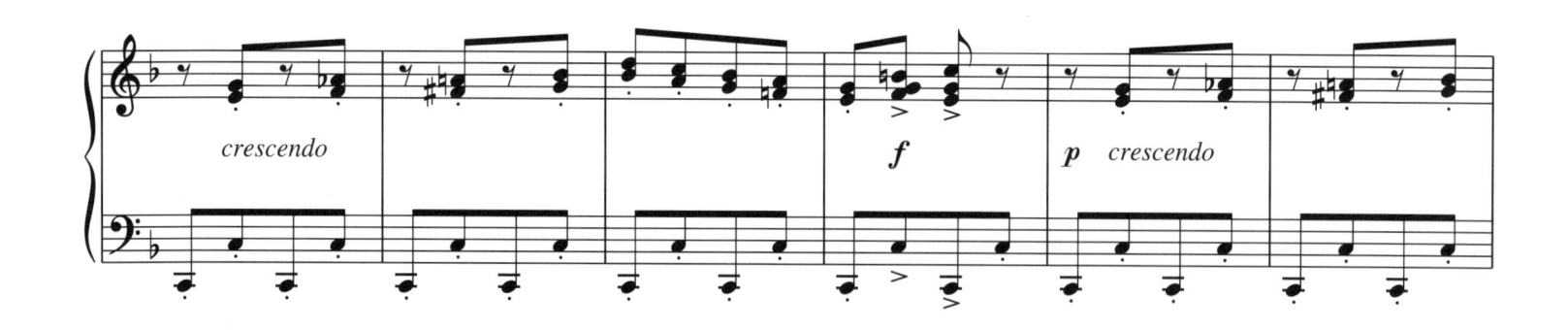

Allegretto

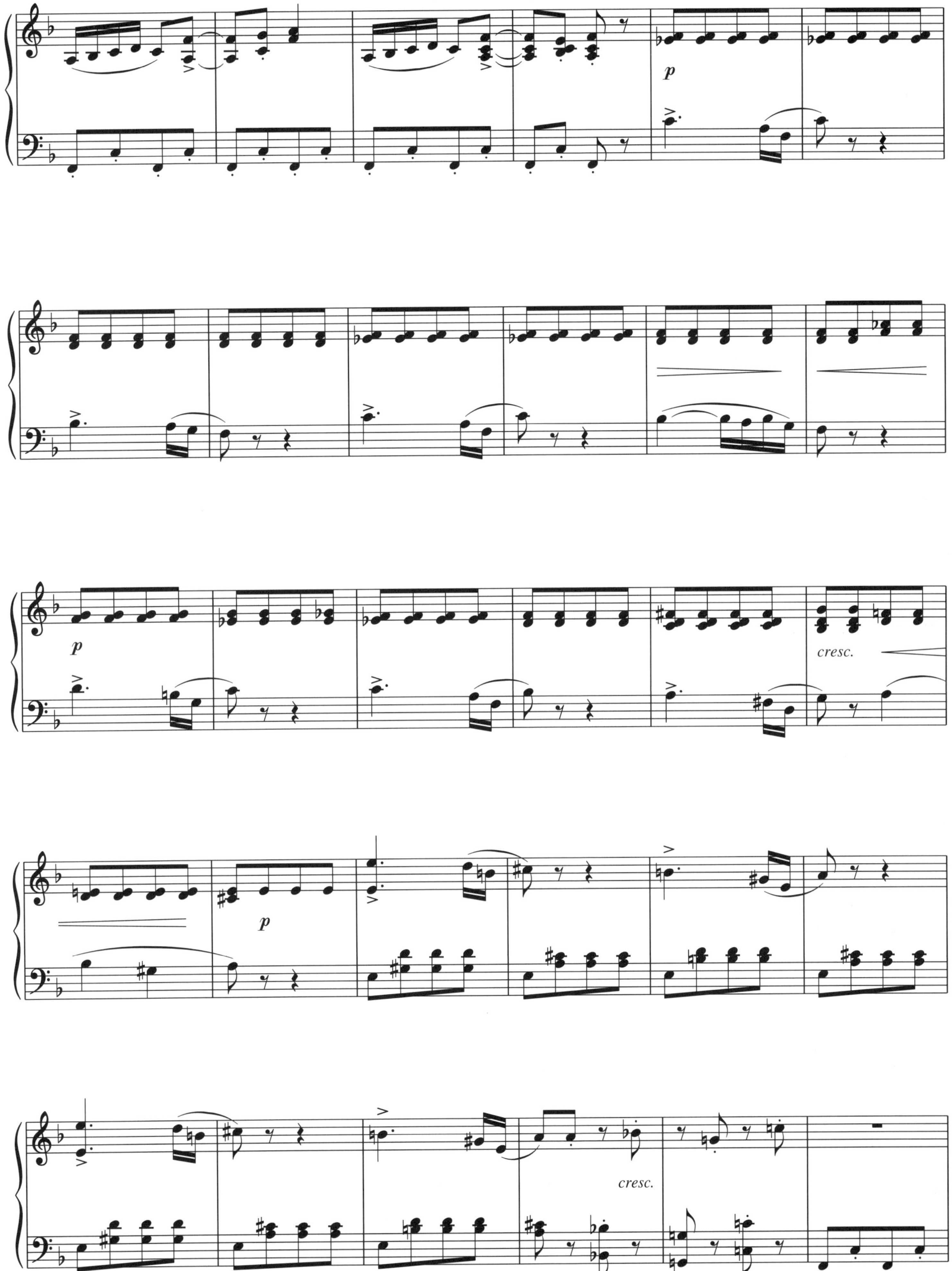
p
p
cresc.
p
cresc.
p

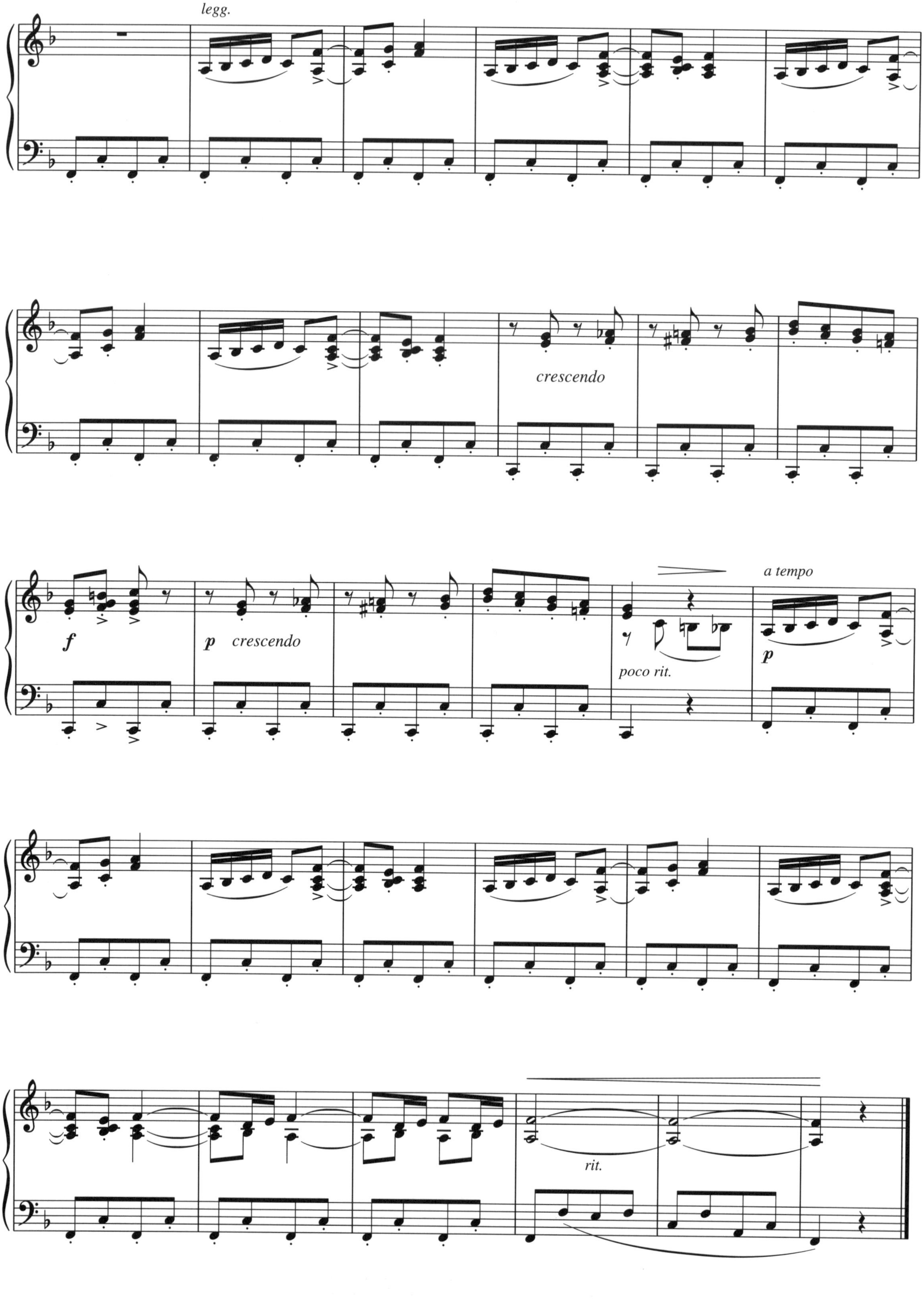
legg.
crescendo
f
p
crescendo
poco rit.
a tempo
p
rit.

M'appari tutt'amor

(Ach, so fromm)
from the opera MARTHA

Friedrich von Flotow
1812-1883

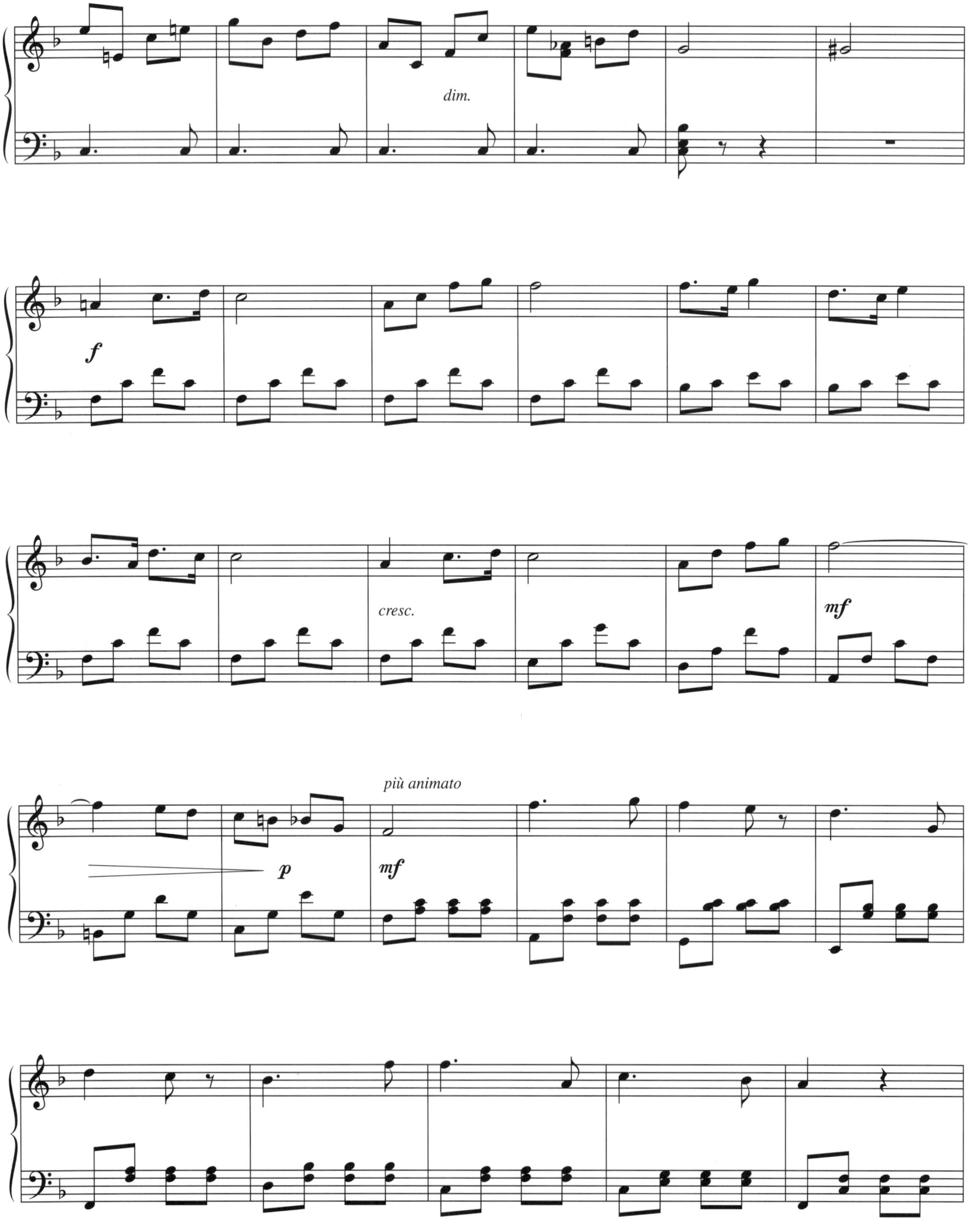
dim.
f
cresc.
mf
più animato
p
mf

143

Après un rêve
(After a dream)

Gabriel Fauré
1845-1924
Op. 7, No. 1
originally for voice and piano

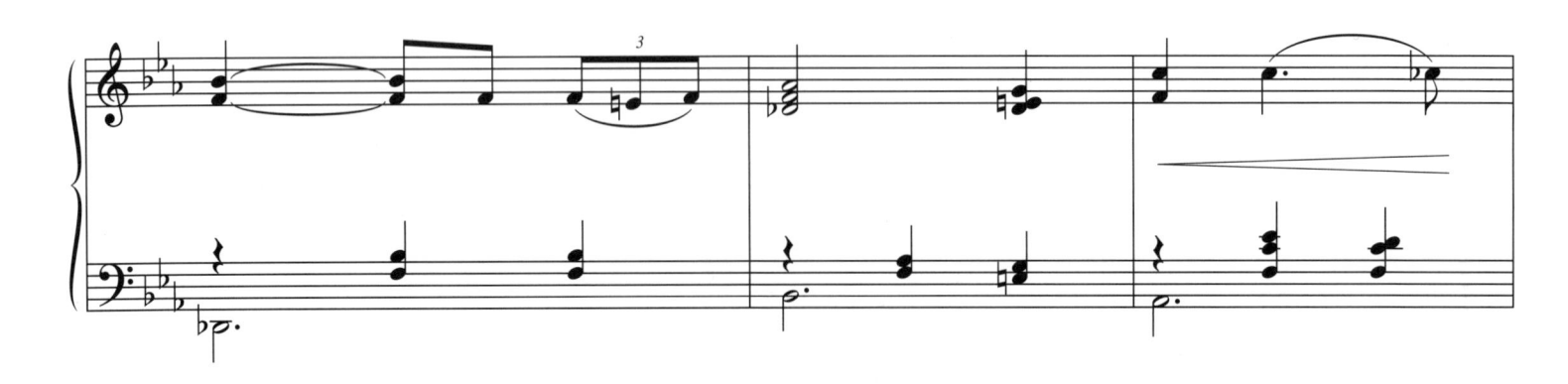

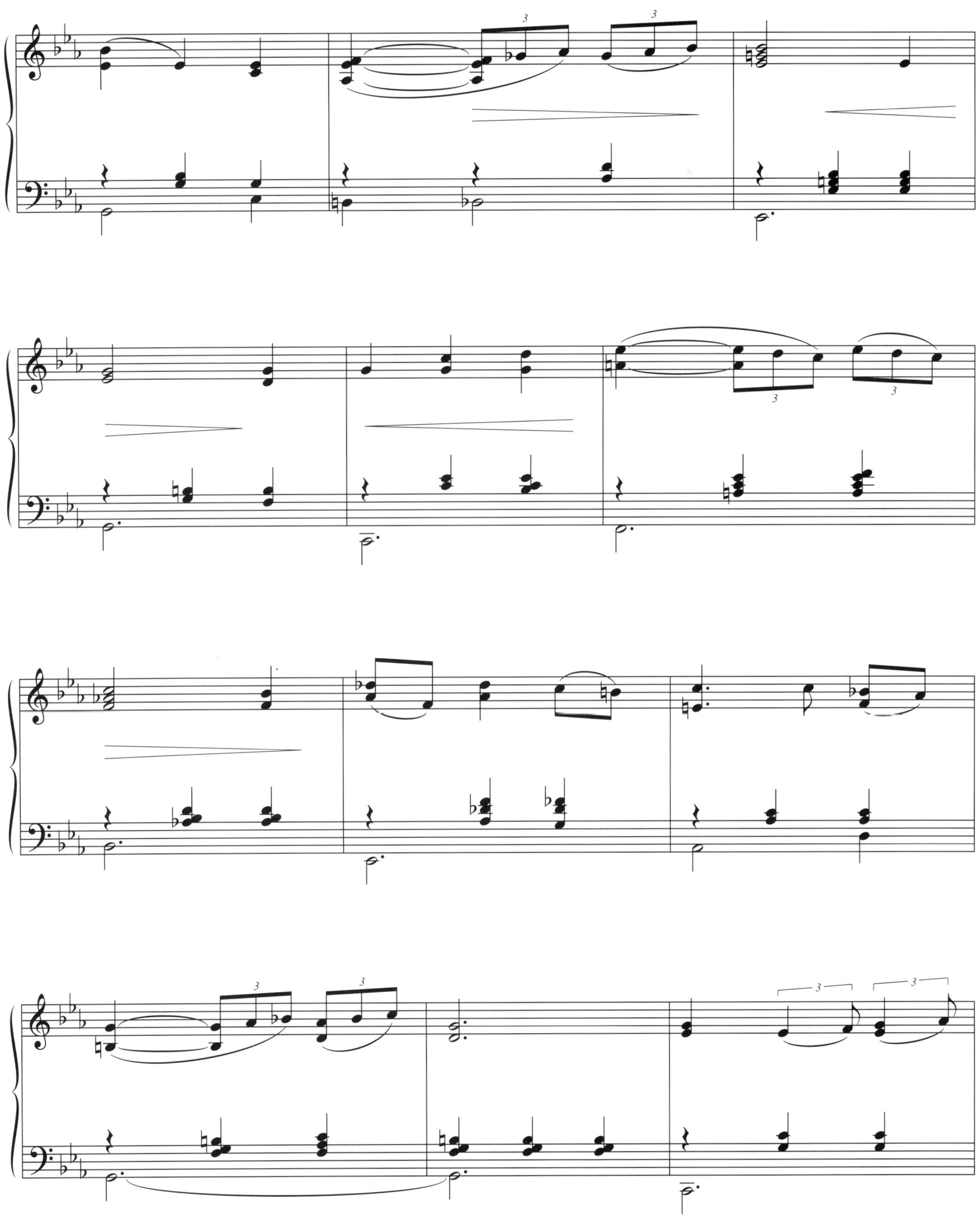
3
3
3
3
3
3
3
3

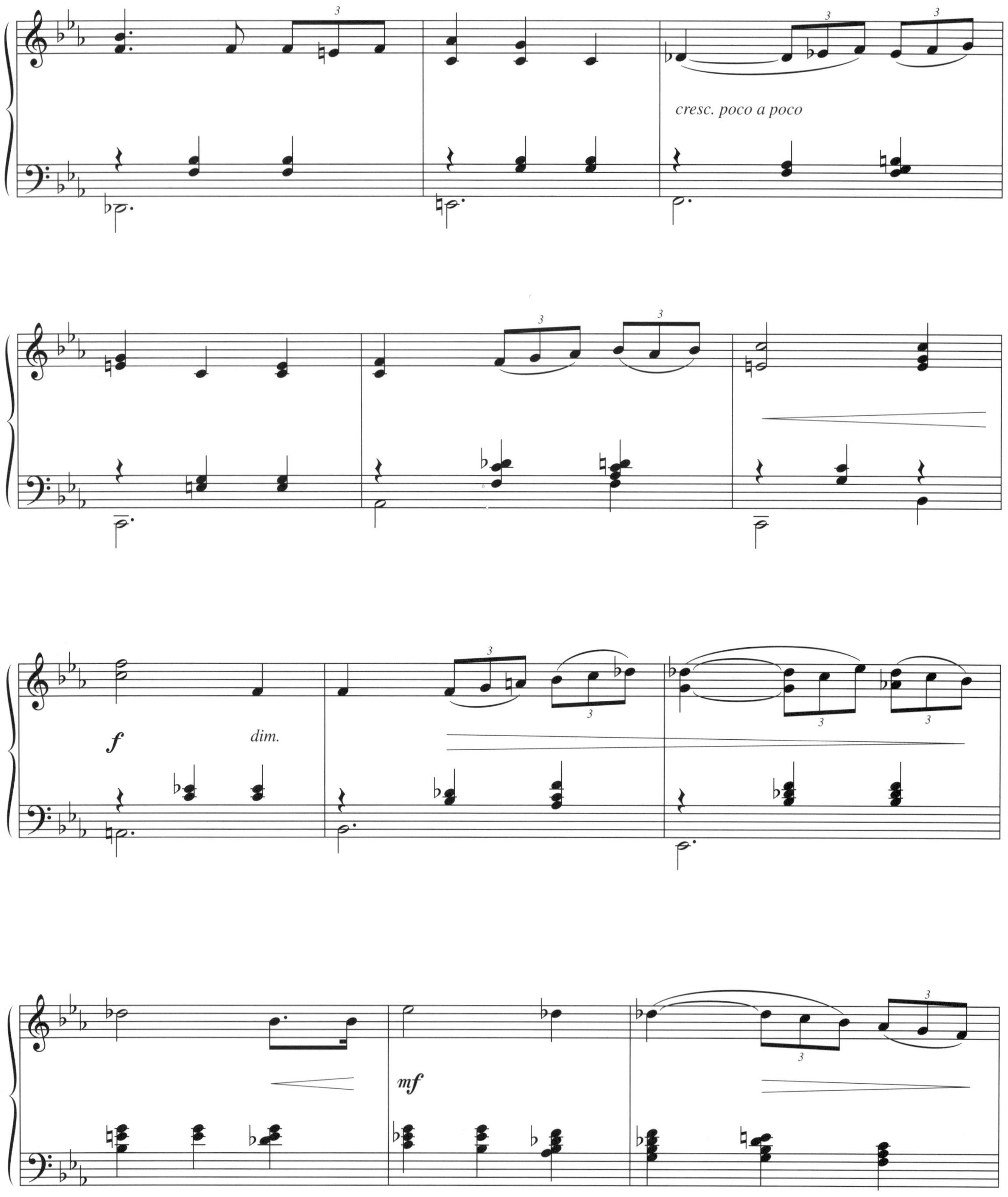
cresc. poco a poco
f
dim.
mf

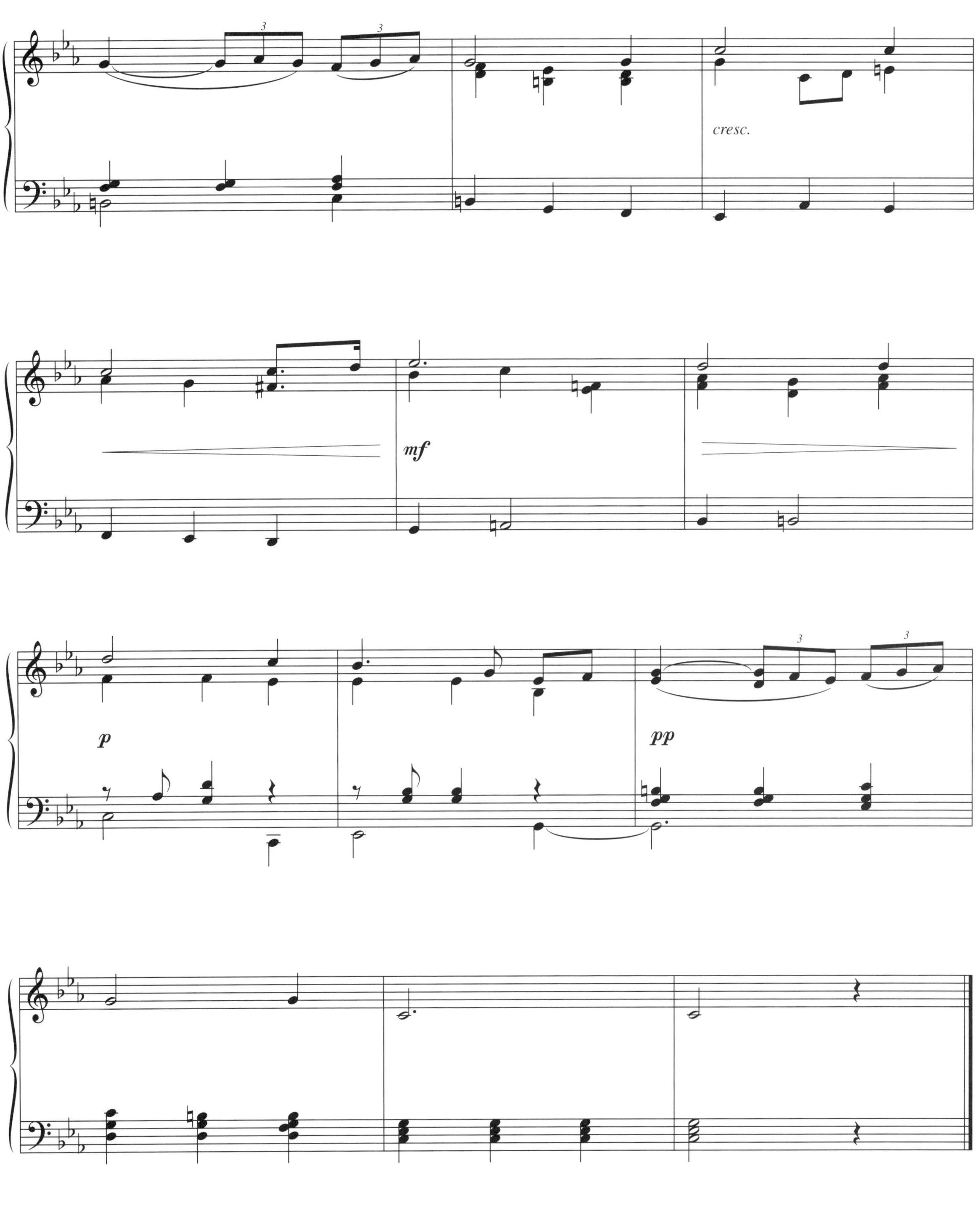
cresc.
mf
p
pp

Panis angelicus

César Franck
1822-1890
originally for tenor and
instrumental ensemble

Poco lento

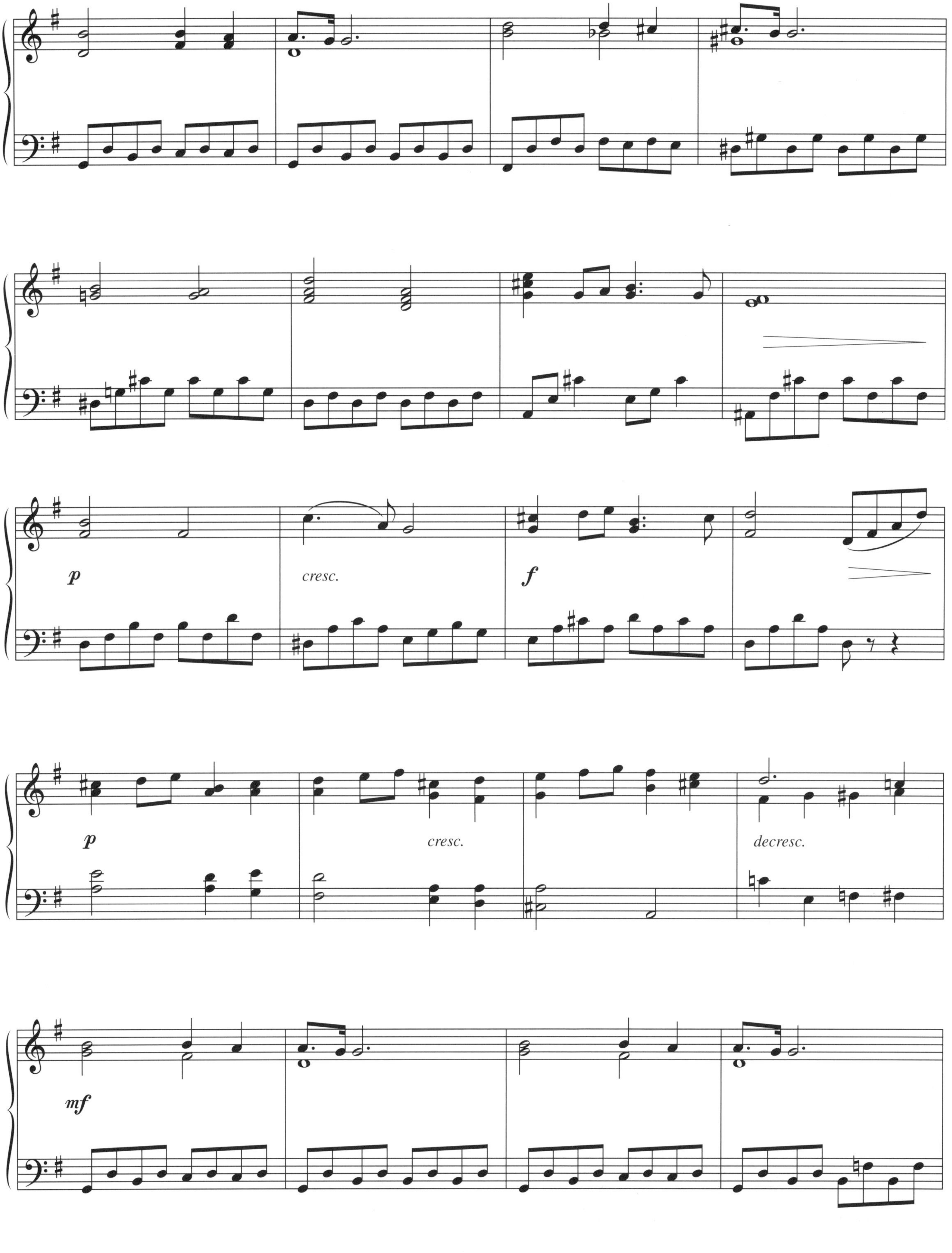
p
cresc.
f
p
cresc.
decresc.
mf

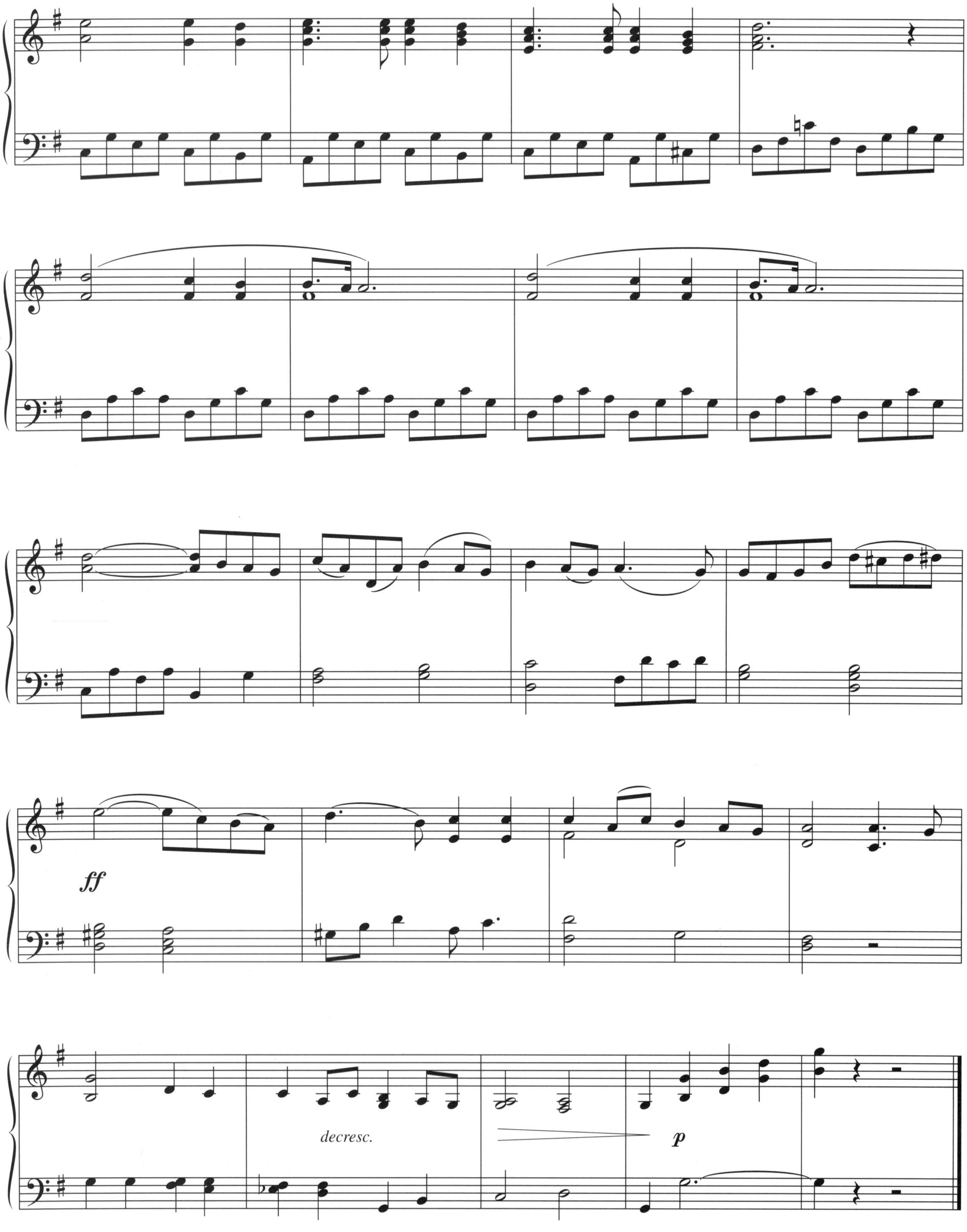
ff
decresc.
p

Gavotte

François-Joseph Gossec
1734-1829
originally for flute and string quartet

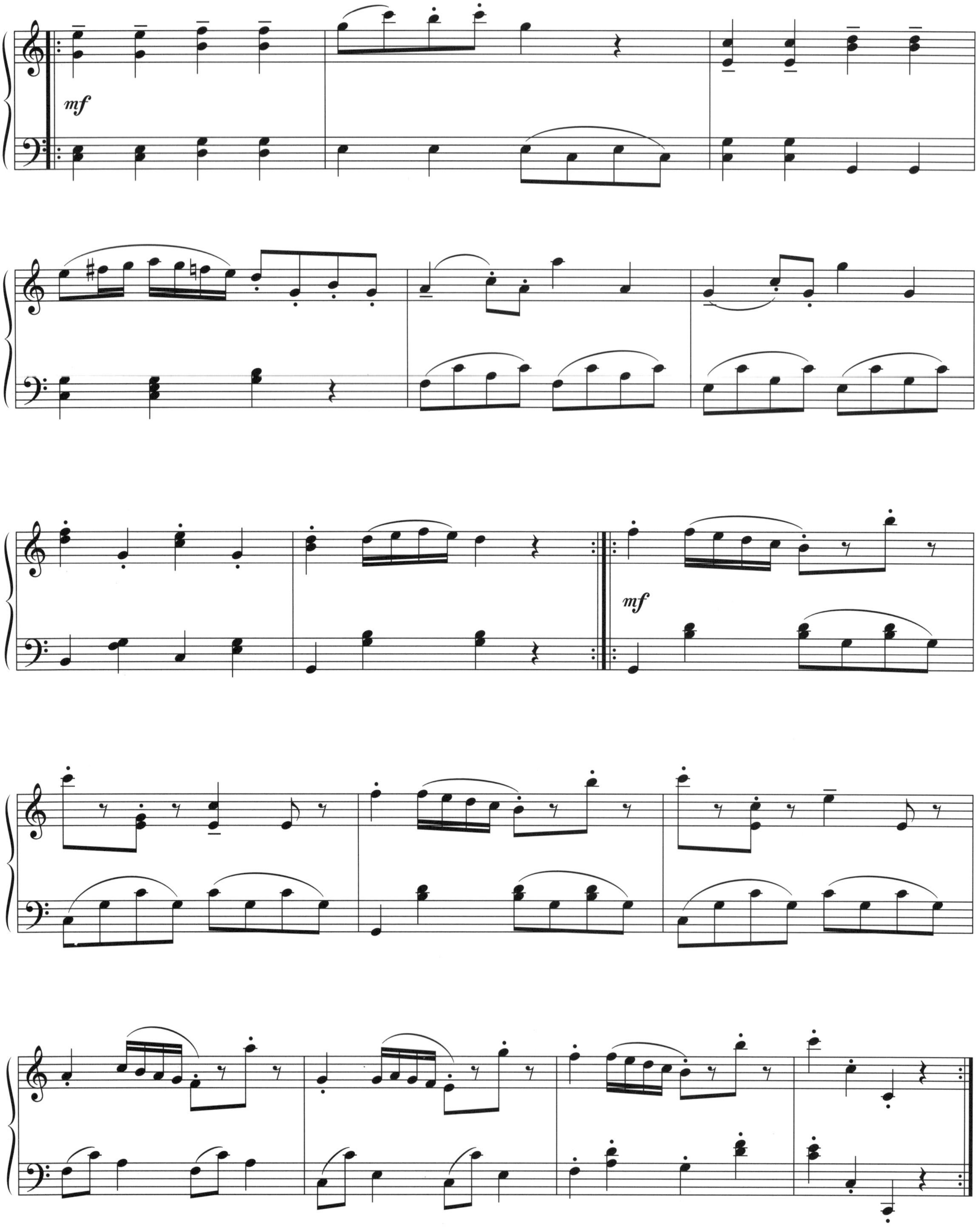
mf
mf

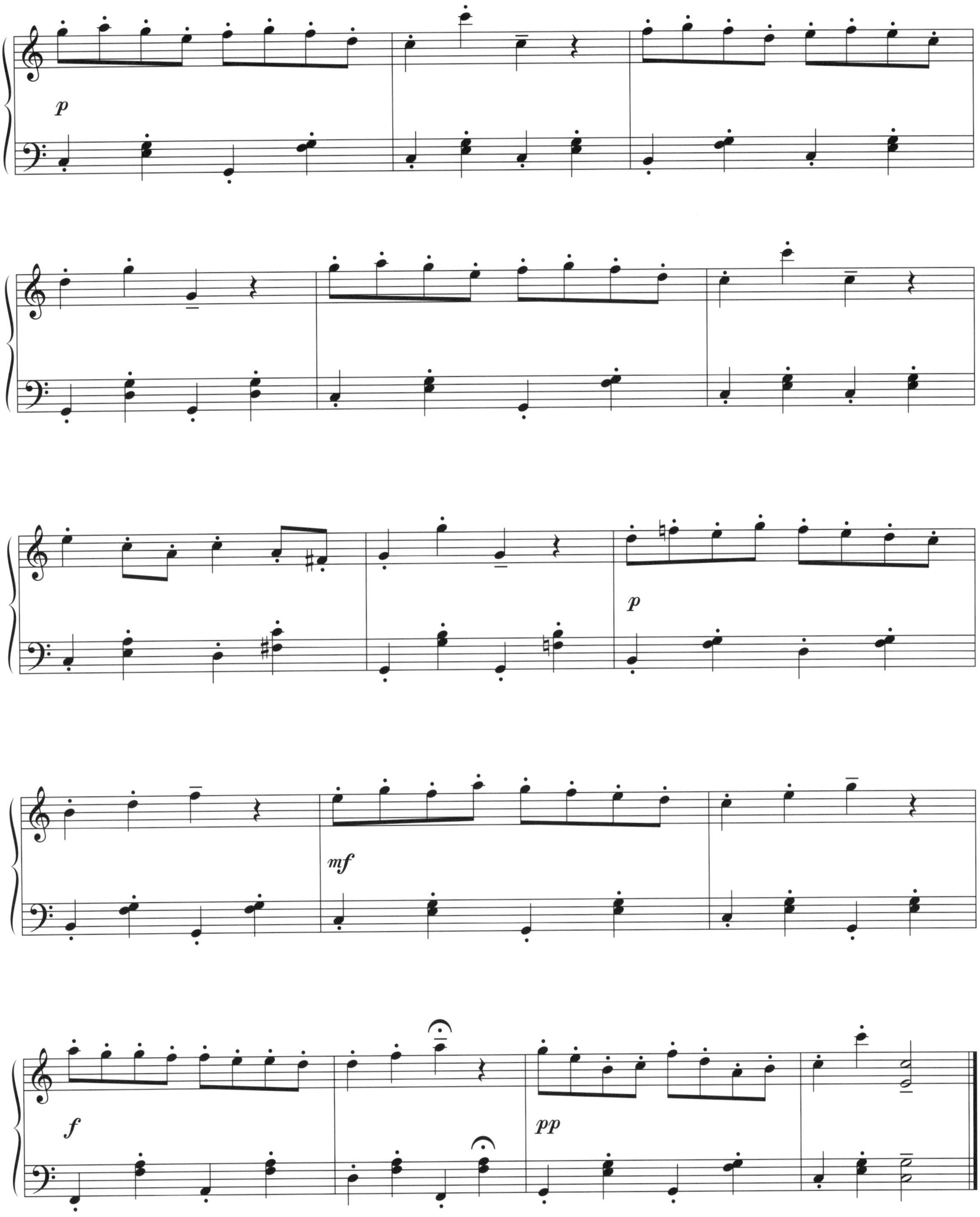
p
p
mf
f
pp

Funeral March of a Marionette

Themes

Charles Gounod
1818-1893
originally for orchestra

Allegretto

155

Ave Maria
based on Prelude in C Major by J.S. Bach

Charles Gounod
1818-1893
originally for chamber ensemble

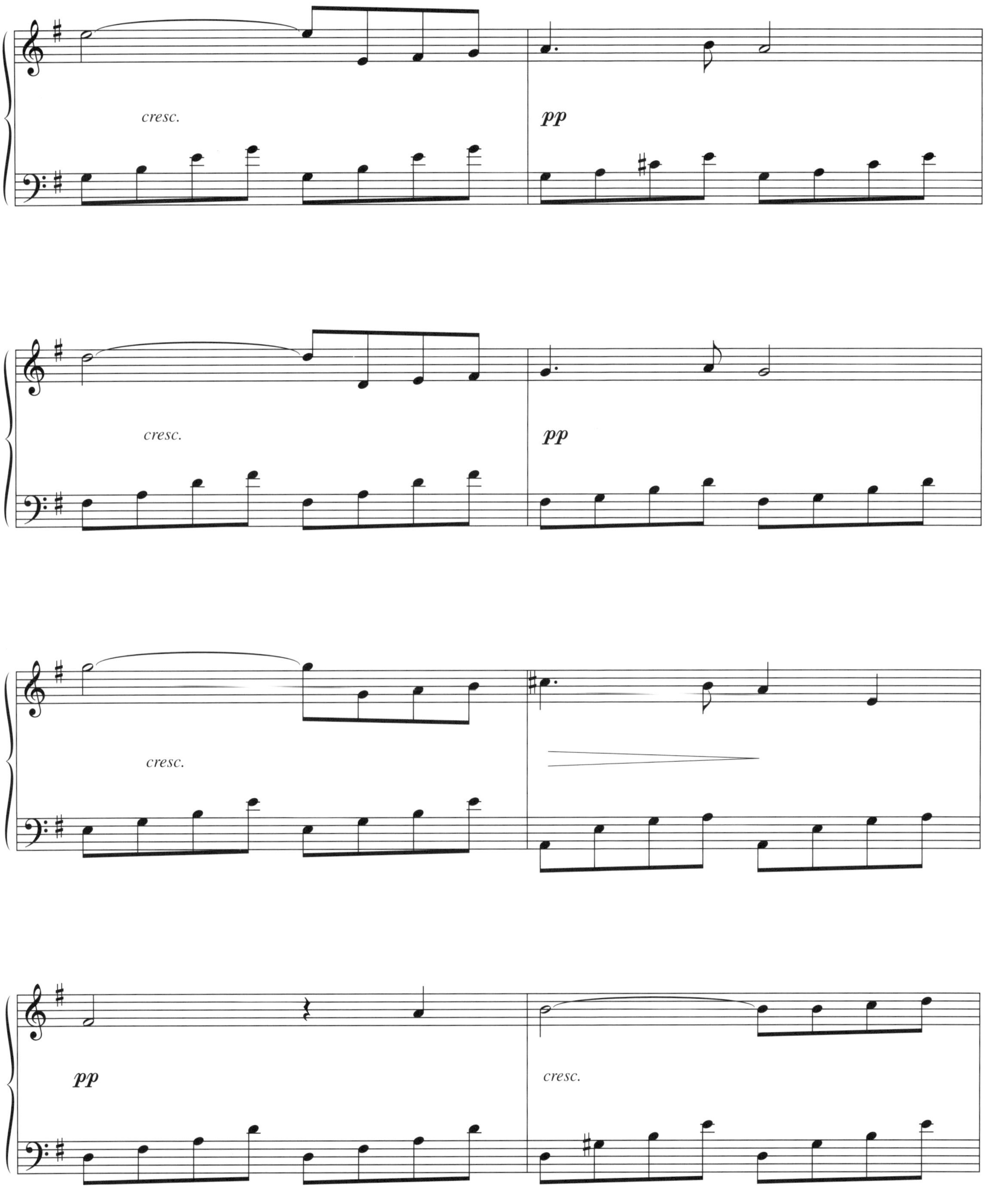
cresc.
pp
cresc.
pp
cresc.
pp
cresc.

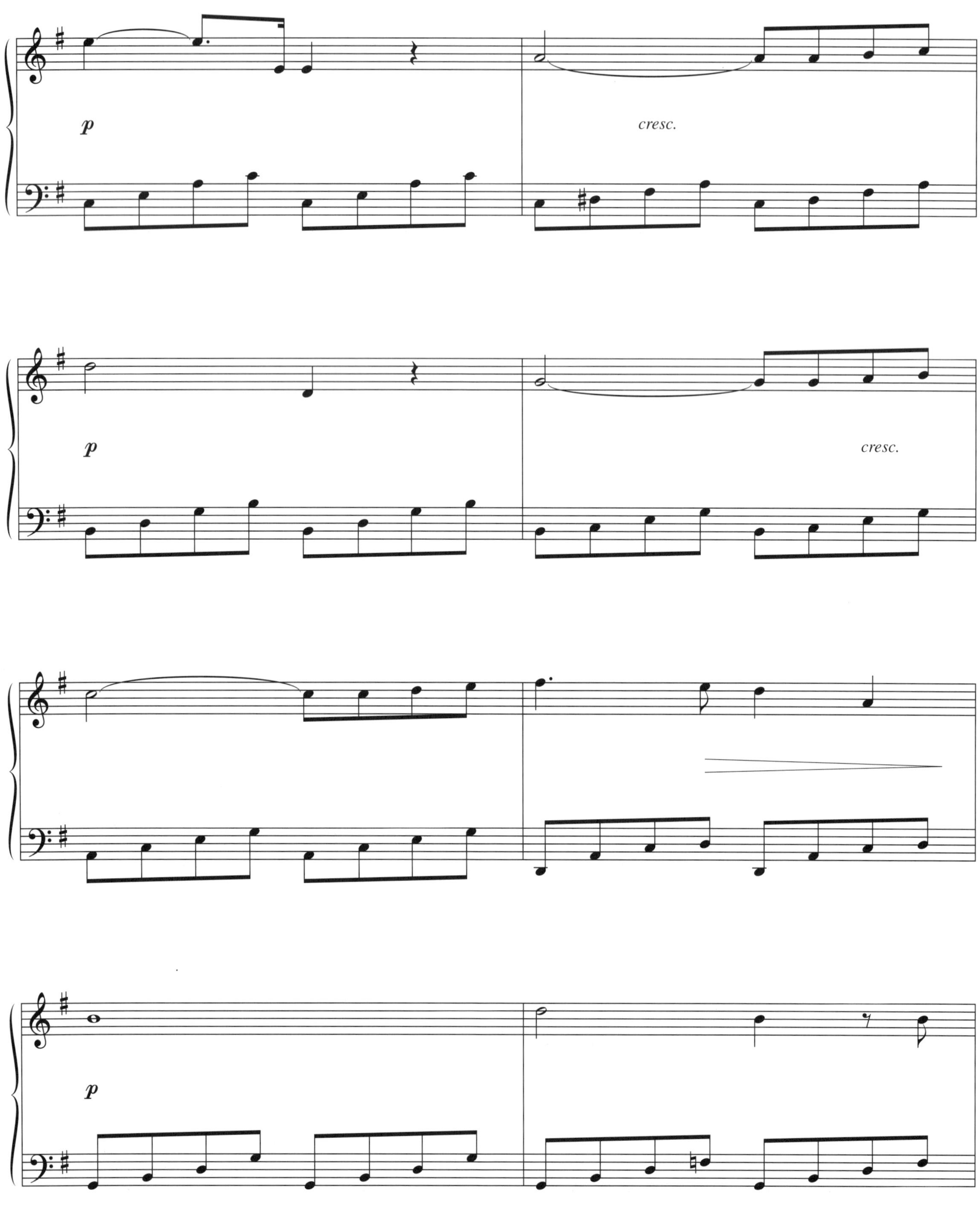
p
cresc.
p
cresc.
p

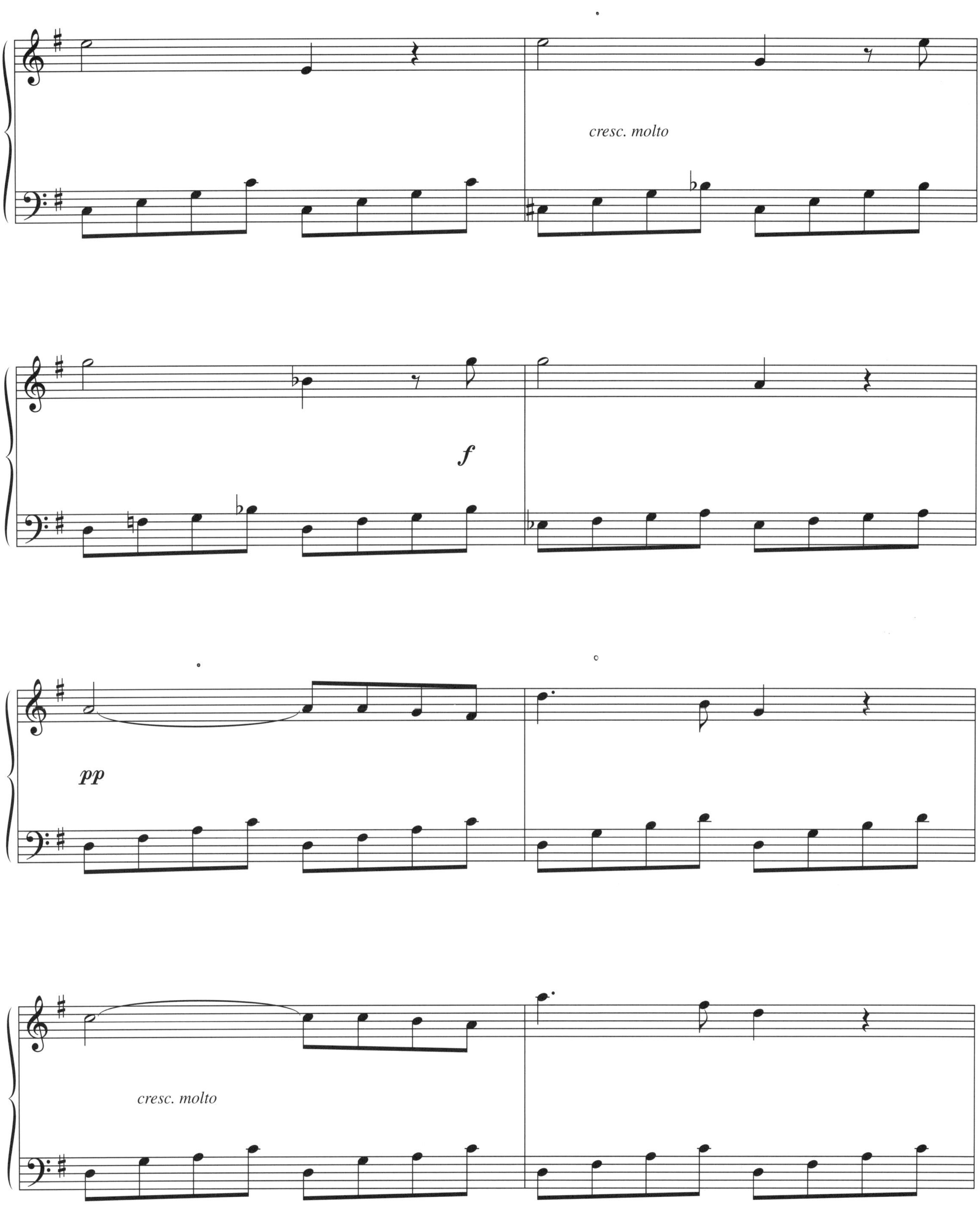
cresc. molto
f
pp
cresc. molto

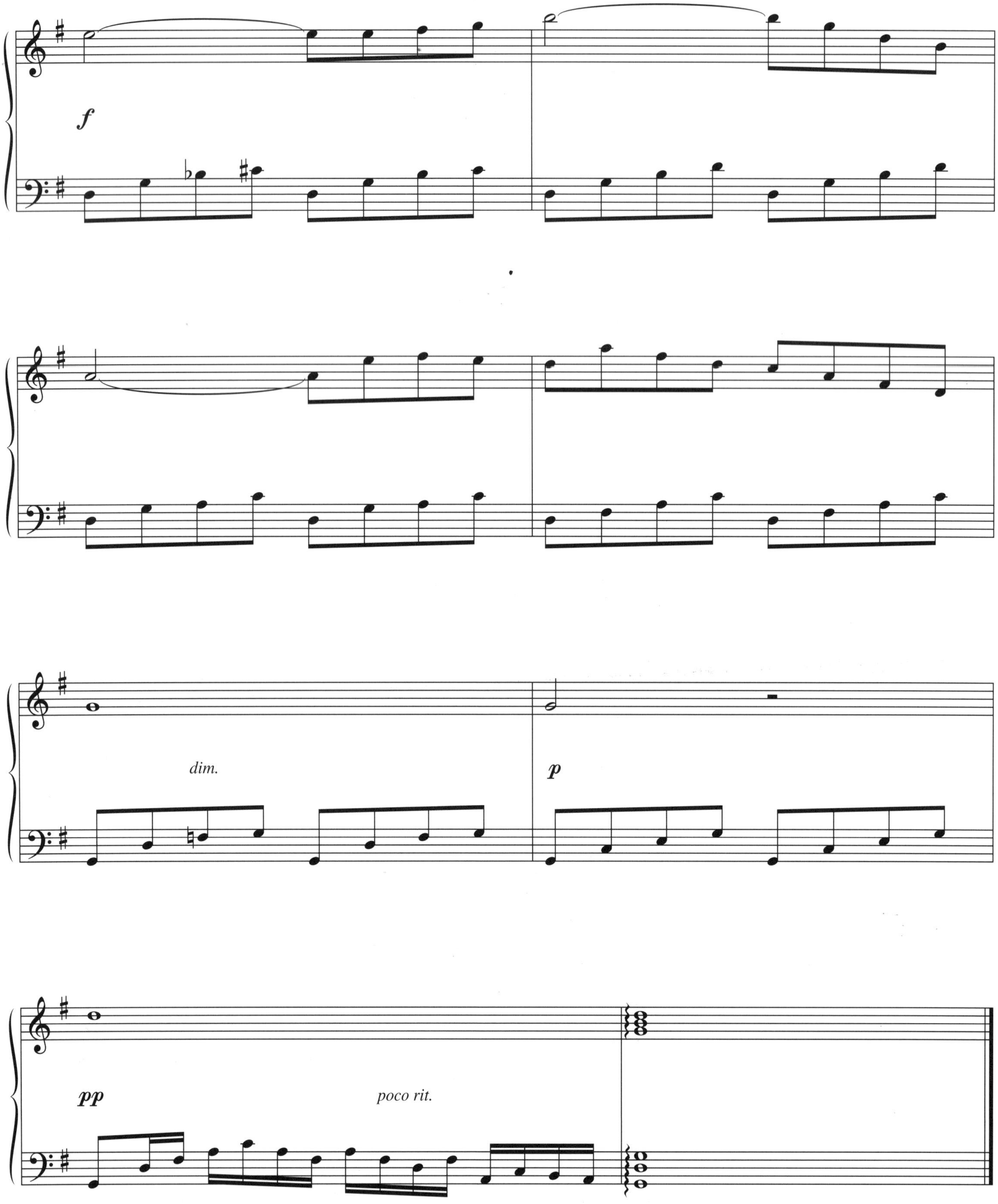
f
dim.
p
pp
poco rit.

In the Hall of the Mountain King
from PEER GYNT

Edvard Grieg
1843-1907
Op. 23, No. 7
originally for orchestra

Alla marcia e molto marcato

pp

sempre staccato e *pp*

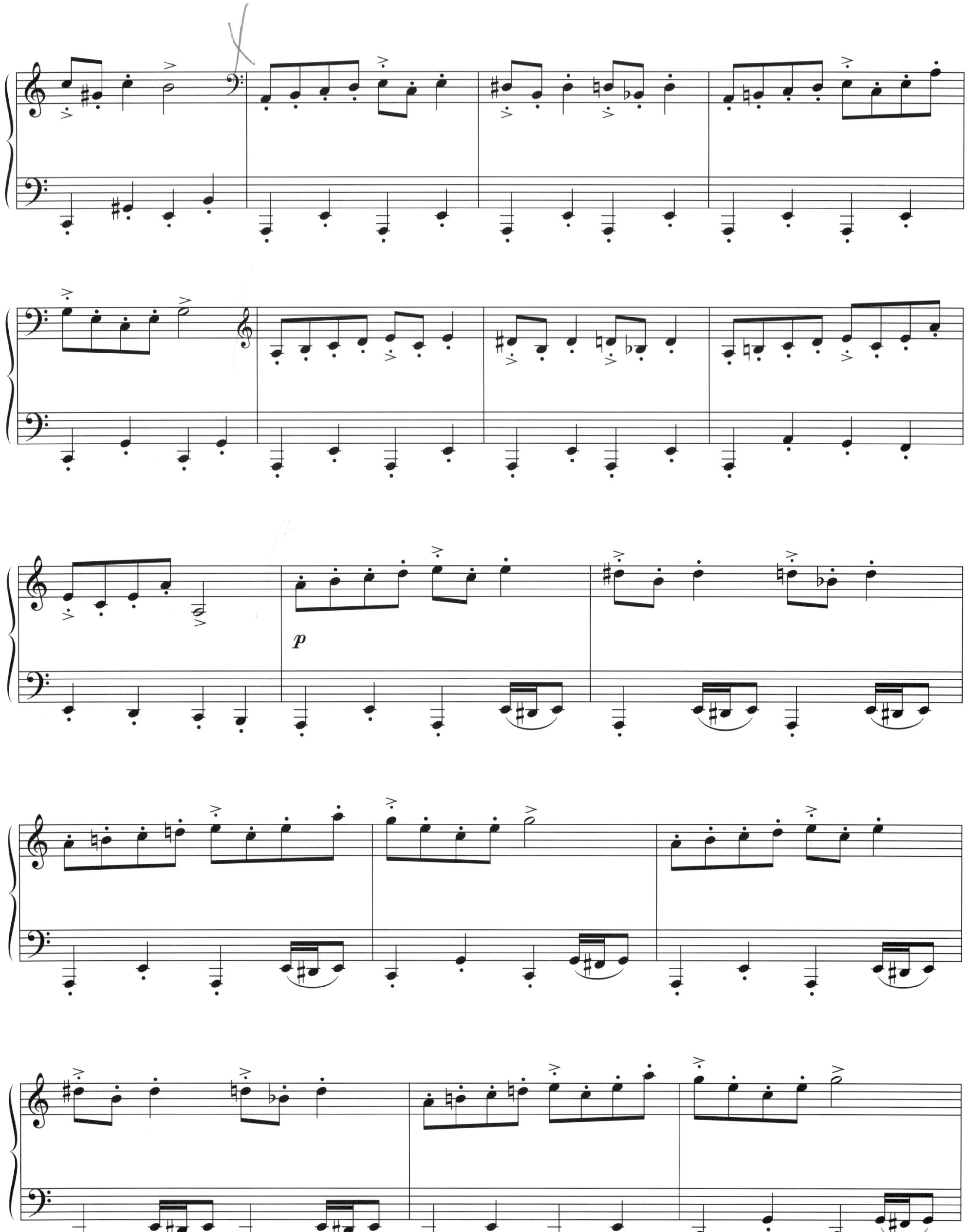
p

poco a poco cresc. e stretto

mf *e sempre cresc.*

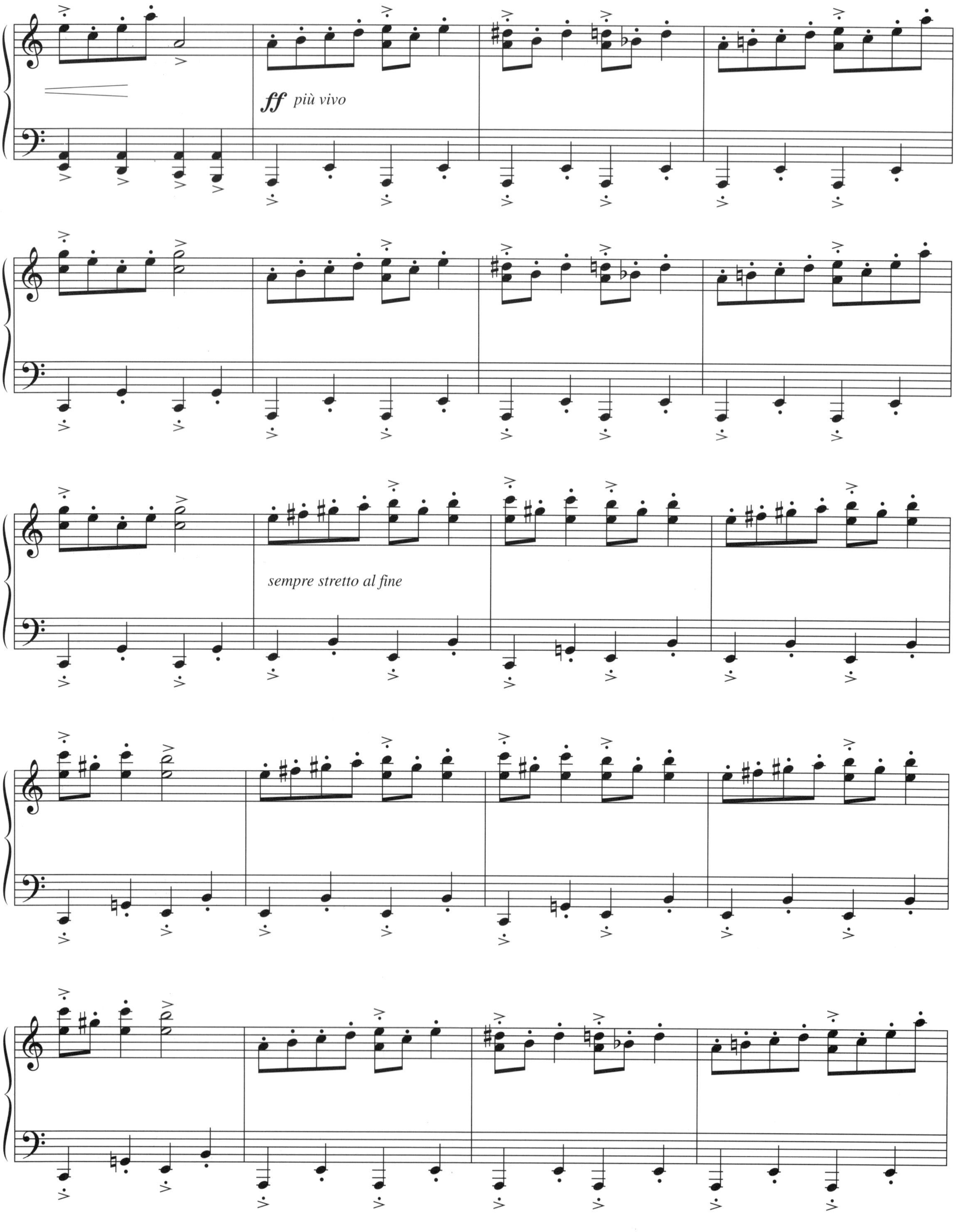
ff più vivo
sempre stretto al fine

165

Solvejg's Song

from PEER GYNT

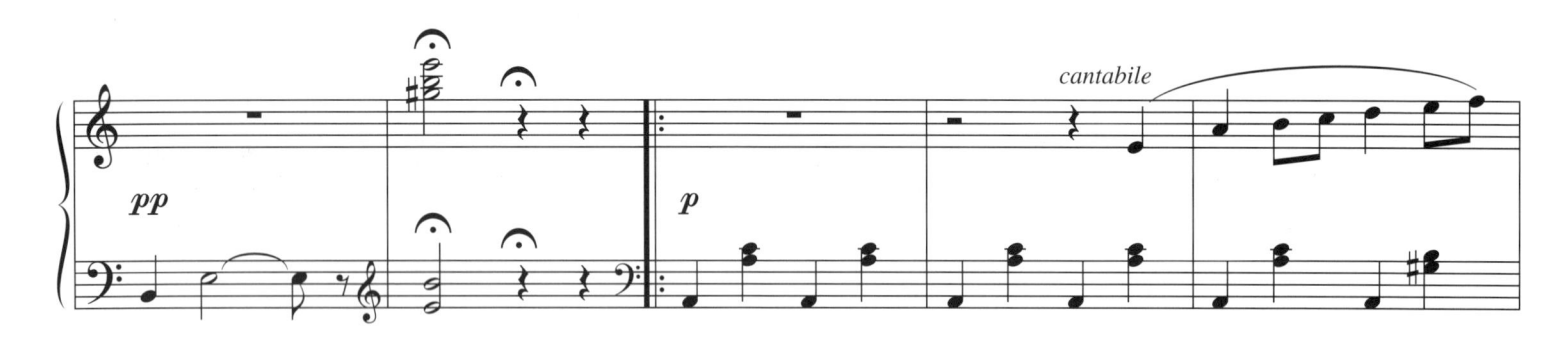

Edvard Grieg
1843-1907
Op. 23, No. 20
originally for soprano and orchestra

Allegretto, tranquillamente
p
pp
poco rit.
Andante
8va
loco
mf
f
p
pp

Morning
from PEER GYNT

Edvard Grieg
1843-1907
Op. 23, No. 13
originally for orchestra

Allegretto pastorale

original key: E Major

169

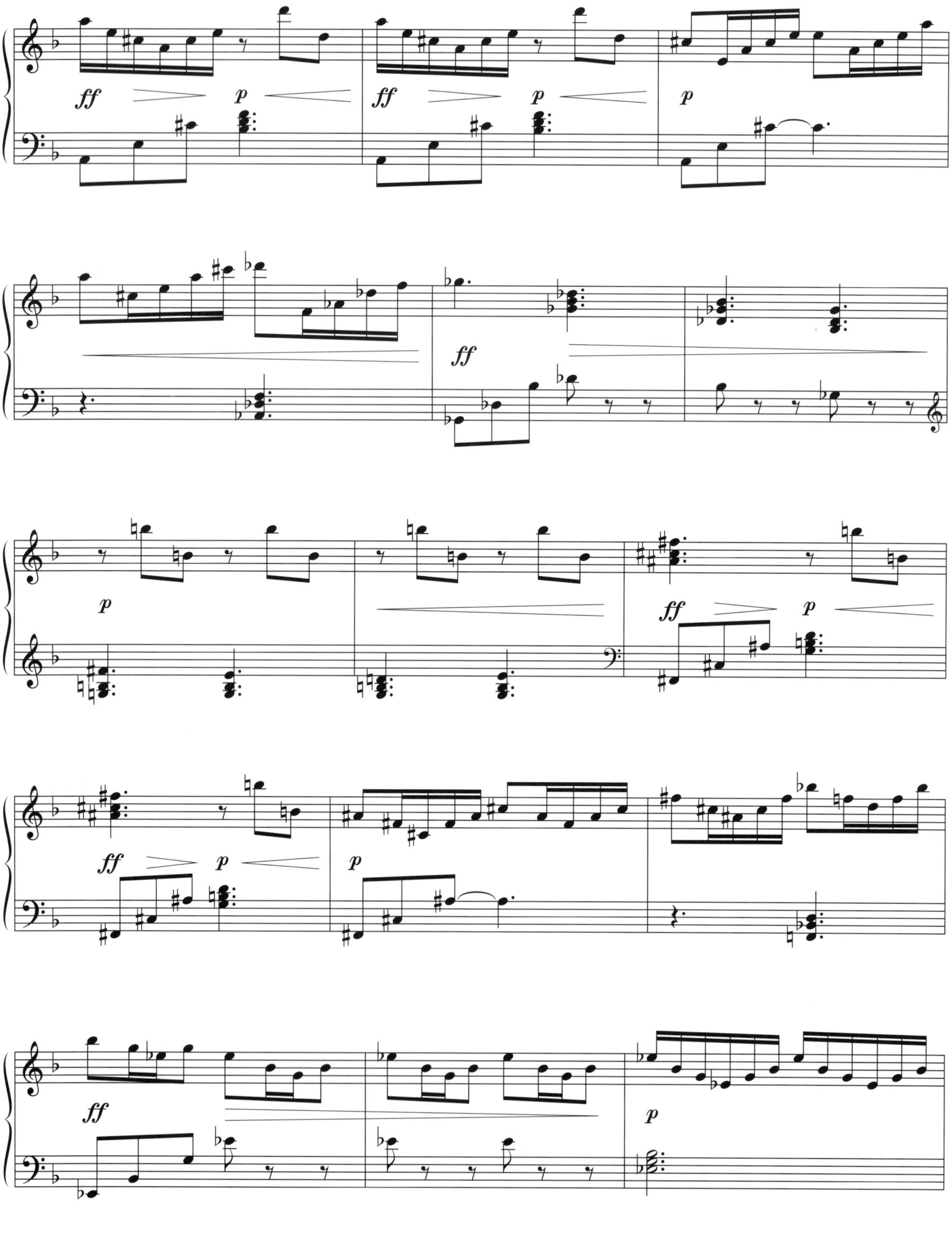
ff
p
ff
p
p
ff
p
ff
p
ff
p
p
ff
p

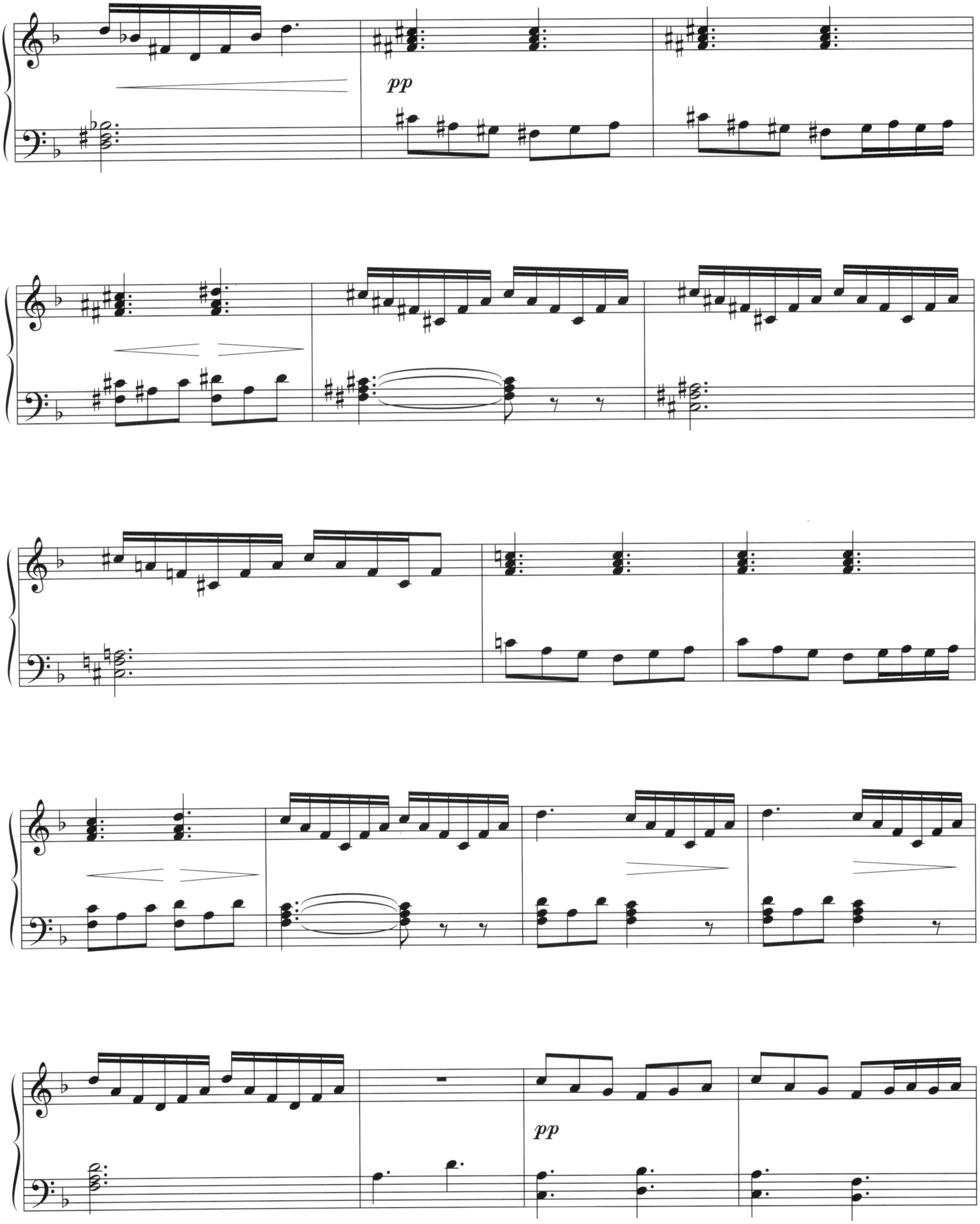
pp
pp

172

Allegro
from WATER MUSIC

George Frideric Handel
1685-1759
originally for orchestra

174

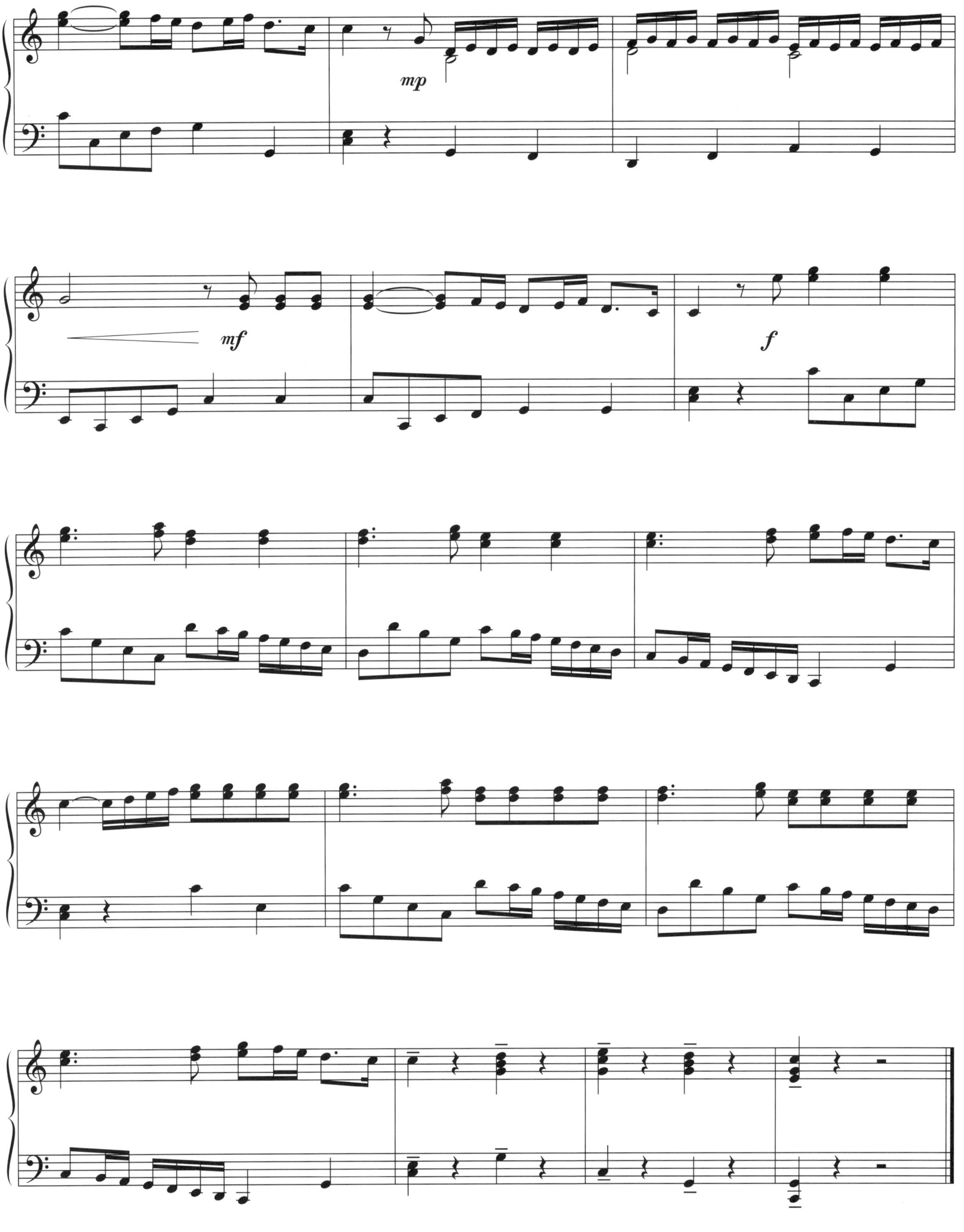
mp
mf
f

Air
from the oratorio WATER MUSIC

George Frideric Handel
1685-1759
originally for orchestra

Andante con moto

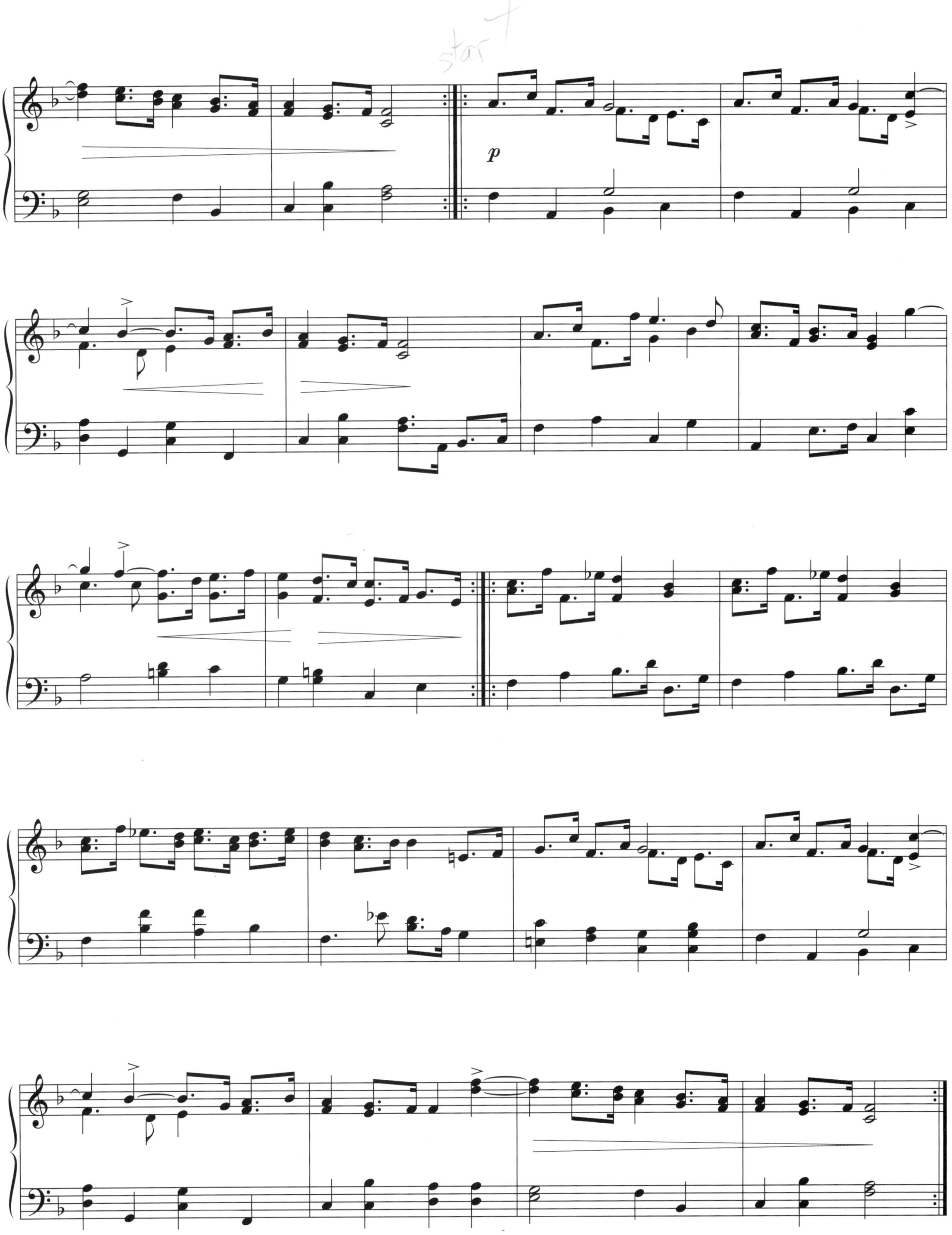

Allegro maestoso
from WATER MUSIC
Excerpt

George Frideric Handel
1685-1759
originally for orchestra

original key: D Major

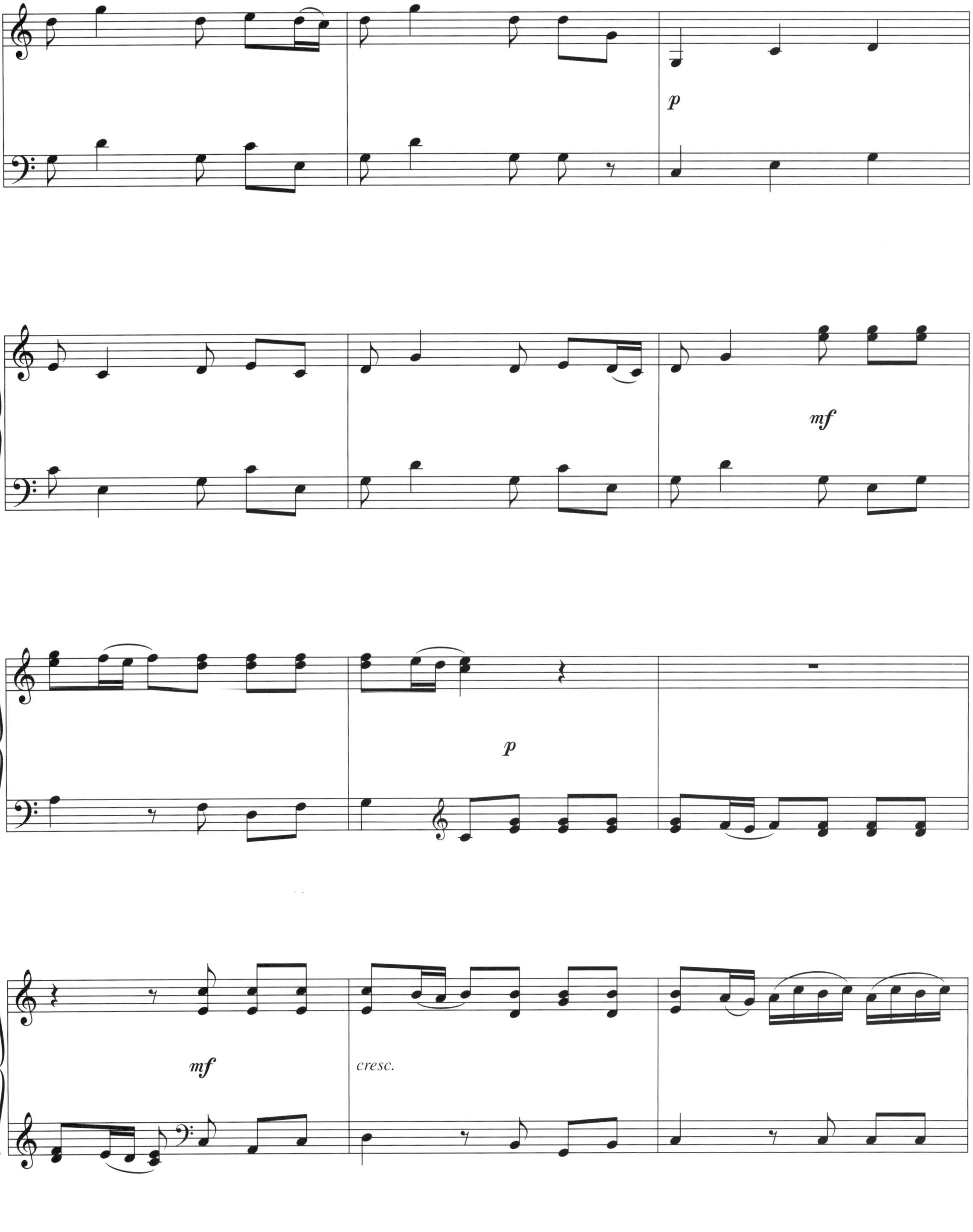
p
mf
p
mf
cresc.

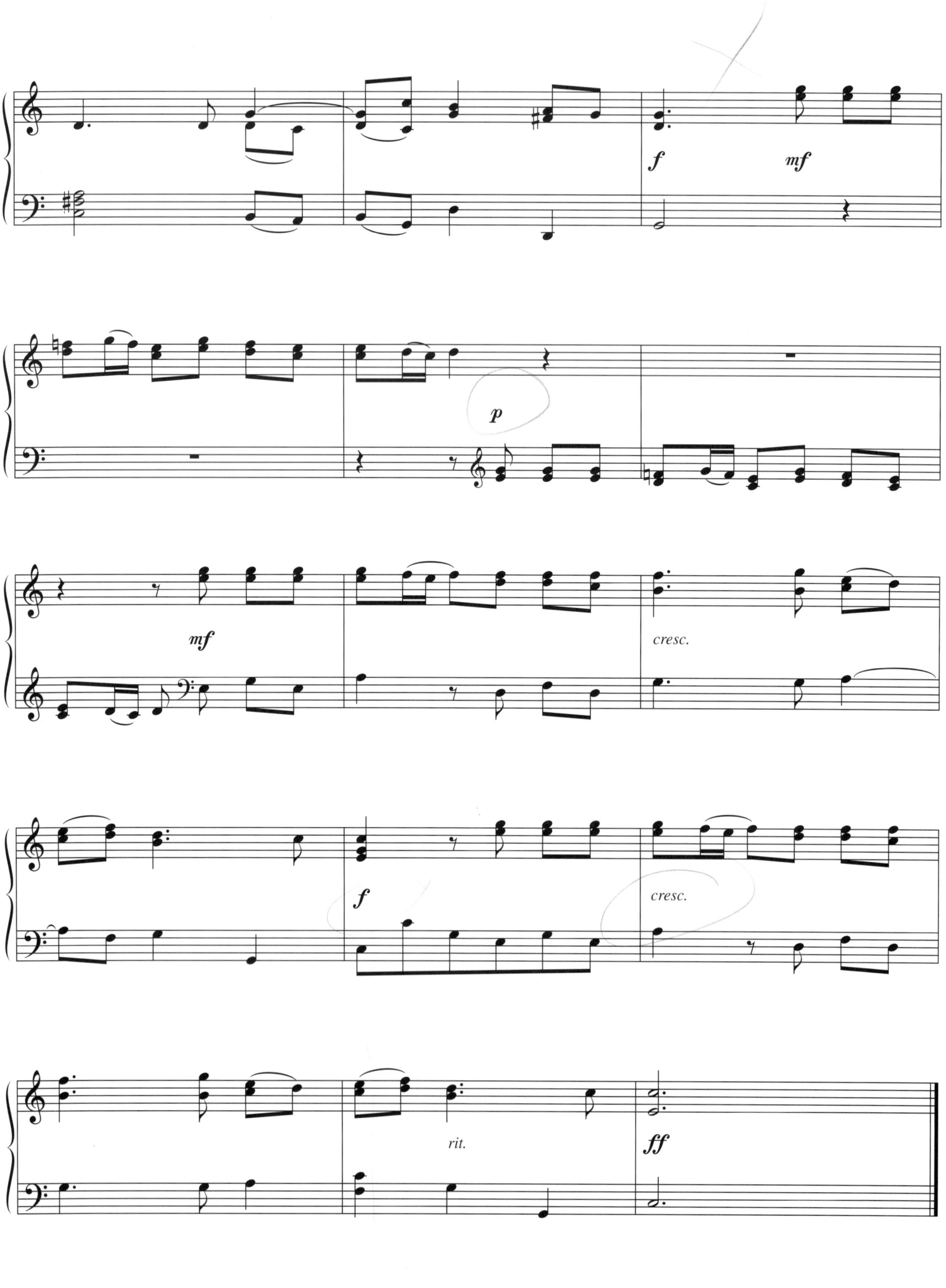
f
mf
p
mf
cresc.
f
cresc.
rit.
ff

The Trumpet Shall Sound
from the oratorio MESSIAH

George Frideric Handel
1685-1759
originally for bass, trumpet and orchestra

Pompaso, ma non allegro

original key: D Major

Copyright © 2000 by HAL LEONARD CORPORATION
International Copyright Secured   All Rights Reserved

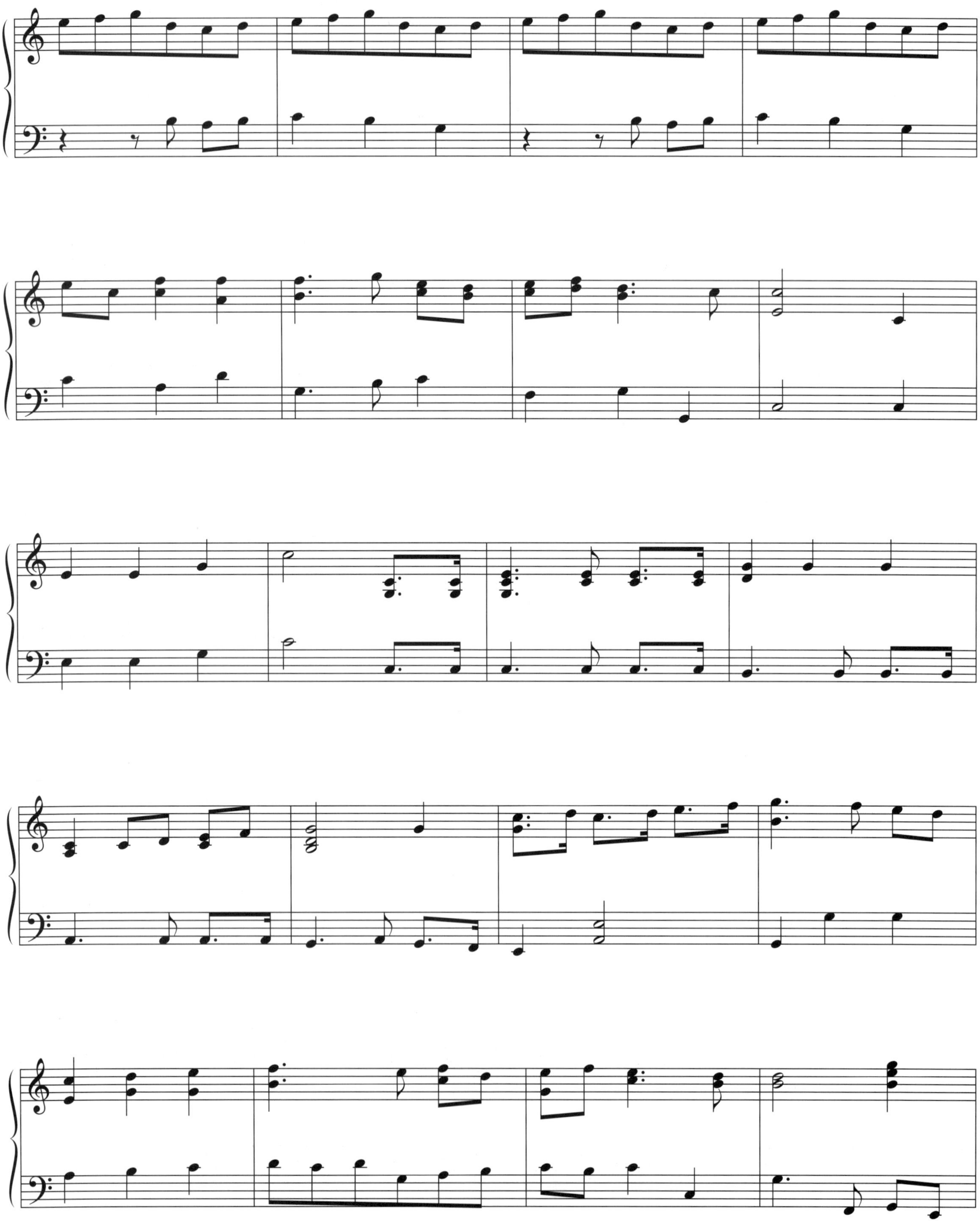

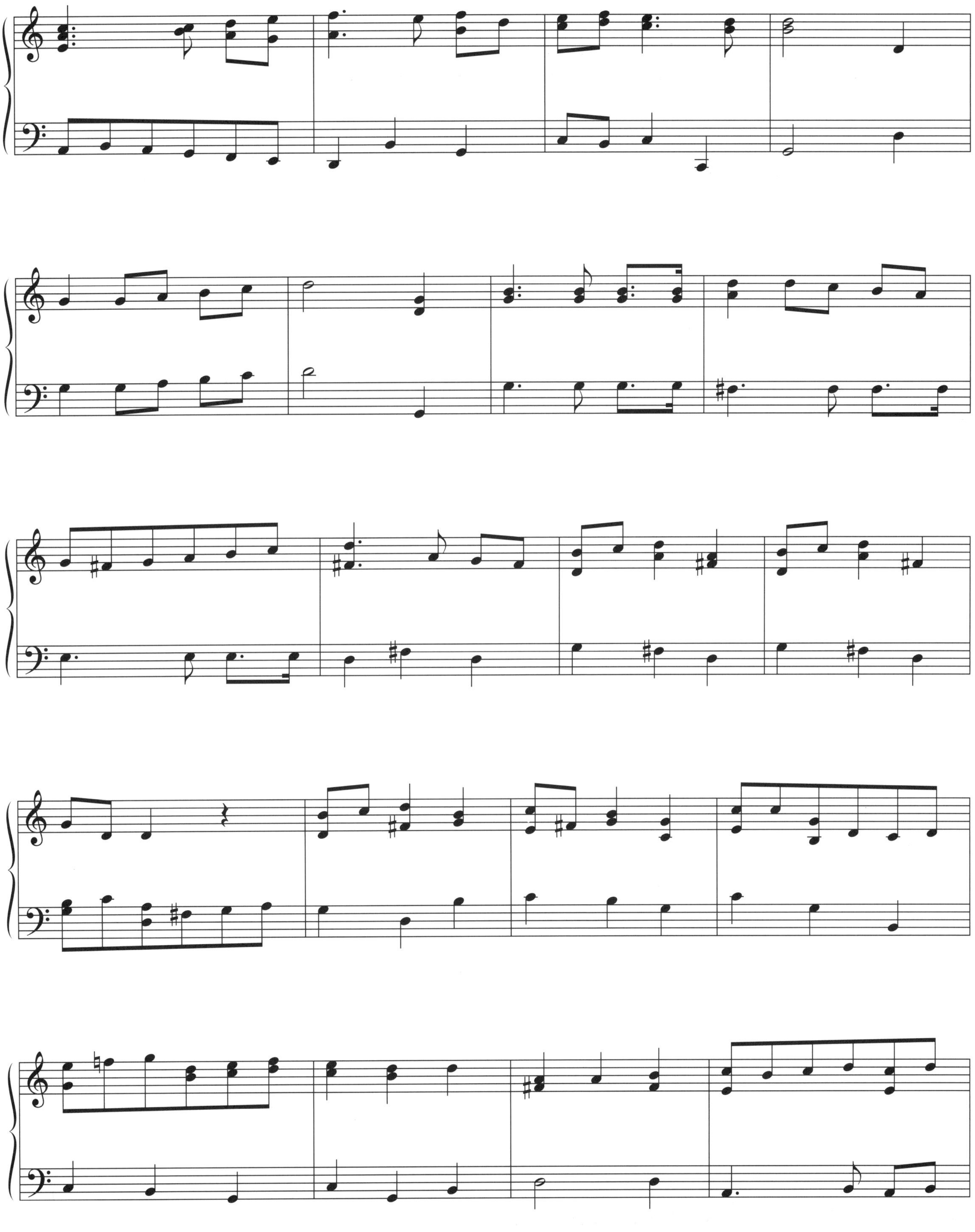

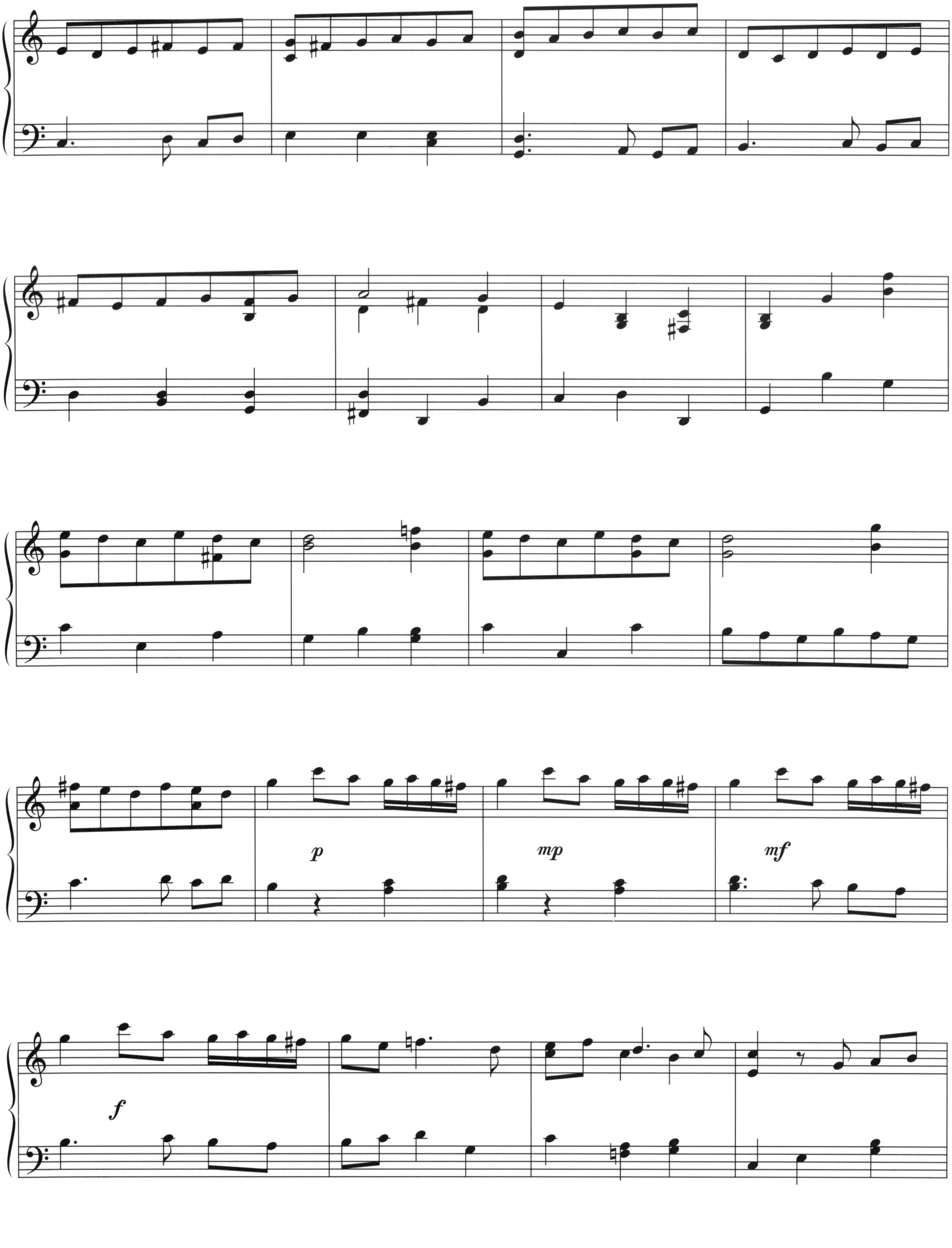
p
mp
mf
f

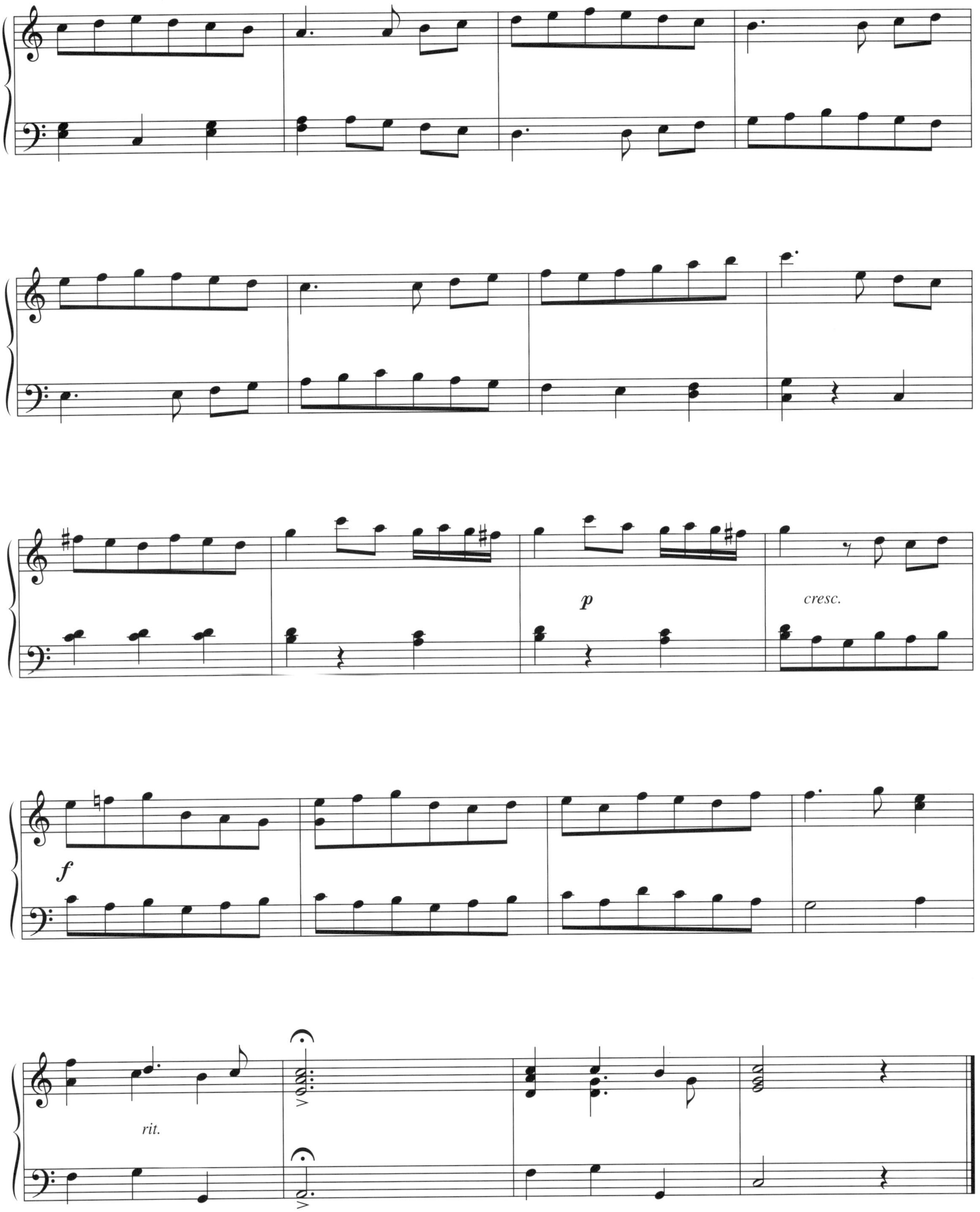
p
cresc.
f
rit.

Pastoral Symphony
from the oratorio MESSIAH

George Frideric Handel
1685-1759
originally for orchestra

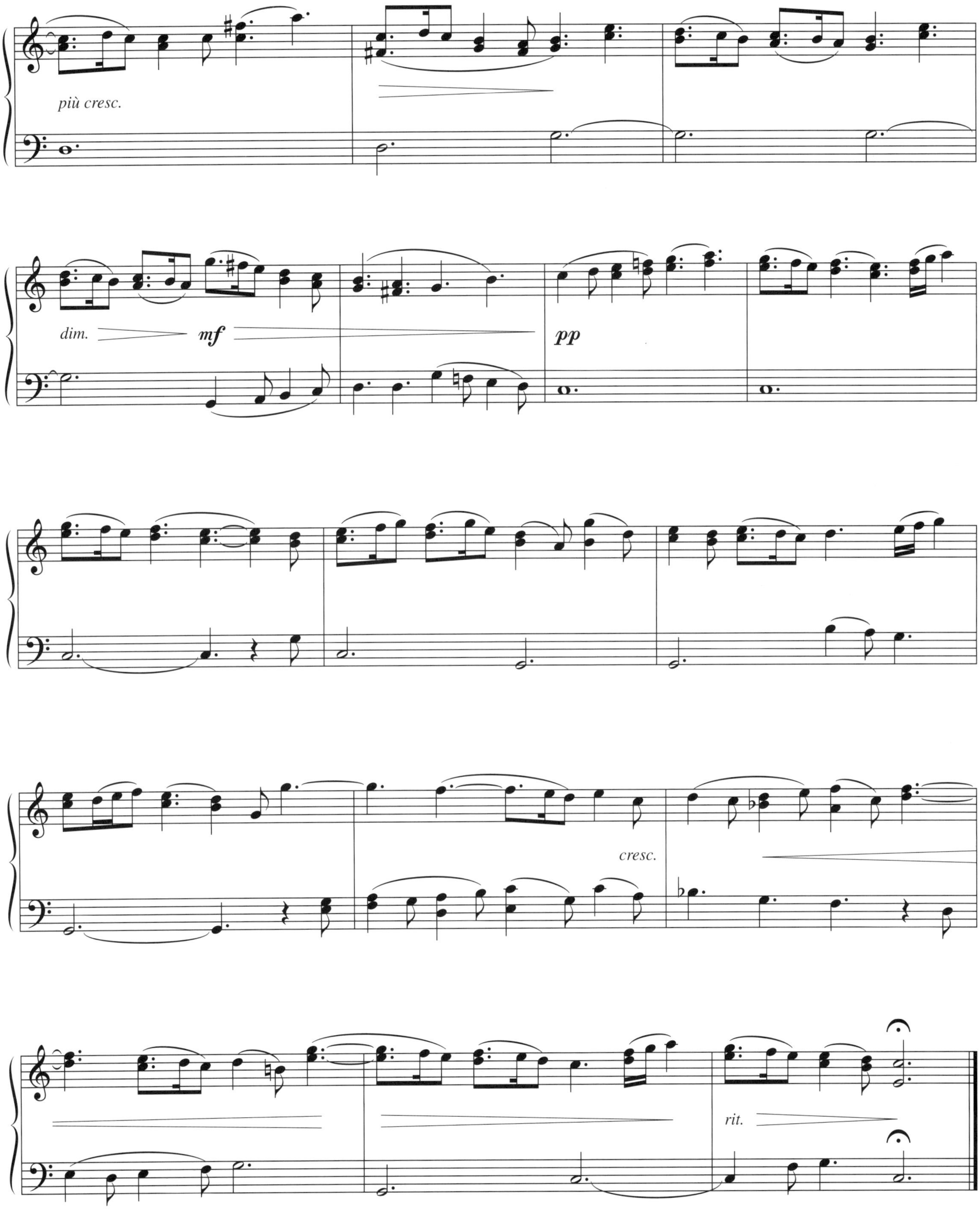
più cresc.
dim.
mf
pp
cresc.
rit.

Hallelujah

from the oratorio MESSIAH
Excerpt

George Frideric Handel
1685-1759
originally for chorus and orchestra

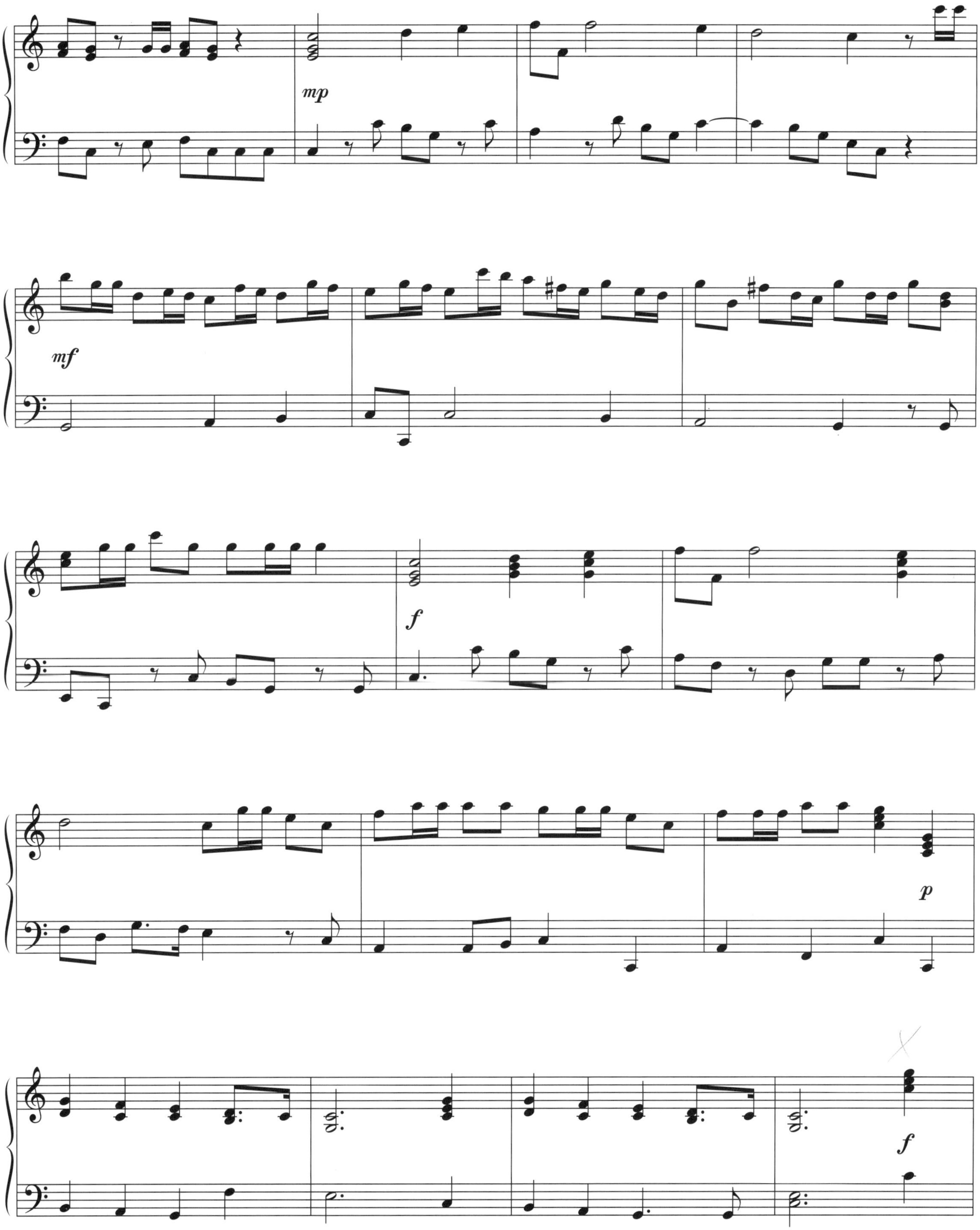
mp
mf
f
p
f

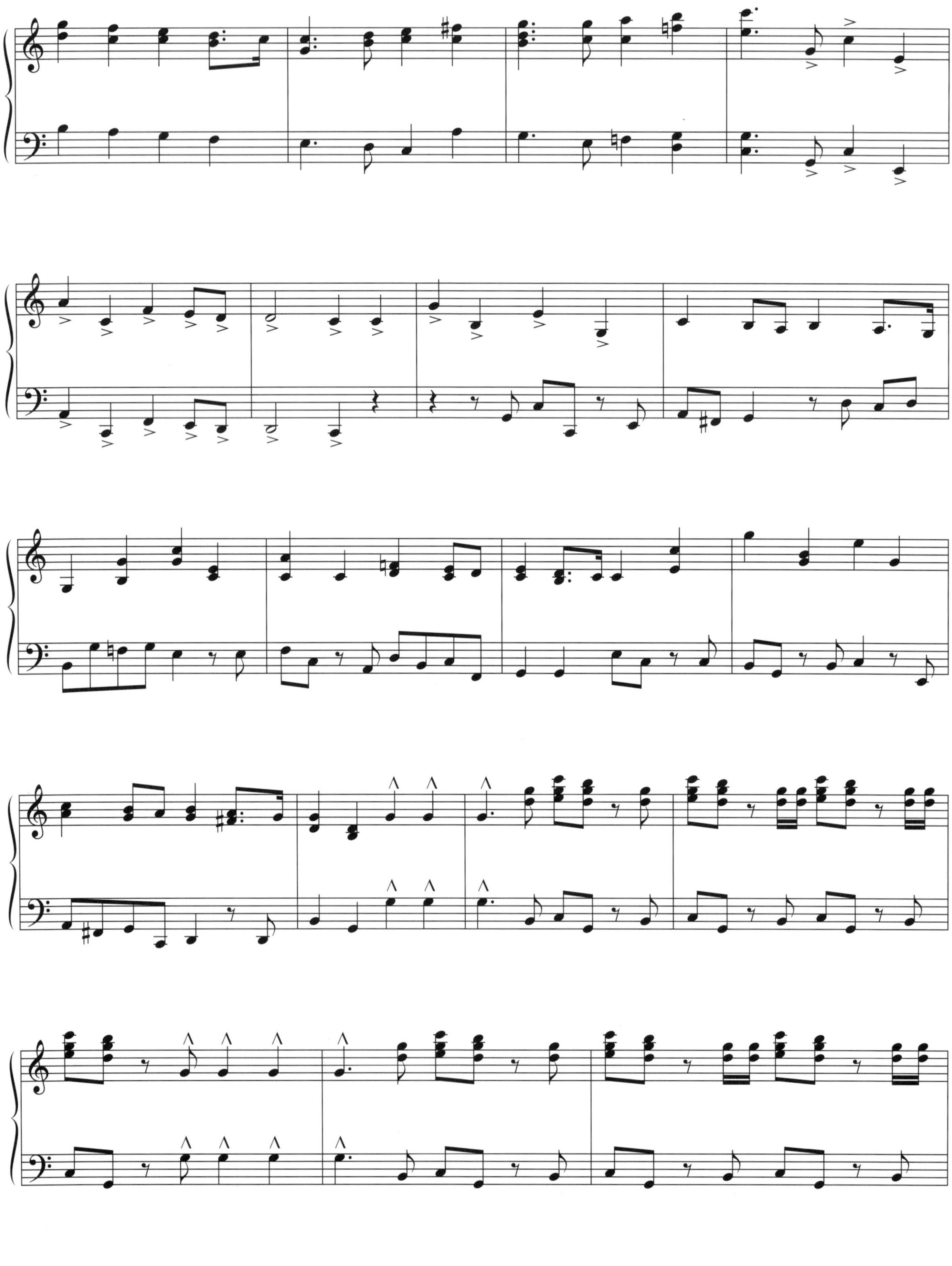

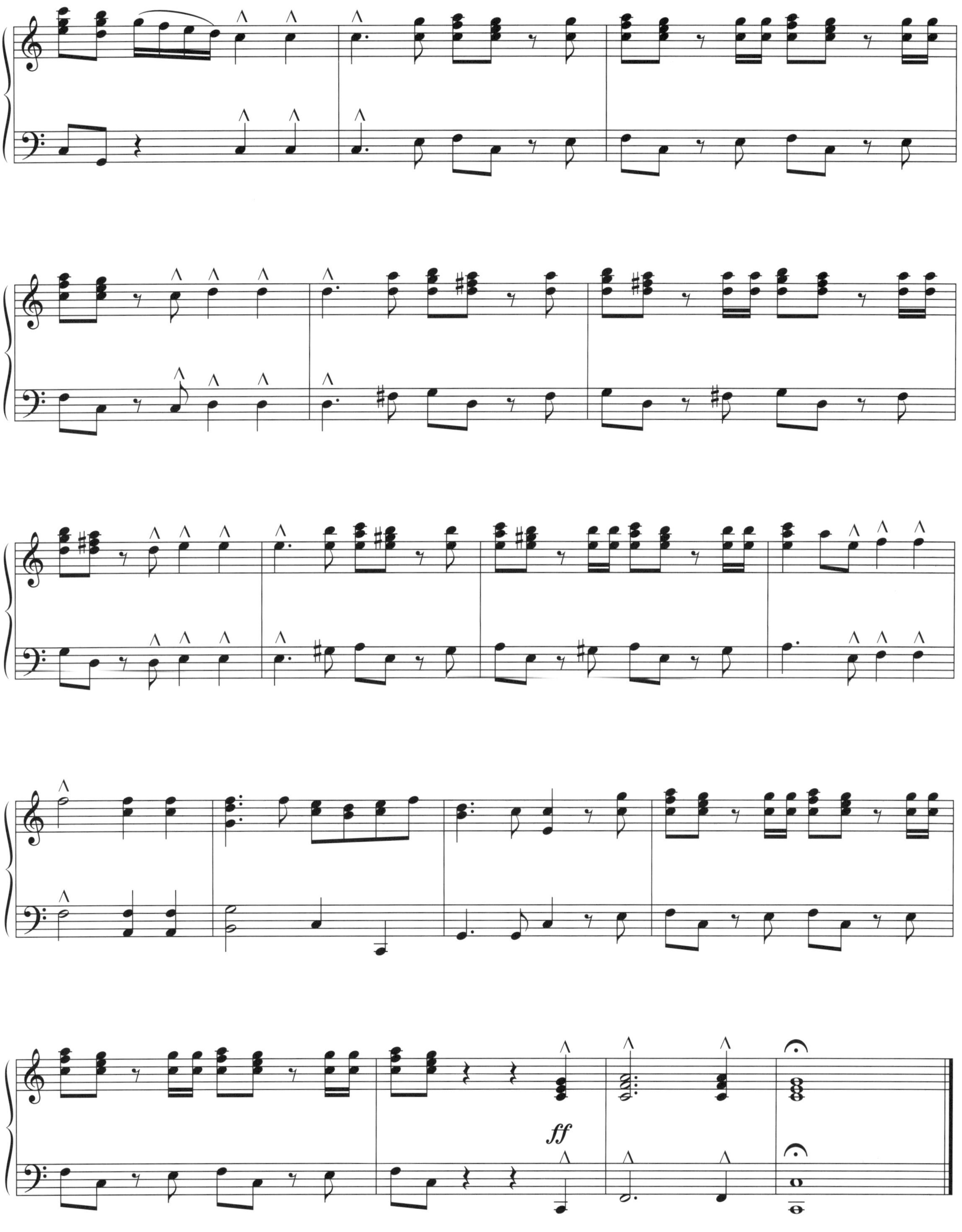
ff

Largo
Ombra mai fù
from the opera SERSE
(Xerxes)

George Frideric Handel
1685-1759

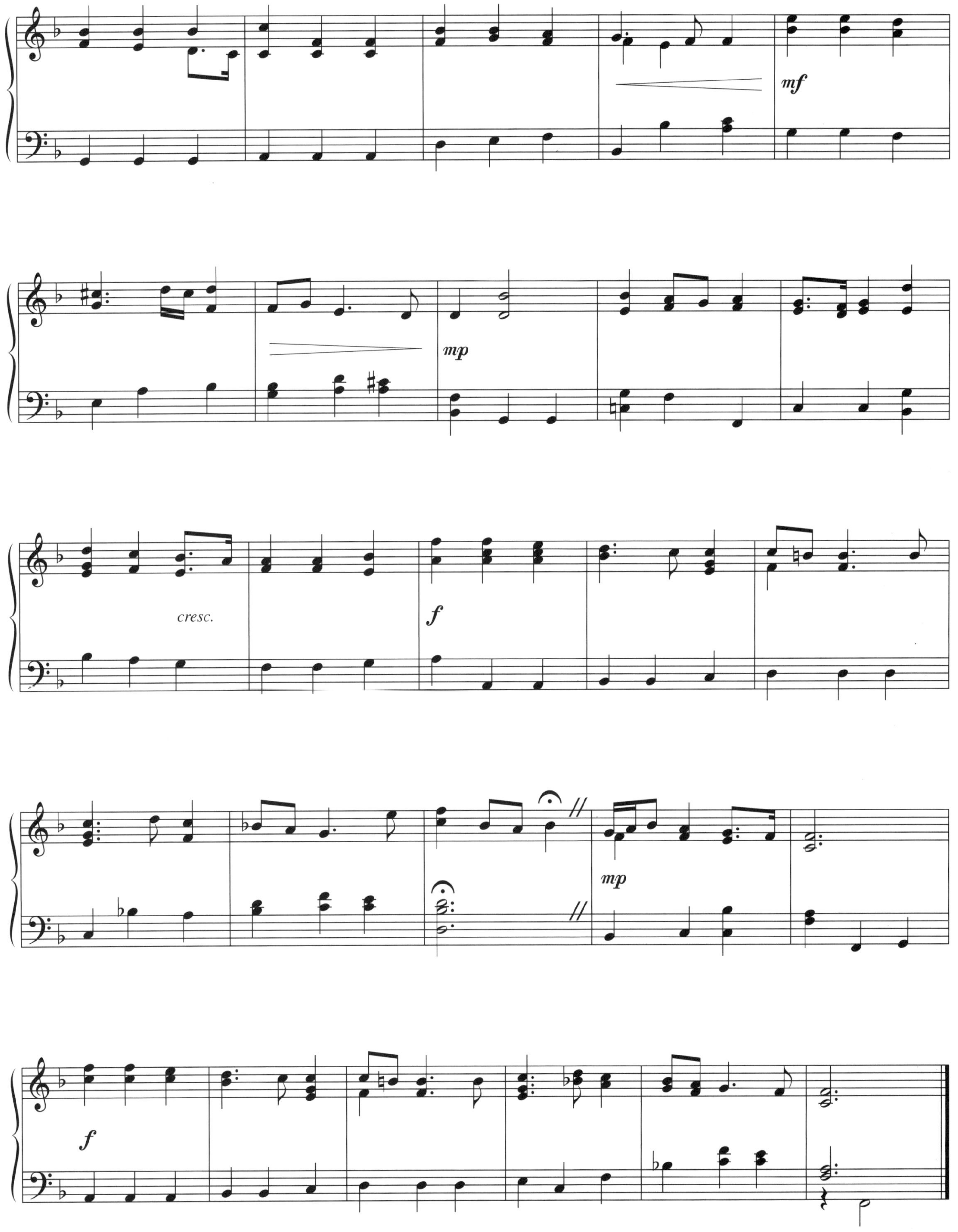
mf
mp
cresc.
f
mp
f

The Heavens Are Telling
from the oratorio THE CREATION

Franz Joseph Haydn
1732-1809
originally for chorus and orchestra

Allegro (♩ = 116)

195

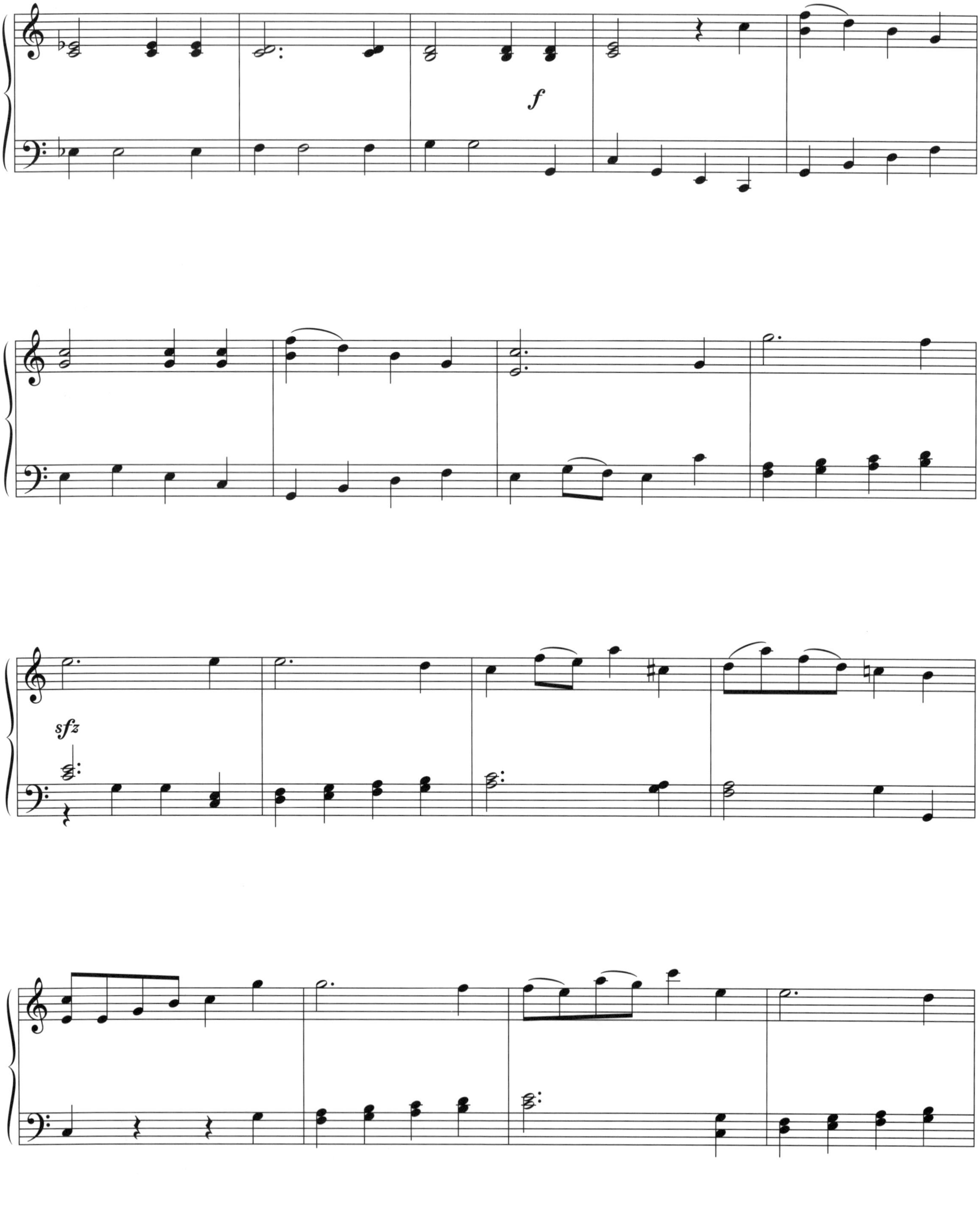
f
sfz

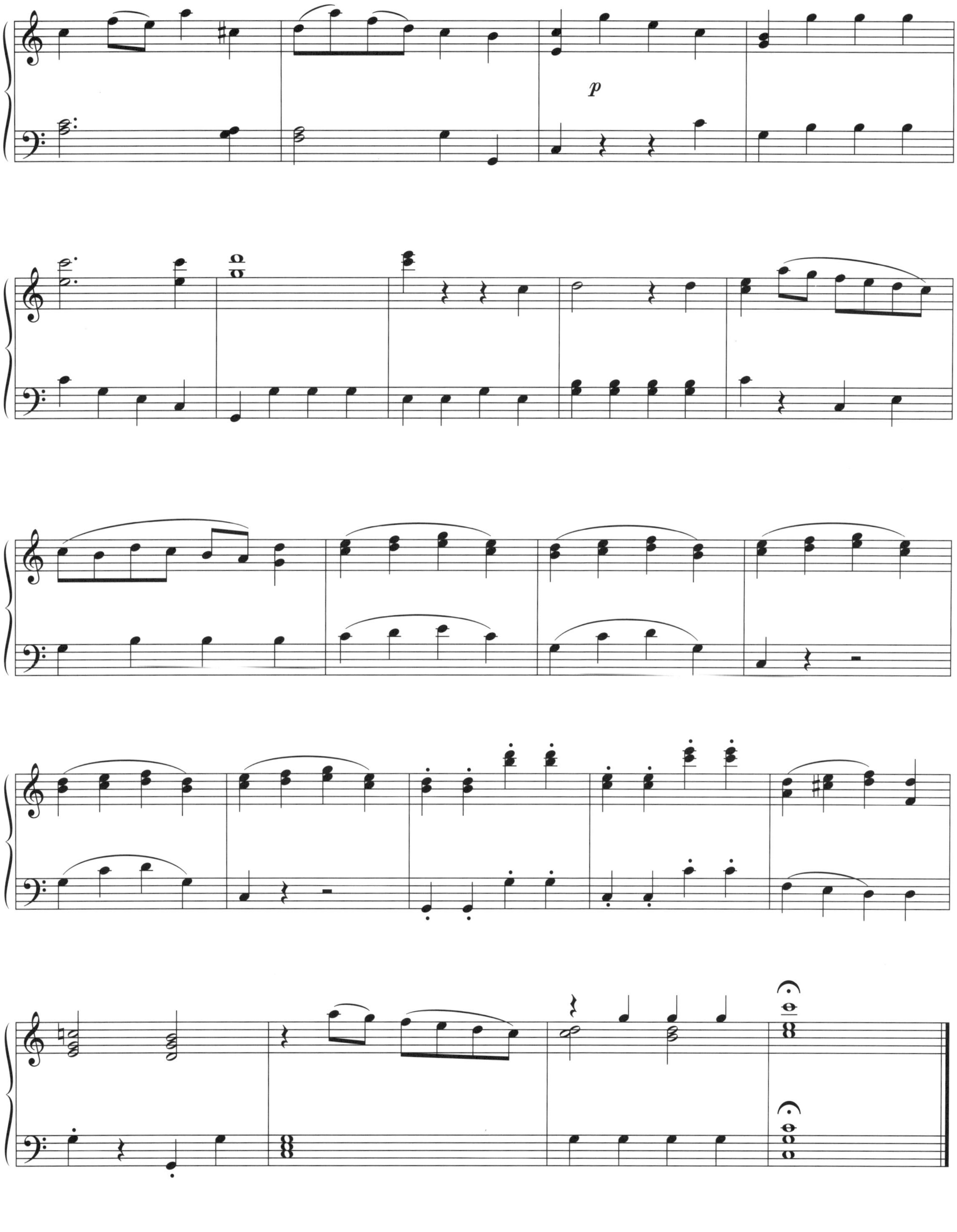
p

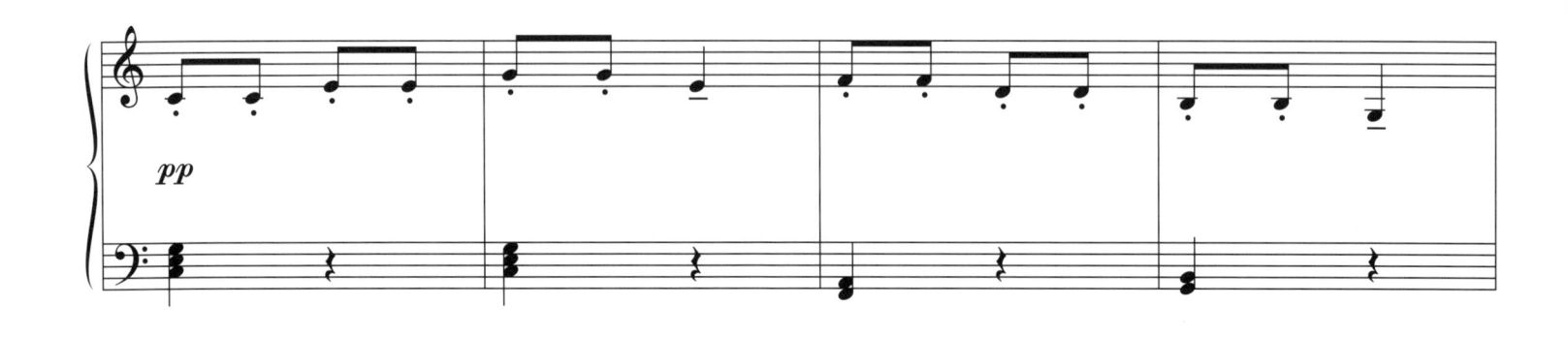

Symphony No. 94

"Surprise"
Second Movement Excerpt

Franz Joseph Haydn
1732-1809
originally for orchestra

199

Symphony No. 101
"The Clock"
Third Movement Excerpt

Franz Joseph Haydn
1732-1809
originally for orchestra

original key: D Major

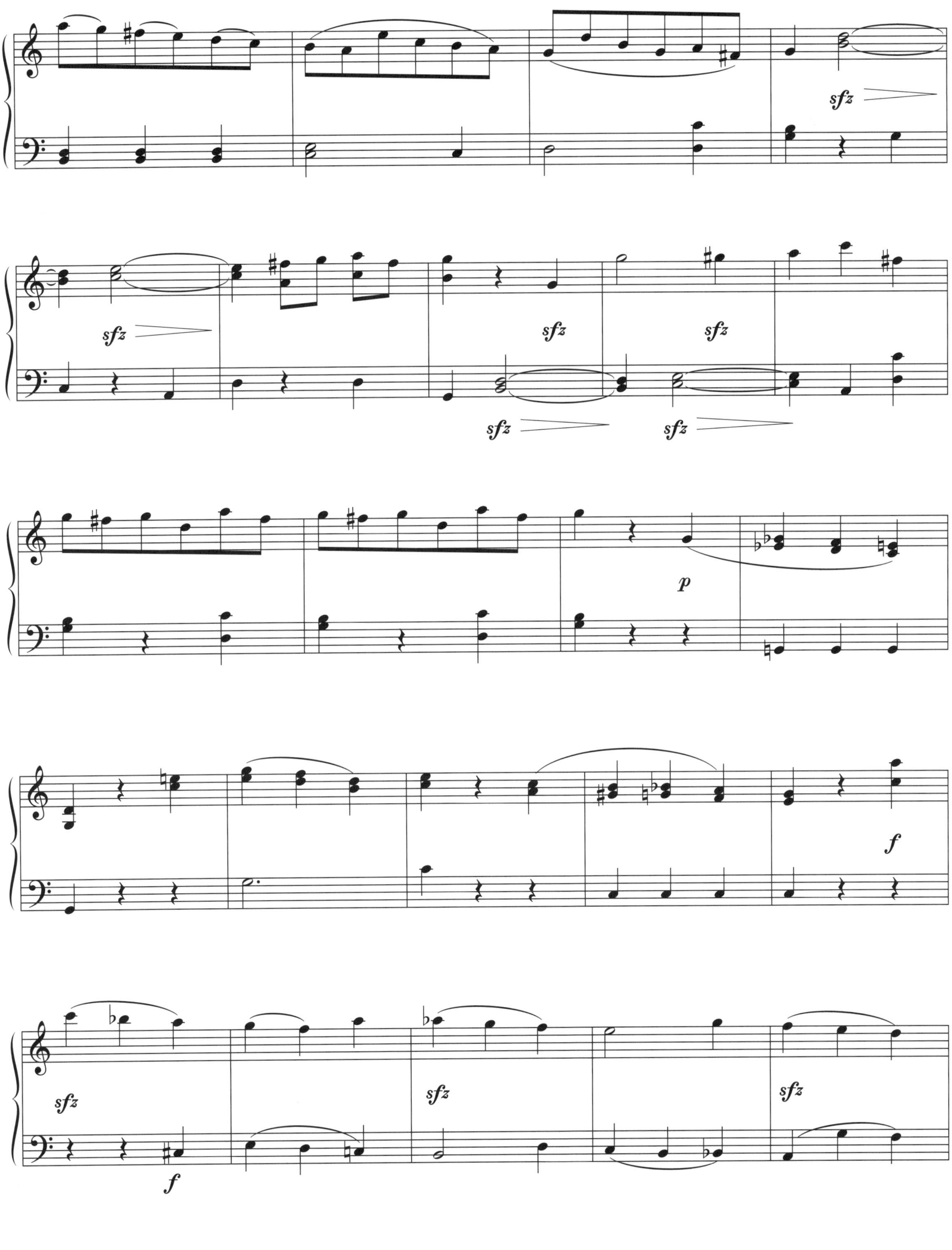
sfz
sfz
sfz
sfz
sfz
sfz
p
f
sfz
f
sfz
sfz

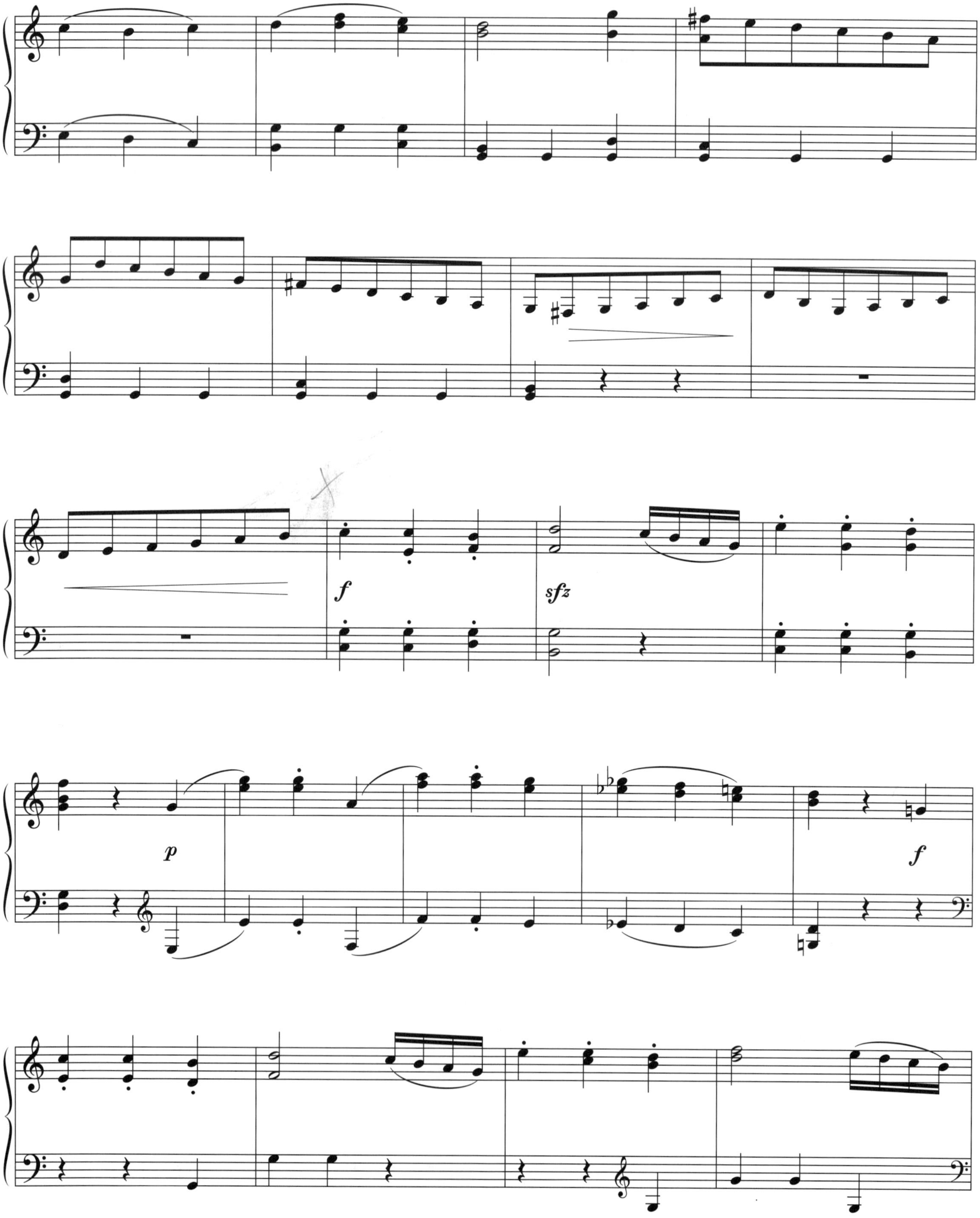
f
sfz
p
f

203

Symphony No. 104
"London"
First Movement Excerpt

Franz Joseph Haydn
1732-1809
originally for orchestra

Allegro

original key: D Major

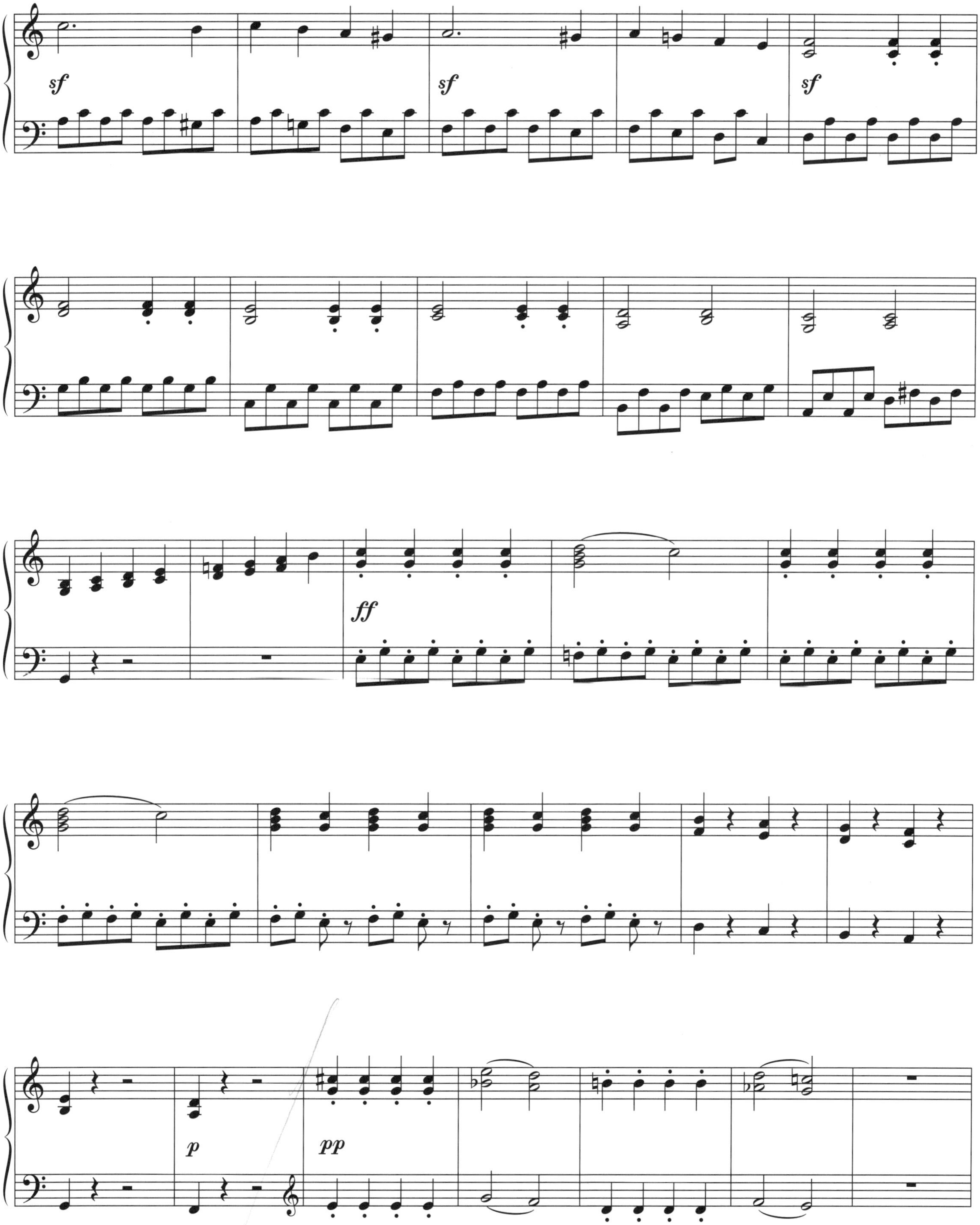
sf
sf
sf
ff
p
pp

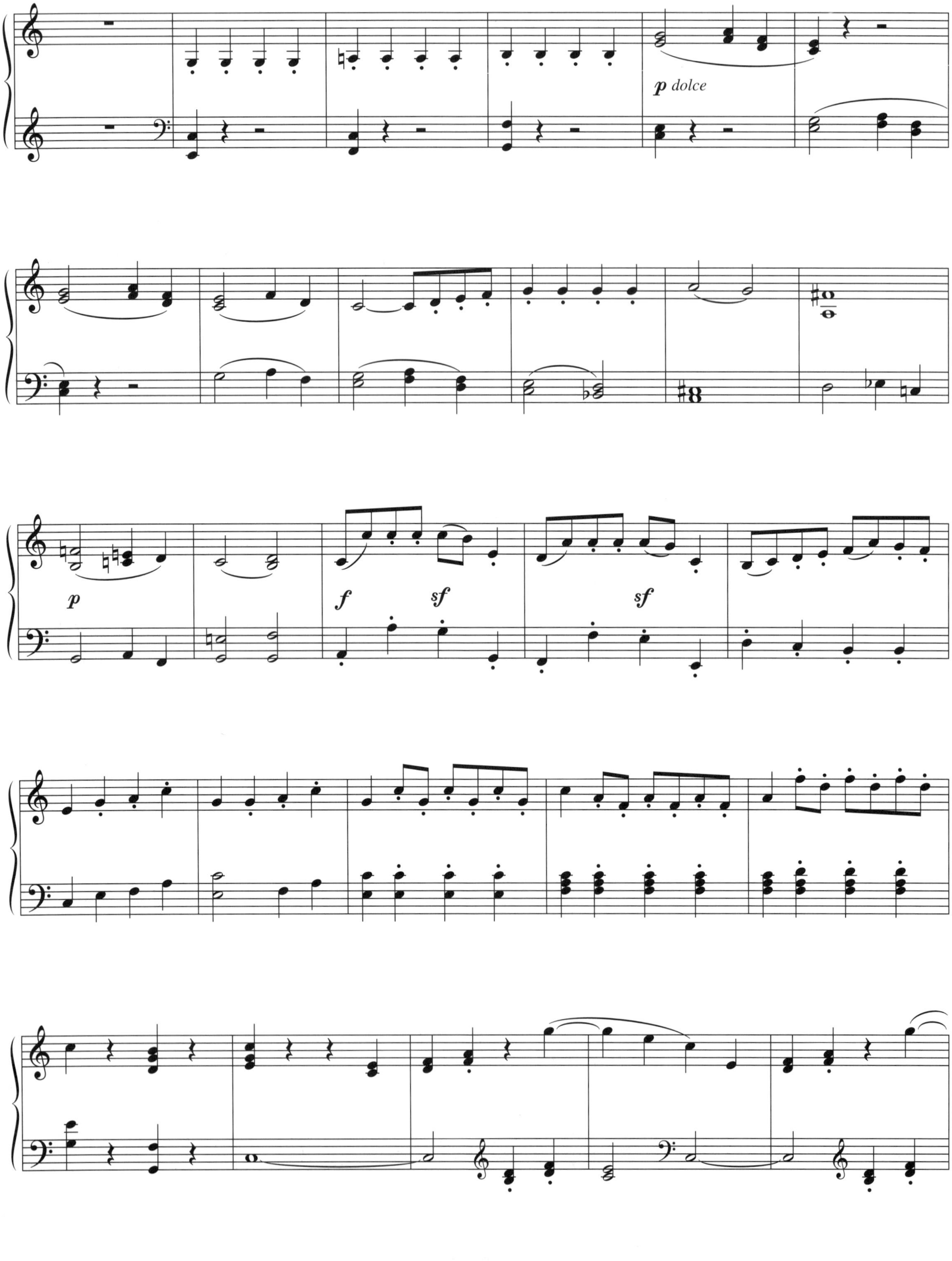
p dolce
p
f
sf
sf

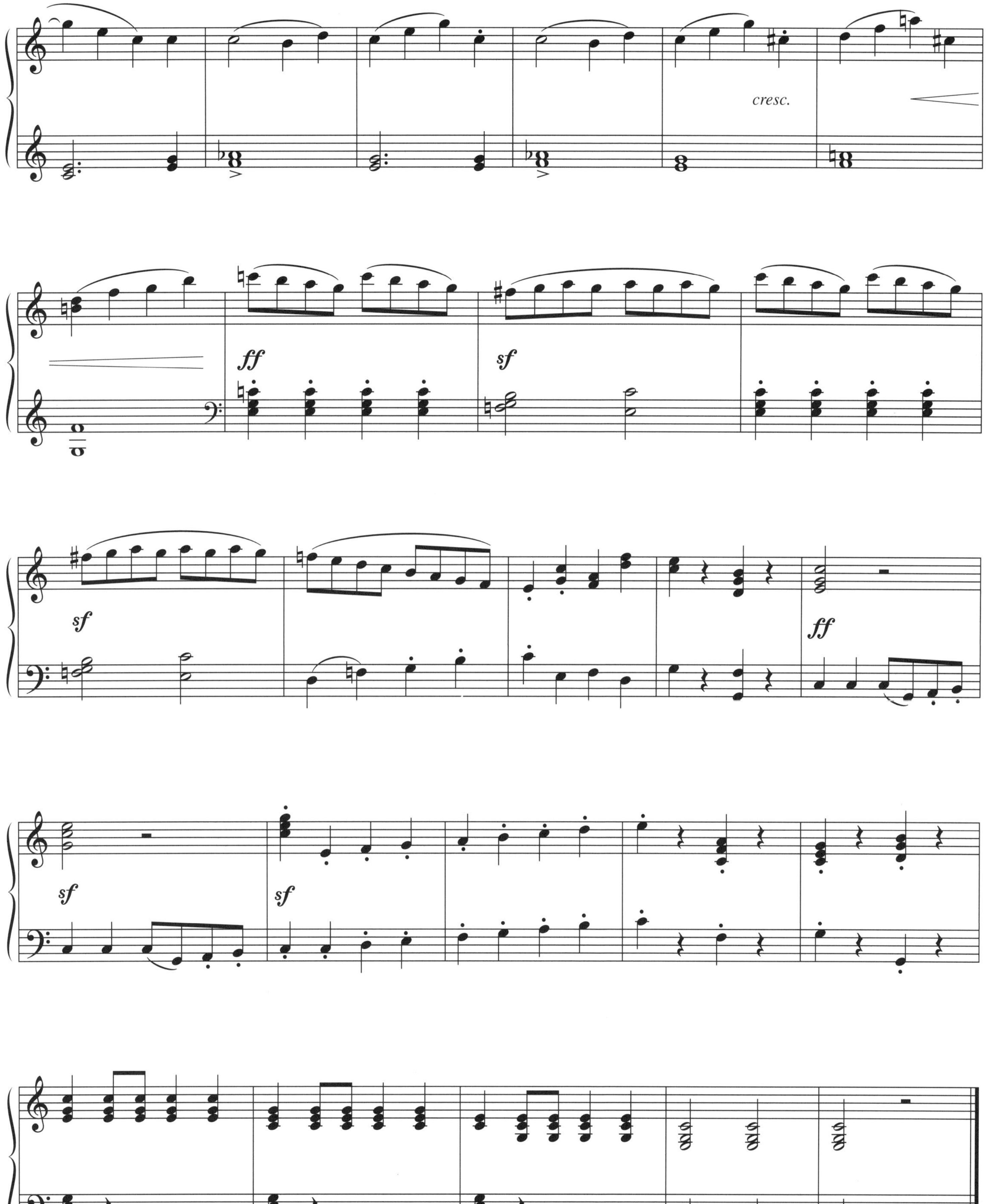
cresc.
ff
sf
sf
ff
sf
sf

Gypsy Rondo

from Keyboard Trio No. 23, in G Major
Third Movement

Franz Joseph Haydn
1732-1809
originally for violin, violoncello, keyboard

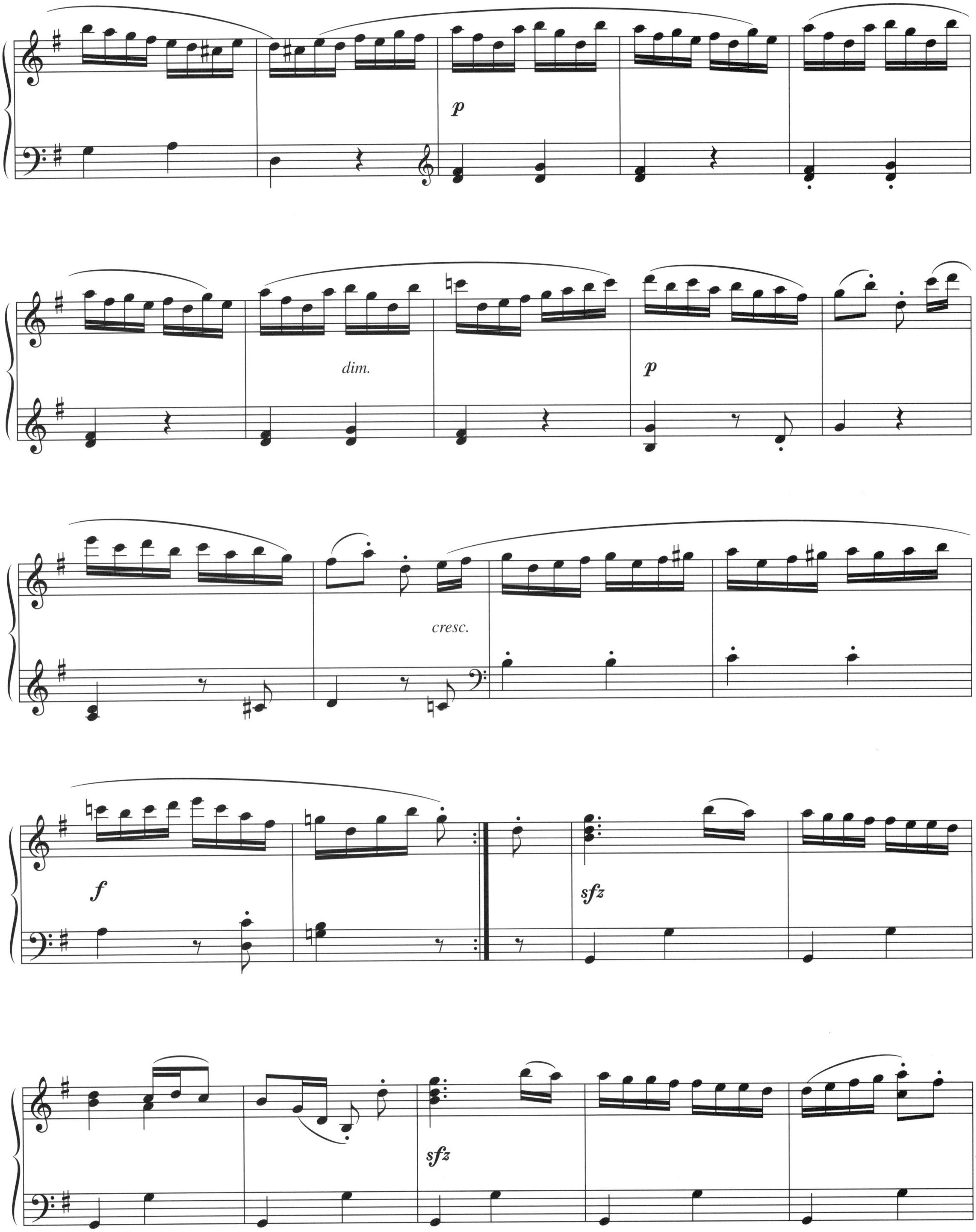
p
dim.
p
cresc.
f
sfz
sfz

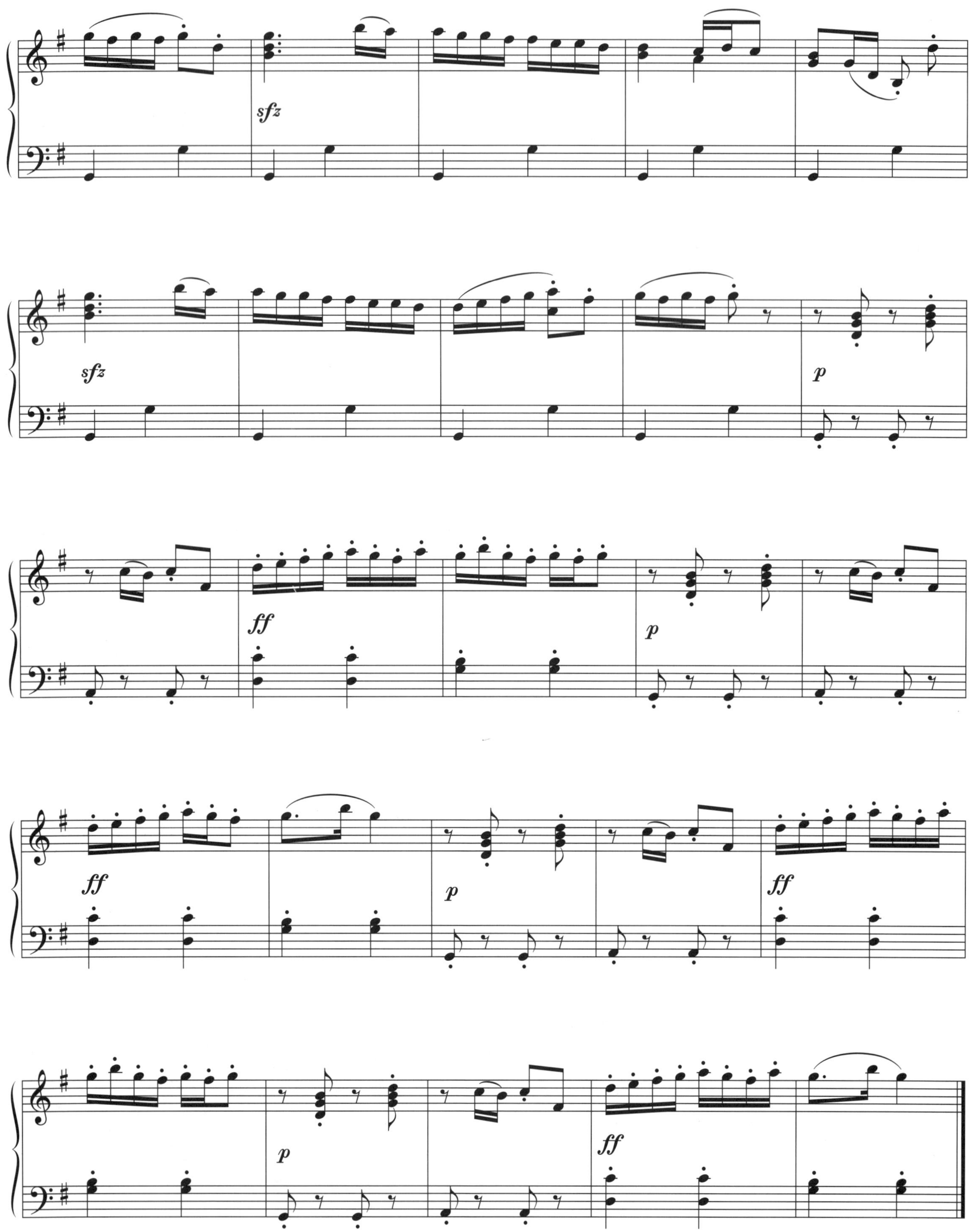
sfz
sfz
p
ff
p
ff
p
ff
p
ff

Maple Leaf Rag

Scott Joplin
1868–1917

212

213

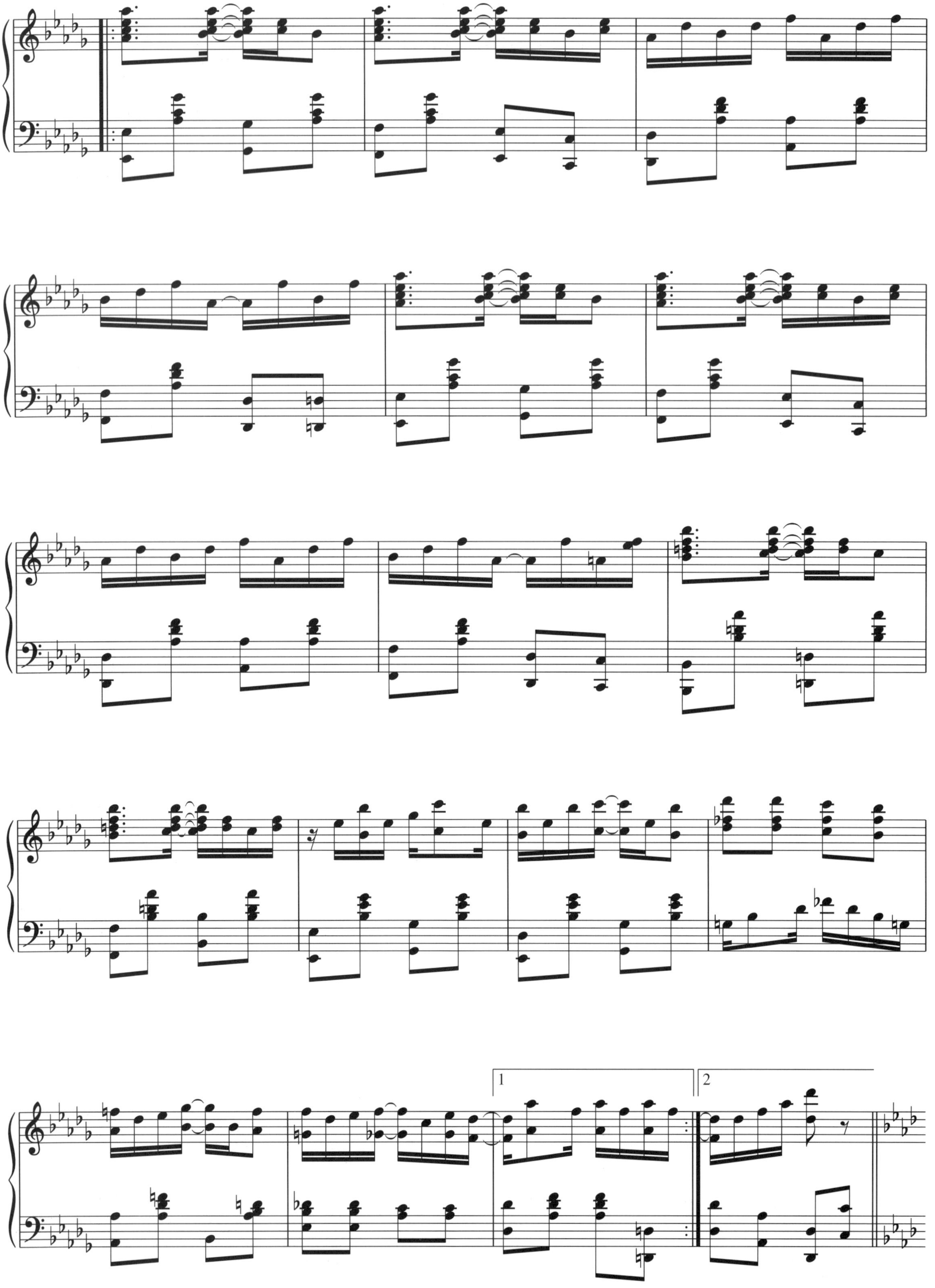
1
2

215

Solace
A Mexican Serenade

Scott Joplin
1868–1917

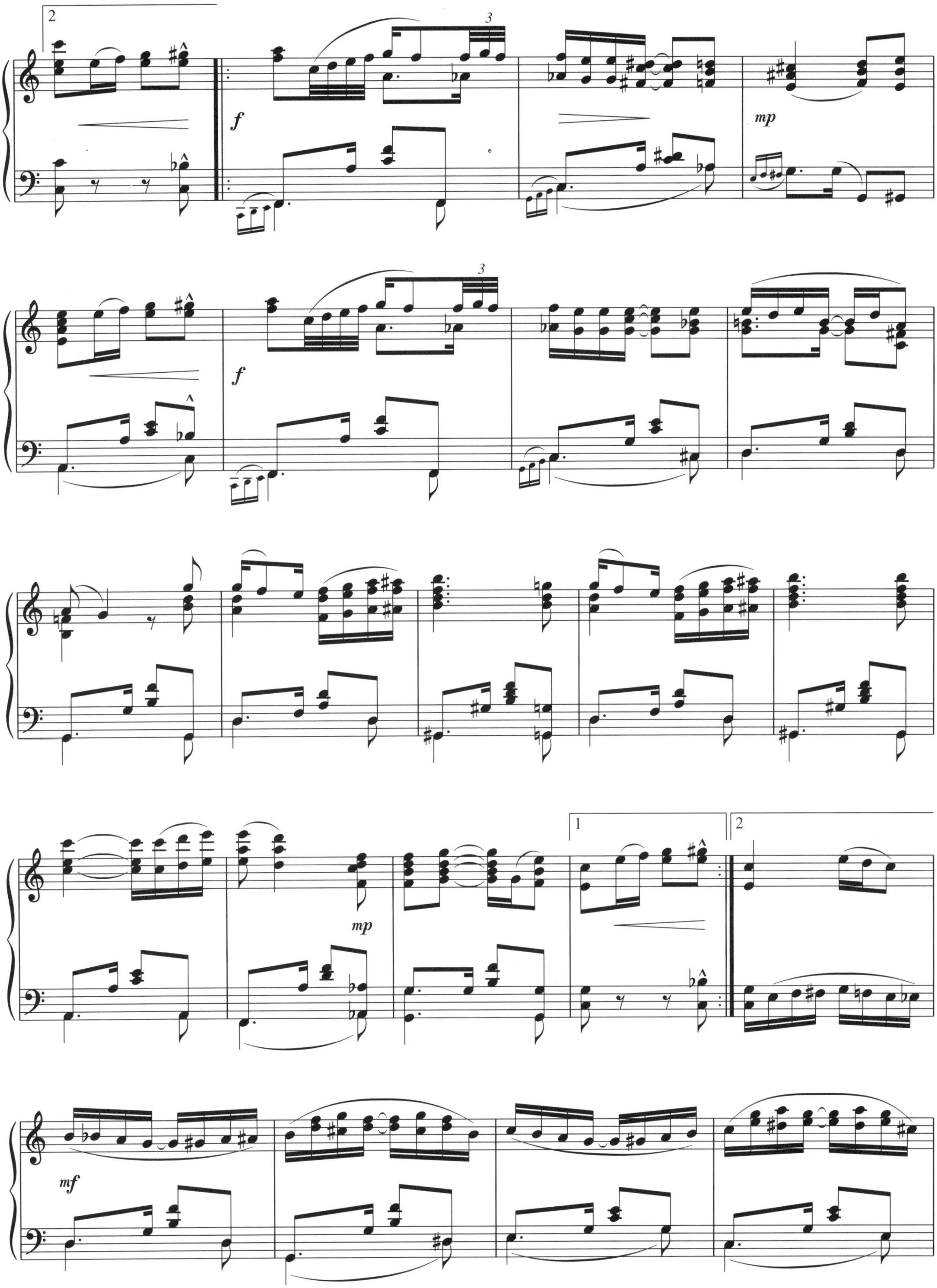
f
mp
f
mp
mf

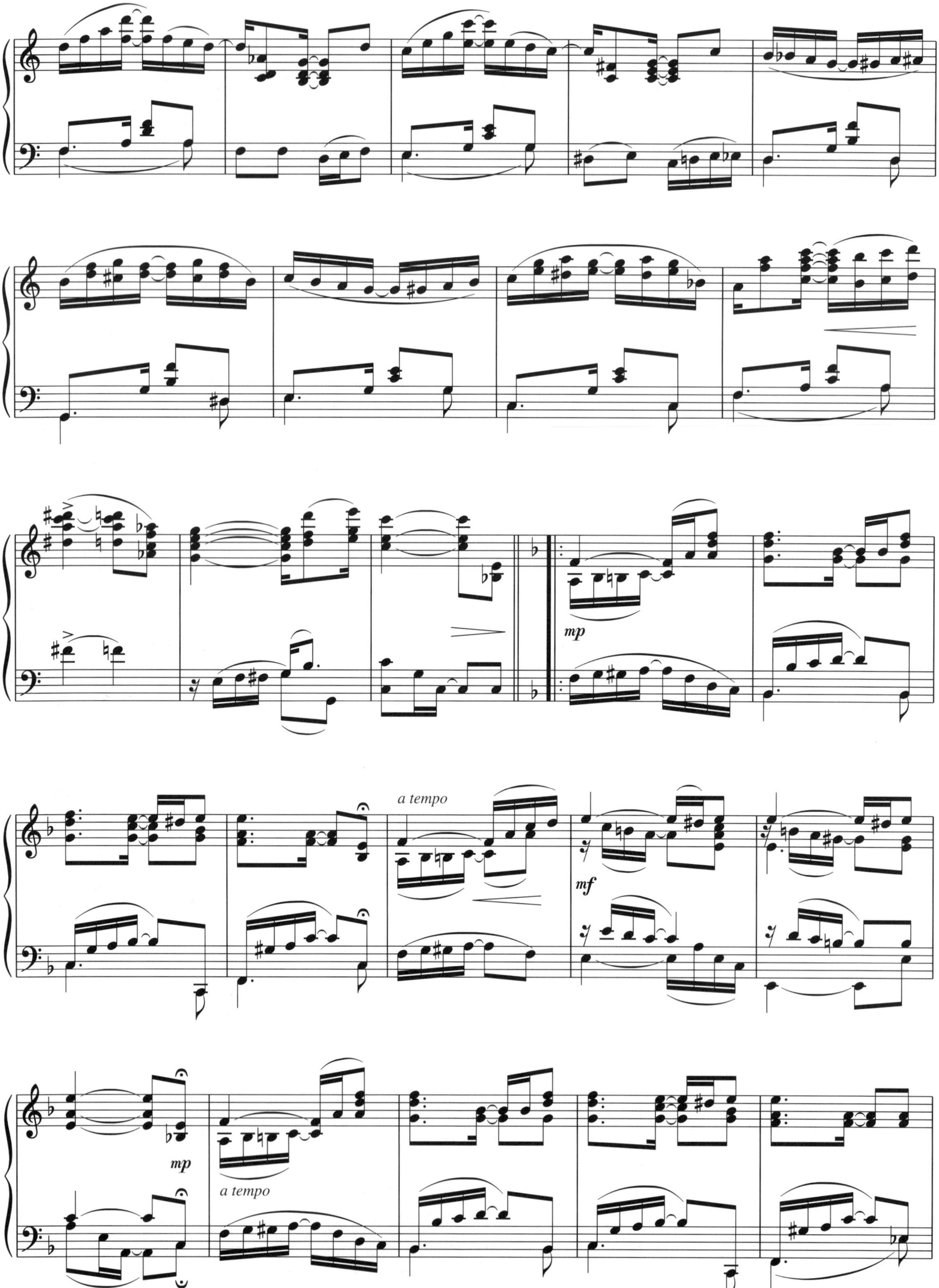
mp
a tempo
mf
mp
a tempo

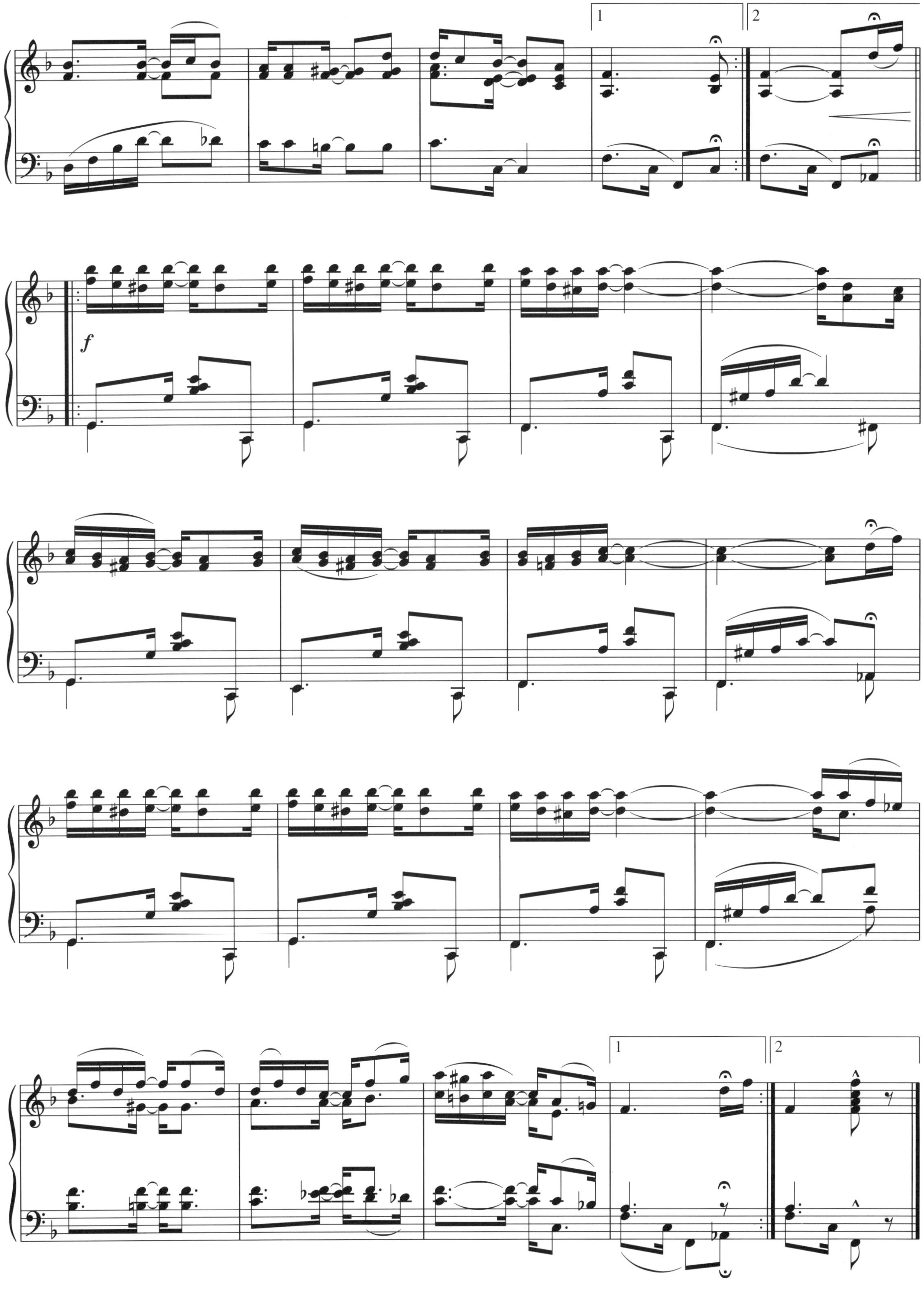
1
2
f
1
2

To a Wild Rose
from WOODLAND SKETCHES

Edward MacDowell
1860-1908
Op. 51

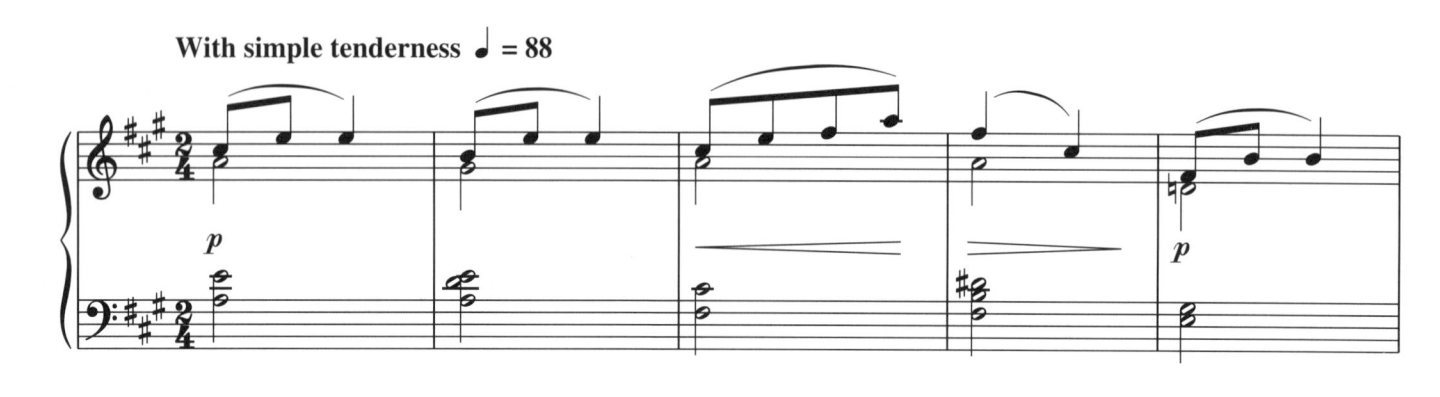

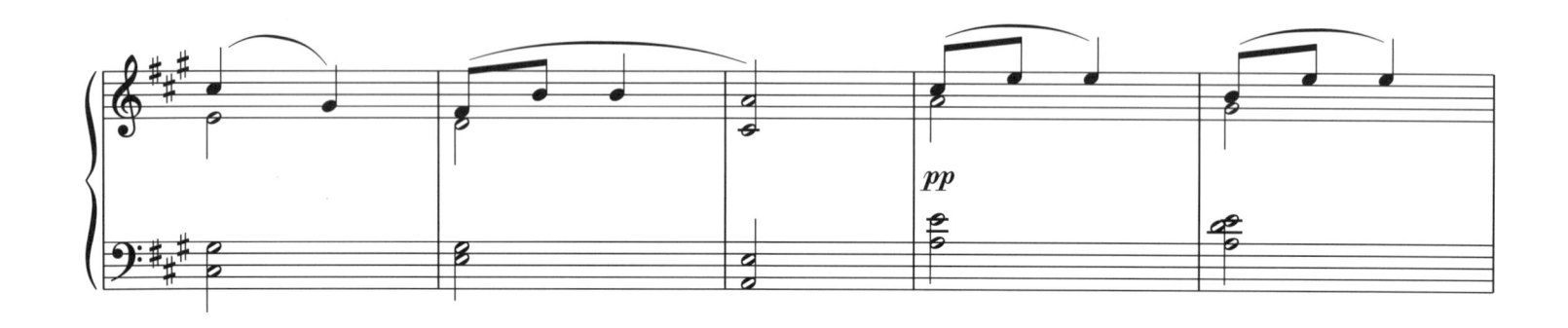

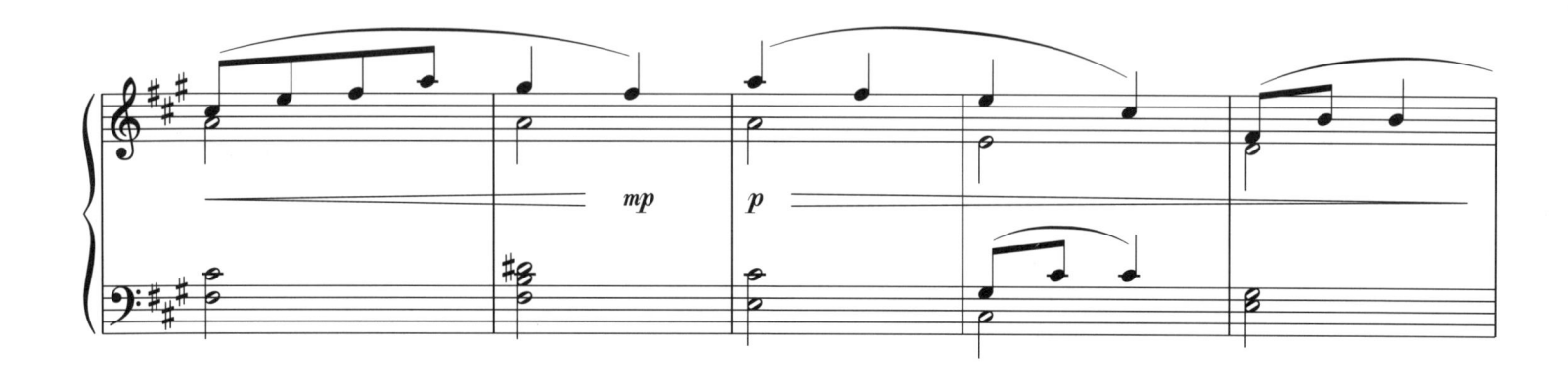

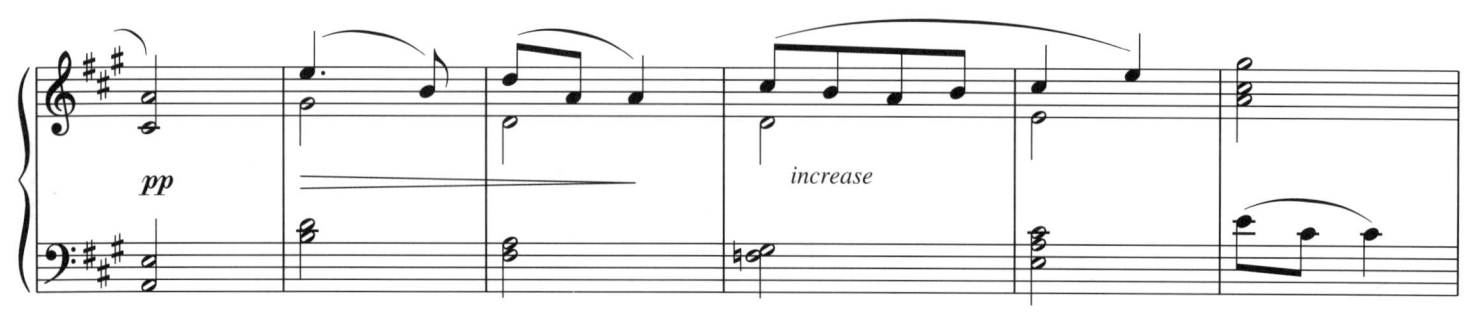

ritard.
still increase
f
diminish
p
p
mp
slightly marked
p
pp
ppp

Symphony No. 1
"Titan"
Third Movement Opening Theme

Gustav Mahler
1860-1911
originally for orchestra

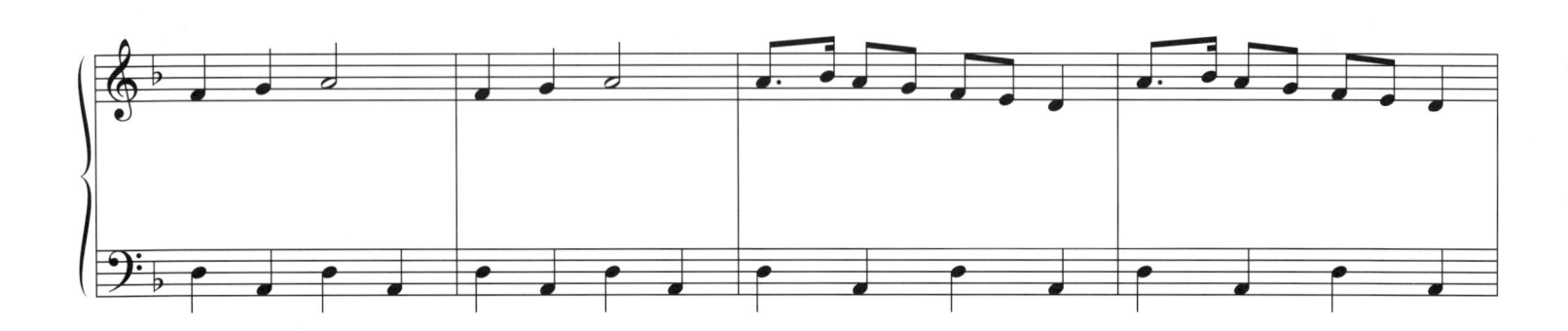

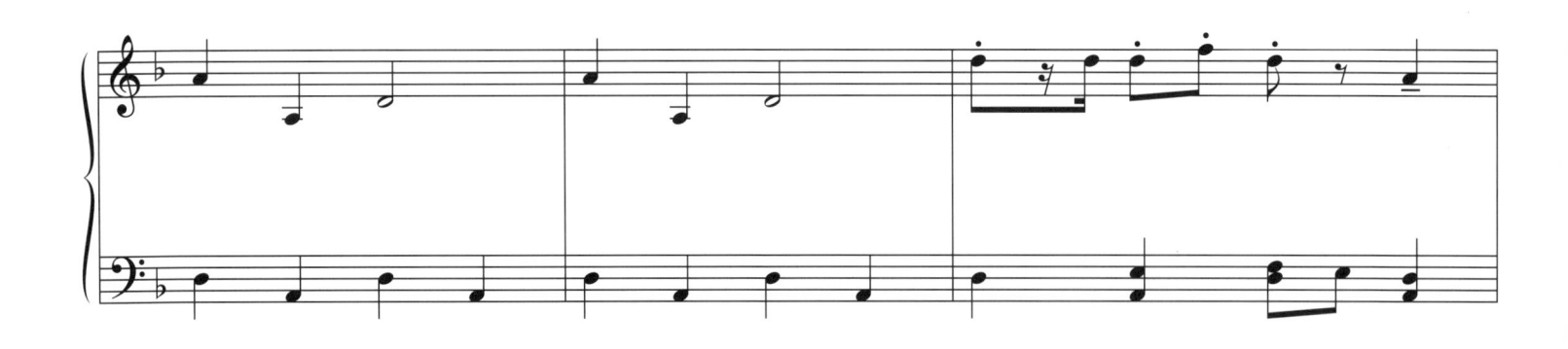

Solemn and steady, without dragging

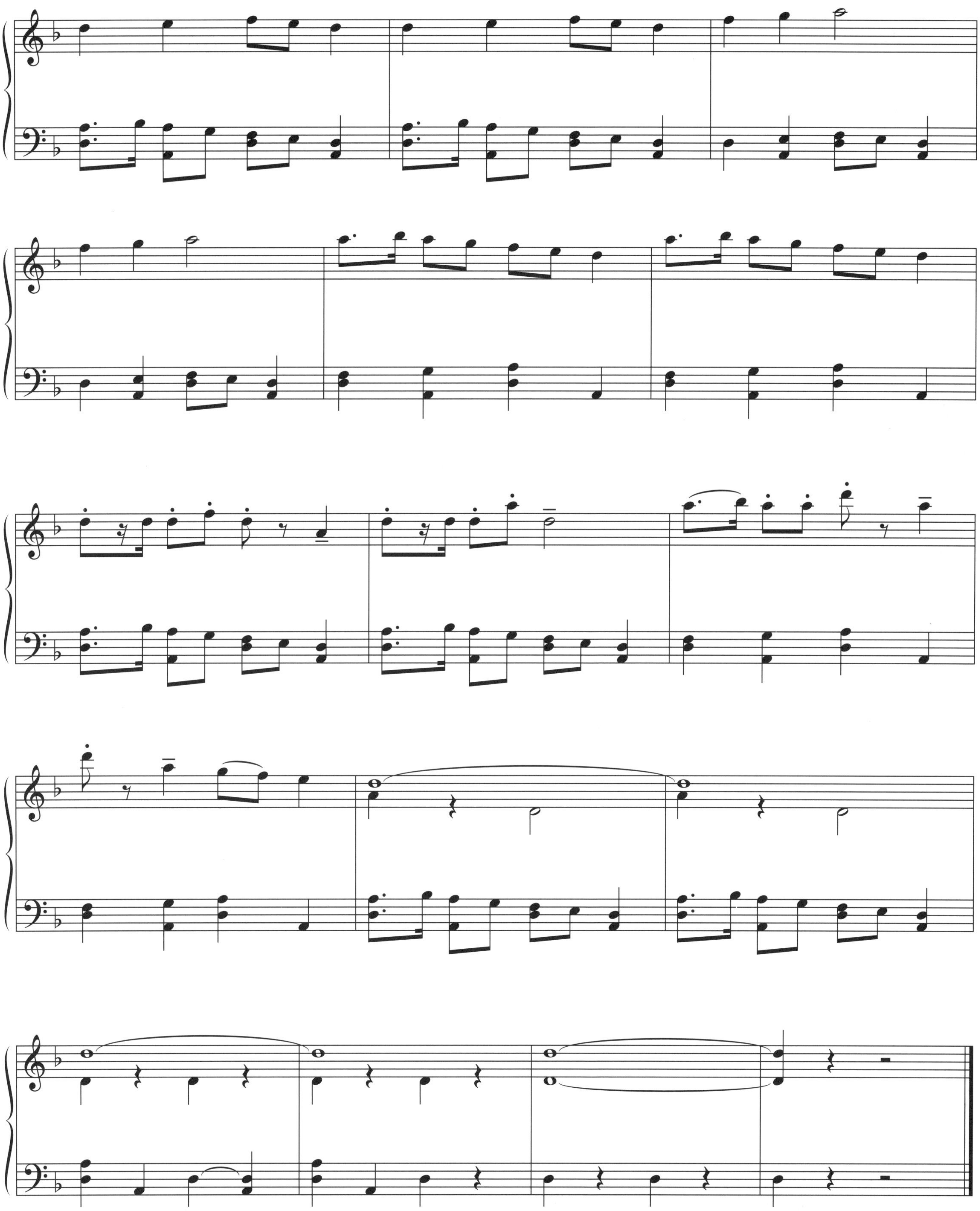

Symphony No. 5
Fourth Movement Excerpt ("Adagietto")

Gustav Mahler
1860-1911
this movement originally
for strings and harp

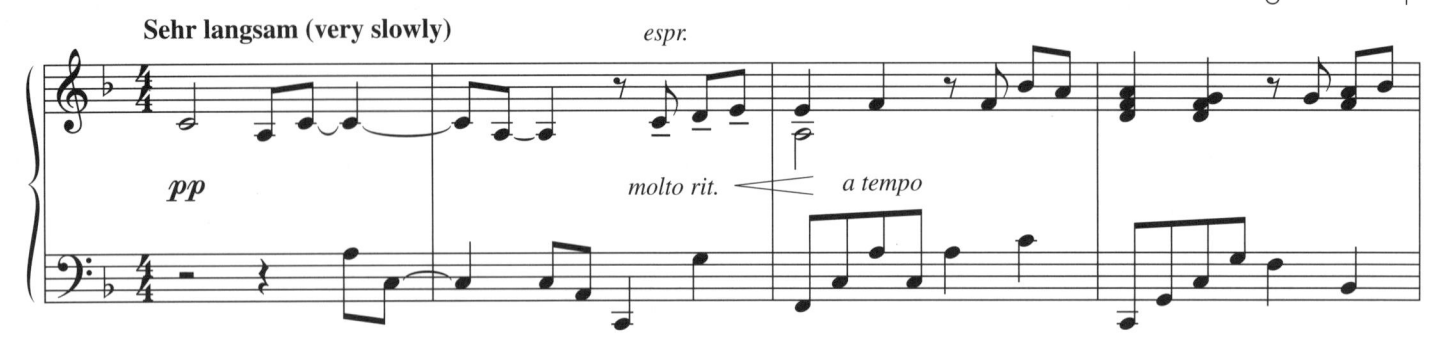

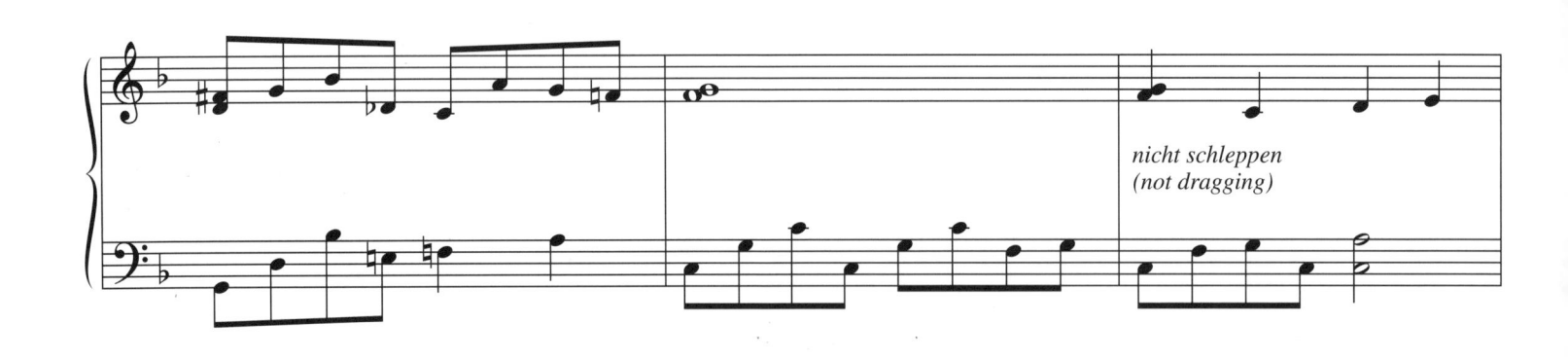

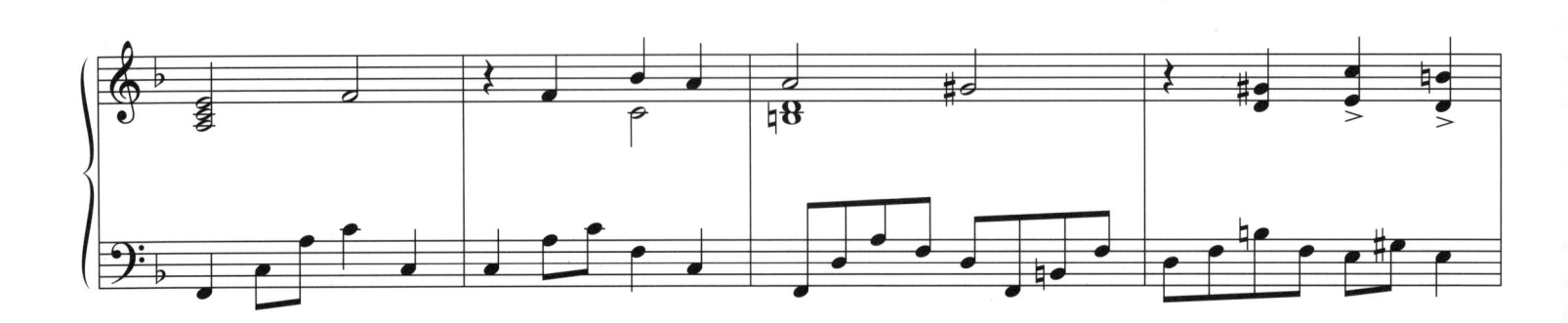

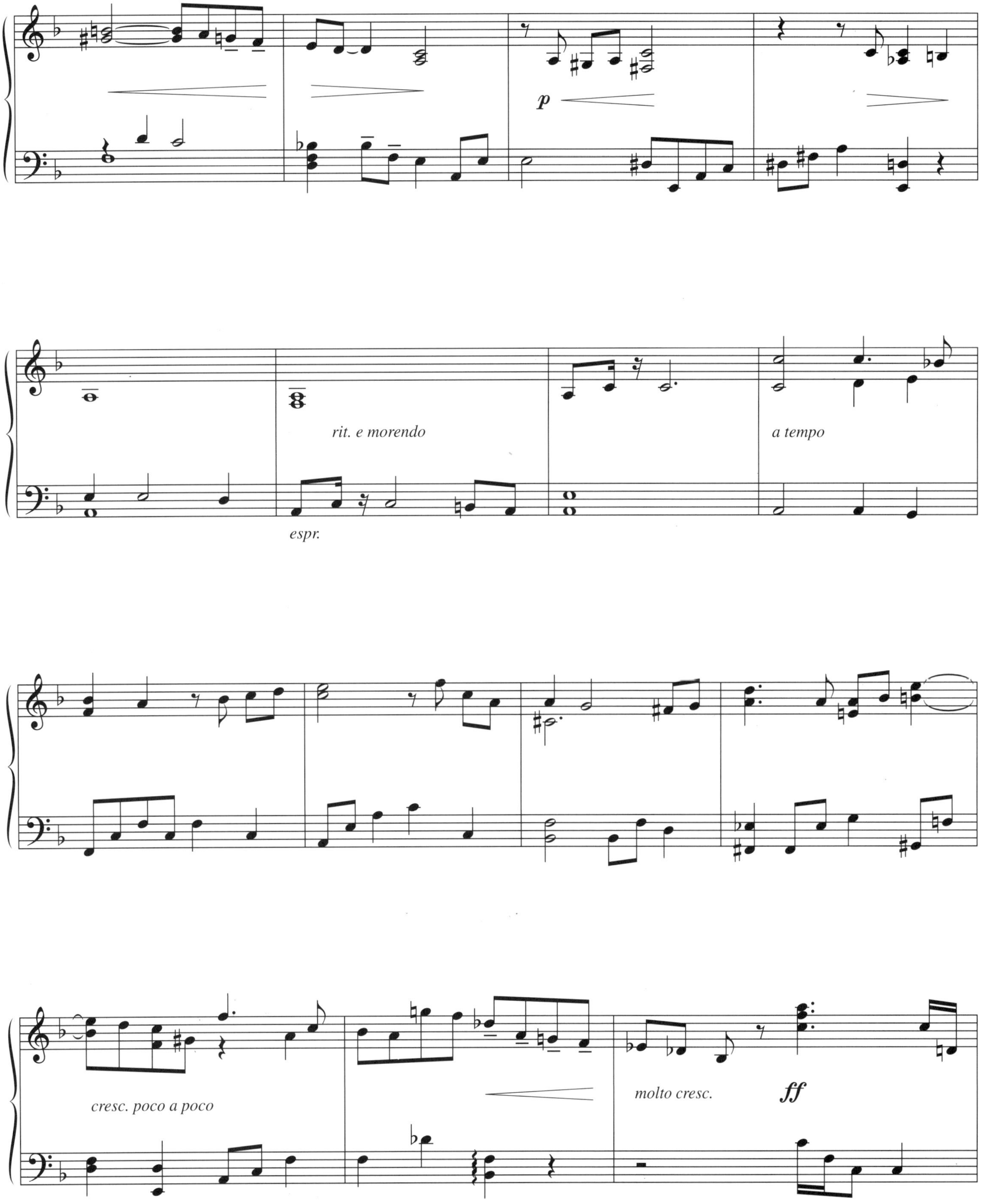
p
rit. e morendo
espr.
a tempo
cresc. poco a poco
molto cresc.
ff

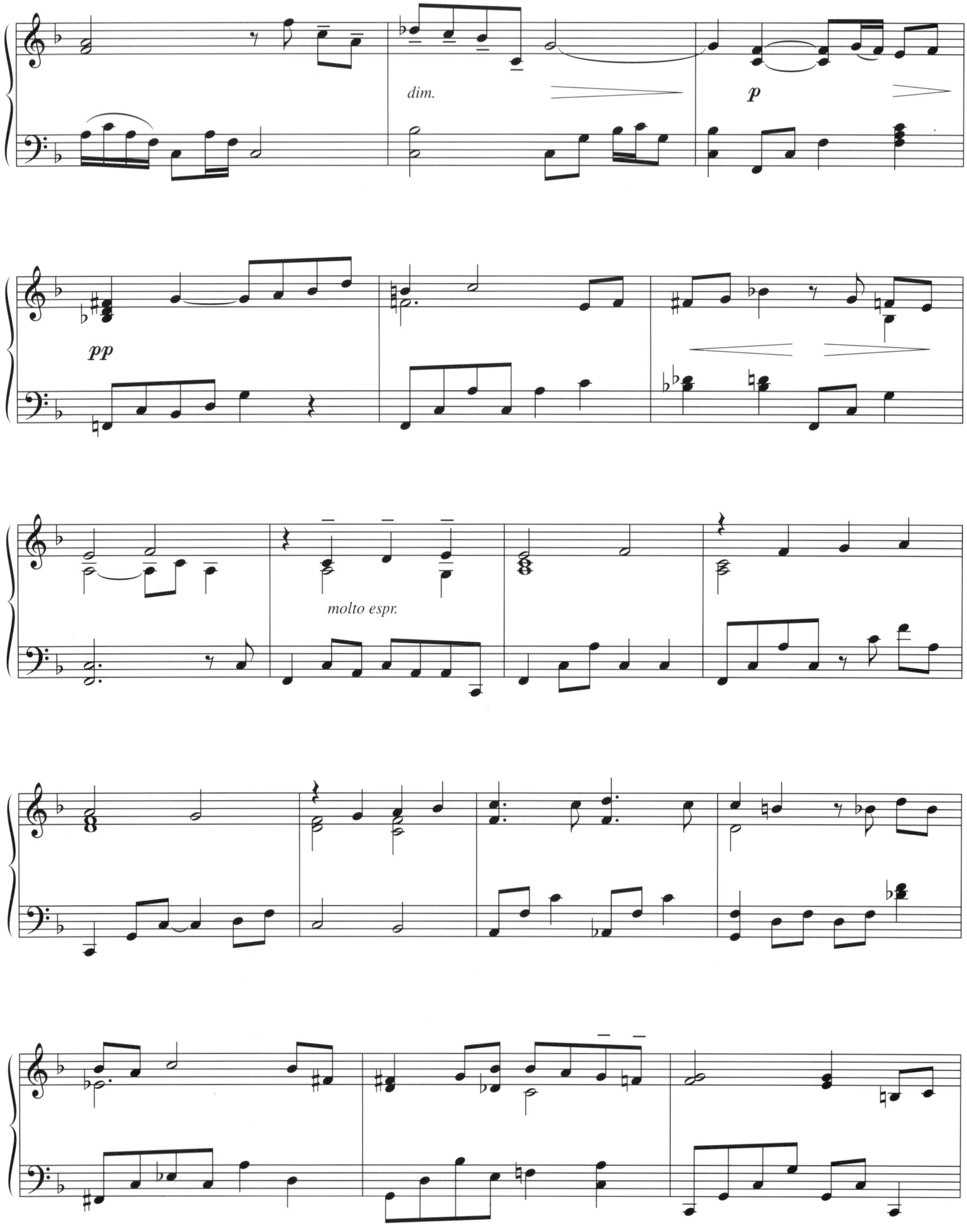
dim.
p
pp
molto espr.

227

Symphony No. 2

"Resurrection"
Fifth Movement Choral Theme

Gustav Mahler
1860-1911
originally for soloists,
chorus and orchestra

Meditation
from the opera THAÏS

Jules Massenet
1842-1912

To Coda
A Tempo più mosso
(♩ = 69)
dolce
cresc.
p rall.
poco a poco appassionato
mf
più f
Calmato
f
p
cresc.
Più mosso agitato
molto espr.
più f
sf

D.C. al Coda
sf
sf
molto espr.
Meno un poco rall.
p
CODA
A Tempo
sfz
dim.
dolce
p
senza affrettare il gruppo
8va
loco
p
sf
sf
p
dim.
Calmato
pp

"Fingal's Cave" Overture
or "The Hebrides"
Themes

Felix Mendelssohn
1809-1847
Op. 26
originally for orchestra

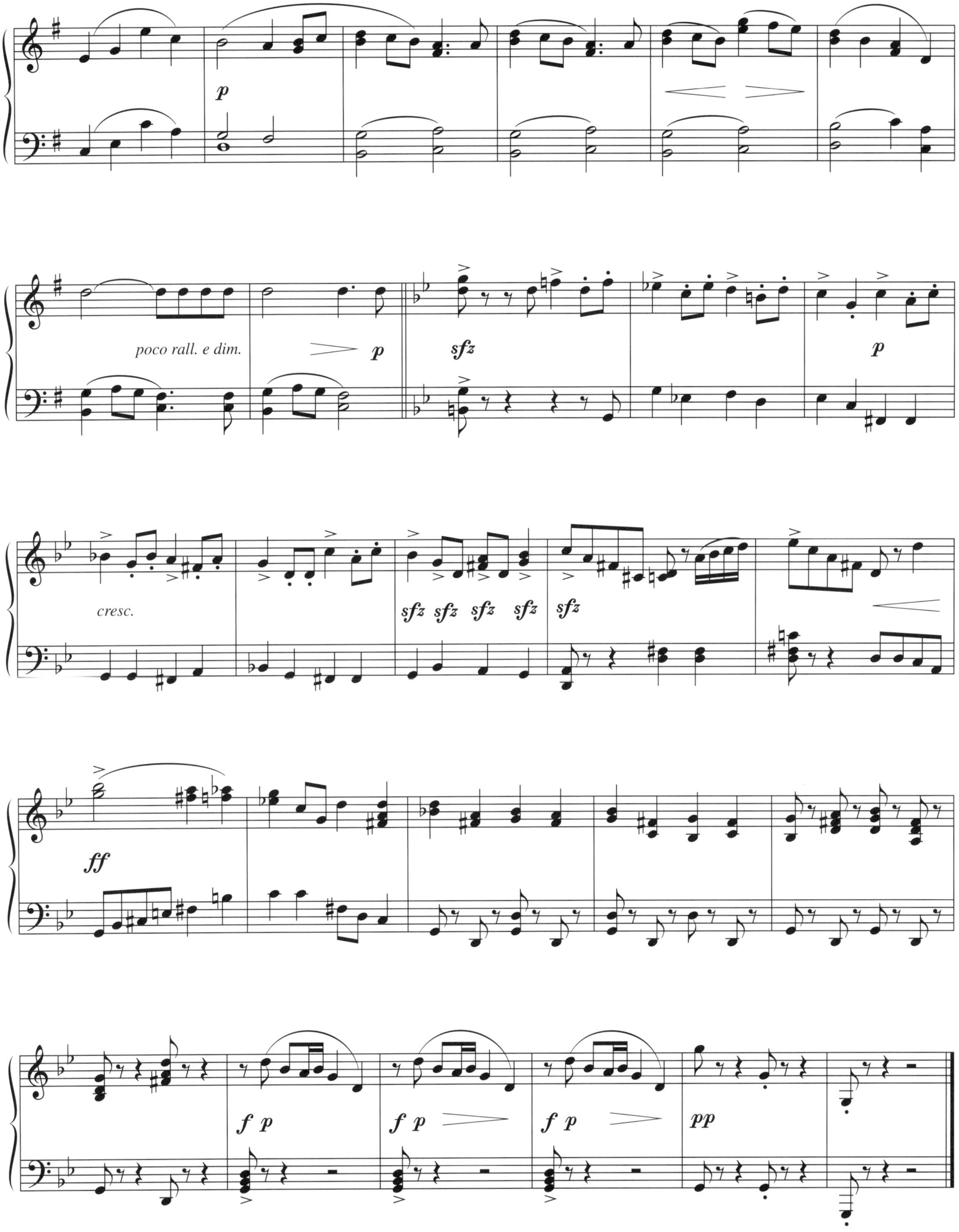
p
poco rall. e dim.
p
sfz
p
cresc.
sfz sfz sfz sfz
sfz
ff
f p
f p
f p
pp

A Midsummer Night's Dream
Overture Themes

Felix Mendelssohn
1809-1847
Op. 61
originally for orchestra

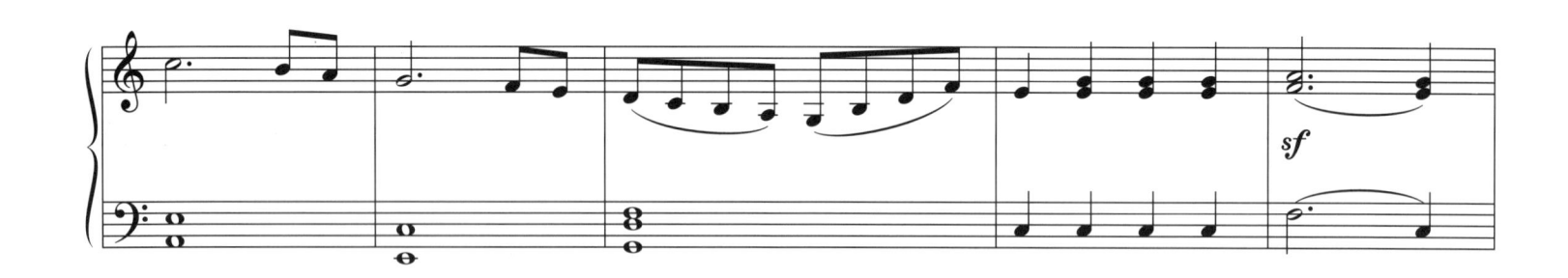

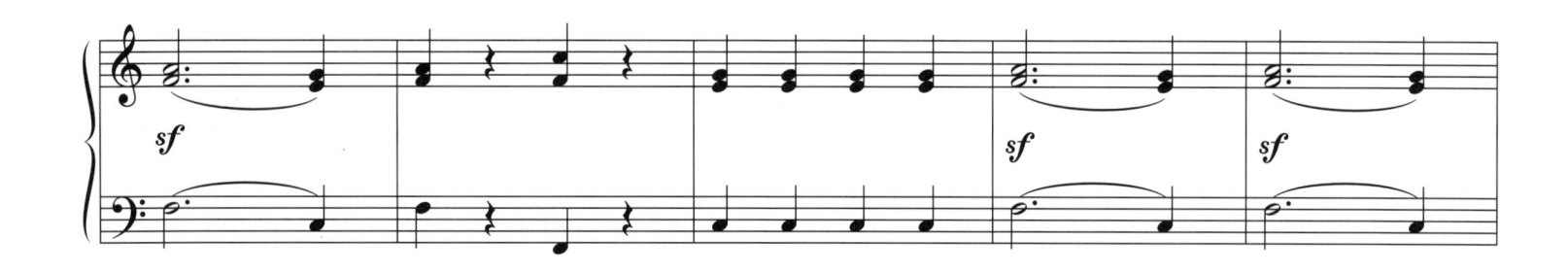

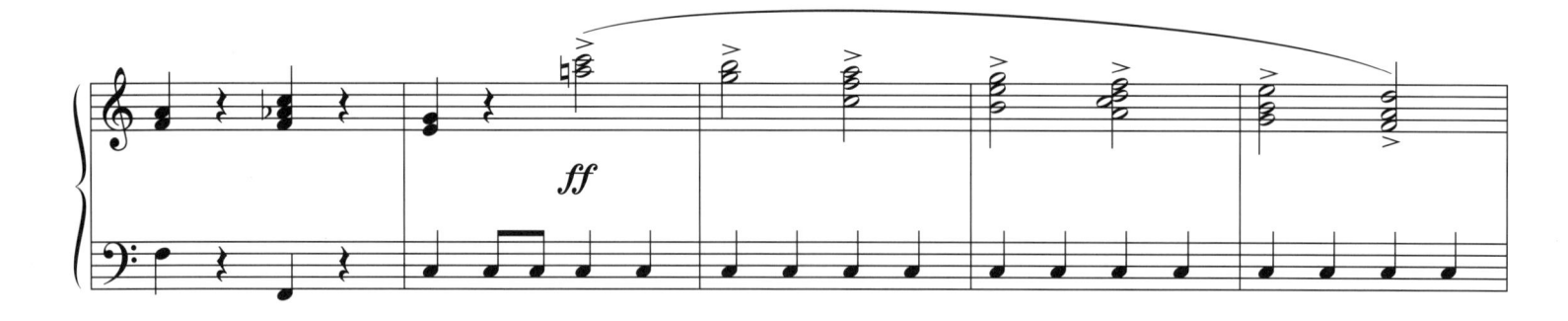

Allegro di molto

original key: E Major

Copyright © 2000 by HAL LEONARD CORPORATION
International Copyright Secured   All Rights Reserved

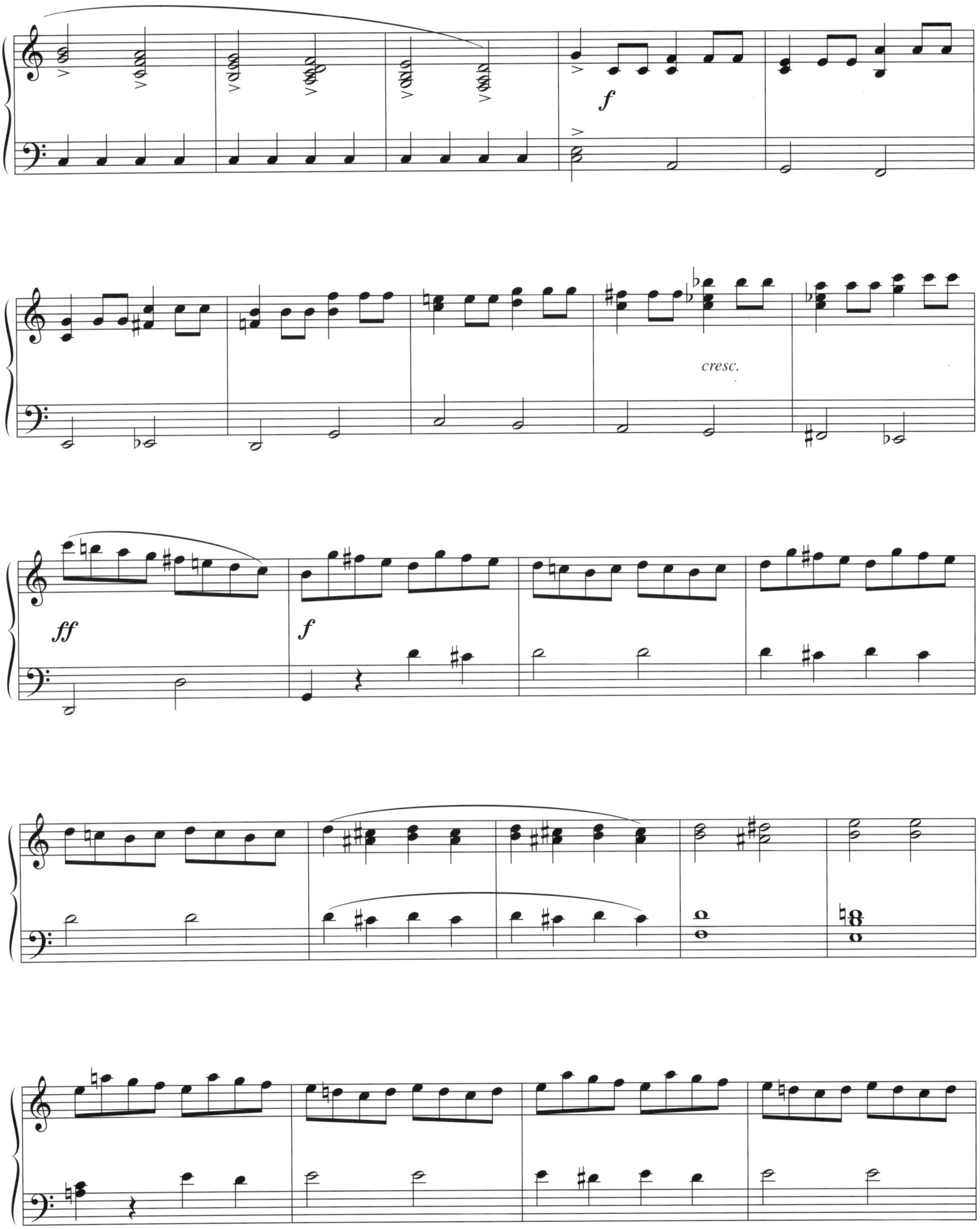
f
cresc.
ff
f

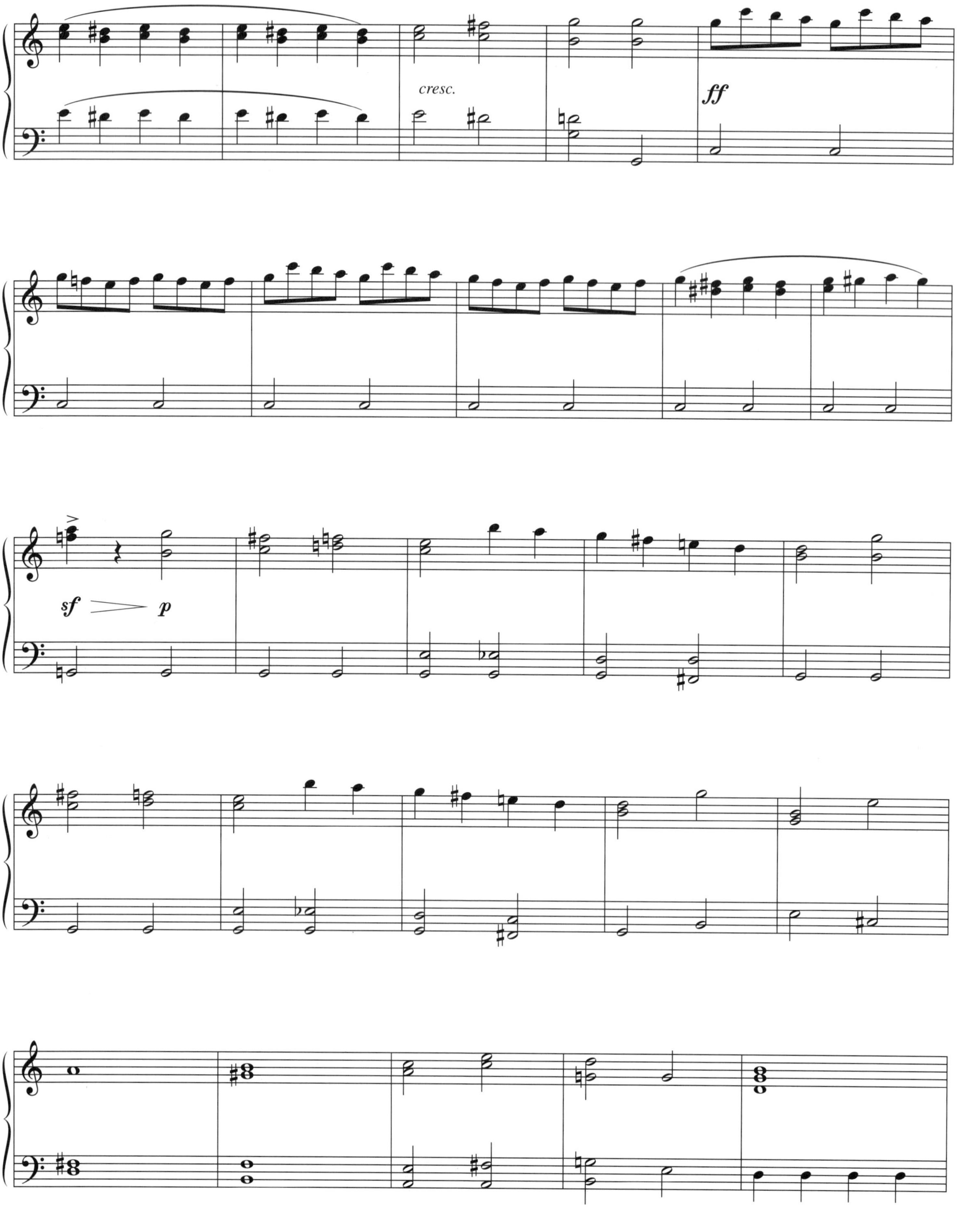
cresc.
ff
sf
p

237

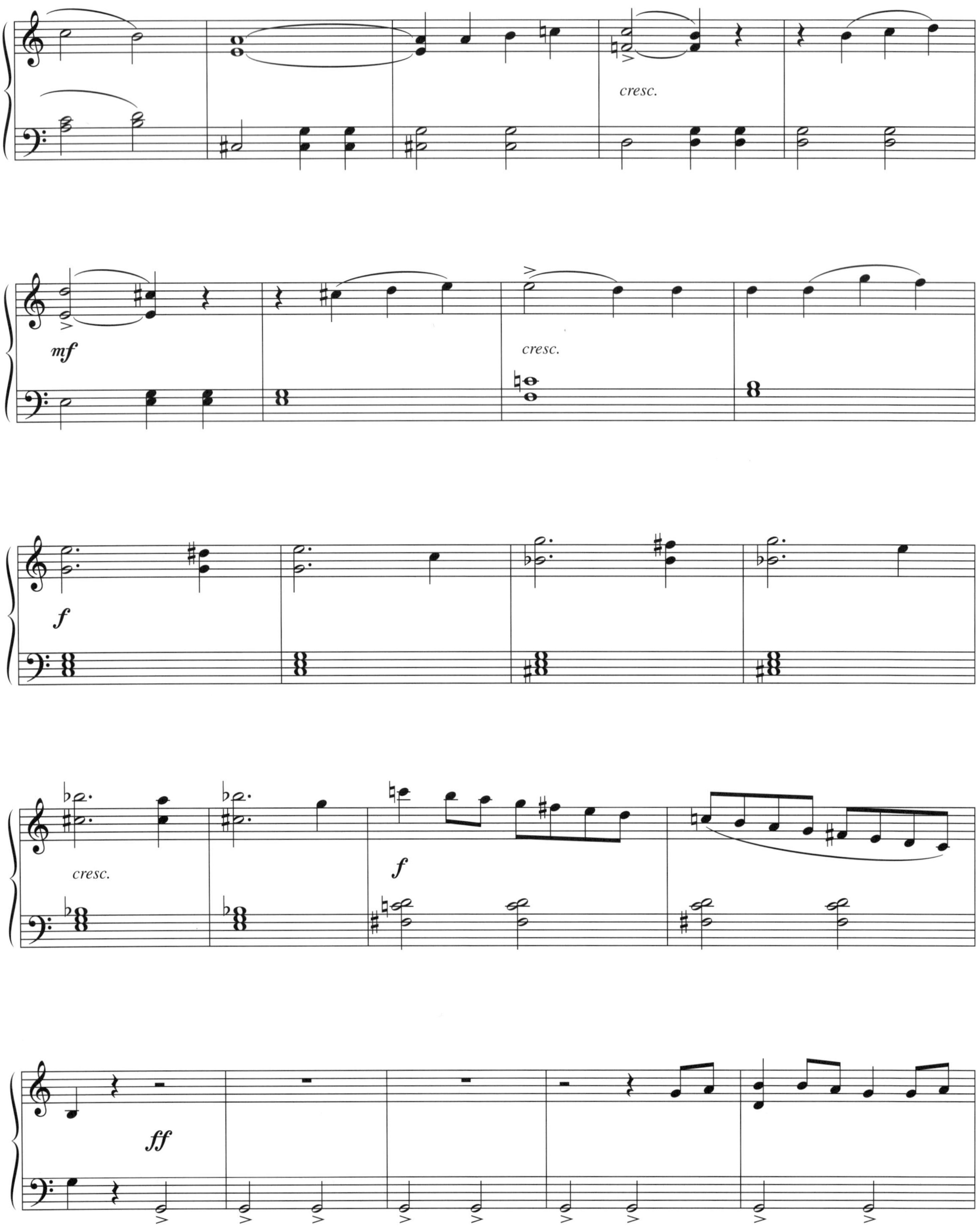
cresc.
mf
cresc.
f
cresc.
f
ff

239

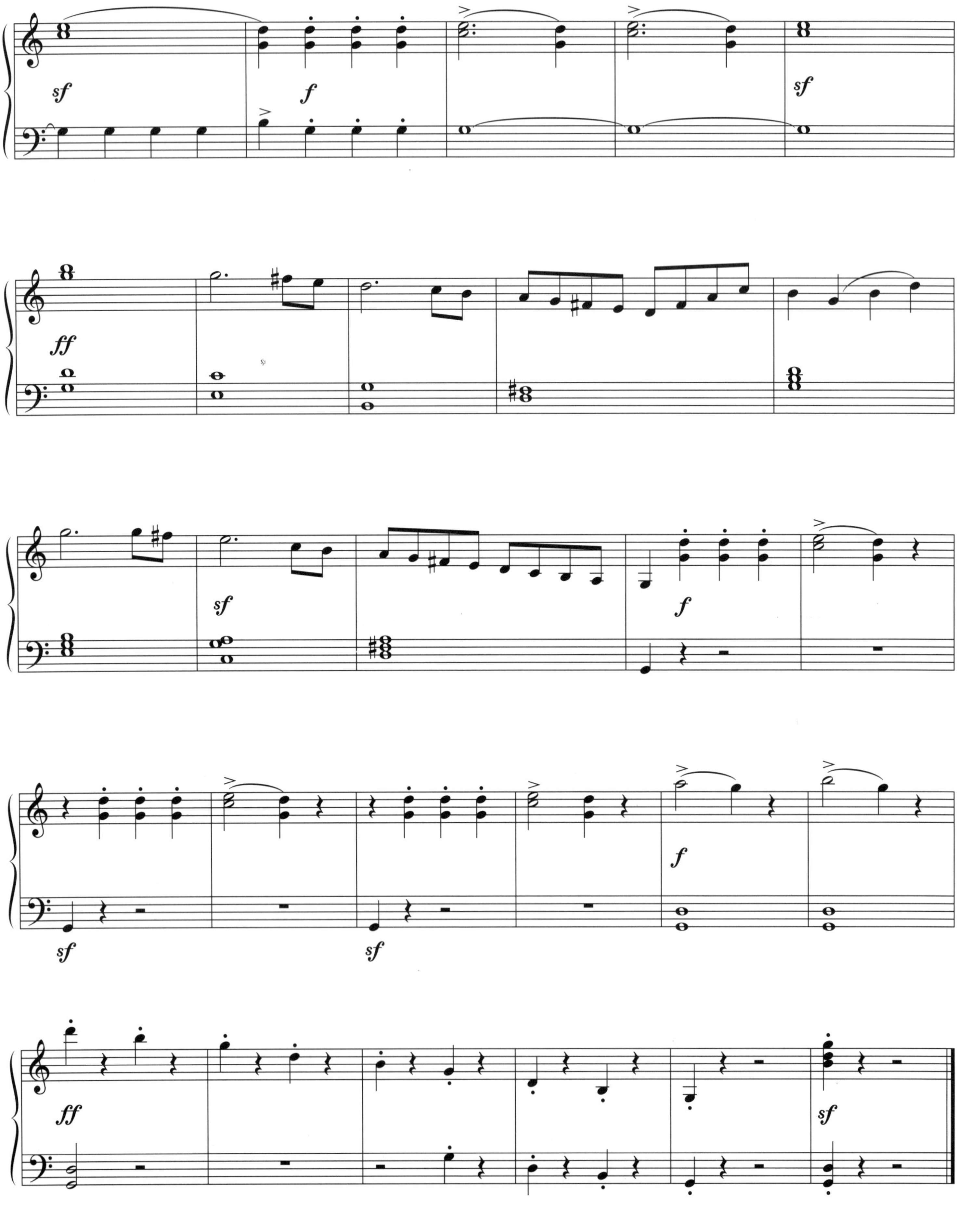

Symphony No. 4

"Italian"
First Movement Excerpt

Felix Mendelssohn
1809-1847
Op. 90
originally for orchestra

Allegro vivace

original key: A Major

Copyright © 2000 by HAL LEONARD CORPORATION
International Copyright Secured All Rights Reserved

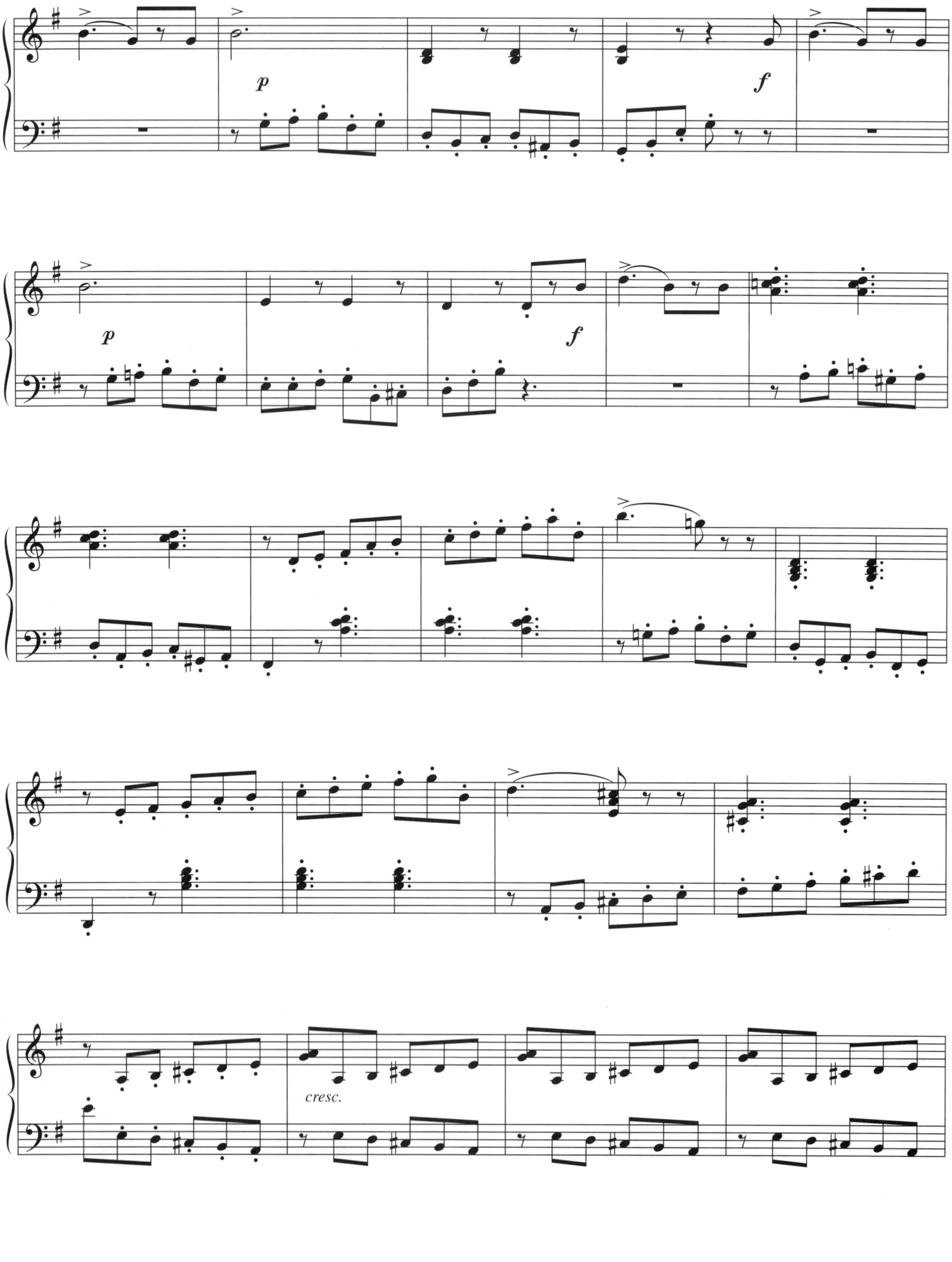
p
f
p
f
cresc.

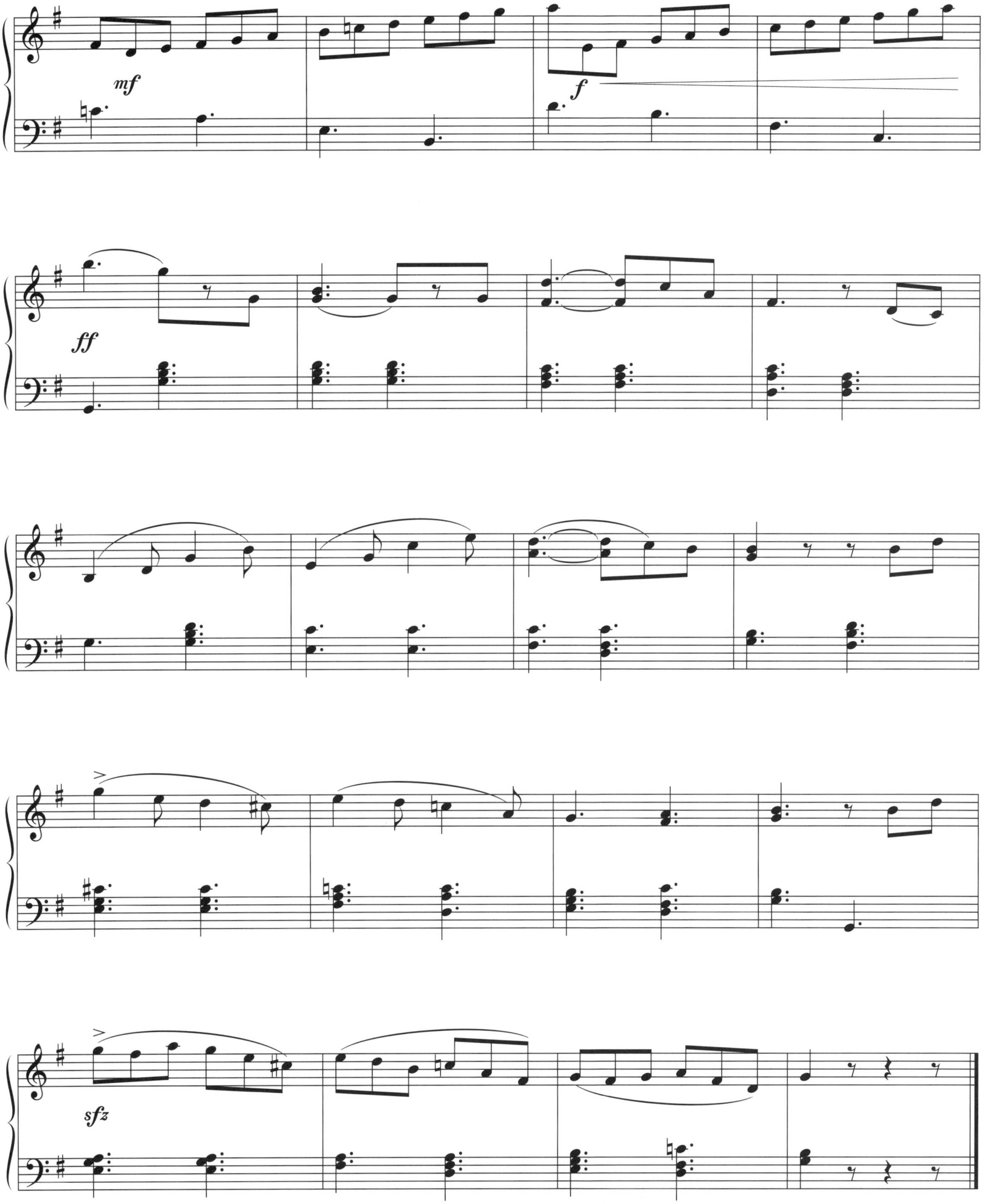
mf
f
ff
sfz

Violin Concerto
First Movement Excerpt

Felix Mendelssohn
1809-1847
Op. 64
originally for violin and orchestra

Allegro molto appassionato

p legato

245

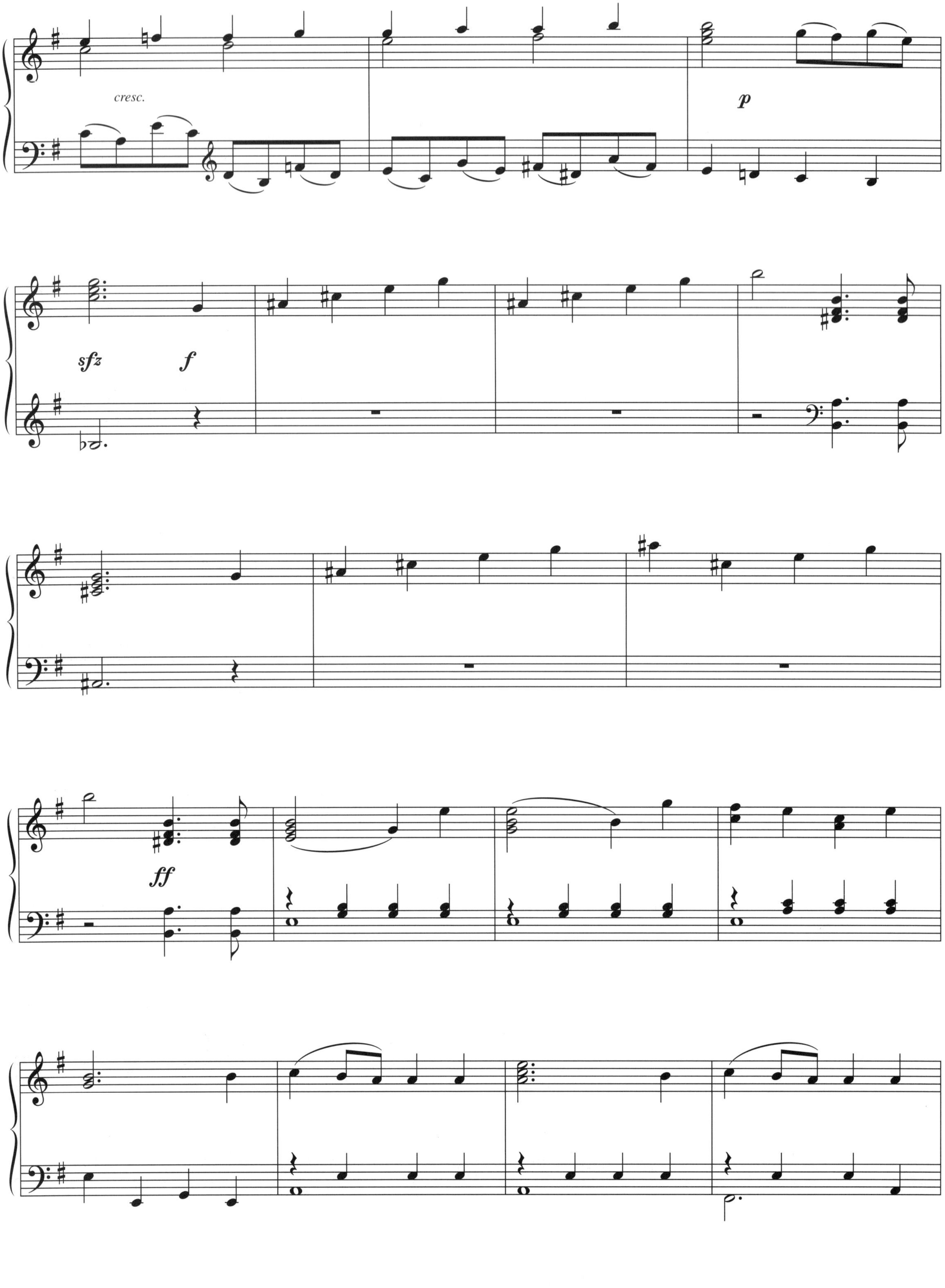
cresc.
p
sfz
f
ff

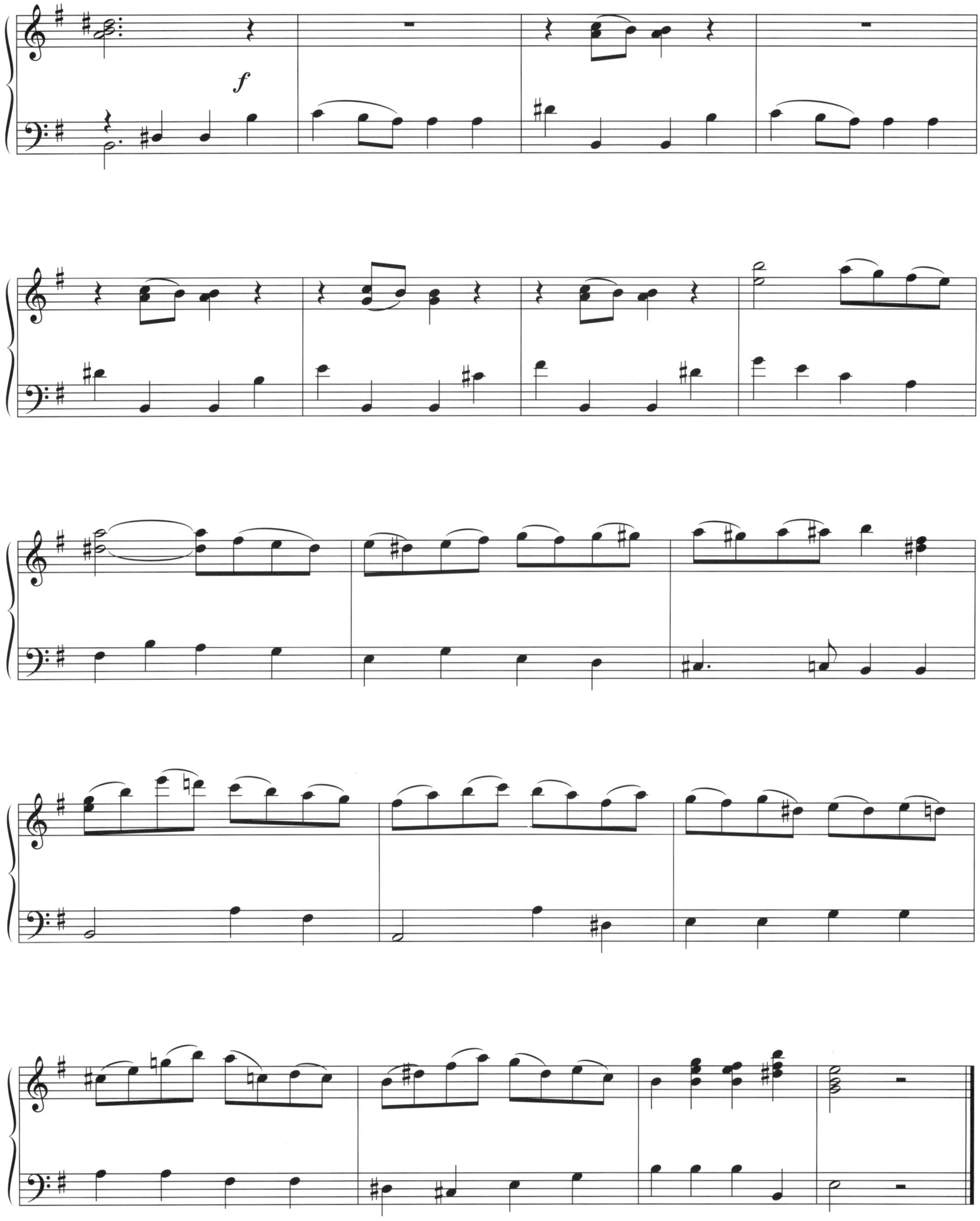
f

Rondeau
Excerpt

Jean-Joseph Mouret
1682-1738
originally for orchestra

249

Alleluia

from the solo motet EXSULTATE, JUBILATE
Excerpt

Wolfgang Amadeus Mozart
1756-1791
K 165
originally for soprano and orchestra

Allegro non troppo

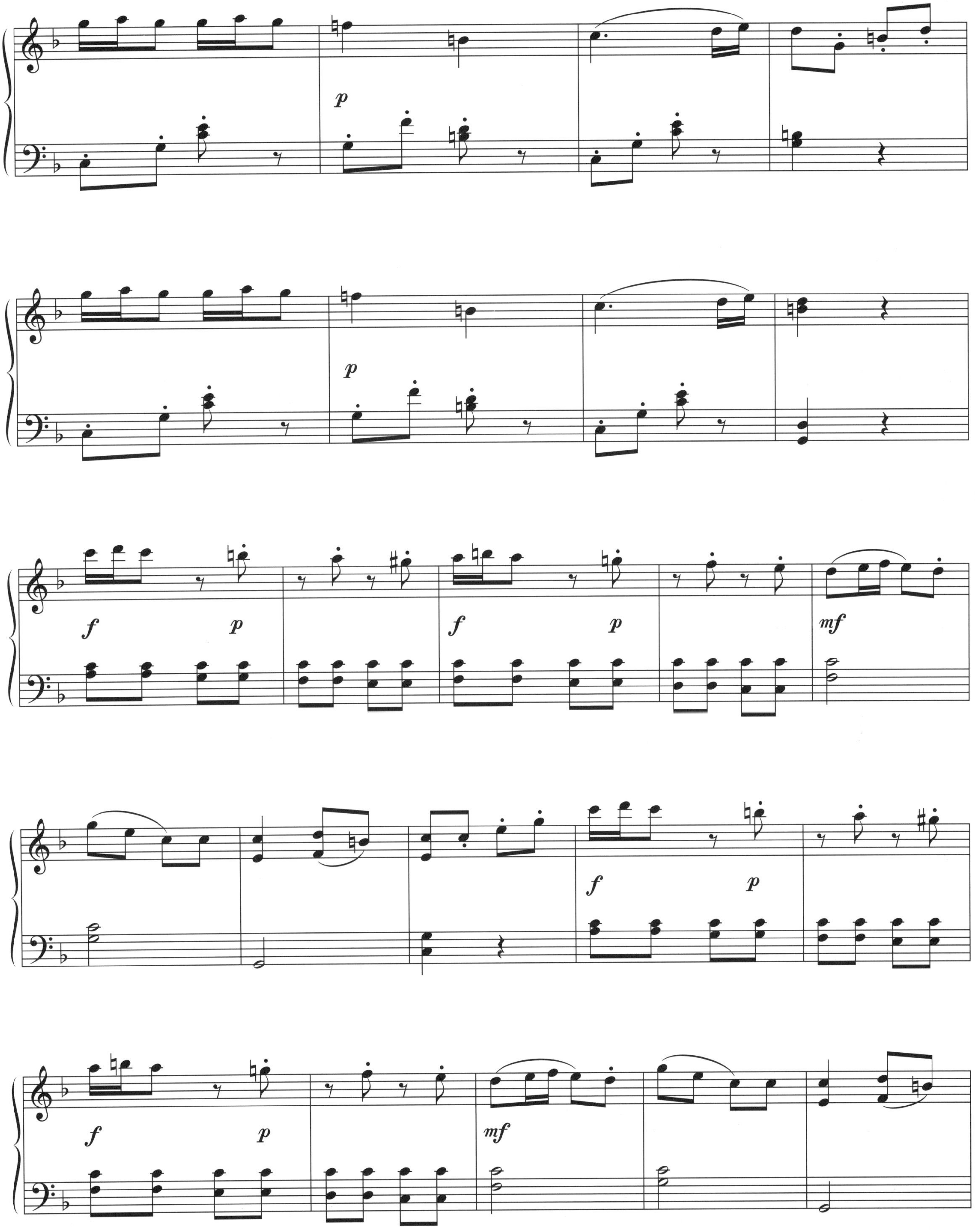
p
p
f
p
f
p
mf
f
p
f
p
mf

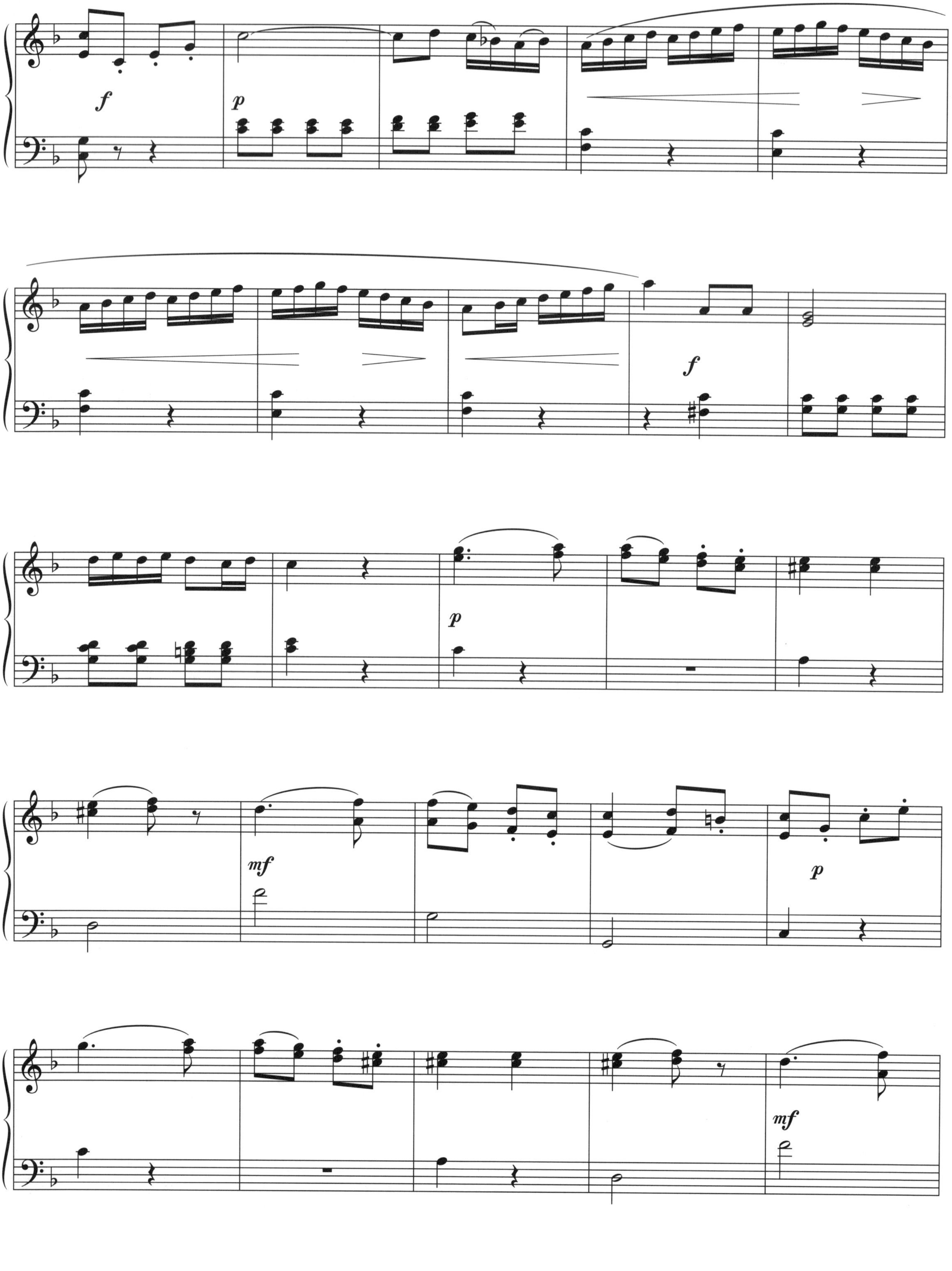
f
p
f
p
mf
p
mf

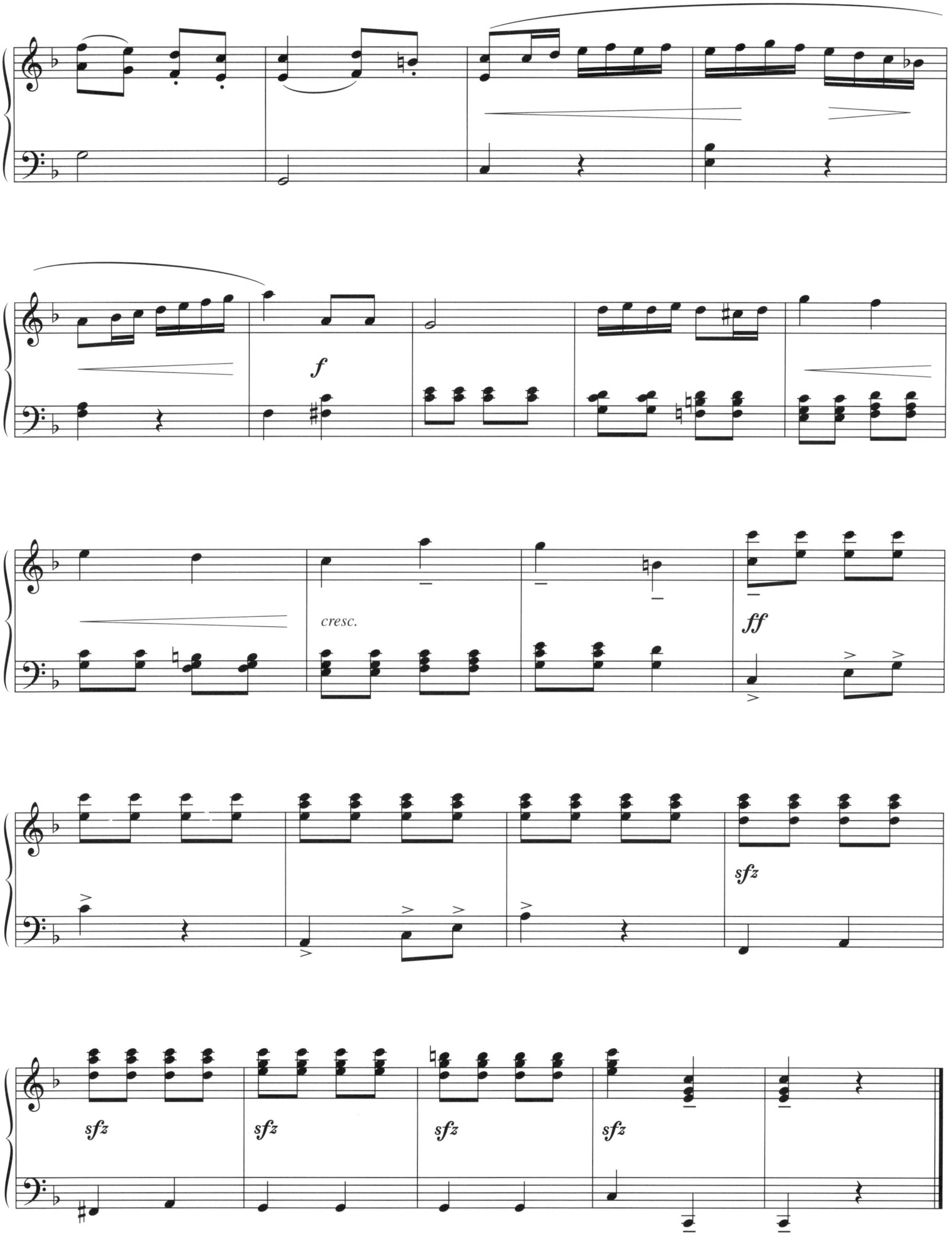
f
cresc.
ff
sfz
sfz
sfz
sfz
sfz

Ave verum corpus

Wolfgang Amadeus Mozart
1756-1791
K 618
originally for chorus and orchestra

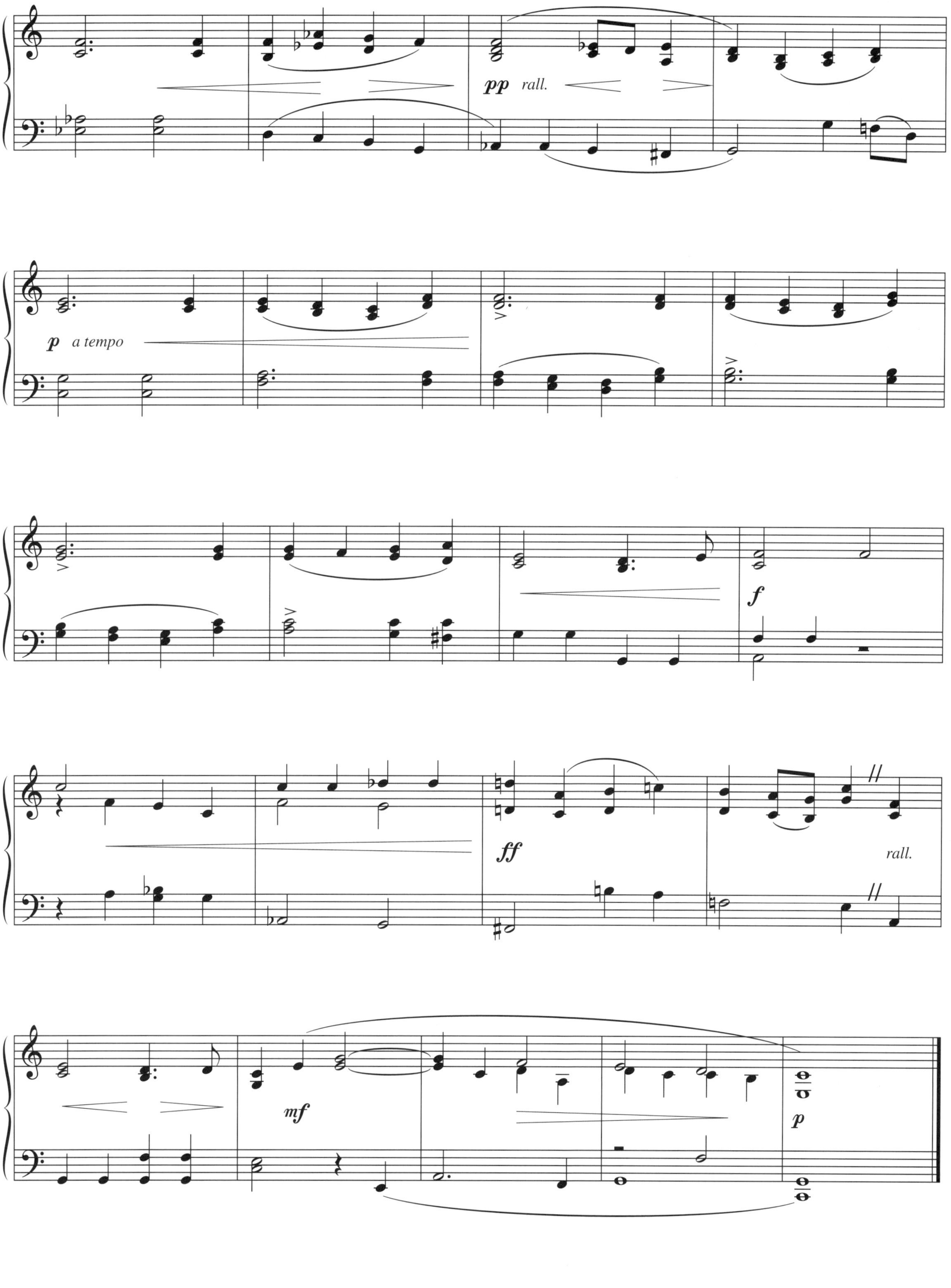
pp
rall.
p
a tempo
f
ff
rall.
mf
p

Là ci darem la mano
from the opera DON GIOVANNI

Wolfgang Amadeus Mozart
1756-1791

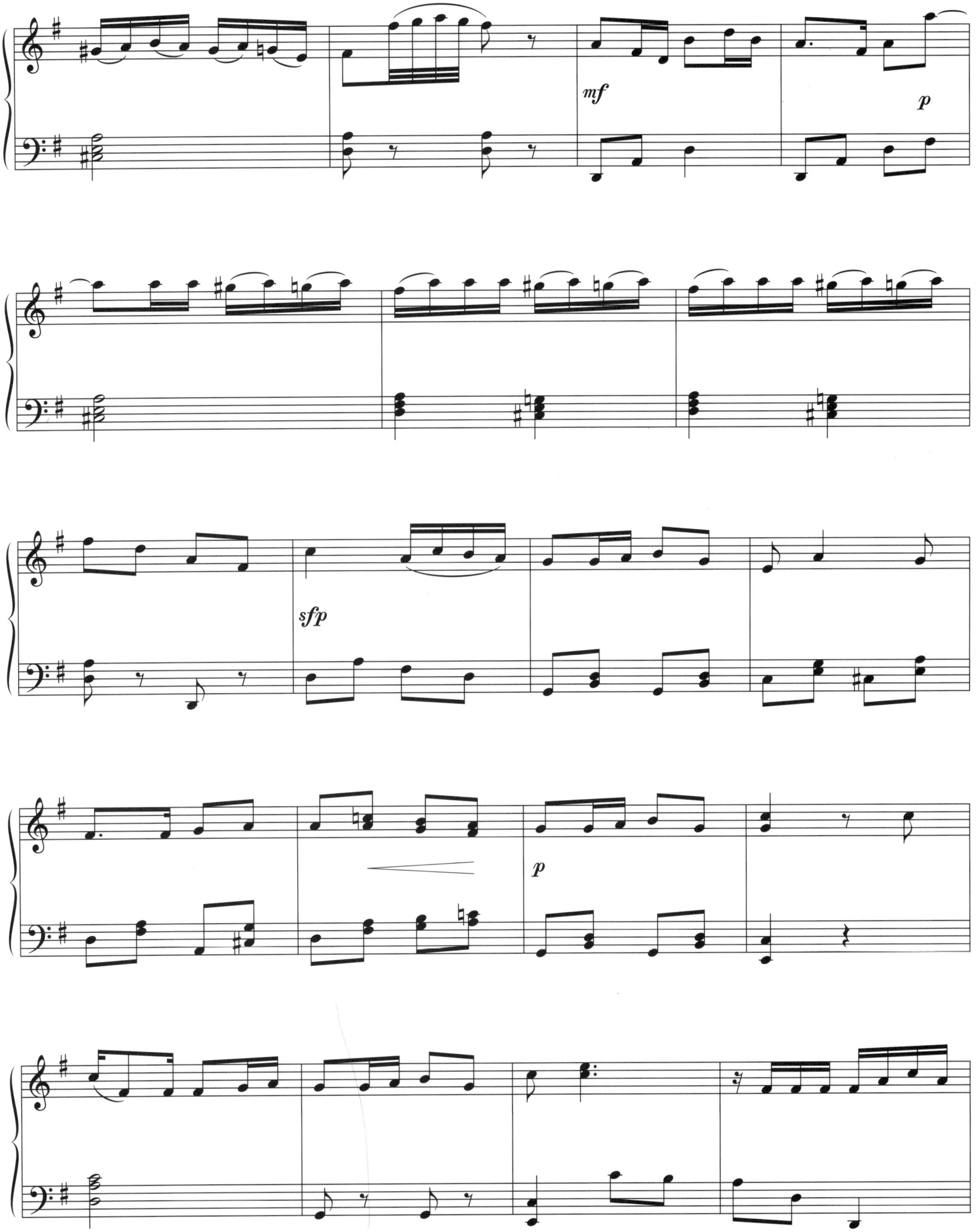
mf
p
sfp
p

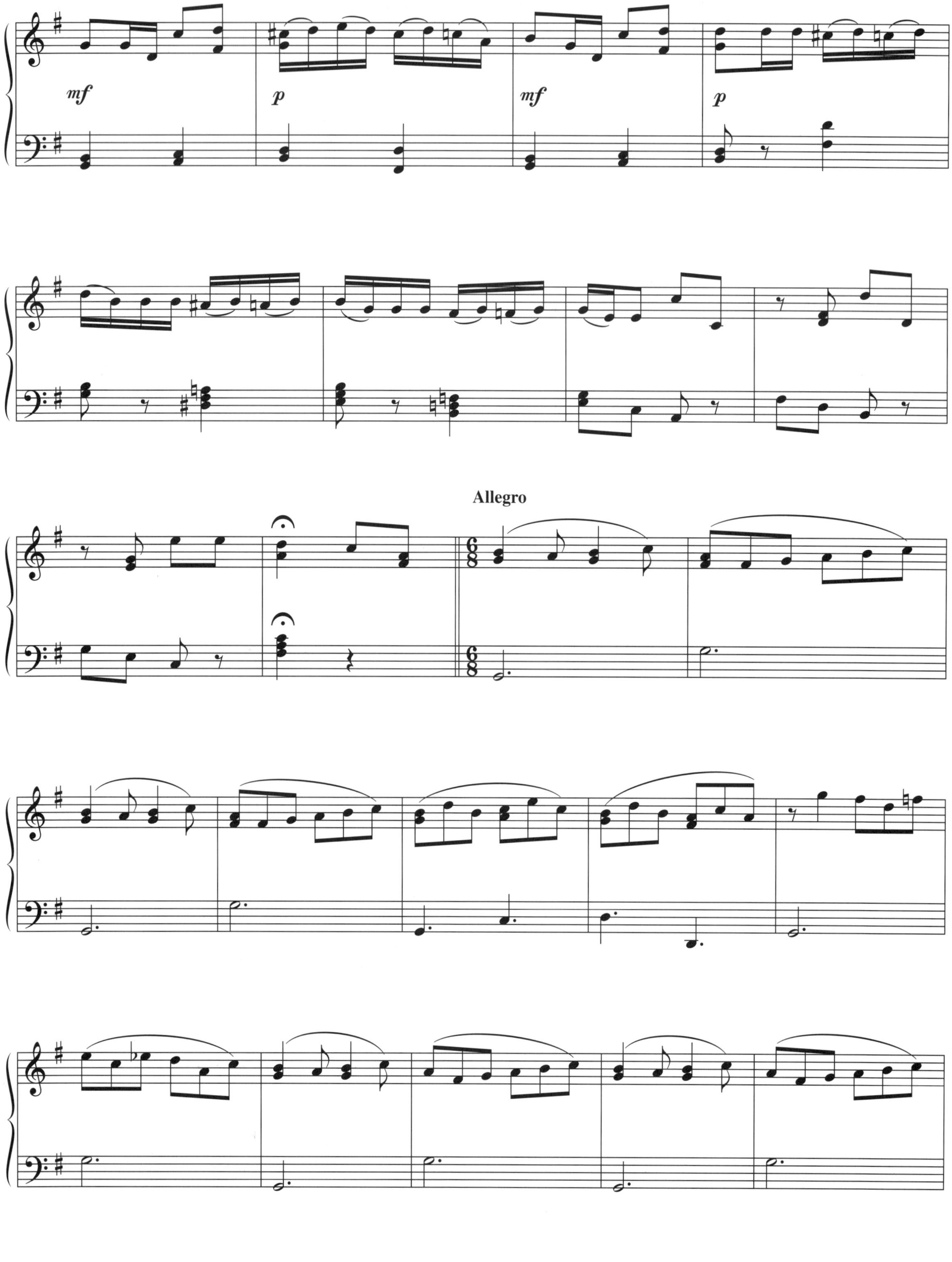

mf
p
mf
p
Allegro

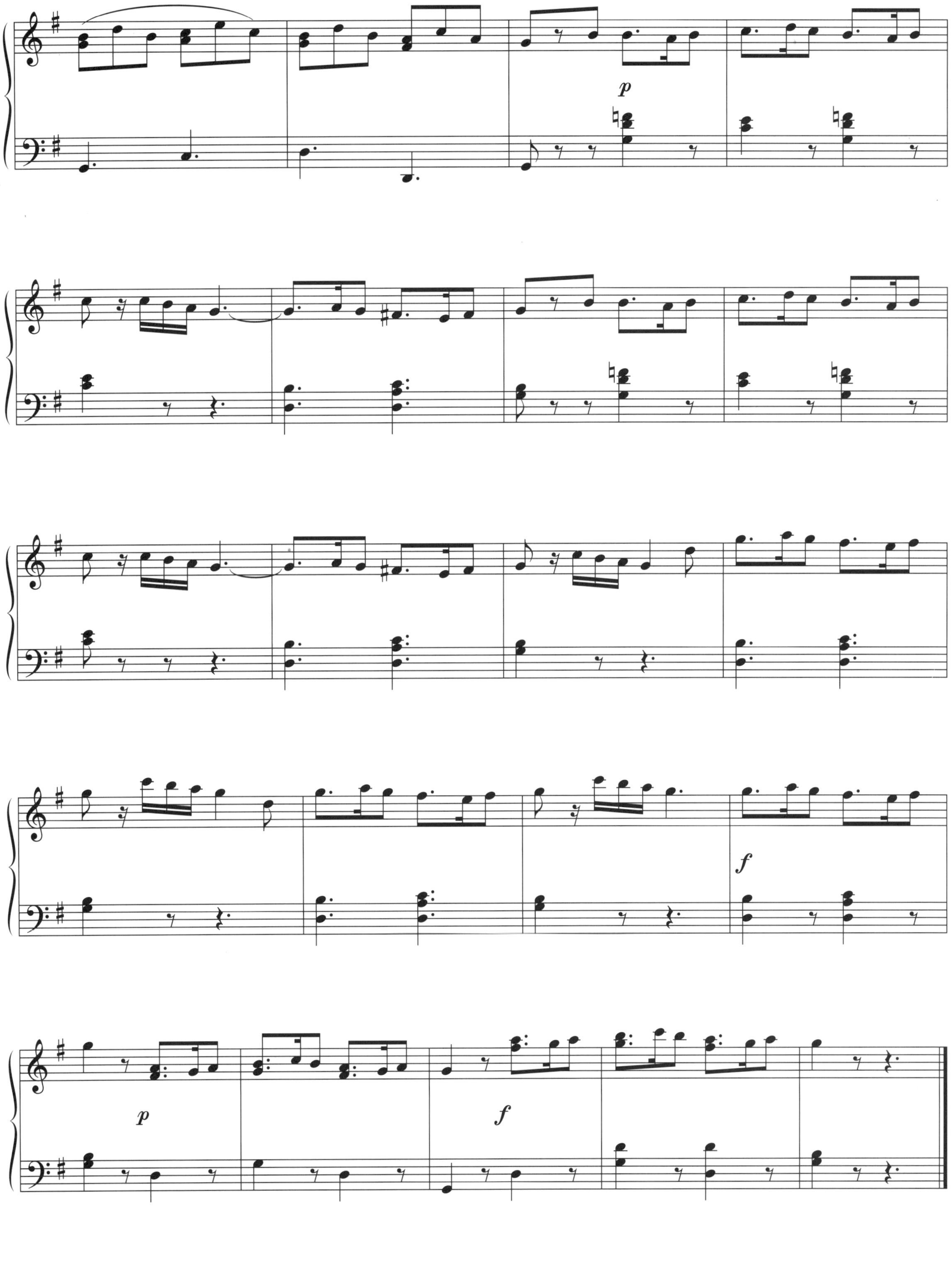
p
f
p
f

Lacrymosa
from REQUIEM

Wolfgang Amadeus Mozart
1756-1791
K 626
originally for chorus and orchestra

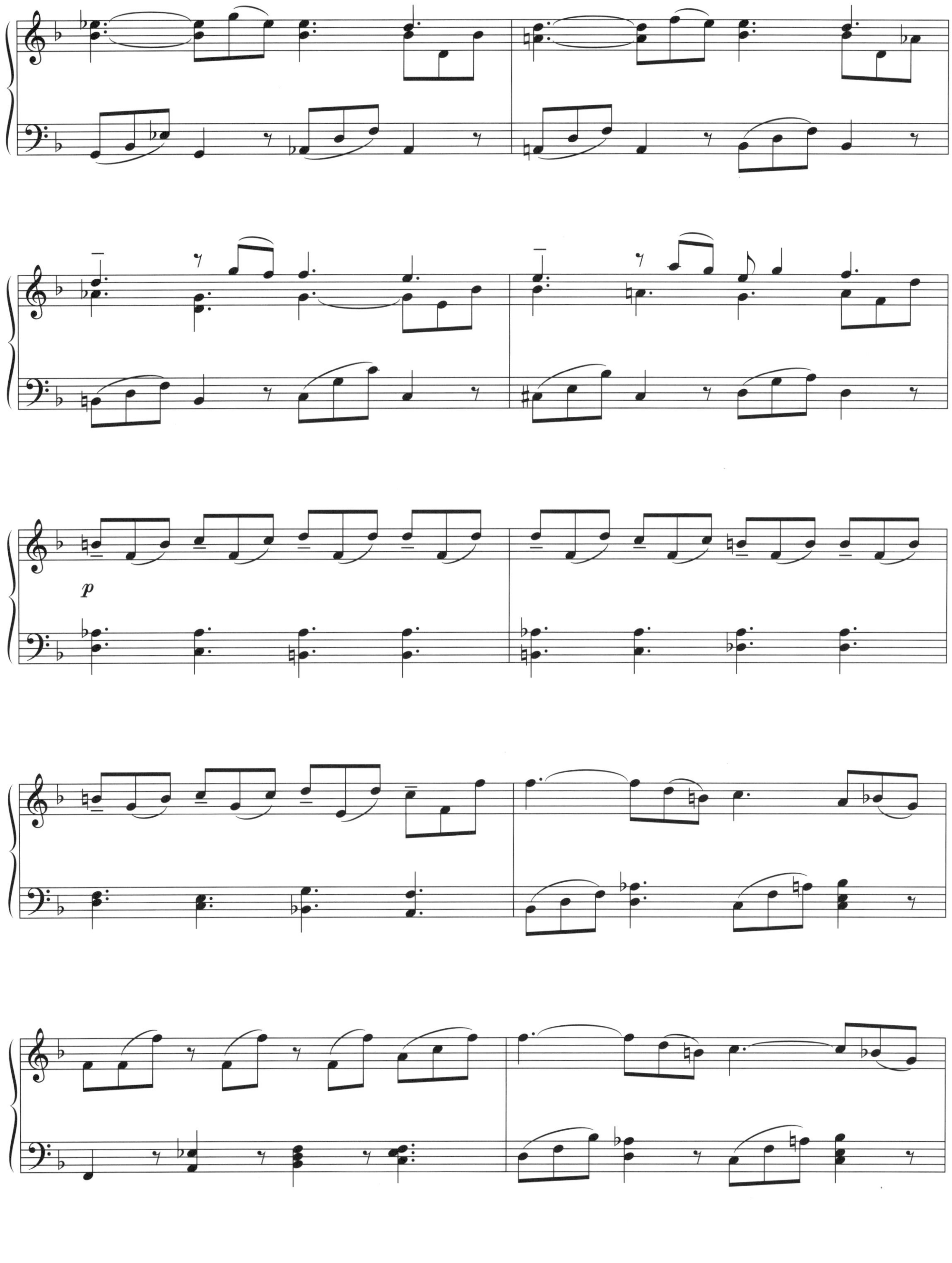
p

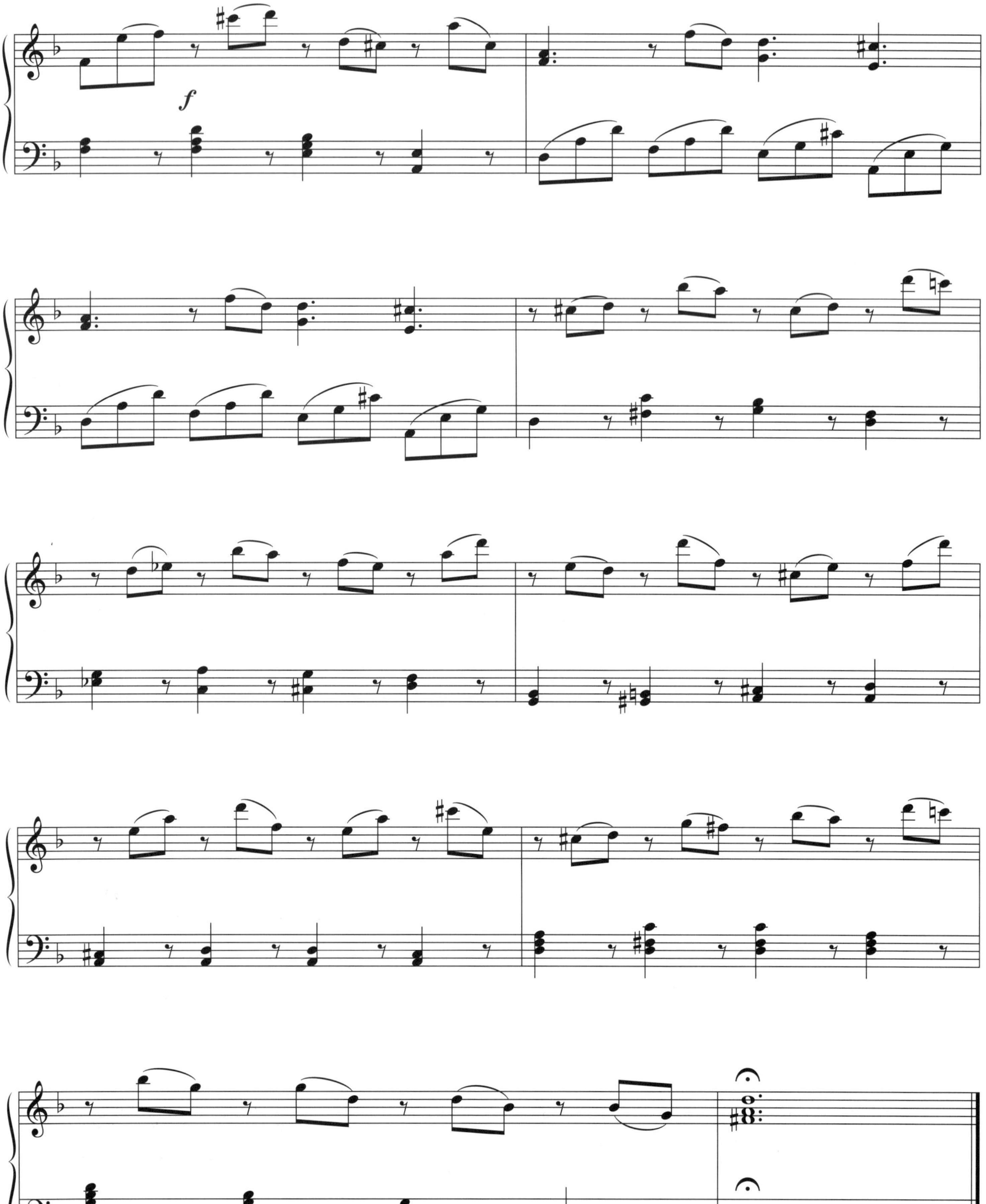
f

Eine kleine Nachtmusik

(A Little Night Music)
First Movement Excerpt

Wolfgang Amadeus Mozart
1756-1791
K 525
originally for string ensemble

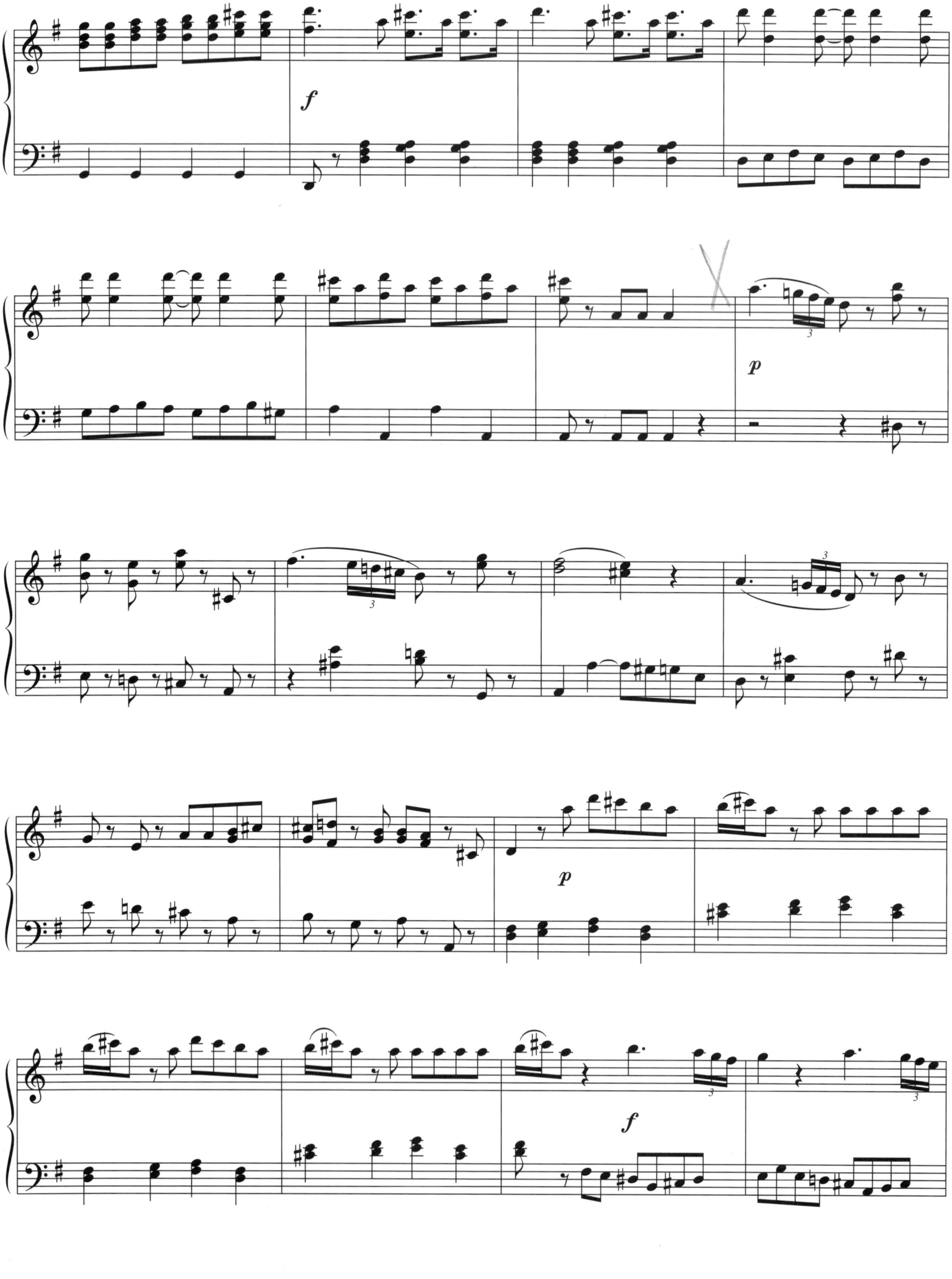

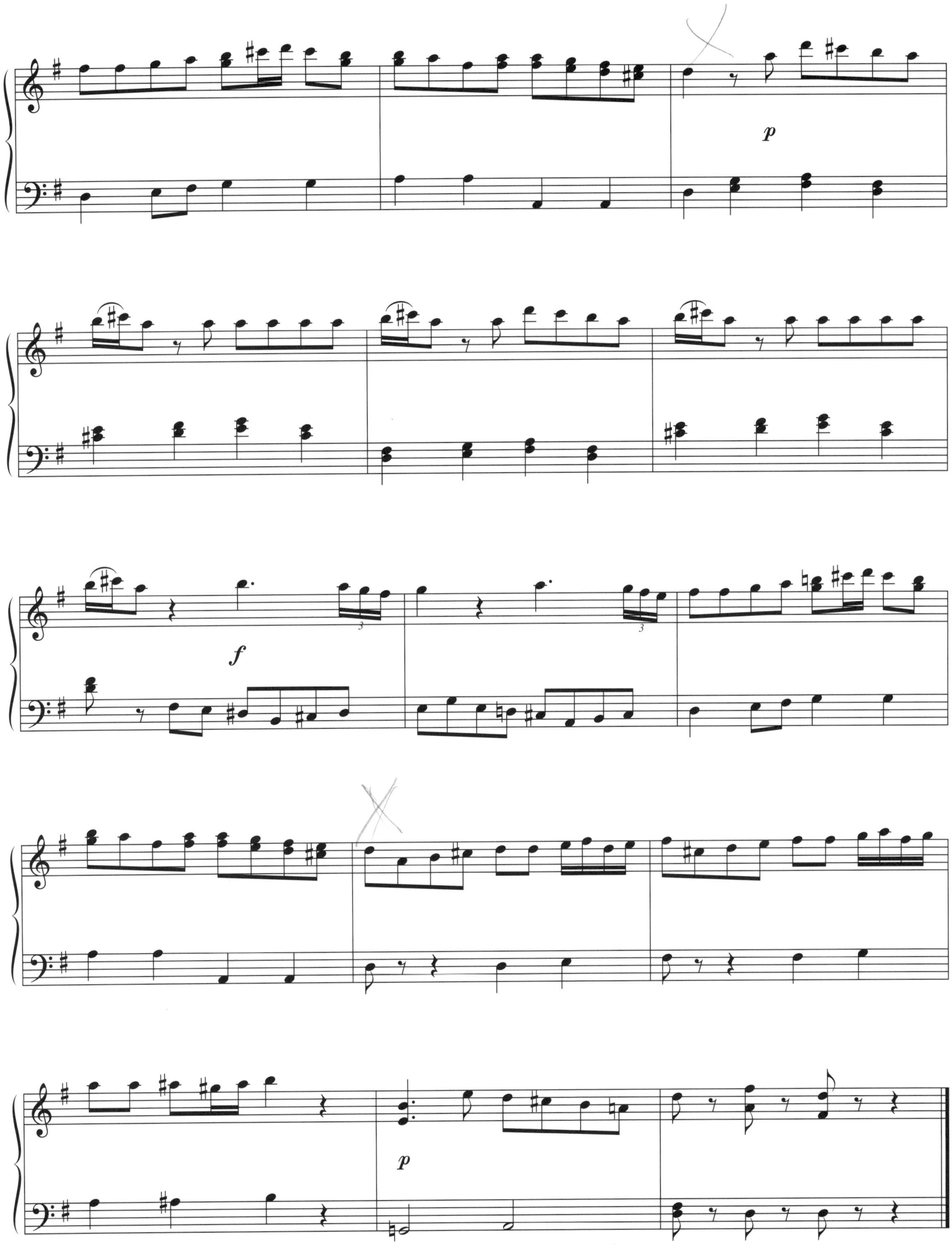
p
f
p

Piano Concerto No. 21

"Elvira Madigan"
Second Movement Excerpt

Wolfgang Amadeus Mozart
1756-1791
K 467
originally for piano and orchestra

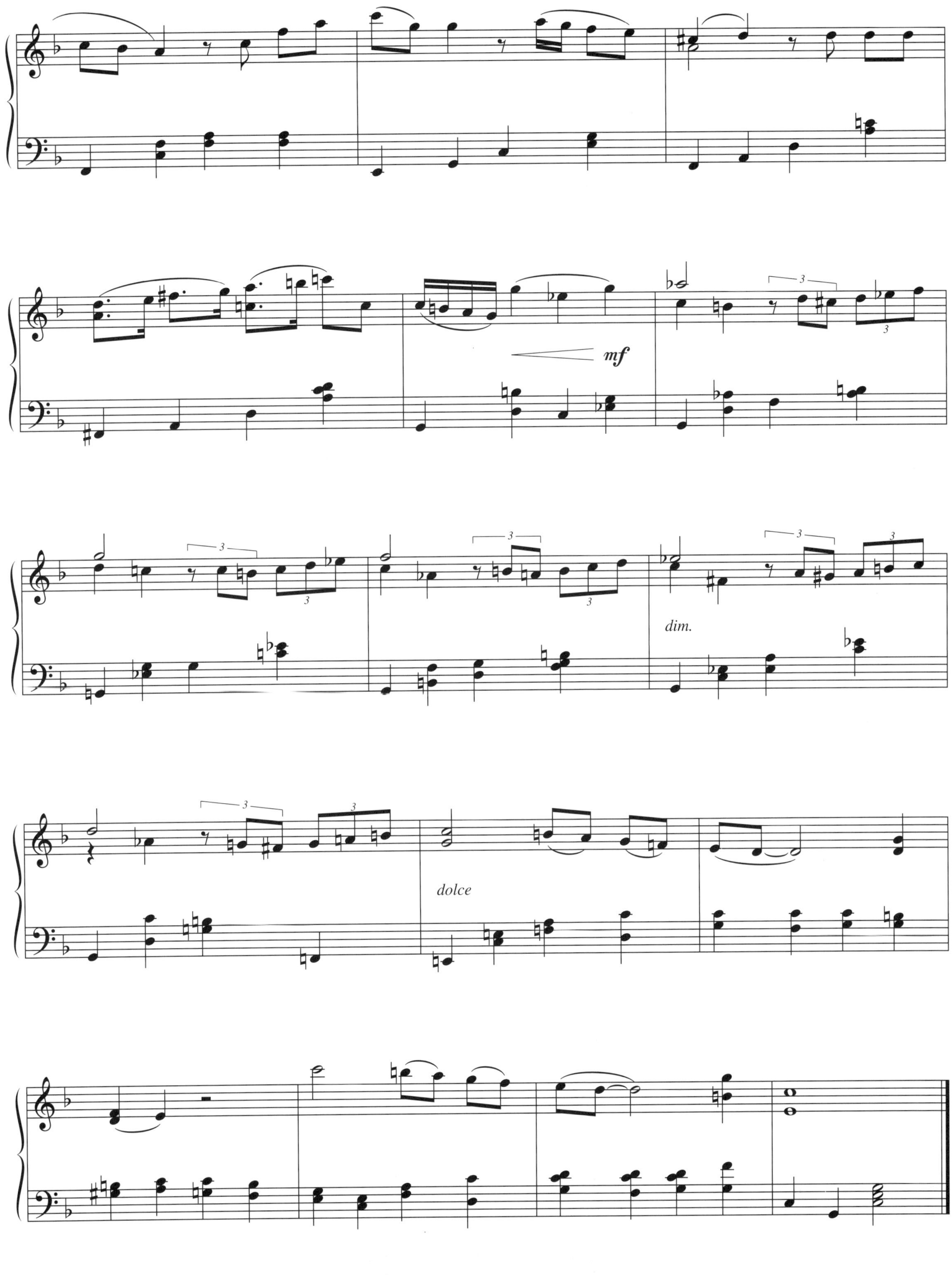
mf
dim.
dolce

Symphony No. 29

First Movement Excerpt

Wolfgang Amadeus Mozart
1756-1791
K 201
originally for orchestra

Allegro moderato

original key: A Major

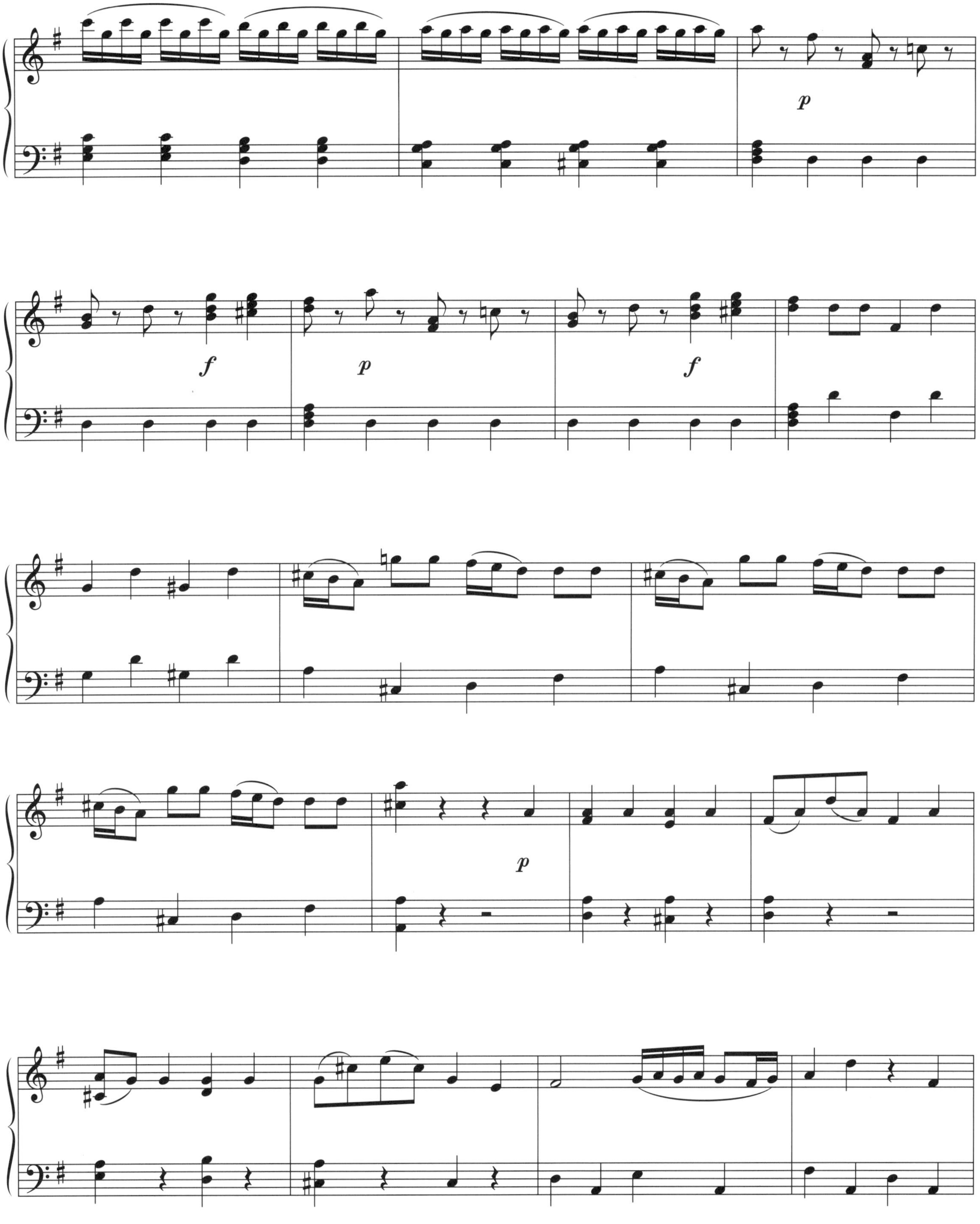
p
f
p
f
p

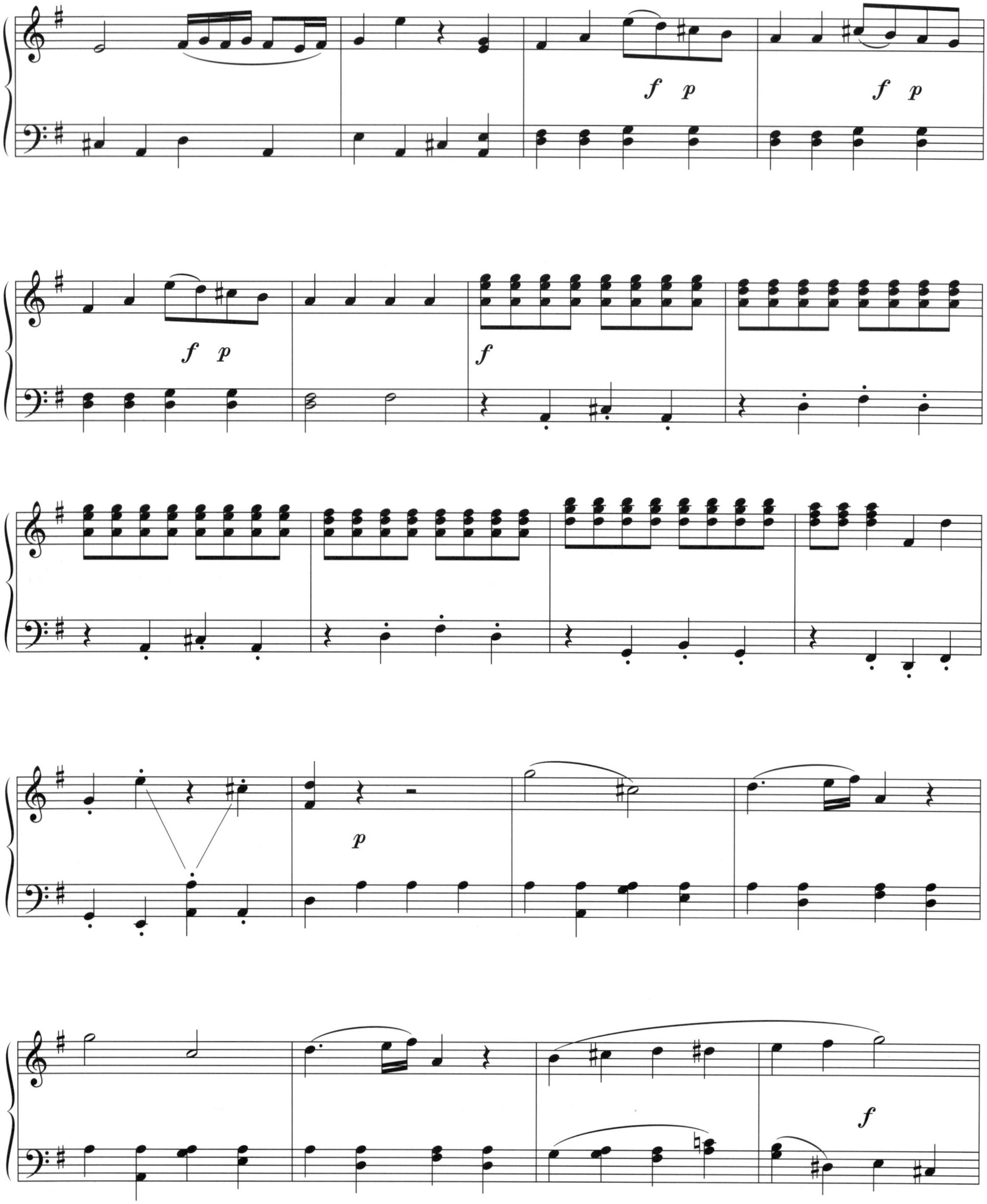
f p
f p
f p
f
p
f

271

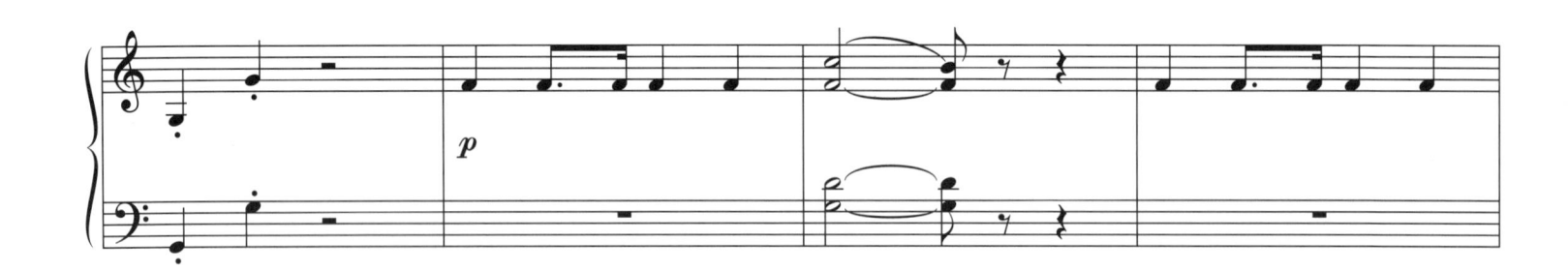

Symphony No. 35

"Haffner"
First Movement Excerpt

Wolfgang Amadeus Mozart
1756-1791
K 385
originally for orchestra

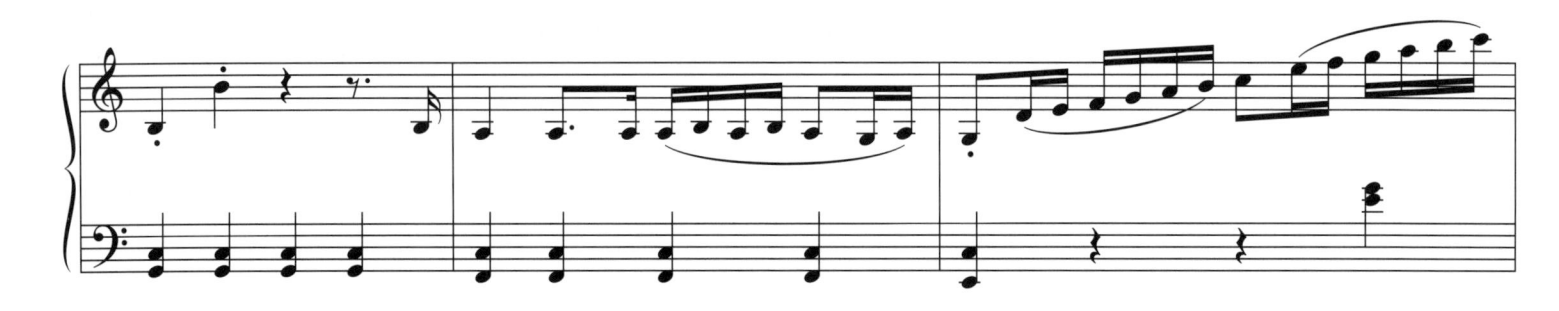

Allegro con spirito

original key: D Major

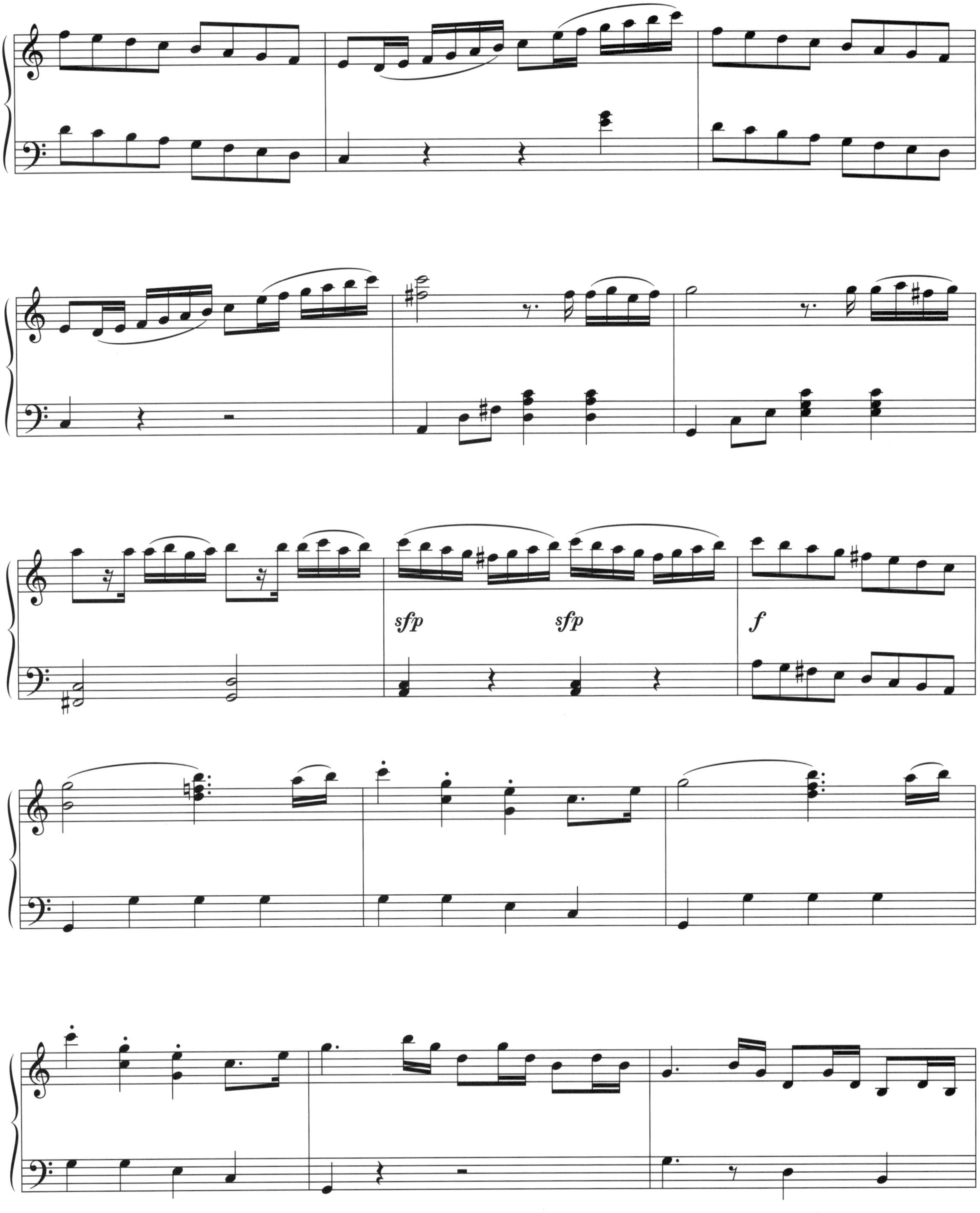
sfp
sfp
f

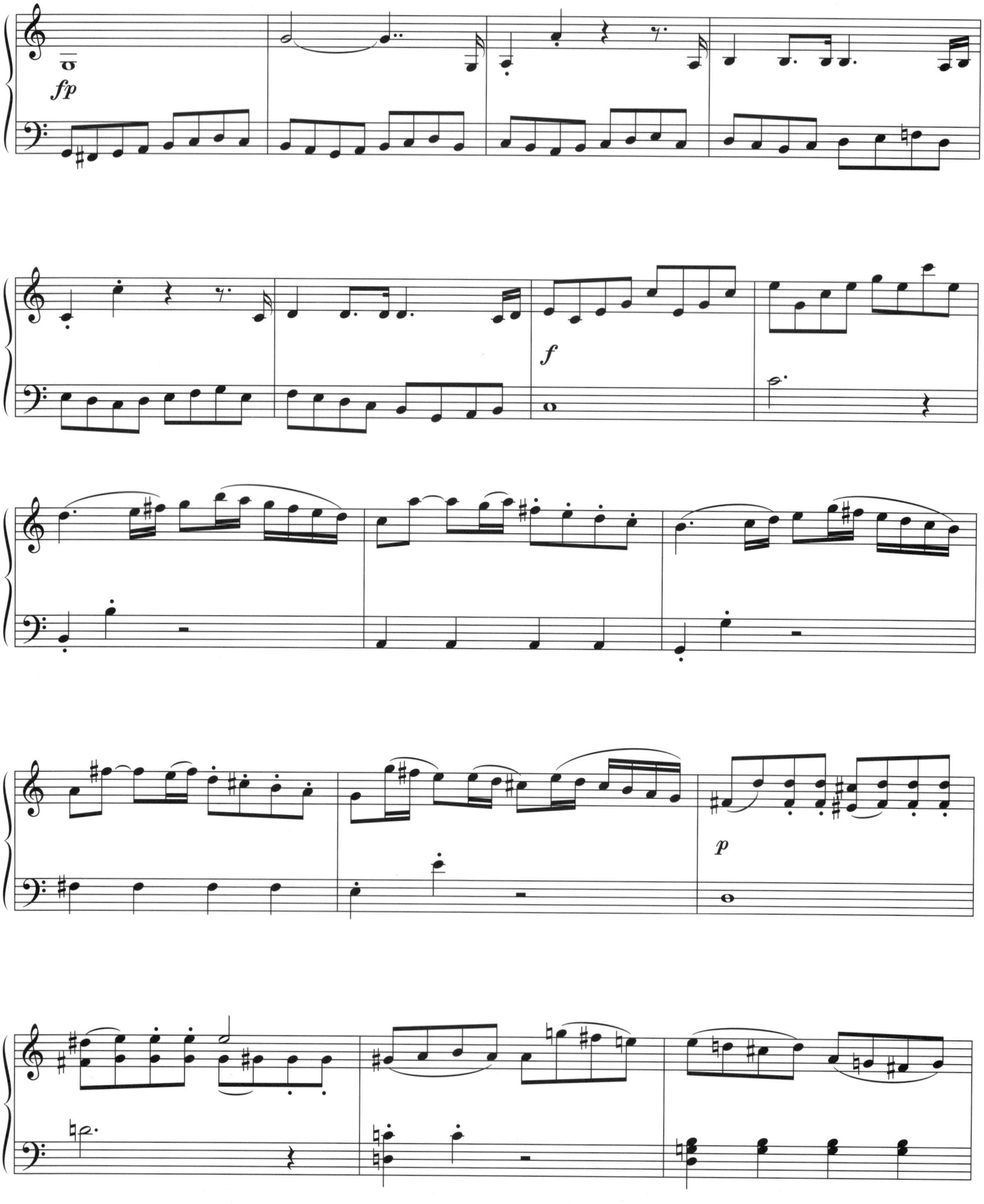
fp
f
p

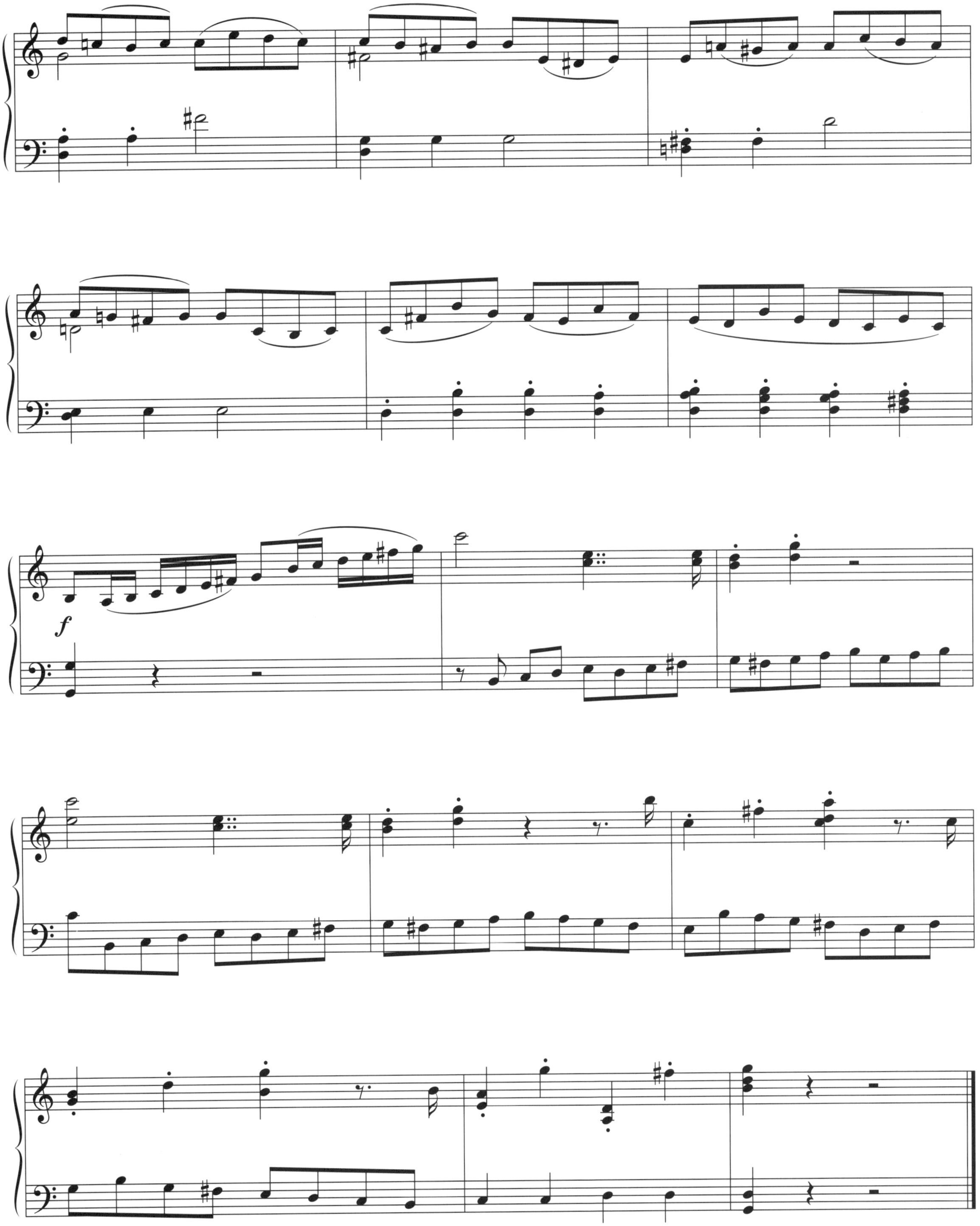
f

Symphony No. 38
"Prague"
First Movement Excerpt

Wolfgang Amadeus Mozart
1756-1791
K 504
originally for orchestra

original key: D Major

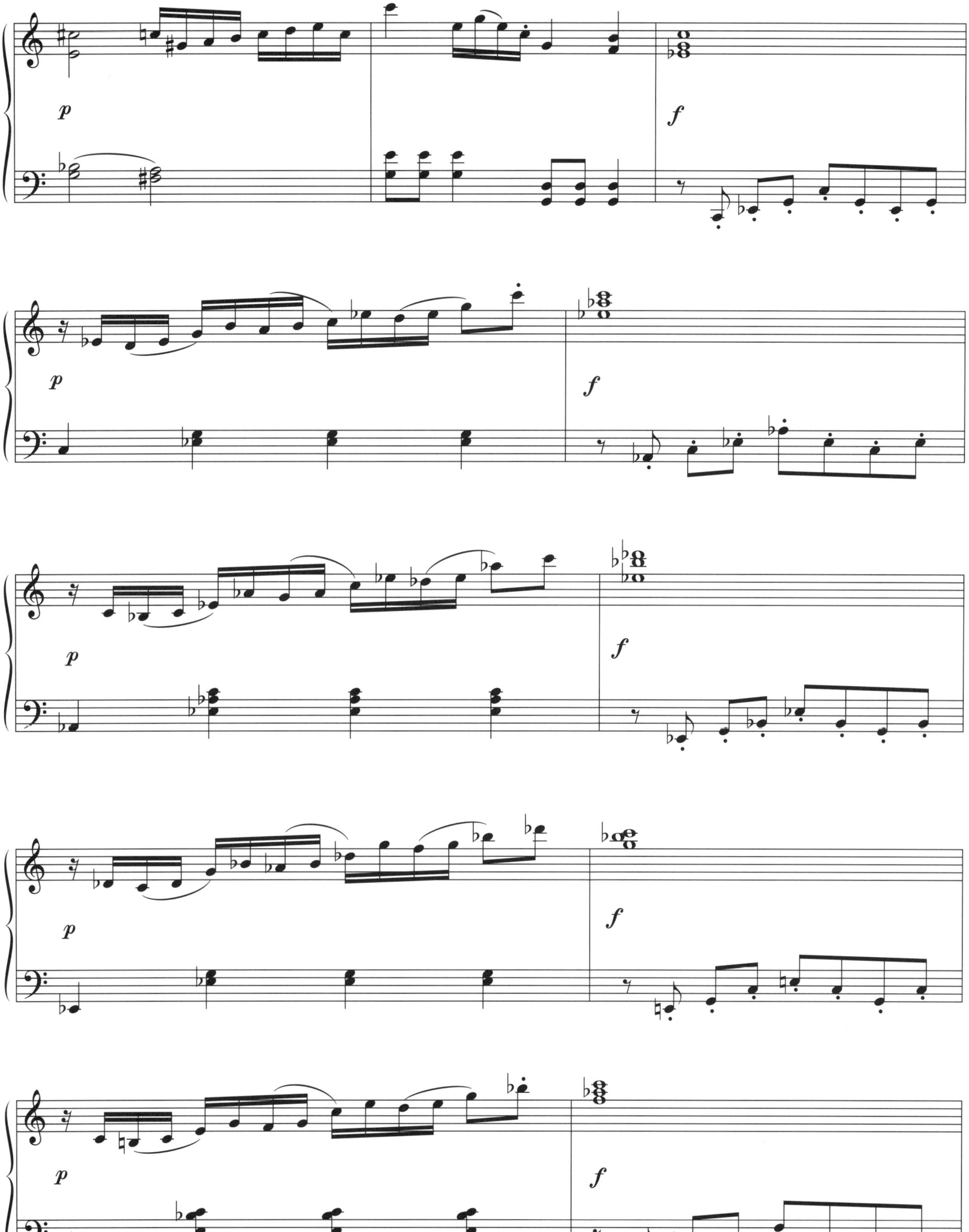
p
f
p
f
p
f
p
f
p
f

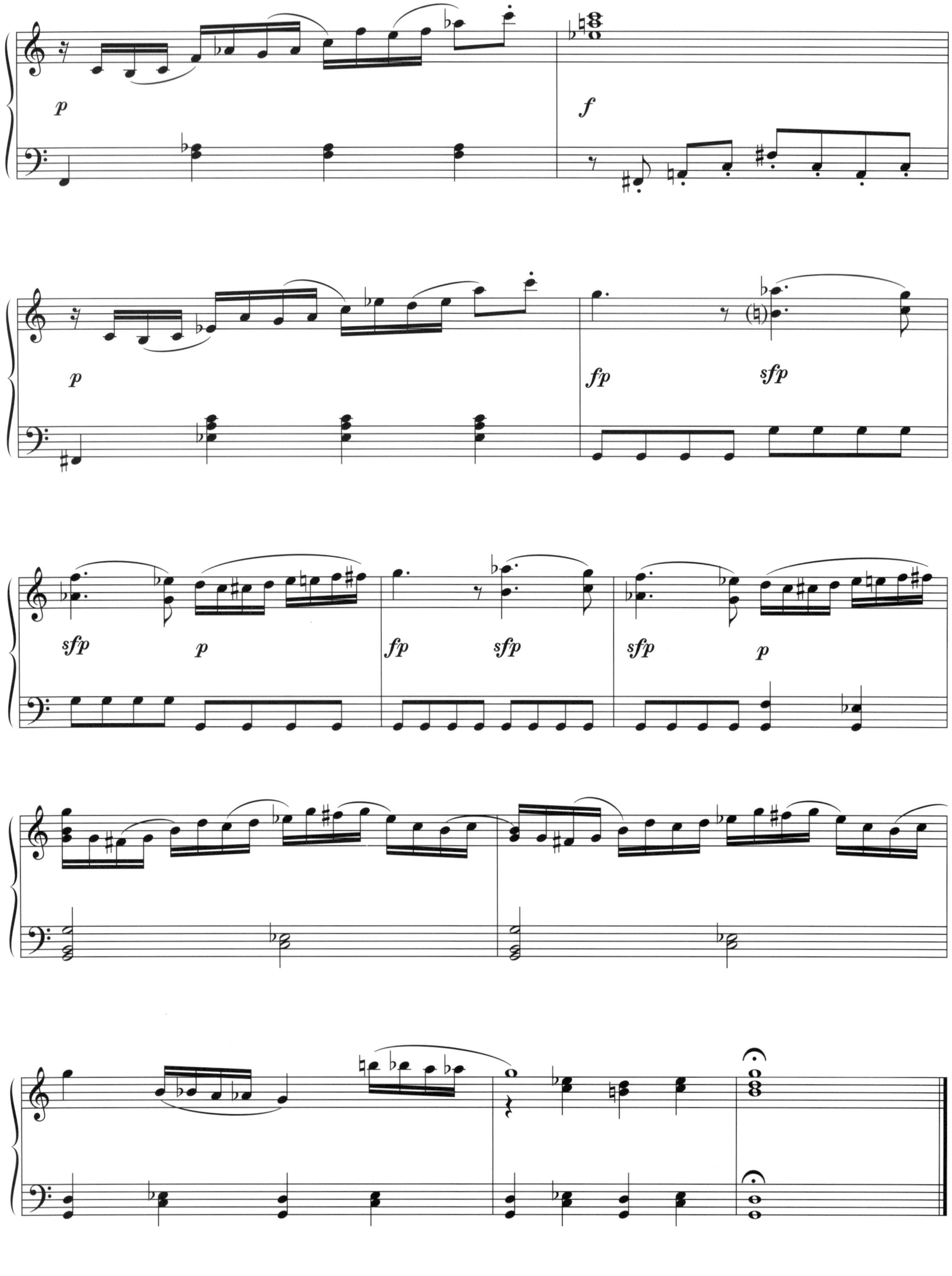
p
f
p
fp
sfp
sfp
p
fp
sfp
sfp
p

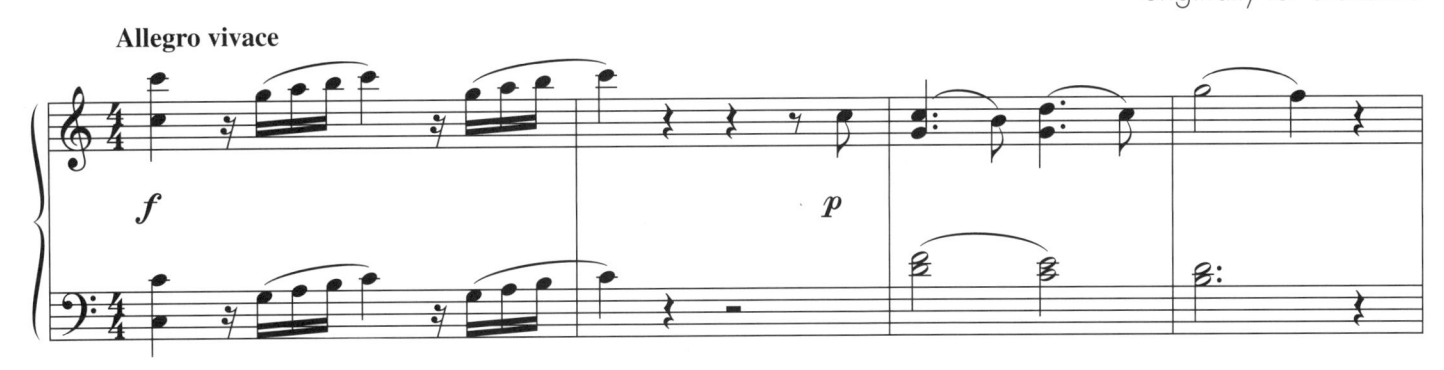

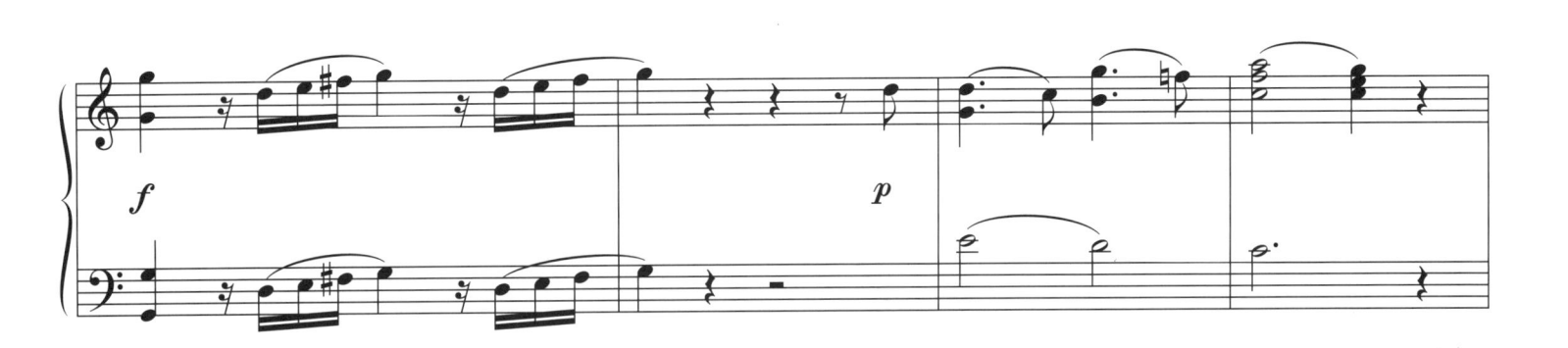

Symphony No. 41

"Jupiter"
First Movement Excerpt

Wolfgang Amadeus Mozart
1756-1791
K 551
originally for orchestra

Allegro vivace

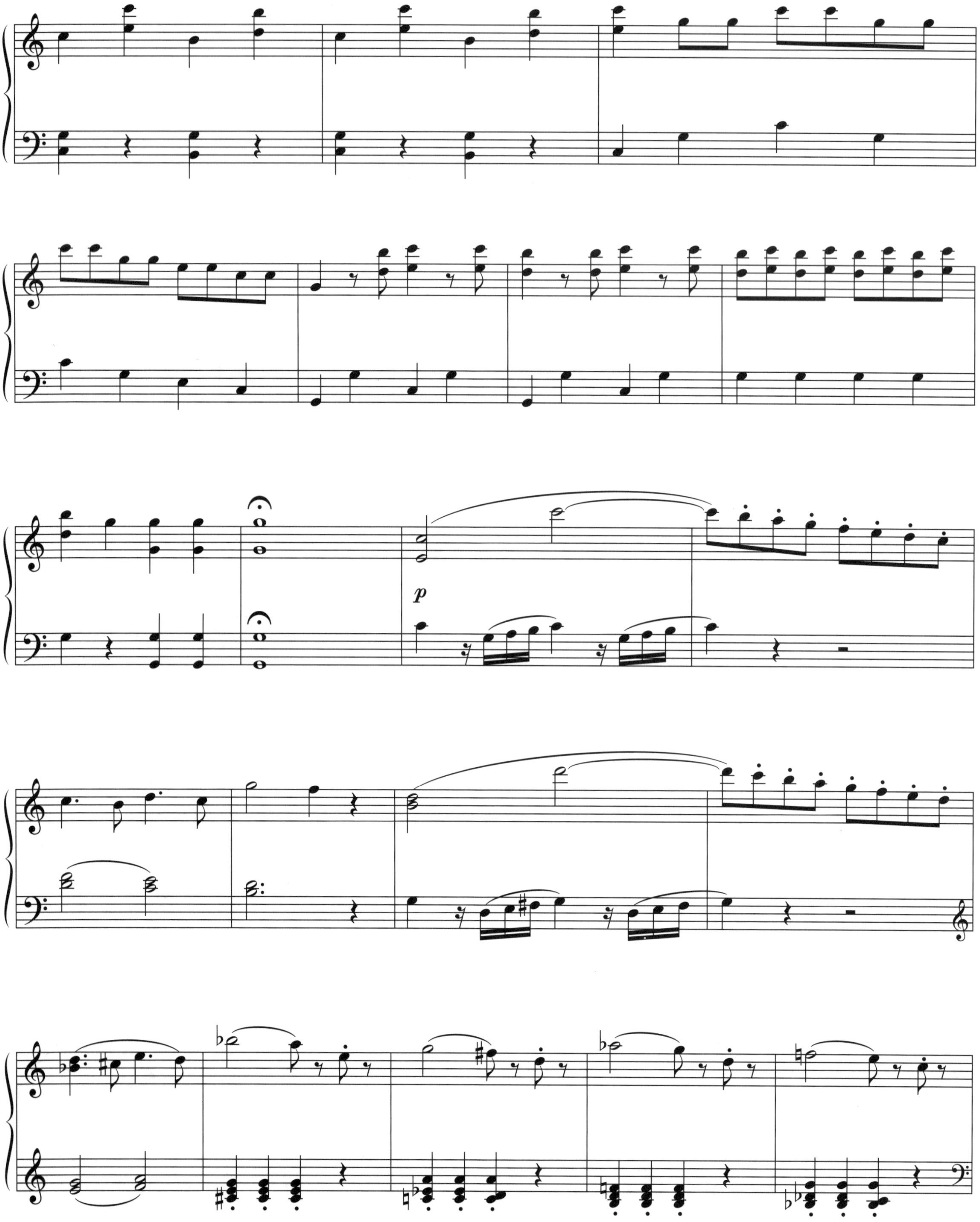
p

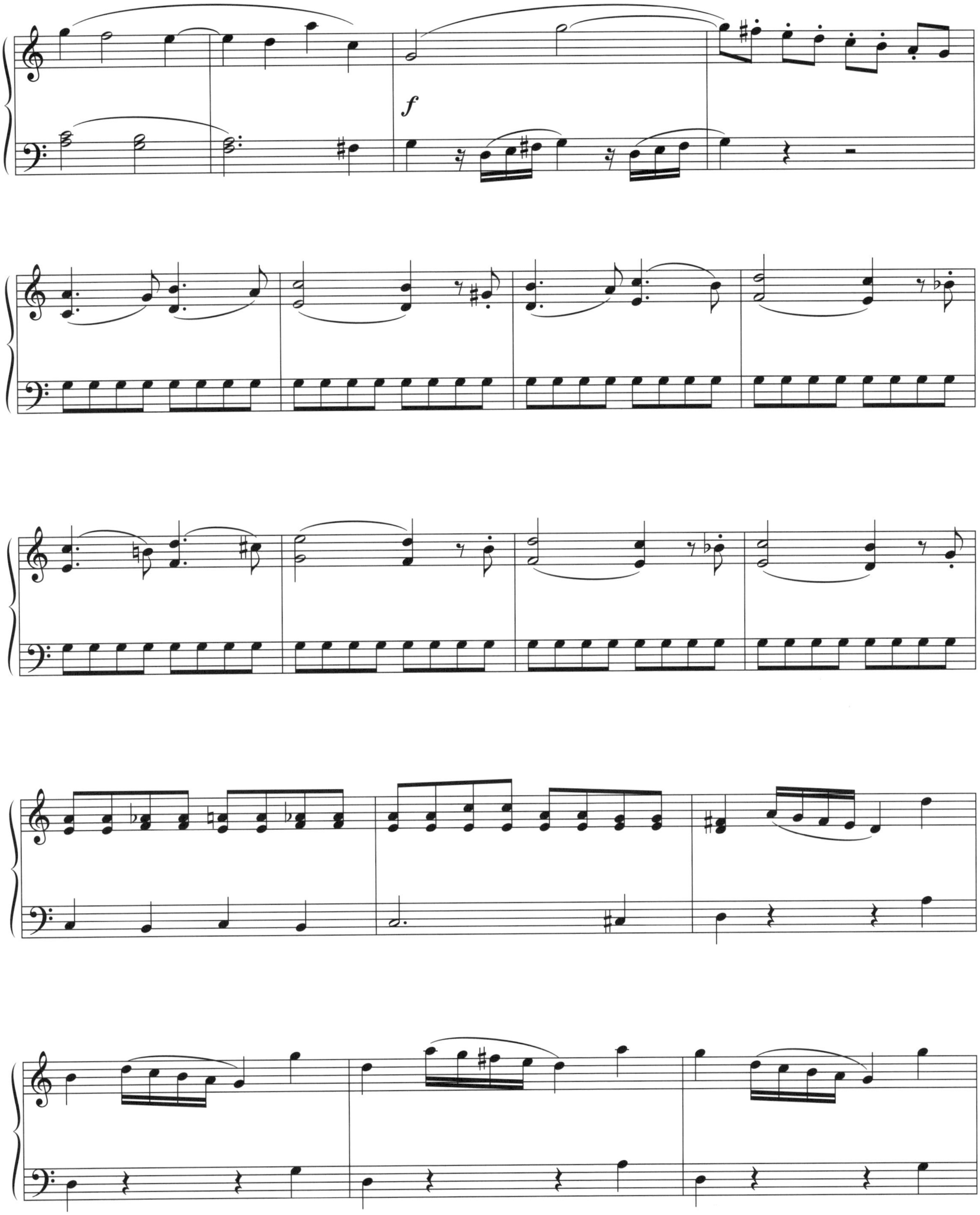
f

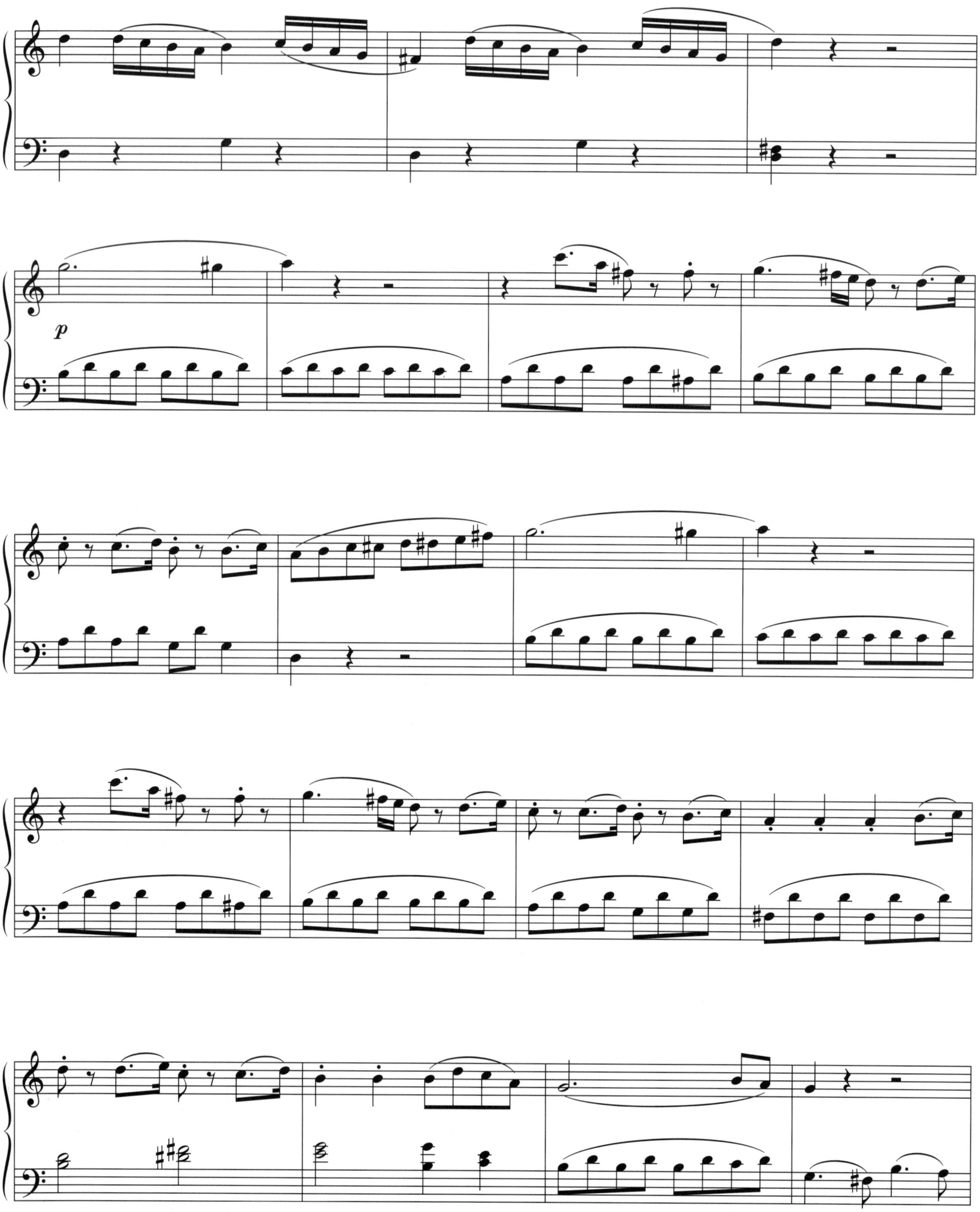
p

283

Symphony No. 40

First Movement Excerpt

Wolfgang Amadeus Mozart
1756-1791
K 550
originally for orchestra

Allegro molto

original key: G Minor

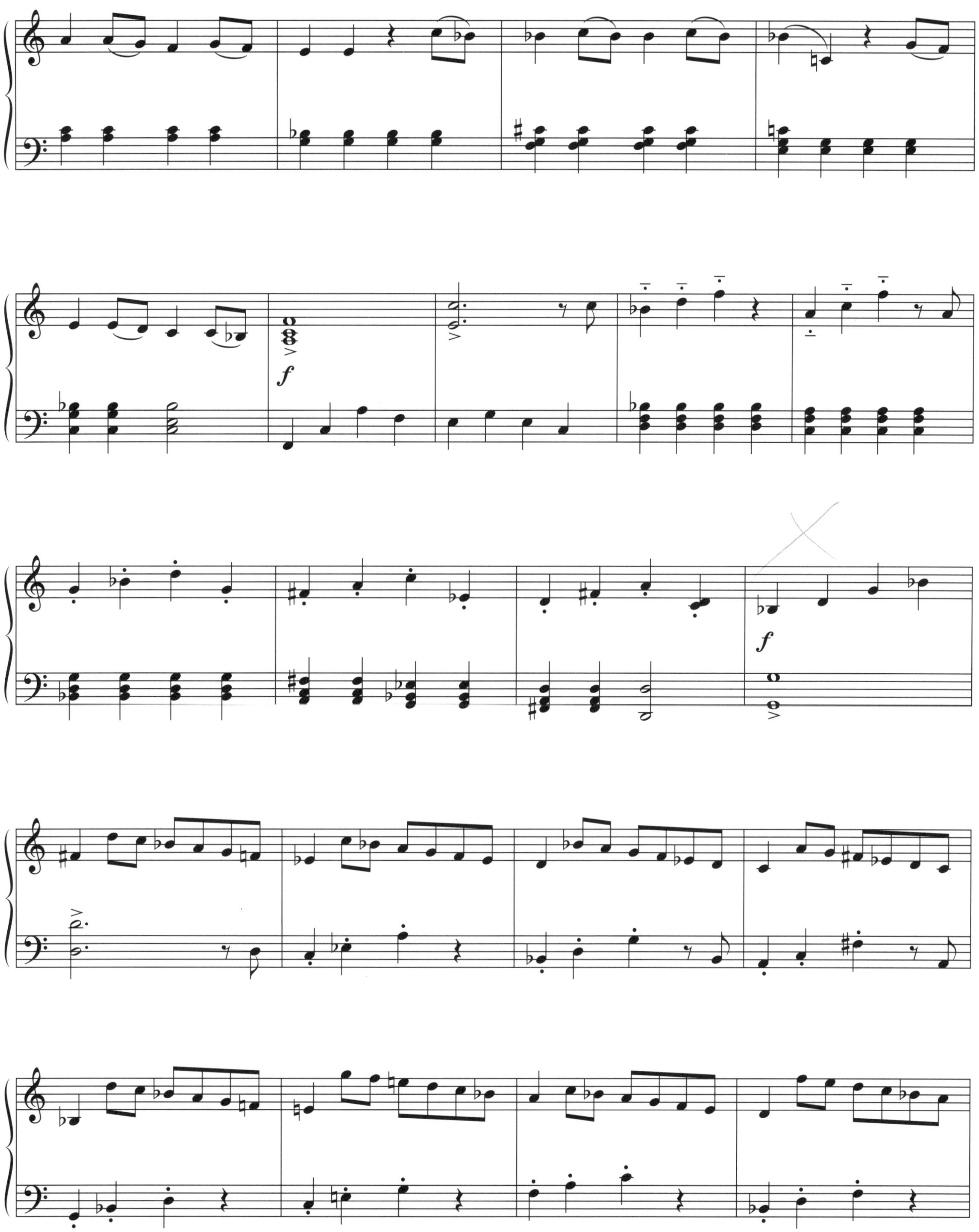
f
f

286

287

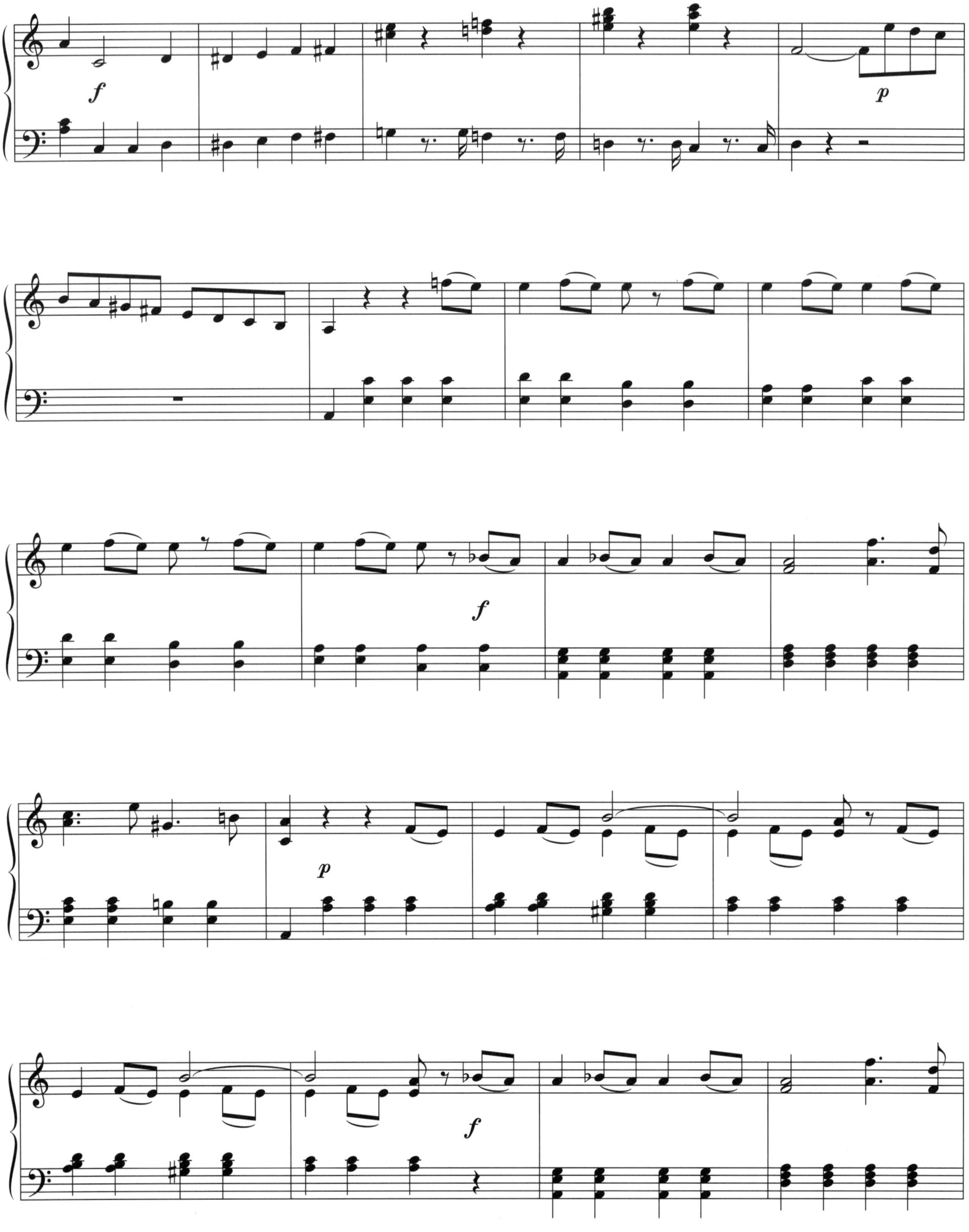
f
p
f
p
f

289

Can Can

from the opera ORPHEUS IN THE UNDERWORLD

Jacques Offenbach
1819-1880
originally for chorus and orchestra

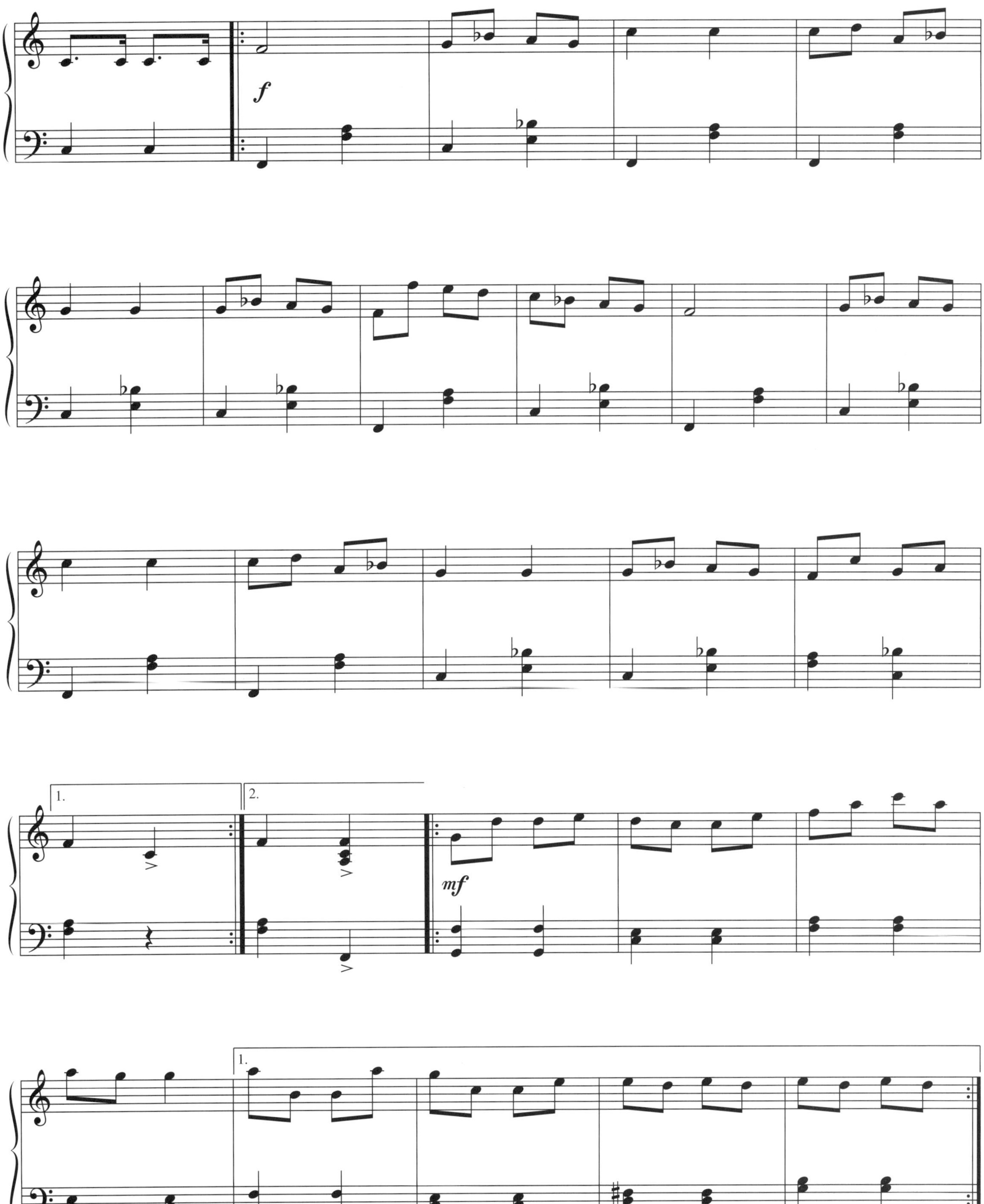
f
1.
2.
mf
1.

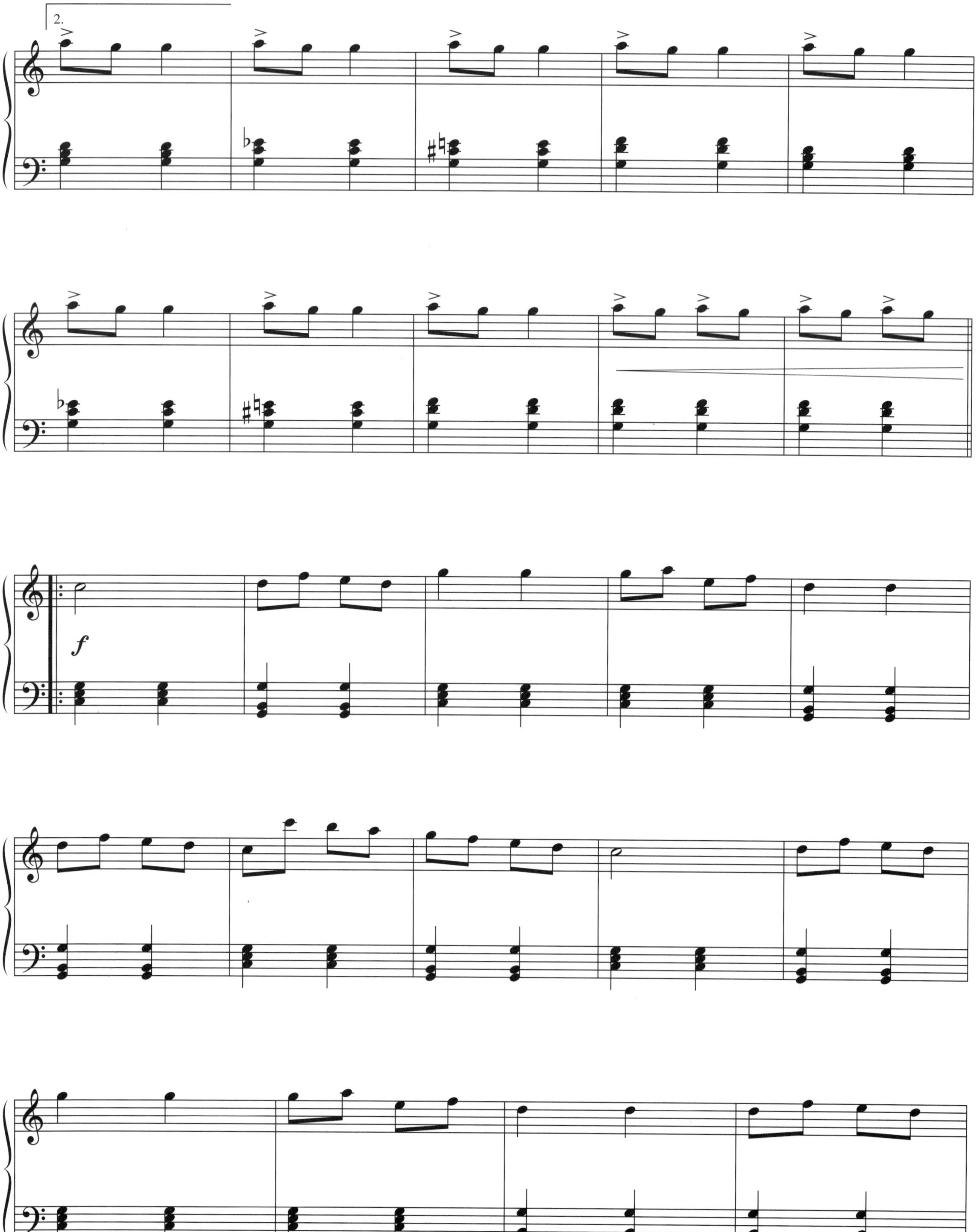
2.
f

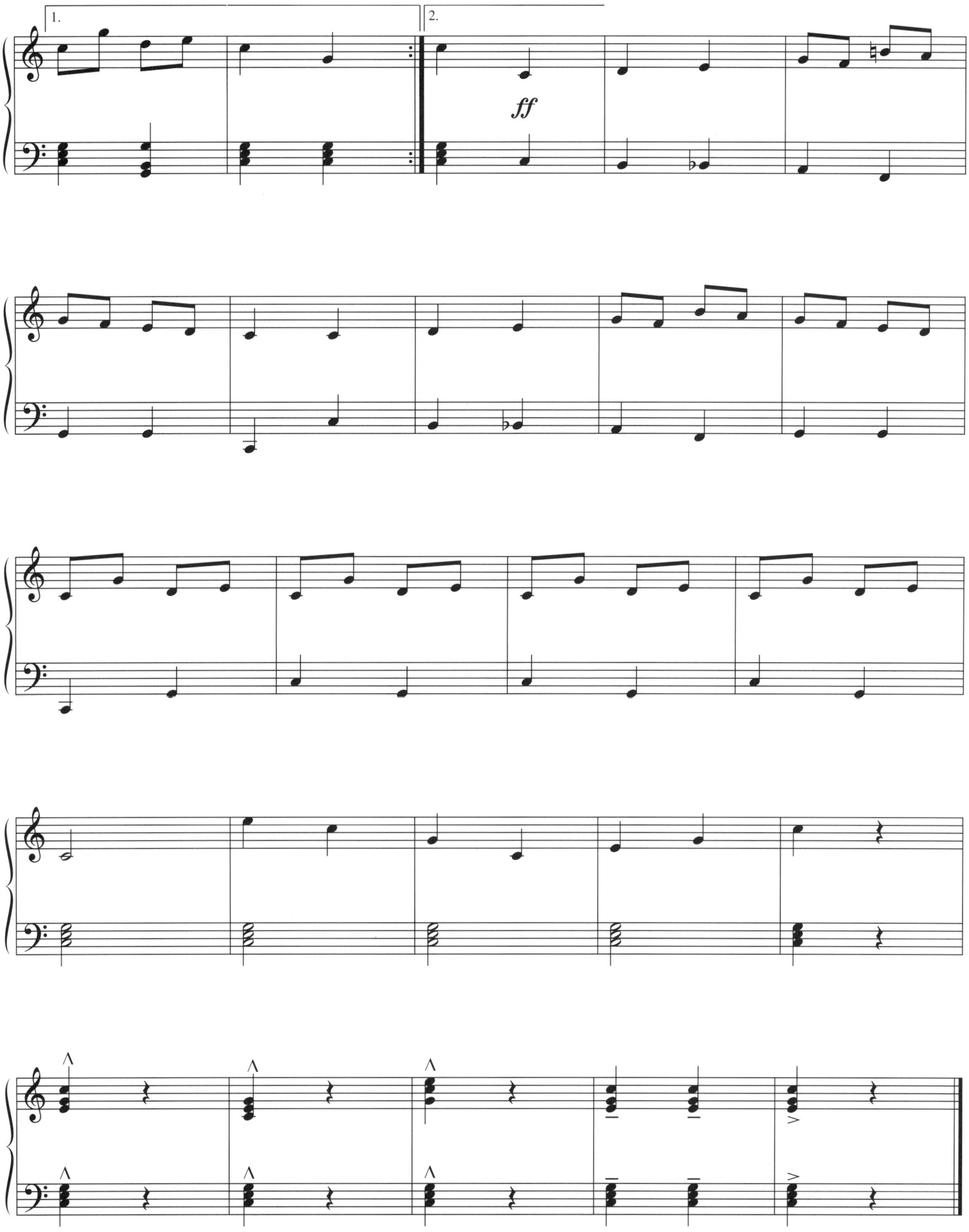
1.
2.
ff

Barcarolle

from the opera THE TALES OF HOFFMANN

Jacques Offenbach
1819-1880
originally for singers, chorus and orchestra

Moderato

pp *molto cantabile*

original key: D Major

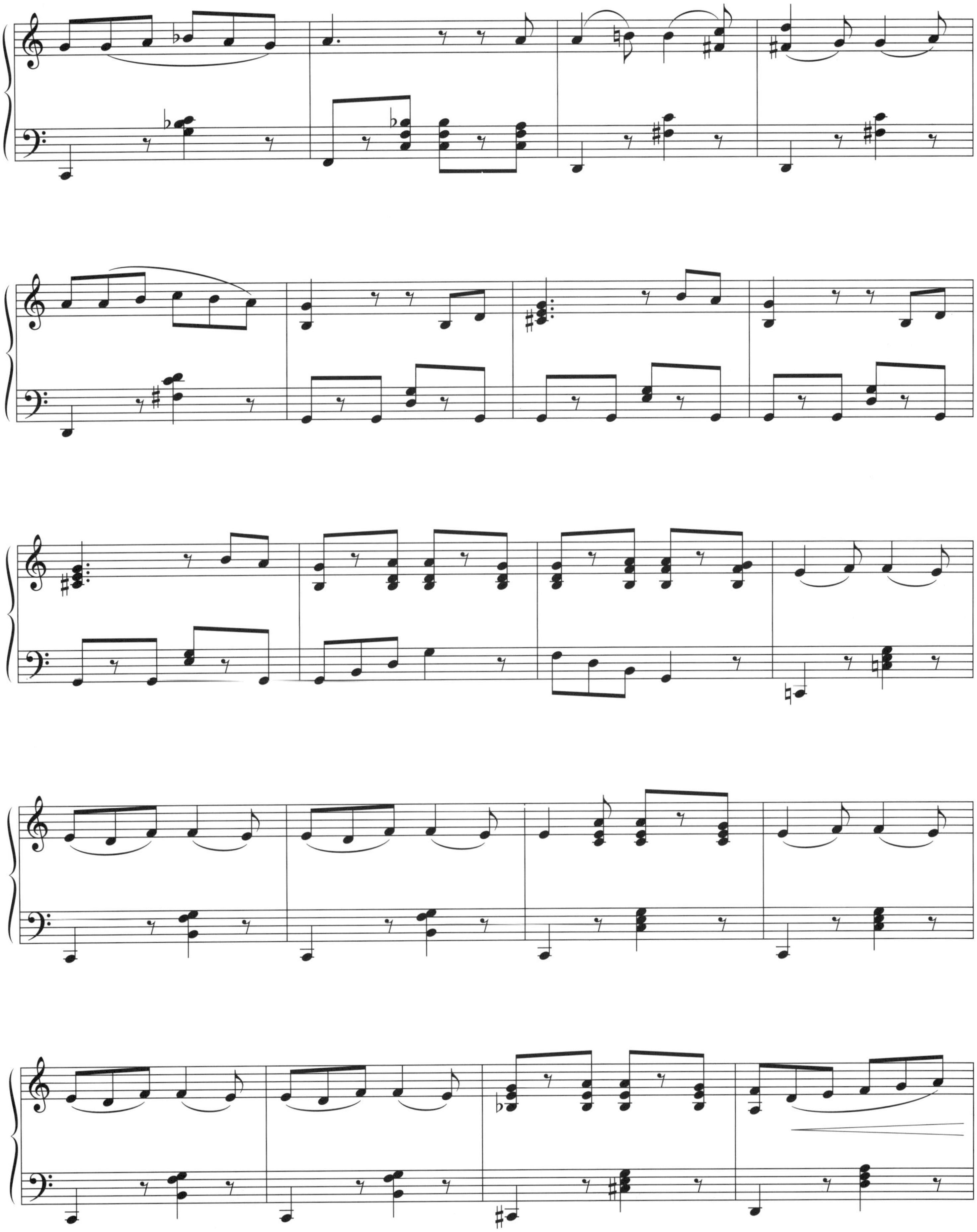

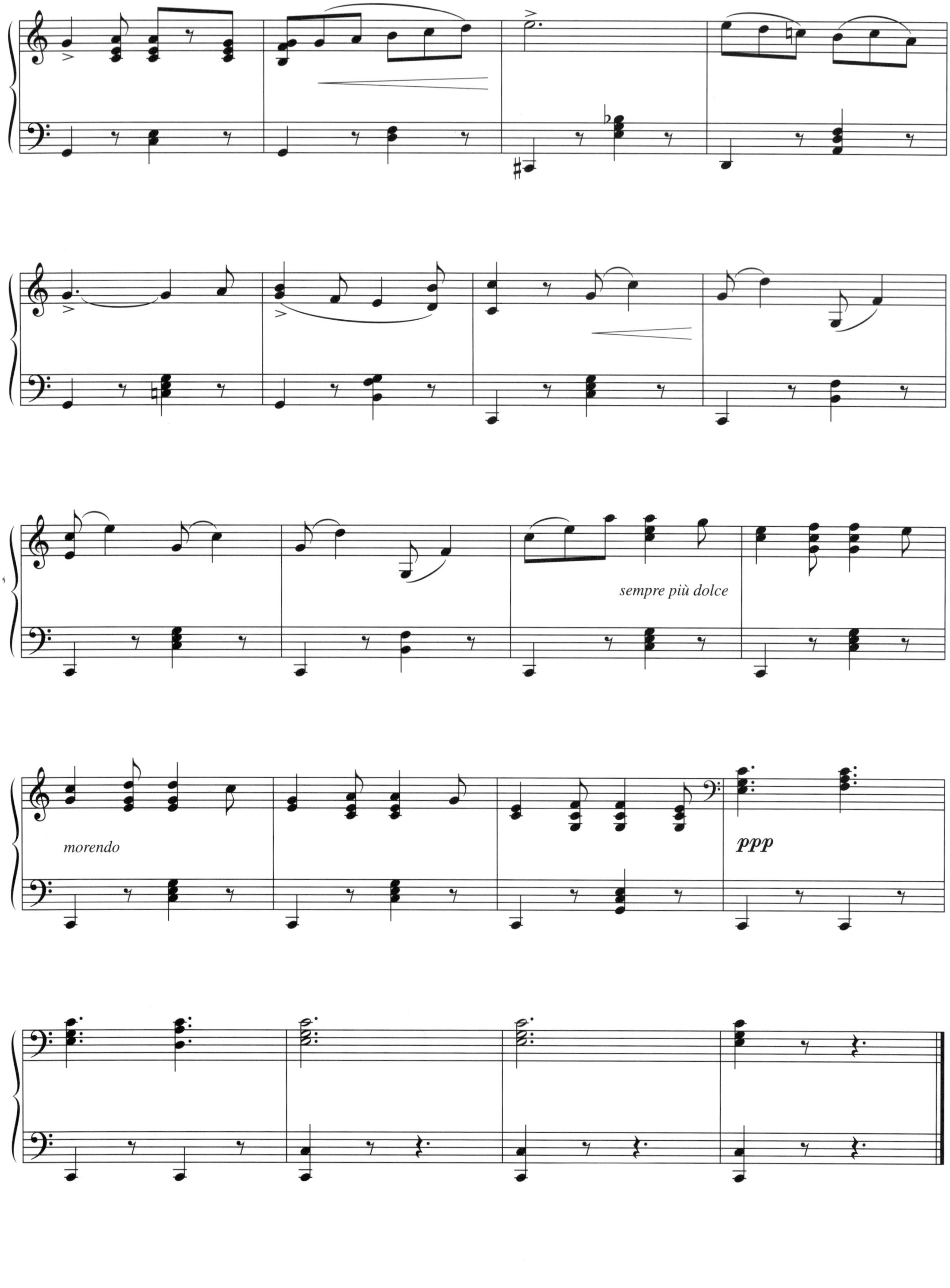
sempre più dolce
morendo
ppp

Jerusalem

Hubert Parry
1848-1918
originally for chorus and organ

Slow, but with animation

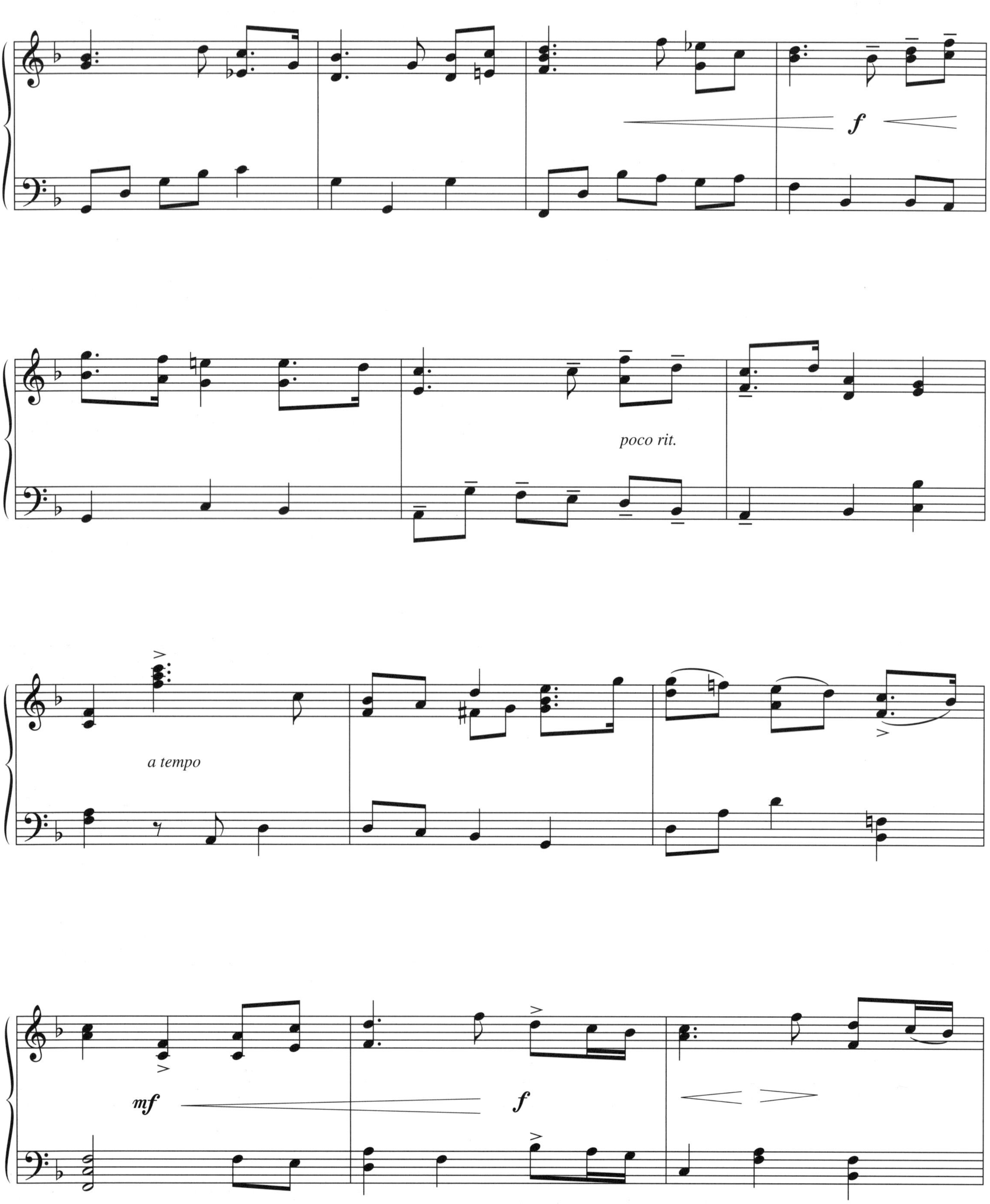
f
poco rit.
a tempo
mf
f

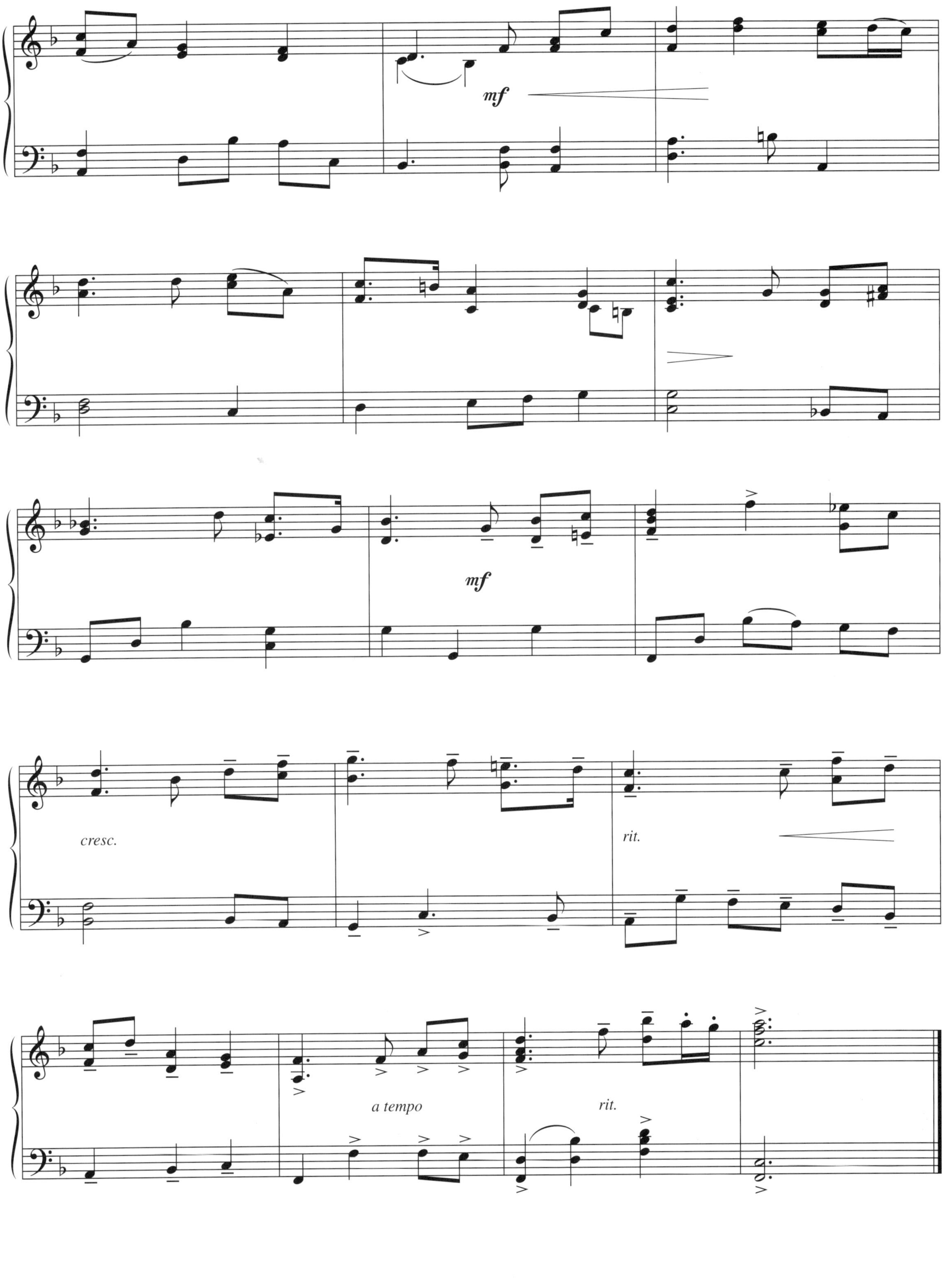
mf
mf
cresc.
rit.
a tempo
rit.

Canon

Excerpt

Johann Pachelbel
1653-1706
originally for 3 violins and continuo

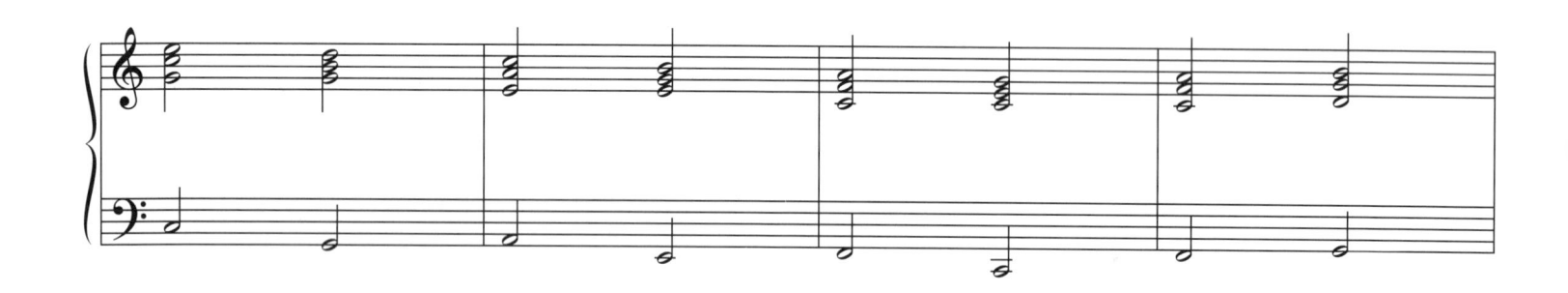

Adagio

p

original key: D Major

301

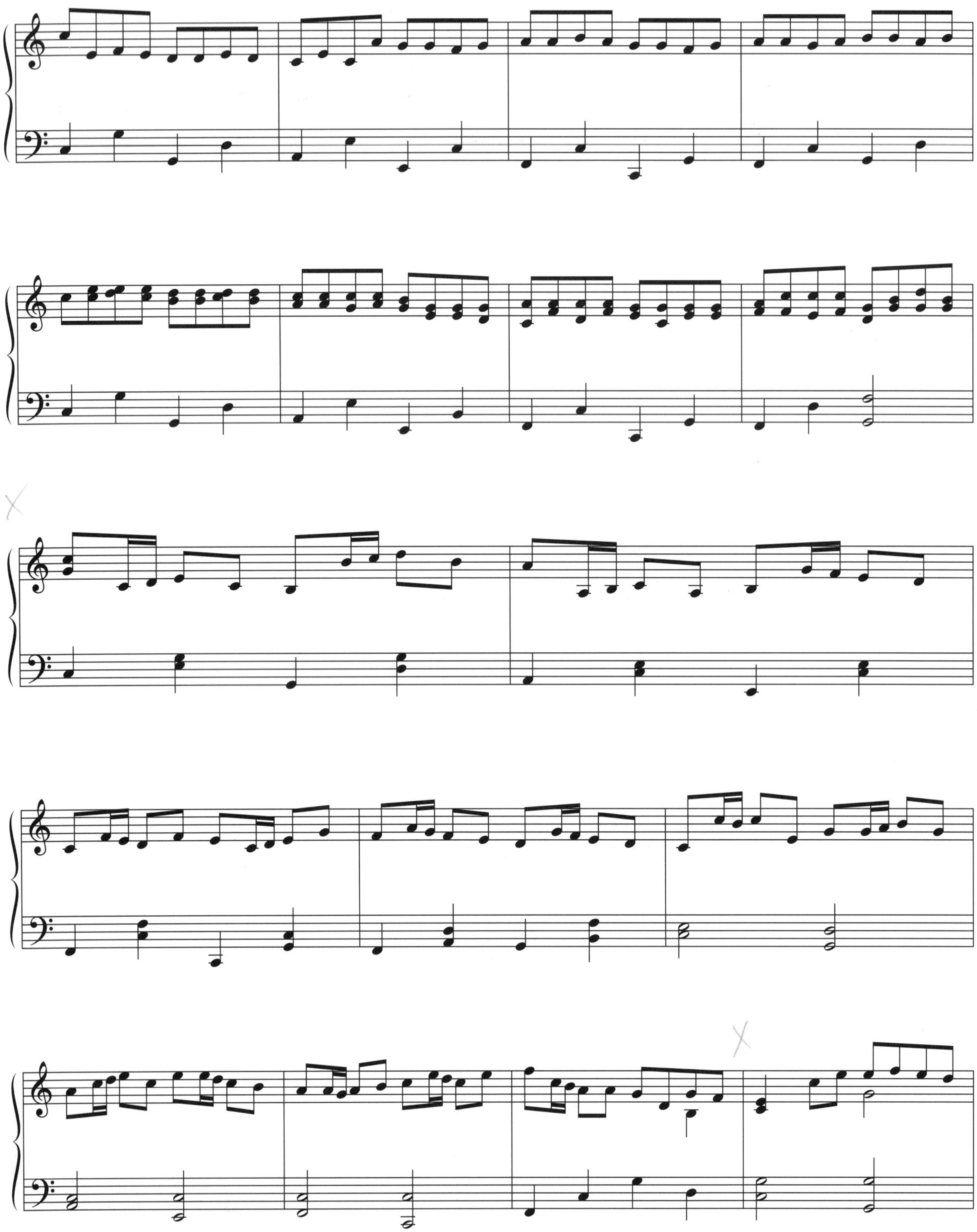

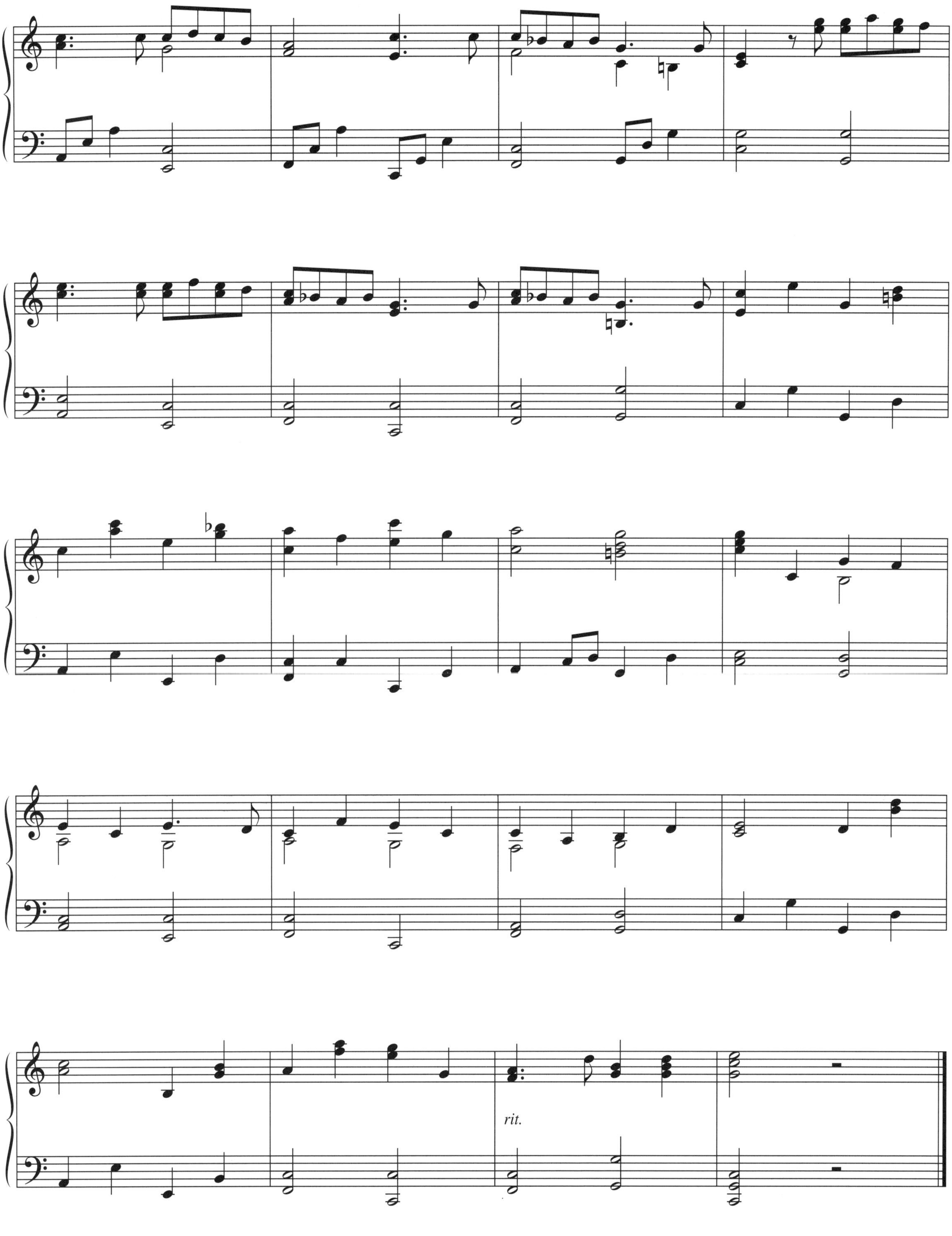
rit.

O mio babbino caro
from the opera GIANNI SCHICCHI

Giacomo Puccini
1858-1924

Andante ingenuo

pp dolce

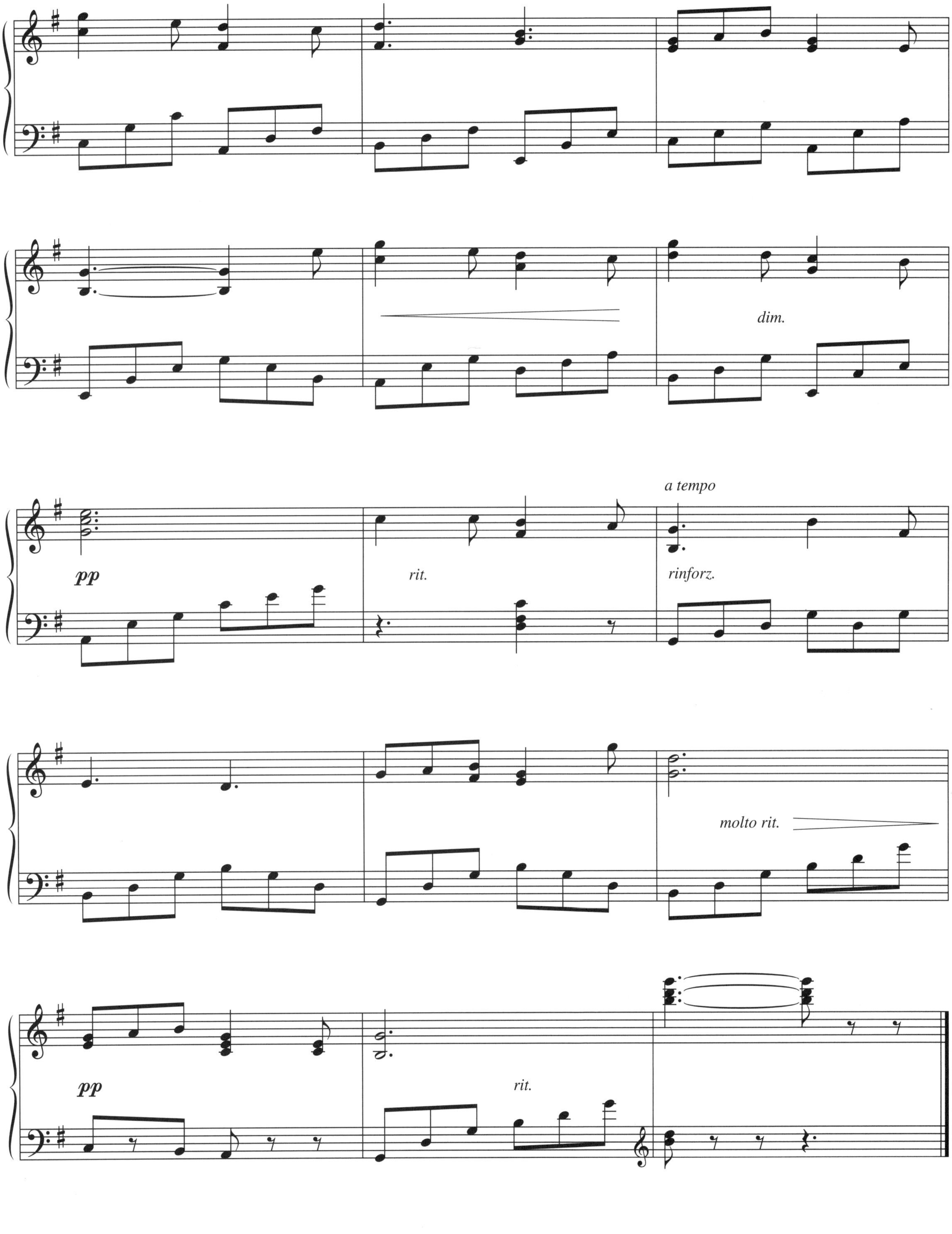
dim.
a tempo
pp
rit.
rinforz.
molto rit.
pp
rit.

Quando men vo

(Musetta's Waltz)
from the opera LA BOHÈME
(The Bohemian Life)

Giacomo Puccini
1858-1924

a tempo
poco rall.
mf a tempo
rit. molto
f
p rall.
morendo
pp a tempo
quasi rit.
a tempo
quasi rit.
a tempo
a tempo
cresc.
poco allarg.
f
p
f
pp

Un bel dì vedremo

from the opera MADAMA BUTTERFLY

Giacomo Puccini
1858-1924

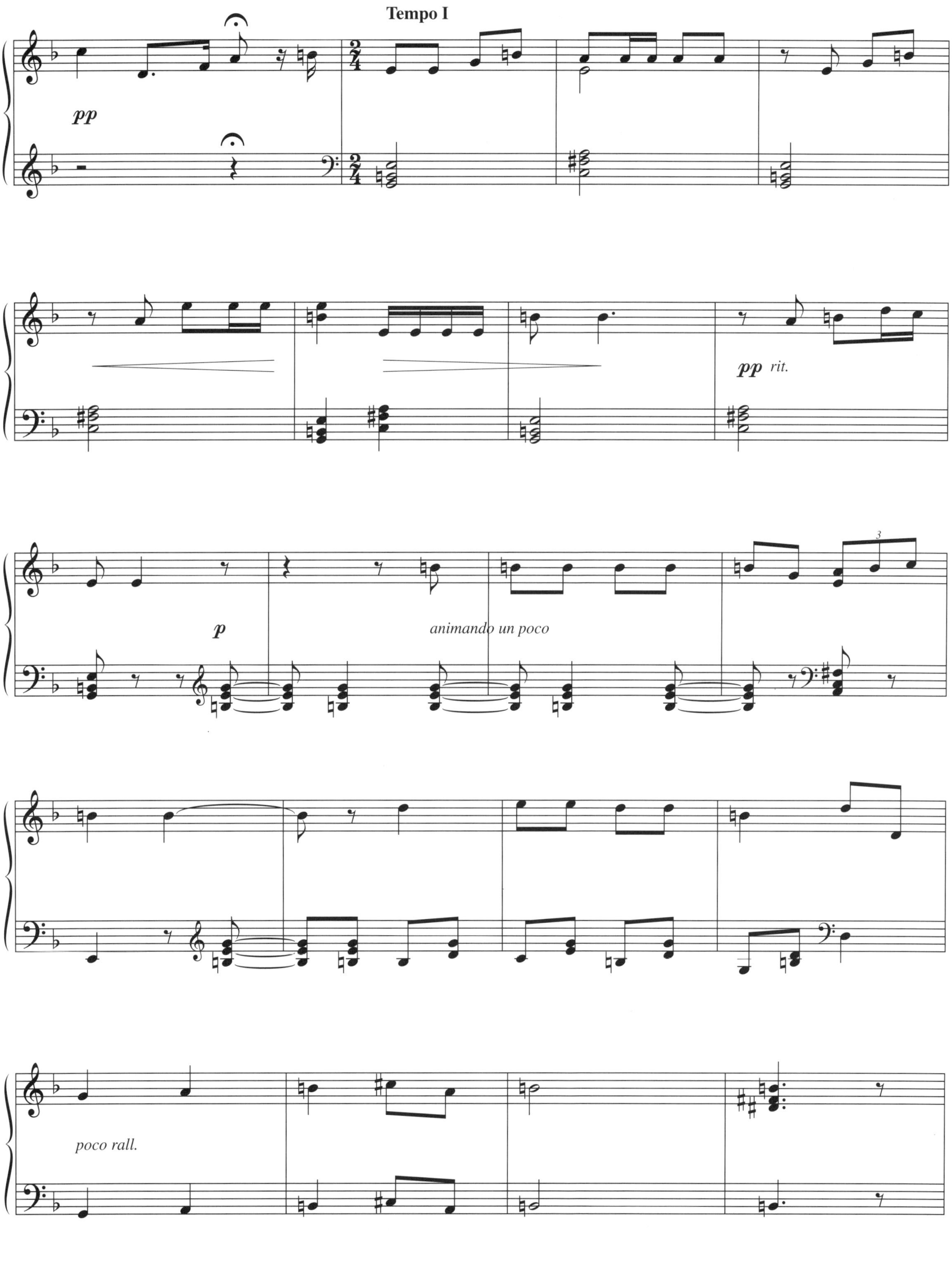
Tempo I
pp
pp rit.
p
animando un poco
3
poco rall.

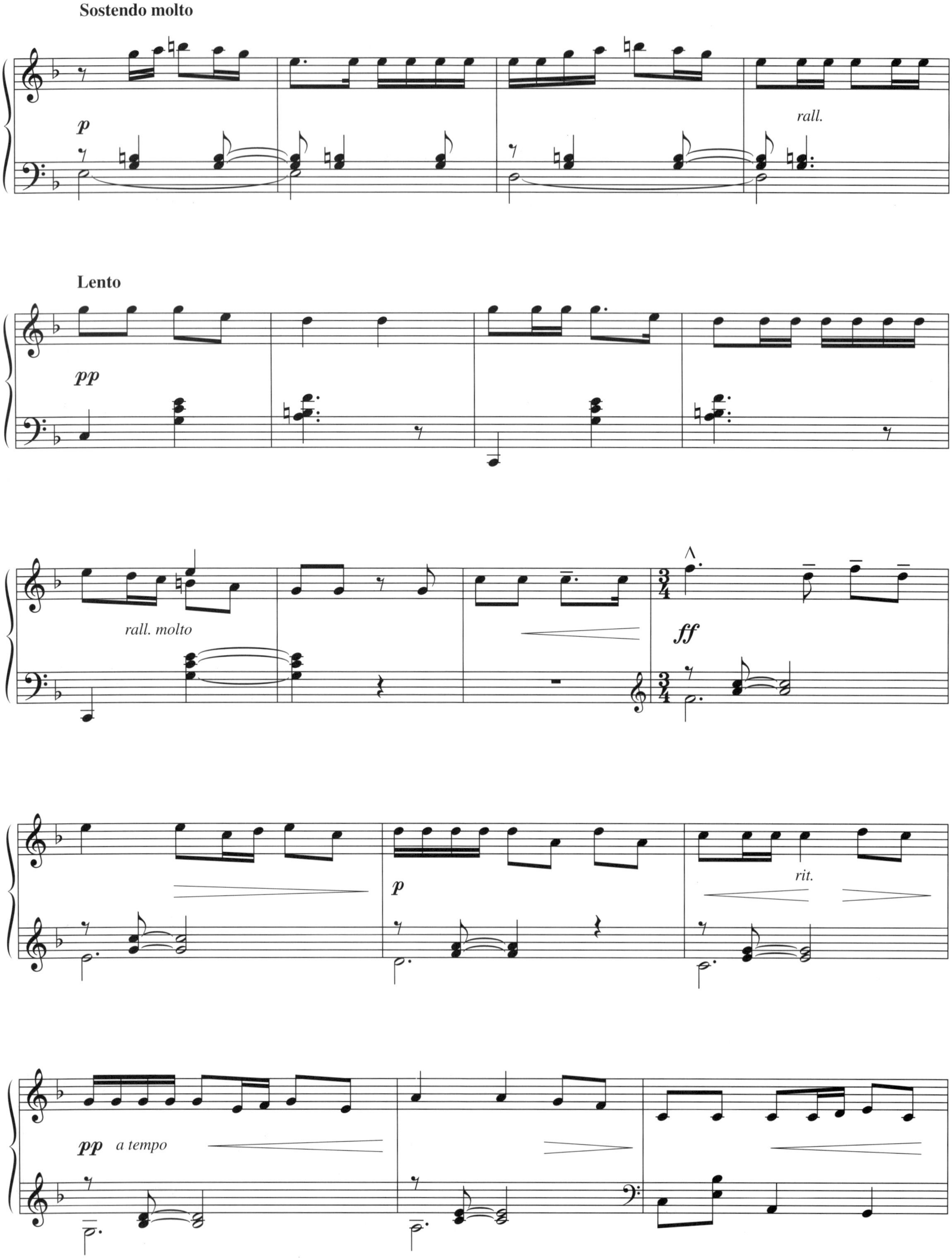
Sostendo molto
p
rall.
Lento
pp
rall. molto
ff
p
rit.
pp a tempo

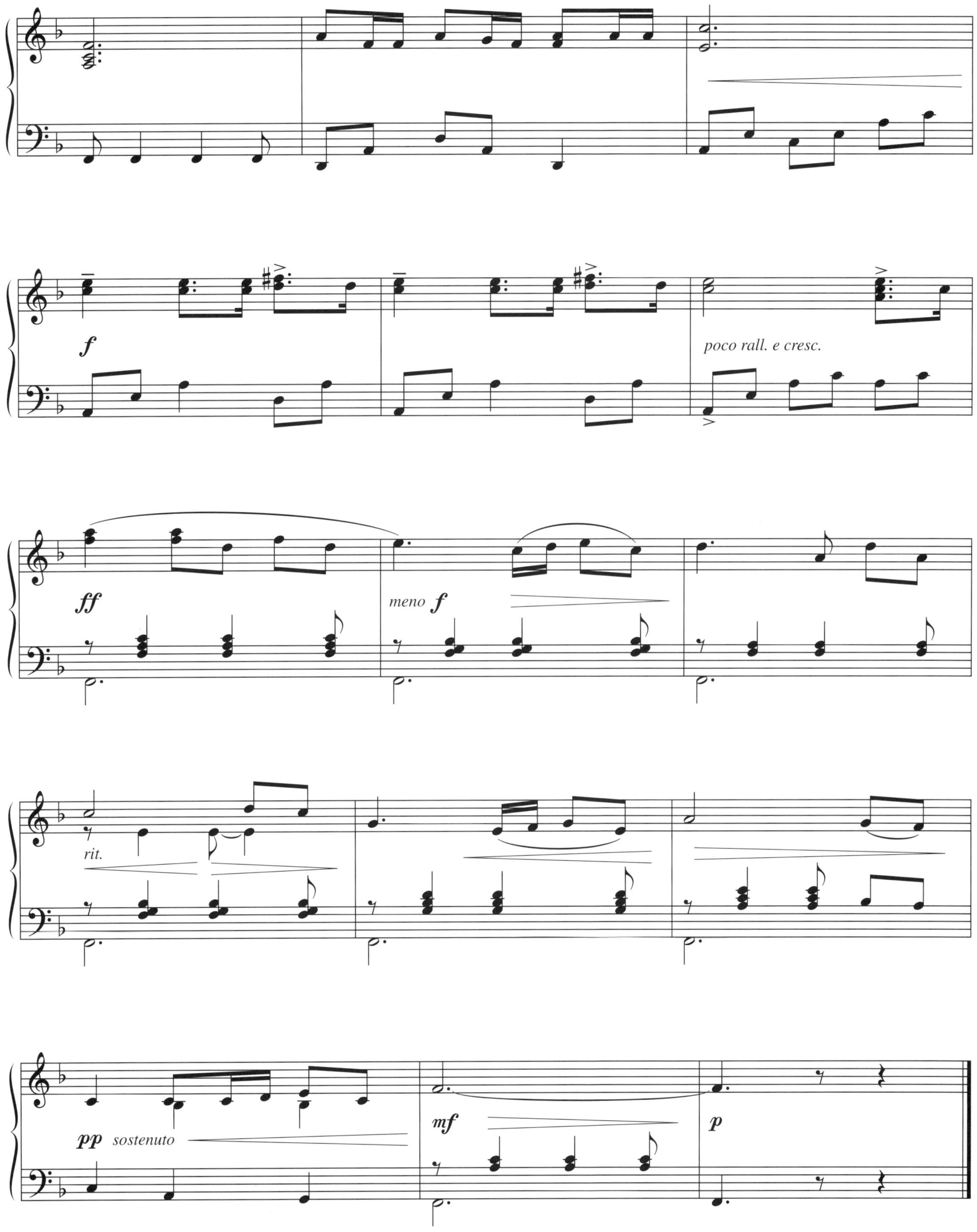
f
poco rall. e cresc.
ff
meno f
rit.
pp sostenuto
mf
p

Vissi d'arte
from the opera TOSCA

Giacomo Puccini
1858-1924

Andante lento appassionato

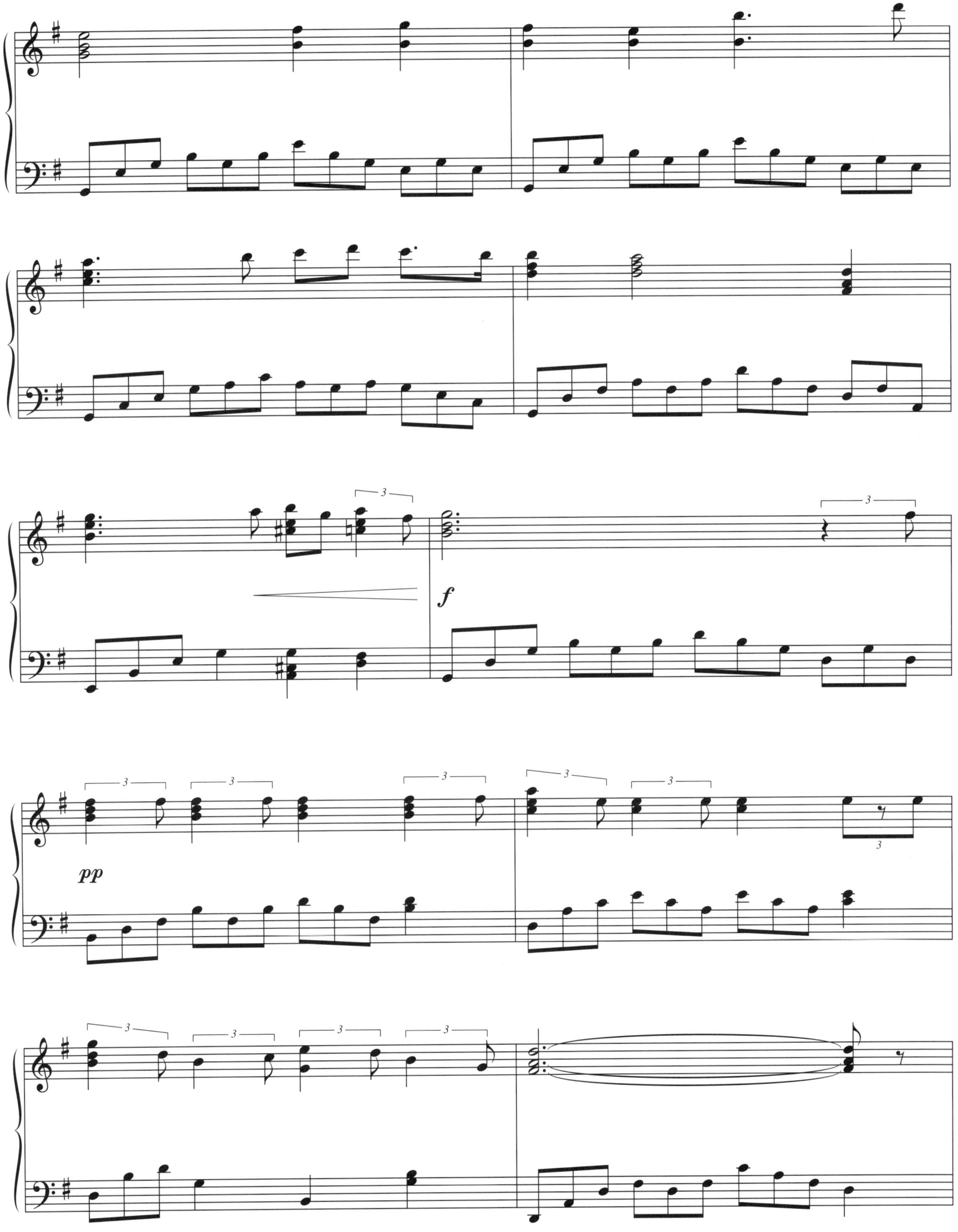
f
pp

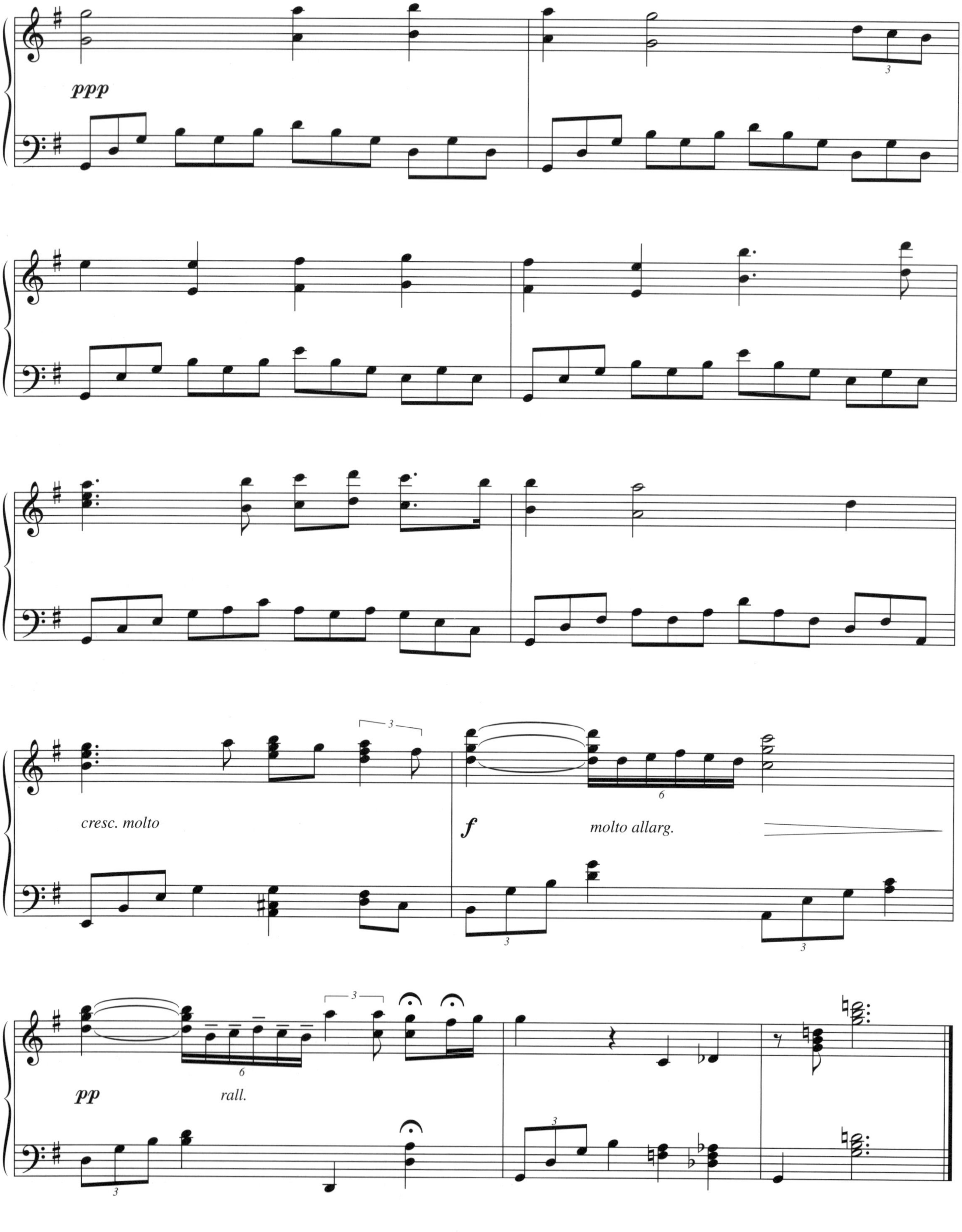
ppp
cresc. molto
f
molto allarg.
pp
rall.

Rondeau

from the theatre music for ABDELAZER

Henry Purcell
1659-1695
originally for orchestra

* Main theme used by Benjamin Britten in his YOUNG PERSON'S GUIDE TO THE ORCHESTRA

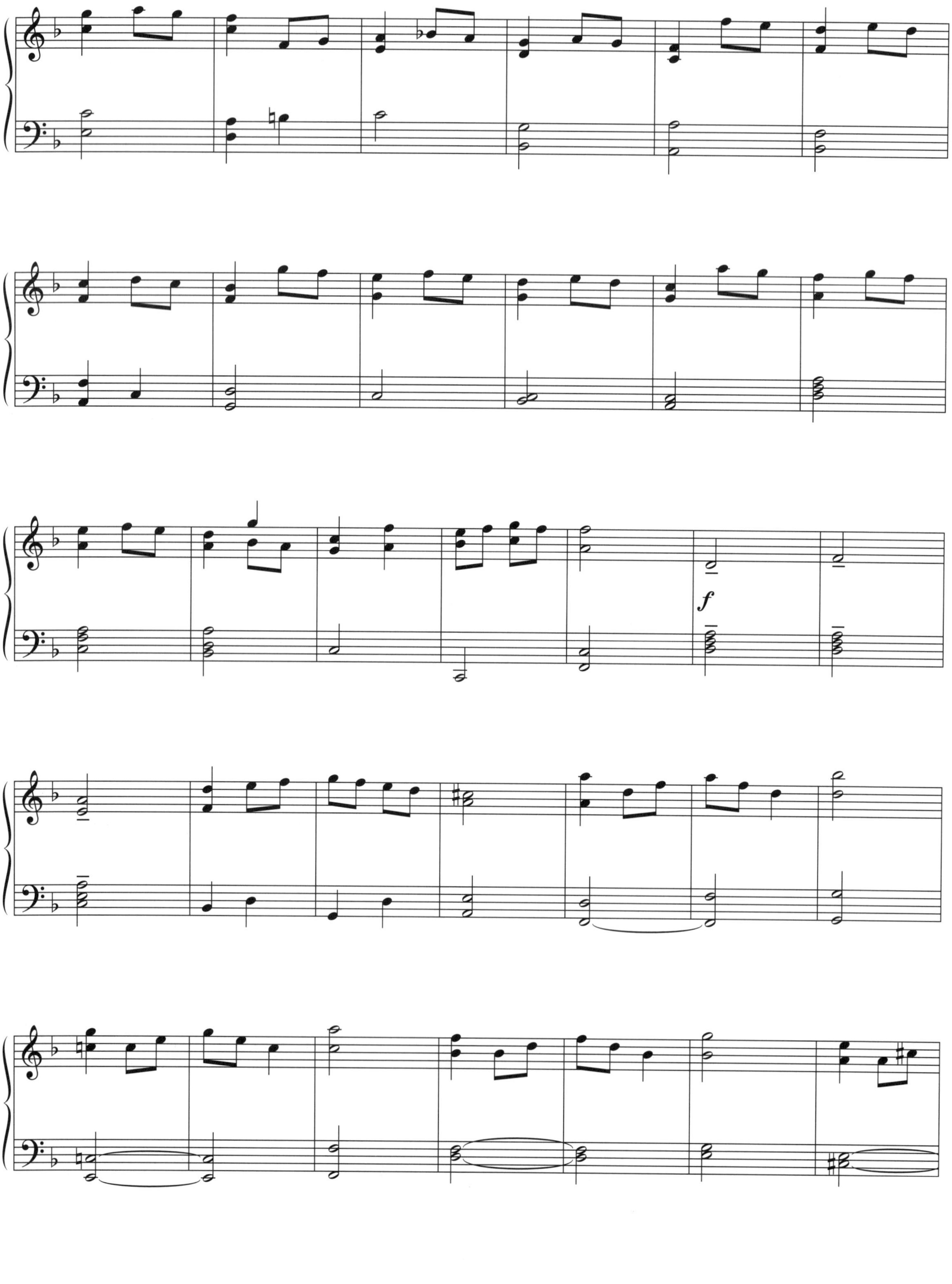
f

317

William Tell Overture

from the opera GUILLAUME TELL
(William Tell)

Gioachino Rossini
1792-1868
originally for orchestra

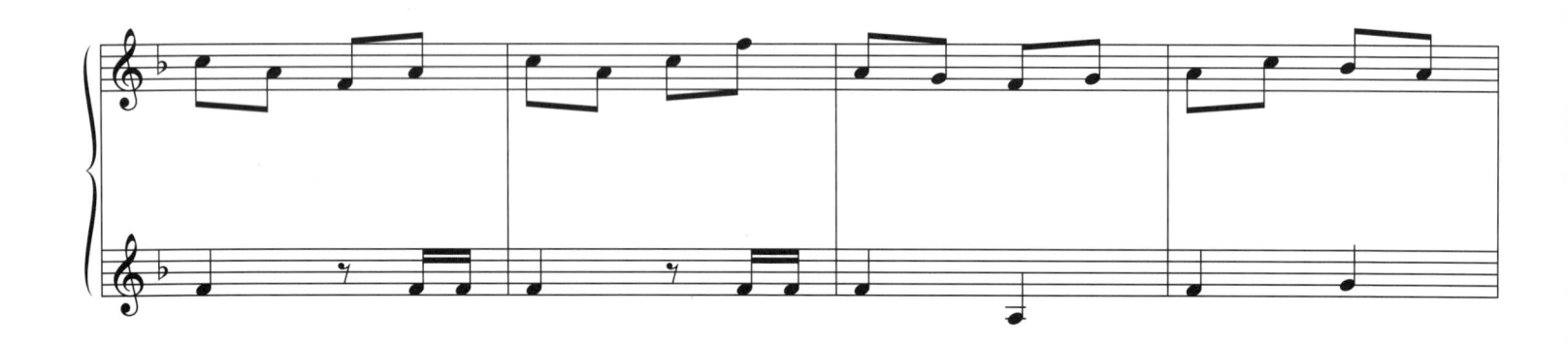

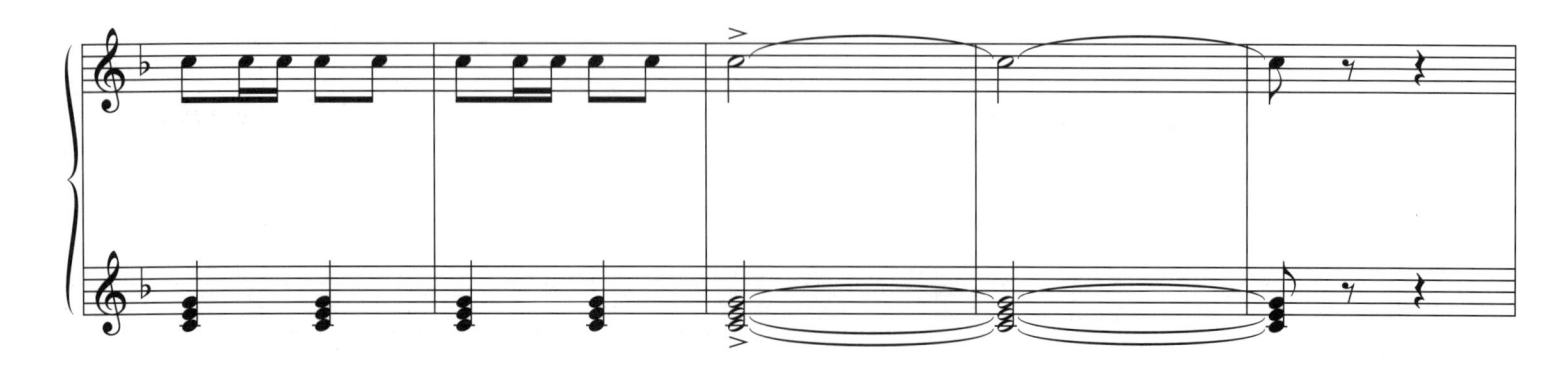

Allegro vivace

original key: E Major

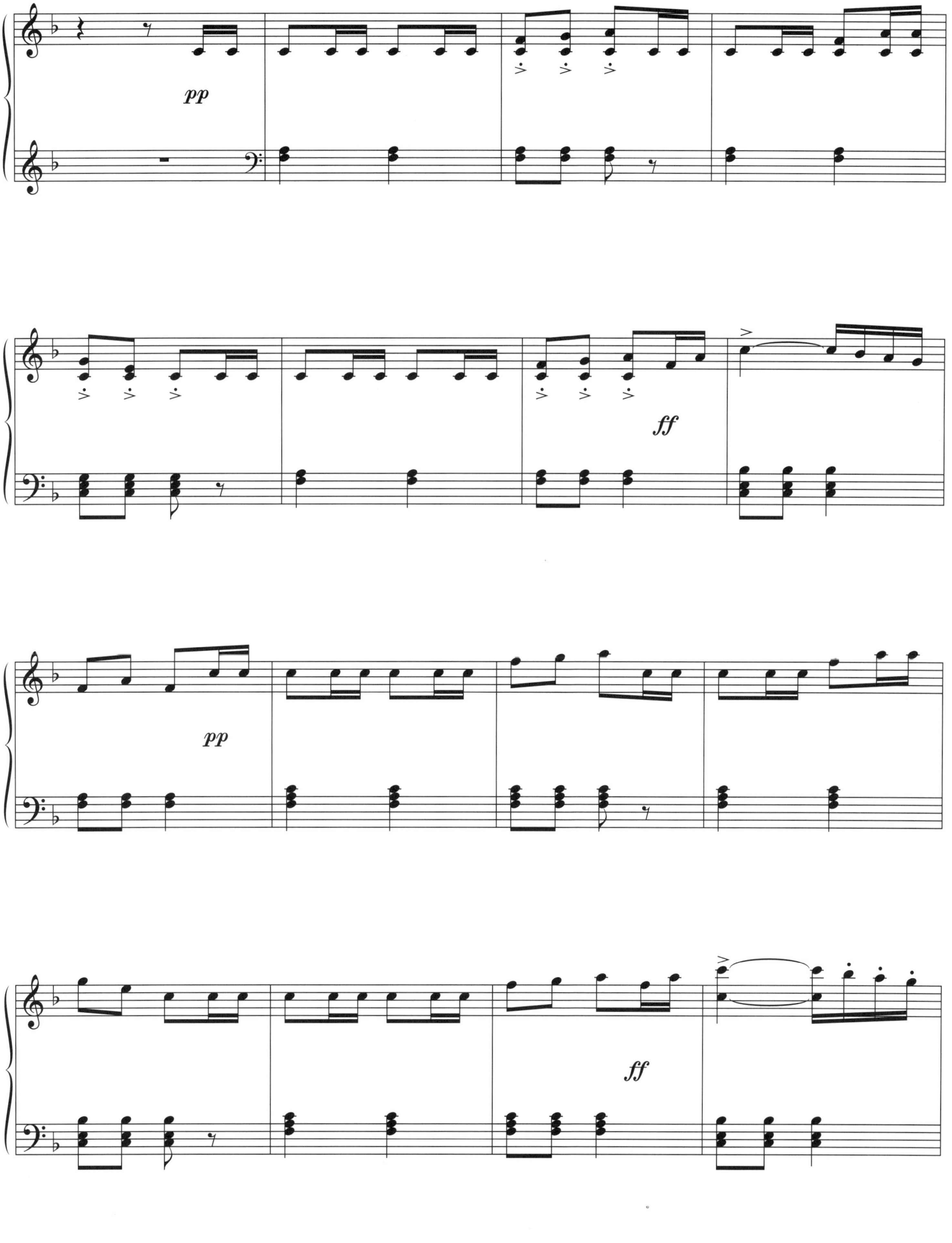
pp
ff
pp
ff

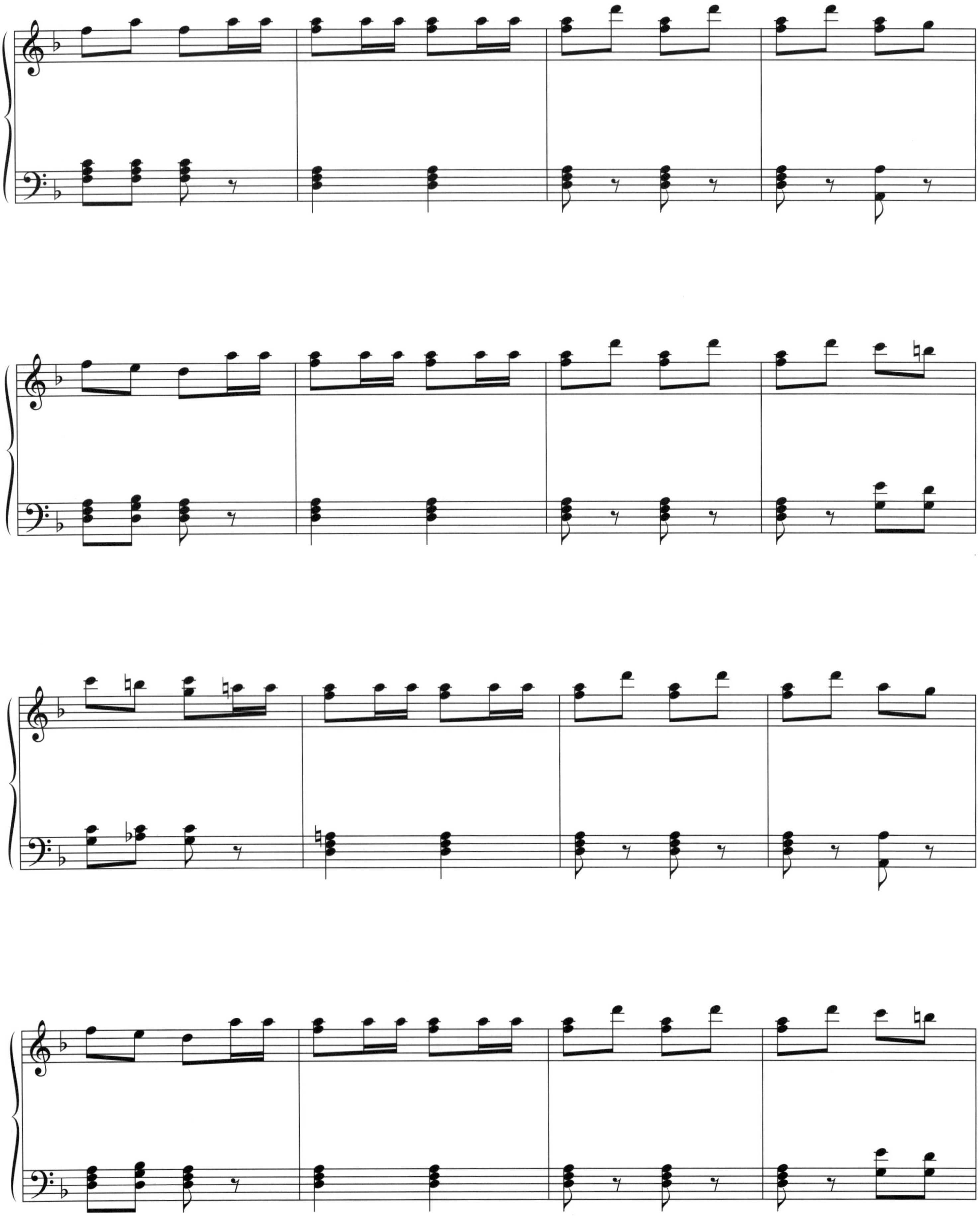

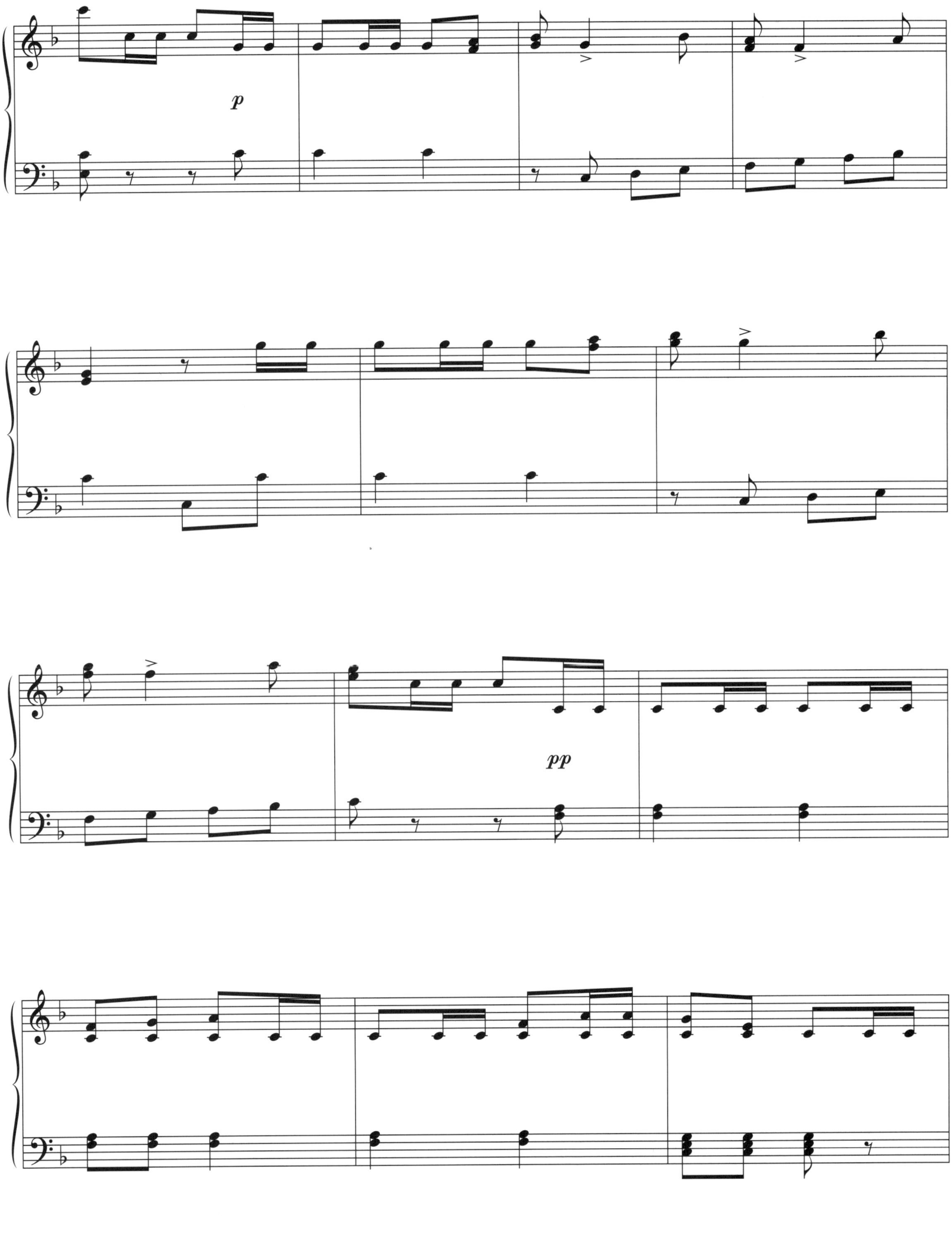
p
pp

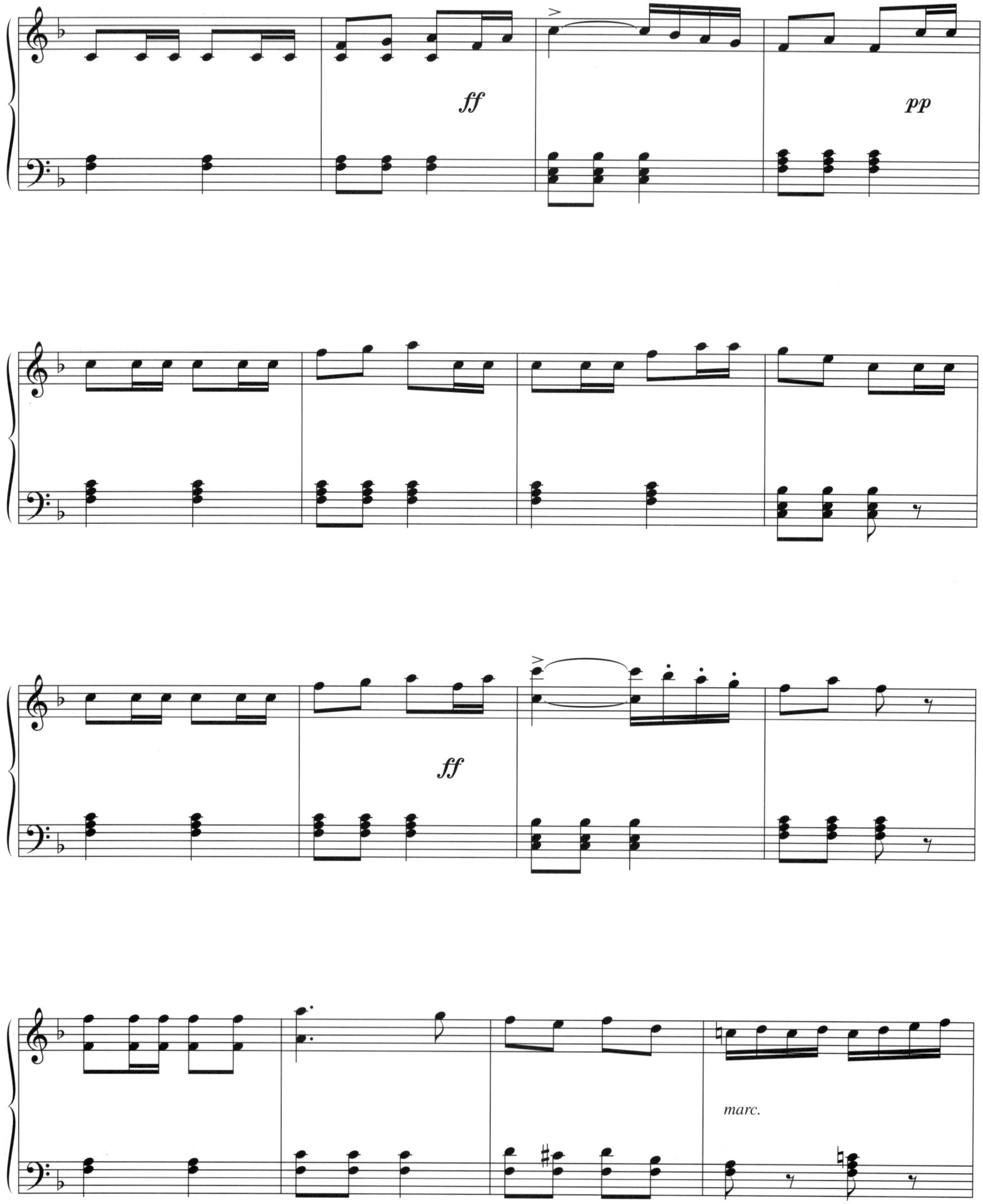
ff
pp
ff
marc.

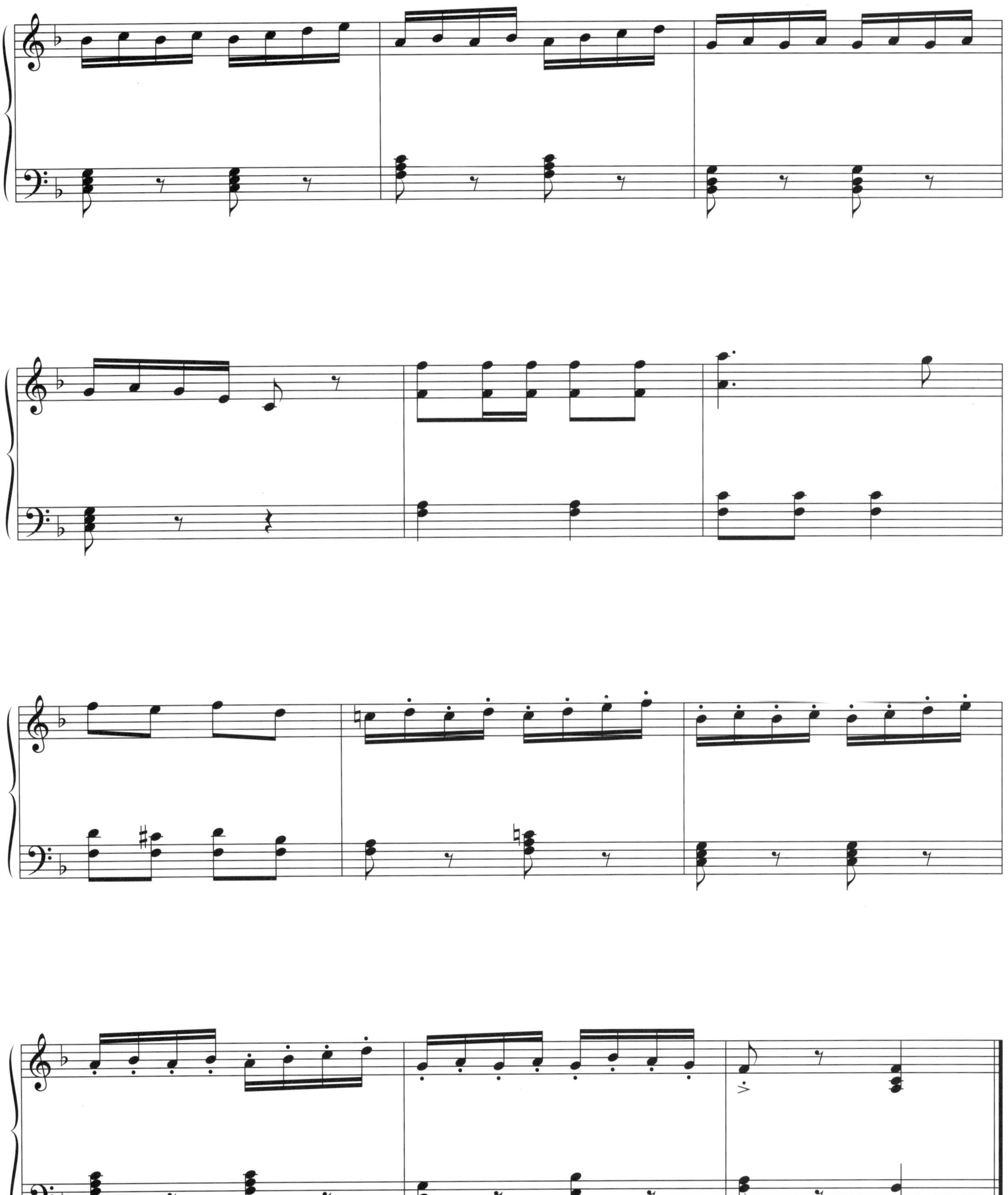

Sheherazade
Themes from Part 1

Nikolay Andreyevich Rimsky-Korsakov
1844-1908
Op. 35
originally for orchestra

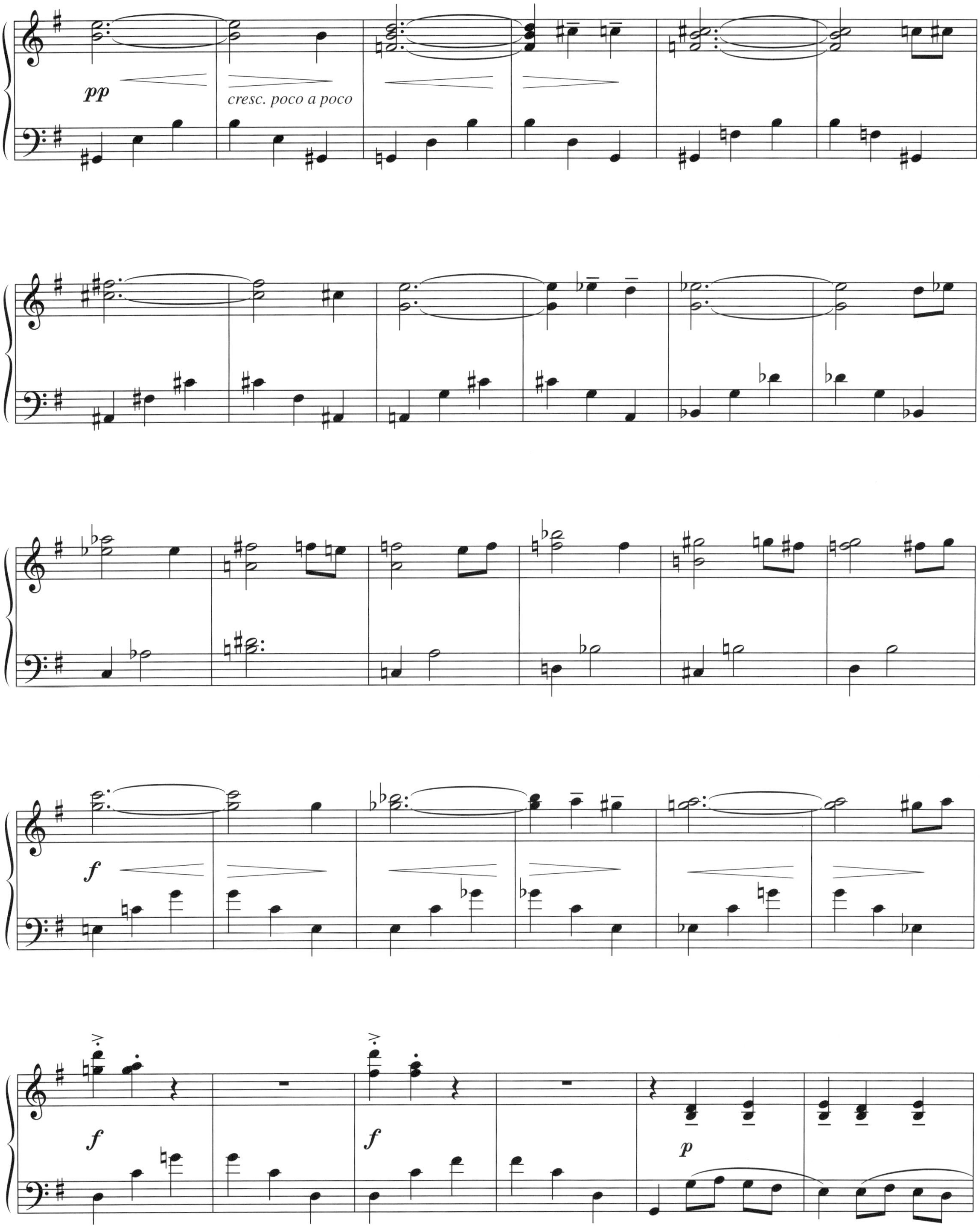
pp
cresc. poco a poco
f
f
f
p

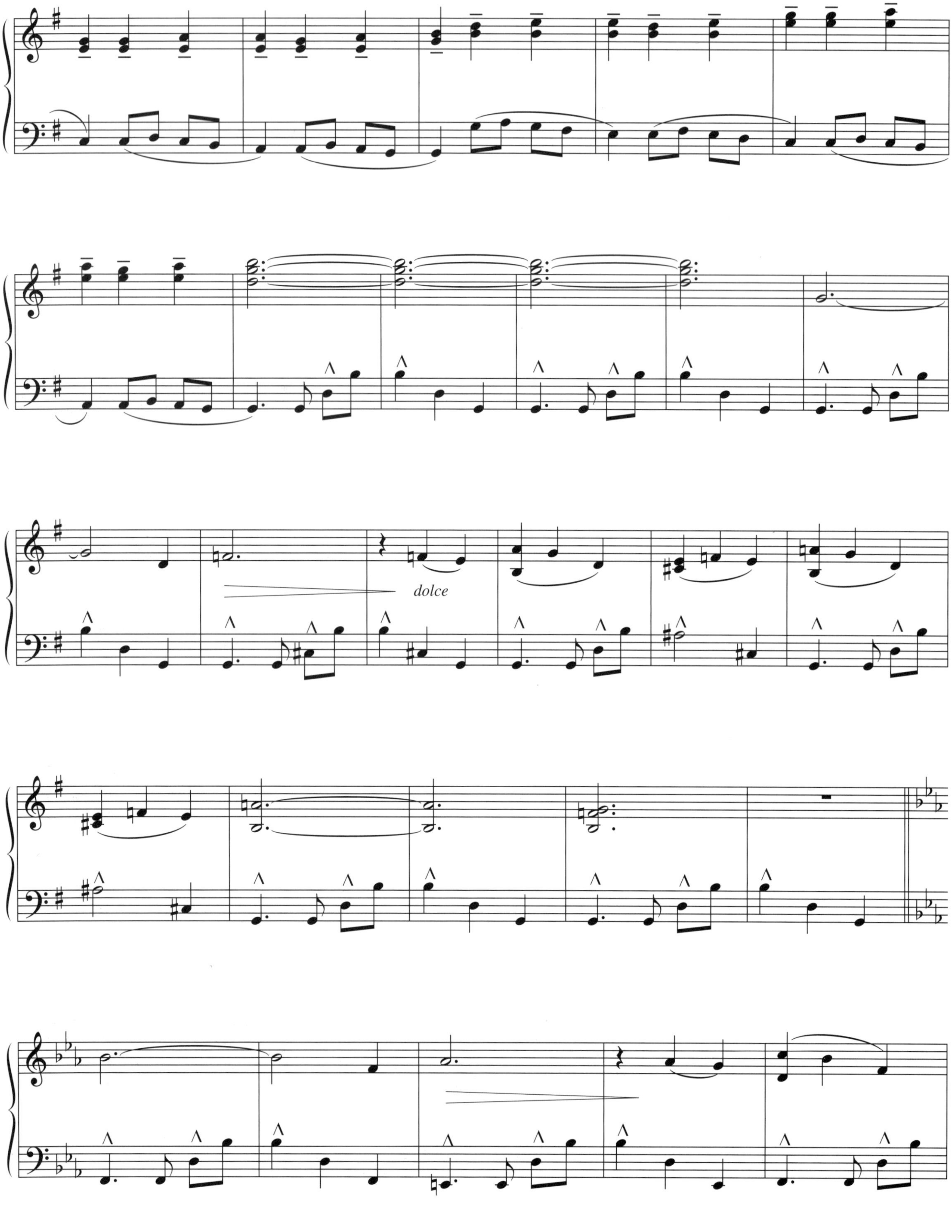
dolce

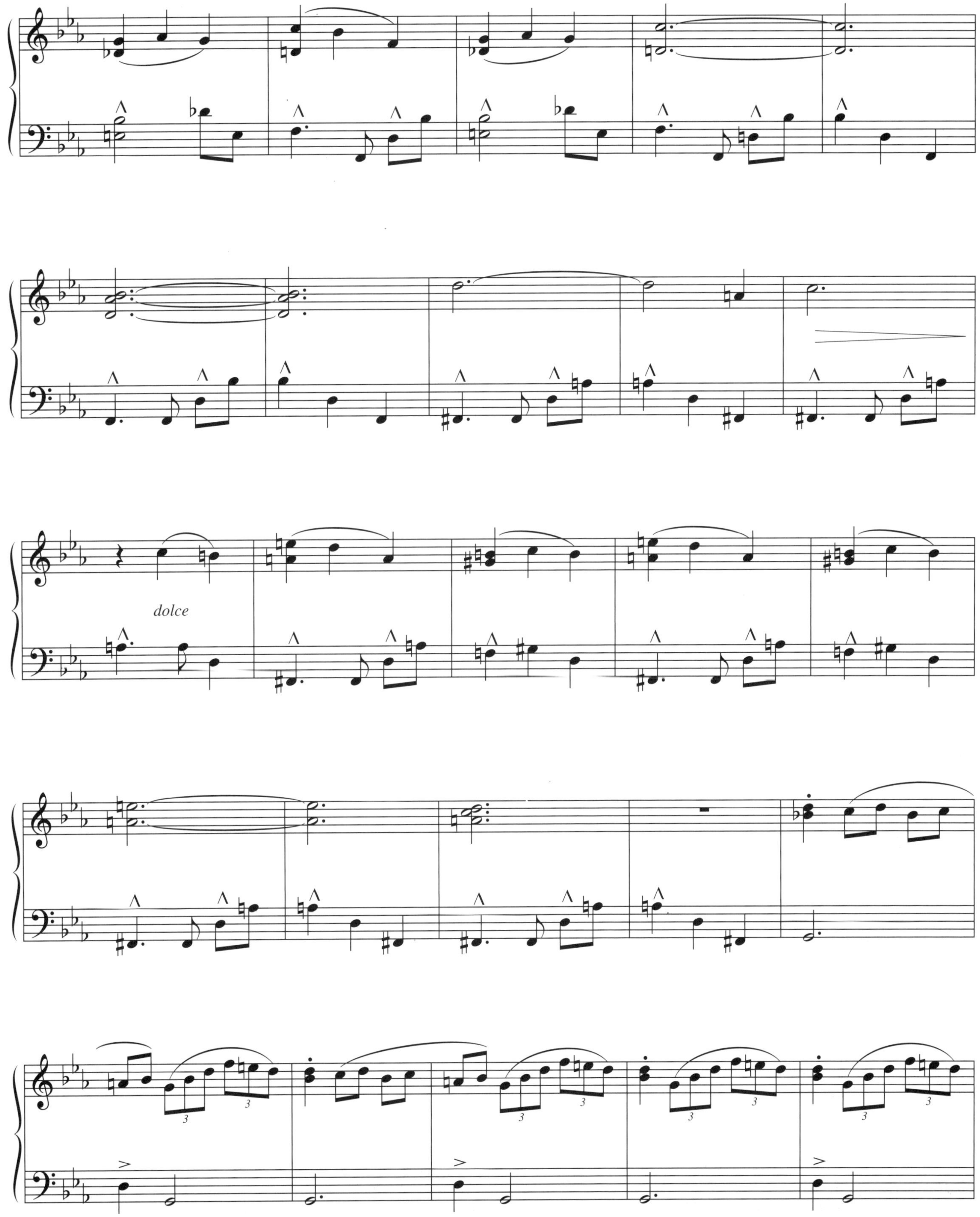
dolce

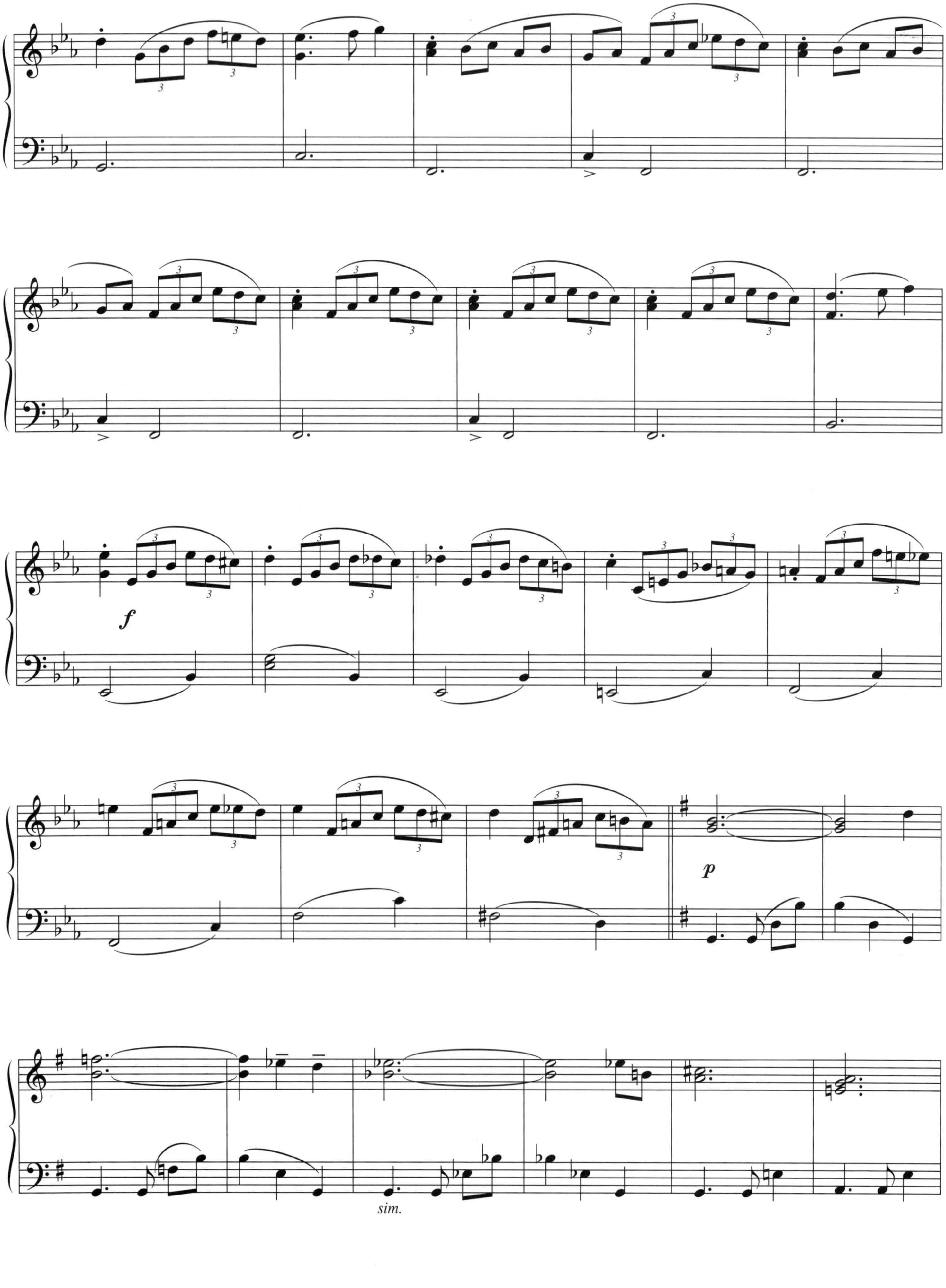
f
p
sim.

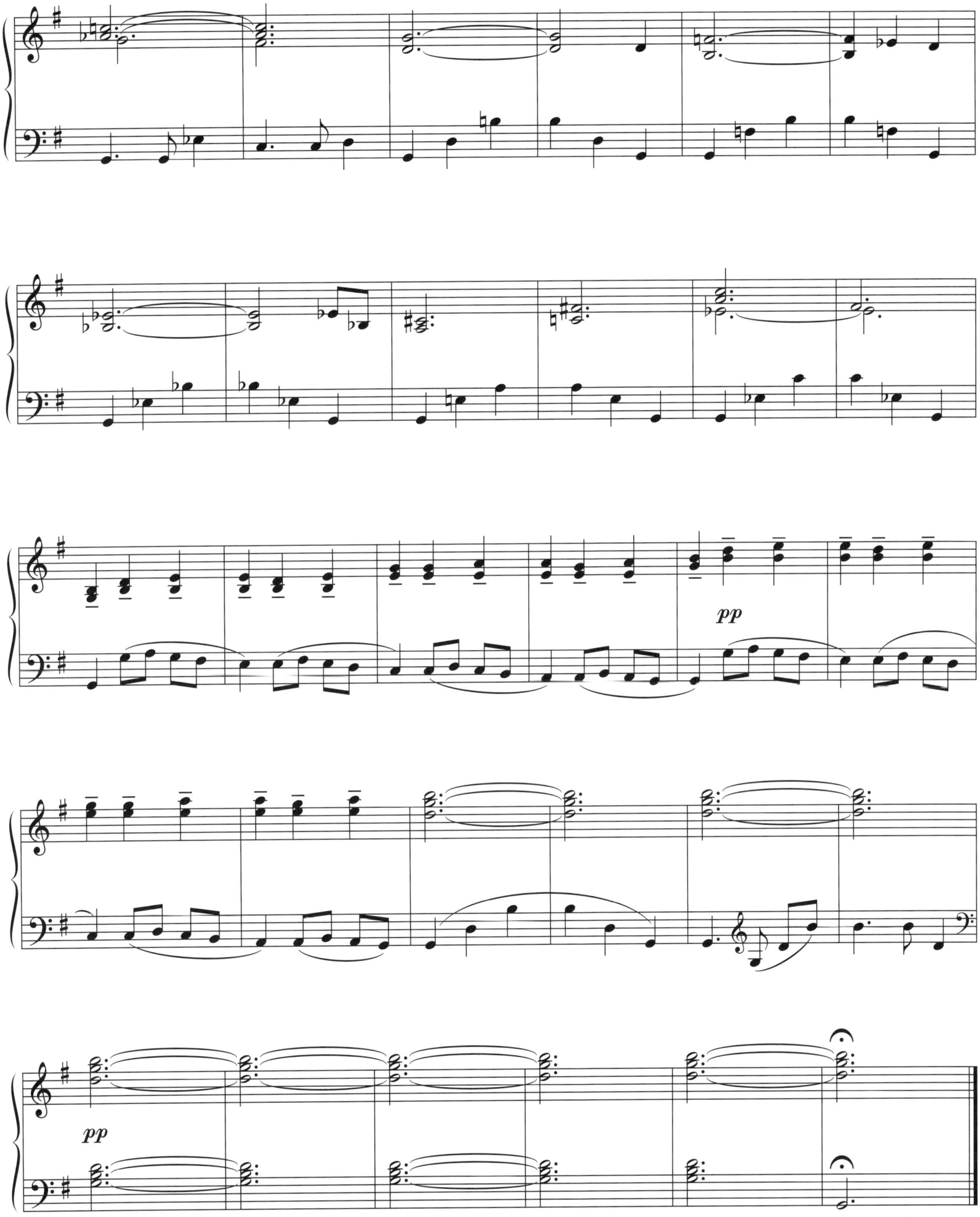
pp
pp

Sadko
"Song of India"

Nikolay Andreyevich Rimsky-Korsakov
1844-1908
Op. 5
originally for orchestra

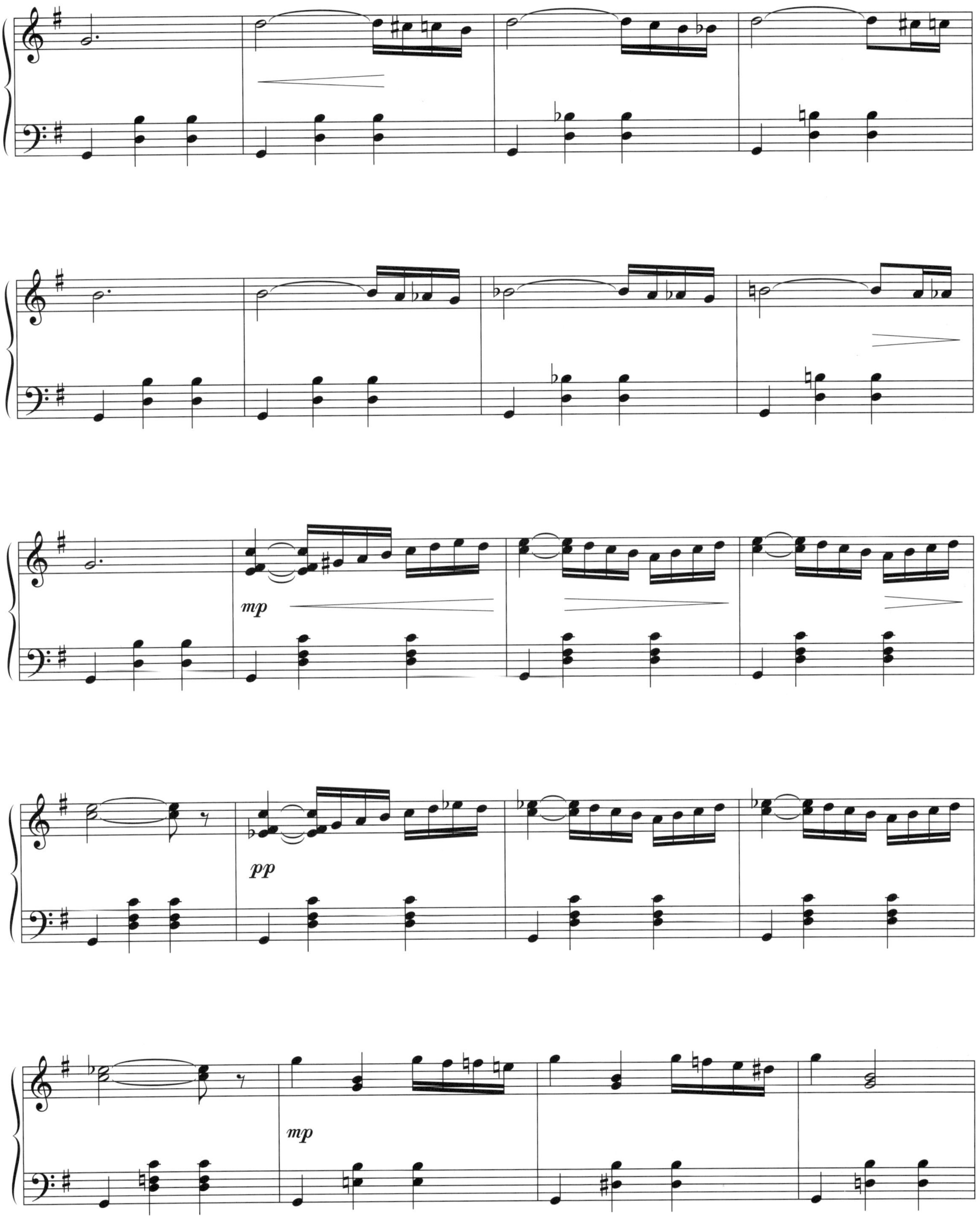
mp
pp
mp

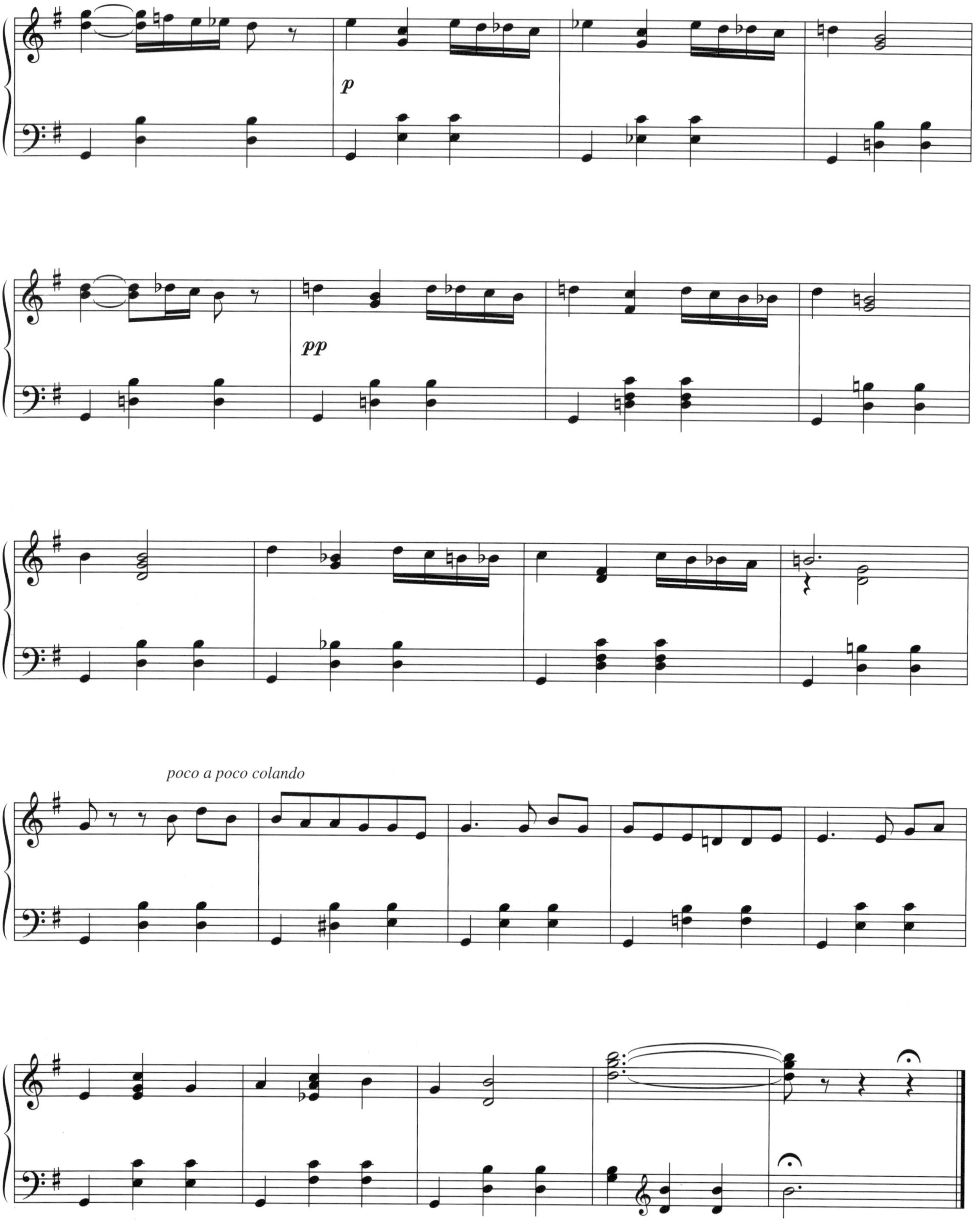
p
pp
poco a poco colando

The Swan
from CARNIVAL OF THE ANIMALS

Camille Saint-Saëns
1835-1921
originally for chamber ensemble

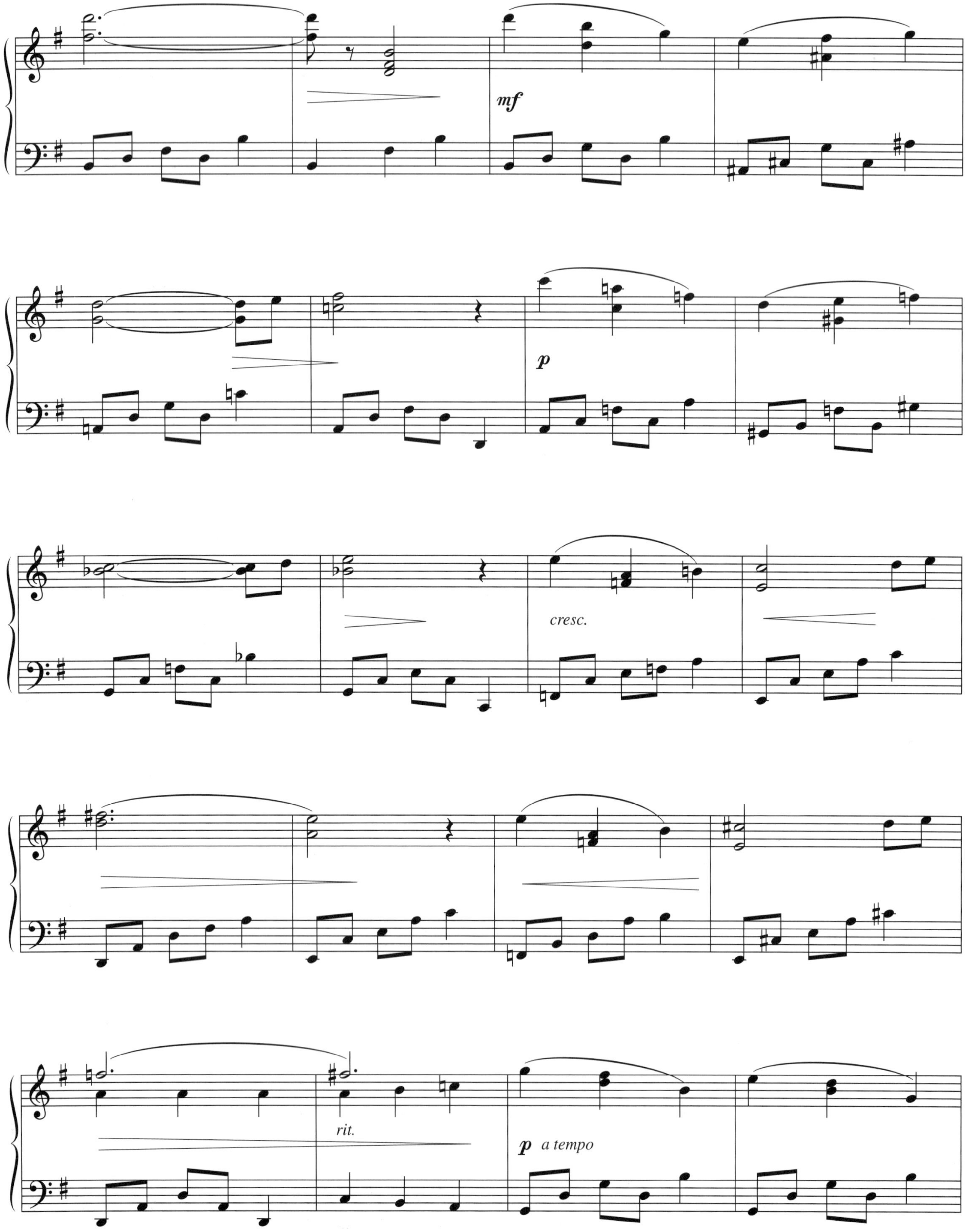
mf
p
cresc.
rit.
p a tempo

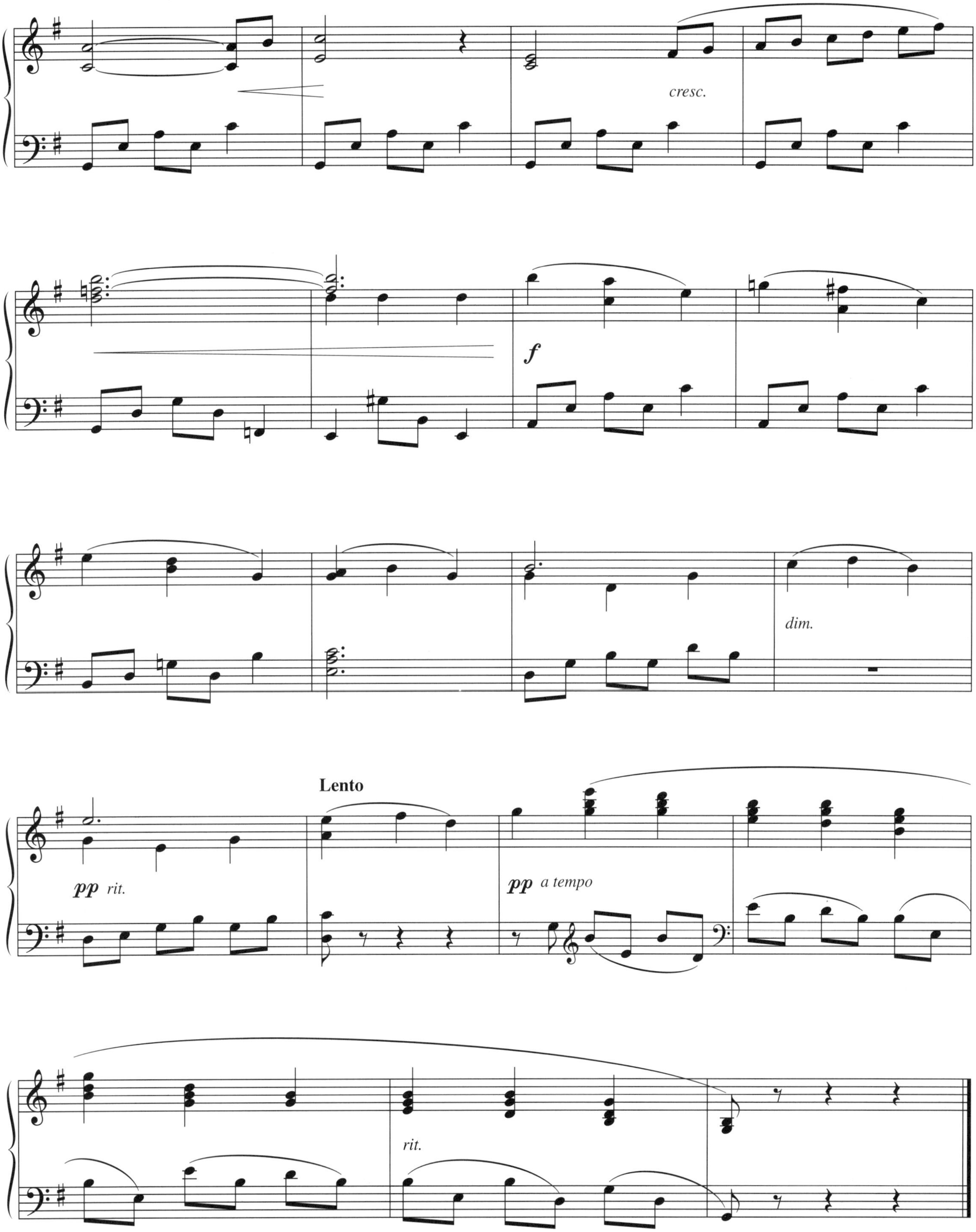
cresc.
f
dim.
Lento
pp rit.
pp a tempo
rit.

Aquarium

from CARNIVAL OF THE ANIMALS

Camille Saint-Saëns
1835-1921
composed 1886
originally for chamber ensemble

337

Gymnopédie No. 1

Erik Satie
1866–1925

Lent et douloureux (slowly and mournfully)

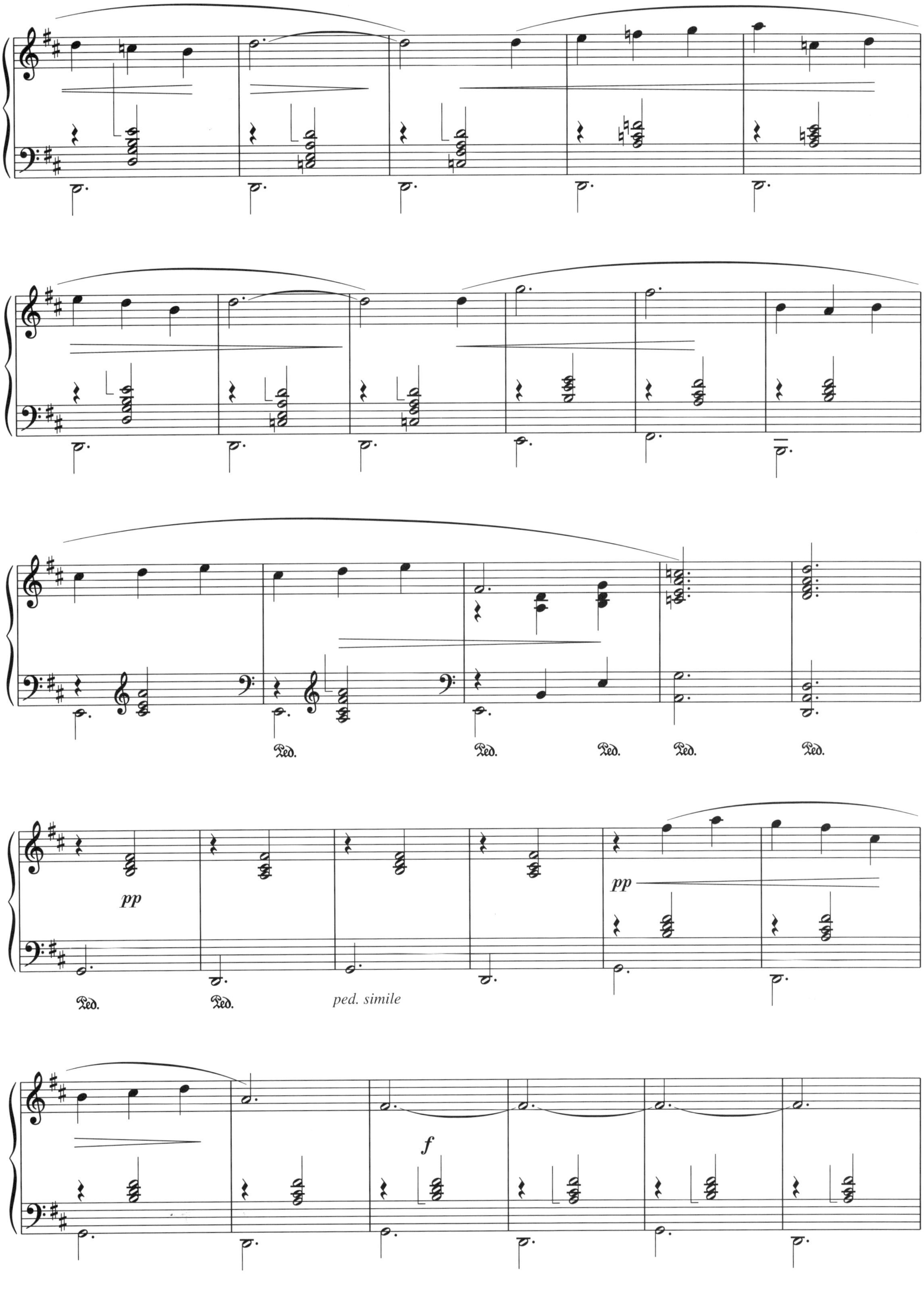
Ped.
Ped.
Ped.
Ped.
Ped.
pp
Ped.
Ped.
ped. simile
pp
f

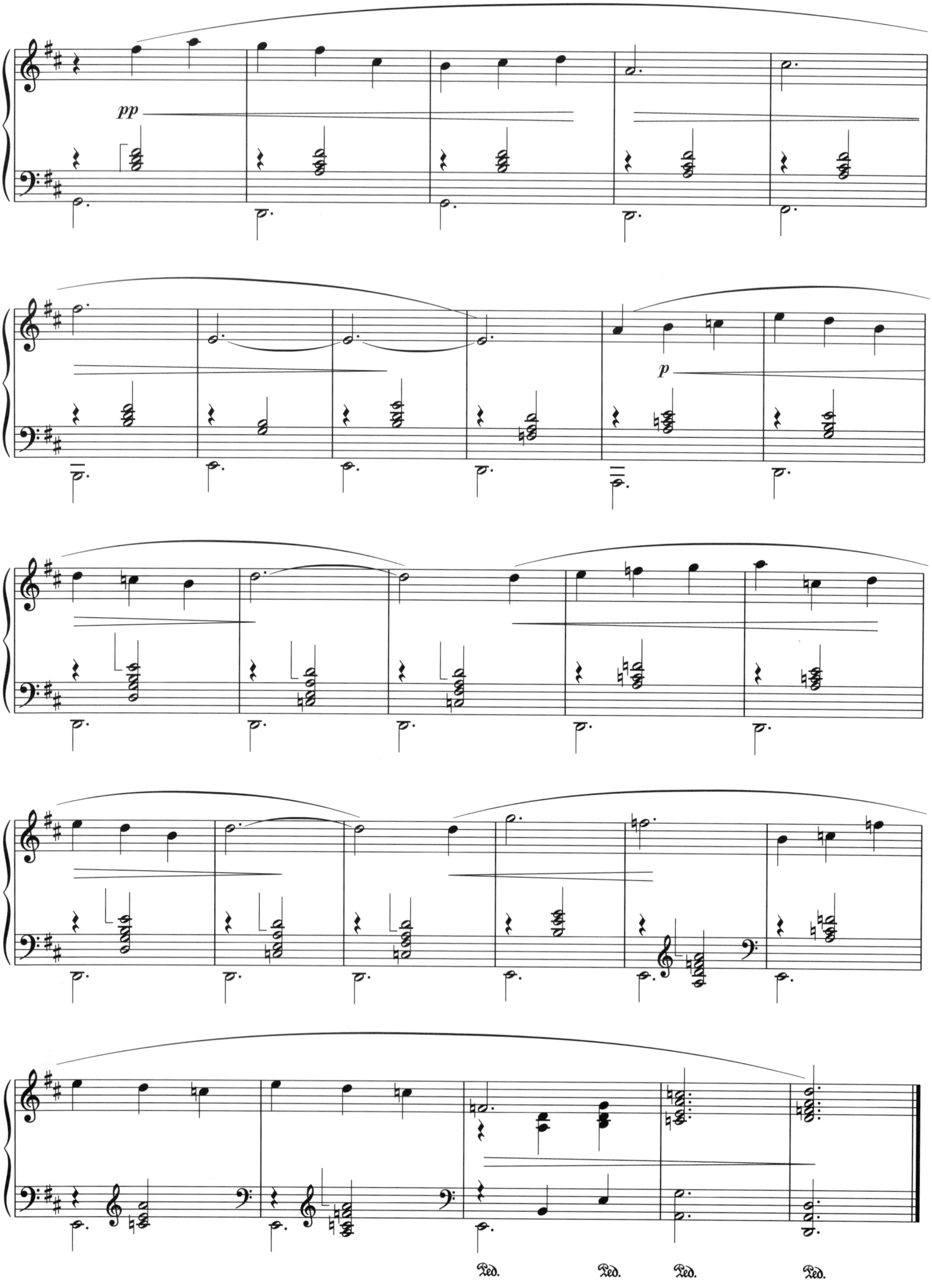
pp
p
Ped.
Ped.
Ped.
Ped.

Die Forelle
(The Trout)

Franz Schubert
1797-1828
D 531
originally for voice and piano

Poco moderato

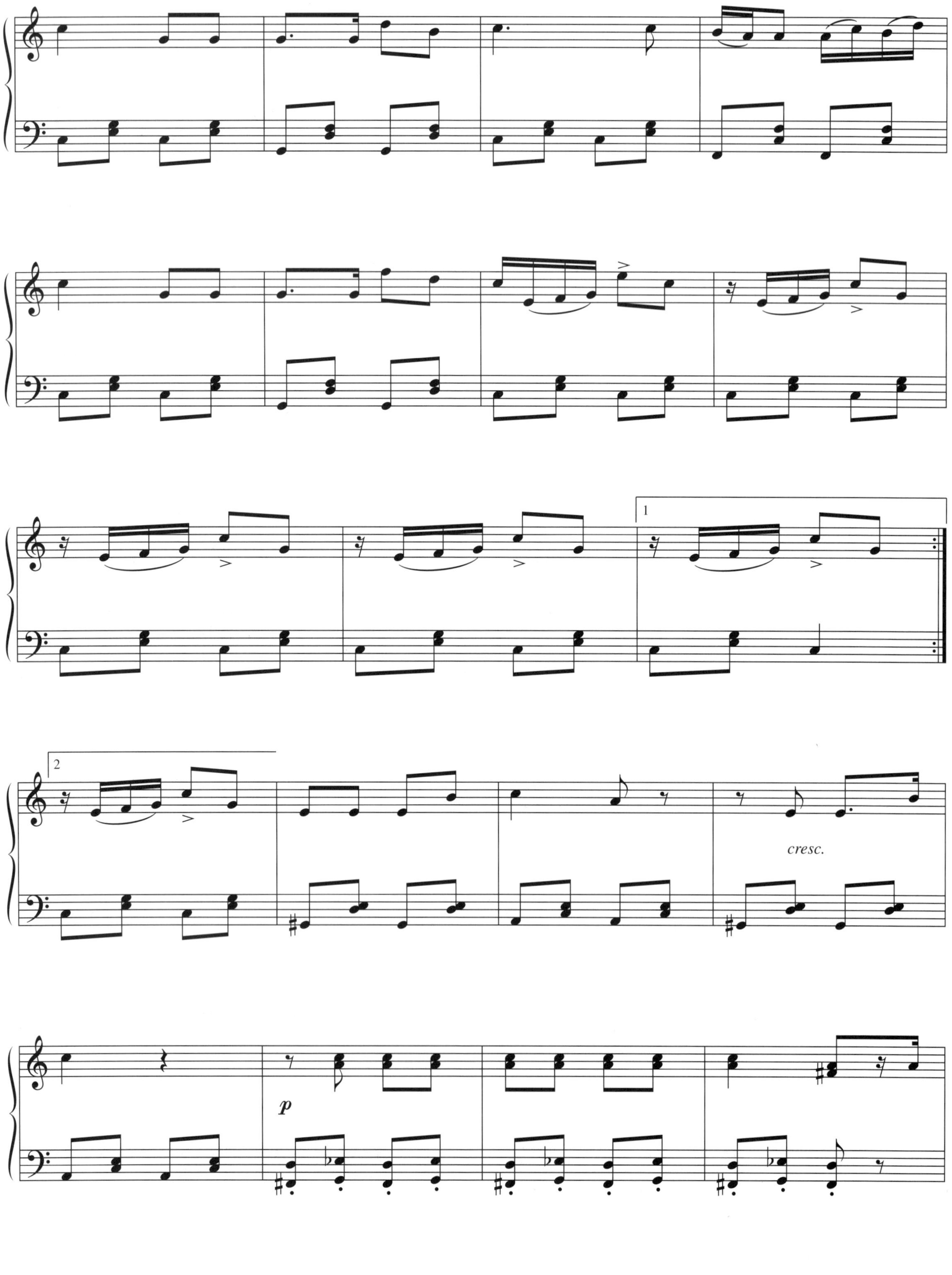
1
2
cresc.
p

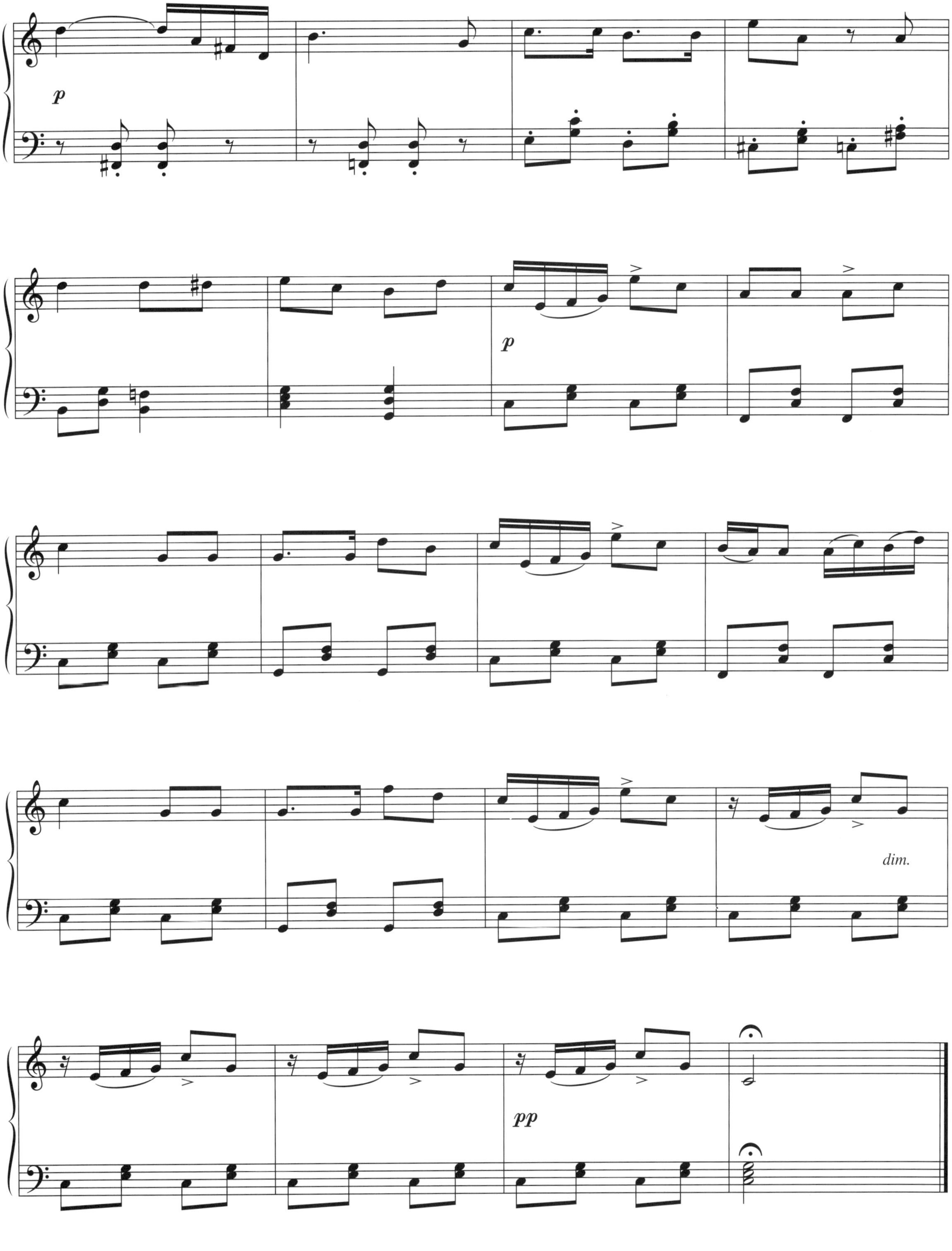
p
p
dim.
pp

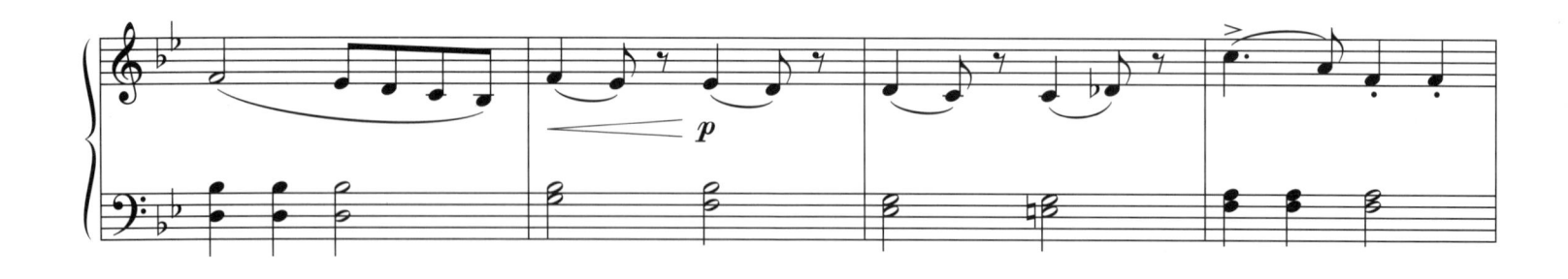

Symphony No. 5

First Movement Excerpt

Franz Schubert
1797-1828
D 485
originally for orchestra

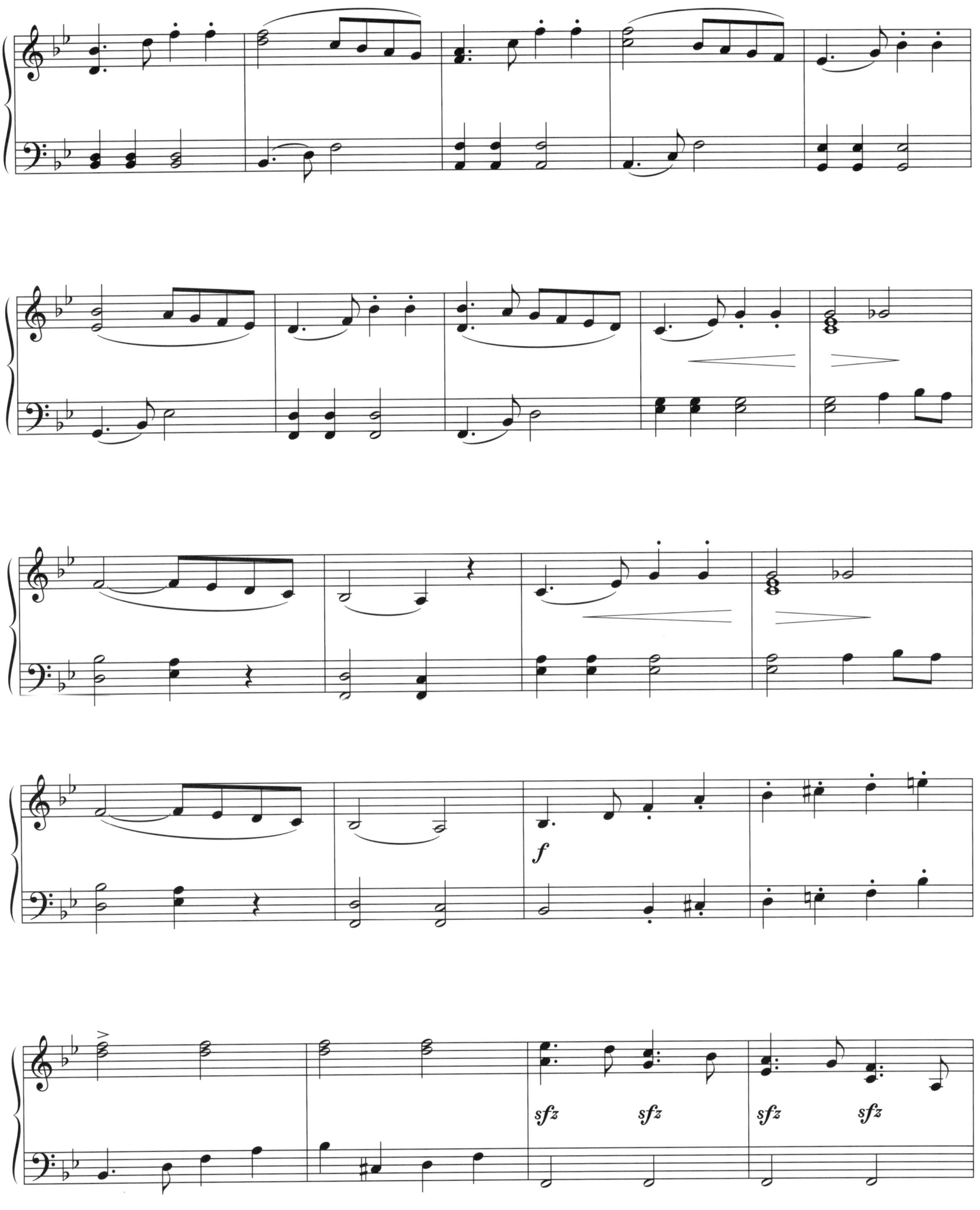
f
sfz
sfz
sfz
sfz

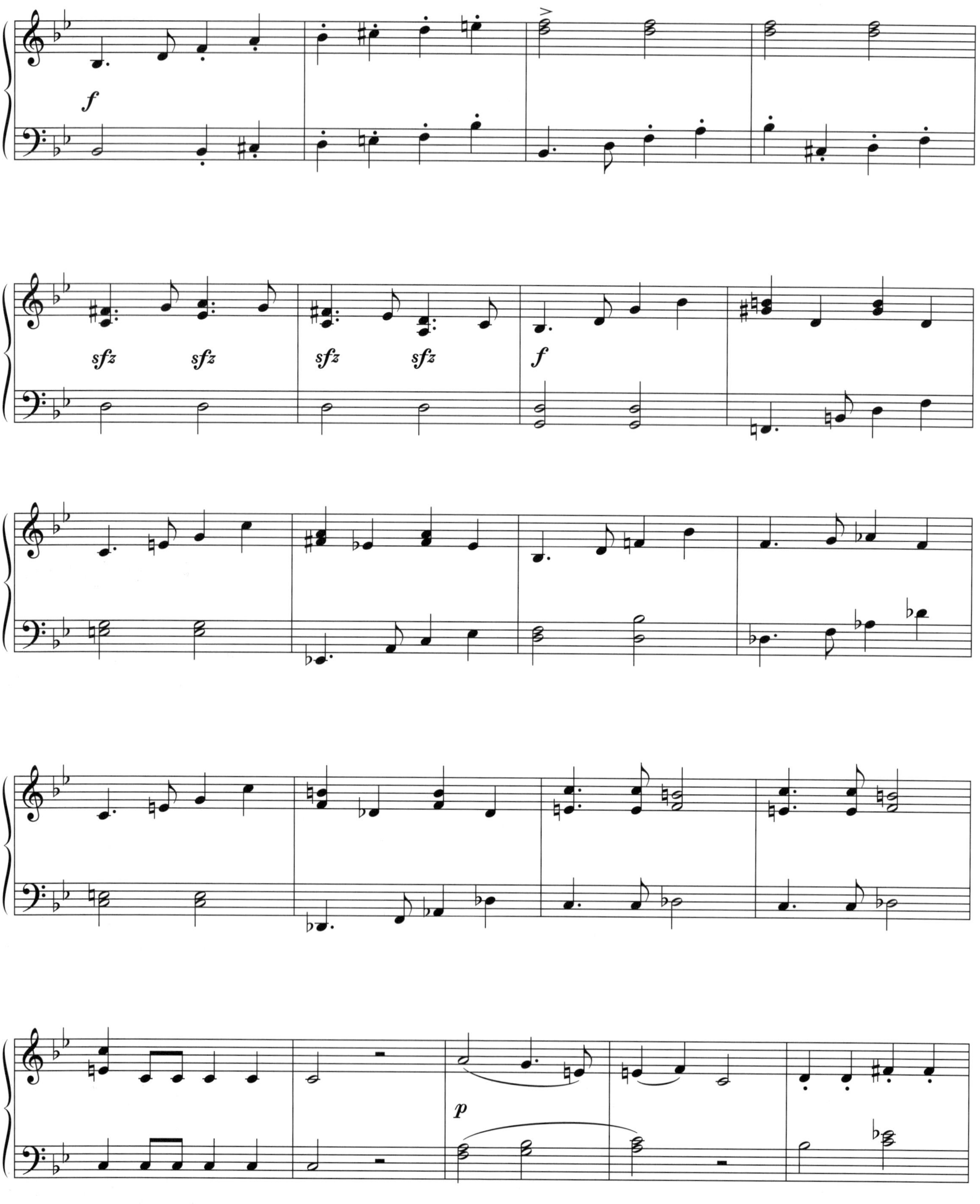
f
sfz
sfz
sfz
sfz
f
p

347

Symphony No. 8

"Unfinished"
First Movement Excerpt

Franz Schubert
1797-1828
D. 759
originally for orchestra

Allegro moderato

original key: B Minor

349

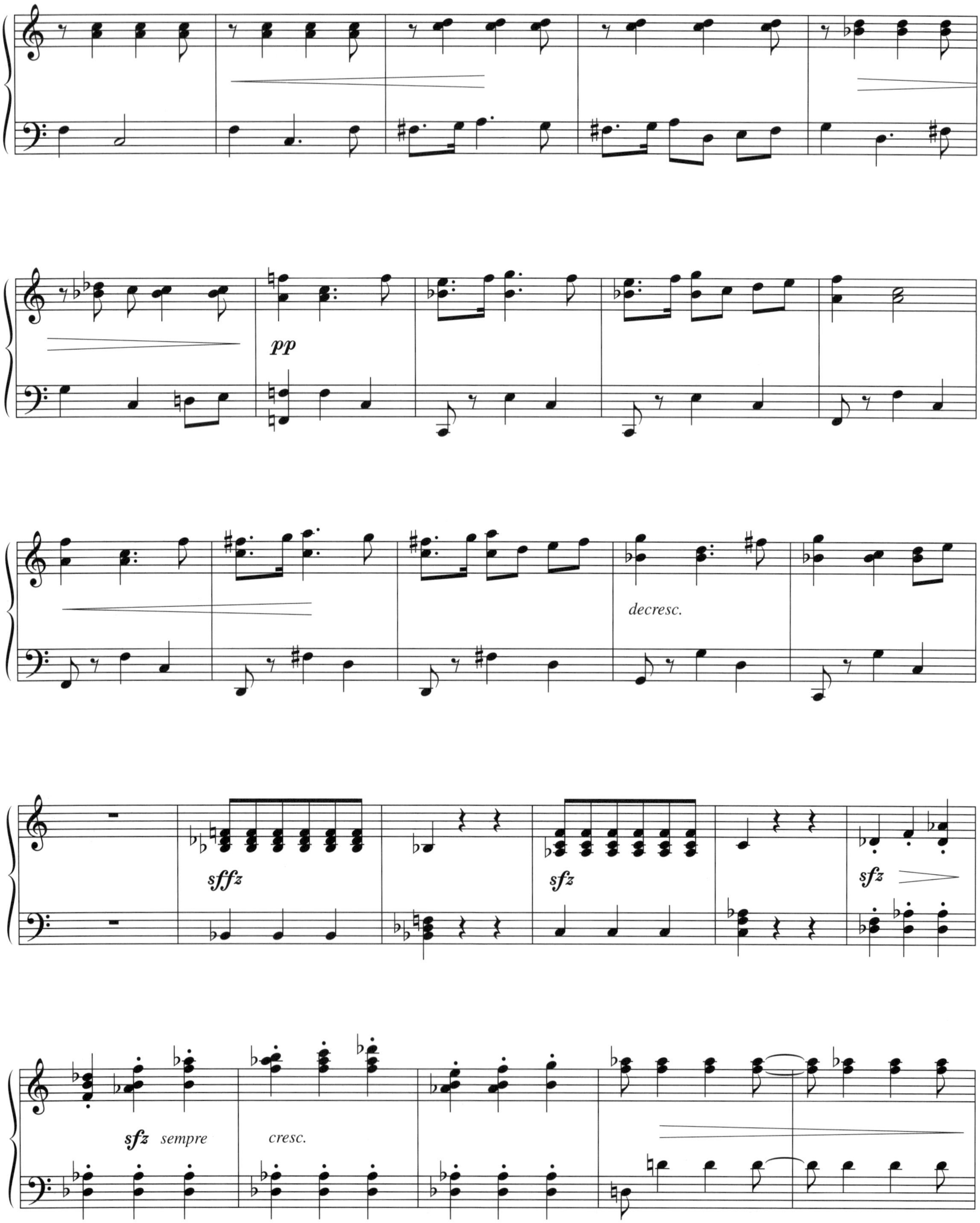
pp
decresc.
sffz
sfz
sfz
sfz sempre
cresc.

351

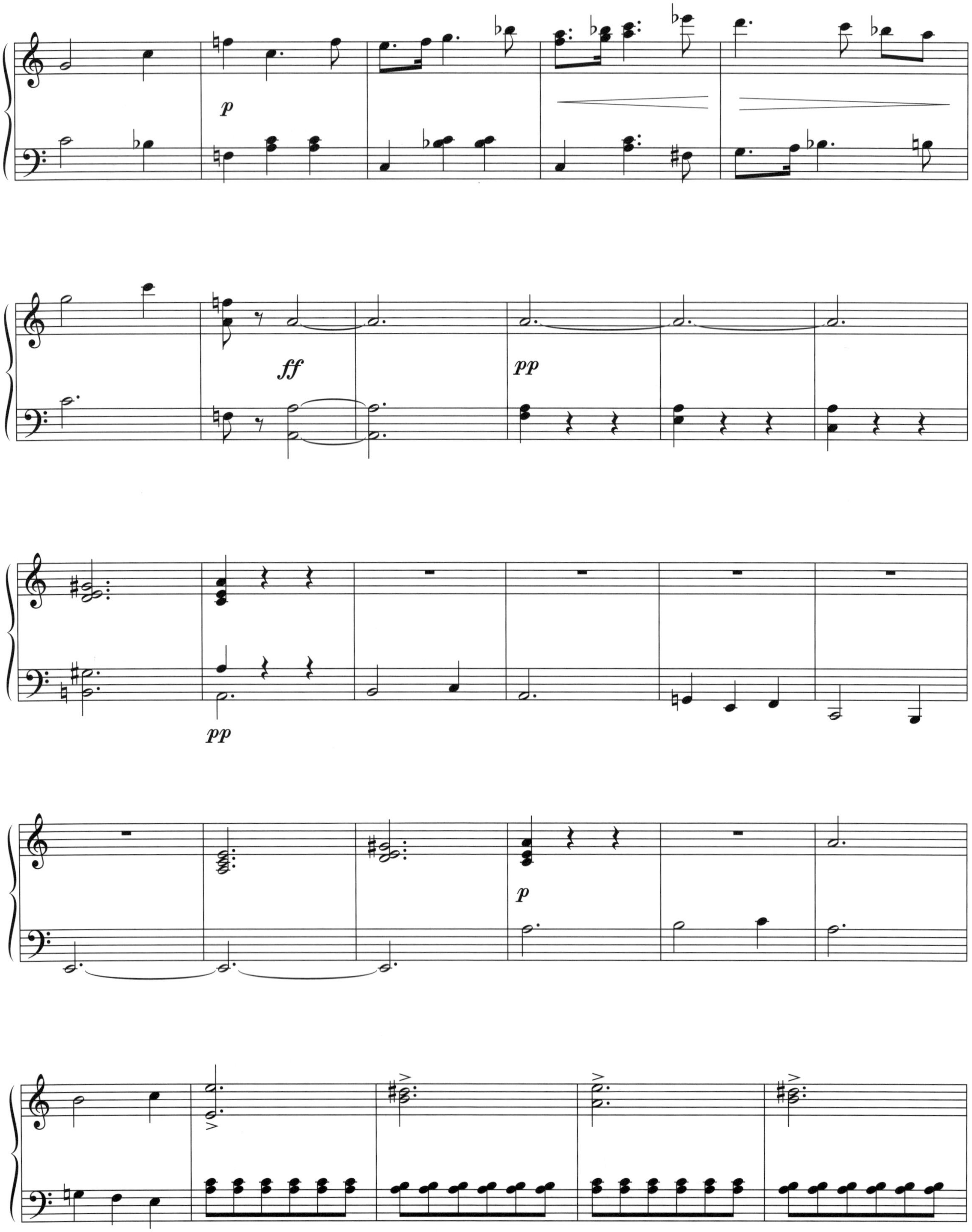
p
ff
pp
pp
p

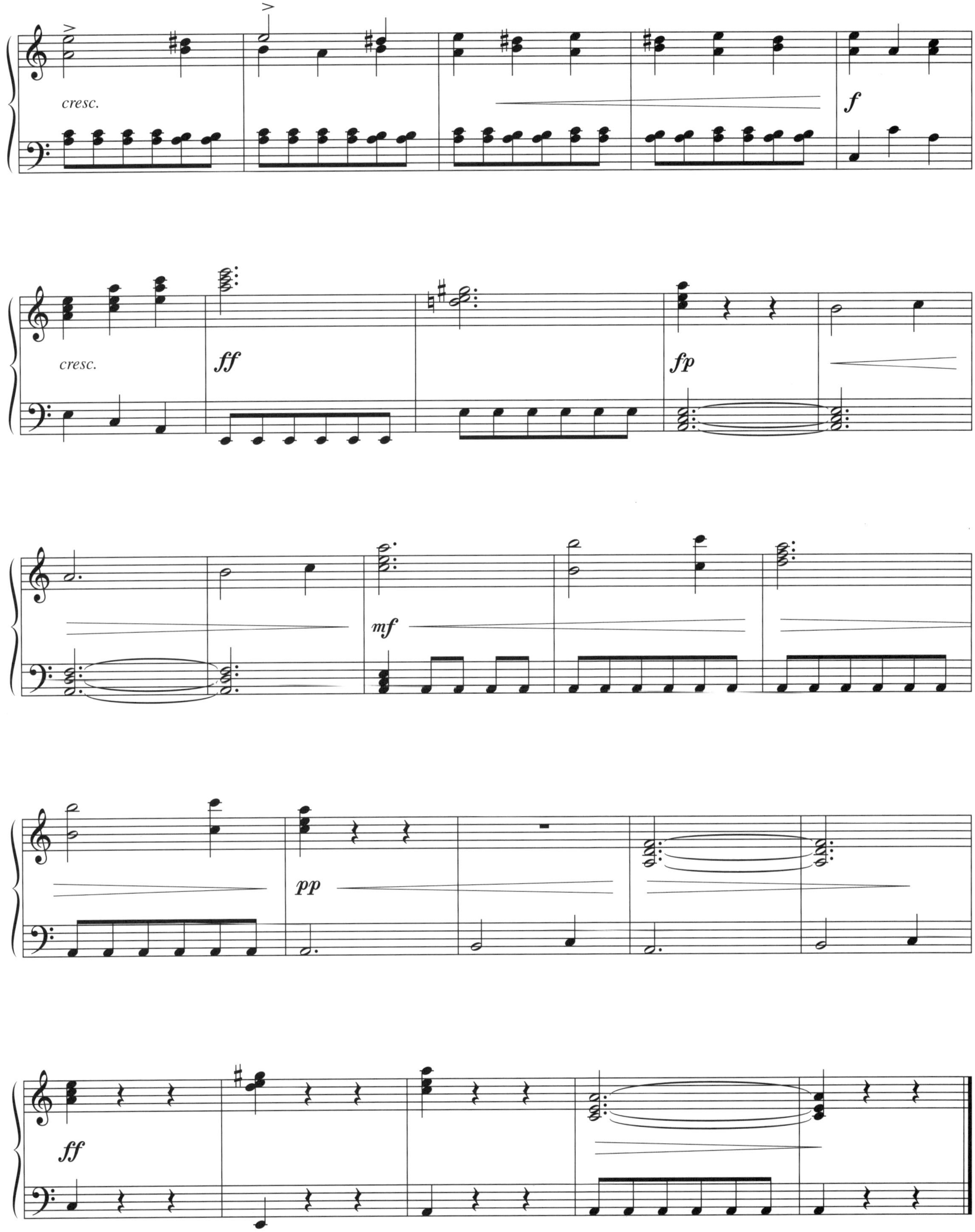
cresc.
f
cresc.
ff
fp
mf
pp
ff

Ave Maria

Franz Schubert
1797-1828
D. 839
originally for voice and piano

Molto lento

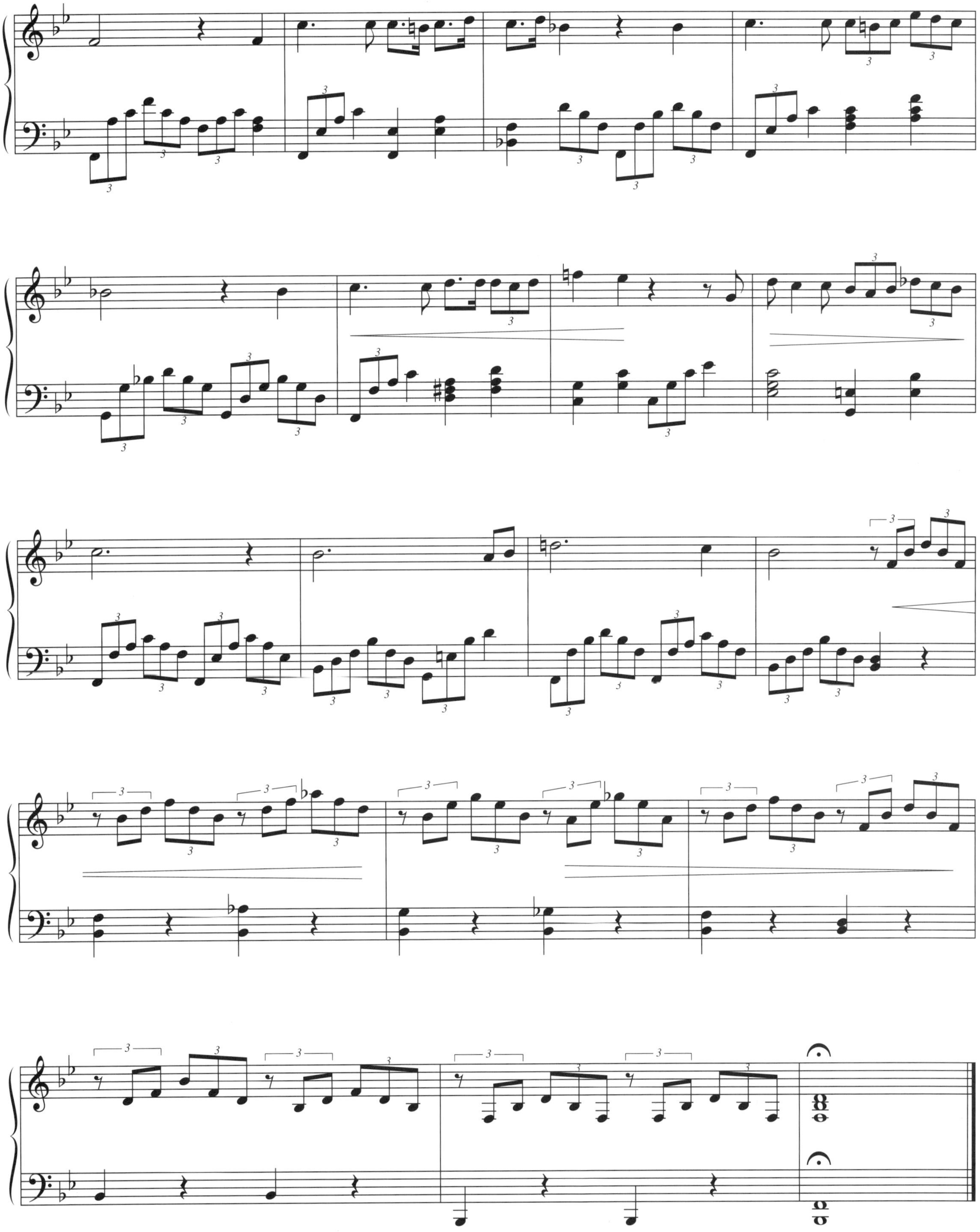

Serenade
(Ständchen)

Franz Schubert
1797-1828
D. 957, No. 4
originally for voice and piano

Moderato

357

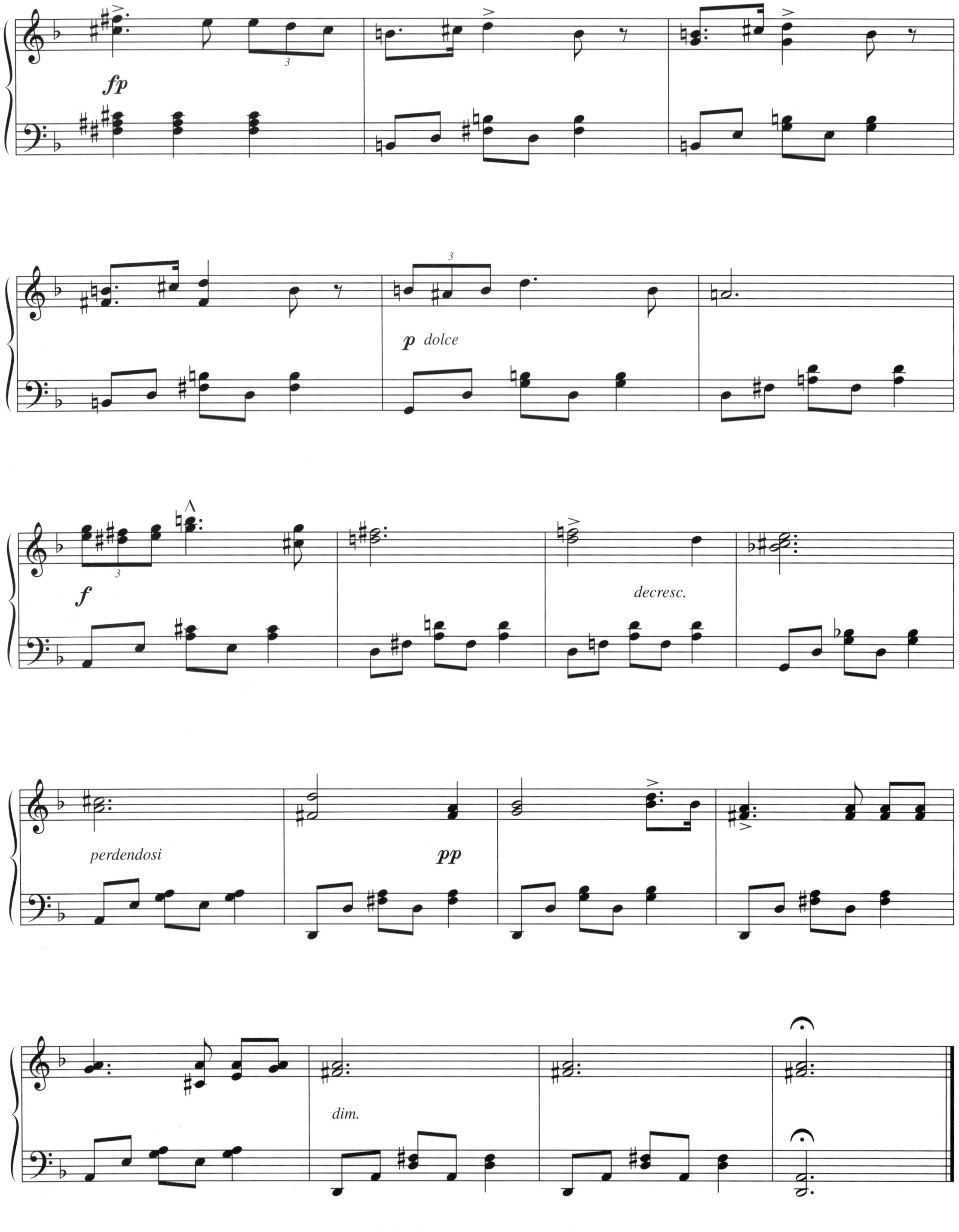
fp
3
3
p dolce
3
f
decresc.
perdendosi
pp
dim.

The Happy Farmer Returning from Work

(Frölicher Landmann, von der Arbeit zurückkehrend)
from ALBUM FÜR DIE JUGEND
(Album for the Young)

Robert Schumann
1810–1856
Op. 68, No. 10

Piano Concerto in A Minor

First Movement Themes

Robert Schumann
1810-1856
Op. 54
originally for piano and orchestra

Allegro affettuoso

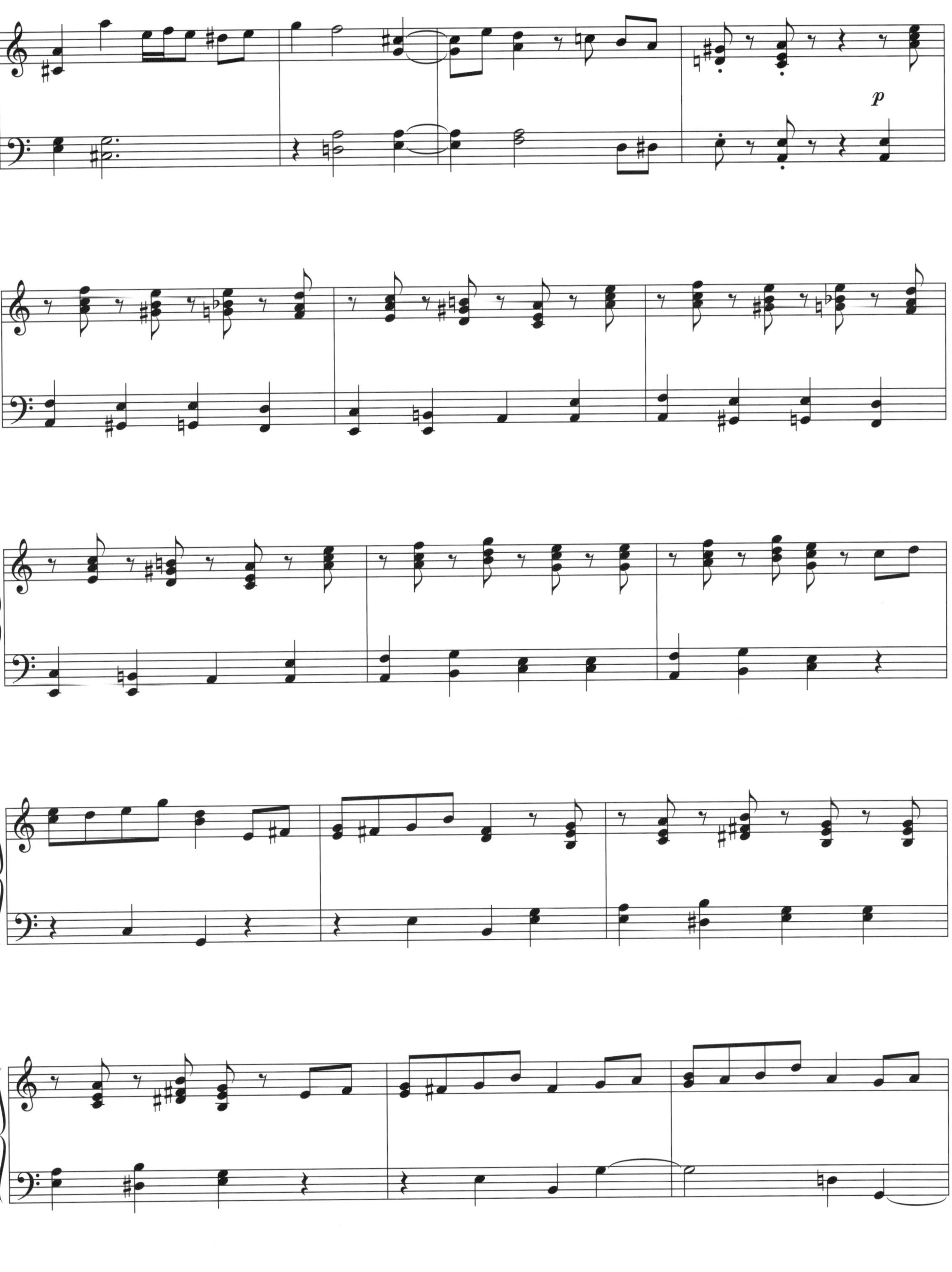
p

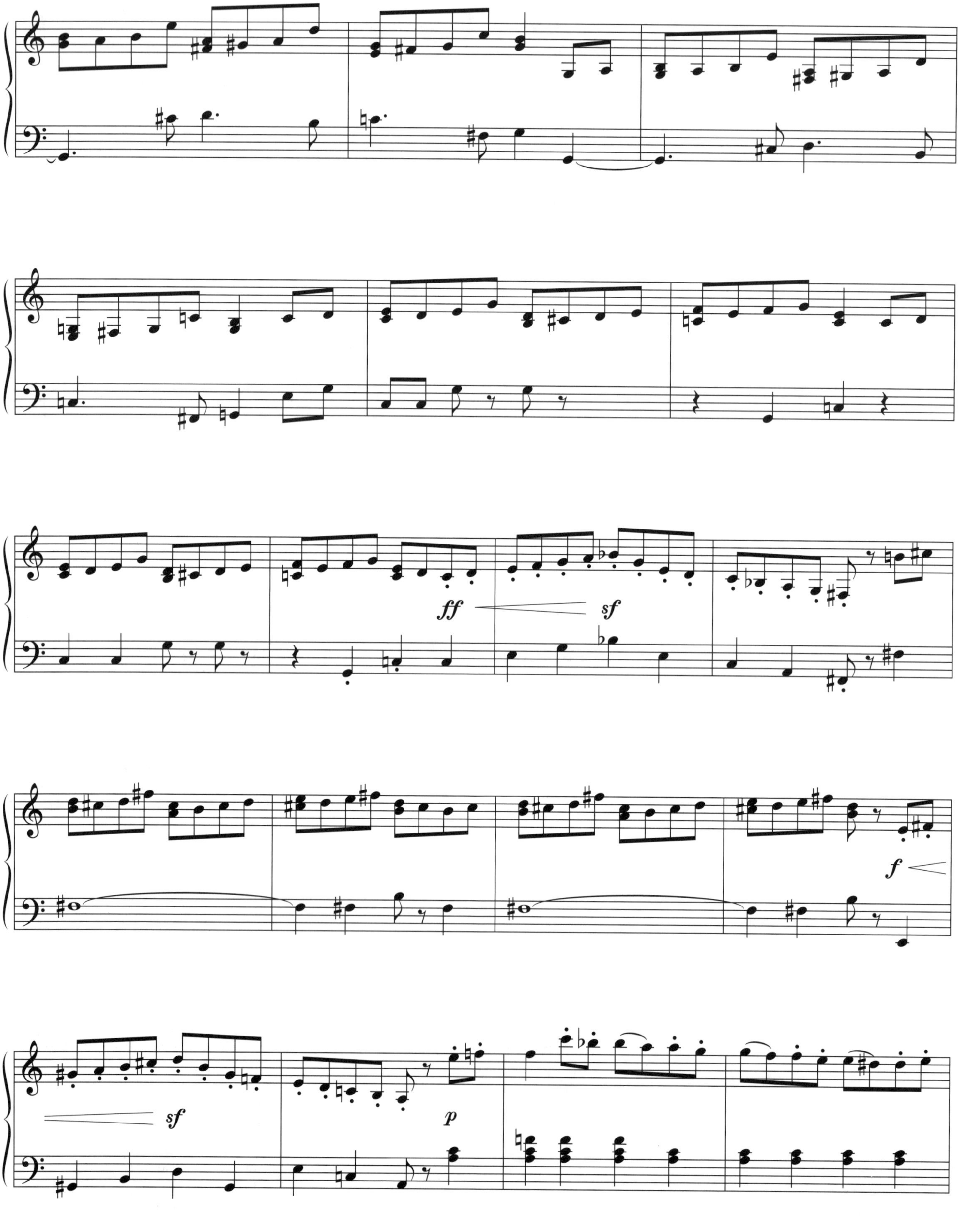
ff
sf
f
sf
p

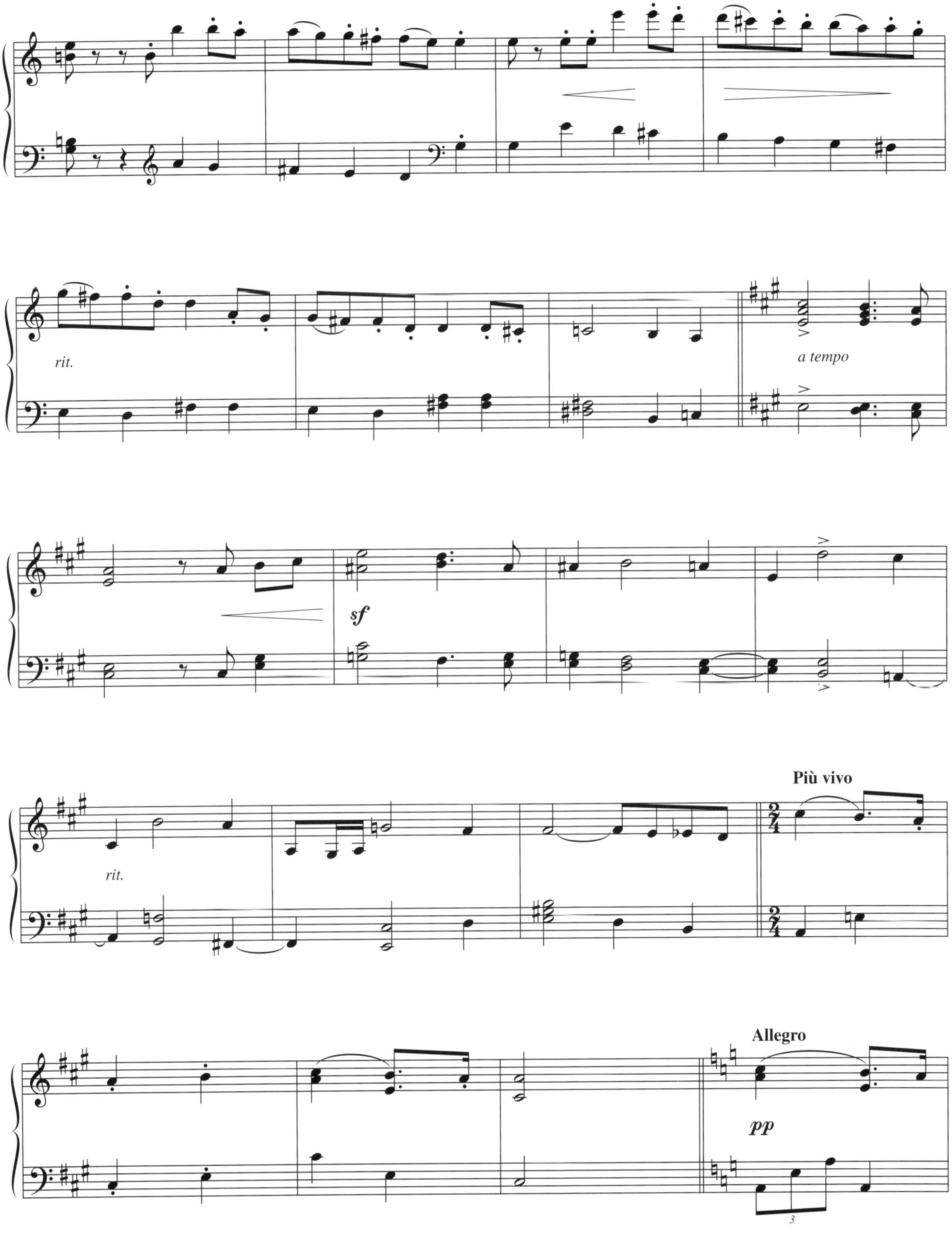
rit.
a tempo
sf
rit.
Più vivo
Allegro
pp
3

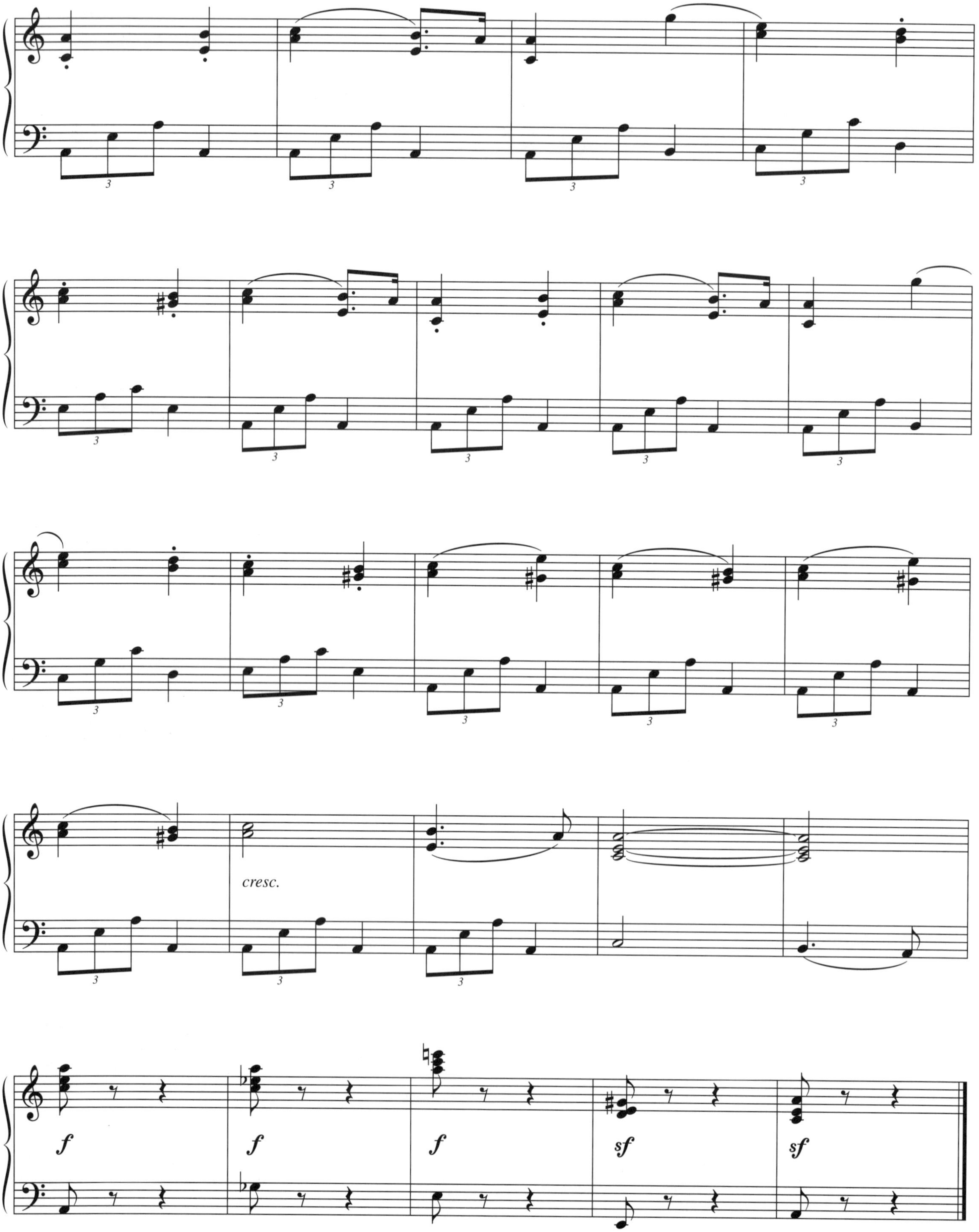
cresc.
f
f
f
sf
sf

Ich grolle nicht
(I bear no grudge)

Robert Schumann
1810-1856
Op. 48, No. 7
originally for voice and piano

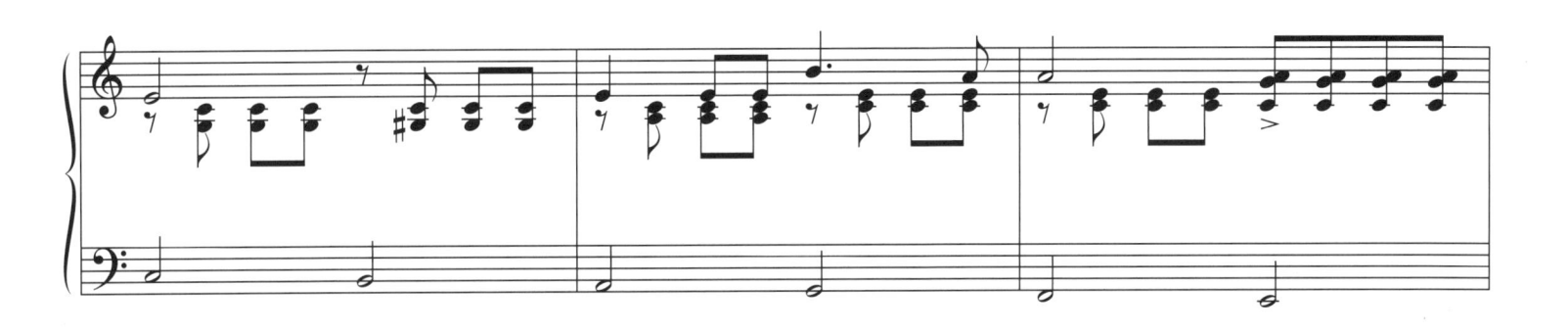

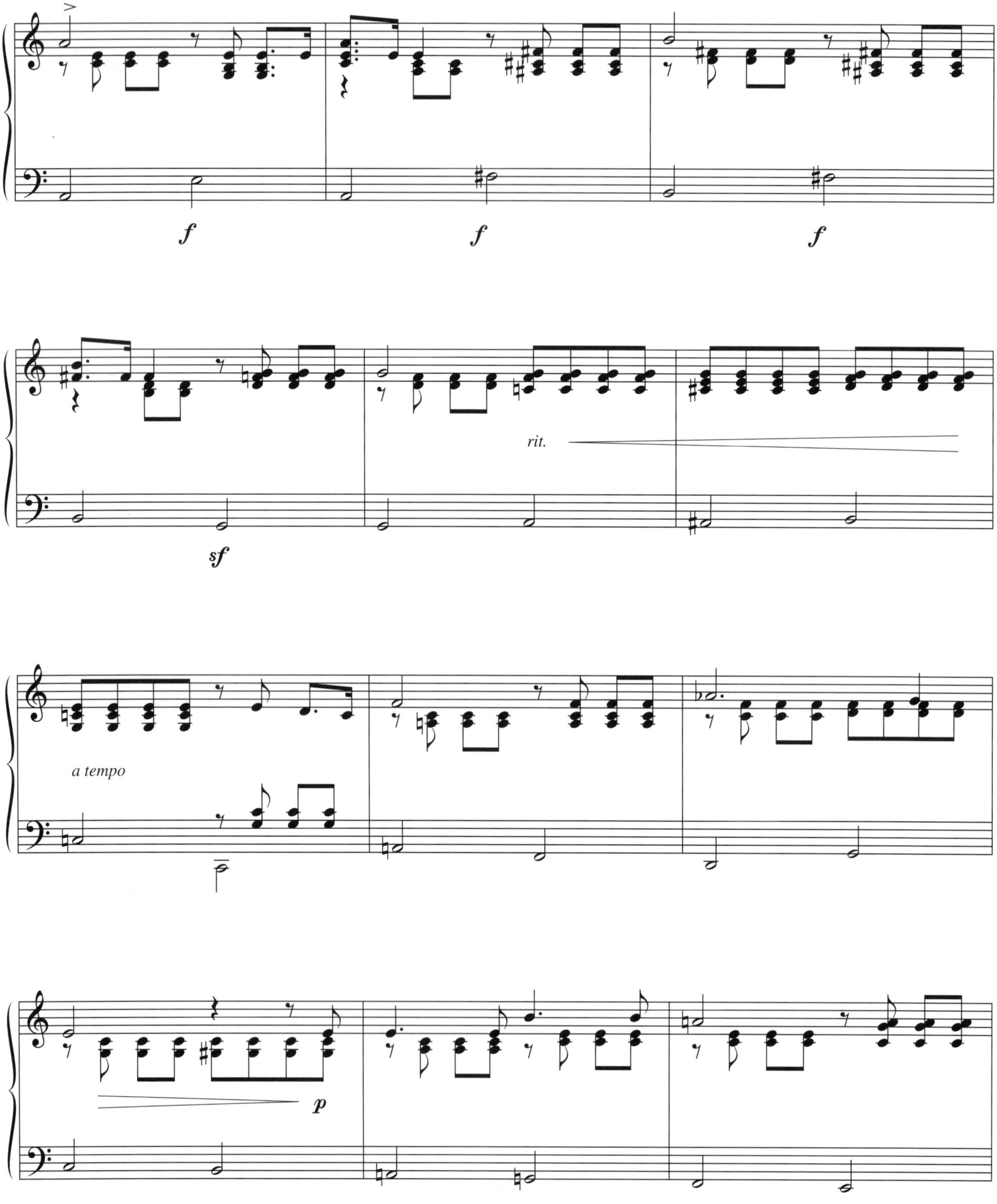
f
f
f
sf
rit.
a tempo
p

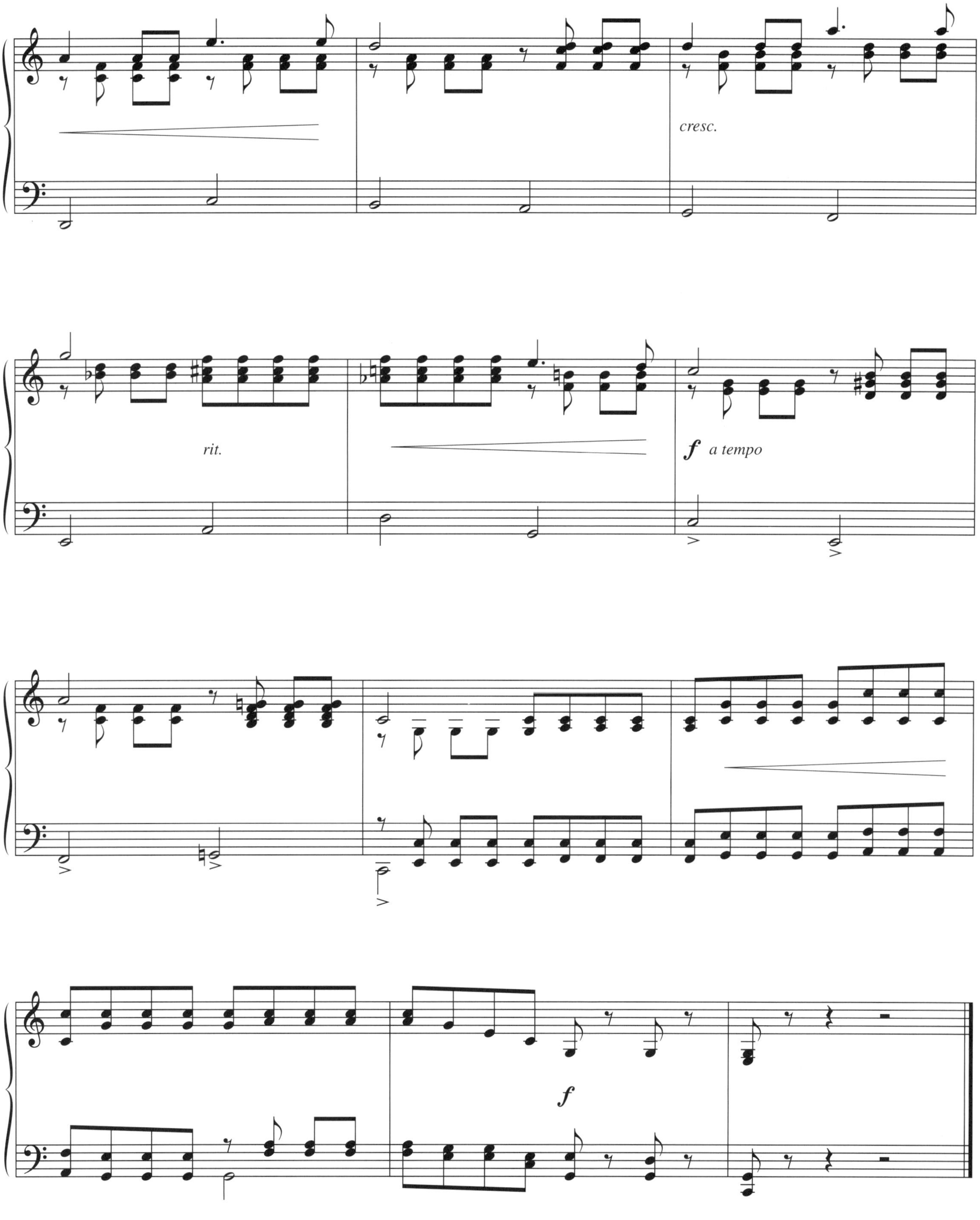
cresc.
rit.
f a tempo
f

Widmung
(Devotion)

Robert Schumann
1810-1856
Op. 25, No. 1
originally for voice and piano

Tenderly, with spirit (♩ = c. 120)

mf

original key: A-flat Major

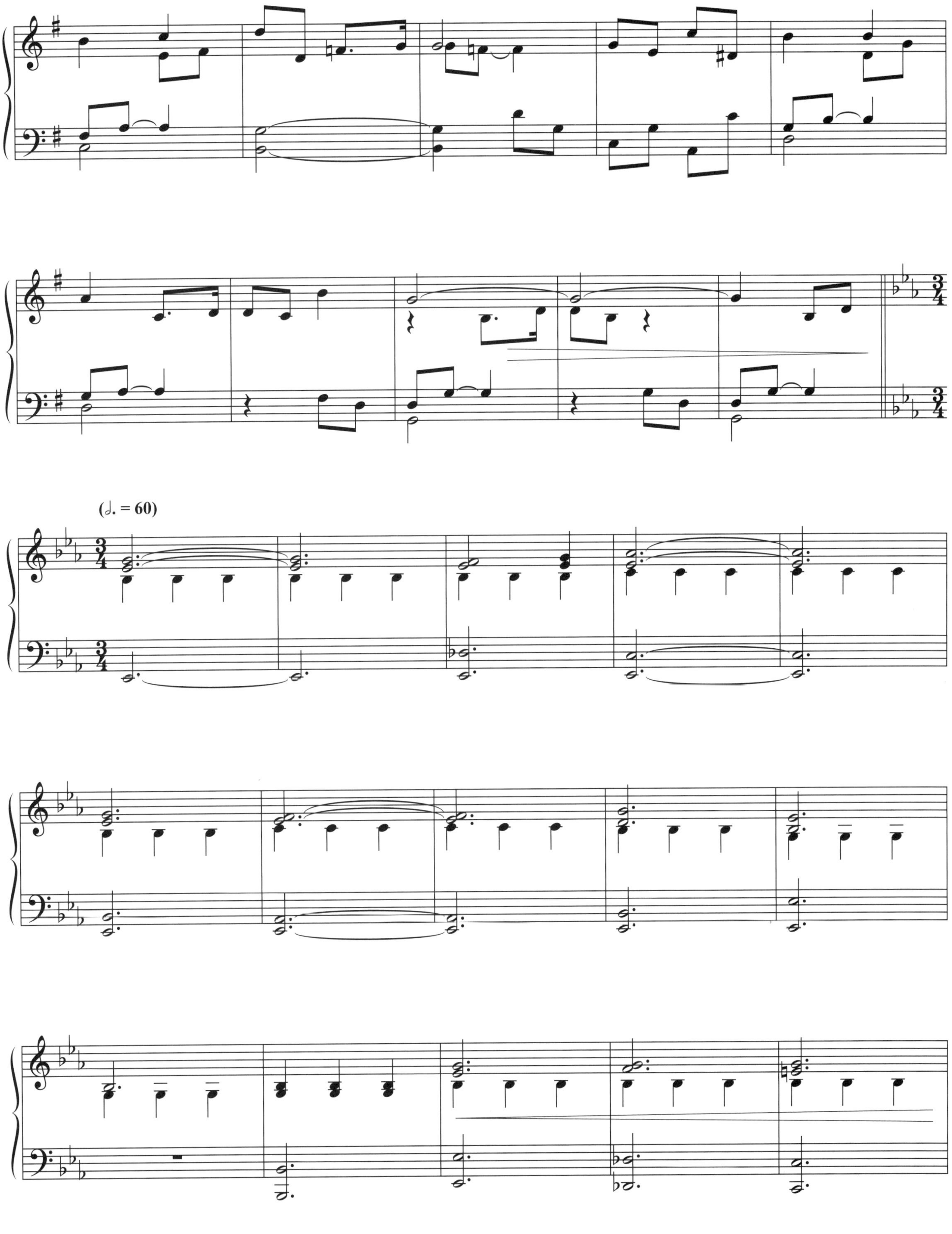
(♩. = 60)

Tempo I ($\quarternote$ = c. 120)

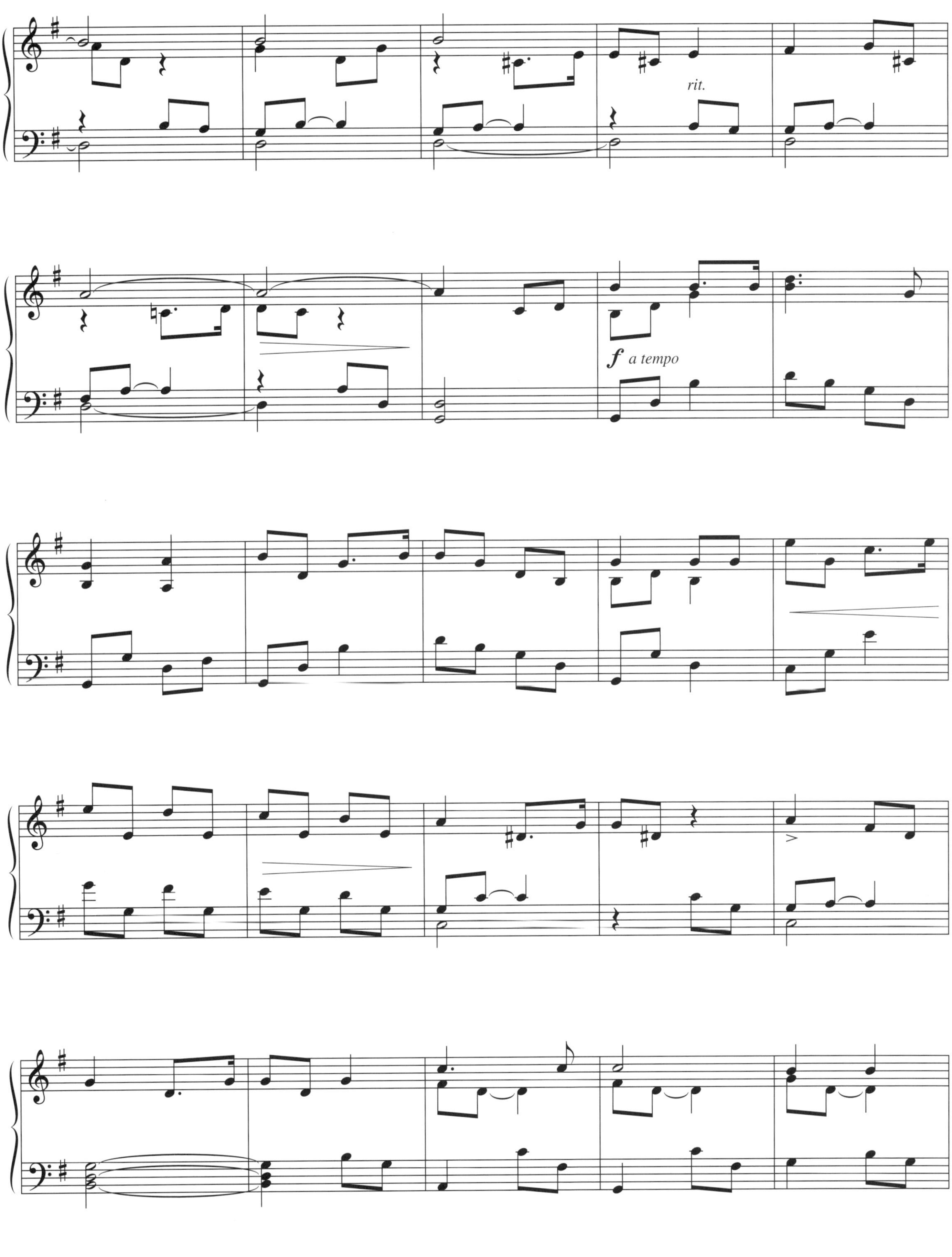
rit.
f a tempo

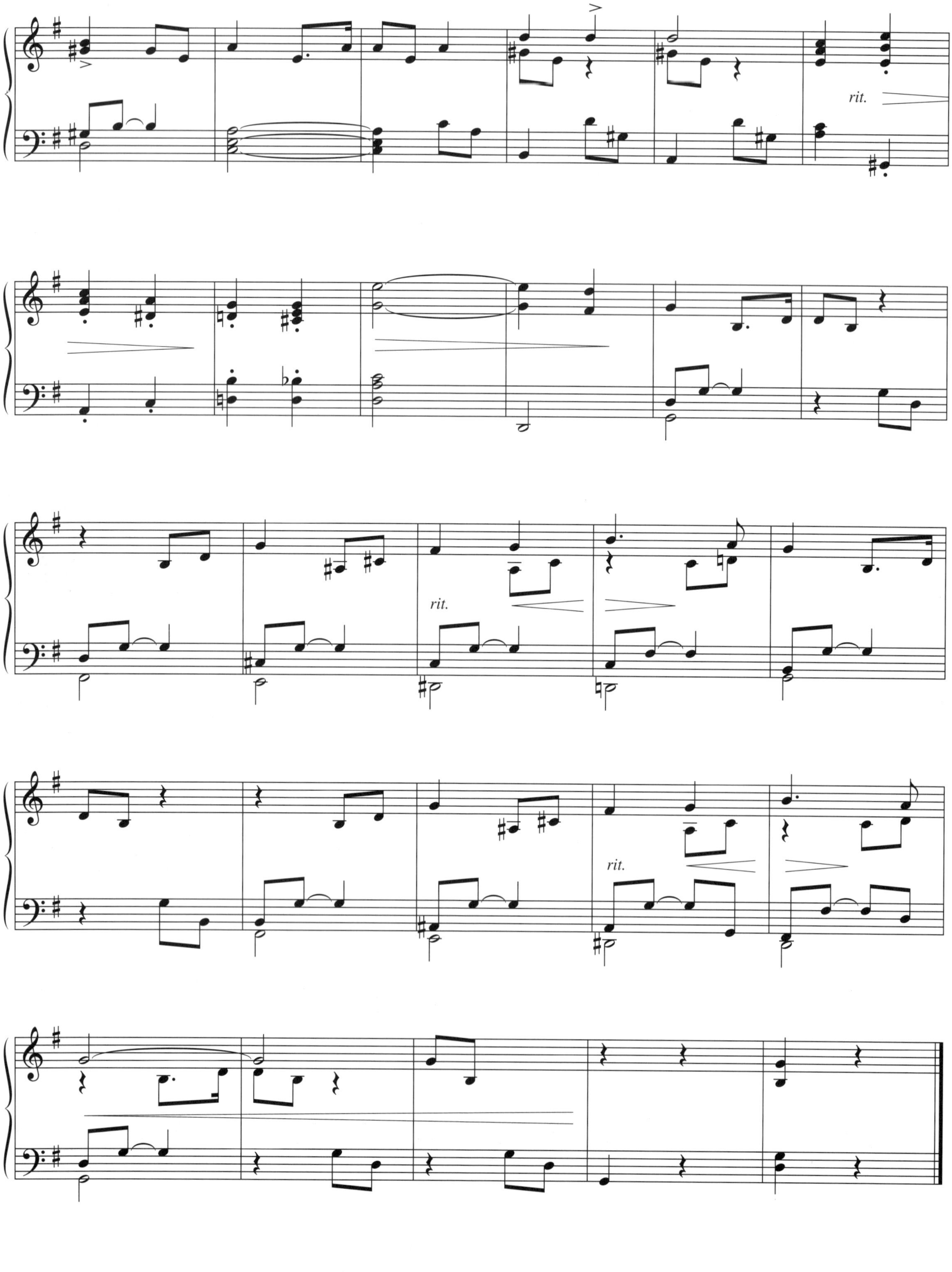
rit.
rit.
rit.

The Moldau

from the symphonic cycle MÁ VLAST (My Fatherland)
Excerpt

Bedrich Smetana
1824-1884
originally for orchestra

Allegro commodo non agitato

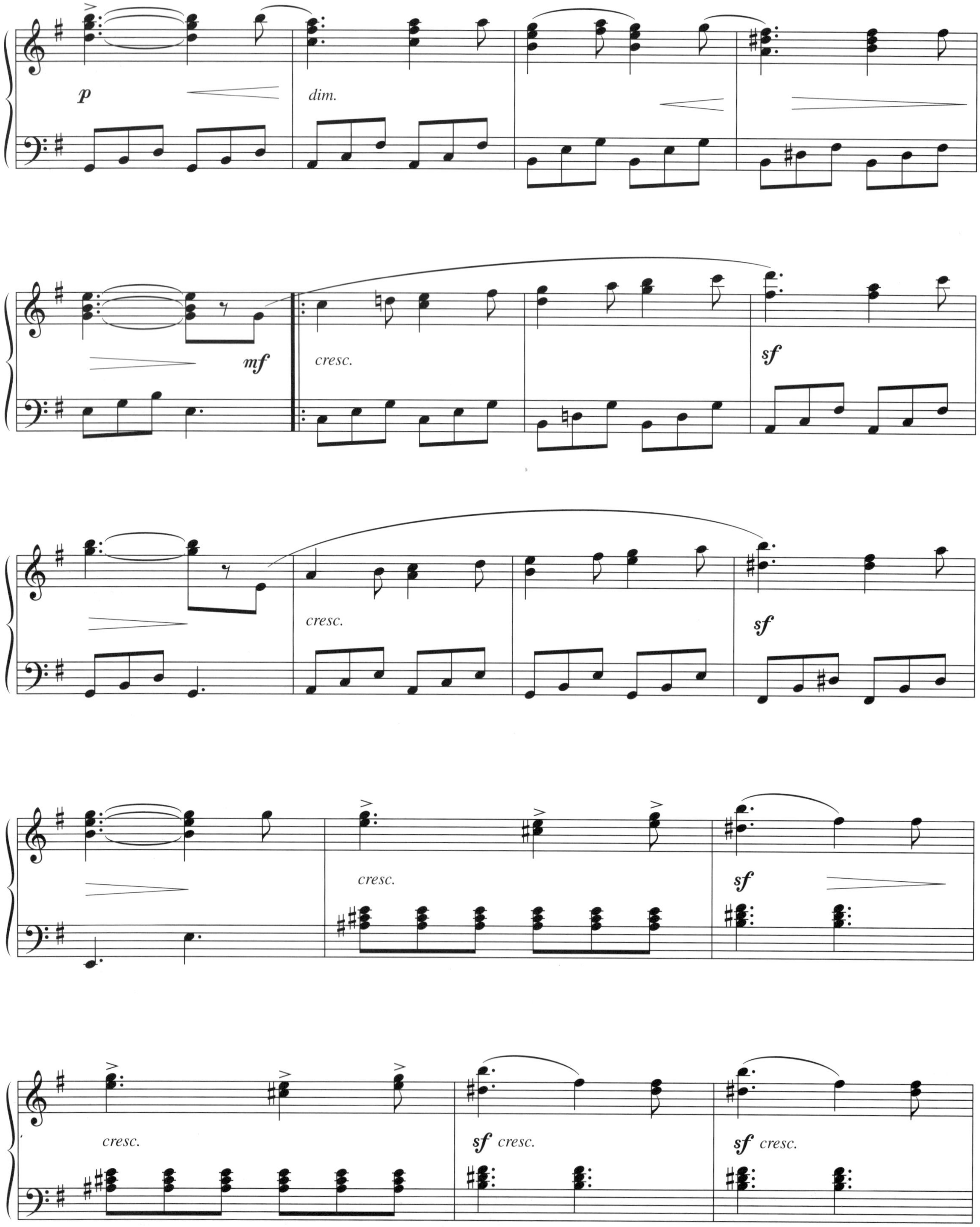
p
dim.
mf
cresc.
sf
cresc.
sf
cresc.
sf
cresc.
sf cresc.
sf cresc.

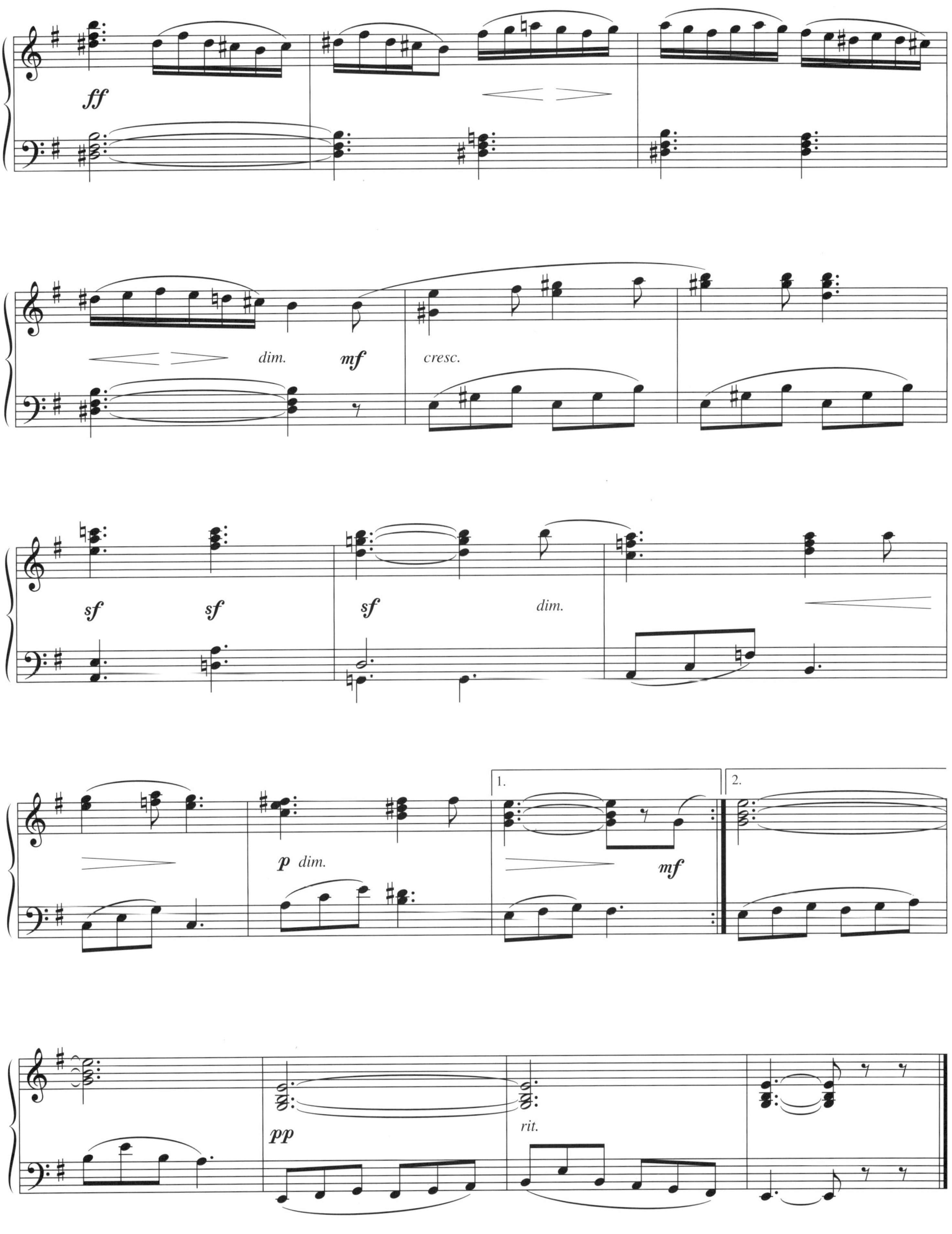
ff
dim.
mf
cresc.
sf
sf
sf
dim.
1.
2.
p dim.
mf
pp
rit.

By the Beautiful Blue Danube

Themes

Johann Strauss, Jr.
1825-1899
Op. 317
originally for orchestra

Tempo di Valse

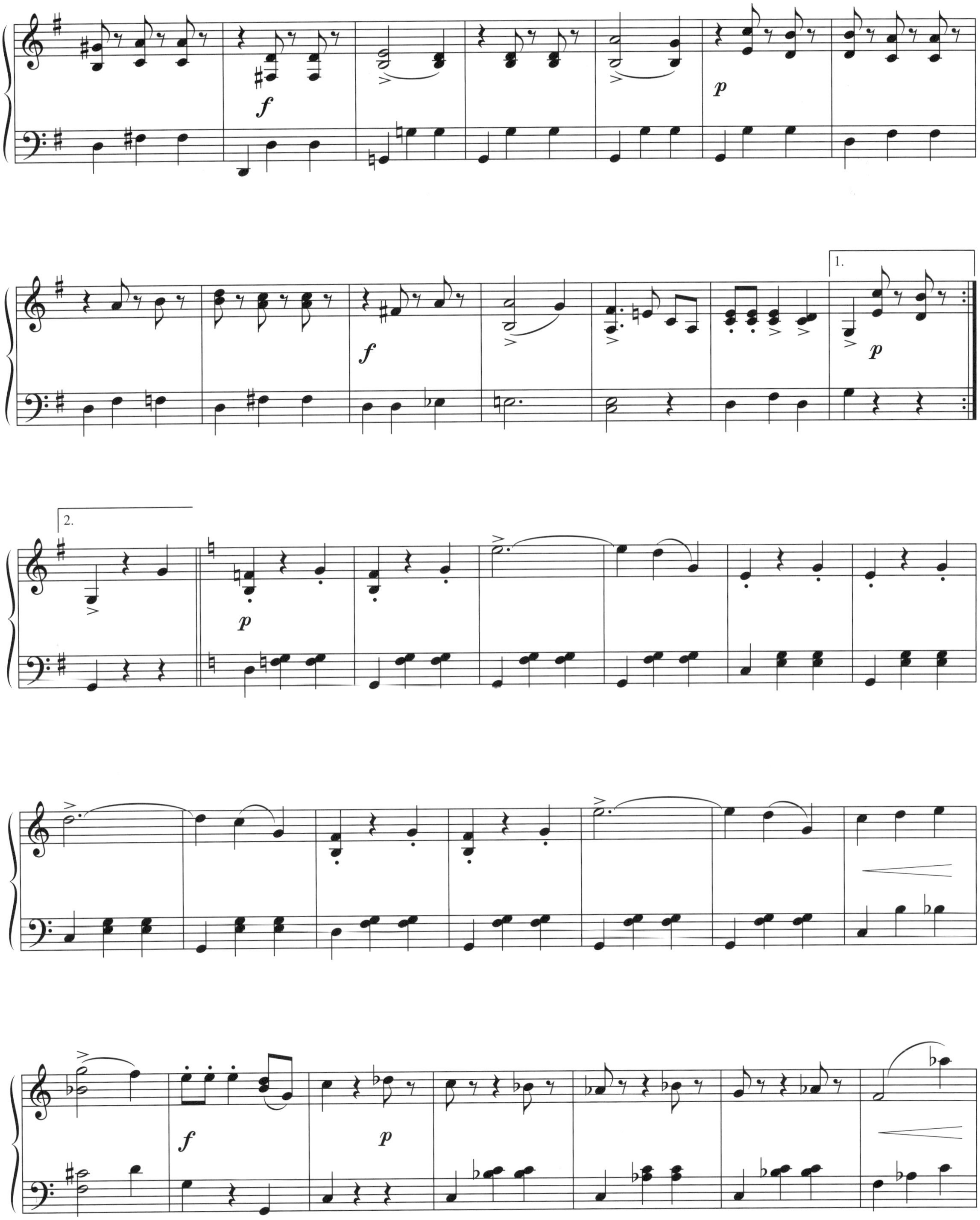

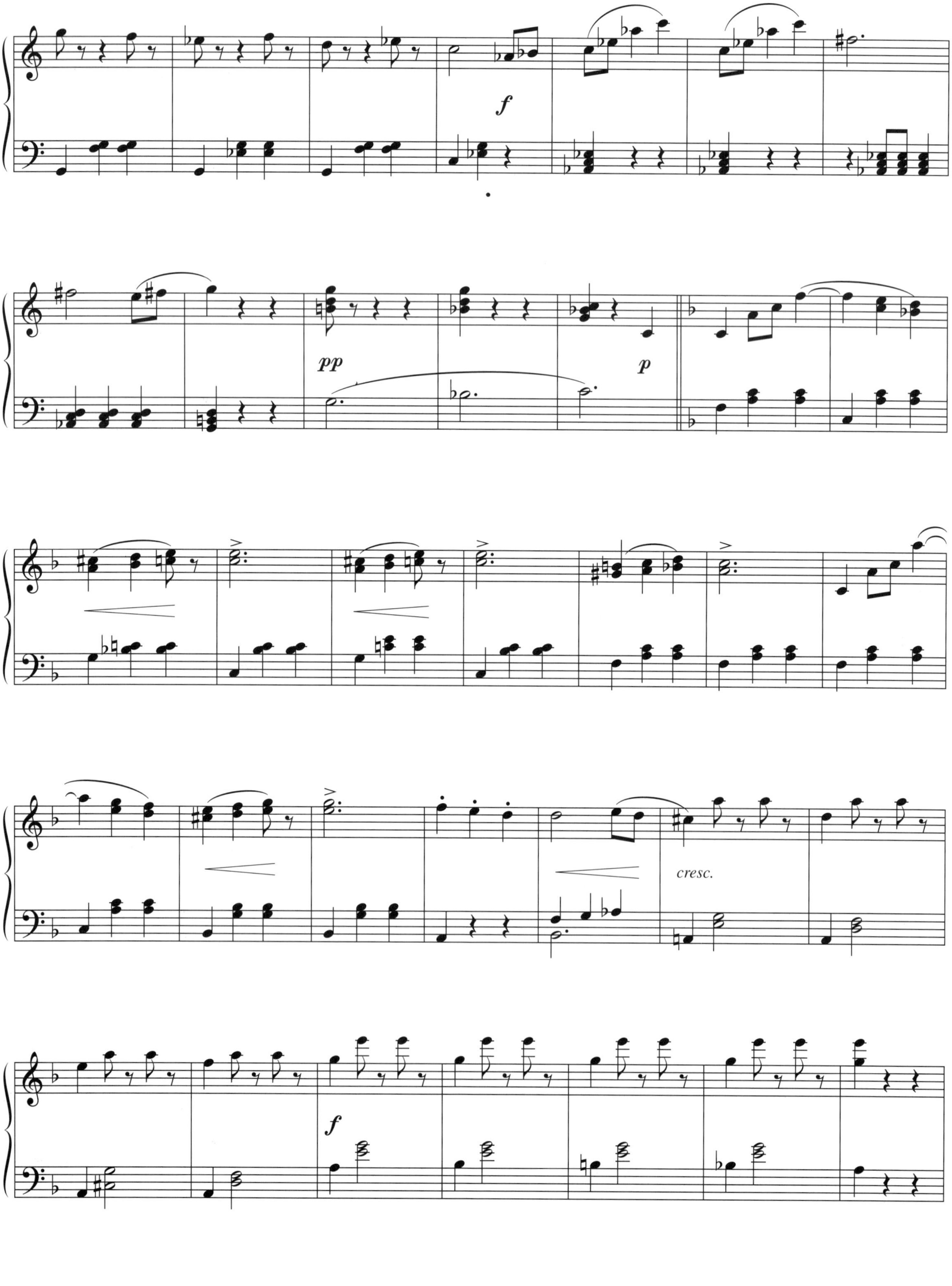
f
pp
p
cresc.
f

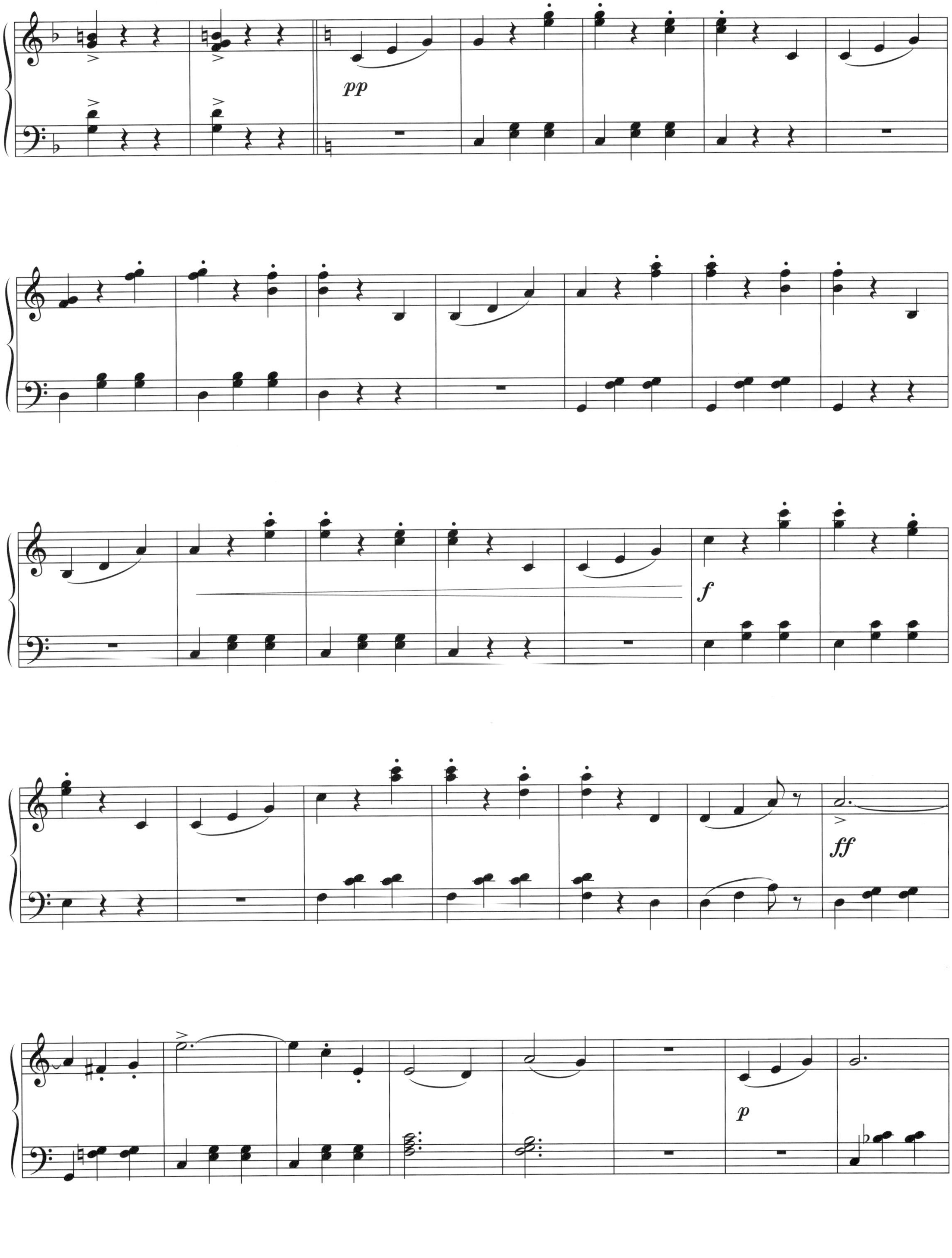
pp
f
ff
p

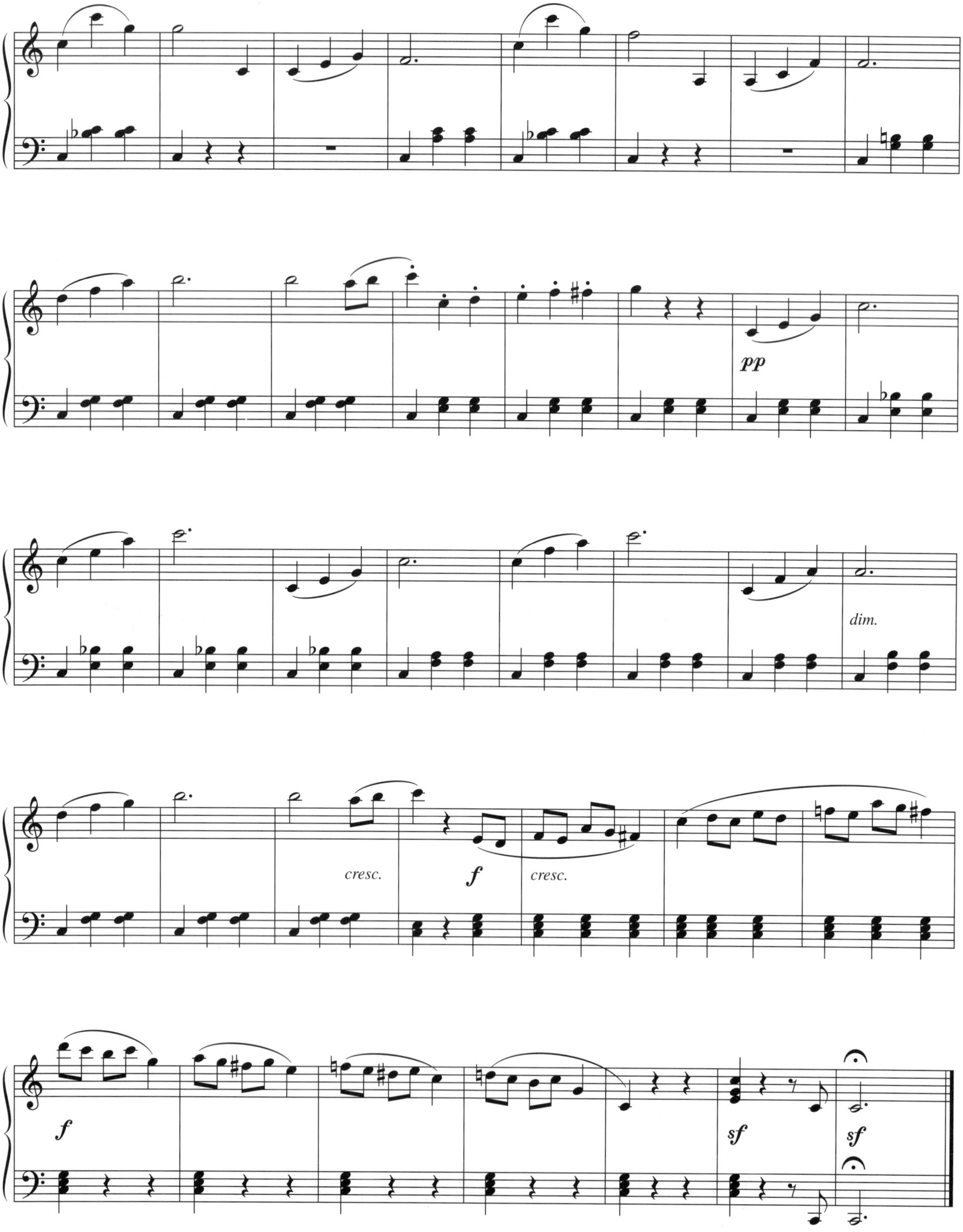
pp
dim.
cresc.
f
cresc.
f
sf
sf

Emperor Waltz

(Kaiser Walzer)
Excerpt

Johann Strauss, Jr.
1825-1899
Op. 437
originally for orchestra

Slow March Tempo

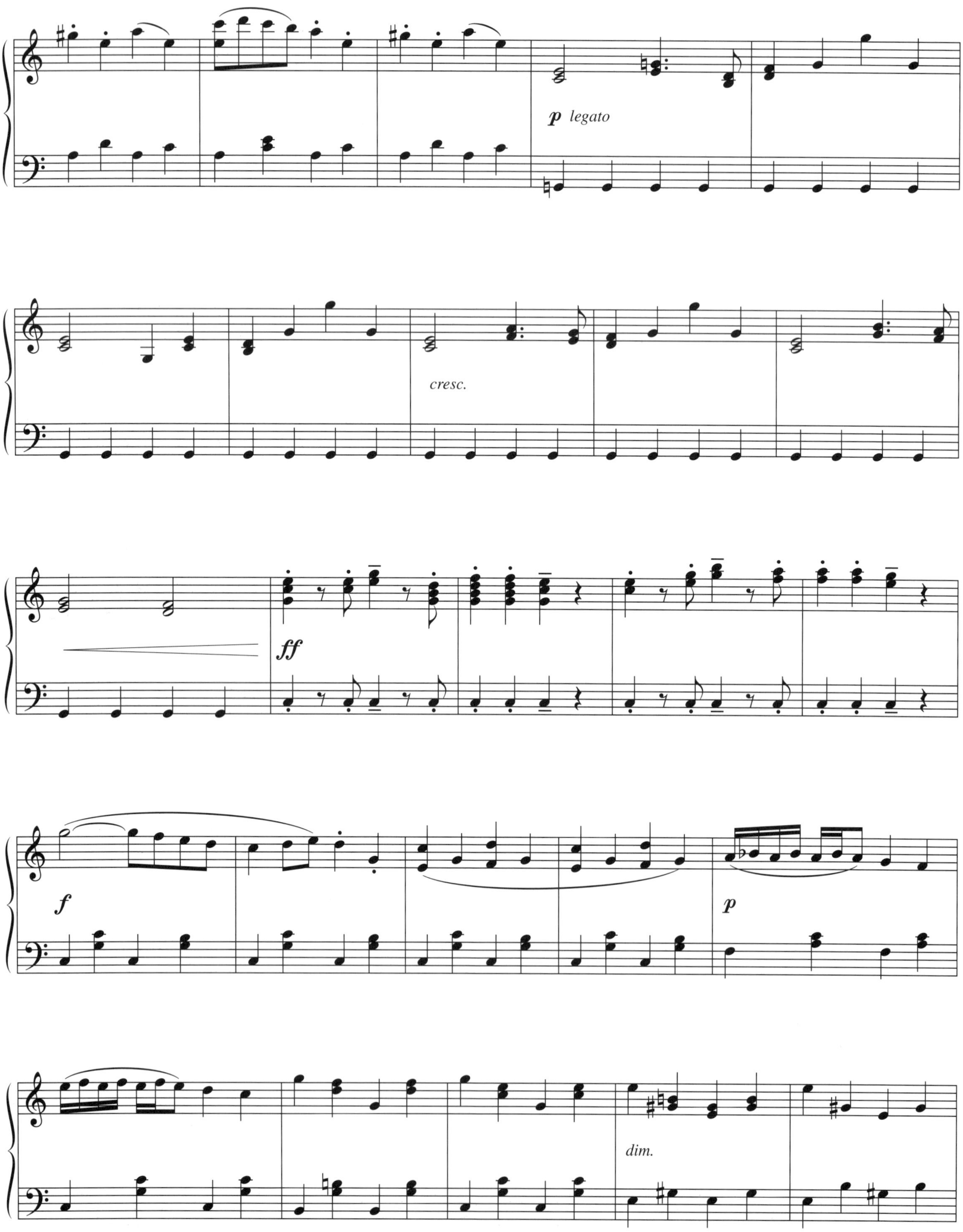
p legato
cresc.
ff
f
p
dim.

Tempo di Valse

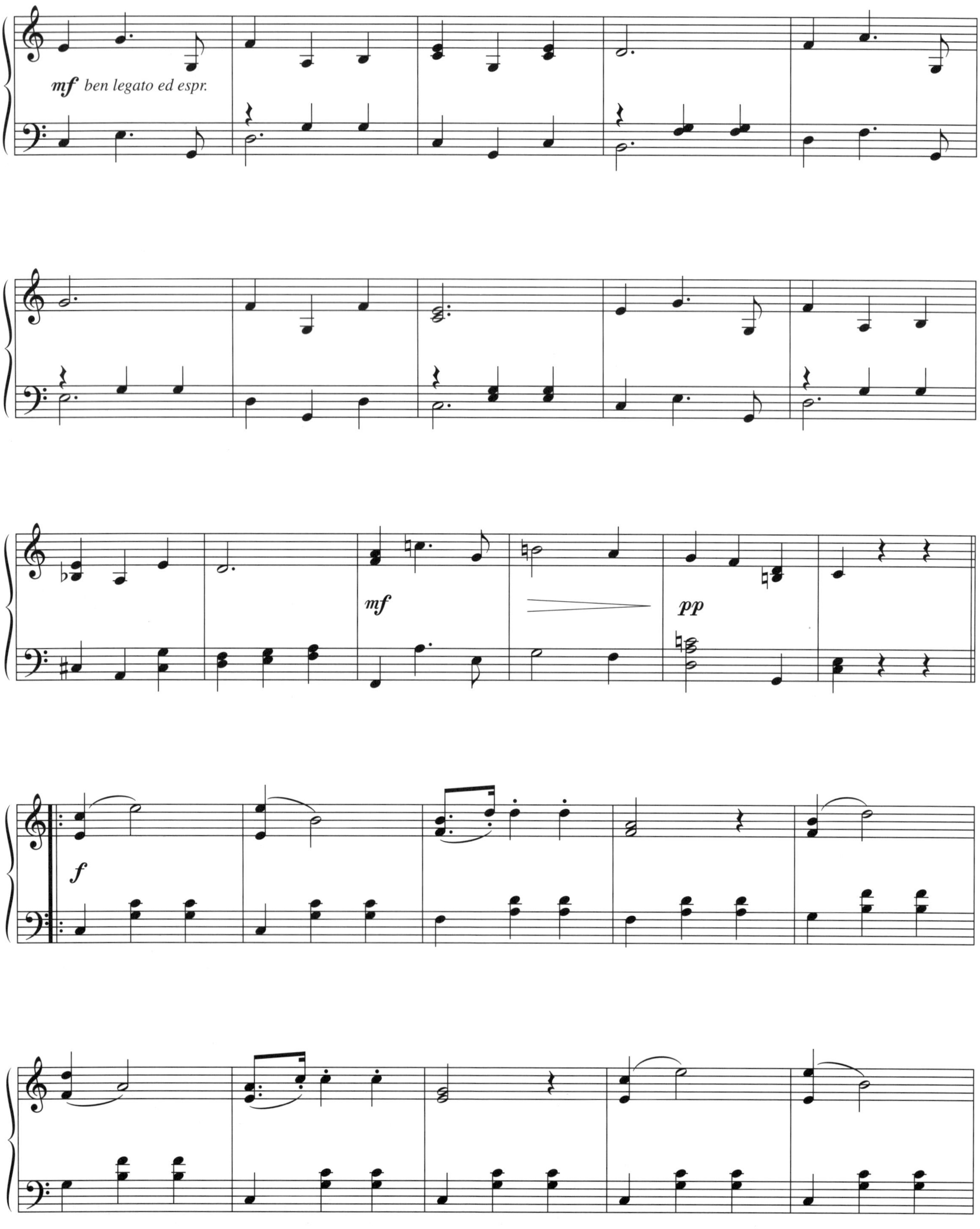
mf ben legato ed espr.
mf
pp
f

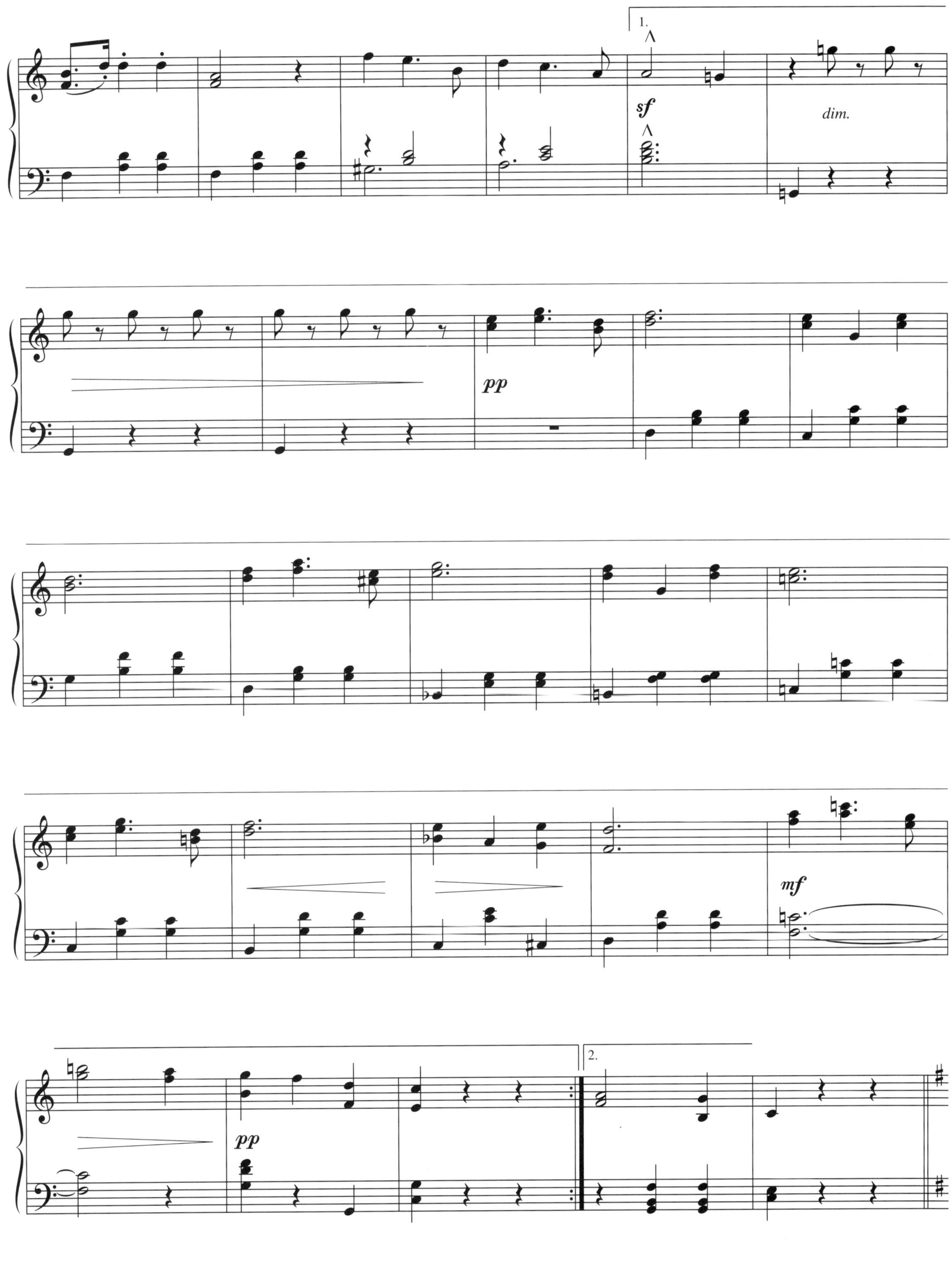
1.
sf
dim.
pp
mf
pp
2.

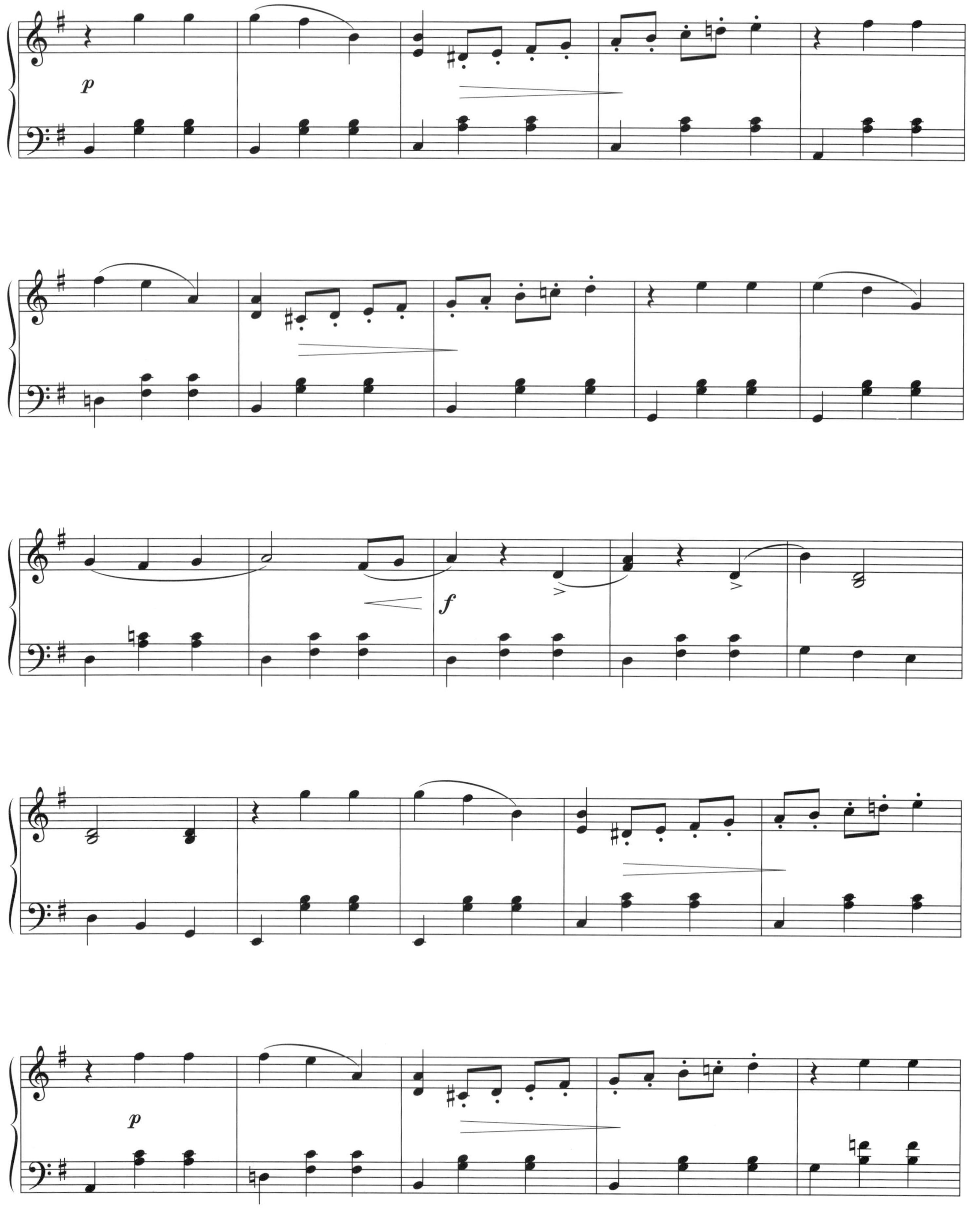

387

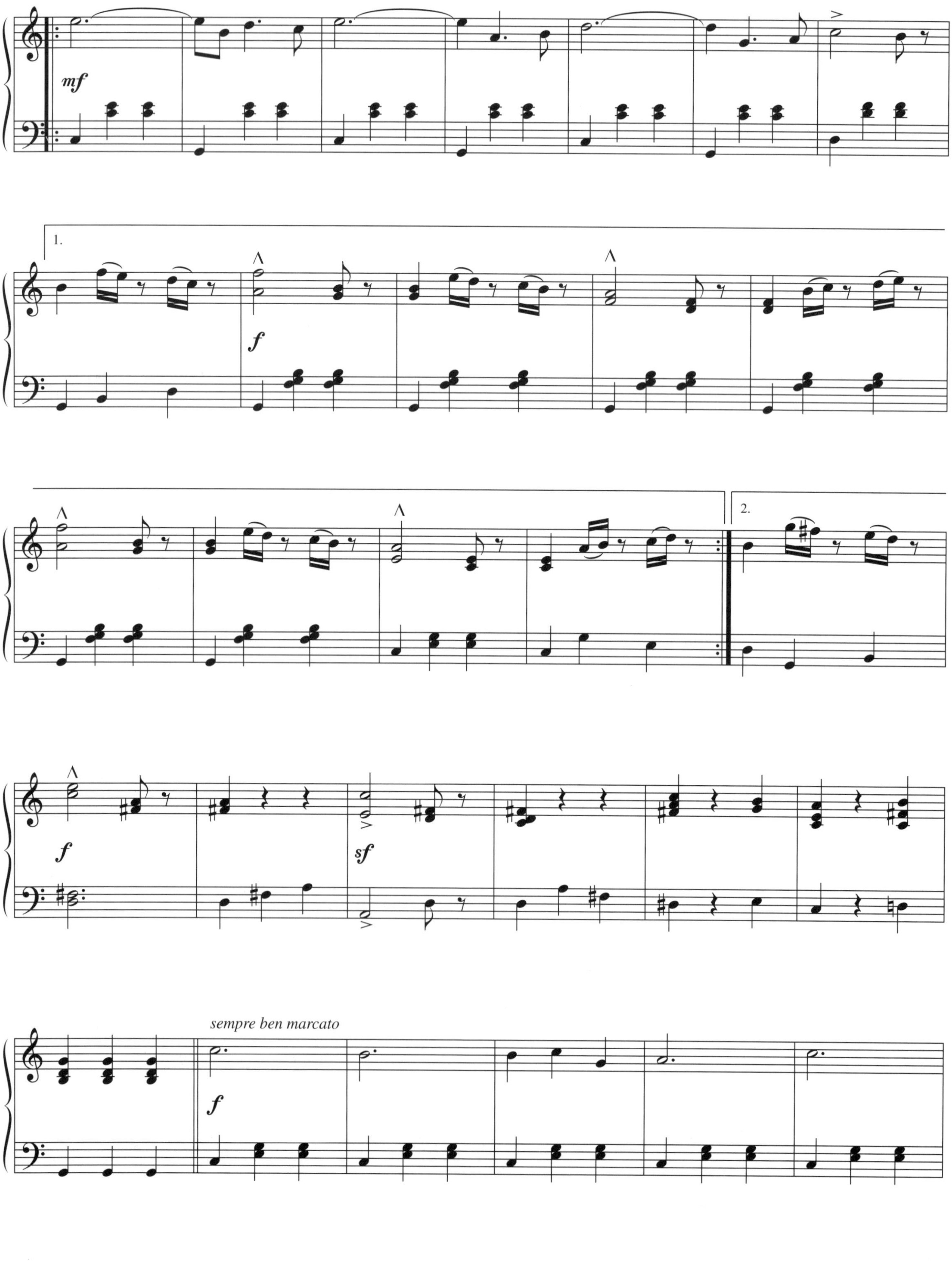
mf
1.
f
2.
f
sf
sempre ben marcato
f

389

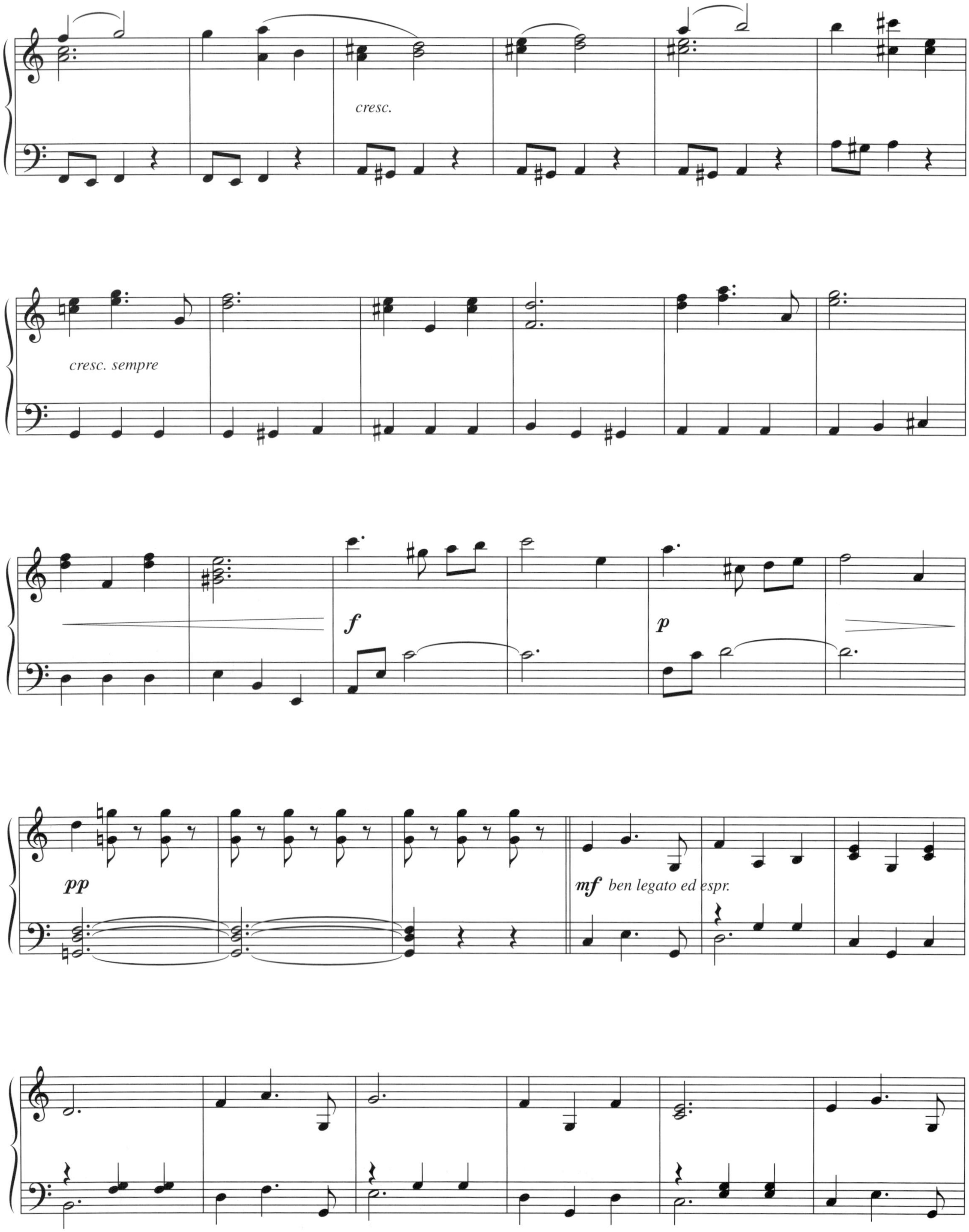
cresc.
cresc. sempre
f
p
pp
mf ben legato ed espr.

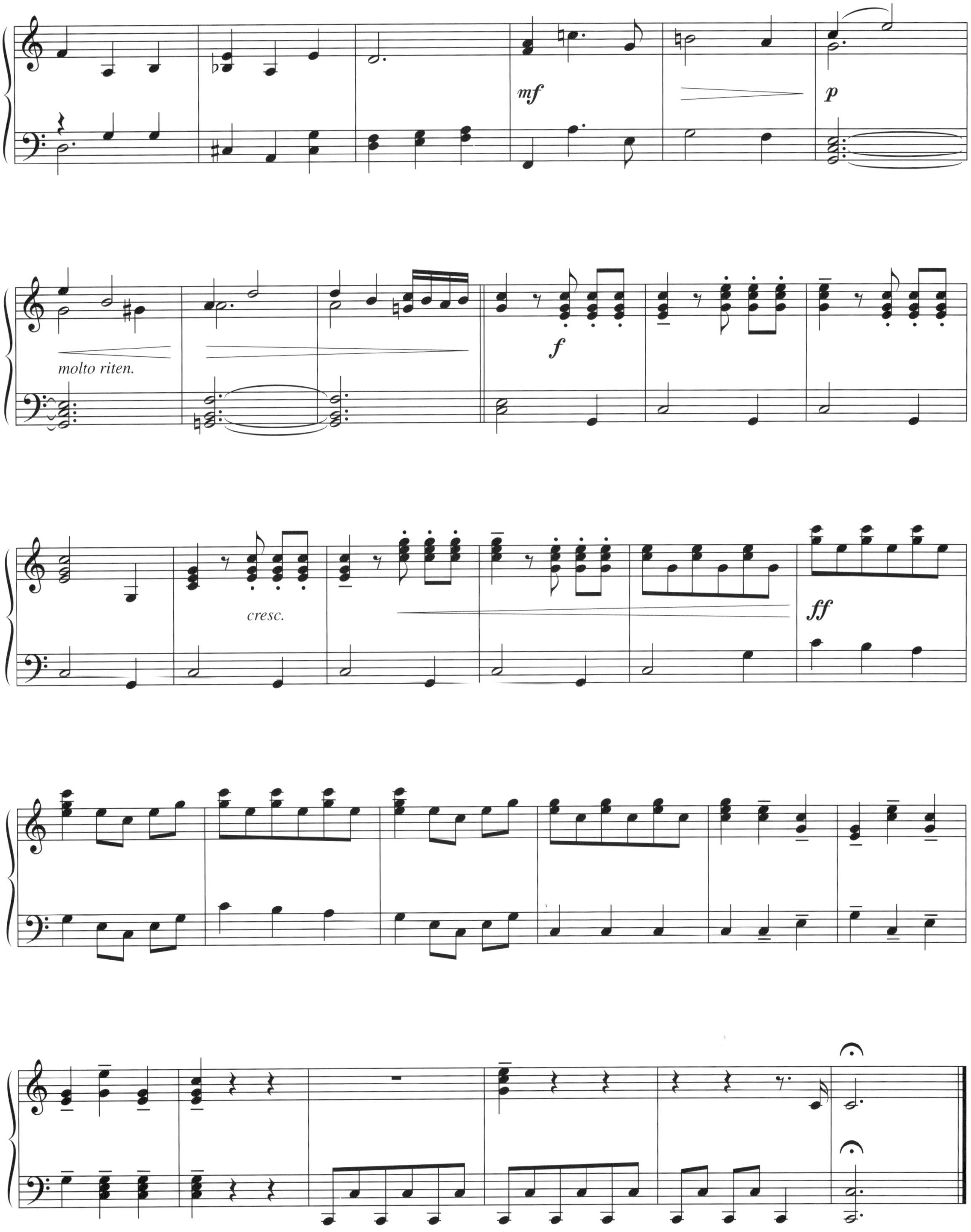
mf
p
molto riten.
f
cresc.
ff

The Fledermaus Waltz

from the opera DIE FLEDERMAUS
(The Bat)

Johann Strauss, Jr.
1825-1899

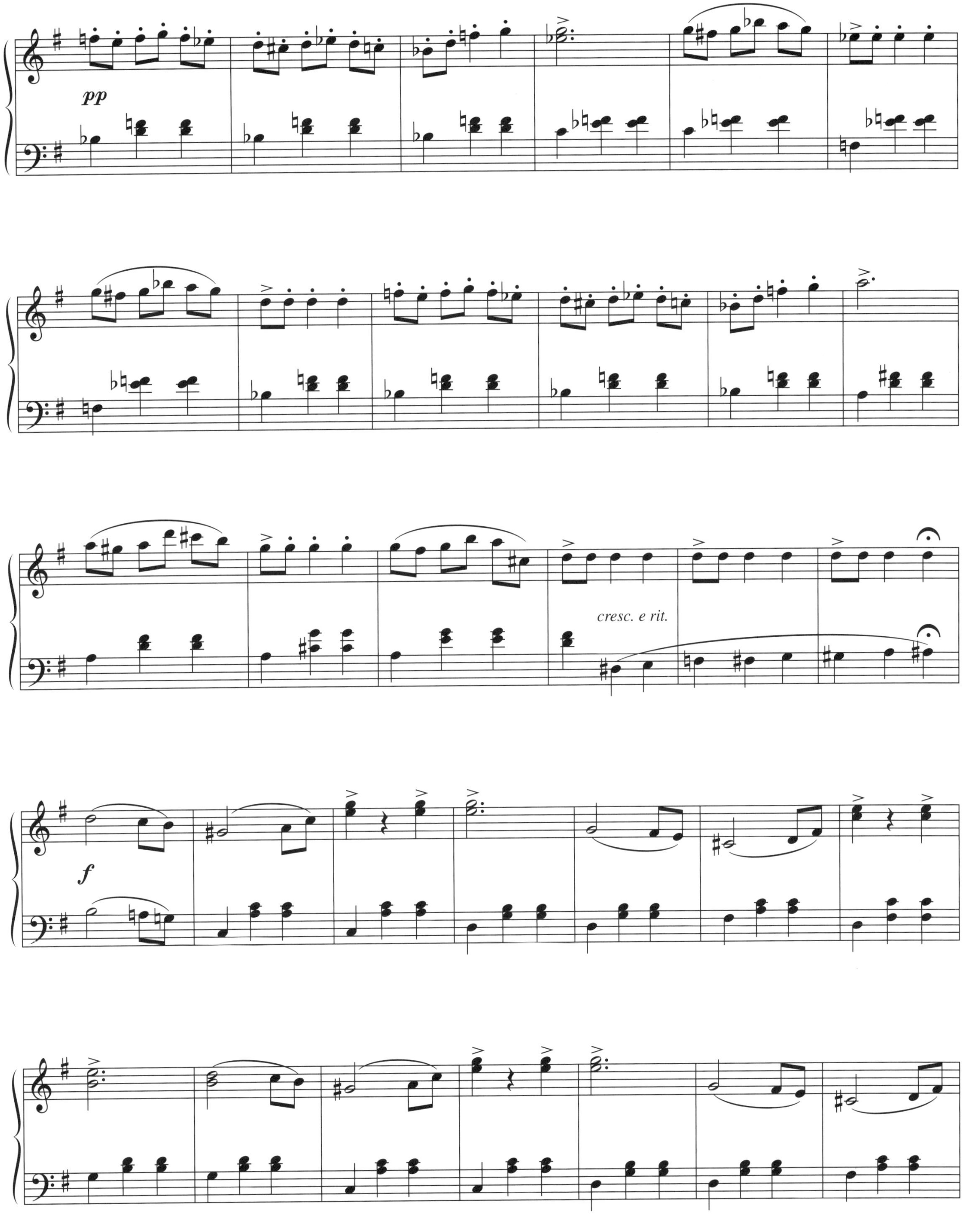
pp
cresc. e rit.
f

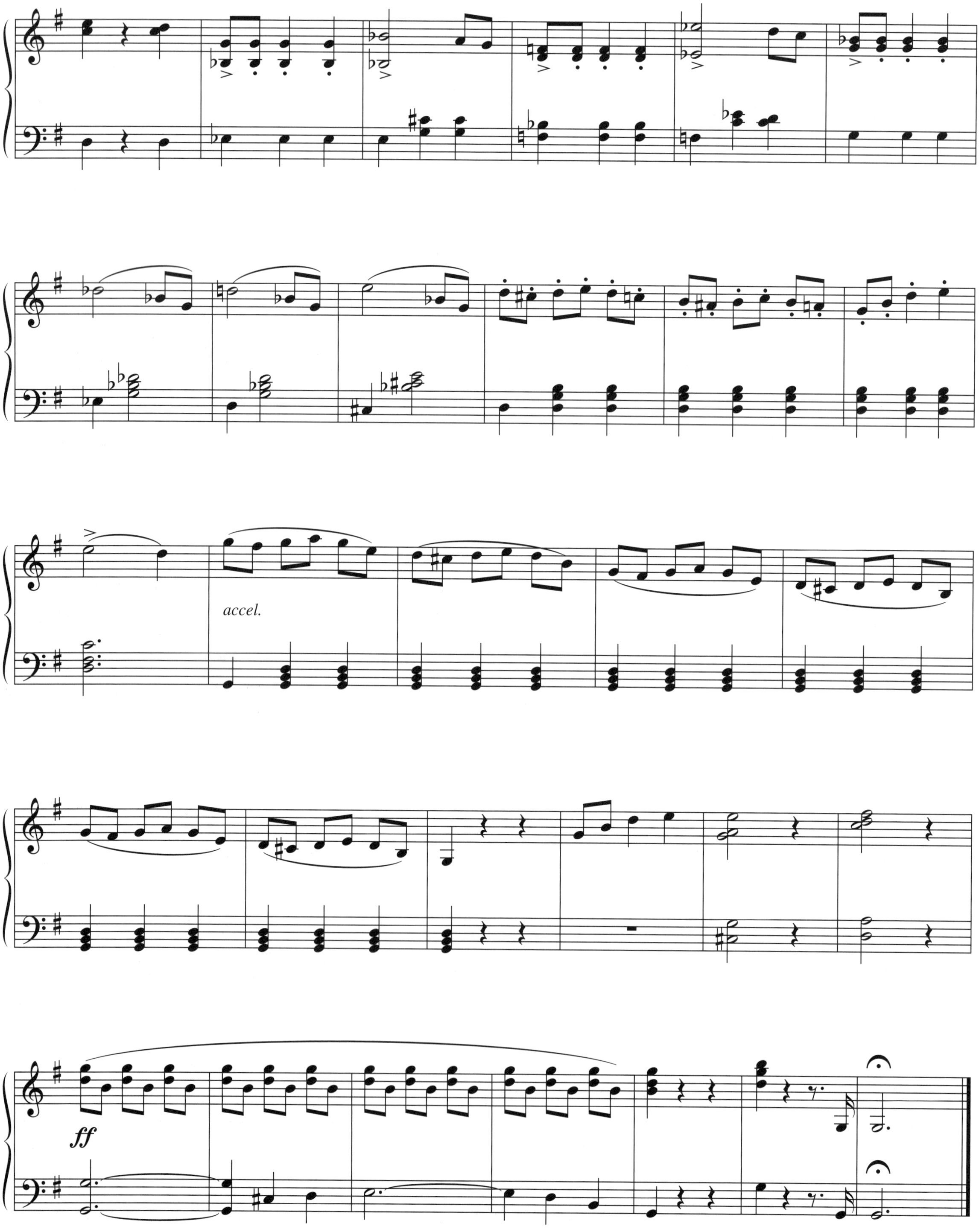
accel.
ff

Tales from the Vienna Woods
Themes

Johann Strauss, Jr.
1825-1899
Op. 325
originally for orchestra

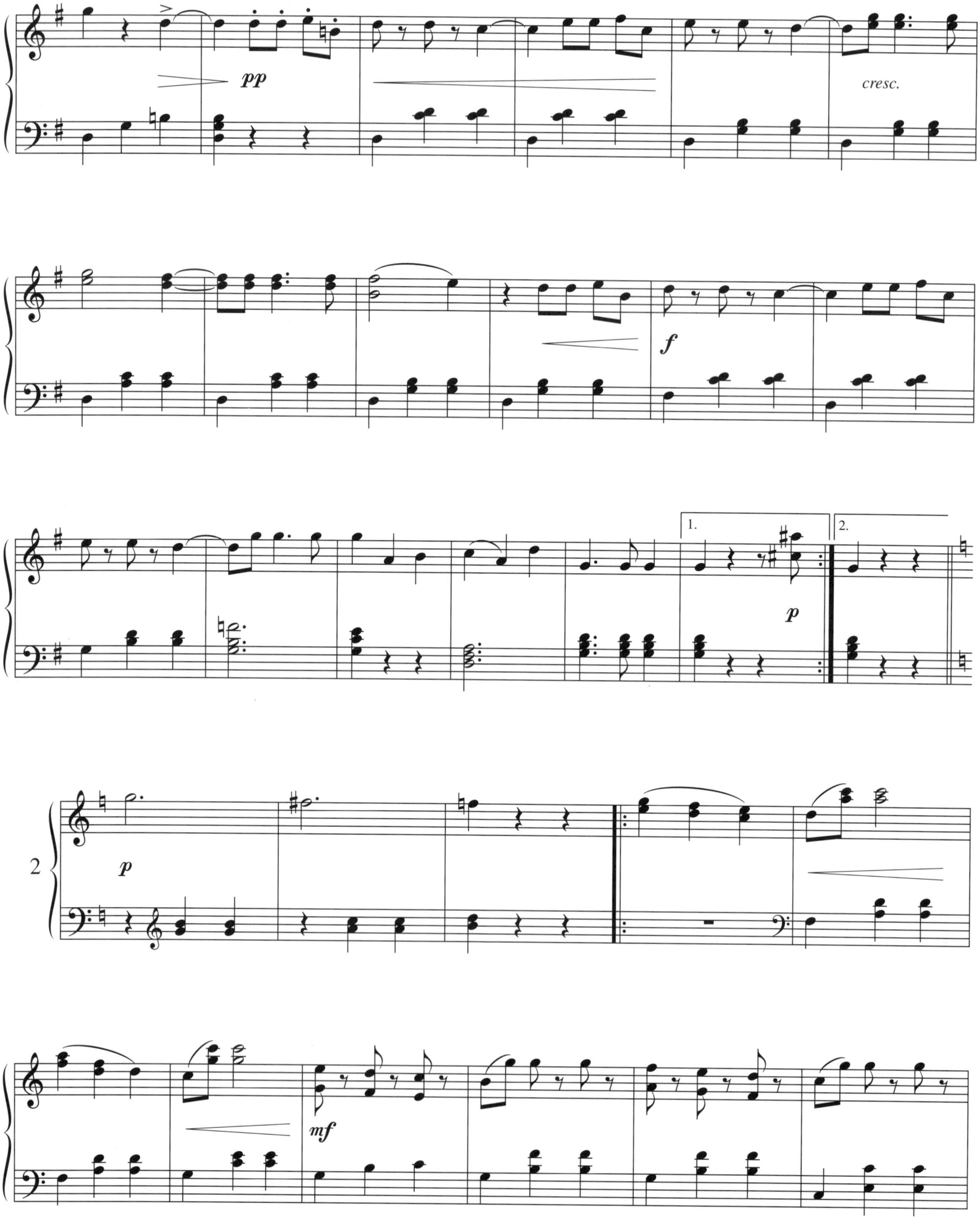
pp
cresc.
f
1.
2.
p
2
p
mf

397

Vienna Life

(Wiener Blut)
Themes

Johann Strauss, Jr.
1825-1899
Op. 354
originally for orchestra

Tempo di Valse

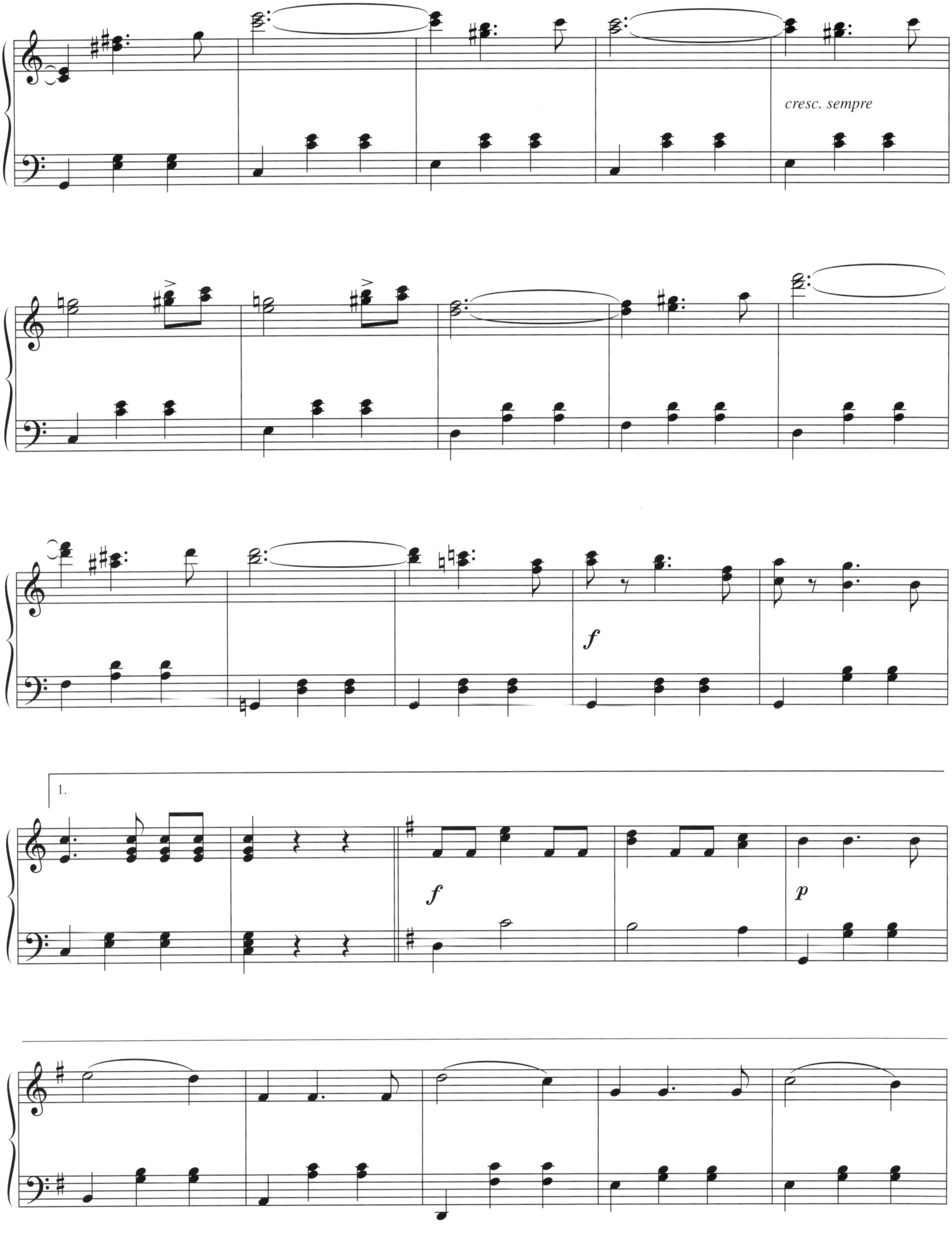
cresc. sempre
f
1.
f
p

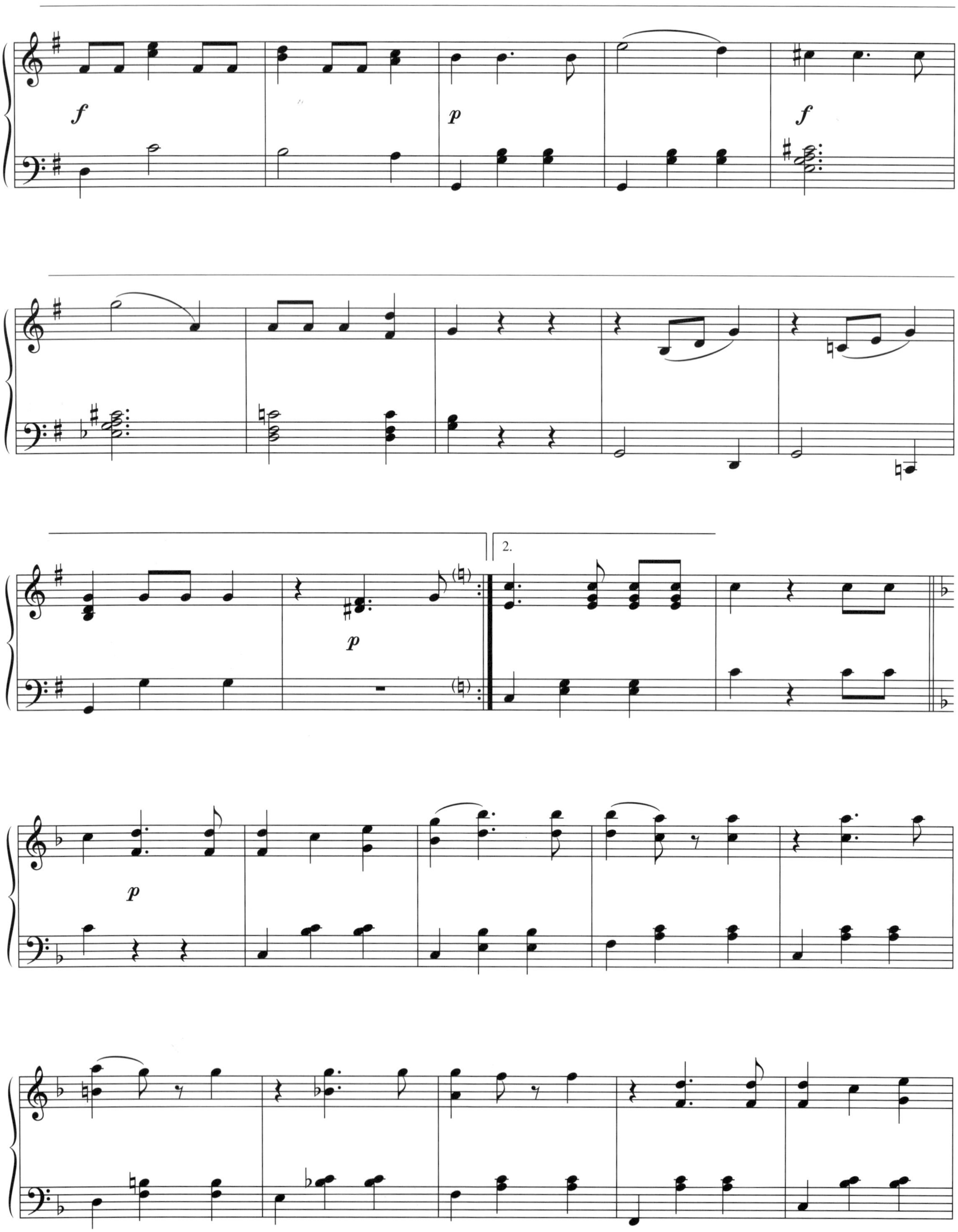
f
p
f
p
2.
p

401

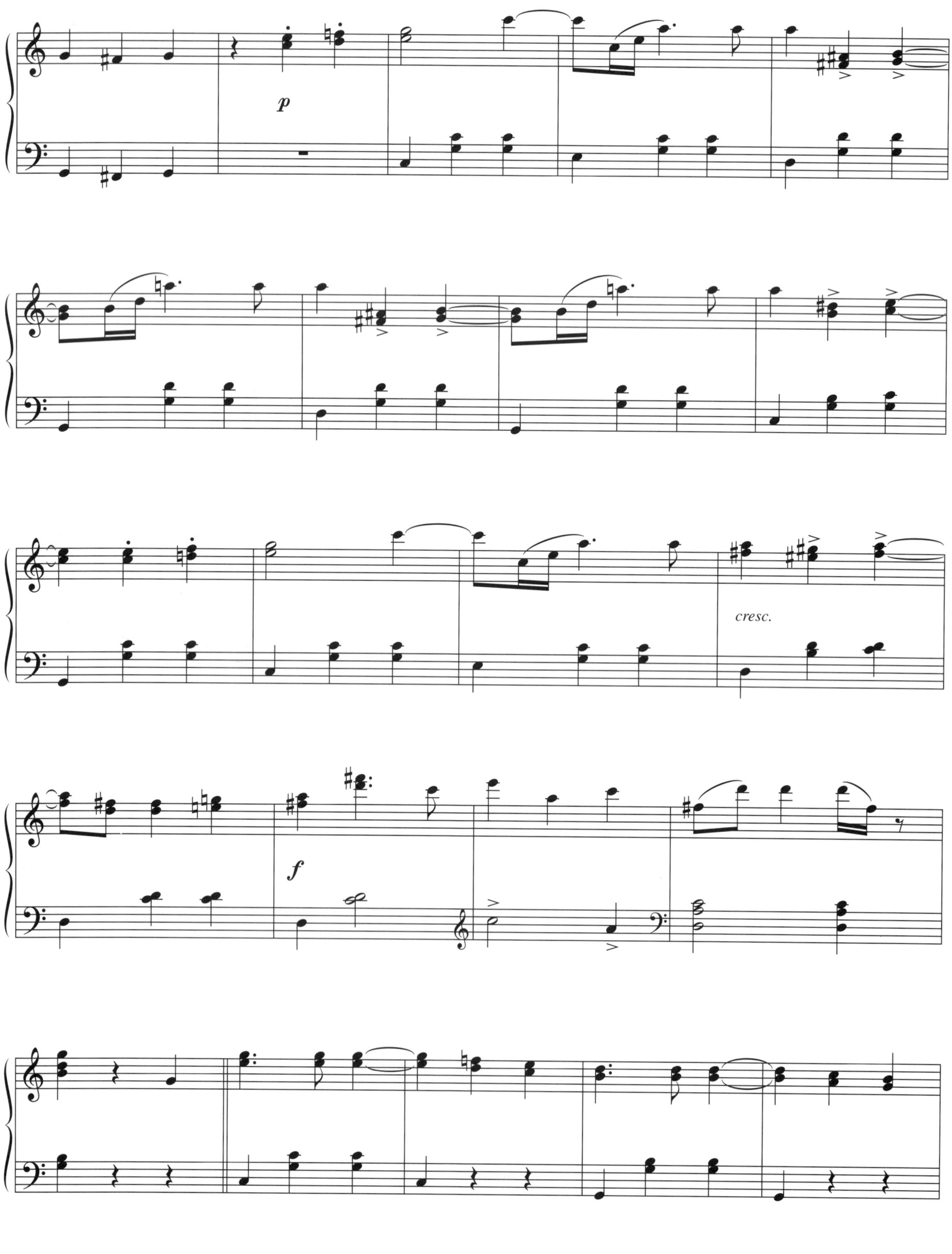
p
cresc.
f

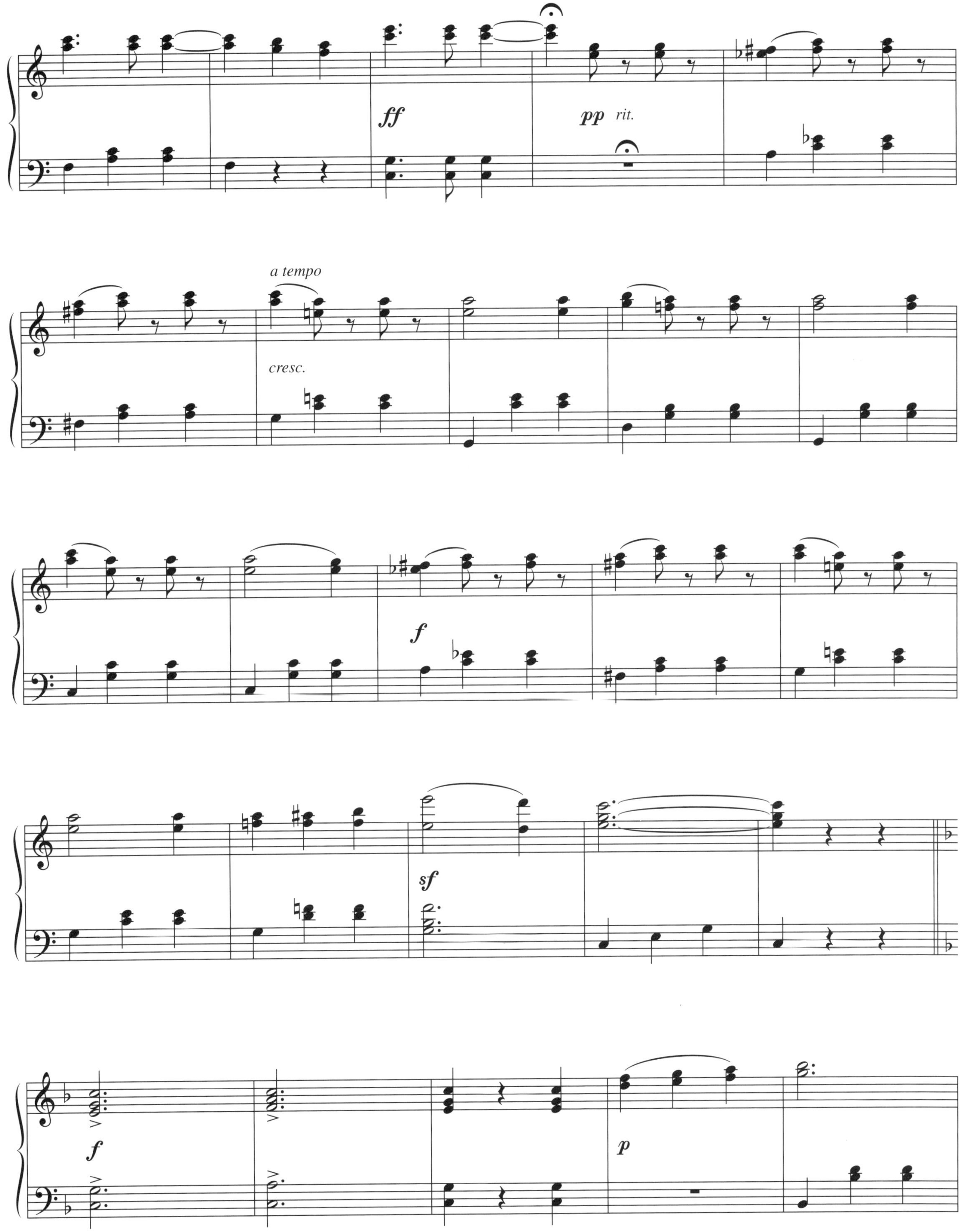
ff
pp
rit.
a tempo
cresc.
f
sf
f
p

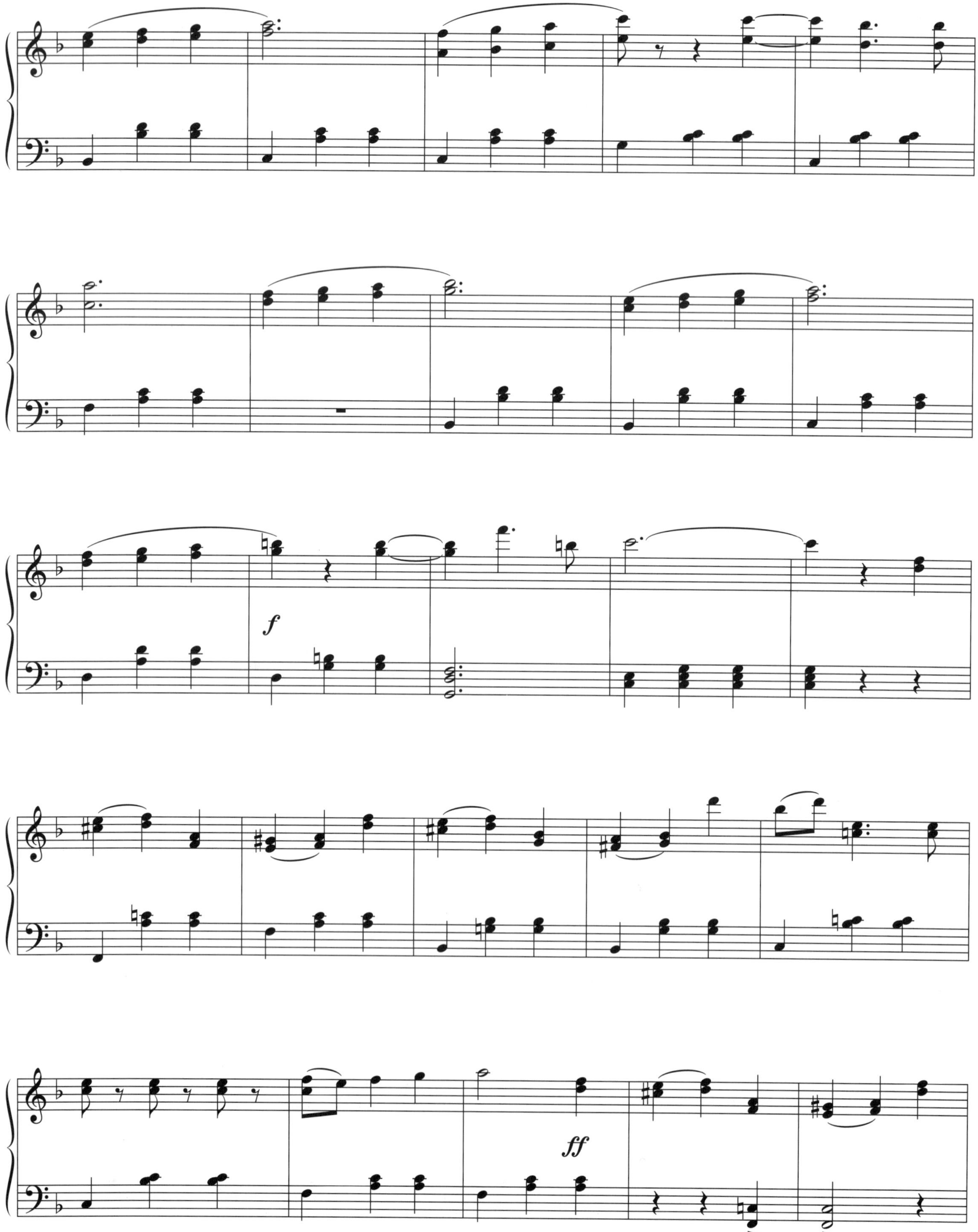
f
ff

405

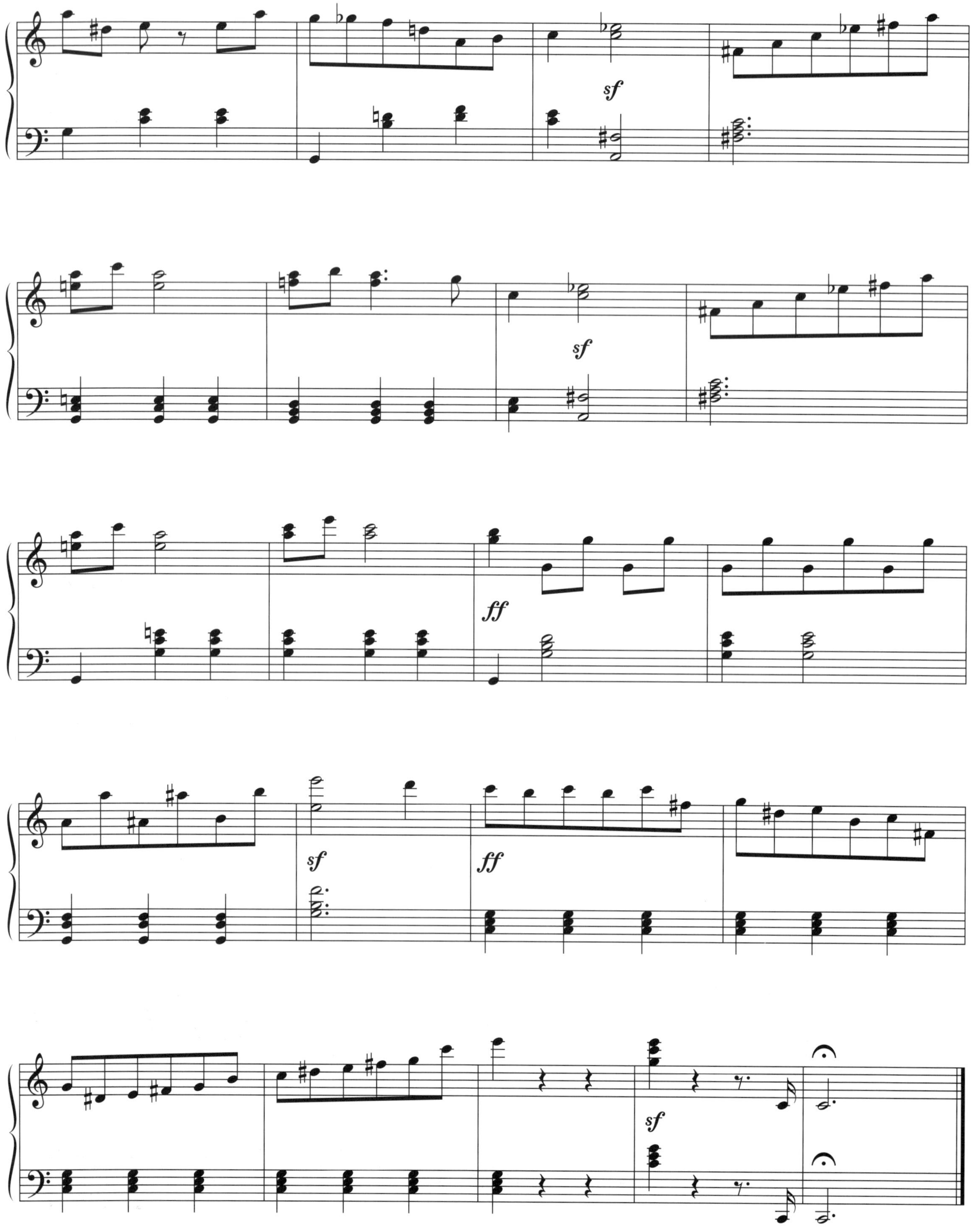
sf
sf
ff
sf
ff
sf

Dance of the Sugar Plum Fairy

from the ballet THE NUTCRACKER

Pyotr Il'yich Tchaikovsky
1840-1893
Op. 71
originally for orchestra

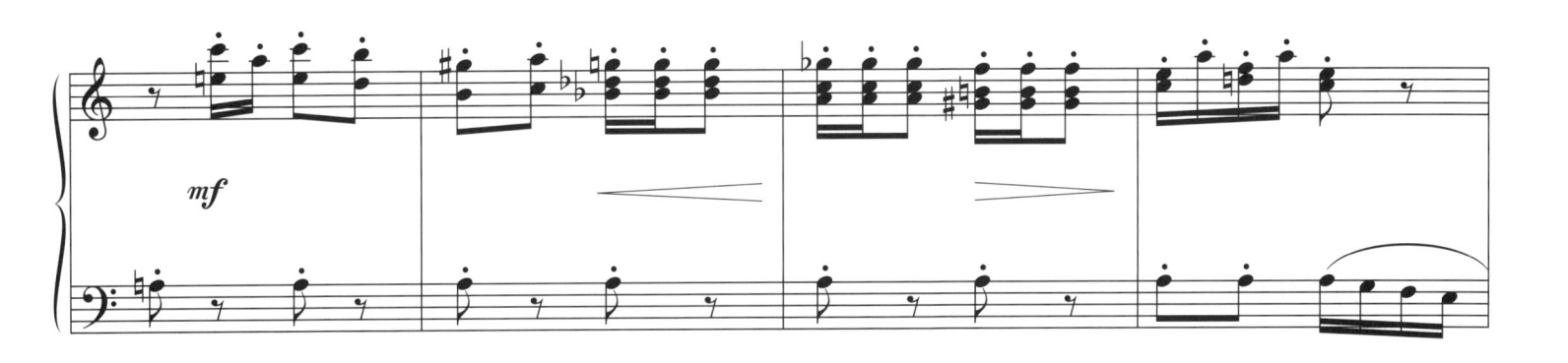

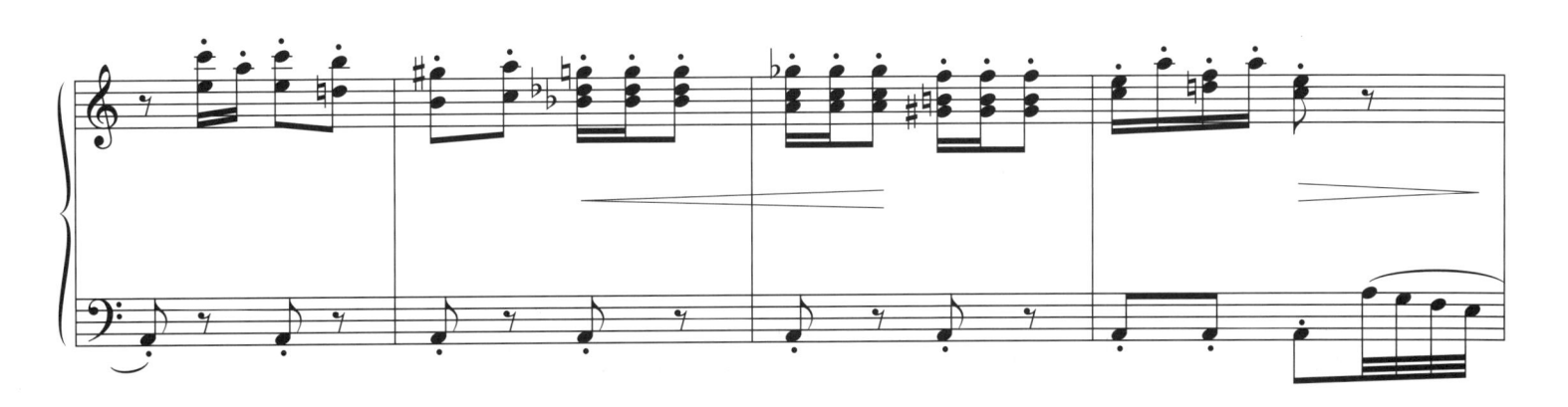

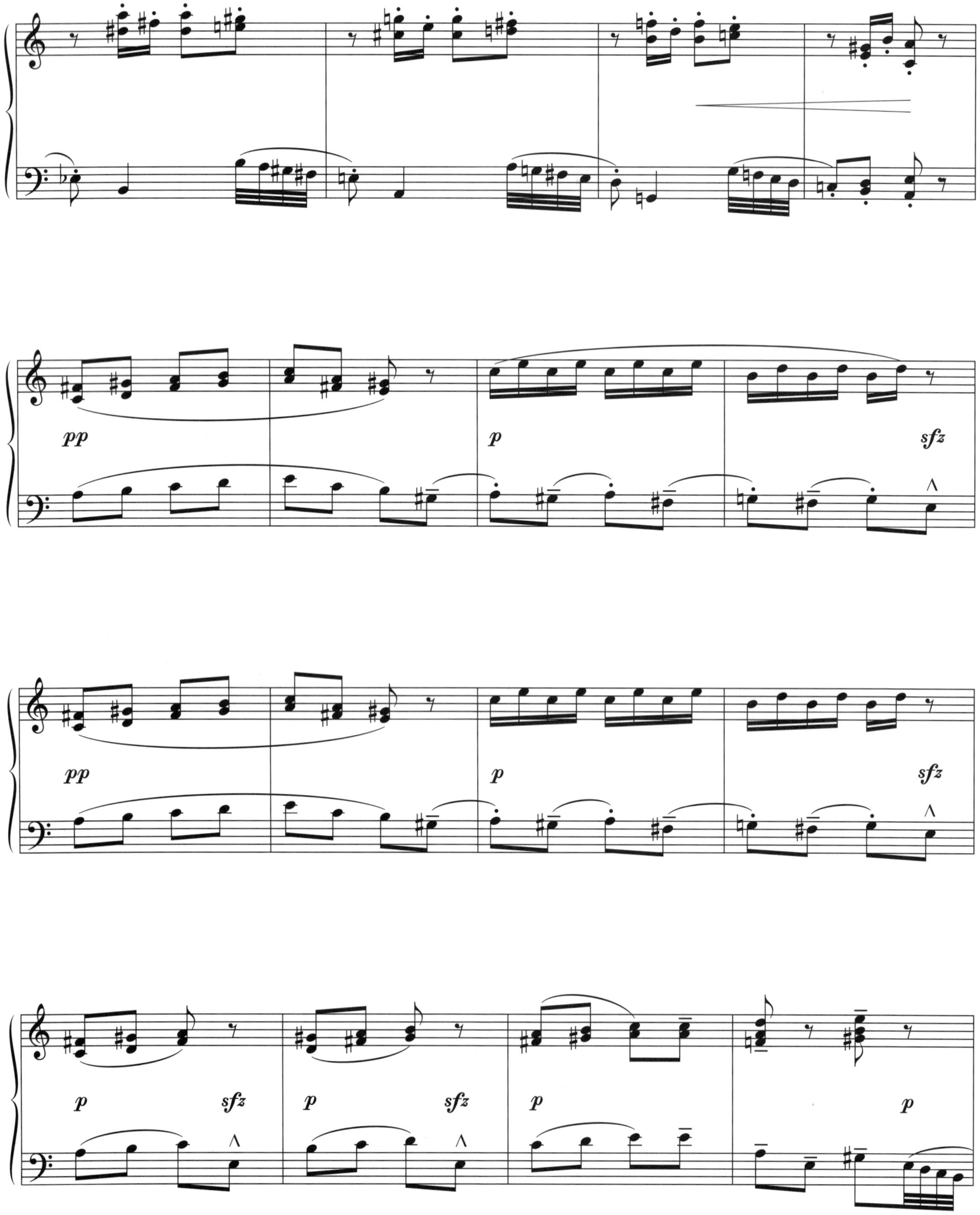
pp
p
sfz
pp
p
sfz
p
sfz
p
sfz
p
p

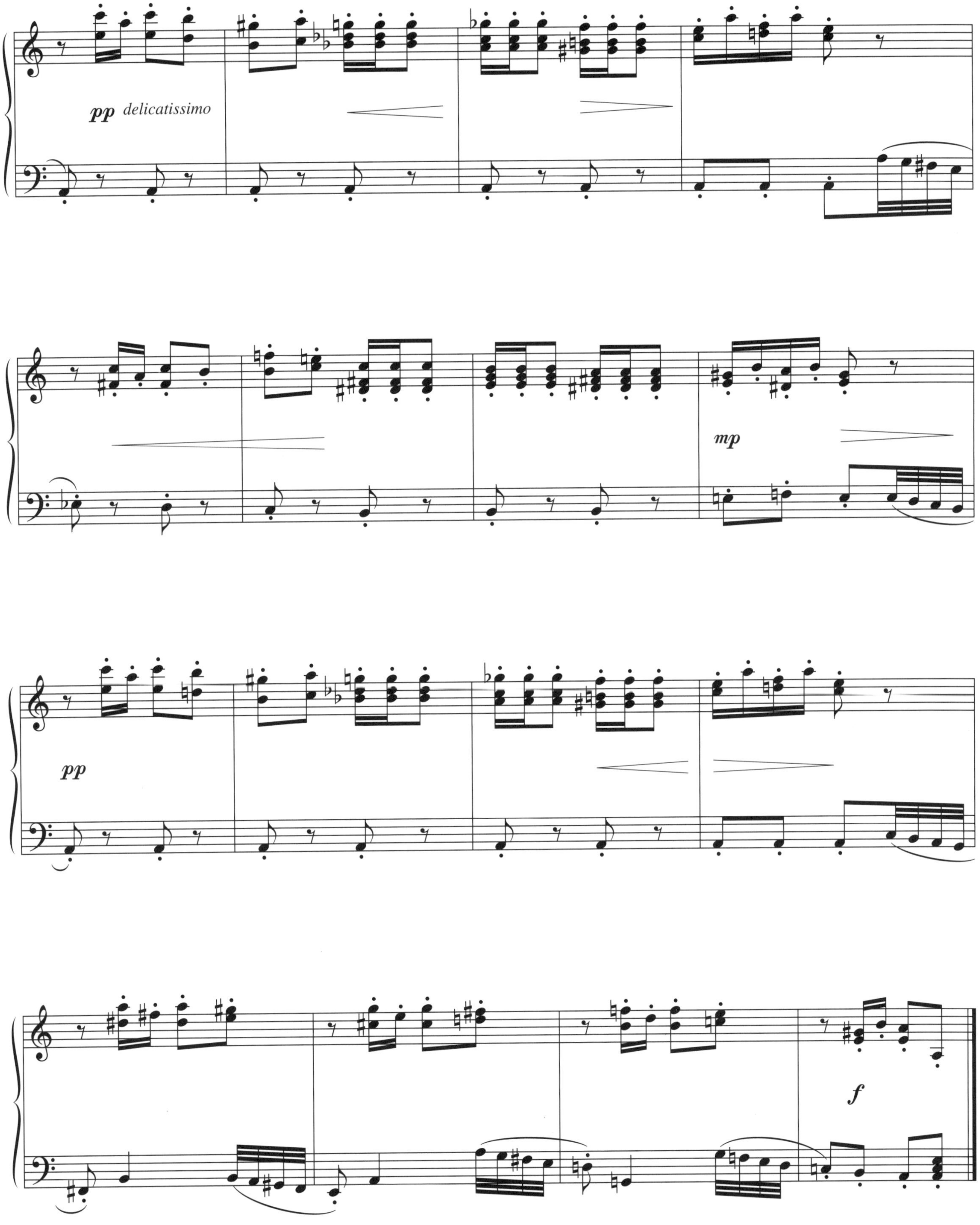
pp delicatissimo
mp
pp
f

Dance of the Reed-Flutes
from the ballet THE NUTCRACKER

Pyotr Il'yich Tchaikovsky
1840-1893
Op. 71
originally for orchestra

Moderato assai

411

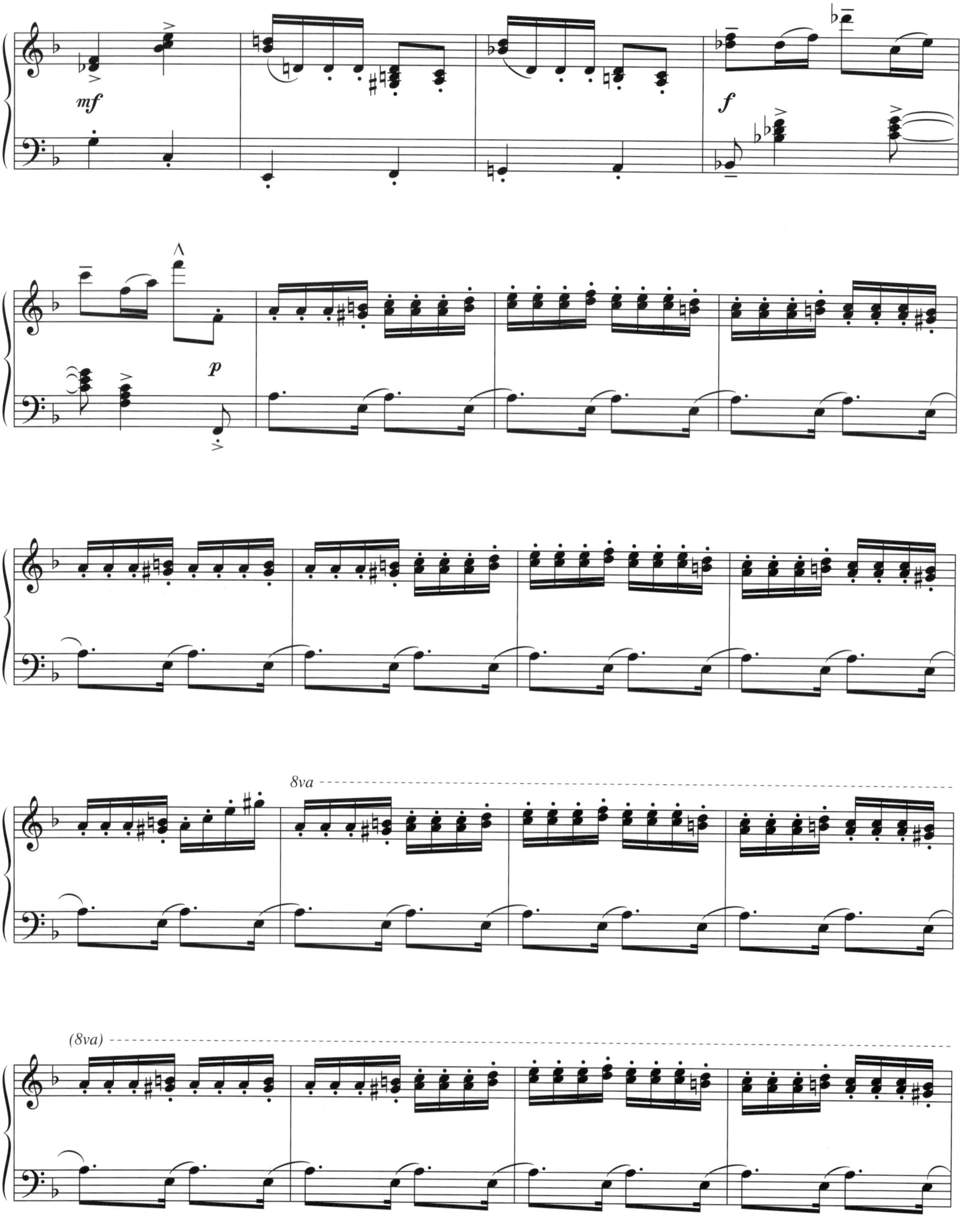
mf
f
p
8va
(8va)

413

Waltz of the Flowers

from the ballet THE NUTCRACKER
Excerpt

Pyotr Il'yich Tchaikovsky
1840-1893
Op. 71
originally for orchestra

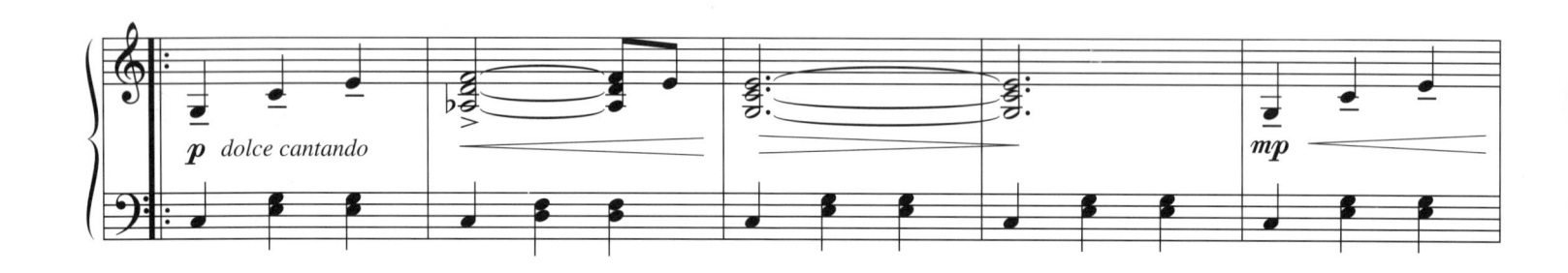

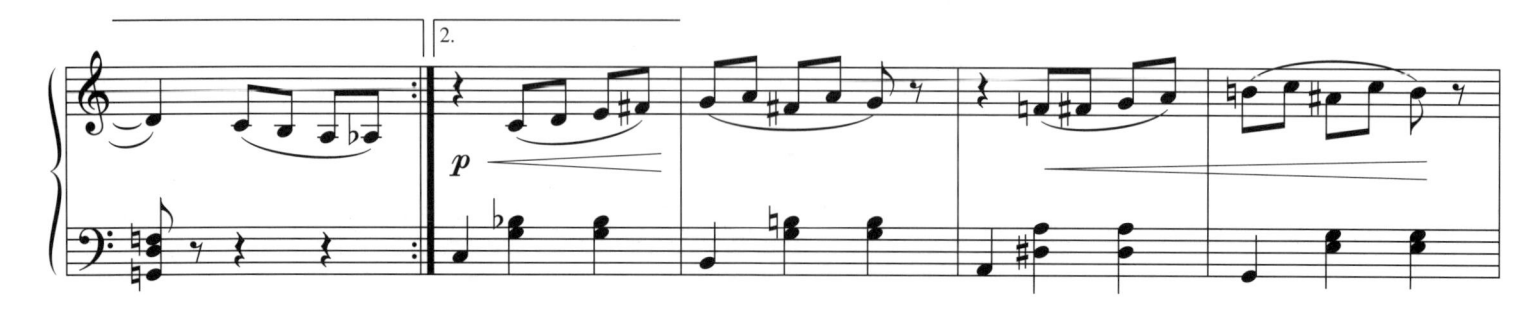

original key: D Major

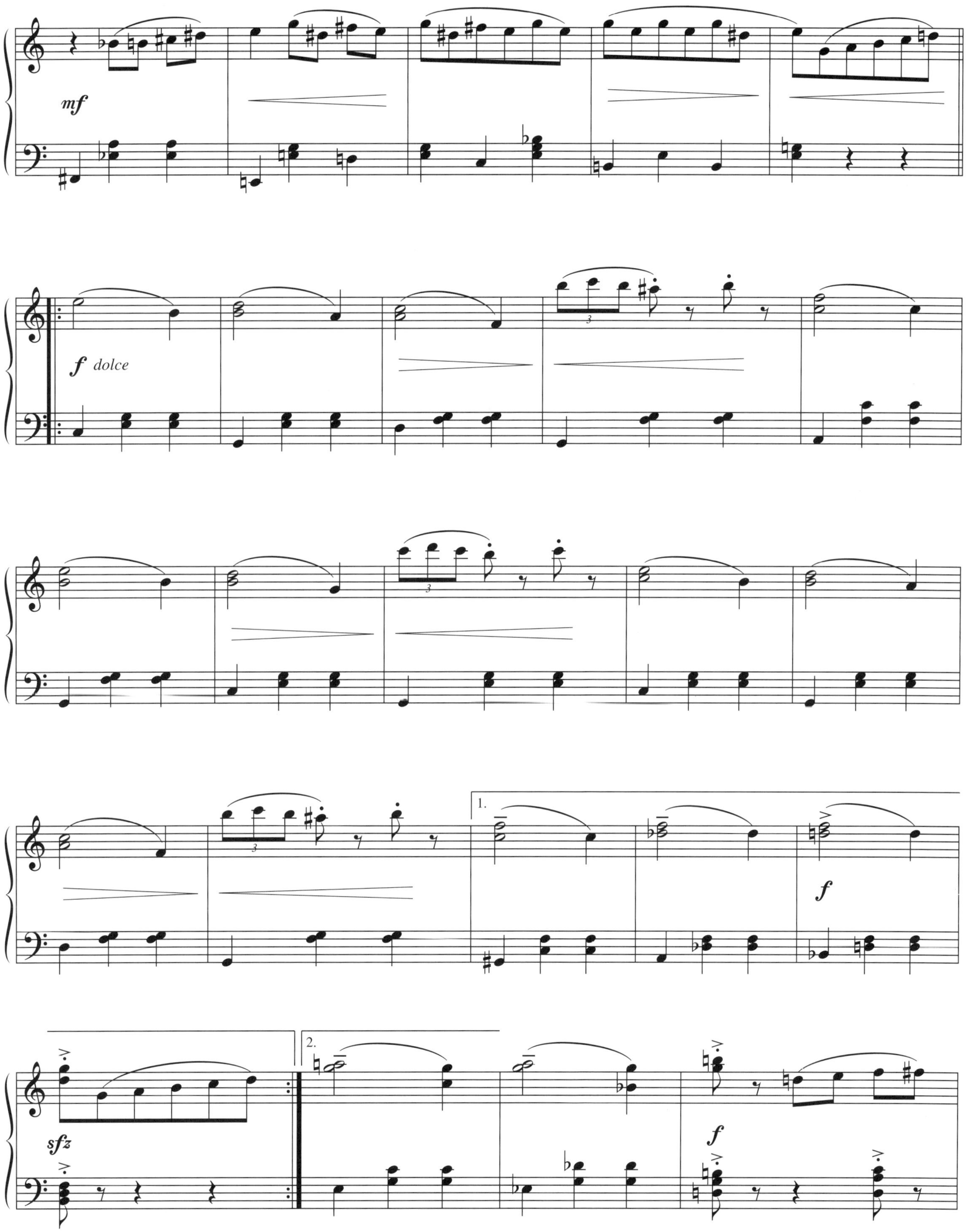
mf
f dolce
1.
f
sfz
2.
f

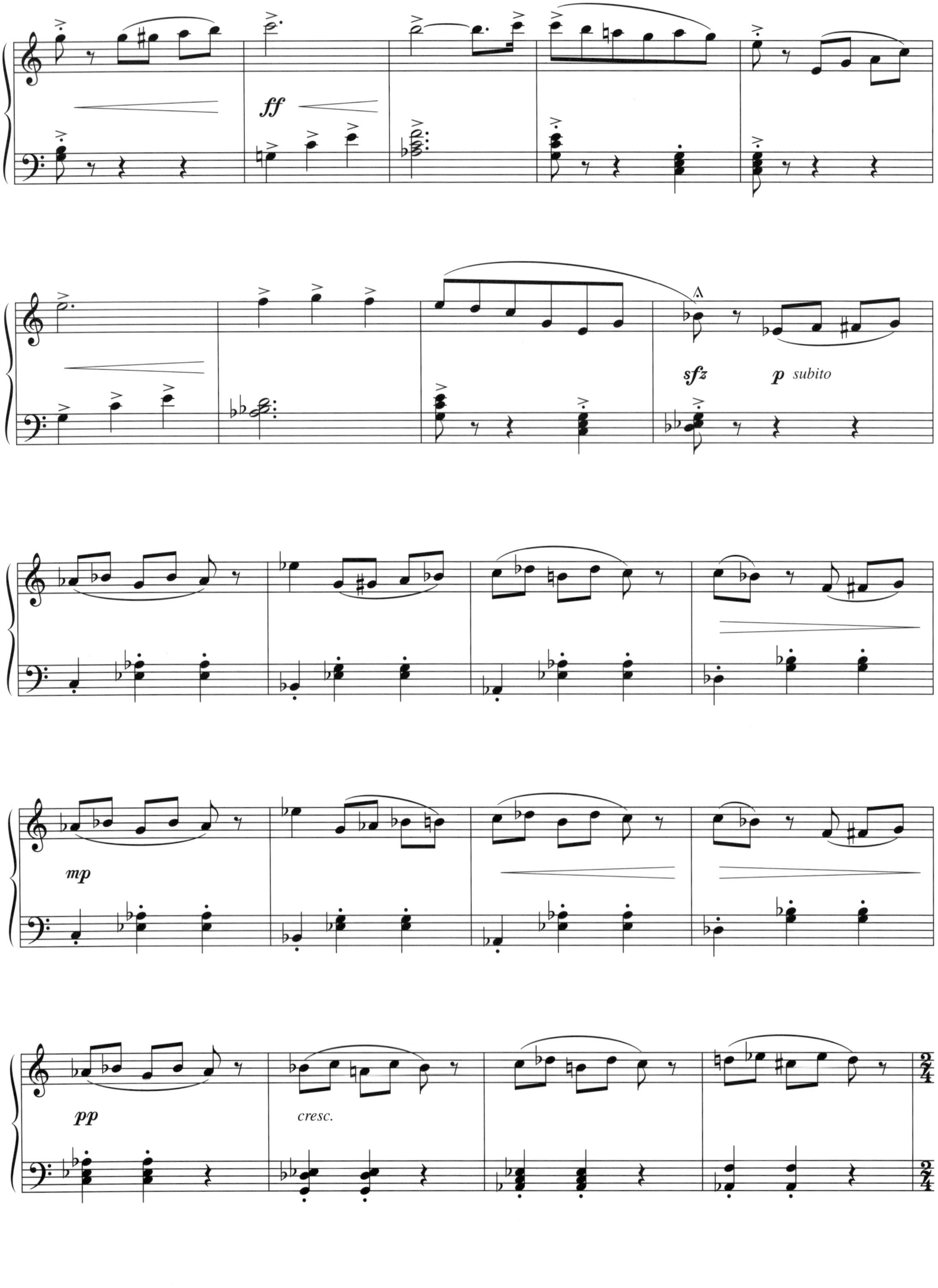
ff
sfz
p subito
mp
pp
cresc.

417

p subito
cresc.
f
ff brillante
sfz
sfz
sfz
sfz
sfz
fff largamente
sfz
rit.
sfz

The Sleeping Beauty Waltz

from the ballet THE SLEEPING BEAUTY
Excerpt

Pyotr Il'yich Tchaikovsky
1840-1893
Op. 66
originally for orchestra

Tempo di Valse

original key: B-flat Major

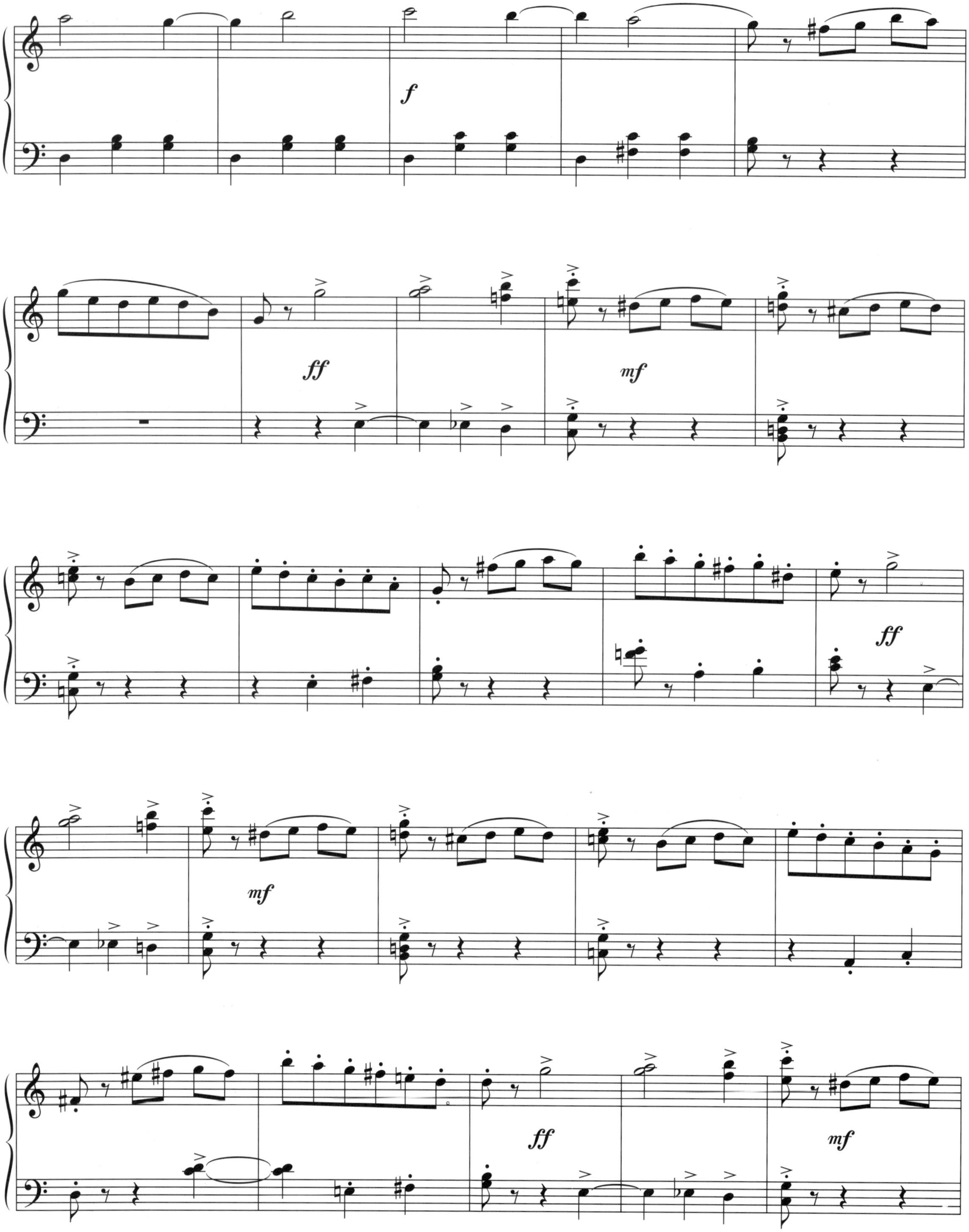
f
ff
mf
ff
mf
ff
mf

421

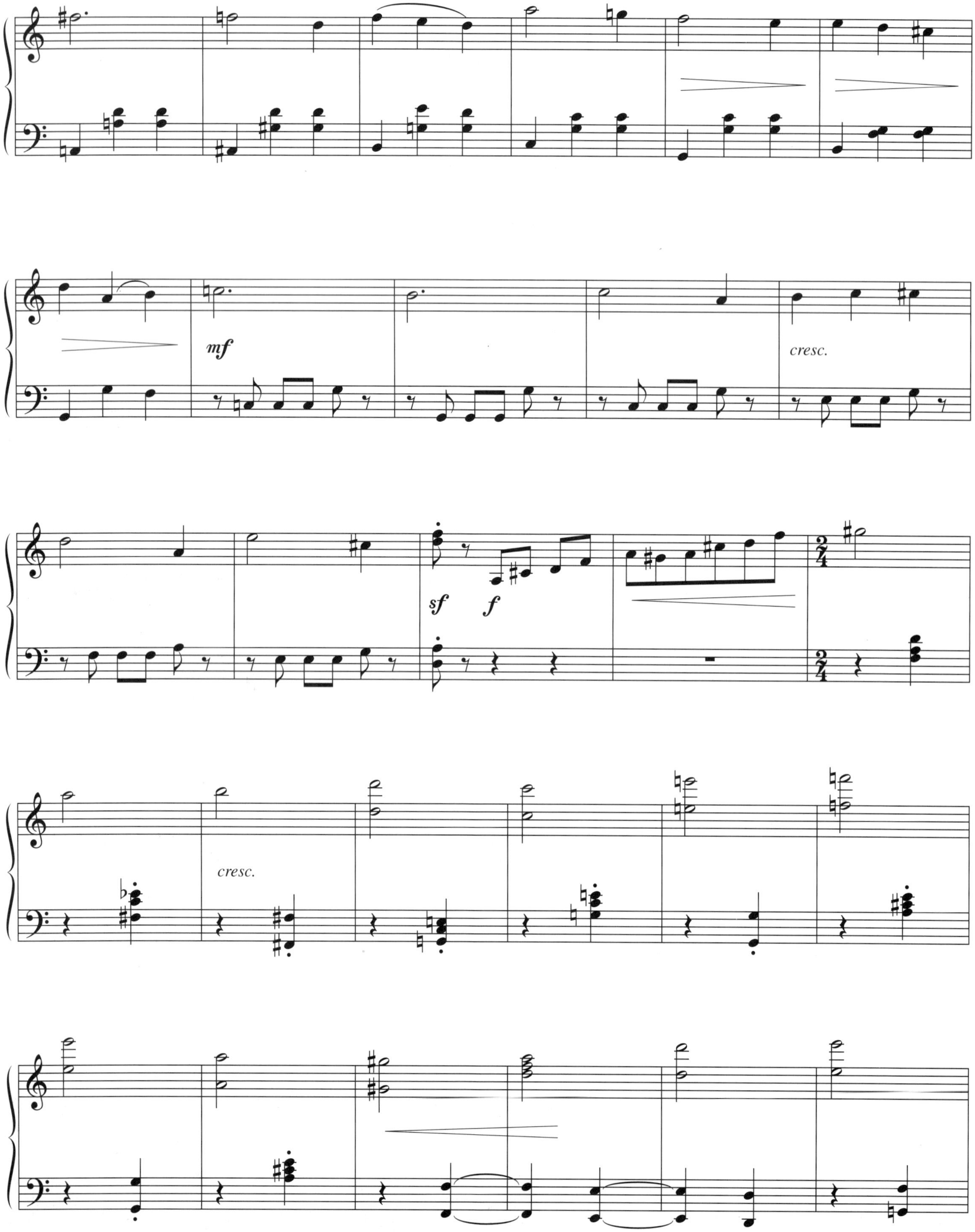
mf
cresc.
sf
f
cresc.

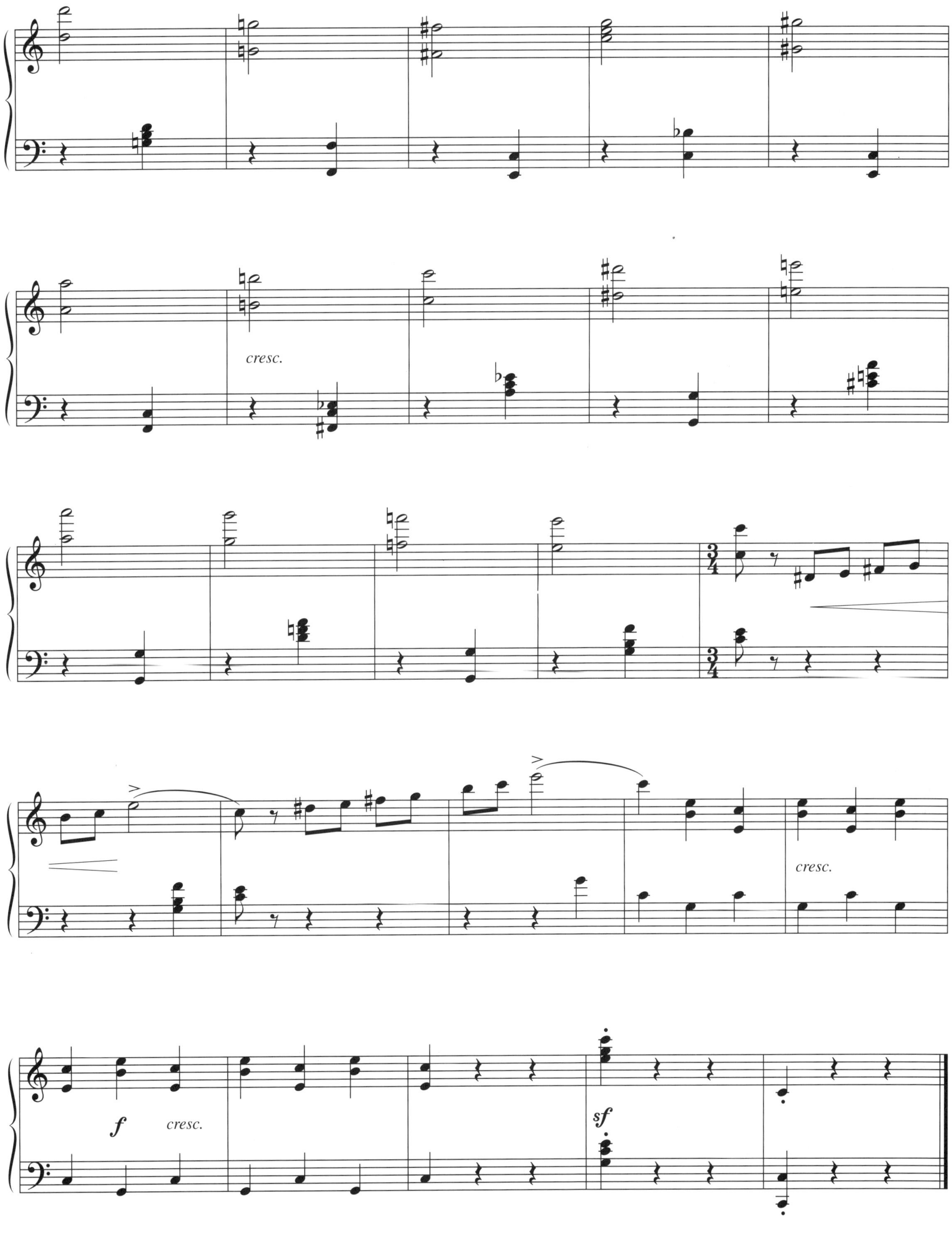
cresc.
cresc.
f
cresc.
sf

1812 Overture

Excerpt

Pyotr Il'yich Tchaikovsky
1840-1893
Op. 49
originally for orchestra

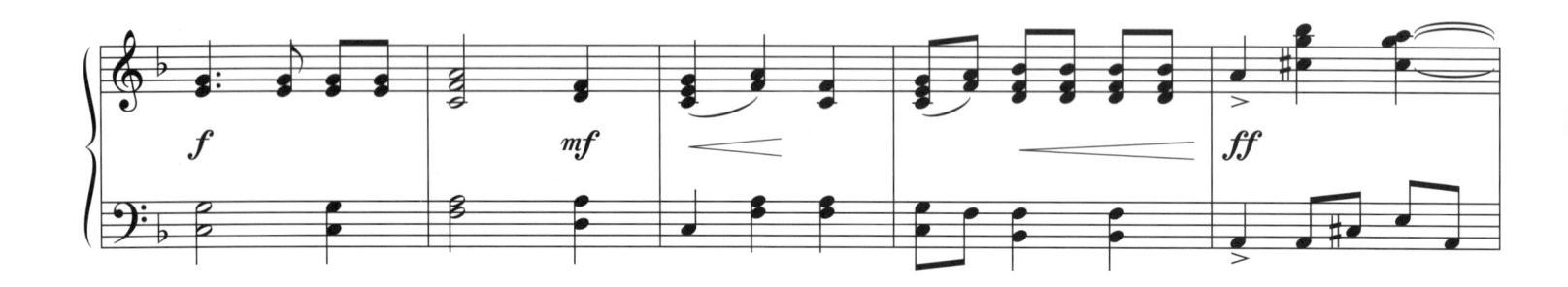

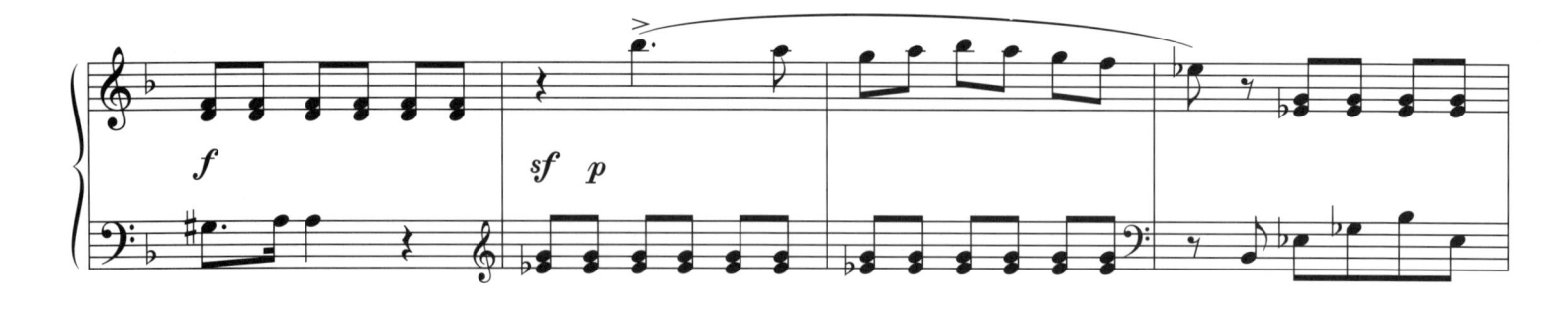

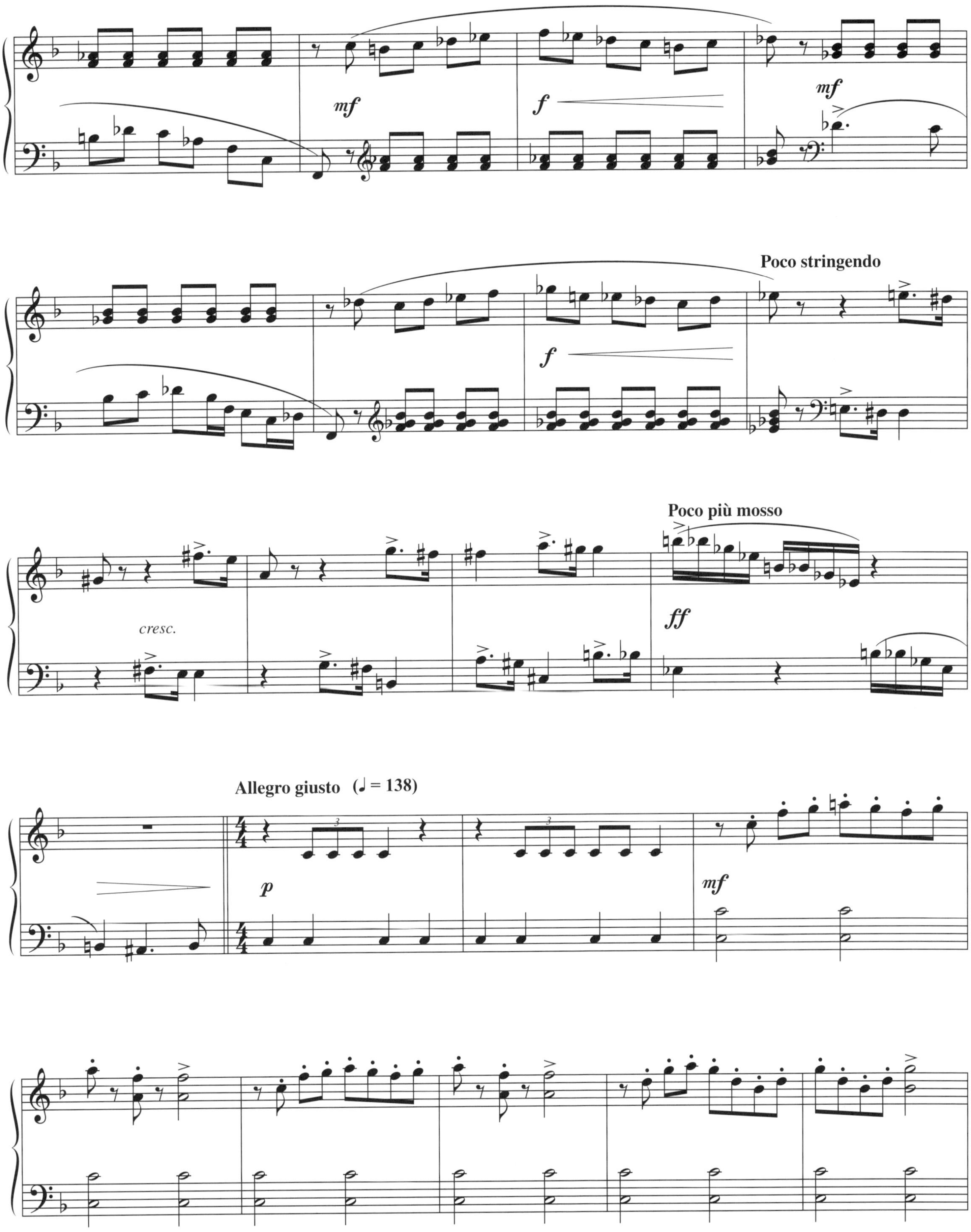
Poco stringendo
cresc.
Poco più mosso
Allegro giusto (♩ = 138)

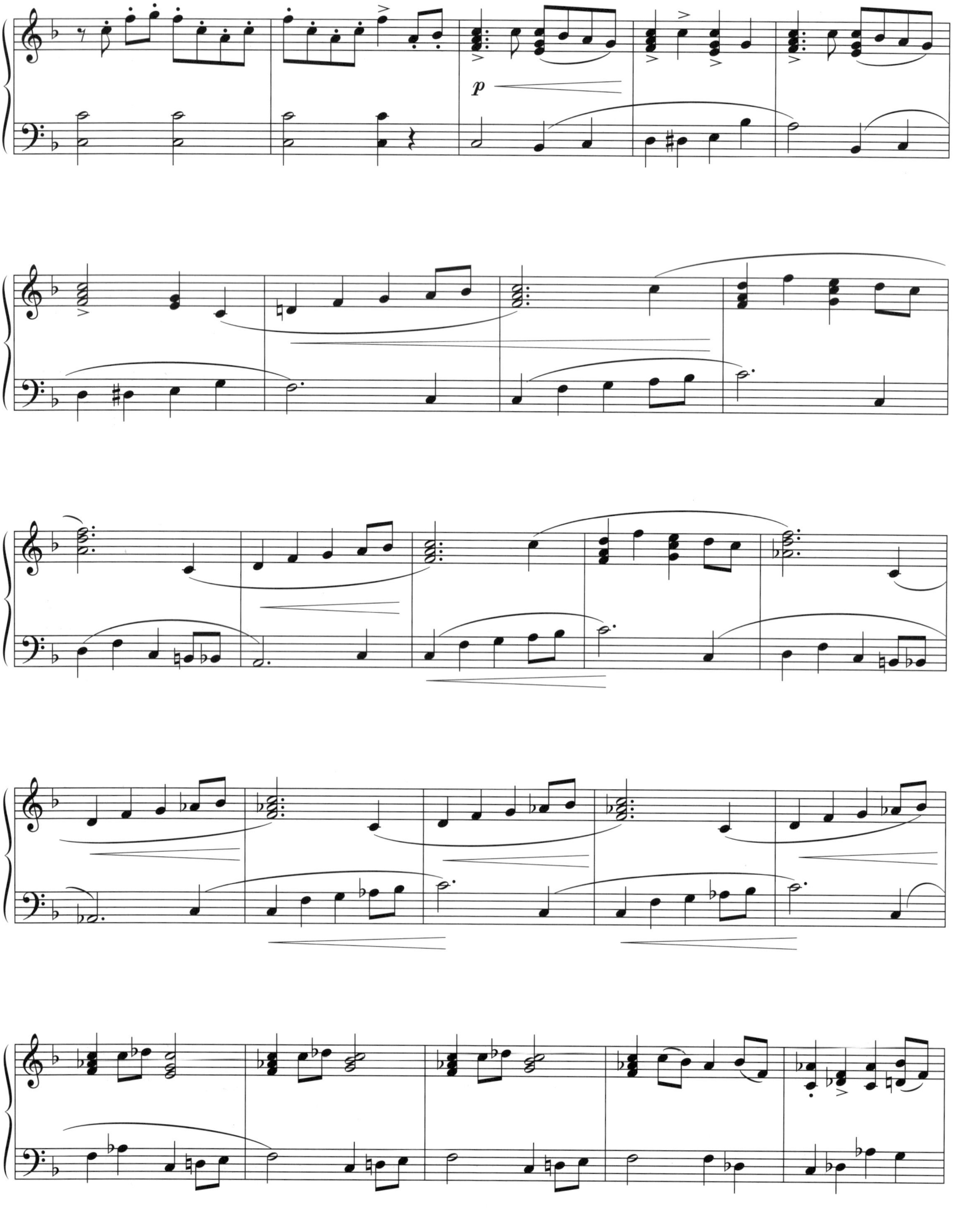

427

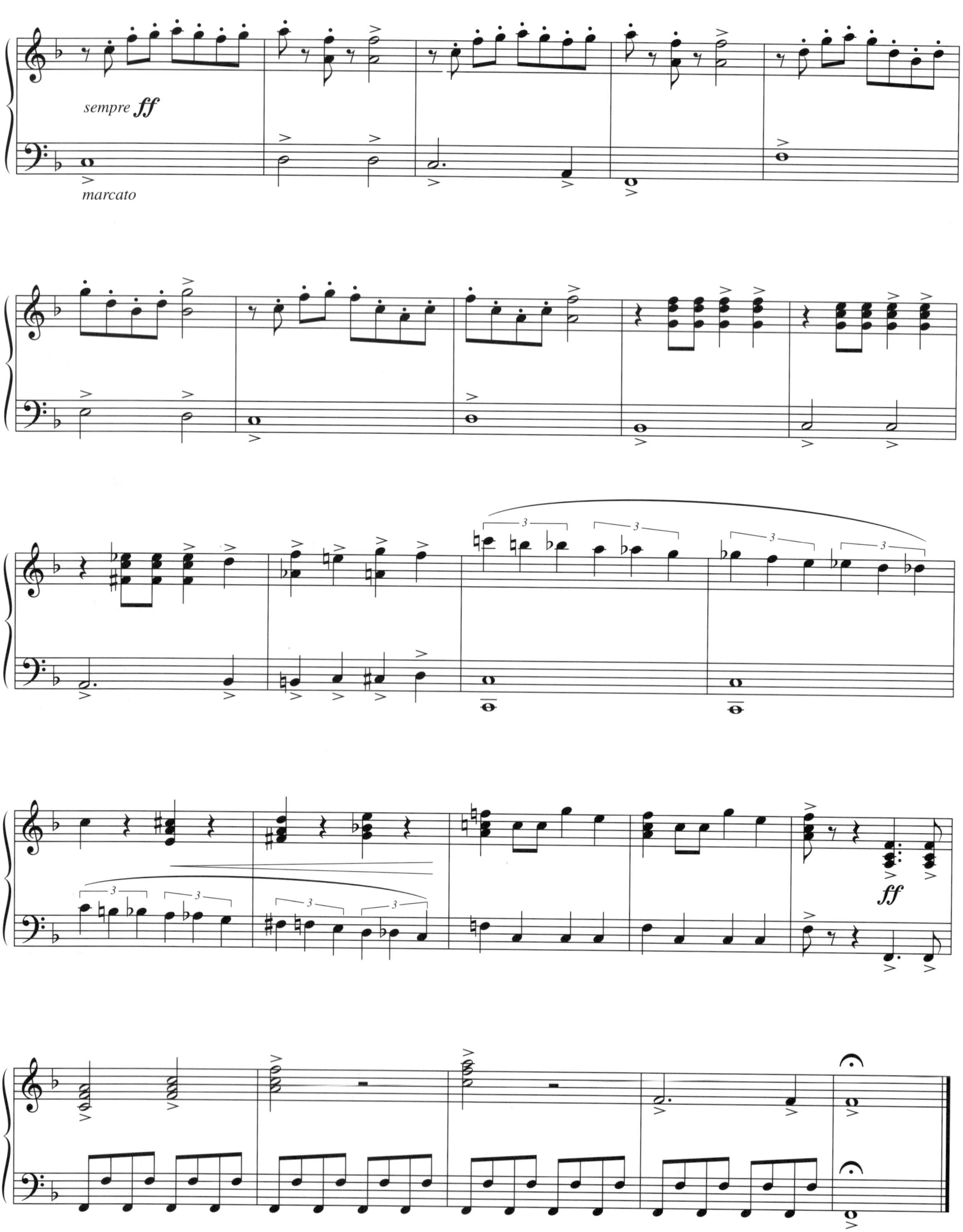
sempre ff
marcato
3
ff

Marche Slav

Themes

Pyotr Il'yich Tchaikovsky
1840-1893
Op. 31
originally for orchestra

Grave quasi marcia funebre

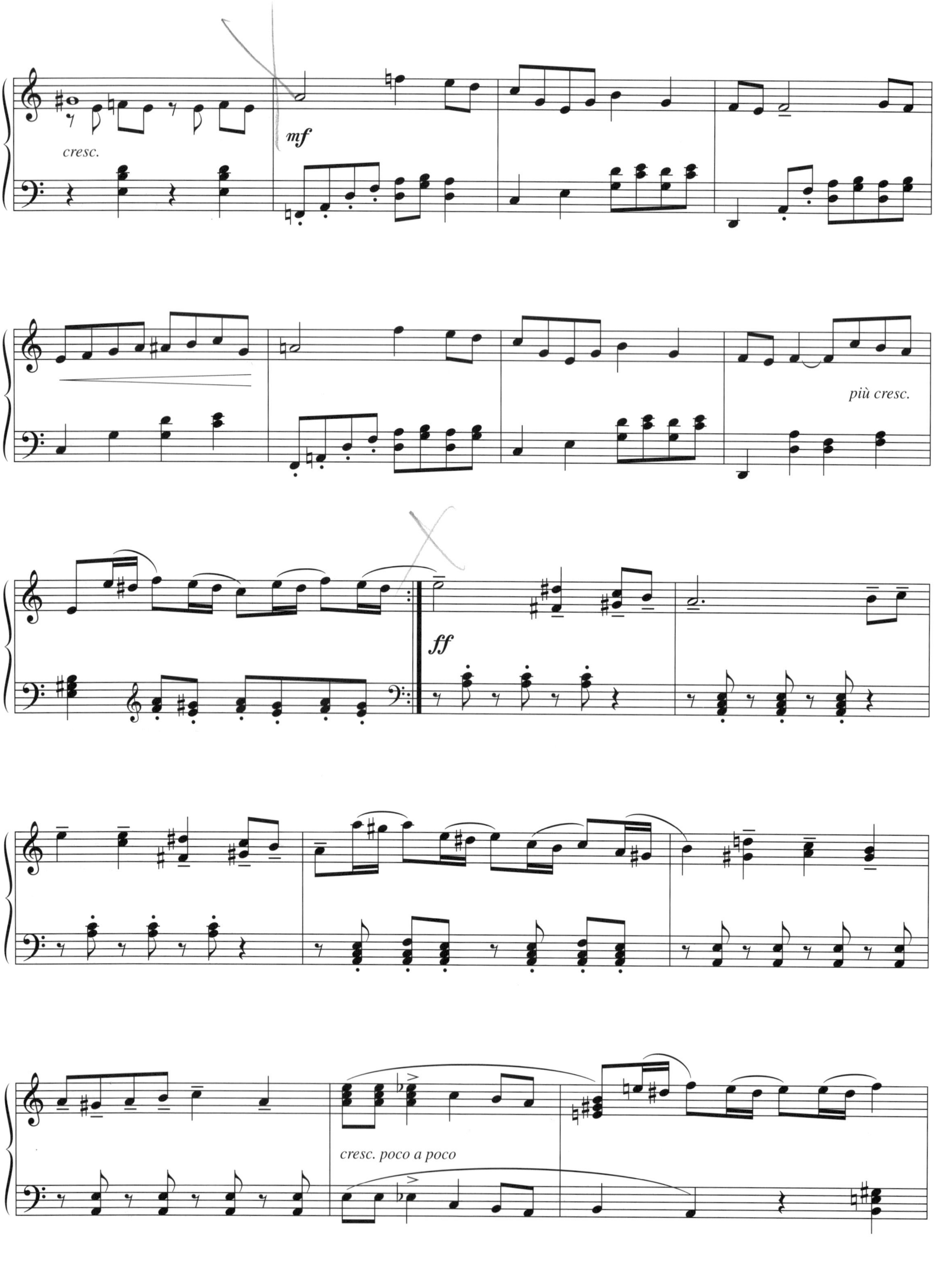
cresc.
mf
più cresc.
ff
cresc. poco a poco

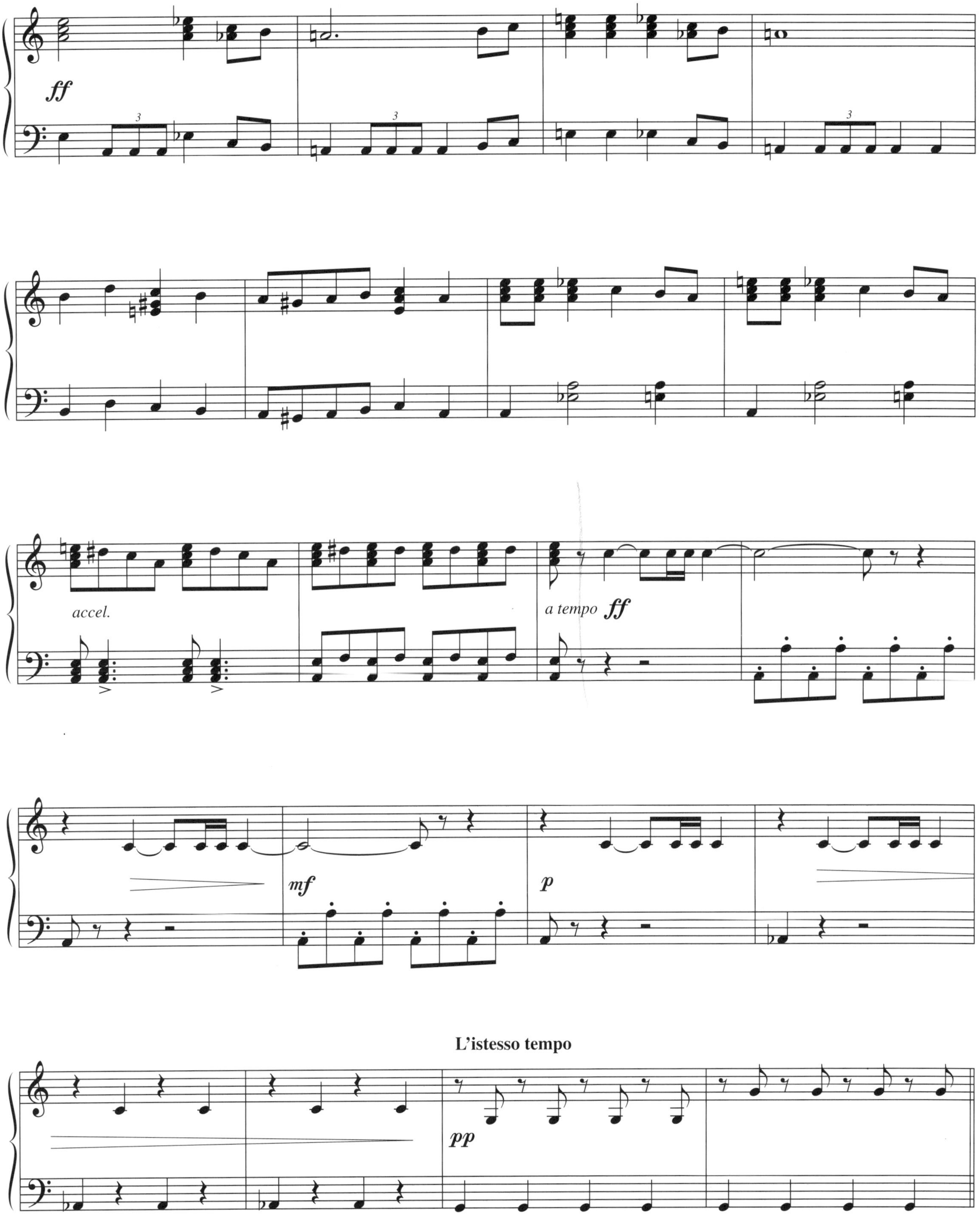
ff
3
accel.
a tempo ff
mf
p
L'istesso tempo
pp

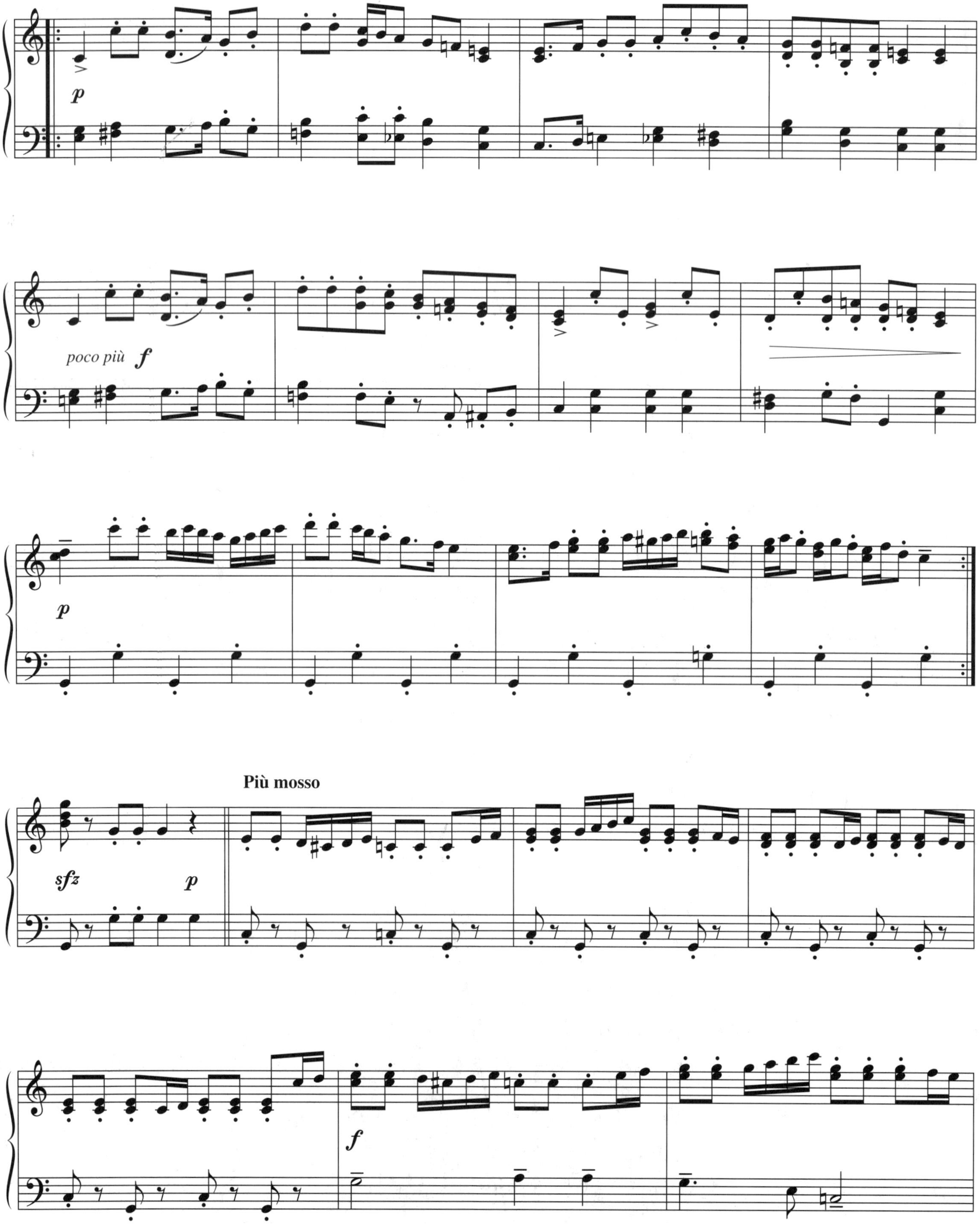
p
poco più f
p
Più mosso
sfz
p
f

433

Piano Concerto No. 1

First Movement Excerpt

Pyotr Il'yich Tchaikovsky
1840-1893
Op. 23
originally for orchestra

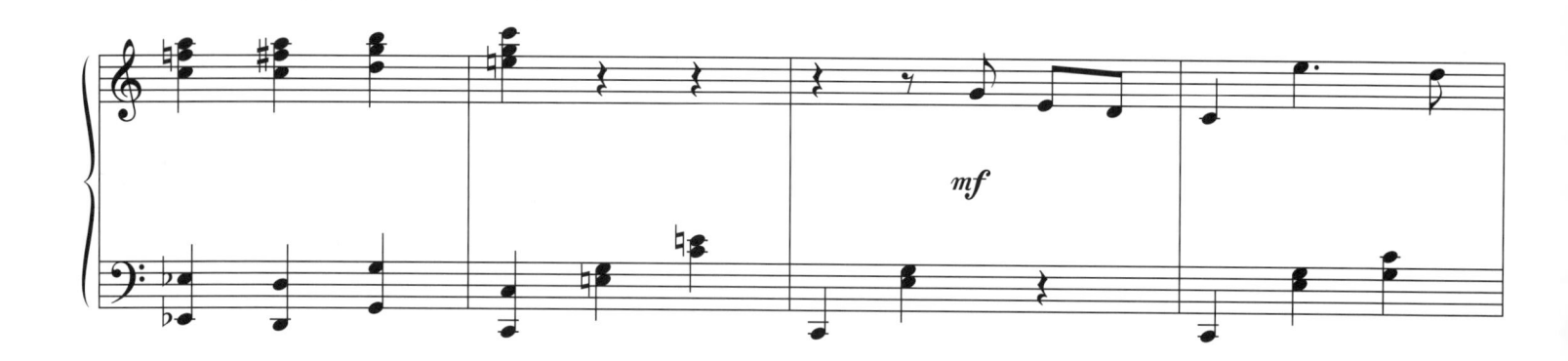

Andante maestoso

original key: B-flat Major

Copyright © 2000 by HAL LEONARD CORPORATION
International Copyright Secured All Rights Reserved

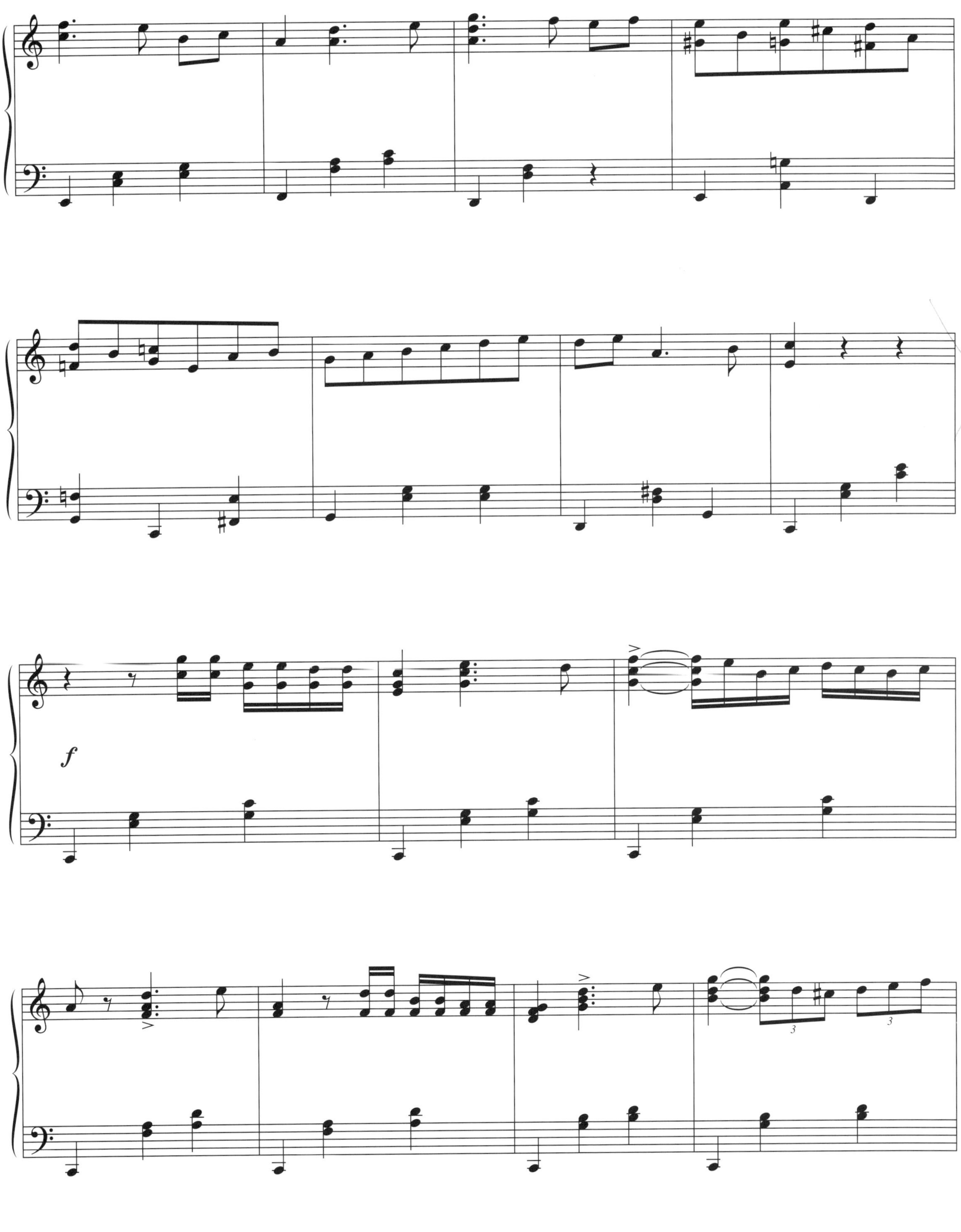
f

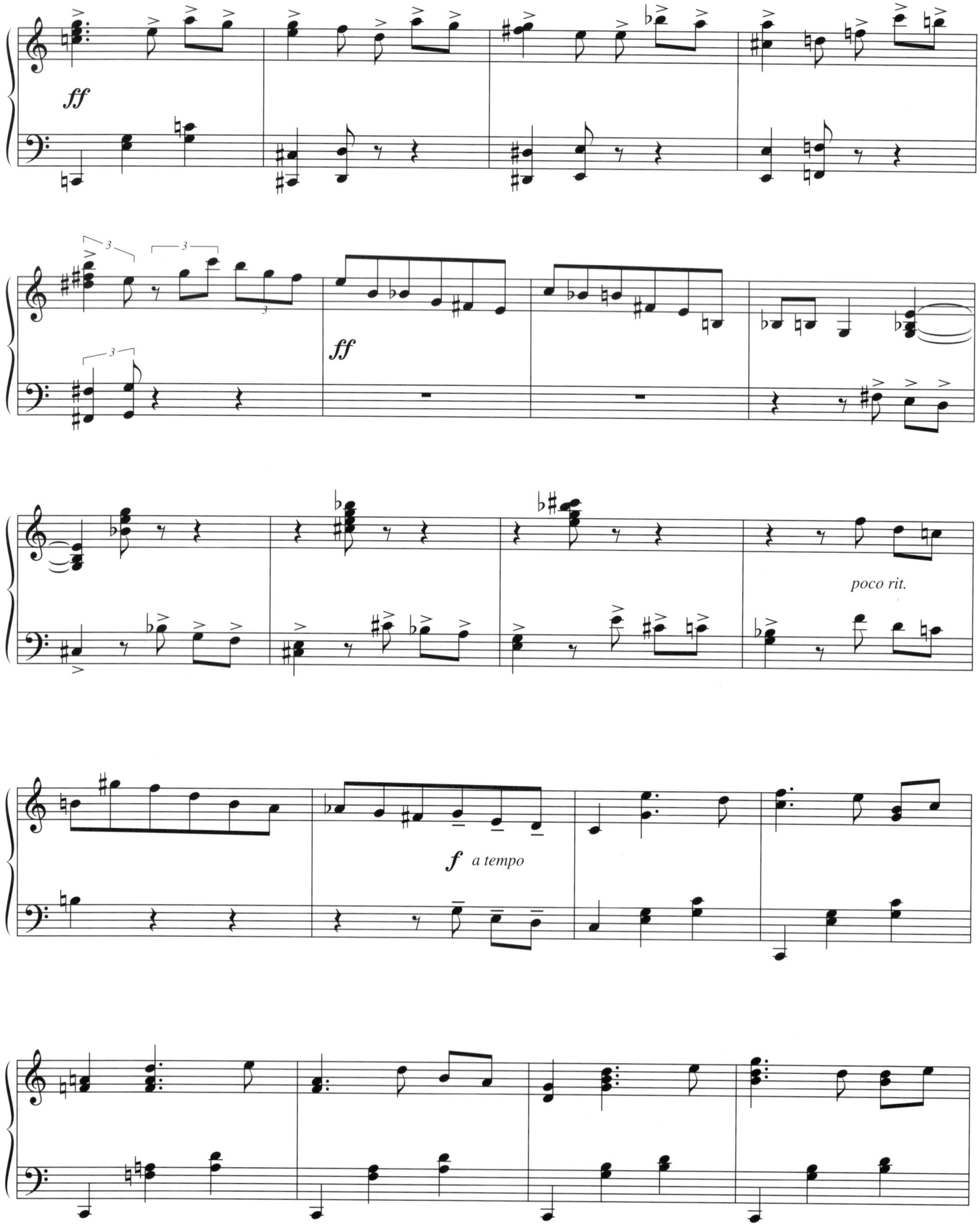
ff
ff
poco rit.
f a tempo

437

Romeo and Juliet

FANTASY OVERTURE
Excerpt

Pyotr Il'yich Tchaikovsky
1840-1893
originally for orchestra

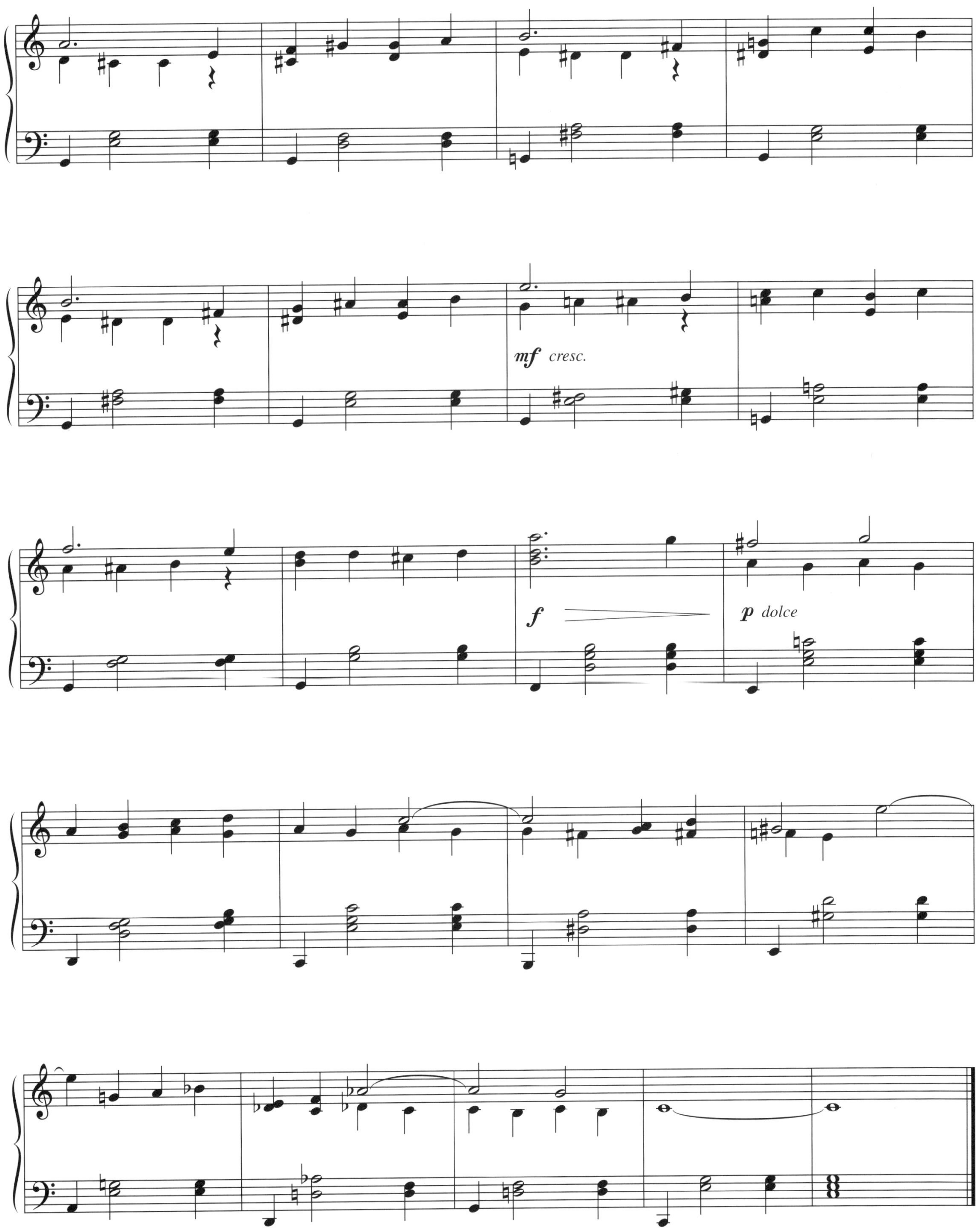
mf cresc.
f
p dolce

ROMEO AND JULIET
Fantasy Overture
"Love Theme"

Pyotr Il'yich Tchaikovsky
1840-1893
originally for orchestra

Allegro giusto, con espressione

mf legato e dolce

pp

sim.

original key: D-flat Major

Copyright © 2000 by HAL LEONARD CORPORATION
International Copyright Secured   All Rights Reserved

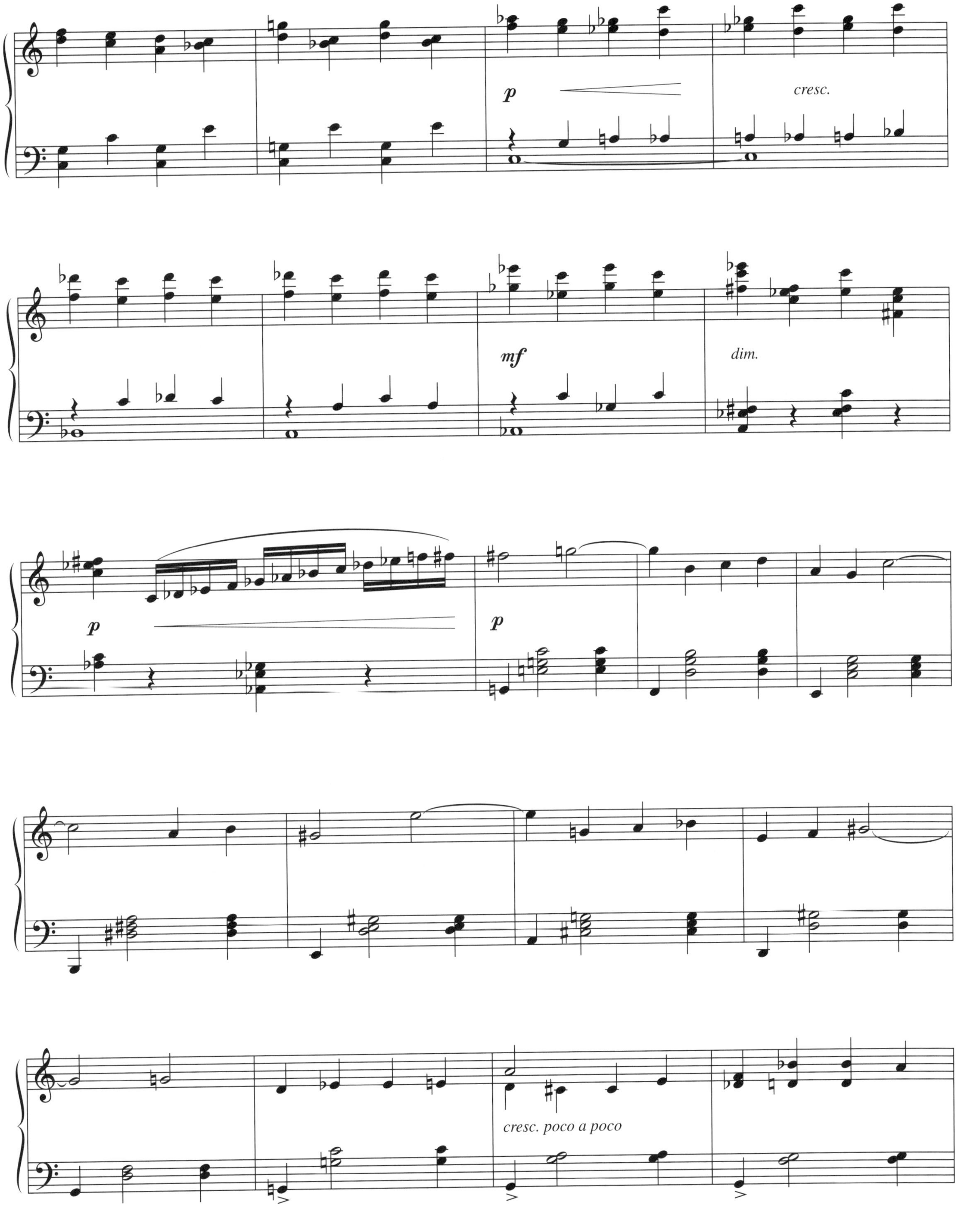
p
cresc.
mf
dim.
p
p
cresc. poco a poco

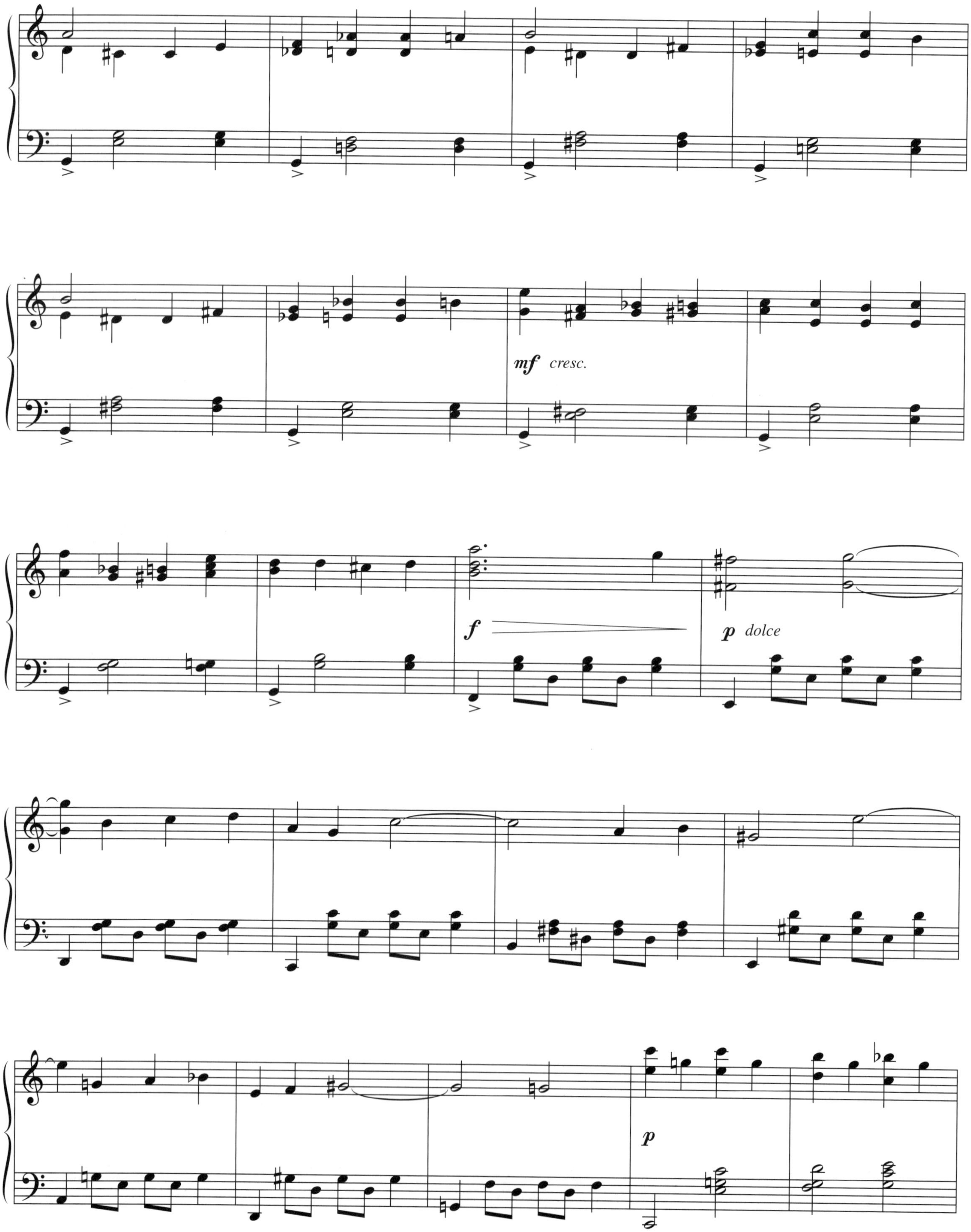
mf cresc.
f
p dolce
p

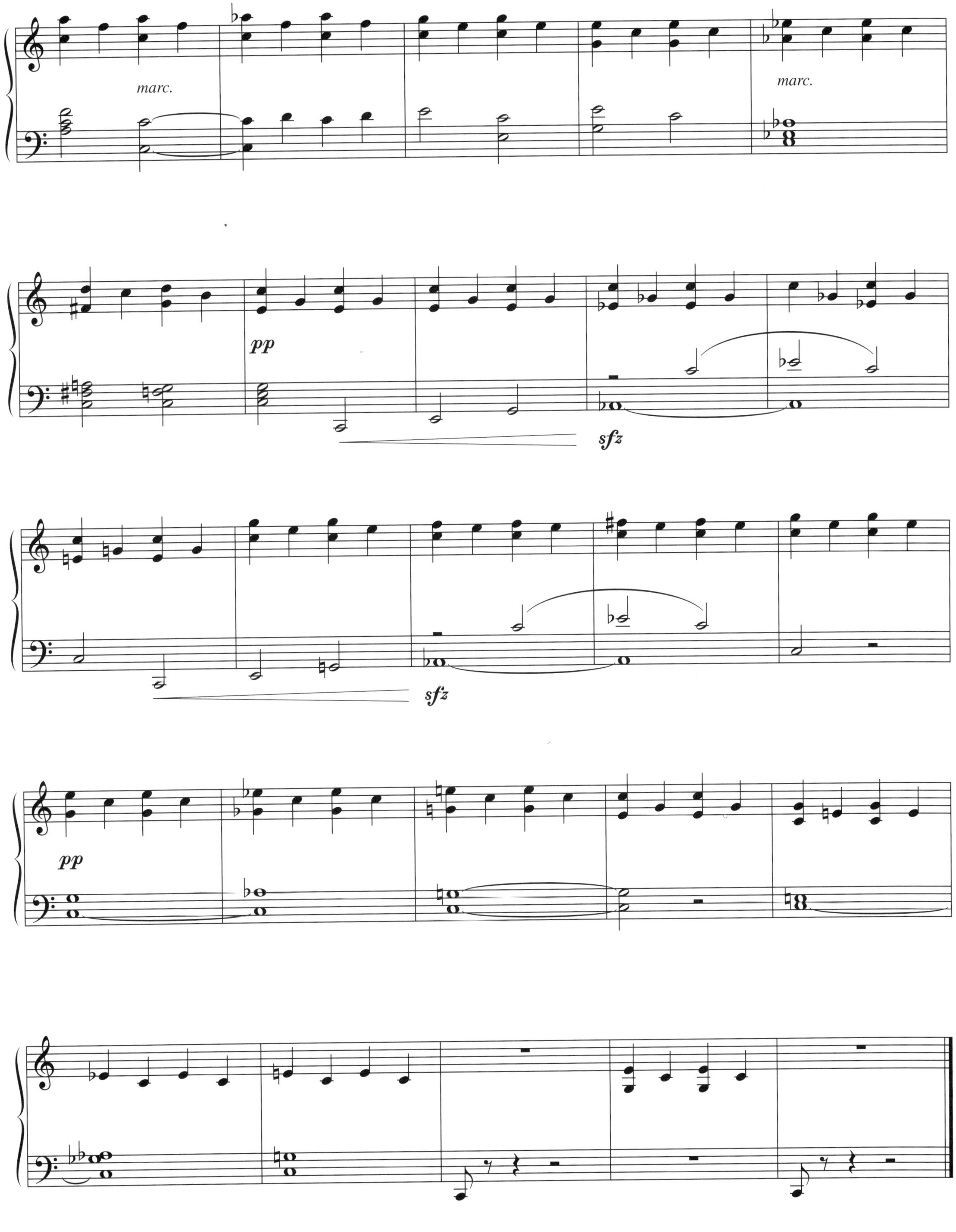
marc.
marc.
pp
sfz
sfz
pp

Symphony No. 6
"Pathétique"
First Movement Excerpt

Pyotr Il'yich Tchaikovsky
1840-1893
Op. 74
originally for orchestra

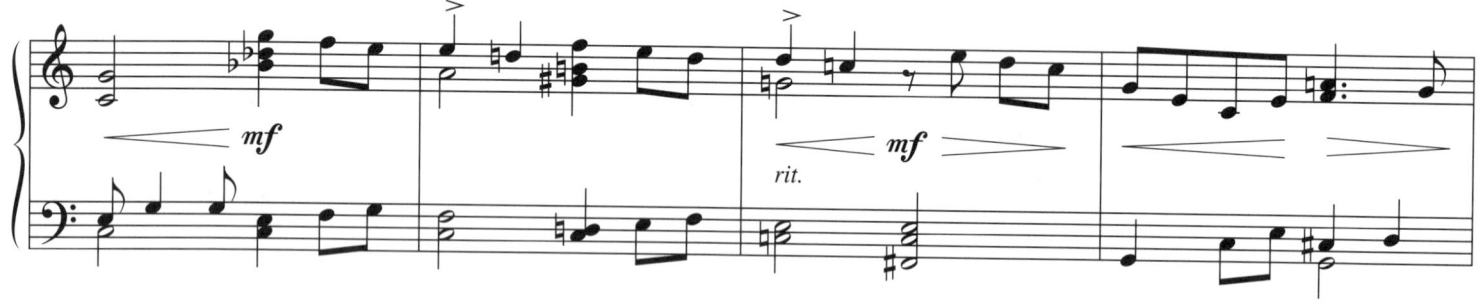

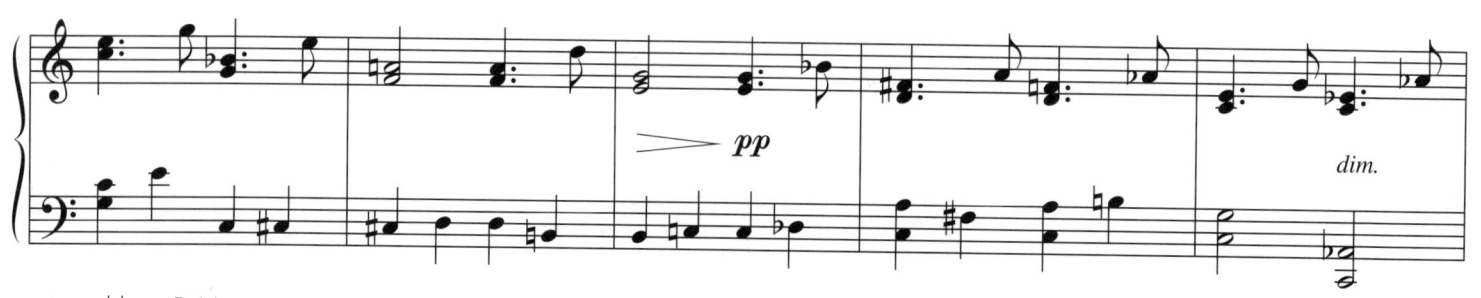

original key: B Minor

Adagio mosso
ppp
rall.
pp
ppp
molto rit.
Andante mosso
p quasi pizzicato
senza Ped.
p
p
dim.
ppp
ppp

Lacrymosa
from REQUIEM

Giuseppe Verdi
1813-1901
originally for soloists, chorus and orchestra

Largo (♩ = 60)

come un lamento

ppp dolciss.

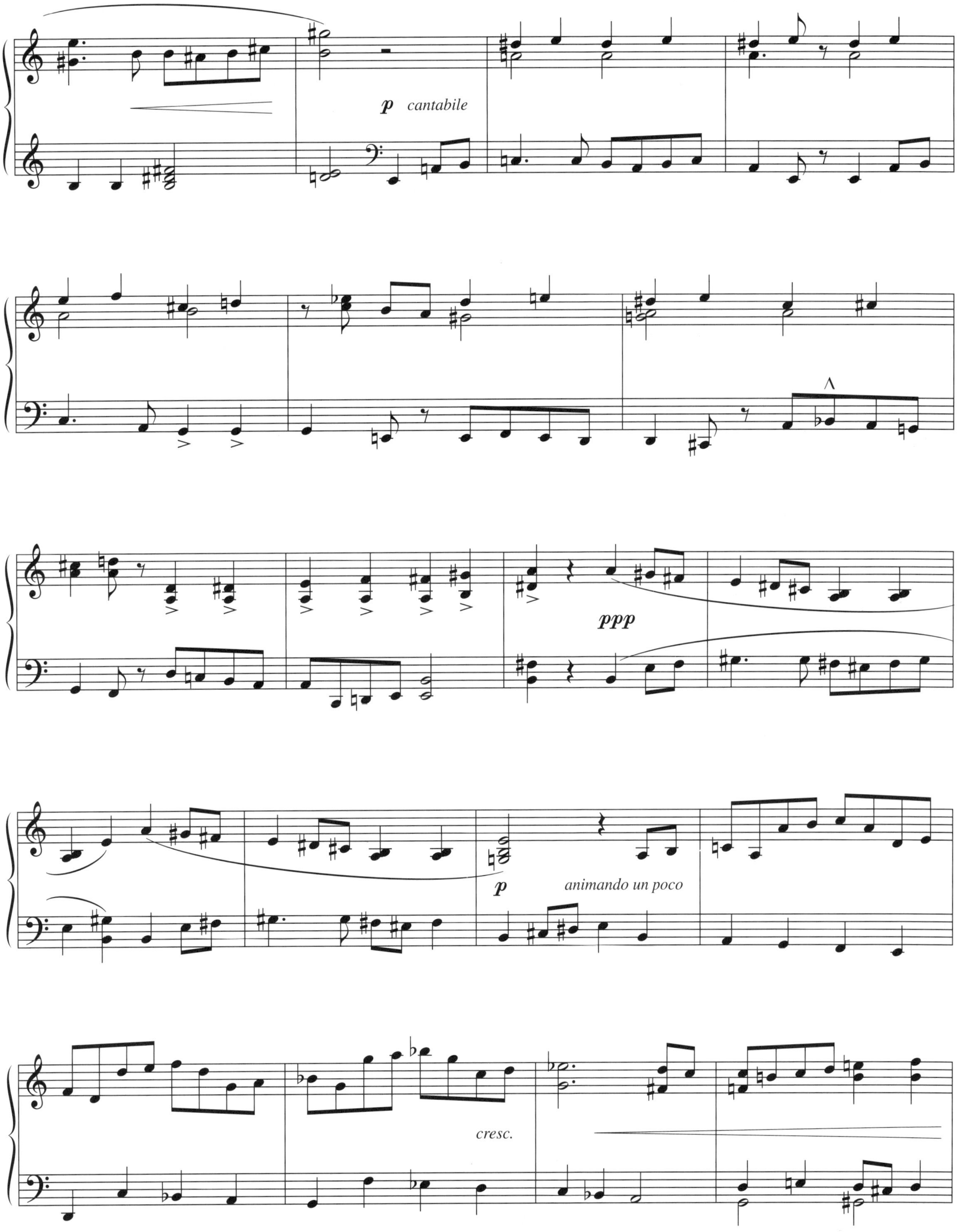
p cantabile
ppp
p
animando un poco
cresc.

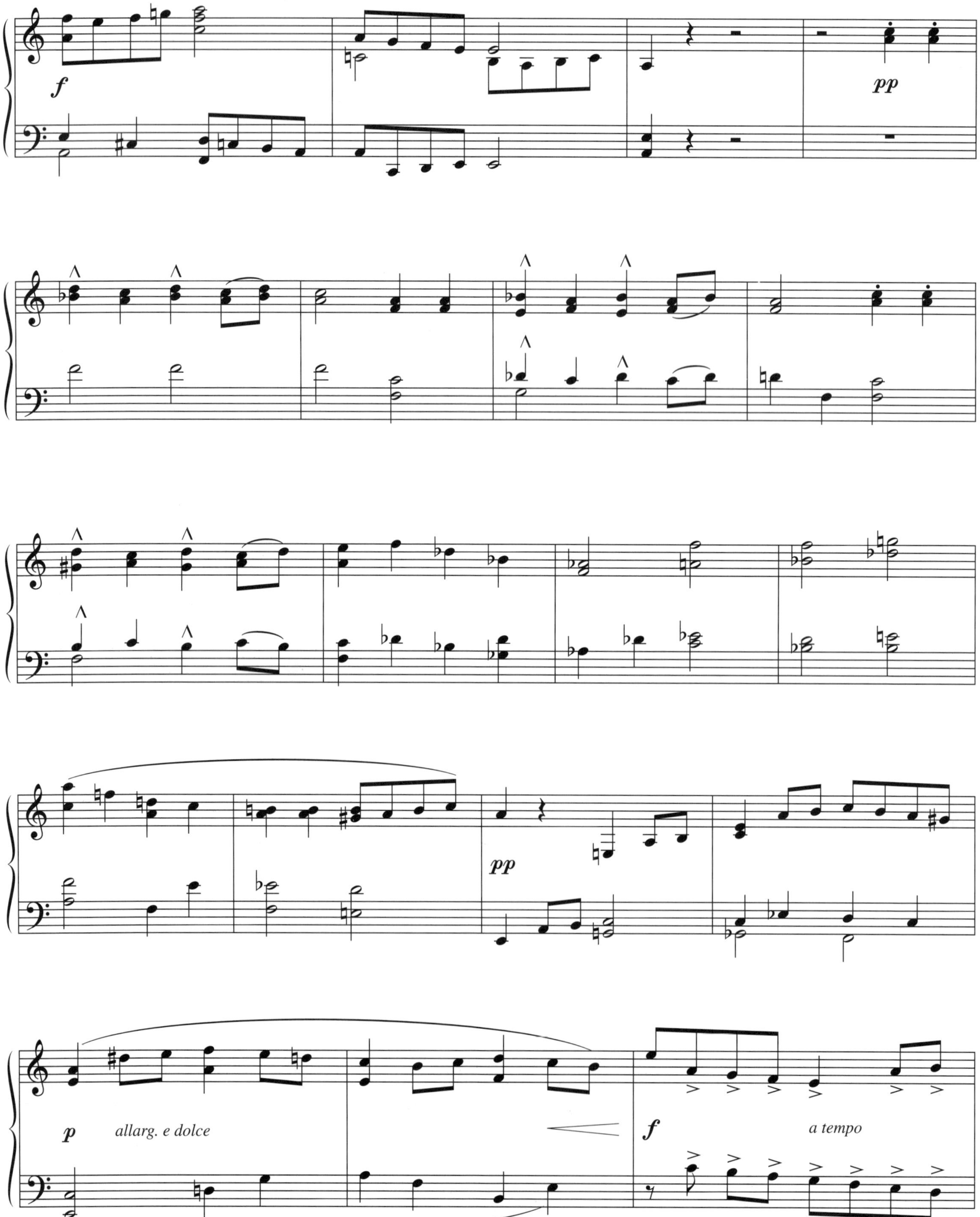
f
pp
pp
p
allarg. e dolce
f
a tempo

449

La donna è mobile

from the opera RIGOLETTO

Giuseppe Verdi
1813-1901

451

Triumphal March
from the opera AÏDA

Giuseppe Verdi
1813-1901

453

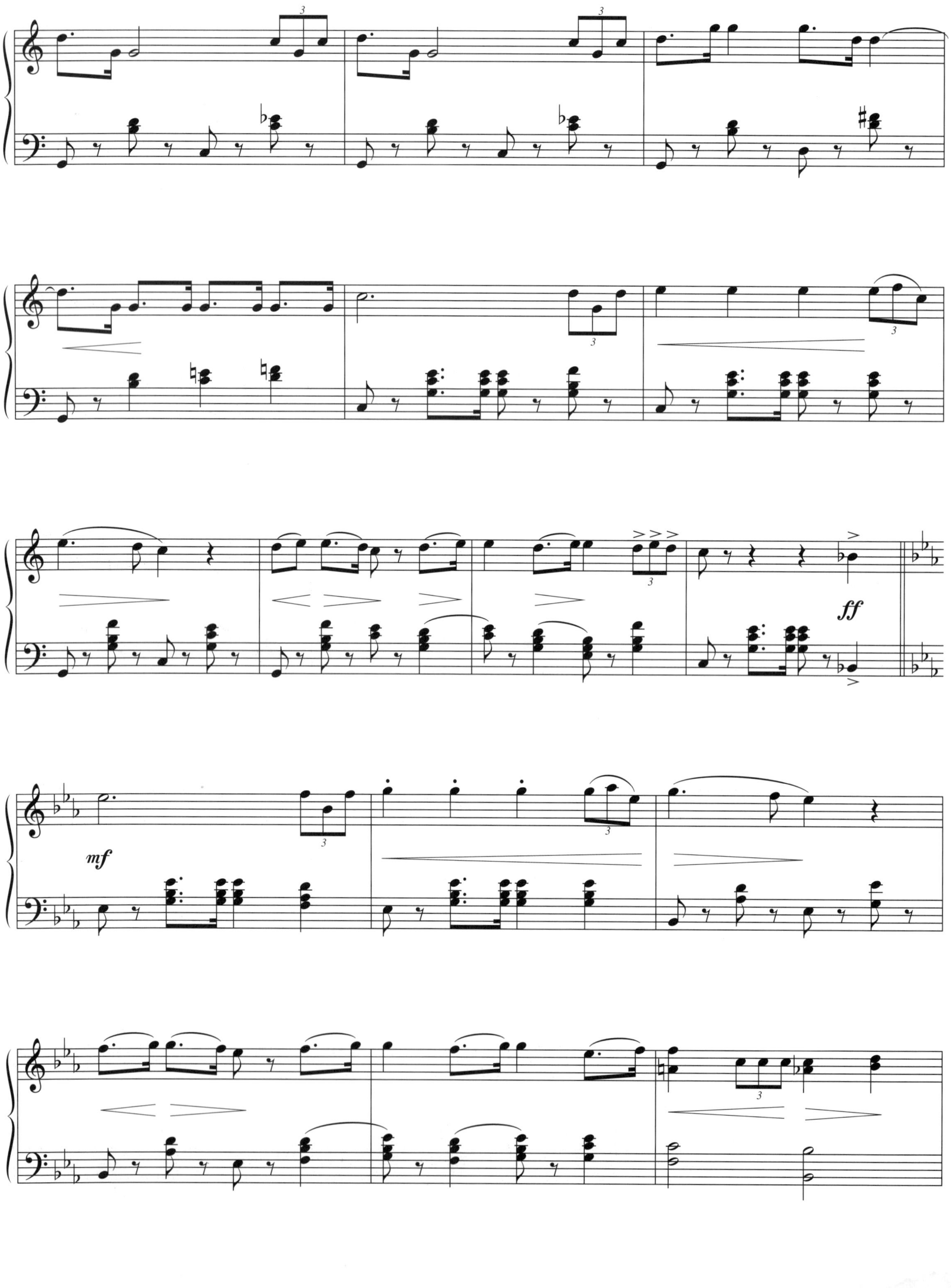
ff
mf

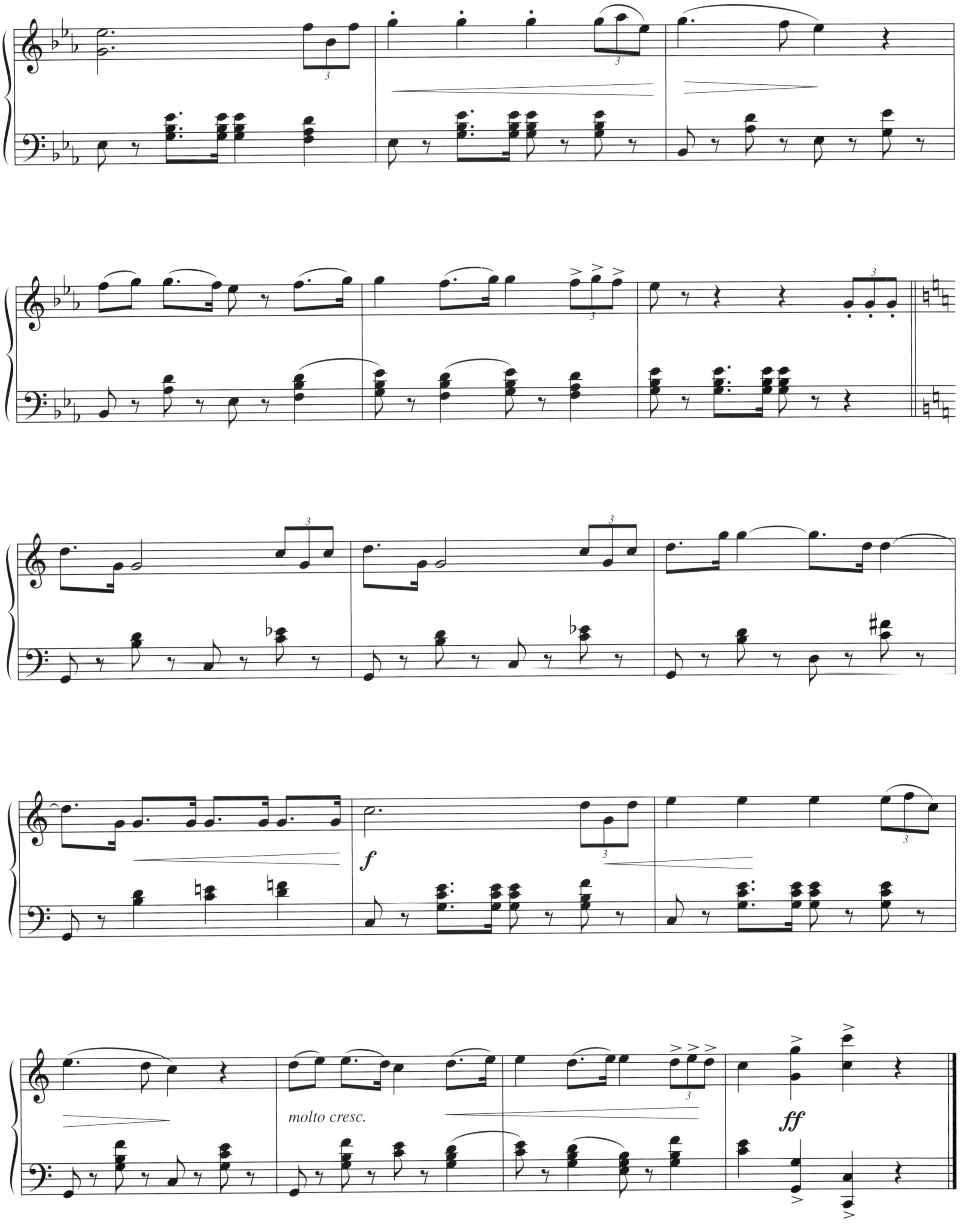
molto cresc.

Autumn

from THE FOUR SEASONS
First Movement Excerpt

Antonio Vivaldi
1678-1741
Op. 8, No. 3
originally for violin and orchestra

Allegro

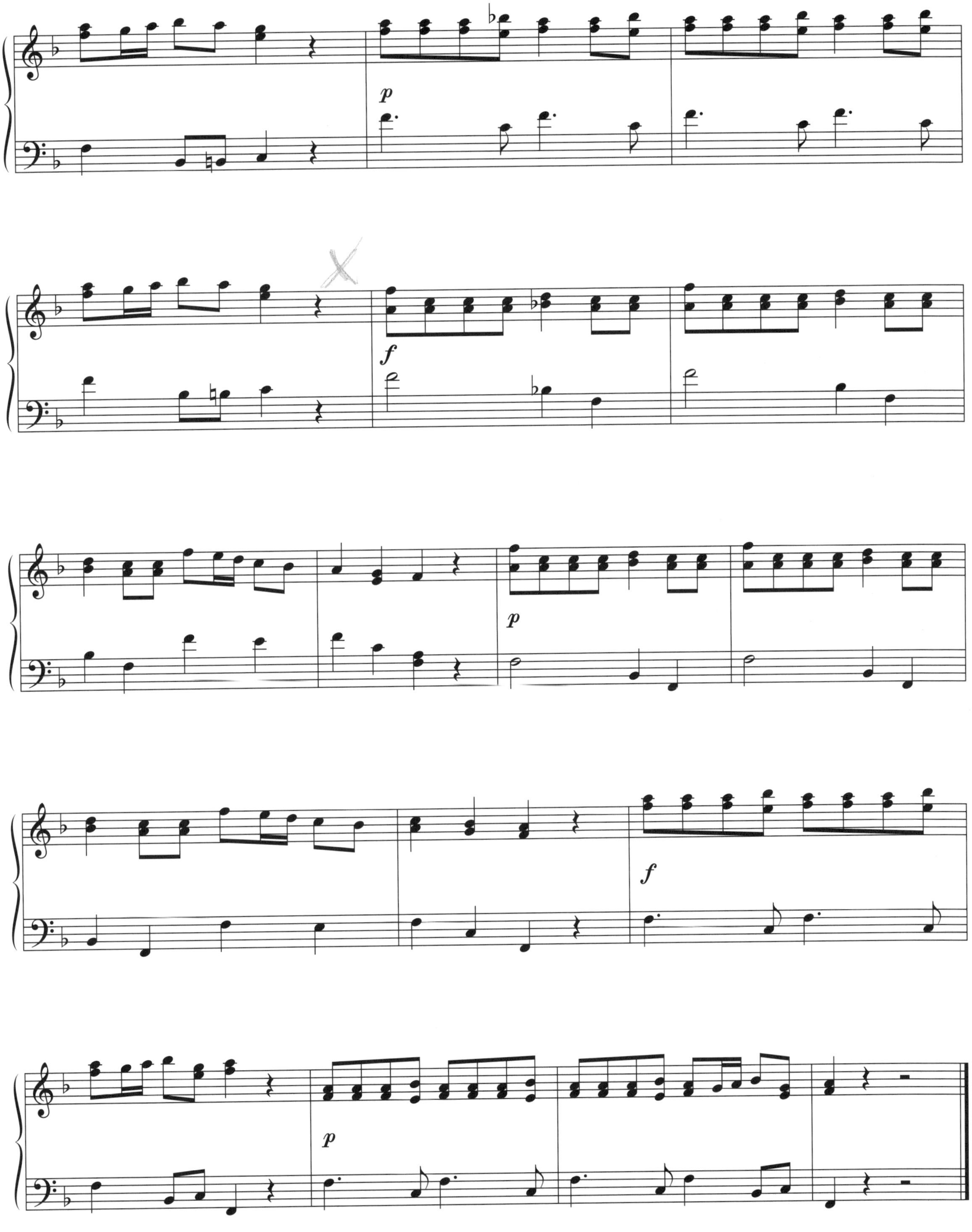
p
f
p
f
p

Autumn
from THE FOUR SEASONS
Third Movement Excerpt

Antonio Vivaldi
1678-1741
RV293, P257, M78, Op. 8, No. 3
originally for violin & string orchestra

Allegro

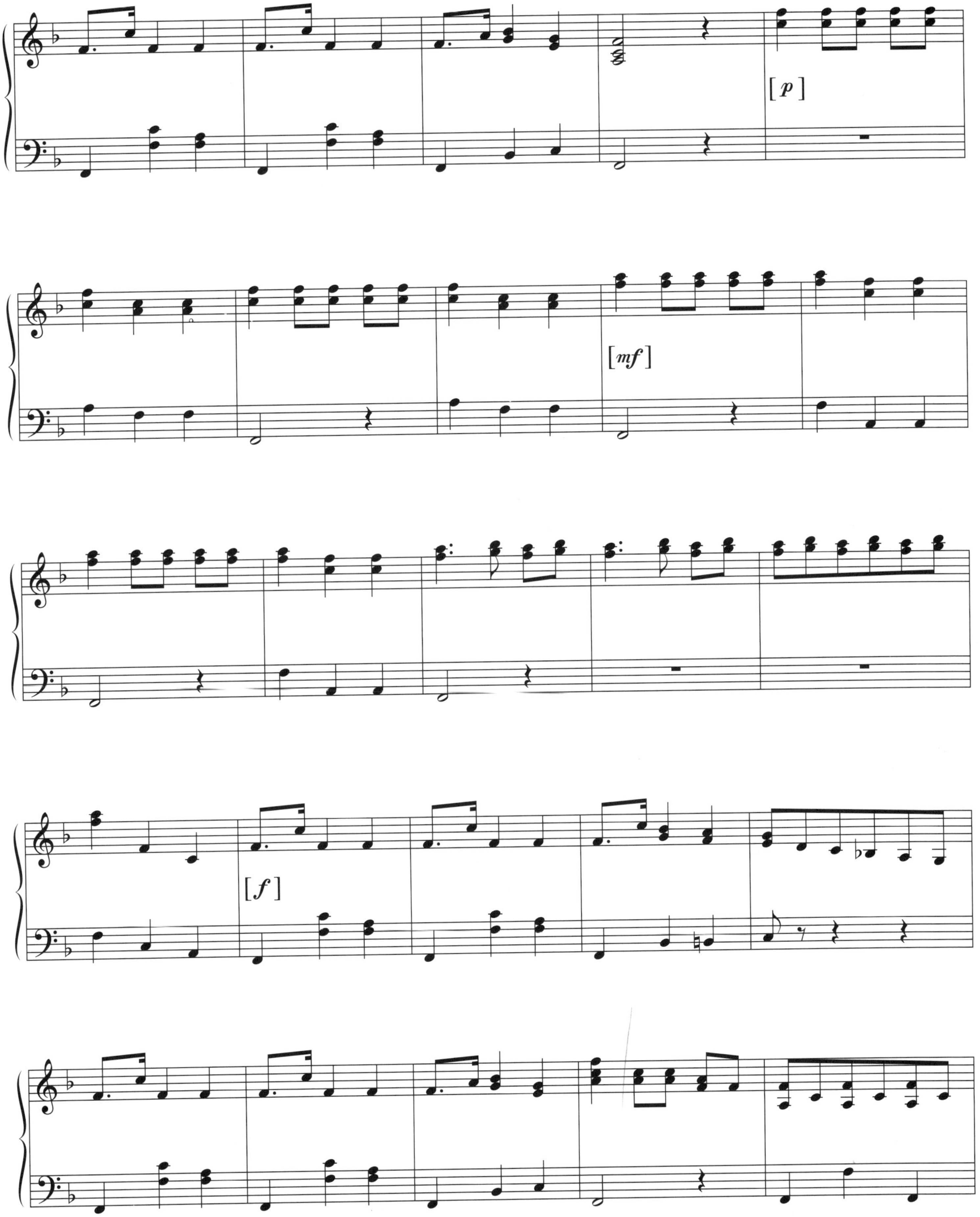
[p]
[mf]
[f]

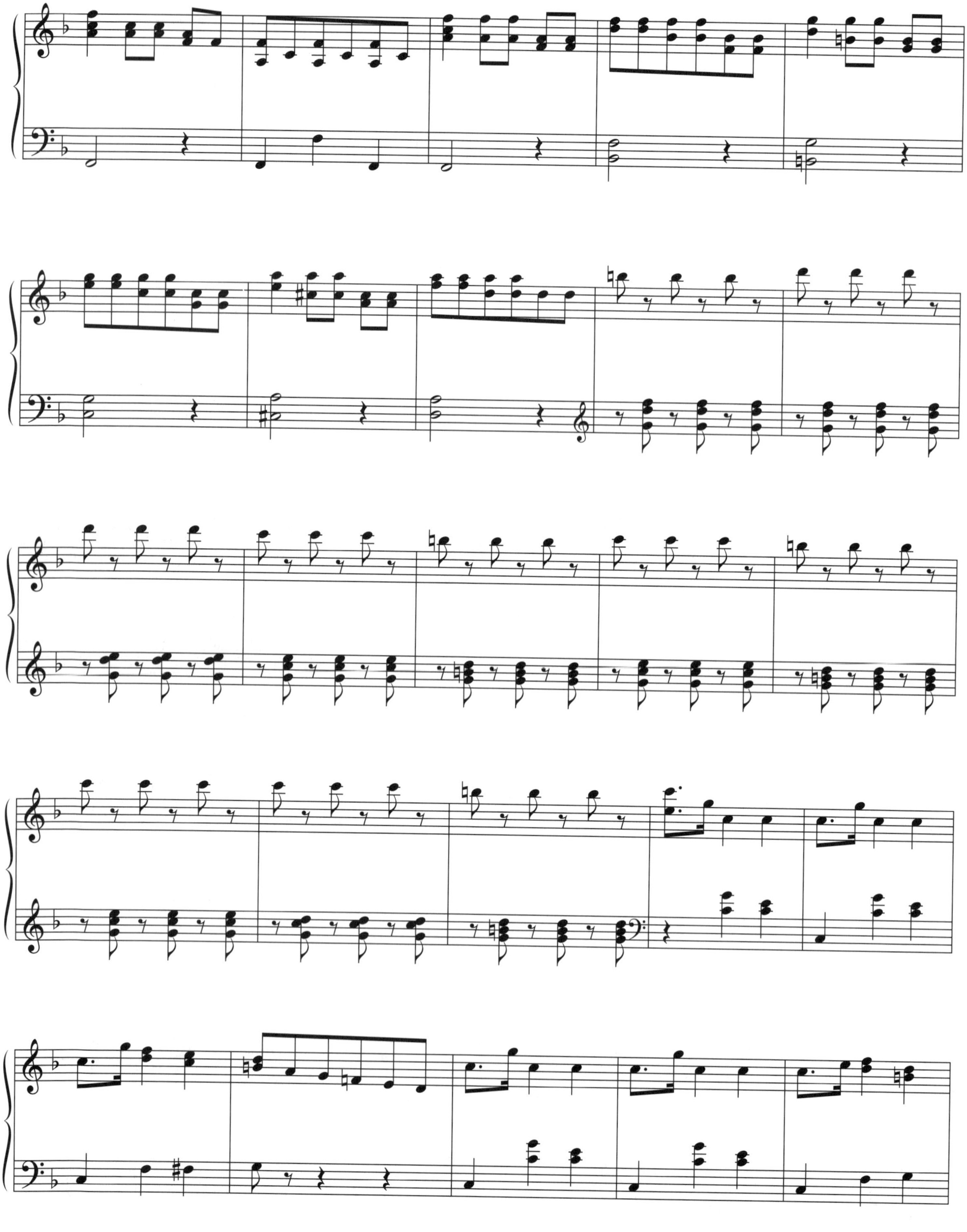

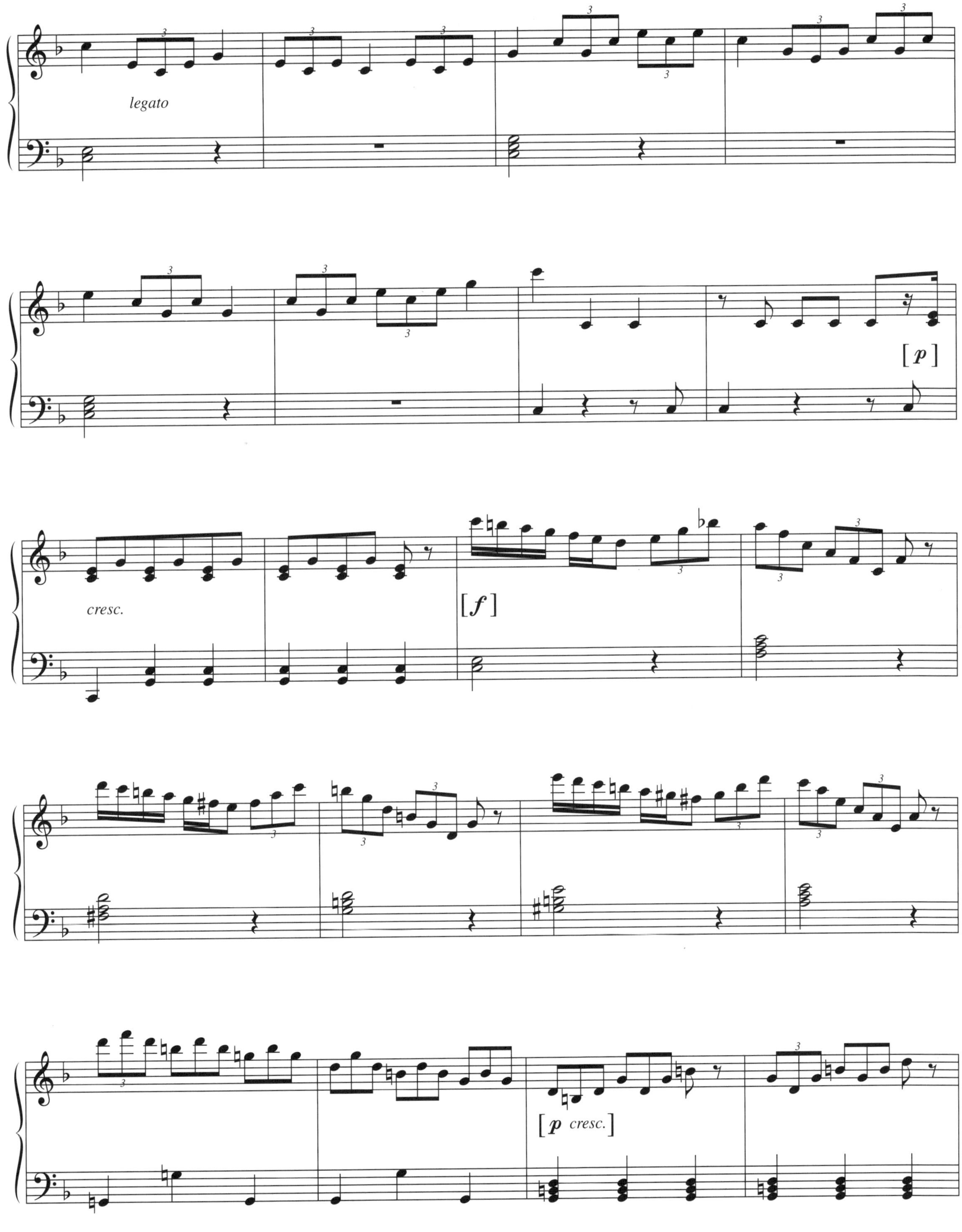
legato
[p]
cresc.
[f]
[p cresc.]

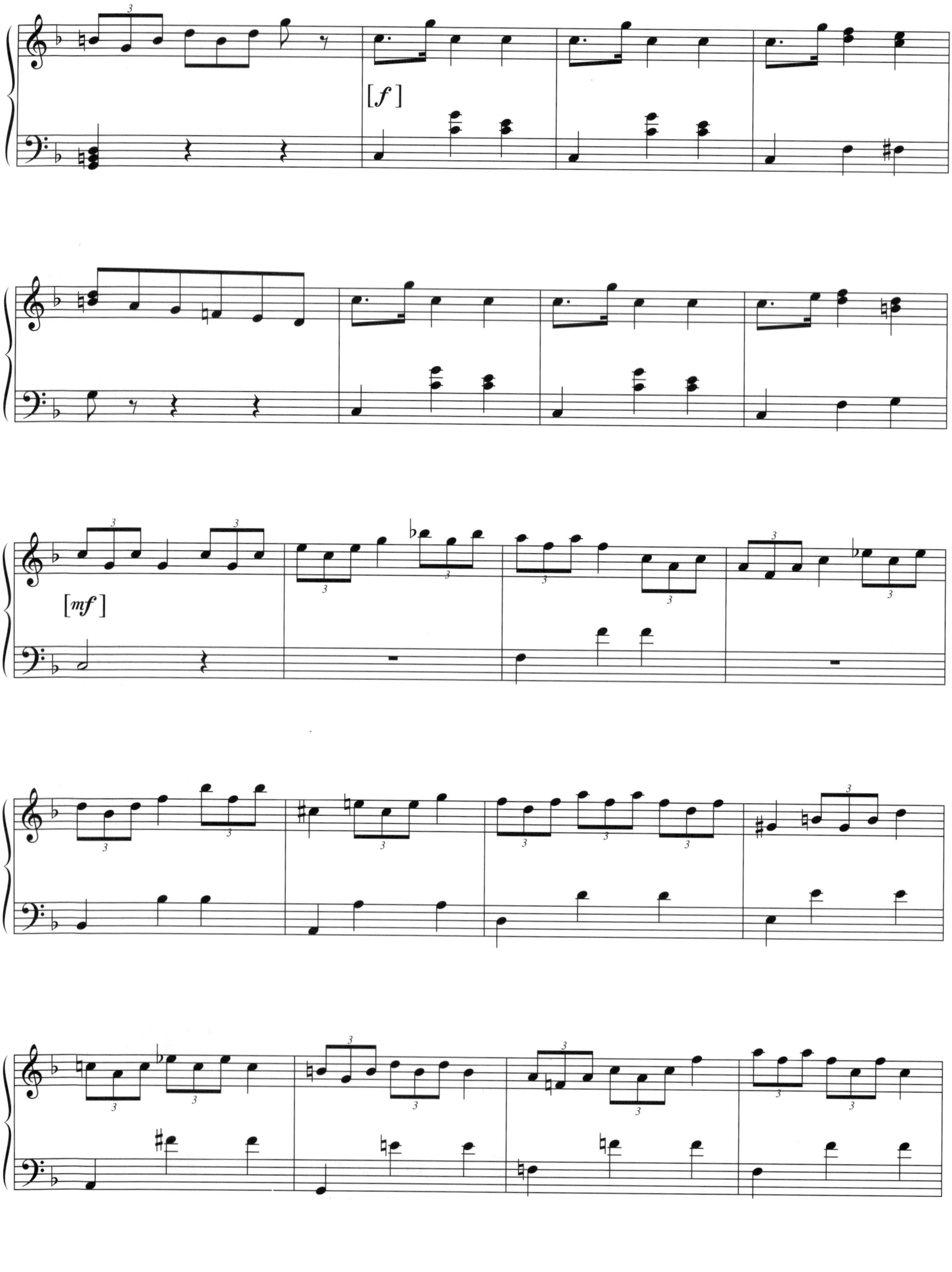
[f]
[mf]

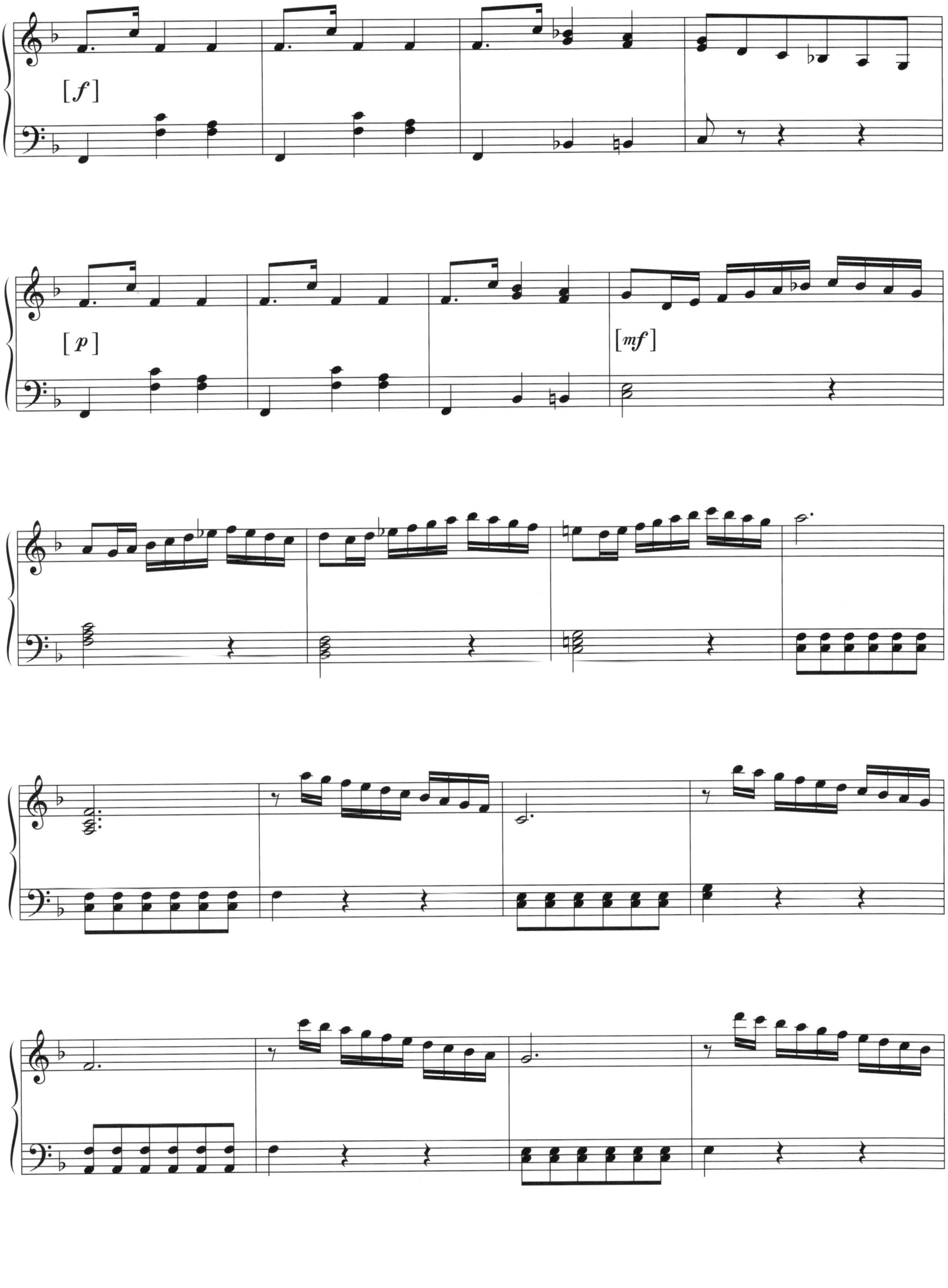
[f]
[p]
[mf]

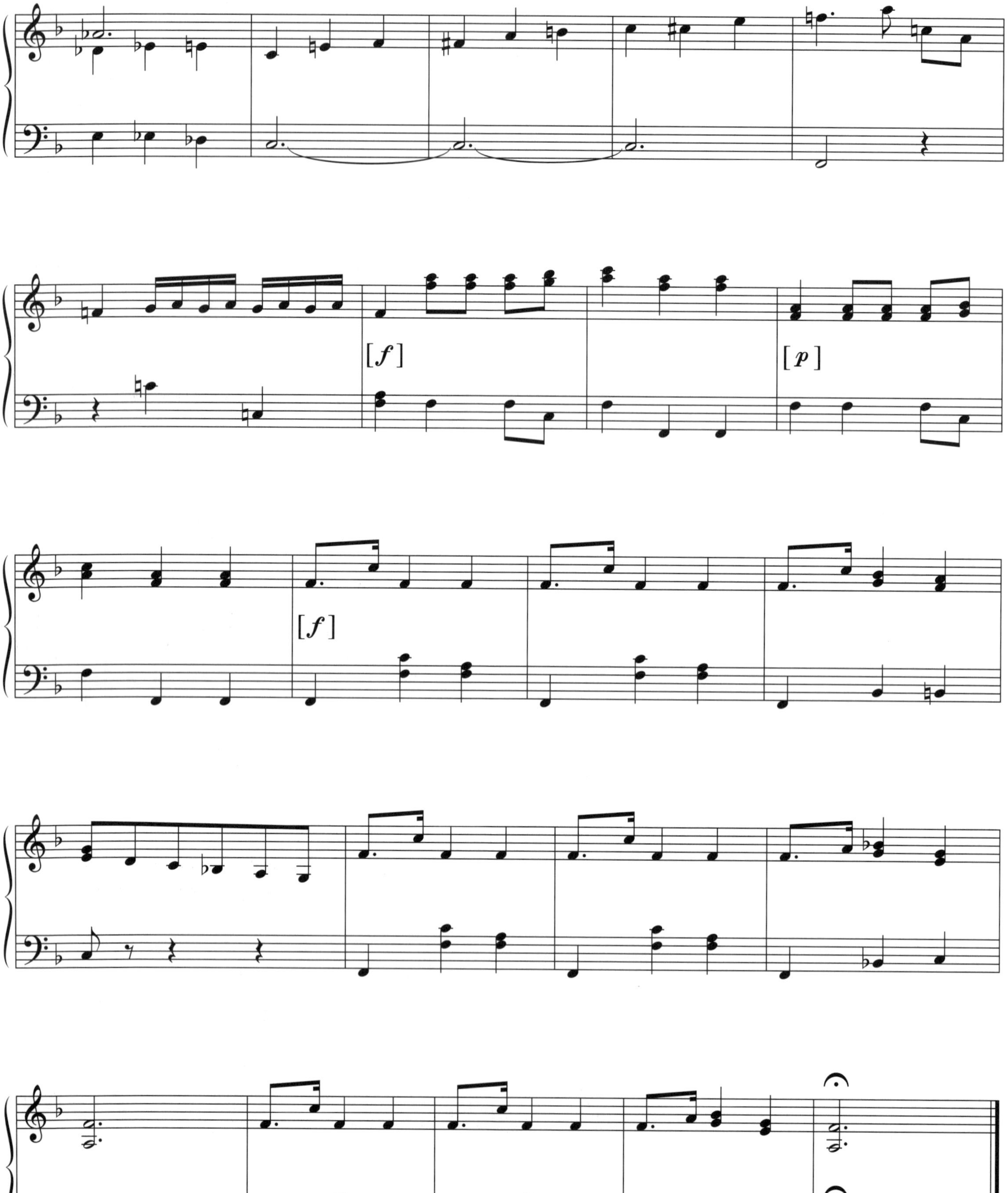
[f]
[p]
[f]

Spring
from THE FOUR SEASONS
First Movement Excerpt

Antonio Vivaldi
1678-1741
RV269, P241, M76, Op. 8, No. 1
originally for violin & string orchestra

original key: E Major

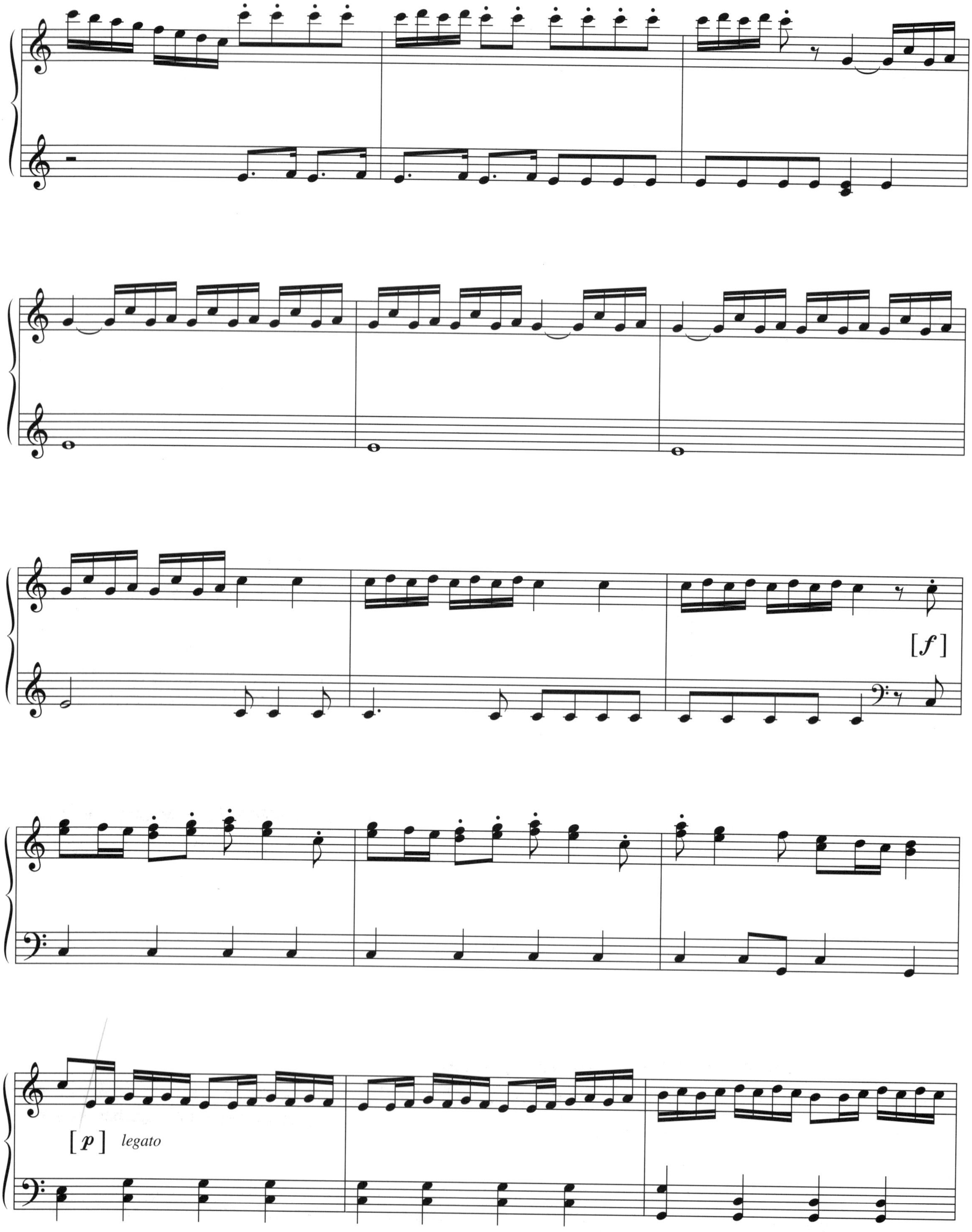
[f]
[p] legato

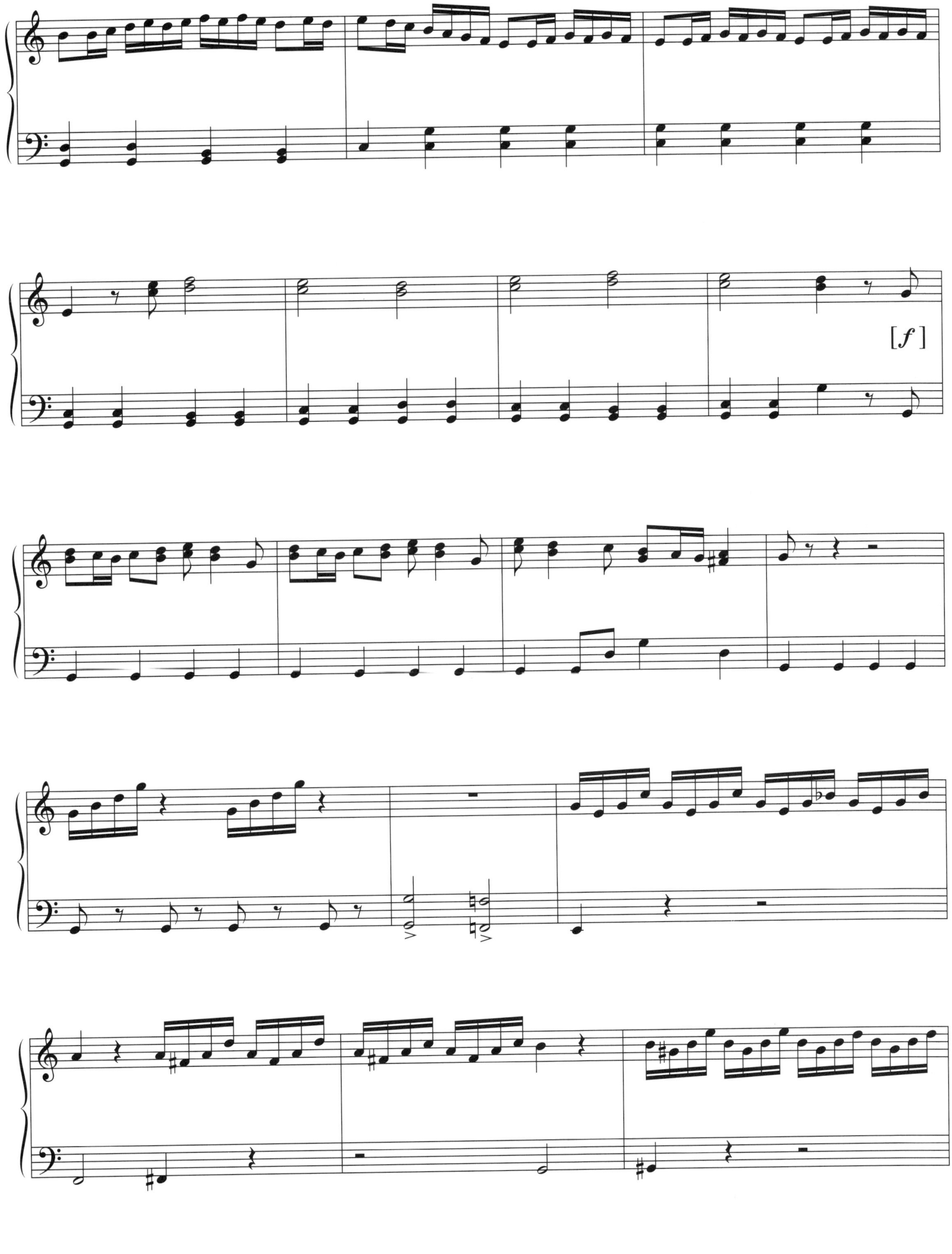
[f]

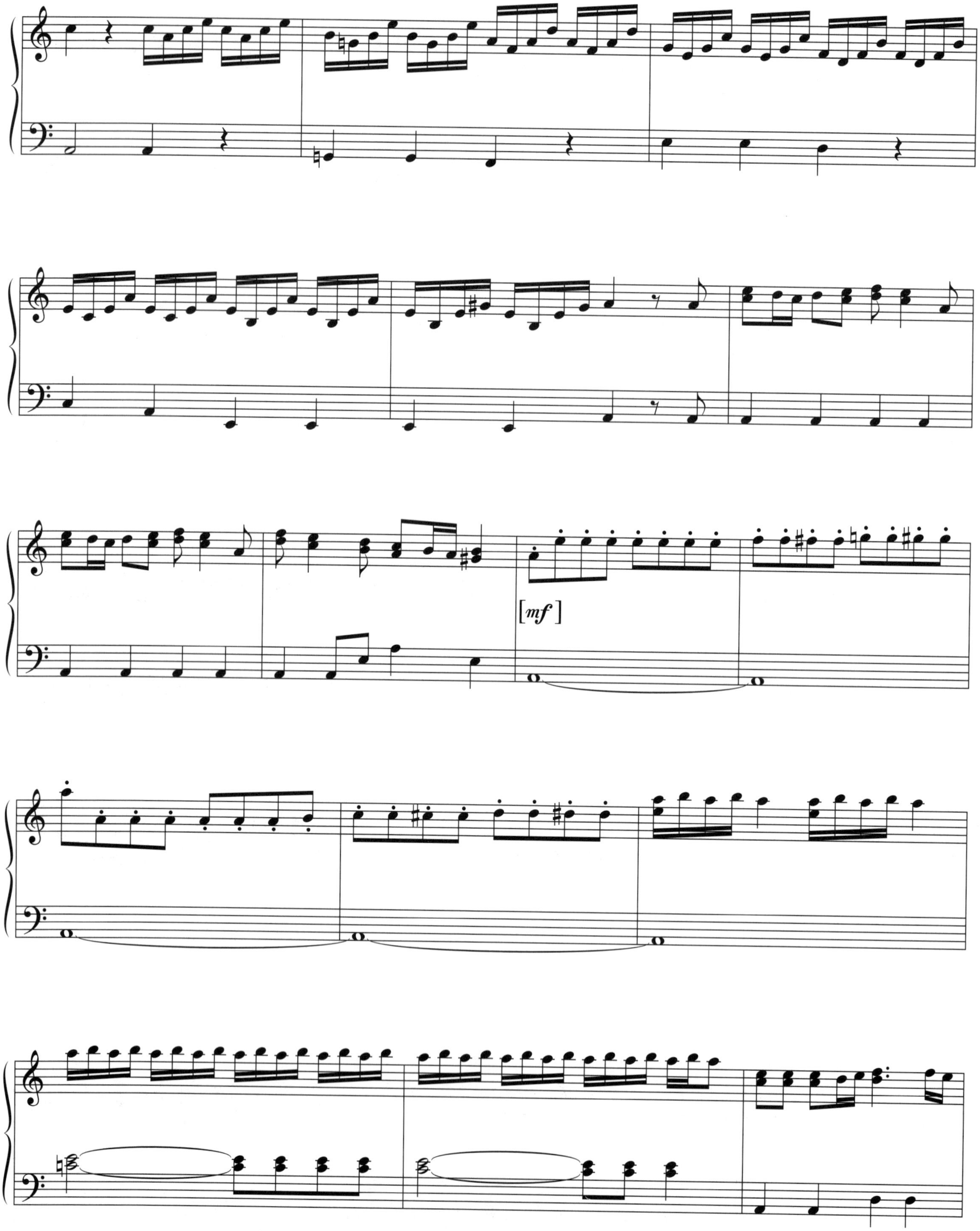
[mf]

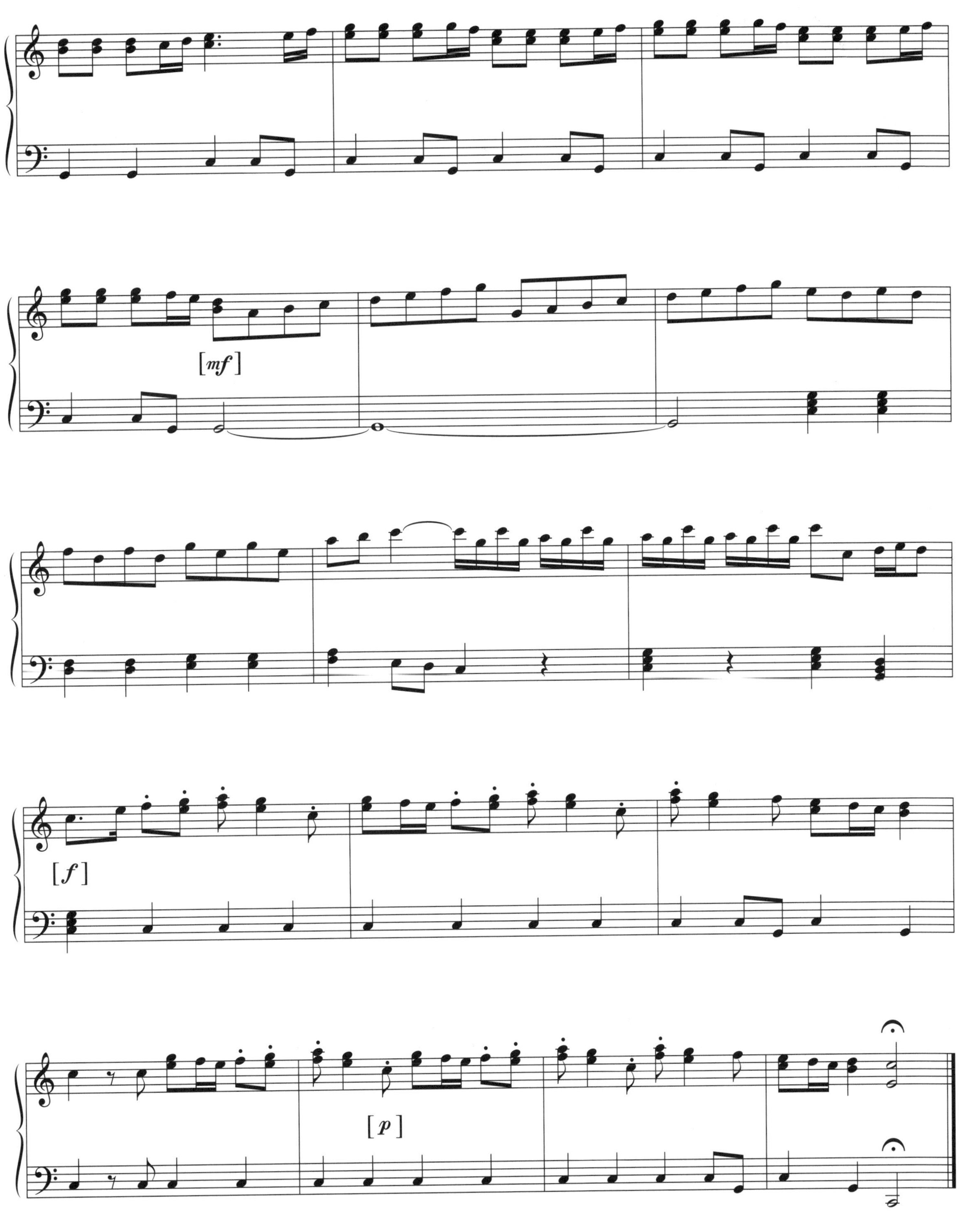
[mf]
[f]
[p]

Mandolin Concerto in C Major
First Movement Excerpt

Antonio Vivaldi
1678-1741
originally for mandolin and orchestra

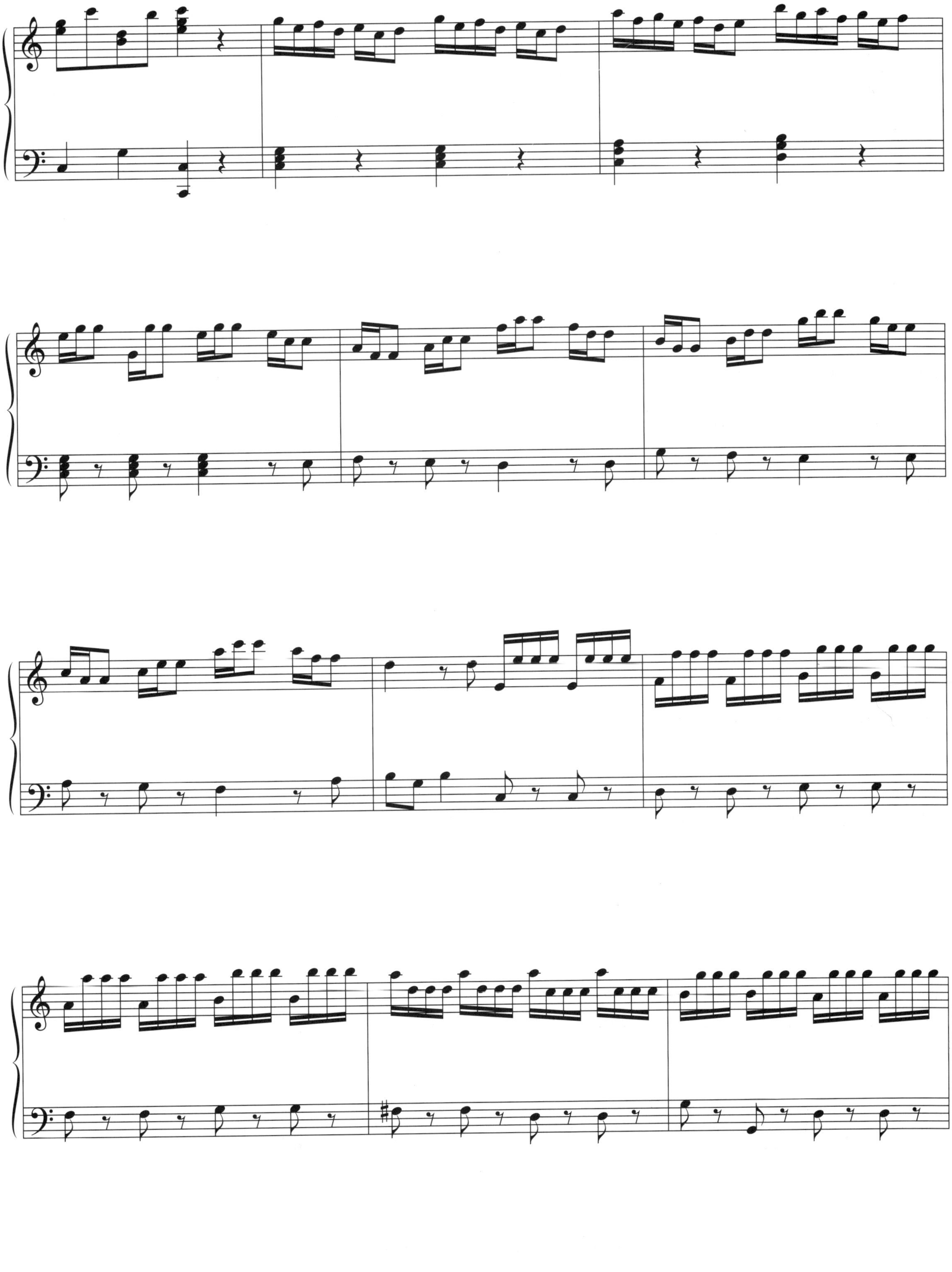

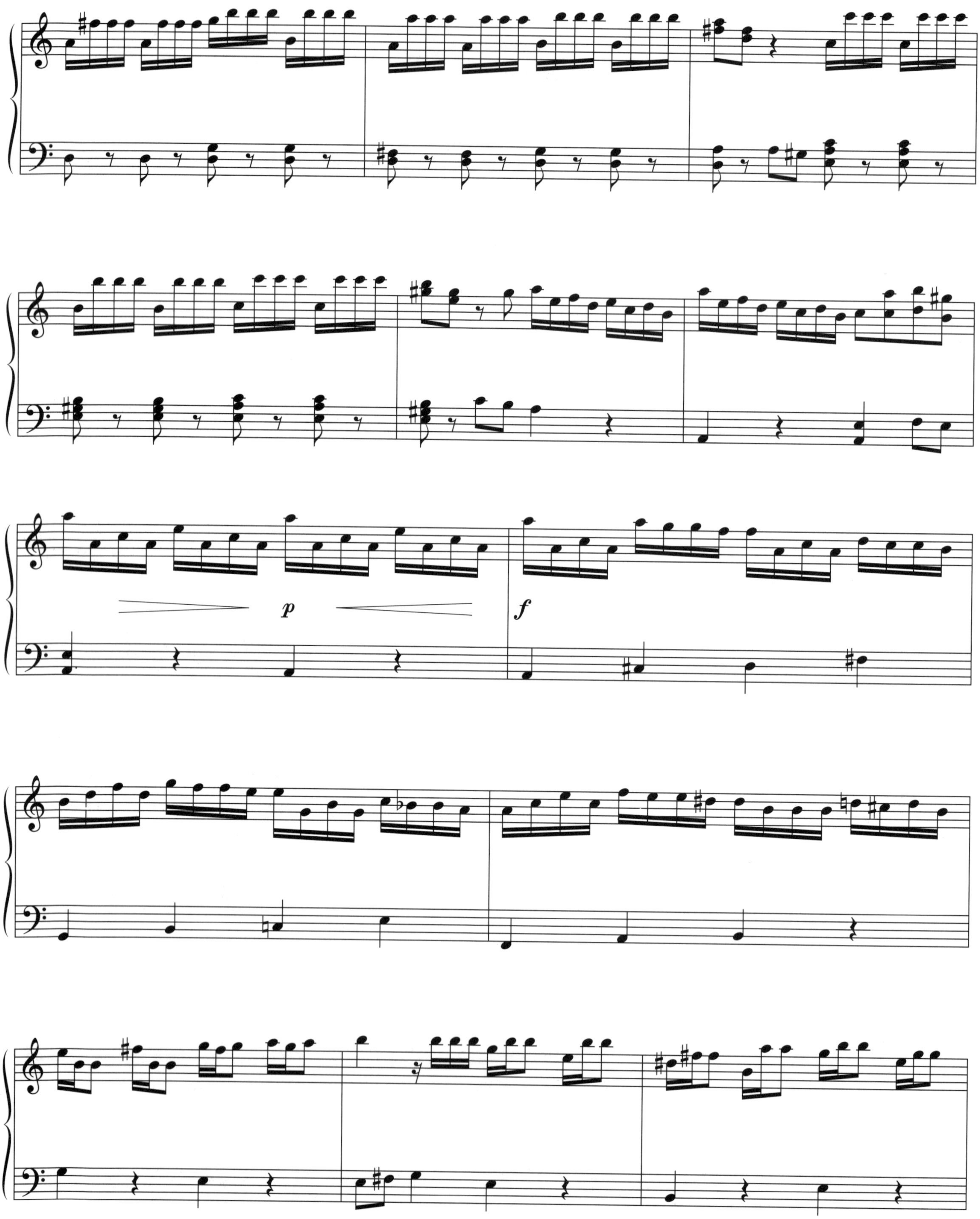
p
f

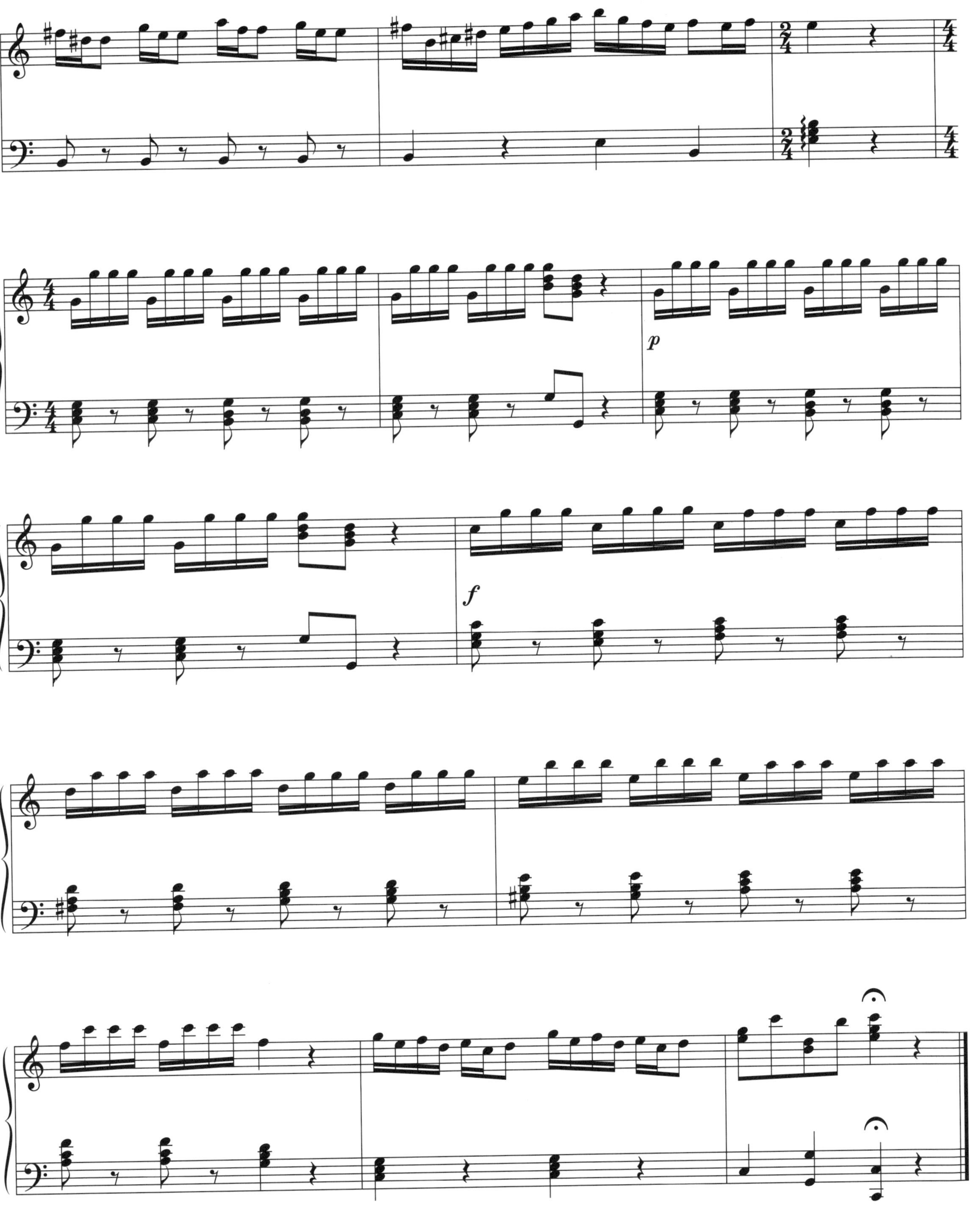
p
f

Pilgrims' Chorus
from the opera TANNHÄUSER

Richard Wagner
1813-1883

Andante maestoso

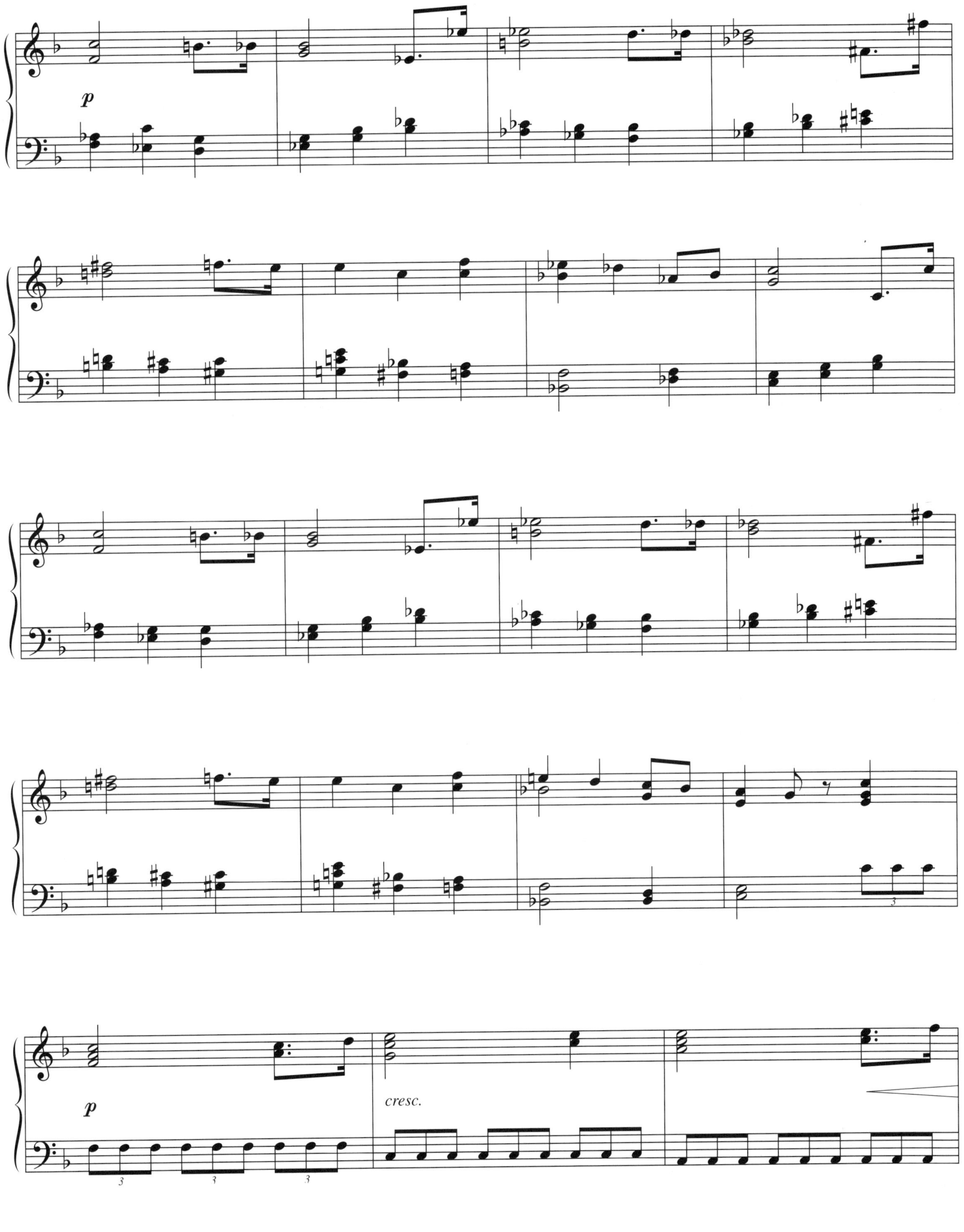
p
p
cresc.

476

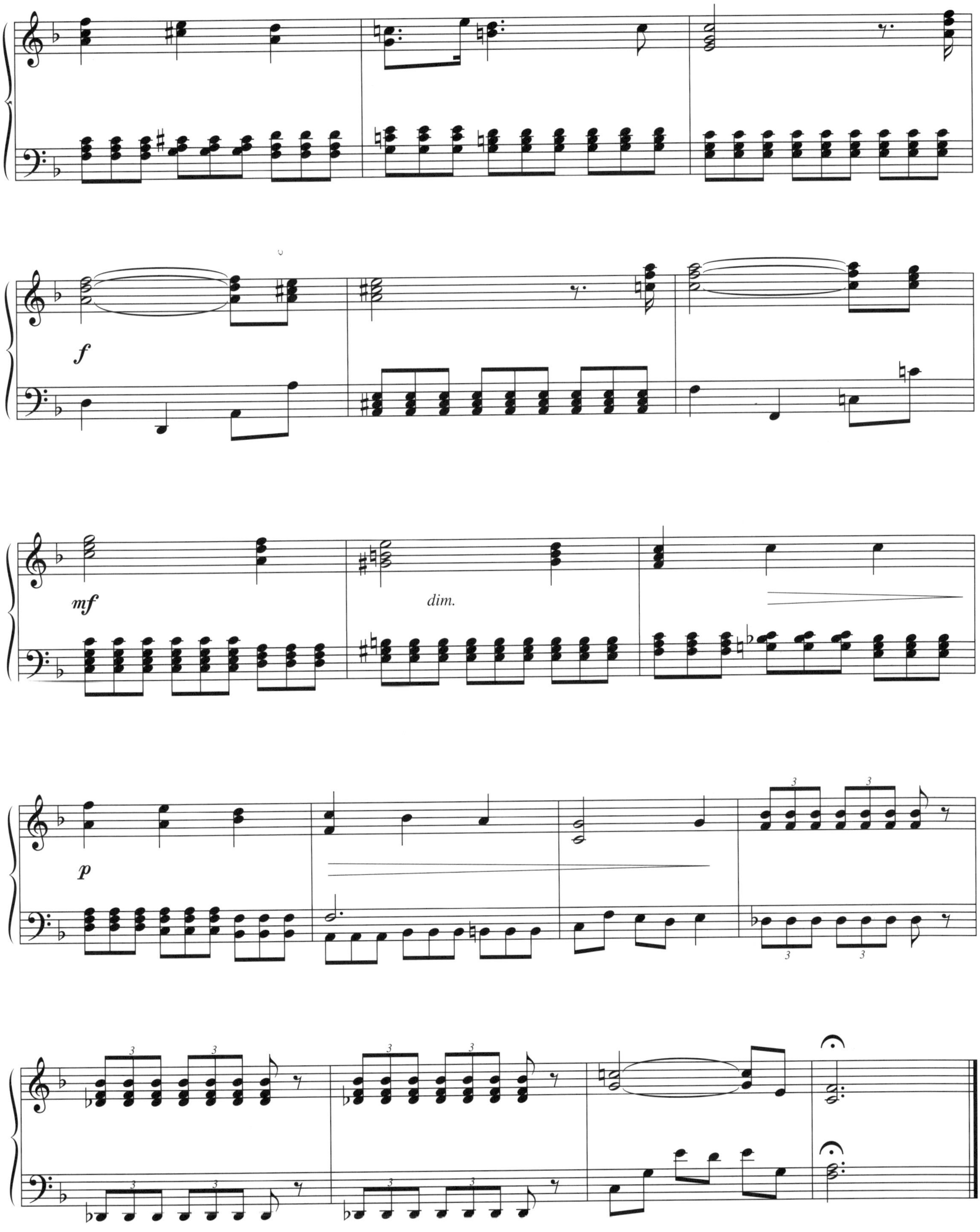
f
mf
dim.
p
3

Bridal Chorus
from the opera LOHENGRIN

Richard Wagner
1813–1883

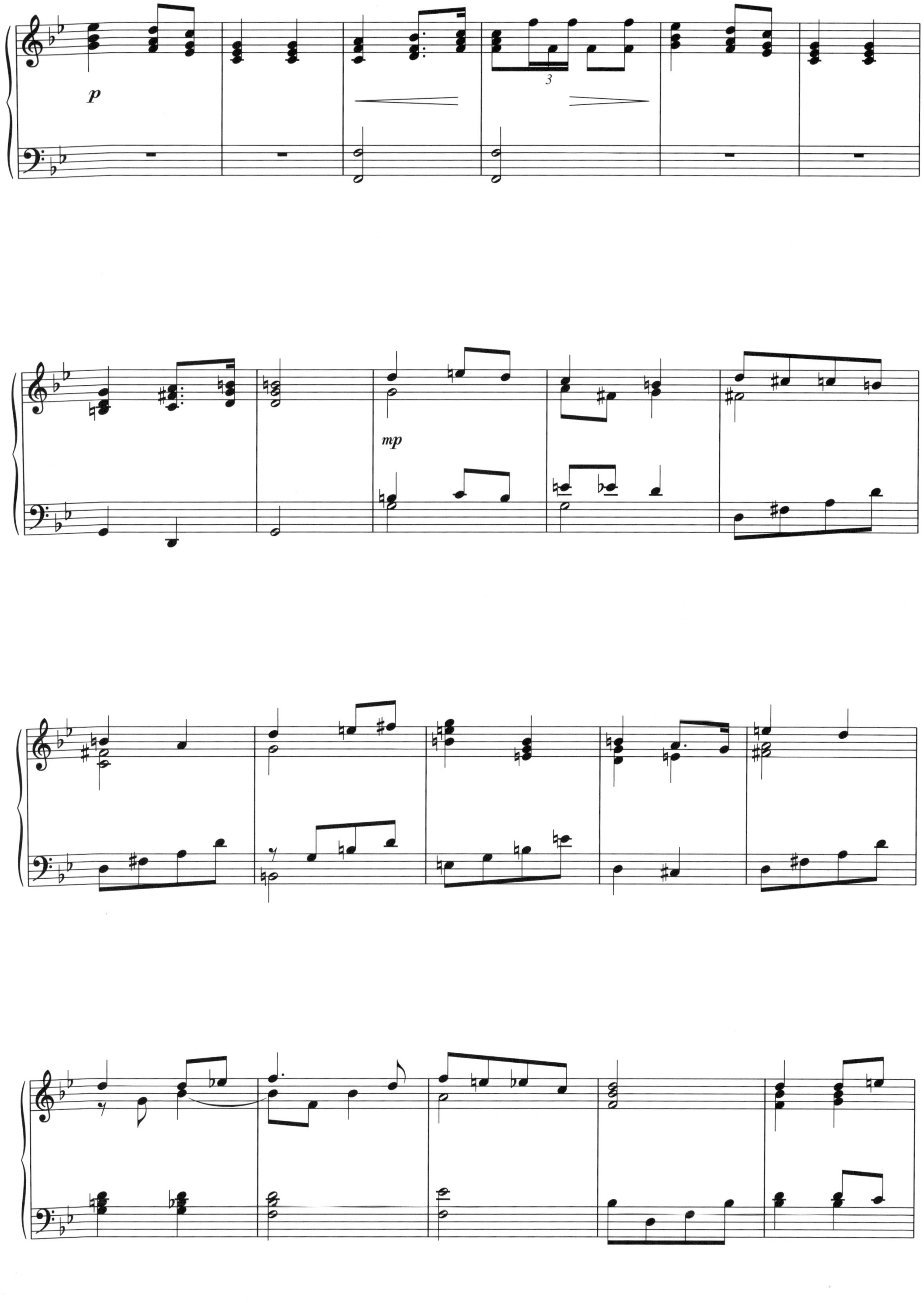
p
3
mp

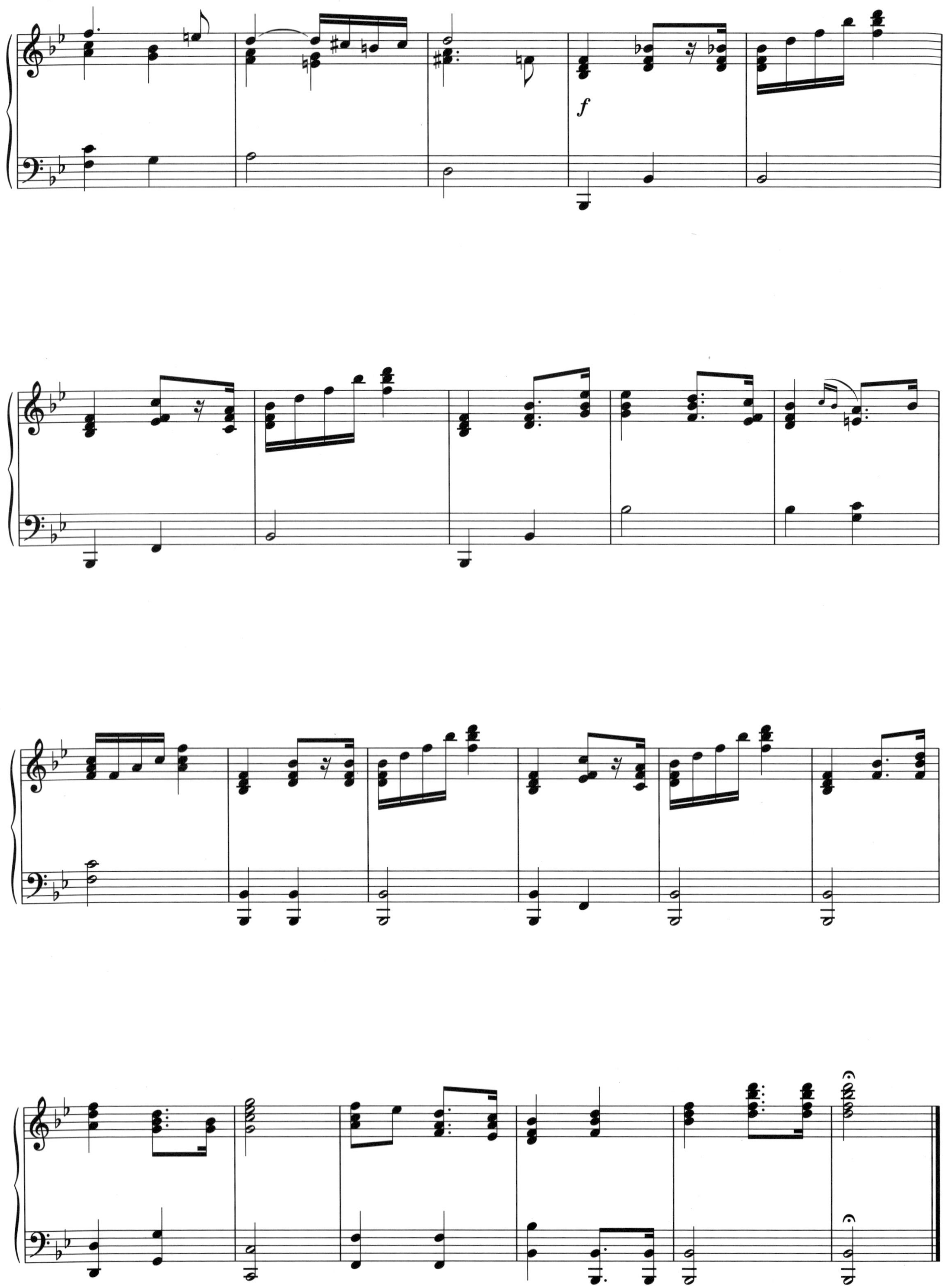
f